MACARTHUR
AT WAR

Also by Walter R. Borneman

*American Spring: Lexington, Concord, and
the Road to Revolution*

*The Admirals: Nimitz, Halsey, Leahy, and King—
The Five-Star Admirals Who Won the War at Sea*

*Iron Horses: America's Race to Bring
the Railroads West*

*Polk: The Man Who Transformed the Presidency
and America*

*The French and Indian War: Deciding the Fate
of North America*

14,000 Feet: A Celebration of Colorado's Highest Mountains
(with Todd Caudle)

1812: The War That Forged a Nation

Alaska: Saga of a Bold Land

A Climbing Guide to Colorado's Fourteeners
(with Lyndon J. Lampert)

MACARTHUR
★ AT WAR ★

WORLD WAR II IN THE PACIFIC

WALTER R. BORNEMAN

Little, Brown and Company

New York • Boston • London

Little, Brown and Company
Hachette Book Group
1290 Avenue of the Americas, New York, NY 10104
littlebrown.com

First Edition: May 2016

Little, Brown and Company is a division of Hachette Book Group, Inc. The Little, Brown name and logo are trademarks of Hachette Book Group, Inc.

The publisher is not responsible for websites (or their content) that are not owned by the publisher.

The Hachette Speakers Bureau provides a wide range of authors for speaking events. To find out more, go to hachettespeakersbureau.com or call (866) 376-6591.

Maps by David Lambert

ISBN 978-0-316-40532-4
Library of Congress Control Number: 2016931808

10 9 8 7 6 5 4 3 2 1

RRD-C

Printed in the United States of America

For Paul L. Miles, PhD, Colonel, USA, Ret.,
soldier, scholar, and friend,

and

for the memory of my father,
who embarked at the age of nineteen to fight in MacArthur's war

Contents

Contents

List of Maps

Pacific Theater
World War II

U.S.S.R.

Sea of
Okhotsk

MONGOLIA

Kuril Islands

Hokkaido

Sea of
Japan

KOREA

JAPAN

Tokyo

CHINA

Yellow
Sea

Kyushu

East
China
Sea

Okinawa

Iwo Jima

INDIA

Hong
Kong

BURMA

INDOCHINA

Formosa

Mariana
Islands

Saipan

Bay
of
Bengal

THAILAND

PHILIPPINES

Guam

Bangkok

Manila

South
China
Sea

Philippine
Sea

Caroline Islands

Truk

Palau
Islands

Singapore

Equator

Borneo

Admiralty
Islands

Sumatra

Balikpapan

Hollandia

Rabaul

Solomo
Island

NEW
GUINEA

Java

NETHERLANDS INDIES

Timor

Port
Moresby

Darwin

Coral
Sea

Townsville

N
Caledo

AUSTRALIA

Brisbane

INDIAN

OCEAN

Perth

Canberra

Melbourne

80°E   100°E   120°E   140°E   160°E

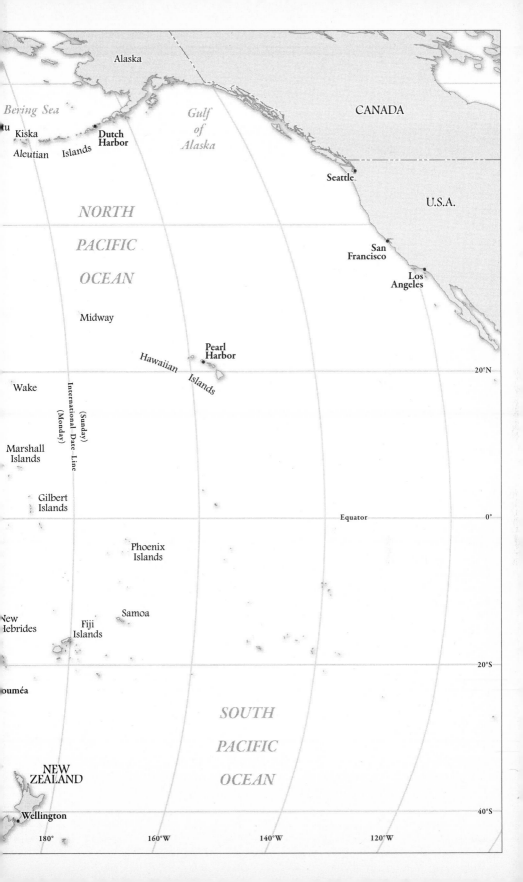

Alaska

Bering Sea

CANADA

Kiska

Dutch
Harbor

Gulf
of
Alaska

Aleutian   Islands

Seattle

U.S.A.

NORTH

PACIFIC

San
Francisco

OCEAN

Los
Angeles

Midway

Pearl
Harbor

Hawaiian   Islands

20°N

Wake

International Date Line

(Sunday)
(Monday)

Marshall
Islands

Gilbert
Islands

Equator   0°

Phoenix
Islands

New
Hebrides

Samoa

Fiji
Islands

20°S

Nouméa

SOUTH

PACIFIC

OCEAN

NEW
ZEALAND

Wellington

40°S

180°   160°W   140°W   120°W

MACARTHUR
AT WAR

Monday, December 8, 1941

In predawn darkness the black telephone rang loudly. The general's wife lifted the receiver from its cradle on the nightstand in the Manila Hotel penthouse suite's master bedroom and hesitantly answered it. Telephone calls in the middle of the night were rarely a good thing. The caller identified himself and said he must speak to the general. She passed the receiver to her husband. "Yes?" he answered as if on duty, which indeed he always was. His face grew increasingly taut and his jaw set as he heard his chief of staff's report. Only then did he show surprise. "Pearl Harbor?" Douglas MacArthur asked incredulously. "It should be our strongest position."[1]

Five thousand miles to the east, across the international date line, it was still December 7 over Hawaii, and hundreds of planes from six Japanese aircraft carriers had just rained destruction on the battleships of the Pacific Fleet. Deployed to Pearl Harbor to bolster American influence and response throughout the Pacific, they had become the target of a devious surprise attack. Suddenly the United States was at war.

In many respects Douglas MacArthur had been preparing for this moment his entire life. First and foremost, he was the consummate soldier, a staunch defender of his country and its honor. But around that core conviction was a complex personality. There was never any middle ground with Douglas MacArthur. He was a study in contradictions, capable of inspiring the very best in some men but also opening himself to ridicule and even inspiring hatred in others.

One either swore by MacArthur or despised him, and MacArthur himself was largely responsible for eliciting those extremes of emotion. He could be competent, caring, and visionary—a leader's leader—but he could also be vain, manipulative, and deceitful, the ultimate backstabber. The only beliefs about which he did not equivocate were his personal sense of mission for the United States and his guiding principles of duty, honor, and country. Always, in his mind, it came back to duty, honor, and country.

As the telephone rang that night, he was about to turn sixty-two years of age—relatively old for the time and just two years shy of the army's mandatory retirement age. One could not tell that by looking at him, however, or by listening to him. His attention to detail was legendary and his memory razor sharp—not just for his own experiences and the grand sweep of history but also for the minutiae of command structures and deployments around the region, those of friend and foe alike. Physically, he was still quite robust, the result of a passion for athletics in his younger days, when what he lacked in raw talent he made up for with gritty determination. His daily exercise regimen still included walks—even if only pacing in his office or on the wide terrace of the penthouse—and a morning set of calisthenics.

In the time-honored fashion of most warriors, MacArthur claimed to eschew electoral politics and know nothing of them, but behind that veneer of feigned innocence he was adroit at political persuasion and theater. Conservatives had floated his name for the presidency in 1940, but that was mostly indicative of the dearth of credible opponents to Franklin Roosevelt.

Indeed, MacArthur and FDR were of similar ilk in more than one significant way: they were sure of themselves and in control even in the face of defeat and error. Roosevelt was a gentleman politician; MacArthur a gentleman soldier. Yet a complete analysis of Douglas MacArthur's character, as well as his effectiveness as a leader, would have been decidedly premature on that December morning in the Philippines. MacArthur was still a military officer of only limited renown.

He had shown bravery and competence in the trenches of France during World War I and breathed new life into a beleaguered West Point afterward, but beyond his rise to army chief of staff at a young age, there was little about MacArthur's career to recommend it to a place of highest honor in history books.

By 1941, Douglas MacArthur had been in the army for forty-two years. Thanks to a combination of family influence and personal skill, he had been a general for twenty-three of those years. This tenure made him one of the stars of the fading World War I generation of leaders, but he was no John J. Pershing. Rather, on the night of the phone call, as he held the receiver to his ear, he was but one of a number of general officers to be remembered but hardly revered.

MacArthur had no particular command following, no loyal band of subordinates to sing his praises. Outside of his immediate family, his closest associates during the previous ten years had been his longtime aide Major Dwight D. Eisenhower and Manuel Quezon, the president of the Commonwealth of the Philippines. MacArthur was cordial in a proper, aristocratic sense to those around him, but he was never "one of the boys." Even his devoted wife usually addressed him as General in public and always referred to him as "my general."

Conservative by nature, and made more so by his military background, MacArthur came slowly to innovation — such as the establishment of an army air corps — as well as to an awareness of the changing political and military realities of Japan's actions in the Far East. Yet he had come to love the Philippines and its people. His father had once served there in the role of conqueror; MacArthur was spending his last professional years there in his chosen role as guarantor of its independence. He had repeatedly assured Quezon and President Roosevelt that the Philippines could be defended against any foe. Although colored by his tendency toward grandiosity and overconfidence, his defense plans for the islands were an impressive blueprint for a citizen army that would defend myriad beaches throughout the archipelago and repel any invasion. Those plans were about to be put to the test.

Early on that December morning, Douglas MacArthur was hardly a household name. Yet within six months' time, he would be hailed as the hero of Bataan and Corregidor—stunning American defeats though they were—and come to personify the war effort in the Pacific in the general public's eyes on two continents. As he returned the telephone receiver to its cradle, one thing was irrevocably clear: Douglas MacArthur was at war.

PART I

ESCAPE

1941–1942

*I wish to reiterate my appreciation of the splendid
support you and the War Department are giving me.
No field commander could ask more.*
                              — MACARTHUR TO CHIEF OF
                         STAFF GEORGE C. MARSHALL,
                                     OCTOBER 28, 1941

*MacArthur in a pretty complete disregard of
everything except his own personal interests has
taken his entire staff away with him from Bataan.*
                         — DIARY OF SECRETARY OF WAR
                                    HENRY L. STIMSON,
                                       MARCH 23, 1942

On his lone visit to Bataan from Corregidor, MacArthur tours the front to visit corps commanders with chief of staff Richard K. Sutherland (over left shoulder), January 10, 1942. *Courtesy of the MacArthur Memorial, Norfolk, VA*

CHAPTER ONE

First Charge, First War

Douglas MacArthur always lived in his father's shadow. It grew long before he was born, when the crisp notes of a bugle sounded the call to advance through the fading light of a November afternoon in 1863. After a week of rain, it was cold and damp—even in southern Tennessee. Union troops under Ulysses S. Grant had encountered tough resistance as they tried to dislodge Braxton Bragg's Confederates from Missionary Ridge and lift the siege of Chattanooga. Grant's plan called for William Tecumseh Sherman to surmount Missionary Ridge from the north while Joseph "Fighting Joe" Hooker swept up its southern flanks, squeezing Bragg between them like a lemon.

But Sherman's divisions bogged down against stout defenses on Tunnel Hill, and Hooker's troops slowed after retreating Confederates destroyed a critical bridge over Chattanooga Creek. That left the remainder of Grant's army hunkered down in a series of newly captured rifle pits directly below the center of the Confederate line. From the slopes above, Bragg's forces poured an unrelenting fire into the massed Union troops.

Quite suddenly, other bugles took up the call to advance. Regiment after regiment from Philip Sheridan's division climbed out of the rifle pits and started up the ridge behind a bright array of fluttering flags. The divisions on either side of Sheridan's followed suit, and soon a line of blue was crawling skyward along a two-mile front. Grant was dumbfounded. "Who gave the order to advance?" he demanded. None of his staff had a ready answer.[1]

At the forefront of Sheridan's effort was an eighteen-year-old captain from Milwaukee—his regiment's adjutant—exhorting his troops with shouts of "On, Wisconsin!" Up Missionary Ridge the 24th Wisconsin went. Its color sergeant fell in a hail of bullets; one color bearer was bayoneted and a second decapitated by a cannonball. The young captain nonetheless unabashedly seized the regimental standard and repeated his cry of "On, Wisconsin!" as the Union line surged toward the top of the ridge.

Which regimental flag reached the summit first was difficult to say, but Captain Arthur MacArthur Jr. waved his banner with all his might as Sheridan's division swarmed up and over the crest. Then young MacArthur, exhausted and covered in the blood of others but, miraculously, unhurt himself, collapsed in a heap. According to MacArthur family lore, Sheridan dismounted, swept the boy adjutant up in his arms, and tearfully commanded, "Take care of him. He has just won the Medal of Honor."[2]

Whether the 24th Wisconsin moved forward at young MacArthur's behest or Sheridan gave a direct order for his division to advance is uncertain. Regardless, those few minutes on Missionary Ridge would forever overshadow Arthur MacArthur's military career. Among the war stories MacArthur later told his sons, the tale of this day in 1863 was oft repeated. For his third child, Douglas, the Missionary Ridge charge was to carry with it the lesson that initiative and aggressiveness—even when unaccompanied by direct orders—were enough to carry the day.

The MacArthurs were of Scottish descent, Arthur MacArthur Sr. having arrived in Massachusetts in 1825 from Glasgow at the age of ten with his widowed mother. Arthur studied law in New York, married Aurelia Belcher, and moved west to Milwaukee, Wisconsin, with a four-year-old son, Arthur junior. The senior MacArthur became enmeshed in Wisconsin politics and, after a brief stint as lieutenant governor, was elected a circuit judge in 1857.

By the time of the Civil War, Arthur junior, not quite sixteen, went to his father determined to enlist. Patience was not a MacArthur family trait, but the judge counseled it anyway—to no avail. When an appointment to the United States Military Academy at West Point proved unattainable in the short term, Arthur junior took matters into his own hands, and on August 4, 1862 — two months after his seventeenth birthday — he marched out of Milwaukee as a first lieutenant and adjutant of the 24th Wisconsin Volunteer Infantry, the judge having relented and lent his political clout, securing Arthur junior his officer position.[3]

The 24th Wisconsin became part of General Philip Sheridan's division in Kentucky and received its baptism by fire at Perryville that October. Neither side could claim victory, but Sheridan noticed Arthur junior's poise under fire and awarded him a brevet promotion to captain. After the Chattanooga campaign and that day on Missionary Ridge, the 24th Wisconsin fought with Sherman to capture Atlanta before coming back to Tennessee for the Battle of Franklin late in 1864. There, Arthur junior suffered wounds to his chest and leg that ended his combat service.

But what a war it had been. Still only nineteen when the Confederacy surrendered, Arthur MacArthur emerged from it an acknowledged leader of men. Having risen to the brevet rank of full colonel, he had commanded the 24th Wisconsin after Missionary Ridge. Recuperating in Milwaukee from his wounds, he studied law for several months to please the judge but quickly determined to make the regular army his career.[4]

Young Arthur's decision led to a string of rather dismal postwar assignments, from dusty army forts in the West to occupation duty in Louisiana. Advancement above his permanent rank of captain appeared unlikely. Past exploits and good looks aside, there wasn't much to recommend him to the ladies, but during a Mardi Gras ball in New Orleans in 1875, he met Mary Pinkney Hardy, a twenty-two-year-old southern belle who was visiting from Norfolk, Virginia. Pinky, as she was known, was taken with this Yankee even though her brothers had fought for the Confederacy and her ancestral home, Riveredge, had suffered under occupation by Union troops. A whirlwind courtship by correspondence ensued, and Pinky and Arthur were married at Riveredge on May 19, 1875, the absence of several of her disapproving brothers notwithstanding.

Fortunately for Pinky, her first assignment as an army wife was in Washington, DC, where Arthur was assigned staff duty. By then,

Arthur senior was on the bench of the United States District Court for the District of Columbia. The first of three sons, Arthur III, was born in 1876 at Riveredge and a second, Malcolm, in 1878, while Pinky was vacationing with the Hardy family in Connecticut.

Meanwhile, Captain MacArthur had been posted back to Louisiana as a company commander and then ordered to Little Rock, Arkansas. Pinky had plans to return to Riveredge for the birth of their third child, but Douglas arrived early, on January 26, 1880, in a two-story former arsenal that had been converted to married officers' quarters. Decades later, with his usual flair for the dramatic, Douglas MacArthur would say that his first recollection was that of a bugle call.[5]

That recollection might also have been of wind and blowing sand, because the MacArthur family spent the next three and a half years at Fort Wingate, in the high desert of New Mexico Territory. Pinky made the best of the post's spartan facilities as she raised three small boys, yet in April of 1883, while the family was on leave to visit her relatives in Norfolk, four-year-old Malcolm succumbed to measles. His loss was a terrible blow, but it seemed only to increase Pinky's devotion to Arthur III and Douglas. "This tie," Douglas later acknowledged, "was to become one of the dominant factors of my life."[6]

In 1889, after twenty-three years as a captain in the regular army, Arthur MacArthur was promoted to major and once again posted to Washington. Judge MacArthur had retired from the federal bench two years before, and this gave him freedom to use his connections to promote Arthur junior's military career as well as his family's social status. Pinky was back in her element, and Washington gave young Douglas his first glimpse at what he called "that whirlpool of glitter and pomp, of politics and diplomacy, of statesmanship and intrigue." He professed it no substitute for "the color and excitement of the frontier West"; but of those worldly characteristics, he would never be able to get enough.[7]

Among the events in which Judge MacArthur had a hand were Arthur junior's assignment to the adjutant general's office, his belated receipt of the Medal of Honor for his dash up Missionary Ridge, and Arthur III's appointment to the United States Naval Academy. According to Douglas, Judge MacArthur also taught him to play poker and administered a life lesson or two along the way. On the last hand the two ever played,

Douglas bet every chip he had on four queens and beamed with confidence until his grandfather quietly laid down four kings and opined, "My dear boy, nothing is sure in this life. Everything is relative."[8]

With Arthur III headed to Annapolis, the other three MacArthurs returned to Texas for duty at Fort Sam Houston, in San Antonio, Texas, in the fall of 1893. Upon his high school graduation four years later, Douglas hoped to enter West Point. Before his death, Judge MacArthur had undertaken a final round of lobbying in support of his progeny and orchestrated letters of recommendation for a presidential appointment for Douglas. Despite these, Democrat Grover Cleveland declined to award him one of his four appointments.

This rejection may have been the first occasion upon which Douglas, who would always be paranoid about the way the powers in Washington treated him, felt a bias against him. But if such a bias then existed, it did not appear to be politically motivated. Another round of recommendation letters the following year also failed to secure him a presidential appointment from William McKinley, a Republican and Civil War veteran.[9]

During these years, Arthur MacArthur Jr.'s star was at last rising through army ranks. Promoted to lieutenant colonel in May of 1896, Arthur was assigned to the Department of Dakota at Saint Paul, Minnesota, the following year. Pinky and Douglas used the occasion to return to Milwaukee—to which Arthur commuted when possible—so that Douglas might establish residency within the congressional district of Theobald Otjen, a faithful and longtime friend of Judge MacArthur. One way or another, Douglas was determined to get into West Point.

When war broke out with Spain over Cuba in 1898, Arthur was appointed a brigadier general of volunteers and initially assigned to expeditionary troops organizing at Chickamauga, Georgia, within sight of Missionary Ridge. Events moved quickly in this ninety-day war, however, and before Arthur could sail for Cuba, he was ordered to the Philippines, where he would soon be made a major general.

The MacArthur who went off to Cuba proved to be Arthur III, who, having graduated from Annapolis in 1896, took part in the naval battle off Santiago along with 1897 Annapolis graduate William D. Leahy. Convinced he was being left out of this family affair, Douglas redoubled his efforts at preparatory study and scored first on Congressman Otjen's competitive exam for the class of 145 plebes entering West Point in 1899.[10]

West Point and its traditions would forever be at the core of Douglas MacArthur's personality, motivation, and ambition. Sworn into the Corps of Cadets on June 13, 1899, MacArthur brought with him two things that would strongly influence his future. One was enormous personal pride—both in himself and in the accomplishments of his father; the other was his mother. Yes, it was true: Douglas MacArthur arrived at West Point accompanied by his devoted mother, who gave no sign of leaving. With Arthur junior still on duty in the Philippines, Pinky moved into the decrepit Craney's Hotel, on the northern edge of the parade ground, and stayed for two years to keep a close eye on her offspring. (Another young man, whose country home was just up the Hudson and who was two years MacArthur's junior, would also remain under his mother's protective eye as he started classes at Harvard the following year; his name was Franklin Roosevelt.)

MacArthur's pride was sorely put to the test during his first summer as a plebe. Vicious hazing was the academy norm, and MacArthur's dashing good looks, his father's notoriety, and the presence of his mother all combined to make MacArthur a ready target. By force of personality, he survived repeated rounds of physical abuse bordering on torture with what one first classman (senior) recalled were "fortitude and dignity."[11]

MacArthur finished his first year at the top of his class and was on his way to a similar finish his sophomore year when his pride almost derailed him in an incident that speaks volumes about his sense of personal honor. Knowing that he held the highest average in mathematics, MacArthur expected to be excused from the final exam, as was the custom. When he nonetheless found his name on the examination list, MacArthur stormed to the personal residence of the department head, Lieutenant Colonel Wright P. Edgerton, a longtime West Point professor who served during the Spanish-American War. Edgerton might have put him on report for this breach of etiquette, but the colonel calmly informed the cadet that in addition to grade average, those exempt were required to have taken two-thirds of the course quizzes. Because of absences for illness, MacArthur was short one quiz.

MacArthur boldly asserted that Edgerton should have informed him of this and given him the opportunity to make up the quiz. Edgerton made no reply, and MacArthur spun on his heel and angrily marched back to his barracks, where, according to his roommate, he grandly declared, "If my name is not off that list before nine in the morning, I'll resign!"

The following day, ten minutes before the scheduled exam, MacArthur received a message from Edgerton excusing him. It is far too much speculation to suggest Pinky's intervention on Douglas's behalf, but she was not above doing so, and there is no better explanation for Edgerton's leniency. According to his roommate, MacArthur believed it his duty to obey an order "no matter how disagreeable," but when he felt he had been treated unjustly, MacArthur considered it an affront to his personal honor. MacArthur would always be quick to paint his disagreements with superiors in such terms.[12]

On the athletic fields, MacArthur won his varsity *A* on the baseball team in the spring of 1901, playing left field in Army's first matchup ever against Navy. Army won 4–3, and by MacArthur's telling, he scored the winning run when, after drawing a walk, he stole second base and went scurrying home on an errant throw into the outfield.

At five feet eleven and a half inches in height but a skimpy 135 pounds, MacArthur was too light for collegiate football, but he lent his enthusiasm to the gridiron team as its manager in the fall of 1902. With President Theodore Roosevelt in attendance at Franklin Field in Philadelphia, MacArthur's Army team beat Navy, 22–8. Navy's regular fullback was injured, and its team was playing with a second-stringer, a third-year cadet and future admiral named William F. Halsey Jr.[13]

It was as a military leader, however, that MacArthur really shined. During his senior year he was appointed first captain of the Corps of Cadets, the highest position in the cadet chain of command. He served as a corporal during his second year and his company's first sergeant his third year, the only year he failed to rank first in his class academically. (He was fourth.) Almost uncannily, he stood second in least number of demerits in each of his first three years. None of his few infractions was particularly egregious, but together they hint at MacArthur's flaunting of his independence as he achieved higher cadet rank:

"long hair at inspection"—personal style in uniforms would be a MacArthur trademark; "slow obeying call to quarters"—taking things in his own time; "trifling with drawn sabre"—always exhibiting theatrical flair.[14]

Despite these minor violations, when MacArthur graduated from West Point on June 11, 1903, he stood academically and militarily at the top of his class of ninety-four newly commissioned second lieutenants. Major General Arthur MacArthur, who had returned from duty in the Philippines and by that time commanded the Department of California, watched with pride as Douglas received his diploma.

Outgoing secretary of war Elihu Root warned the graduates that another war was "bound to come," adding, "Prepare your country for that war."[15]

Having been assigned to the Army Corps of Engineers, as was the norm for graduates who ranked at the top of their class, Douglas MacArthur embarked for the Philippines with the Third Engineer Battalion in September of 1903. Landing in Manila after a thirty-eight-day voyage, the shiny new second lieutenant inspected his father's old haunts and immediately felt at home. "The Philippines charmed me," MacArthur later recalled, and "fastened me with a grip that has never relaxed." His posts included Tacloban, on the island of Leyte, and Manila, where two newly minted law school graduates, Manuel Quezon and Sergio Osmeña, were reportedly among his Filipino acquaintances.[16]

By the spring of 1904, MacArthur was a first lieutenant. After a year in the Philippines, which included an almost ritual bout with malaria, he returned to the United States and was soon appointed acting chief engineer of the Department of California, his father's command. Whether Arthur MacArthur, who was then serving as a military observer in Manchuria as the Russo-Japanese War wound down, had a hand in his son's assignment is unknown, but three months later, as the general prepared to embark from Yokohama for a grand tour of the Far East, he requested that Douglas accompany him as his aide-de-camp.

The following nine months gave Lieutenant MacArthur invaluable lessons in the history, politics, and military preparedness of the Far East.

The MacArthurs' itinerary—Pinky was along, too, to make it even more of a family affair—led them from Japan to Shanghai, Hong Kong, Java, Singapore, and Burma. By January of 1906, they were in Calcutta, and a two-month tour of India took them all the way to the Khyber Pass. Then it was eastward to Bangkok, Saigon, and more of China before returning to Japan. Among General MacArthur's observations were that Japan's imperialist ambitions posed "the problem of the Pacific" and that stronger Philippine defenses were necessary to prevent the archipelago "from becoming a liability rather than an asset to the United States."[17]

By the time of this tour, Arthur MacArthur, the aging veteran of the charge up Missionary Ridge, had been causing President Theodore Roosevelt and his new secretary of war, William Howard Taft, a good deal of angst. Taft and MacArthur first crossed swords in 1900 in the Philippines over the differing roles of civilian and military authority when Taft was civilian governor of the islands. Before MacArthur's Far East tour, the general had been critical of plans to form an American general staff modeled after the German army and gone so far as to predict a war with Germany. "Recently I had to rebuke MacArthur for speaking ill of the Germans," Theodore Roosevelt wrote Taft. "Our army and navy officers must not comment about foreign powers in a way that will cause trouble."[18]

Arthur MacArthur's extended tour throughout the Far East may even have been Roosevelt and Taft's way of getting him out of the mainstream. Despite a promotion to lieutenant general that many viewed as something of a sop, MacArthur was not made chief of staff even as he became the army's highest-ranking officer. Instead he was ordered to Milwaukee to await a future assignment that never came.

The result was that Arthur MacArthur retired from his beloved army in 1909, shortly after Taft's inauguration as president, with a bad taste in his mouth, going so far as to instruct Pinky that he should not be buried in his uniform. But there was to be a silver lining to his father's retirement for Douglas. Many of the men coming into the army's top ranks, including then chief of staff J. Franklin Bell and future chiefs Leonard Wood and Peyton C. March, owed a great deal to Arthur MacArthur for nurturing their careers. They in turn would do the same for his son.[19]

That son loved the army as much as his father had, but two examples of his behavior—acts that smacked of his father's independence—threatened to derail Douglas's career. They occurred not because of lack of competence but because of his insistence on setting his own priorities. While posted to Washington to attend an engineering school, Douglas was also appointed a social aide-de-camp at the White House. MacArthur found this far more interesting than engineering school and ignored his studies so much that the chief of engineers wrote, "His work was far inferior to that which his West Point record shows him to be capable of."[20]

Douglas didn't do any better at a subsequent assignment in his hometown, Milwaukee. He was supposed to be developing harbors on Lake Michigan, but he preferred spending long hours with his father discussing military strategy, the Far East, and the inadequacies of William Howard Taft. Then, too, there was Pinky. She wanted to show off Douglas to the Milwaukee social set. Douglas could never say no to his parents and often chose these commitments over his duties.

When his commanding officer wrote that MacArthur's "duties were not performed in a satisfactory manner," MacArthur judged the report—despite its truth—one of those affronts to his personal honor against which he often railed. He protested "the ineradicable blemish" placed on his record and argued his belief that "my presence in the office was not regarded as a matter of much practical importance." Then, in typical fashion, MacArthur sent his response not to his immediate superior but directly to the chief of engineers, who reprimanded him for doing so and noted that MacArthur's ignorance of proper channels and his indelicate words were themselves justification for his superior's assessment.[21]

Lieutenant MacArthur was momentarily silenced, but as usual he shared the exchange with his mother. Pinky was furious. How dare they treat her boy that way? She went so far as to write E. H. Harriman of the Union Pacific Railroad about a job with greater promise for Douglas. But it was one of his father's friends who saved him.

In the midst of the row over MacArthur's performance in Milwaukee, army chief of staff J. Franklin Bell, who had served under Arthur MacArthur in the Philippines, signed orders sending Douglas to the garrison at Fort Leavenworth, Kansas, then the center of the army's junior officer training. Suddenly back in his element, MacArthur took command of Company K of the Third Engineer Battalion and transformed it from the lowest-rated of the twenty-one companies at the post to the champions. Later he was made an instructor in the Field Engineer School.[22]

His record at Fort Leavenworth got him promoted to captain and again noticed in Washington. Meanwhile Arthur, his recent disappointment with the army aside, had been giving a speech to a reunion of the 24th Wisconsin in Milwaukee on September 5, 1912, when he suffered a stroke and died at the podium. "My whole world changed that night," Douglas later wrote. "Never have I been able to heal the wound in my heart."[23]

Within weeks of Arthur's death, another of his protégés, then chief of staff Major General Leonard Wood, tapped Douglas for duty with the General Staff of the War Department, and the general's widow took up residence with her son at his new Washington assignment. For once, Pinky felt that her youngest was being fully appreciated, as Wood rated him "a highly intelligent and very efficient officer."[24]

General Wood's confidence in Captain MacArthur was at the core of a secret mission MacArthur undertook to Veracruz in May of 1914. A change of government in Mexico had resulted in a perceived insult to the American flag, and the United States Navy and Marines occupied the port of Veracruz on the Gulf of Mexico in response. Wood prepared to take the field with an army expeditionary force, but he needed intelligence on the state of Mexican railroads beyond Veracruz. Rather than involve the local American commander, he dispatched MacArthur.

Arriving in Veracruz, MacArthur slipped behind the Mexican lines and located a number of locomotives that could be commandeered. Whether he went beyond his orders by personally undertaking this mission rather than simply interviewing locals became a matter of some debate, because American troops had been explicitly restricted to Veracruz to minimize the chance of deadly incidents. As it was, MacArthur and his bribed Mexican companions from the Veracruz and Alvarado Railway exchanged gunfire with locals that may have left as many as seven of them dead. Even MacArthur, writing about his decision to undertake the mission personally, acknowledged, "I may have been right or I may have been wrong."[25]

19

MacArthur made his report to Wood, and that might have been the end of the matter, except that one of the officers in Veracruz wrote Wood suggesting that MacArthur be awarded the Medal of Honor for his exploits. Wood made the recommendation, citing MacArthur's own initiative, the risk to his life, and "an amount of enterprise and courage worthy of high commendation." Harboring visions of his father's Medal of Honor for his dash up Missionary Ridge, MacArthur eagerly watched the progress of Wood's recommendation through the War Department bureaucracy.

A review board of the General Staff recommended against the award. The majority questioned the advisability of the reconnaissance without the knowledge of the local commander, and a minority report—also declining the award—noted "nothing unusual in combat, nothing extraordinary and such as clearly to distinguish him for gallantry and intrepidity above his comrades." Again, that might have been the end of the matter.

But Douglas MacArthur was by then on his high horse—certain that his personal honor had been impugned and that behind-the-scenes powers on the General Staff were out to deny him due recognition. Before the board's judgment was final, MacArthur wrote a blistering memorandum to the new chief of staff, Major General Hugh L. Scott, citing the review board's "rigid narrow-mindedness and lack of imagination."

This almost insubordinate missive took even MacArthur's staunchest supporters by surprise. Scott circulated MacArthur's memo to the three men responsible for passing final judgment on the board's recommendation, and any hope that they might overrule the board was put to rest by MacArthur's own arrogance. Thus MacArthur managed to turn what should have been a star on his record—Medal of Honor or not—into a blemish that marked him difficult and mercurial in the eyes of many on the General Staff.[26]

What made Douglas MacArthur's pursuit of the Medal of Honor all the more misguided was the fact that by then Europe was embroiled in war. German and Austro-Hungarian armies were bogged down in trenches opposite British, French, and Italian armies in France and Italy, while

German victories on the eastern front pushed Russia down the road to revolution. The United States remained ostensibly neutral until April of 1917, when Germany's unrestricted submarine warfare prompted President Woodrow Wilson to ask Congress for a declaration of war.

By then, Major Douglas MacArthur, still on the General Staff, had spent a year as press liaison for secretary of war Newton D. Baker. When Major General Frederick Funston, the presumed head of any expeditionary force, dropped dead of a heart attack several months before the declaration of war, it was MacArthur who interrupted a dinner party that Secretary Baker was giving for President Wilson with the news.

According to MacArthur's account, Wilson asked Baker who would take over the army, and Baker in turn asked MacArthur whom the army would choose. He could not speak for the army, MacArthur replied, "but for myself the choice would unquestionably be General Pershing." Wilson supposedly acknowledged, "It would be a good choice."[27] Major General John J. Pershing, another Arthur MacArthur protégé, indeed became head of the American Expeditionary Force and later in 1917 was made a full (four-star) general.

Douglas MacArthur's relationship with Newton Baker paid its own dividends. Scrambling to organize American troops, Baker asked MacArthur how National Guard units might best be utilized. MacArthur suggested taking small units from many states and forming a composite division. Brigadier General William A. Mann, chief of the War Department's militia bureau, concurred, and MacArthur replied, "Fine; that will stretch over the whole country like a rainbow." Thus the Forty-Second "Rainbow" Infantry Division was formed.[28]

Baker chose Mann to command the new division, but because Mann was approaching retirement age, MacArthur suggested that the most experienced colonel on the General Staff become the division's chief of staff. Baker replied that the post was already filled and put his hand on MacArthur's shoulder. MacArthur mildly protested that he was only a major, but Baker assured him that his promotion to colonel would be forthcoming. When asked whether he wanted his new commission to continue in the Engineers, MacArthur declined. "Dazed as I was," he recalled, "I could think only of the old 24th Wisconsin Infantry, and answered, 'No, the Infantry.'"[29]

*   *   *

Twenty-seven-thousand men from twenty-six states assembled at a training center at Mineola, New York, on Long Island, and the Rainbow Division embarked for France in mid-October of 1917. But upon its arrival, all was not well. Pershing and his staff planned to break it up and use the pieces as replacement units for other divisions. So much for the rainbow!

Mann and MacArthur howled in protest all the way from Pershing's headquarters in Chaumont to Washington. Mann used his political connections, and MacArthur reached out to press contacts he had made while working for Secretary Baker, to plead for public support to keep the division intact. MacArthur also appealed to Pershing's chief of staff, Brigadier General James G. Harbord, and asked him to review the division and judge its merits for himself. Harbord did so, and the result—quite possibly encouraged by Baker—was that the Forty-Second remained a separate combat division.[30]

But MacArthur was not the only one with an agenda. His dear mother, Pinky, at a spry sixty-five and no less protective of him than ever, had been lobbying Baker for Douglas's promotion to brigadier general even before the Rainbow Division sailed from Long Island. Claiming to Baker, "It is only through you that he can ever hope to get advancement of any kind," Pinky assured the secretary that even men as able as her Douglas "must first get the opportunity in order to achieve success, and it is this opportunity I am seeking from you."[31]

Pinky spent the winter of 1917–18 in Santa Barbara with Arthur III's family; he was at sea in command of the cruiser *Chattanooga*. The following June, she took up residence in a Washington, DC, hotel and pressed her case more aggressively. With Pinky almost on his doorstep, Baker reminded her that she knew his "personal affection for Colonel MacArthur too well to doubt" but asserted that the matter of promotions rested with General Pershing. The next day, Pinky turned her pen to Pershing.[32]

"My dear General Pershing," Pinky's syrupy letter began. "I am taking the liberty of writing you a little heart-to-heart letter embolden[ed] by the thought of old friendship for you and yours, and the knowledge of my late husband's great admiration for you." Unabashedly stressing her connections to Secretary Baker—however tenuous—Pinky went on to note that three officers junior to Douglas had already been appointed brigadier generals. Playing her own age card, she confessed that her one ambition was "to live long enough to see this son made a General Officer."[33]

The truth of the matter was that Pinky's boy was well on his way to a general's star on his own. The Rainbow Division had completed its field training and entered the trenches in March of 1918, becoming the first American division to be responsible on its own for an entire sector. Heavy defensive fighting against German attacks followed east of Reims. Despite his position as chief of staff, MacArthur was everywhere along the front lines. Fearless, flamboyant, and egotistical to a fault, he led from the front and gave no quarter to friend or foe alike.

"MacArthur is the bloodiest fighting man in this army," the Rainbow's new commander, Major General Charles T. Menoher, reported. "I'm afraid we're going to lose him sometime, for there's no risk of battle that any soldier is called upon to take that he is not liable to look up and see MacArthur at his side."[34]

On June 29, 1918, much to his mother's pride, MacArthur's name appeared in the *New York Times* on a list of forty-three colonels appointed to brigadier general. It is likely that Pershing had not yet received Pinky's latest plea and unlikely that it would have had much impact in any event. Far more likely is that Secretary Baker and Arthur MacArthur protégé Peyton C. March, who had recently become army chief of staff, saw to it that Douglas was included. The result was that when Pershing received Pinky's letter, he was able to cable her "my sincere congratulations upon his advancement."[35]

The Allied offensive north of Château-Thierry put the Rainbow Division in a seesaw battle for Sergy. In the thick of the fighting, General Menoher relieved the commander of the division's Eighty-Fourth Brigade and put MacArthur in command. After six of what MacArthur called "the bitterest days and nights of the war for the Rainbow," the new brigade commander conducted a stealthy reconnaissance with only an aide into the no-man's-land between the lines and found that the Germans had withdrawn. MacArthur, who had not slept in ninety-six

23

hours, reported the news to Menoher and then collapsed into an exhausted sleep. When he awoke, he learned that Menoher had recommended him for the Silver Star.[36]

By mid-September, the Rainbow was engaged, along with more than six hundred thousand American and French infantrymen, in attacking the bulge in the German line at the Saint-Mihiel salient. As the Germans fell back, MacArthur made another behind-the-lines reconnaissance and discovered the rail junction of Metz largely undefended. He pleaded for the Eighty-Fourth Brigade to lead an assault, but the high command went ahead with its long-planned Meuse-Argonne offensive and suffered staggering losses. MacArthur wrote in his memoirs that he learned from his superiors' ill-fated "pursuit of previously conceived ideas."[37]

Pulled out of the line and deployed westward, the Rainbow Division endured the thickest of the fighting in the Argonne forest. As the advance along the American front stalled, the Eighty-Fourth Brigade gathered below the dense woods of the hill known as the Côte de Châtillon. When General Menoher asked MacArthur if his brigade could take the hill, MacArthur was unusually candid and voiced doubt. On the evening before the scheduled attack, the corps commander, Major General Charles P. Summerall, appeared at the Rainbow's headquarters looking like he was down to his last hope.

Clutching a steaming cup of black coffee, Summerall suddenly turned to MacArthur and pleaded, "Give me Châtillon, MacArthur. Give me Châtillon, or a list of five thousand casualties."

"All right, General," MacArthur replied theatrically. "We'll take it, or my name will head the list."[38]

The hill was taken, but at a horrific cost. Out of one battalion of 1,450 men and twenty-five officers, only three hundred men and six officers survived. A grateful Summerall recommended MacArthur for the Medal of Honor and the second star of a major general. The awards board at Pershing's headquarters granted neither but bestowed a second Distinguished Service Cross, second only to the Medal of Honor, in consolation. "On a field where courage was the rule," the citation read, "his courage was the dominant factor."[39]

Throughout his time at the front, MacArthur's personal eccentricities and nonregulation dress also attracted considerable attention. He dressed in a turtleneck sweater and muffler—his excuse: he was susceptible to tonsillitis—carried a riding crop, and declined both a helmet and a pistol. Criticism of his behavior by Pershing's staff became the norm. MacArthur's response was vintage MacArthur—he had an answer for everything: "I wore no iron helmet because it hurt my head. I carried no gas mask because it hampered my movements. I went unarmed because it was not my purpose to engage in personal combat, but to direct others. I used a riding crop out of long habit on the plains. I fought from the front as I could not effectively manipulate my troops from the rear."[40]

Nonetheless, Pershing recommended MacArthur for promotion to major general and command of his division. Then came the Armistice, on November 11, 1918, and promotions were placed on hold. In short order all division commands reverted to existing major generals. Brigadier General MacArthur's record as one of the fighting generals could not, however, be denied. He had been awarded seven Silver Stars, two Distinguished Service Crosses, the Distinguished Service Medal, two Purple Hearts, and a number of French decorations. The Rainbow Division paid for them and the other awards its members received with the third-highest casualty count among American divisions: 14,683 killed and wounded.[41]

Rumors circulated that MacArthur would be assigned to postwar duty in France, but he was anxious to return to America. As was his custom, he informed the adjutant general of a personal exigency: "My mother's health is critical," MacArthur cabled, "and I fear [the] consequences [of] my failure to return as scheduled." Whatever else the powers in the War Department thought of one of their youngest brigadiers, they were not about to trifle with the health of the widow of Arthur MacArthur. Her Douglas arrived in New York with his division on schedule, on April 25, 1919, to await his next assignment.[42]

As it turned out, he was going back to West Point. Never mind that, increasingly flamboyant in dress, he would return to the storied plain nattily attired in a raccoon coat and looking more like a Roaring Twenties fraternity brother than a military academy superintendent.

CHAPTER TWO

West Point to the Philippines

Douglas MacArthur always made it seem as if General John J. Pershing was one of his biggest supporters. Pinky's missives on her son's behalf notwithstanding, MacArthur wrote gushy letters to Pershing, praising him despite evidence that the general and his staff were less than enamored with the flamboyant brigadier. It's possible that Pershing was a true MacArthur fan and that the hints of coolness that whiff across their relationship are a result of Pershing's own austere personality. But as MacArthur returned from France in the spring of 1919, it was chief of staff Peyton C. March, always the loyal Arthur MacArthur protégé, who remained Douglas's greatest champion and ordered his assignment to West Point.[1]

Reporting to Washington, MacArthur professed surprise with his new post, telling March, "I am not an educator. I am a field soldier. Besides there are so many of my old professors there. I can't do it." March assured MacArthur that he not only could do it but also would do it. March's orders were simple and direct: revitalize the academy and bring it into the twentieth century.[2]

In truth, March was doing MacArthur a huge favor on two fronts: first, despite the dispirited state in which World War I had left West Point, its superintendency remained a plum assignment, and in that position March could make MacArthur's temporary rank of brigadier general permanent, giving him a decided leg up on his contemporaries. As for his professors, MacArthur indeed would be one of the youngest

26

superintendents in West Point history, but his age would be the least of his problems in convincing the old guard that changes were necessary.[3]

The old guard wanted less exposure to the real world, but, having seen that world up close, MacArthur believed there should be much more exposure to it. Calling West Point "cloistered almost to a monastic extent," MacArthur instituted weekend leaves for upperclassmen, started a cadet newspaper, formed a cadet honor committee to enact and enforce a code of ethics, allowed the entire corps to attend away football games, and issued each cadet an allowance of five dollars per month to spend as he pleased.[4]

If he found anything that didn't fit his concept of military life as he had experienced it in France, MacArthur changed it. He ordered the corps to Camp Dix, in New Jersey, to receive training in weapons and tactics from tough regular army sergeants, many of whom had been with MacArthur in the trenches in France. On the curriculum side, MacArthur broadened exposure to the humanities, particularly history, English, composition, and speech, telling critics that part of being an effective leader was the ability to communicate articulately. He urged less emphasis on the age-old technique of rote recitation and placed more emphasis on discussion.[5]

MacArthur also became a champion of athletics, both for the physical conditioning and the esprit de corps it promoted, and he required every cadet to take part in an intramural sport. He wrote the words that he ordered chiseled into the stone of West Point's gymnasium: "Upon the fields of friendly strife are sown the seeds that, upon other fields, on other days, will bear the fruits of victory." Still, at the intercollegiate level, despite his sideline cheering and gift of tickets to General Pershing, MacArthur endured three straight years of Army football losses to Navy at the Polo Grounds in New York City: 6–0, 7–0, and 7–0.[6]

Two things, however, didn't change at West Point. The first was MacArthur's flair for exhibiting his personal taste in fashion, and the second was Pinky. The superintendent still removed the wire brace from his cap, carried a well-worn riding crop, and wore a short overcoat despite the full-length models then prescribed. And, as she had done when he was an underclassman, Pinky moved with him to West Point. This time, however, instead of the dismal Craney's Hotel, she occupied the two-story superintendent's house and served as his official hostess.[7]

As usual, the widow of General Arthur MacArthur did not shy away from asserting command. On one occasion Douglas happened to engage several plebes in conversation as they passed his residence while returning to their quarters with a carton of ice cream—thanks to his practice of providing allowances. Pinky opened an upstairs window and called out, "Douglas! You must stop talking to those boys and let them go. Don't you see that their ice cream is beginning to melt?"[8]

MacArthur's responsibilities included testifying before congressional committees about West Point's reforms and budget needs. He wasn't always successful. He asked for an expansion of the cadet corps from 1,300 to 2,500 men and proposed a vigorous capital construction program. Congress, fully embracing the country's postwar isolationism and budget constraints, granted neither, although it reestablished the academy's four-year program, which had been shortened during the war.[9]

Even when he wasn't successful before Congress, MacArthur had plenty of cover on his flanks as long as Newton Baker was secretary of war and Peyton March was chief of staff, but with the Harding administration's arrival in March of 1921, that changed. John W. Weeks became secretary of war, and John J. Pershing succeeded March as chief of staff. It was no secret that MacArthur had zealously supported his old commander, Leonard Wood, for the Republican presidential nomination, and between the old guard at West Point criticizing his reforms—including a group of alumni that MacArthur's adjutant dubbed DOGS, for "disgruntled old grads"—and Pershing's staff, which remained largely the same as the clique from Chaumont, MacArthur's position was soon exposed.[10]

MacArthur had expected to serve a four-year tour at West Point, but in November of 1921 he received a letter from Pershing notifying him of a War Department policy that made foreign service mandatory for the entire officer corps. MacArthur's name, Pershing warned, was "high up for this," and his successor at West Point would be named soon so that the new superintendent could relieve MacArthur "immediately after graduation in June, 1922."[11]

This may well have been a simple matter of postwar shuffling, but then an event occurred that carried personal overtones and whetted the appetites of gossips far and wide: General MacArthur heard wedding bells.

Henrietta Louise Cromwell Brooks — she detested her given first name and was known by her middle name, Louise, for most of her life — was ten years Douglas MacArthur's junior, recently divorced, the mother of two young children, fabulously wealthy, and by all accounts the epitome of a liberated Roaring Twenties woman racing at breakneck speed to embrace far more rights than those granted by the recently ratified Nineteenth Amendment.[12]

Petite, dark-eyed, with a stylish bob of hair, Louise exuded a sensual sexuality that drew MacArthur to her like a moth to a flame. But she was equally attracted to him. "I had never before met so vivid, so captivating, so magnetic a man," newspaperman William Allen White wrote of MacArthur after interviewing him in France at the close of the war. "He stood six feet, had a clean-shaven face, a clean-cut mouth, nose, and chin, lots of brown hair, good eyes with a 'come hither' in them that must have played the devil with the girls."[13] If that was how a veteran no-nonsense Kansas newspaper publisher felt, then it was no wonder that Louise was smitten.

For her part, Pinky was aghast, but her boy was charging harder than his father had up Missionary Ridge. Having met in the fall of 1921, Louise and Douglas announced their engagement in the *New York Times* on January 15, 1922, and they were married a month later, on Valentine's Day, in Palm Beach, at El Mirasol, the Spanish-style villa of Louise's stepfather. MacArthur wore his uniform bedecked with medals and stood before an altar flanked by the flags of the Rainbow Division and West Point. Louise's colors — she was trying very hard at this point — were red, white, and blue. Pinky, perhaps recalling her own wedding and following the family custom of disapproval, stayed away, and even Douglas's best man was from the bride's side — Louise's brother James.[14]

In the interim, however, a tantalizing rumor circulated that General Pershing had exiled MacArthur to foreign duty in the Philippines because the chief of staff was upset over the dashing bachelor's sudden interest in Mrs. Brooks. Whether the sixty-two-year-old Pershing had his own designs on her or was merely promoting a relationship between Louise and one of his closest aides in a fatherly way is not entirely clear.

Pershing called the story "all damn poppycock without the slightest foundation." There were even rumors that MacArthur would resign to avoid the Philippines assignment. Pershing said he did not believe such rumors and went out of his way to call MacArthur "one of the most splendid types of soldiers I have ever met."[15]

This made a gossipy story in print, and it may have had a whiff of truth to it, but a more likely reason behind MacArthur's Philippines assignment was the appointment of one of the old guard who eschewed MacArthur's reforms to succeed him as West Point superintendent. "I fancy it means a reversal of many of the progressive policies which we inaugurated," MacArthur told his adjutant—and it was. Among the casualties were MacArthur's summer training camp and expanded privileges for upperclassmen.[16]

On September 5, 1922, MacArthur, Louise, and her two children sailed from San Francisco for the Philippines. By all accounts, the general was relaxed and pleased. He truly felt at home amid the archipelago's laid-back atmosphere and friendly people, and he appeared relieved to leave the fast pace of Louise's flamboyant lifestyle. But for exactly that reason, Louise viewed the assignment as one of exile— whatever Pershing's motives. She sought solace in the small cadre of Manila's American officials, while MacArthur socialized with rising Filipino leaders such as Manuel Quezon, who had become president of the Philippine Senate.[17]

Barely had they settled into Manila, however, when word came that Pinky, who was living with Arthur III's family, in Washington, DC, in Douglas's absence, was critically ill. Pinky's health had a tendency to fluctuate depending on its value as either an excuse to help her younger son or a lever she could use to attract his attention. "Mother critically ill—come home at once," read the cable from his sister-in-law that sent Douglas, Louise, and the children hurrying home by the next steamer. Pinky recovered, but the visit was the last time Douglas saw his brother, by then a navy captain, as Arthur III died of appendicitis the following December.[18]

In this instance, Pinky and Louise were unwitting allies. While Louise's first wish was that Douglas take advantage of her wealth and become a stockbroker on Wall Street, her more realistic quest—since he adamantly refused to leave the army—was to arrange for Rainbow Division veterans to lobby Secretary Weeks to make him a major general. Pinky wholeheartedly concurred and took her campaign to Pershing, who, she believed, had "never failed" her yet.

Telling Pershing, who was completing his chief of staff tour, that it was "a real joy to see you on Saturday looking still so young and wonderfully handsome," Pinky pleaded with him to be "the 'Dear Old Jack' of long ago" and give her some assurance that he would approve her son's "well earned promotion" before Pershing left the army. As Douglas had done on occasion in his letters to both Pershing and Leonard Wood, she ended her missive asserting that if it were in her power, she would "crown your valuable life by taking you to the White House."[19]

This lobbying by both mother and wife probably had little effect, but in January of 1925—a few months after Pershing's retirement—MacArthur received his second star and became the youngest major general in the American army. Louise's Philippine exile ended, and MacArthur returned to the United States, first to a short stint in Atlanta in command of the IV Corps and then to III Corps territory, around Washington, DC. They settled into Louise's estate of Brookfield—quickly renamed Rainbow Hill—near Baltimore, conveniently close to the powers in Washington, including his mother.[20]

It should have been a fully celebratory time, but the powers soon gave him what MacArthur later called "one of the most distasteful orders I ever received." He was appointed to the board of judges for the court-martial of Billy Mitchell. In his crusade for airpower, Mitchell had become increasingly critical of his military and civilian superiors in the War Department, going as far as to charge them with negligence. For this he was charged with insubordination. As Louise watched from the audience, MacArthur kept an uncharacteristically low profile during the seven-week trial. Hindsight might suggest that he agreed with

Mitchell's advocacy even as he admitted that Mitchell was "wrong in the violence of his language." But at the time, he was likely being careful not to make waves that might affect his own future.

No record remains of MacArthur's vote—inferences vary with whoever is telling the story. MacArthur himself was unusually circumspect, saying only, "I did what I could in his behalf and I helped save him from dismissal." But that refers to Mitchell's punishment—a five-year suspension without pay—rather than the guilty verdict. Many years later, after he had long practiced speaking his own mind, MacArthur wrote in his memoirs: "It is part of my military philosophy that a senior officer should not be silenced for being at variance with his superiors...."[21]

If the Mitchell court-martial was the most disagreeable professional incident of his years at Rainbow Hill, the most pleasant occurred when MacArthur, while still on active duty, was permitted to serve as head of the American Olympic Association after the unexpected death of its president. The general brought the same vigor and concept of total victory to international athletics as he had to war. "We are here to represent the greatest country on earth," he told the American track team during the 1928 summer games in Amsterdam. "We did not come here to lose gracefully. We came here to win...and win decisively." The United States finished first in gold medals and in total medal count. Germany was a distant second and Finland third.[22]

The one person who might truly have been in her element alongside MacArthur in Amsterdam was not in Europe that summer. Things had not been going well for the MacArthurs on the domestic front. The year before, Louise had moved with her children from Rainbow Hill to the entire twenty-sixth floor of a mid-Manhattan hotel and thrown herself full tilt into the "roaring" part of the 1920s. Upon his return from the Amsterdam games, MacArthur was ordered back to the Philippines to fill the top post of department commander. Once again he sailed for Manila, but this time he went alone.[23]

Douglas MacArthur's third arrival in the Philippines, in the fall of 1928, was bittersweet. He seems to have truly missed Louise's children, and perhaps he even missed the better points of Louise herself.

But once again, the Philippines took him in and gave him respite. And once again, MacArthur sought close association with a potential champion. Henry L. Stimson was already a veteran American politician, having served William Howard Taft as his secretary of war. In 1928, Stimson was completing a brief stint as governor-general of the Philippines. According to MacArthur, the two "became fast friends."[24]

But as with General Pershing, warm accolades of friendship flowed more freely from MacArthur's side than they did from Stimson's. When President Herbert Hoover appointed Stimson secretary of state in 1929, MacArthur used the occasion to congratulate Stimson and — as was his mother's custom when dealing with men of power — express his hope that the position was "but a stepping stone to that last and highest call of America, the Presidency."[25]

MacArthur's own name was mentioned as a possible successor to Stimson's in the Philippines. His most vocal supporter, aside from himself, appears to have been Manuel Quezon: the two were becoming friends and mutual allies in the frequently painful process of moving the Philippines toward independence. In a cable to the *New York Times* that was datelined Manila, "certain high circles here, which cannot be named now," reported that the governor-generalship was MacArthur's "if he really wants it." The cable — which seems unlikely to have originated without the acquiescence of those high circles — went on to quote "close friends" of MacArthur who said that the general had "his eyes on the White House...eight or twelve years hence," after four years as governor-general and "four years in a Cabinet post, either as Secretary of State or Secretary of War."[26] It was all a bit premature but nonetheless indicative of MacArthur's ambitions.

Perhaps Louise might have paid attention to MacArthur's name being linked to the White House — however remotely — but she was soon in Reno, where on June 18, 1929, she was granted a divorce on the grounds of MacArthur's failure to provide for her support. Louise would be quoted — and likely misquoted — on the subject of their relationship over the ensuing years, but MacArthur always remained tight-lipped and stoic about it, as he usually did about all personal matters. Years later, in his memoirs, he addressed his seven years with Louise in a single sentence: "In February 1922 I entered into matrimony, but it was not successful, and ended in divorce years later for mutual incompatibility."[27]

Shortly after receiving news of the divorce, MacArthur learned that President Hoover wanted to appoint him chief of engineers so that he could oversee the flood-control system being planned throughout the Mississippi Valley in response to the horrendous 1927 floods. MacArthur was dubious, claiming he lacked engineering skill but also worrying that the post might deny him the chance to become chief of staff. On the other hand, refusing a proffered presidential appointment might in itself be a professional misstep. MacArthur gambled and declined the post to remain in the Philippines.[28]

But that didn't mean that MacArthur wasn't thinking about Washington, particularly as chief of staff Charles Summerall's term was due to expire in the fall of 1930. In the time-honored method of army seniority, Peyton March's early appointment of MacArthur to the rank of permanent brigadier general was about to pay huge dividends. At the age of fifty, MacArthur stood seventh on the list of eligible major generals, but none of the six ranking above him had the time remaining before mandatory retirement at age sixty-four to serve a full four-year term. On the other hand, there were ten other major generals junior to MacArthur (several by a matter of days and months) with at least four years left to serve, including Pershing's reported favorite, Fox Conner.[29]

Pershing, however, was occupied in France with a war monuments commission. Summerall, still grateful for the Rainbow's response to his plea of "give me Châtillon," favored MacArthur. Secretary of war Patrick J. Hurley was in receipt of an ingratiating letter from MacArthur profusely praising — almost to the point of embarrassment — Hurley's grasp of Philippine policy. And President Hoover had already recognized MacArthur's talents.

In the end, even though the *New York Times* wished there had been a closer scrutiny of other candidates, it was an easy decision. "It gives me great pleasure," Hoover announced on August 5, 1930, "to promote so brilliant a soldier." He had "searched the Army for younger blood," Hoover recalled years later, "and finally determined on General Douglas MacArthur. His brilliant abilities and his sterling character need no exposition from me."[30]

Rather disingenuously, MacArthur wrote in his memoirs, "I did not want to return to Washington, even though it meant the four stars of a general, and my first inclination was to try and beg off." MacArthur claimed that his mother persuaded him otherwise, saying that his father "would be ashamed if [he] showed timidity."[31] It makes a humble story, but it is ridiculous. MacArthur aspired to be chief of staff at least from his cadet days at West Point, especially after his father had been denied the post. Now he had the prize that had eluded his father. He certainly would not refuse it.

About to reach the zenith of an enviable military career, Douglas MacArthur nonetheless made an egregious error in personal judgment. Returning to Washington to take up residence with his mother in Quarters One at Fort Myer—the official residence of army chiefs of staff since 1908—the general also arranged for a young Filipina, Isabel Rosario Cooper, who had been his mistress for around a year in Manila, to follow him and surreptitiously take up residence at his expense in a Washington apartment.

On November 21, 1930, Douglas MacArthur was sworn in as chief of staff of the United States Army. Given the military demobilization since the end of World War I, he commanded a peacetime force of only twelve thousand officers and 125,000 enlisted men with an overall budget of approximately $300 million. On two trips to Europe during the following two years, MacArthur would be feted for the American effort in the recent war, but on a global scale the United States Army ranked behind those of Portugal and Greece.[32]

The 1920s had ceased to roar, and the country was rapidly descending into the depths of the Great Depression. Its collective mood—in part because of the domestic gloom—was decidedly isolationist, so much so that senior military officers stationed in Washington dressed in civilian clothes so as not to attract unwelcome attention.

Central to MacArthur's years as chief of staff were monetary battles with a Congress trying to drastically reduce the federal budget. The allocation of limited funds within the army appropriation became heated and put MacArthur in the middle between traditional manpower requirements and the need to develop new weapons systems, particularly aircraft and tanks. Airpower advocates lumped him among those who had cashiered Billy Mitchell, but his first priority was to protect the officer corps. Even so, headquarters staffs were reduced and minor posts closed, along with the army's experimental armored unit.

Already there was talk of creating a separate air force then combining all three services — army, air force, and navy — into one department of national defense. Proponents cited economies of scale and command and control efficiencies, but MacArthur clung to the army tradition he had known since childhood. He called the status quo "the strongest possible organization for war." Tampering with it, he warned, would be "inefficient, uneconomical, and uselessly cumbersome."[33]

Not only did MacArthur want to keep the army as independent as possible, but faced with budget cutbacks, he also wanted to shackle the growth of the air corps, a sentiment shared by a number of his contemporaries. MacArthur went so far as to tell the head of the American delegation to the 1932 World Disarmament Conference in Geneva that its "ultimate aim should be to obtain an agreement... to give up military and naval aviation in their entirety and not to subsidize directly or indirectly civilian aviation."[34]

Between the army and navy, however, MacArthur wanted the army to be the dominant service in the air. After MacArthur and the chief of naval operations, Admiral William V. Pratt, agreed that airborne coastal defenses would be the responsibility of the army and naval aviation would content itself with training and scouting operations, MacArthur learned that the navy was developing torpedo planes. Because they delivered a type of bomb, he demanded that the army have its share of the planes. Ultimately, MacArthur's insistence on controlling coastal defenses backfired and undermined his tight rein on air corps spending, because advocates of airpower used the air corps' mission of coastal defense to argue for the development of a long-range bomber. In 1935, Boeing introduced the first experimental model of an airplane that MacArthur would come to know well — the B-17.[35]

MacArthur's role as army chief of staff was considerably different from that of his navy counterpart. MacArthur's responsibilities and concomitant authority ran to all army operations in the field as well as the air corps, training programs, and matters of materiel and supply, although in practice certain specialized areas, such as the Corps of Engineers, were given wide latitude in their operations. But on the navy side, the chief of naval operations operated as a "first among equals" in coordinating the activities of eight independent bureaus, including ordnance and aeronautics. Fleet operations were separate and under the command of the commander in chief of the United States Fleet. If the United States went to war, MacArthur—short of a presidential decision otherwise—would command the army, while the navy chain of command would be split.[36]

Throughout his career, MacArthur had long displayed his conservative stripes. That inclination wasn't unique for a military officer, and it was one of the reasons why Hoover had shown an interest in promoting him to the Corps of Engineers post. MacArthur definitely stood out, however, in the public manner in which he espoused his political beliefs. Most senior officers religiously recognized the clear line between the military and the political, but, as MacArthur's soon-to-be aide, Major Dwight D. Eisenhower, recalled, "if General MacArthur ever recognized the existence of that line, he usually chose to ignore it."[37]

Increasingly, in the spring of 1932, MacArthur confronted the waves of domestic unrest sweeping the country, particularly among its labor force. When the University of Pittsburgh invited the chief of staff to speak at its commencement and receive an honorary degree that June, liberals among the faculty and student body protested loudly. MacArthur took up the challenge and managed to deride "pacifism and its bedfellow, Communism," while asserting, "Any nation that would keep its self-respect must be prepared to defend itself."[38]

A few weeks after the Pittsburgh speech, MacArthur faced what he called his "most poignant episode during my role as Chief of Staff."[39] At issue was the extra compensation, or bonus, Congress had promised World War I veterans. Passed during the boom of the 1920s, the provision was in many respects a harbinger of Social Security. Individual amounts were prorated according to service but averaged around one thousand dollars—a significant sum as the Depression deepened and unemployment soared. Initially, these bonuses were to be redeemable in 1945, but faced with economic ruin, veterans demanded them in 1932. Despite legislation allotting one-half of each bonus early, many recipients were still not satisfied.[40]

An army of veterans, many with their families, descended on Washington and made camp in abandoned buildings along Pennsylvania Avenue near the Capitol and in a larger encampment to the south, across the Anacostia River. On July 28, 1932, President Hoover directed the army to assist District of Columbia police in maintaining order and ultimately ejecting the Bonus Marchers, as they were known, from their encampment. Amid clouds of tear gas and lines of fixed bayonets, MacArthur insisted on taking the field in person to supervise the operation.

His chief aide at the time, Major Eisenhower, strongly advised MacArthur against appearing in person, telling him it was "highly inappropriate for the Chief of Staff of the Army to be involved in anything like a local or street-corner embroilment." MacArthur ignored this advice, as well as Eisenhower's later caution against talking to the press about what Eisenhower thought should be cast as a political rather than a military matter.[41]

Taking to the streets of Washington against former comrades in arms was an uncharacteristic thing for MacArthur to do. His experiences with the Rainbow Division in France suggest that, if anything, he should have marched down to the Anacostia camp alone and talked his way around the fires of the veterans gathered there. The chief factor in his personal involvement and subsequent actions was that MacArthur believed that most of those gathered in and around Washington were not veterans at all but Communist-inspired insurgents who hoped, in MacArthur's words, "to incite revolutionary action." MacArthur believed that "the movement was actually far deeper and more dangerous than an effort to secure funds from a nearly depleted federal treasury."[42]

Most evidence suggests otherwise. By one Veterans Administration survey, it was estimated that out of perhaps as many as twenty-five thousand Bonus Marchers, 94 percent had army or navy records and two-thirds had served overseas. Around one-fifth were disabled as a result of their service. Of this entire number, less than two hundred were active Communists, and while they indeed might have hoped to foment a clash, their influence was relatively small.[43]

Believing otherwise, MacArthur showed a definite defiance and aloofness that he had not exhibited with the rank and file in the trenches of France or, subsequently, with the cadets at West Point. Once the veterans had been dispersed, the Bonus March incident became not only a black mark on MacArthur's career but also evidence in the minds of his friends and foes alike of a certain detachment on his part.

Sitting in his office in Albany, the governor of New York and Democratic presidential nominee, Franklin D. Roosevelt, hung up after a ranting call from Louisiana's firebrand former governor and then US senator, Huey P. Long, and admonished his aides "to remember all the time that [Long] really is one of the two most dangerous men in the country." Asked if the other was the conservative radio priest Father Charles Coughlin, Roosevelt shook his head. "Oh, no," he answered. "The other is Douglas MacArthur."[44]

Recorded by Rexford Tugwell, a member of the New Deal intelligentsia, this quotation has been repeated in numerous accounts of the Roosevelt-MacArthur relationship without much scrutiny of its historical or editorial context. According to Tugwell, Roosevelt went on to express concern that many people mired in the Great Depression wanted strong military leadership bordering on totalitarianism and were "willing to trade liberty for it." Roosevelt stopped short, however, of suggesting that Americans were ready to embrace MacArthur as the man on horseback and charge the barricades behind him.

If Roosevelt indeed considered MacArthur "one of the two most dangerous men in the country," he offered that view while still a Washington outsider. Nominated but not yet elected, he as yet had no experience working with MacArthur as chief of staff. Besides, it was the highly charged summer of the Bonus March—hardly the shining moment of MacArthur's career by any standard.

There must also be some scrutiny of Rexford Tugwell as the sole source for this characterization. Tugwell was a self-appointed guardian of the New Deal legacy. MacArthur, particularly in the shadow of the Bonus March, was a handy symbol—"well endowed with charm, tradition, and majestic appearance," as Tugwell characterized him—for those stoking fears of military dictatorship prior to Roosevelt's own aggressive leadership. Nonetheless, the "dangerous men" quotation is repeated in many secondary sources at face value. If indeed Roosevelt said it, it wasn't indicative of their total relationship. That was to prove far more complex.[45]

If the dismal state of the nation's economy had not already done so, the dispassionate routing of the Bonus March destroyed any remaining hope for Herbert Hoover's reelection. In March of 1933, with the retired hero Pershing ailing and unable to do the honors, Douglas MacArthur led Franklin D. Roosevelt's inaugural parade down the same Pennsylvania Avenue from which he had ousted the Bonus Marchers.

The general's relationship with the president-elect went back to their pre–World War I days, when MacArthur was a junior officer on the General Staff and Roosevelt was assistant secretary of the navy.[46] Poles apart politically, they were uncannily alike in other areas: both had protective and domineering mothers, were masters of the theatrical moment, and carried an unwavering sense of destiny for themselves and the country.

It seems clear from both sides' later telling that FDR usually addressed MacArthur as Douglas, a familiarity that did not exist between the president and some of his other military subordinates, most notably George C. Marshall, who bristled the one reported time Roosevelt called him George instead of General. MacArthur was enough of a soldier — as well as a politician — to address his superior as Mr. President.[47]

Budget battles were still at the forefront. Within days of Roosevelt's inauguration, Congress passed the army's appropriations bill for 1934. Totaling $277 million, it was less than what was proposed by the outgoing Hoover administration, but then Roosevelt ordered another $80 million trimmed. MacArthur went ballistic, calling the proposal "a stunning blow to national defense." Next came 15 percent pay cuts for all federal workers, cuts to veterans benefits, and a proposed House of Representatives measure to furlough members of the armed forces at Roosevelt's discretion.[48]

MacArthur repeatedly appeared before congressional committees and at the White House to oppose these actions. He graphically recalled in his memoirs one of the most heated exchanges with Roosevelt early in FDR's first one hundred days. Arguing that "the country's safety was at stake" because of Roosevelt's proposed cuts, MacArthur remembered that he told the president "something to the general effect that when we lost the next war, and an American boy, lying in the mud with an enemy bayonet through his belly and an enemy foot on his dying throat, spat out his last curse, I wanted the name not to be MacArthur, but Roosevelt."

FDR responded with equal passion before MacArthur offered his resignation as chief of staff and stormed toward the door. "Don't be foolish, Douglas," Roosevelt said, declining to accept it as he smoothly tried to defuse the moment. "You and the budget must get together on this." But MacArthur kept on going. By the time he reached the steps at the North Portico, secretary of war George Dern caught up with him and asserted that the general had "saved the Army" — FDR would indeed slightly reduce some of his cuts in 1934. MacArthur, however, was feeling differently. A paralyzing nausea gripped him, and he vomited on the steps of the White House.[49]

Given such exchanges, one might assume that Roosevelt would gladly have seen MacArthur's term as chief of staff come to an end on schedule in the fall of 1934. But Roosevelt was first and foremost a political animal not above using his opponents to his advantage. MacArthur's apparent choice to succeed him was his former war plans chief and then head of the Army War College, George S. Simonds. Roosevelt was reportedly partial to IX Corps commander Malin Craig. There was a political solution: if Roosevelt stalled for a year in replacing MacArthur, four years hence would take Simonds into retirement and thus remove any competition to the president's choice of Craig.

Although military glory was in short supply in Washington during the 1930s, MacArthur would have delighted in another four-year term as chief of staff. He was only fifty-four and had no worries about retirement age. If he moved to another army assignment, it would be anticlimactic. Politics was a possibility, or a cabinet appointment, but the latter wasn't likely to come from Roosevelt.

Throughout the fall of 1934, Roosevelt stalled when the press asked him about the chief of staff position. Finally, on December 12, 1934, the president announced that MacArthur would be retained as chief of staff until his successor was named. This supported his strategy of appointing Craig in due course, but Roosevelt announced that he was doing so "in order to obtain the benefit of General MacArthur's experience in handling War Department legislation in the coming session."[50]

In retaining MacArthur through the 1935 budget negotiations with Congress — during which the 1936 army budget rose to more than $355 million and authorized enlisted strength increased to 165,000 men — Roosevelt was taking his first small steps toward preparing the country for war and covering his own political flanks by having a well-known conservative make his national defense arguments.

MacArthur's political profile throughout his tenure as chief of staff left him exposed to the sort of media attacks generally reserved for politicians, not military officers. No one came out more aggressively against him than columnist Drew Pearson. Later one of the most widely read political commentators in America, Pearson was then a thirty-eight-year-old still trying to make his name. Beginning with two anonymously coauthored books and continuing with his Washington Merry-Go-Round syndicated column, Pearson caricatured MacArthur's manner and motives as deplorable examples of the military establishment.

Pearson's information was fueled at least in part by vengeful tidbits of MacArthur's personal habits provided by his ex-wife, Louise. She was by then on her third marriage — it was already unhappy — and seemed to relish the role of gossip. Finally, in May of 1934, MacArthur had enough of Pearson's rants and filed a $1.75 million libel suit against him, charging that the "column gave the impression he was guilty of conduct unbecoming an officer, or held him up to ridicule and contempt."[51] This only served to bring Pearson more of the notoriety he sought, and it ultimately brought home to roost the poor judgment MacArthur had used in bringing Isabel Rosario Cooper to the United States.

Regular trysts between MacArthur and Isabel had come to an end sometime in the spring of 1934, and MacArthur bought Isabel a return ticket to Manila. She didn't go. When Louise clammed up on the eve of the libel trial and refused to offer corroborating testimony in Pearson's defense, Pearson thought he was finished. But another of MacArthur's bitter enemies, Congressman Ross Collins of Mississippi, a Democrat and chairman of the House subcommittee on military appropriations, came to Pearson's rescue. Collins lived in the same Washington hotel in which MacArthur had lately kept Isabel, and he found her only too happy to cooperate. Just before the trial, when MacArthur's attorney asked him why someone named Isabel Rosario Cooper was on Pearson's witness list, her name hit like an unexpected artillery barrage in the night.

Opposing counsel conferred, and MacArthur agreed to settle the suit for one dollar in damages from Pearson. In exchange for returning her trove of MacArthur's letters, postcards, and telegrams and promising never again to ask him for money, Isabel received fifteen thousand dollars from MacArthur.

Some were mystified by MacArthur's prompt retreat. He was a bachelor at the time, and while his conduct was perhaps unseemly, he might have shrugged and said, "So what?" According to Admiral William D. Leahy, who had attended Annapolis with MacArthur's brother, the reason for MacArthur's reversal was the other woman in his life. MacArthur simply couldn't bear to have his mother learn the torrid details of his affair with his mistress.[52]

Faced with the end of his high-profile tenure as chief of staff and relieved to escape the vengeful women in his life, Douglas MacArthur was only too pleased when Manuel Quezon, about to be inaugurated as the first president of the Commonwealth of the Philippines, made him an offer that he couldn't refuse.

CHAPTER THREE

Manila Before the Storm

One of the most contentious episodes in American foreign policy occurred when the United States became involved militarily in a fragmented country in Southeast Asia and attempted to steer it on a path to democracy. Vast numbers of the local population resisted the American efforts, and many in America protested that their nation had no business being there. Political leaders in the United States were subjected to criticism in the press and in the streets. The intervention became an undeclared war in which 125,000 American troops were deployed with upwards of seven thousand casualties. This was not the 1960s, and the country was not Vietnam. Rather, it was the early 1900s, and the loosely federated country was the Philippines.

Great Britain ostensibly won the Philippines from Spain during the final round of the Seven Years' War in 1762, but controlling the country beyond Manila and Cavite proved impossible. Britain was relieved to relinquish its tentative conquest back to Spain with the resulting peace treaty. At the time of the Spanish-American War, in 1898, Filipinos, led by Emilio Aguinaldo, were fighting Spain for their independence.

Meanwhile, "that Cuba should be free" became the American chant of the short-lived war, and in 1902, after a brief stint as an American protectorate, Cuba got its independence — however rocky the road ahead was to be. After initially allying his anti-Spanish forces with invading American troops around Manila, Aguinaldo was led to believe that the Philippines would quickly achieve the same result, and he became the leader of the First Philippine Republic. But the United States chose to view the Philippines differently from the way it viewed Cuba.

Two American presidents — William McKinley and Theodore Roosevelt — decreed that the polyglot Philippines was not ready for independence and must take that road slowly. The result was a three-year war between Filipinos fighting for independence under Aguinaldo and American troops seeking to administer the Philippines as an overseas colony. This war ended soon after Aguinaldo's capture in 1901, but guerrilla activity in the islands beyond Manila continued until 1913.

If this seems like irrelevant history, it must be remembered that Douglas MacArthur and most leaders of the American army and navy who would be his contemporaries in World War II came of age at West Point and Annapolis in the shadow of the Spanish-American War and the larger but lesser-known conflict they termed the Philippine Insurrection. American influence throughout the Pacific was increasingly important, and an American presence in the Philippines — hard-won though it turned out to be — was considered vital to those interests.

MacArthur's first deployment to Manila, in 1903, had come just after the cessation of major hostilities, and by the time of his 1922 and 1928 postings, the country under the leadership of Manuel Quezon was slowly moving toward independence with an American governor-general but an elected Filipino legislature. In 1934, the US Congress passed the Tydings-McDuffie Act, which, upon acceptance by Filipinos, provided for a transition to commonwealth status followed by full independence in ten years. This not only raised the question of how the Philippines was to defend itself upon independence, it also raised the question of how the islands and America's continuing interests there were to be defended during the interim. Enter Quezon's offer of military employment to MacArthur.

As MacArthur's tenure as chief of staff came to an end, he asked himself what was left for someone at the age of fifty-five who had no desire to see the colors fade. Reverting to the rank of major general and commanding one of the United States' corps areas would have been a huge letdown—besides, he had already done that. The Philippines provided him a comfortable stage far removed from his home turf where he could assume the role of the region's number one soldier and benefit from his long association with Quezon.

They had become an interesting pair. Francis Bowes Sayre, Woodrow Wilson's son-in-law and later high commissioner of the Philippines, remembered Quezon as "one of the most colorful figures in the Far East." Sayre described Quezon as "impulsive, daring, charming beyond words to all whom he set out to win; he was adroit, keen-witted, ambitious and always dramatic. He had outwitted and out-maneuvered all his rivals and stood clearly at the forefront, the unquestioned political boss of the Philippines."[1]

Sayre recalled MacArthur as "sharp and observant [but] always indrawn and playing his part as an actor." To average Americans in Manila, MacArthur was "inscrutable and enigmatic" because they only saw him from a distance, "for he held himself aloof from the crowd." MacArthur's personality, Sayre claimed, lacked "the open, democratic, American approach."[2]

The first step in a MacArthur-Quezon partnership was for Quezon to ask the United States to provide a military mission to his new commonwealth government, much as it had been doing for a number of Latin American countries. The relationship was fuzzy, because on the one hand American troops still in the Philippines were directly responsible to the War Department, but on the other hand, Quezon needed to develop an independent defense force responsible to the commonwealth.

When Congress approved the military-mission legislation, it was common knowledge that Quezon wanted MacArthur to head it and that the general would quite willingly do so. In fact, MacArthur appears to have crafted the legislation for secretary of war Dern and drafted—at Quezon's request—Quezon's subsequent letter requesting MacArthur's services.[3]

As part of the establishment of the military mission, the legislation provided that MacArthur would be able to continue to draw his salary as a major general while at the same time receiving compensation from the Philippine government. It was a very generous double-dip that provided MacArthur with $7,500 annually from the United States Army and a handsome package from Quezon of $18,000 per year in salary, an additional $15,000 annual personal allowance, and the use of a seven-room, fully air-conditioned suite atop the Manila Hotel, all worth around $650,000 today.[4]

MacArthur's first preference through all this would have been to be named high commissioner of the Philippines, the top American position in the islands after the post of governor-general was abolished under the country's commonwealth status. Despite his assurances to Quezon that "the great work involved as your Military Adviser seems to me to transcend in ultimate importance anything else that is conceivable," MacArthur waged an active campaign for the commissionership with Franklin Roosevelt and a less-than-subtle campaign against Frank Murphy, a former governor-general then filling the high commissioner seat.[5]

According to MacArthur, Roosevelt agreed to name him to the high commissioner post at a private dinner between the two at Hyde Park, New York, on September 3, 1935. Then when MacArthur discovered that he would have to resign from the army in order to hold this civilian position, he suggested special legislation to fix the matter. Clearly he did not intend to resign from the army, and he concluded that should Roosevelt decide "to abandon either now or in the future your purpose in making the appointment...I will conform instantly to the revised plan."[6]

But did Roosevelt have a devious political motive for packing MacArthur off to the Philippines in one role or another? MacArthur certainly had his share of political enemies as well as the baggage of a divorce and his liaison with Isabel, but some Republicans were enamored with him as presidential material—particularly as no front-runner had yet emerged against Roosevelt in 1936. Rather than have MacArthur, an ambitious former chief of staff with time on his hands, flitting around Washington or New York, Roosevelt may have wanted him out of the country.

When Frank Murphy finally stepped down as high commissioner the following year, Major General Hugh Drum, then commander of the army's Hawaiian Department, suggested to MacArthur that he "could really do both" jobs—high commissioner and military adviser— adding: "The combination would have many advantages." Drum reminded MacArthur, "I have not changed my views as given to you in Washington one afternoon relative to 1940. Such a possibility is in the offing through the background you have created."[7] However veiled the message, this suggests that Drum and MacArthur had had some level of conversation about the possibility of MacArthur's presidential candidacy in 1940.

In response to MacArthur's request, Roosevelt said he was "inclined to hope that there will be little or no trouble on the Hill" in resolving the prohibition against MacArthur's holding both a civilian post and a military rank. But in the meantime, secretary of war Dern issued orders commanding MacArthur to "act as the Military Adviser of the Commonwealth Government in the establishment and development of a system of National Defense."[8]

As MacArthur understood the plan, he would arrive in Manila wearing the four stars of a full general and holding the title of chief of staff. His stature as America's top soldier would make for a triumphant return to the country his father had once governed, provide prestige for Quezon as the newly elected president of the commonwealth, and underscore America's commitment to the defense of the archipelago. On December 15, 1935—thirty days or so after his arrival—his term as chief of staff would come to an end and Roosevelt would announce his successor. To the surprise of MacArthur, as well as Secretary Dern, it didn't happen that way.

Roosevelt, never one to shy away from reminding all comers that he alone was the keeper of the powers of the presidency, made a different decision midcourse. On October 2, as MacArthur and Major Dwight Eisenhower, who was to accompany him to the Philippines as his chief of staff, were speeding west through Wyoming on a Union Pacific train bound for San Francisco, where they would then board a ship bound for Manila, the general received a telegram from the assistant secretary of war, who was acting in Dern's absence. It announced that Roosevelt had appointed Malin Craig chief of staff effective immediately and that MacArthur would revert to the rank of major general.

MacArthur's reaction was loud enough to be heard across Wyoming. "It was," Eisenhower recalled of MacArthur's tirade, "an explosive denunciation of politics, bad manners, bad judgment, broken promises, arrogance, unconstitutionality, insensitivity, and the way the world had gone to hell."[9] Then, his rant finished, MacArthur, in characteristic fashion, dictated politically correct telegrams: to Roosevelt, praising the president's appointment of Craig as "splendid"; to the assistant secretary of war, asking him to convey further to Roosevelt that Craig's appointment was "not only admirable but timely"; and to Craig himself, expressing "keen anticipation to what cannot fail to be a successful tenure of office." But then, in what was also characteristic MacArthur fashion, the general sent one more telegram. It went to the press-relations section of the War Department, asking that his magnanimous telegrams be given "immediate publicity."[10]

Wearing the two stars of a major general, Douglas MacArthur embarked from San Francisco for Manila on the liner *President Hoover*. The most important member of his contingent was his mother. Mary Pinkney Hardy MacArthur was then eighty-three and finally failing for real. Her son arranged to have the family's longtime physician, Major Howard J. Hutter, assigned to his staff, but by the time they arrived in Manila, Pinky's situation was grim. Five weeks later, she succumbed to a cerebral thrombosis, and, as MacArthur sadly recalled, their "devoted comradeship of so many years came to an end."[11]

But just as the most dominant woman in his life was departing, another, who would come to take Pinky's place in importance and influence, made her appearance. Like Pinky, Jean Marie Faircloth was a southern girl, born in Nashville, Tennessee, on December 28, 1898. A spinster of thirty-six when she met MacArthur, Miss Faircloth was hardly spinsterish in personality. Lively, engaging, and usually beaming with a smile, Jean was a petite, brown-eyed brunette who exuded confidence. She was also something of a fashion hound. But where Louise had focused on getting, Jean's priority was giving.

Her father, Edward C. Faircloth, was a wealthy banker and businessman. When Jean was eight, her parents divorced, and her mother, Sallie Beard, took Jean and her two brothers back to her birthplace,

Murfreesboro. Like Pinky's Hardy clan, the Beards were a family of Confederate veterans. Jean was a member of both the Daughters of the American Revolution and the United Daughters of the Confederacy, and her fellow members recalled that "every time Jean Faircloth heard a Fourth of July firecracker go off, she jumped to attention and saluted." Young men who came courting were advised, "If you want to win Jean Marie, you better get a uniform."[12]

Jean attended Ward-Belmont College in Nashville for a year and eventually graduated from Soule College in Murfreesboro. She was not close to her father when she was growing up, but as both grew older, Edward Faircloth took his only daughter on trips and cruises throughout the world. After he died, she was left with a substantial inheritance that she determined to use continuing those travels. It was just such a trip that found her a passenger on the *President Hoover* bound for the Far East in the fall of 1935.

MacArthur was attentive to his ailing mother on that voyage, but after being introduced to Jean, he ordered flowers delivered to her cabin when the ship called in Honolulu. They were a pair from the beginning, although without the public attention and rush to the altar that had characterized his courtship of Louise. Jean chose to stay in Manila when the *President Hoover* docked, and they began a ritual of evening movies and dinners overlooking Manila Bay.

When both returned to the United States in 1937 for a visit, MacArthur went about army business and arranged for Pinky's burial in Arlington National Cemetery next to his father, while Jean quietly visited family in Murfreesboro and Louisville. Hearing about what had become her plans to marry the general, Jean's aunt remarked, "The people of America will certainly be surprised." Jean flashed one of her trademark smiles and replied, "Well, the people in Manila won't!"[13]

They married in the Municipal Building in New York City on the morning of April 30, 1937. The only witnesses were two of MacArthur's aides. Shortly afterward, MacArthur took Jean on her first visit to West Point, showing her the place to which he was so firmly attached.

Back in Manila several months later, they settled into MacArthur's penthouse suite atop the new five-story wing of the Manila Hotel, which afforded panoramic views of Manila harbor and the vibrant sunsets that silhouetted the island of Corregidor to the west. Their only child, Arthur MacArthur IV, would be born early the following year, on February 21, 1938. It was all very peaceful, genteel, and romantic. But there were alarming indicators afoot that this tranquillity was about to be shattered for the MacArthur family and for all of the Philippines.[14]

The United States had assumed that Japan would be its foe in the Pacific since Theodore—not Franklin—Roosevelt had warned of sooner or later having to fight that empire. But despite the significant amount of resources and attention—as well as a certain degree of angst—that had been invested in the Philippine archipelago over the course of four decades, there had never been an unequivocal strategy about how the islands were to be defended. Some maintained they neither would be nor could be. "I doubt very much," former governor-general W. Cameron Forbes told army chief of staff Summerall in 1927, "if any real effort will be made to defend the Philippine Islands as such. They are indefensible and from a military point of view not worth defending. The main thing is to make any interference with them as costly as possible."[15]

Any American defense of the Philippines was rooted in Plan Orange, a blueprint for war with Japan that was one of a series of color-coded military plans devised to protect the United States against likely and—in the case of Plan Red against Great Britain—unlikely opponents. The Joint Planning Committee of the Joint Army and Navy Board, which was essentially a limited forerunner of the Joint Chiefs of Staff, had been routinely developing and revising such plans since around 1904. They formed the basis of countless war games at both the army and navy war colleges and informed—as well as biased—a generation of officers.

Initially, Plan Orange envisioned an American fleet sailing from the West Coast to the Philippines and defeating the main Japanese fleet either en route or shortly after marshaling in Manila Bay, which the army was charged with holding. This smacked of the old saw about preparing to fight the last war, à la Admiral George Dewey sailing to Manila Bay to defeat the Spanish in 1898, although he did so from

Hong Kong, not California. Such a West-Coast-to-Far-East naval rescue was made more problematic after World War I by Japan's wartime
acquisition—as a nominal member of the Allied powers—of German
territories in the Mariana, Caroline, and Marshall Islands. They strad-
dled the direct Hawaii-to-Manila route and provided Japan with naval
bases as well as opportunities to deploy land-based airpower.

In its 1924 version of Plan Orange, the Joint Planning Committee
advocated offensive sea and air operations against Japan's naval forces,
to be followed by the rapid deployment of at least fifty thousand
troops from the West Coast of the United States to Oahu within ten
days. They were to be prepared to depart Hawaii for Manila Bay four
days later. Given daunting logistics and the fact that this was roughly
one-third of the strength of the entire American army, it was totally
unrealistic.

The 1924 version was, however, prescient in one key recommendation: planners were insistent that both army and navy forces operate
under one unified command. The generals and admirals of the Joint
Army and Navy Board balked and agreed only to mutual cooperation
between the services, while maintaining separate army and navy commands. A few years later, though, this was revised to provide an initial
period after the commencement of hostilities for unified command
under the navy, which was acknowledged to have the "paramount
interest" given the watery expanses of the Pacific. Complete and continuing unity of command would become a critical concept in the years
ahead.[16]

By the 1930s, Plan Orange had evolved with the realization that only
a slower deployment of troops was practical. Rather than rushing to the
Philippines, troops were charged with first ejecting Japanese forces
from the Marshall and Caroline Islands to protect their advancing lines
of communication and supply. In 1936, the Joint Board reduced the
mission of American troops in the Philippines from defending Manila
and its environs to holding only the entrance to Manila Bay in expectation of the navy's arrival.

Finally, by 1937, with Japan aggressively renewing its attacks in
China, the Joint Board came to the realization that US forces could not
hold the Philippines against a serious Japanese attempt long enough for

the United States Fleet to arrive. Since increasing defenses in the islands was out of the question given public sentiment and other priorities closer to home, the board called for withdrawing to a defensive Alaska-Oahu-Panama line in the eastern Pacific and employing economic pressure to force Japan's collapse while a sufficiently large army was mobilized.[17]

As the man on the scene, Douglas MacArthur had never put much faith in the quick-relief component of Plan Orange, although, as we shall see, by 1942 that is exactly what he expected. Instead, during the 1930s, he promoted a largely volunteer army of citizen soldiers built around a cadre of regular officers and NCOs. Upon MacArthur's arrival in 1935, the Philippine National Assembly appropriated $8 million for these purposes with the expectation of expending similar amounts annually during the decade leading to full independence, at which time the country's military would be fully developed.

It didn't work out that way. MacArthur's grand plans aside, this amount of funding was a pittance compared to the needs of maintaining an eleven-thousand-man force of regular troops, providing five and a half months of training annually for forty thousand citizen soldiers, building a fleet of fifty torpedo boats, and purchasing an air force of 250 planes, not to mention creating a Philippine military academy, lesser service schools, and more than 120 training camps.[18]

Even after it took more than a year to get the first contingent of twenty thousand trainees into camps — they would not report until early 1937 — and after trainees showed little retention of military skills when called out on subsequent maneuvers, MacArthur clung to the citizen-army concept. "The result," MacArthur told Quezon in his first official report, "is that in the world today there is no other defensive system that provides an equal security at remotely comparable cost to the people maintaining it." But that was precisely the problem: you get what you pay for. "Though we worked doggedly through 1936 and 1937," recalled Dwight Eisenhower, "ours was a hopeless venture. The Philippine government simply could not afford to build real security from attack."[19]

While the American War Department "loaned" the Philippine

defense forces largely obsolete stocks of munitions, substantial reinforcements and armaments for American troops remaining in the army's Philippine Department (not under MacArthur's command) were not forthcoming. Universal shortages aside, by 1938 a large part of the rationale for this meagerness was that under Plan Orange as it was then conceived, a prolonged, self-sustained defense of the Philippines was no longer considered viable.

Brigadier General Walter Krueger, chief of the army's War Plans Division, warned chief of staff Malin Craig in February of 1938 that it was "highly improbable, as matters now stand, that expeditionary forces will be sent to the Philippines in the early stages of an Orange war. Even if the dispatch of such forces were contemplated, it would be impossible to predict, with any degree of accuracy, the time when they would arrive." Krueger advised Craig to tell the Philippine Department's commander to "accomplish his mission for the maximum time possible with the personnel and reserves then available to him."[20]

Other than wrangling a few officers from the army's Philippine Department to serve on his military adviser staff, MacArthur stayed focused on the Sisyphean task of building a viable Philippine military. Few doubted, as he had assured Quezon before taking the post, that MacArthur was "prepared to devote the remainder of my life if necessary to securing a proper defense for the Philippine Nation." But his promise to forge Quezon "a weapon which will spell the safety of your nation from brutal aggression until the end of time" was clearly standard MacArthur hyperbole.[21]

And, as usual, MacArthur's continuing rhetoric and military programs did not play well with the liberal press and isolationist and pacifist policy makers, with which Washington in the 1930s was rife. Many people in the United States were still critical of MacArthur over his role in the Bonus March and convinced that he was needlessly militarizing the Philippines and antagonizing Japan in the process. Reports drifted back to Manila that there was a growing movement to recall him as military adviser.

In early August of 1937, chief of staff Craig cabled MacArthur the antithesis of the message MacArthur had once received from Pershing detailing him to foreign service. This time, it was said that MacArthur

54

had been away too long, and after two years overseas, he was to be brought home for duty in the United States. MacArthur responded graciously and professed to look forward "to whatever duty the War Department may have decided I should now undertake in the service of my country."[22] But for the next few weeks, his pacing on the terrace of his Manila penthouse became more intense. He was definitely in a quandary. What should he do?

He finally cabled Craig on September 16, 1937: he would retire from the army. Citing poor health—which certainly wasn't true—and other fabricated reasons, from his work as military adviser being completed to his wish to open up the promotion ladder to younger men, MacArthur chose December 31, 1937, as his final day in the uniform he had worn so proudly since arriving on the plain at West Point thirty-eight years earlier.

In truth, of course, the primary reason for his retirement was that after being chief of staff and enjoying the subsequent grandeur of his position in the Philippines—however hollow his command—he simply could not bear to serve under anyone and retire as a mere corps commander or occupy a similar subordinate post. He found that thought, as he candidly told Craig, "repugnant."[23] From his perspective, MacArthur would go out on top on his own terms.

Besides, he still had the Philippines and his exalted rank as field marshal of the Philippine army. While never in use in the American military, the rank of field marshal among international forces was generally thought to outrank that of four-star generals and admirals. Conferring the rank on MacArthur in 1936 as part of the Philippines' National Defense Act appeared to be Quezon's idea, but much later Quezon acknowledged to Eisenhower that the suggestion had been MacArthur's. At the time, Eisenhower tried to talk MacArthur out of accepting the rank, later saying he had thought it "pompous and rather ridiculous to be the field marshal of a virtually non-existing army."[24] MacArthur demurred, took up his field marshal's baton, and that was that.

But not quite. The War Department made it clear in 1936 that no matter what rank the Philippine government chose to bestow on MacArthur or any other American officer serving in the capacity of military adviser, the American military would consider Philippine forces analogous to a national guard until the commonwealth achieved full independence. As such, it would not render any honors or salutes and certainly no command deference simply because of a rank conferred by the Philippine government.[25]

Further, after MacArthur's retirement—Philippine field marshal though he might still be—the War Department went to great lengths to explain that the retired general would no longer represent the United States as a military adviser to the Philippines. He was not to exercise command of any American forces, and any requests from the Philippine government for personnel, materiel, or services were to be transmitted through the army's Philippine Department, not MacArthur.[26]

By January of 1938, fully retired and perhaps feeling a little out of the mainstream, MacArthur came up with one of his patented ideas, calculated to be showy and grandiose, with plenty of the pageantry he craved. He ordered Eisenhower and Lieutenant Colonel James Ord, who had remained as his aides in the military adviser's office, to plan large-scale maneuvers near Manila. They were to culminate with a massive parade that MacArthur thought would showcase the country's developing military, building pride and support in the process. Given the limited budget of the Philippine forces, Eisenhower and Ord were appalled at the cost of bringing thousands of troops from throughout the islands to the capital, but they began to make the plans.

When President Quezon got wind of the proposed troop movements and asked Eisenhower about it, Eisenhower was astonished to learn that MacArthur had not cleared the event with Quezon. The Philippine president got upset with MacArthur and angrily called a halt to the maneuvers. MacArthur then called Eisenhower and Ord on the carpet and denied he had ever given orders for them to proceed—he merely wanted them to investigate the possibility, he said. This was "certainly news to us," Eisenhower recalled, and from then on "never again" were he and MacArthur "on the same warm and cordial terms."[27]

The parade episode also struck a sour note into the mutual admiration society that had theretofore been established between MacArthur and Quezon. Part of the problem was that Quezon was flexing his political muscle. He had begun to call for full independence earlier than 1946, but at the same time, he questioned the effectiveness of MacArthur's plans for a citizen army. In the fall of 1939, Quezon told a large gathering in Manila on the anniversary of the founding of the commonwealth, "The Philippines could not be defended even if every last Filipino were armed with modern weapons." He shut out MacArthur, going so far as to have his secretary, Jorge Vargas, tell MacArthur that Quezon was too busy to see him. Uncharacteristically, MacArthur seems to have taken this in stride and calmly told Vargas, "Jorge, some day your boss is going to want to see me more than I want to see him."[28]

At the same time, MacArthur was also losing Eisenhower. After seven years with MacArthur, four of them in the Philippines, Eisenhower finally prevailed upon the general to approve his transfer back to the States, where he was anxious to get a troop command in light of the gathering war clouds over Europe. When the two parted in Manila, in December of 1939, each had occasionally rankled the other during their association, but MacArthur had generally held Eisenhower in high esteem, and, later frustrations aside, Eisenhower would reflect that he was always "deeply grateful for the administrative experience he gained under General MacArthur."[29] When they next met, it was in Japan in 1946, and both were five-star generals.

Eisenhower's replacement as MacArthur's chief of staff and right-hand man was Lieutenant Colonel Richard K. Sutherland, who had joined the staff after Ord's death in a plane crash the previous year. A Yale graduate who had gotten his commission by competitive exam, Sutherland was brash, hard-edged, and frequently unpleasant with his subordinates. He was, however, devotedly loyal to MacArthur, and the general considered him invaluable in return.

Lieutenant Colonel Richard J. Marshall became MacArthur's other key aide, charged with the thankless tasks of procurement and supply. He was a graduate of Virginia Military Institute and had been a battery commander in the artillery before transferring to the Quartermaster Corps. While neither Sutherland nor Marshall could claim the West Point pedigree that MacArthur held so dear, they became the first members of the group of insiders that would come to be called MacArthur's Bataan Gang.[30]

There was another Marshall—also a graduate of VMI—who would come to figure heavily in MacArthur's future. This was George

Catlett Marshall, who had briefly been part of Pershing's headquarters staff at Chaumont. His path and MacArthur's had first crossed at Fort Leavenworth prior to that war, and whatever else George Marshall thought of Douglas MacArthur, he had supported MacArthur's attempt to press on to capture Metz even as some on Pershing's staff questioned MacArthur's frontline antics. Marshall's specialty was in administration and training, but when he was promoted to colonel in September of 1933, he hoped for command of an infantry regiment. Instead he was assigned to be a senior instructor for the Illinois National Guard.

Years later, those looking to magnify every slight tension in the MacArthur-Marshall relationship would be quick to say that MacArthur, as chief of staff, had exiled Marshall to the Illinois National Guard. But MacArthur's oft-quoted opinion that Marshall had "no superior among infantry colonels" was sincere, and MacArthur wanted to provide top training to a politically sensitive command. Pershing, and by some accounts Marshall himself, appealed to MacArthur, but he refused to assign Marshall otherwise or promote him to brigadier general. MacArthur may have been saving Marshall for a temporary major generalship as chief of infantry when that position opened up, but before that happened MacArthur was out as chief of staff.[31]

Finally, the floodgates opened for George Marshall, and he was promoted to brigadier general in October of 1936. After a stint commanding an infantry brigade at Vancouver Barracks in Washington State, he moved to Washington, DC, first briefly as chief of the War Plans Division and then as deputy chief of staff. He got on well with Franklin Roosevelt during their early encounters and seems to have impressed the president by speaking his mind. The result was that on September 1, 1939, George Marshall became chief of staff and a four-star general. On that same day, Adolf Hitler invaded Poland.

For a man whose strengths usually included the ability to see the sweep of geography and its relationship to any battlefield, Douglas MacArthur gave little advice on the early phases of the new war in Europe. To be sure, the United States was not yet in the conflict, but a key reason for MacArthur's reticence was his preoccupation with the situation in the Philippines. Prior whimsical whispers of his possible candidacy for the presidency in 1940 proved just that—whimsy. Besides, Roosevelt shocked observers and defied convention by announcing his run for an unprecedented third term. Consequently MacArthur once again focused on obtaining appointment as high commissioner.

In March of 1941, MacArthur wrote presidential press secretary Stephen Early asking for the position in anticipation of Francis Bowes Sayre being recalled to the State Department. Telling Early that he held "the complete confidence of the Filipinos," MacArthur went on to assert, "From Vladivostok to Singapore I am thoroughly familiar with the most intimate details, political, military and commercial. I have a personal acquaintance with everyone of importance in the Orient and I believe no American holds the friendship and respect of this part of the world more than myself." As was his custom—and despite their prior fencing—MacArthur closed with a glowing tribute, calling FDR "not only our greatest statesman but what to me is even more thrilling, our greatest military strategist."[32]

Franklin Roosevelt, himself a master of effusive praise, was the least likely person to be swayed by it. Determined to keep MacArthur on the military side, Roosevelt had his military aide, Edwin "Pa" Watson, assure MacArthur that "in all discussions as to the availability of various active and retired officers, your name is always outstanding and most seriously considered."[33] Just what role he might fill was clarified two months later, when chief of staff Marshall informed MacArthur unofficially that he would be "the logical selection as the Army Commander in the Far East should the situation approach a crisis."[34] Two days after Marshall wrote this, it did.

On June 22, 1941, Hitler sent three million troops on a massive invasion of the Soviet Union, his former ally. His turnabout momentarily gave leaders in Japan pause. Because American code breakers were already deciphering some Japanese intercepts, Roosevelt was able to gauge the debate within the Japanese government. He characterized it as "a real drag-down and knock-out fight among themselves...to decide which way they are going to jump—attack Russia, attack the South Seas (thus throwing in their lot definitely with Germany) or whether they will sit on the fence and be more friendly with us."[35]

Japan chose to continue its attacks in China and pursue its long-range goal—to secure natural resources in the East Indies and on the Malay Peninsula. All maps showed the Philippines to be between Japan and that goal. In mid-July of 1941, with Vichy France essentially a puppet state of Germany, Japanese forces completed the occupation of French Indochina (present-day Vietnam, Laos, and Cambodia), partially encircling the Philippines and coming within striking distance of Singapore and Borneo. Roosevelt's reaction on July 26 was to freeze Japanese assets in the United States, close the Panama Canal to Japanese shipping, and, along with the British and Dutch, create an economic blockade of Japan.

Once again Japan faced a critical decision. It could consolidate its gains to date and negotiate with the United States and its allies for oil and other resources in amounts that would sustain it but not allow the pursuit of further conquest, or it could continue its expansion. Largely as a matter of saving face, militarists in its government prevailed and chose the latter.

On July 26, as part of the American reaction, the president nationalized the Philippine army into the service of the United States, and the War Department established a new Far Eastern command. Acting on his unofficial statement to MacArthur of the month before, Marshall recalled him to active duty as a major general and designated him "Commanding General, United States Army Forces, Far East" (USAFFE).[36] A day later, Roosevelt appointed him to the temporary rank of lieutenant general.

Suddenly, Manuel Quezon was only too happy to see him—just as MacArthur had predicted. Quezon wrote MacArthur the next day expressing his full confidence that MacArthur would "attain in this difficult assignment the same success that has crowned your every endeavor in the past."[37] No doubt thinking of the MacArthur allure that the general himself went out of his way to promote, Quezon felt assured that if Roosevelt was appointing MacArthur to this position, it was evidence of a major American commitment to the defense of the Philippines and, if necessary, interdiction against Japanese aggression throughout the Far East.

It was a sign of his long-standing personal affection for Quezon that MacArthur appears to have welcomed him back into the fold. But

MacArthur could afford to be magnanimous. He suddenly had much of what he wanted: Roosevelt had given him supreme US Army authority in the Far East; Quezon again looked to him as the savior of the Philippines; and the Philippine Department of the US Army, which had occasionally bedeviled him with its chain of command running to Washington, was firmly under his control.

Paying more attention to these largely cosmetic changes around him than to the strength and intentions of Japan's military, MacArthur was his optimistic self. Writing John C. O'Laughlin, a staunch Republican and the publisher of the *Army and Navy Journal,* about the mood in the Far East, MacArthur asserted: "President Roosevelt's action… completely changed the picture and an immediate and universal feeling of confidence and assurance resulted." Tokyo, MacArthur claimed, "was dumbfounded and depressed."[38]

Even as he wrote these lines, MacArthur received word that the planning gurus in the War Department had once again been tinkering with Plan Orange. In fact, in recognition of the likelihood that any future conflict would be against multiple foes, the color-coded, single-foe plans originally devised decades earlier had been replaced with a rainbow scheme. Part of this scheme was a plan called Rainbow 5, which contemplated a two-ocean global war in alliance with Great Britain against both Germany and Japan.

Rainbow 5 had grown out of joint British-American talks—dubbed ABC for "American-British conversations"—which in many respects were the forerunner of the deliberations of the wartime Combined Chiefs of Staff. Of central importance to the Philippines were the salient points that any war in Europe would take precedence over Pacific operations—a strategy quickly termed Germany First—and that the key line of defense in the Pacific would be the previously delineated Alaska-Hawaii-Panama axis. Any operations in the Philippines were to be conducted with existing forces and then only with the aim of holding Manila Bay and its immediate environs.[39]

While he had disregarded much of Plan Orange and its subsequent revisions, MacArthur reacted angrily to Rainbow 5. What had he been working for these last six years if the Philippines were to be presumptively abandoned? Forcefully, he lobbied Marshall and insisted that the

Philippines should and could be held, and in late November of 1941, the Joint Army and Navy Board amended Rainbow 5 to approve MacArthur's recommendation that the Philippine Sea Frontier be expanded from Luzon to include such land and sea areas necessary to defend the entire Philippine archipelago.

Under the amended Rainbow 5, in the event of hostilities MacArthur was further assigned the tasks of supporting the US Navy in raiding Japanese sea communications, conducting air raids against Japanese forces and installations within range of his available bases, including Formosa, and cooperating with British and Dutch allies in defense of their territories. With British agreement, the joint ABC-1 plan added Luzon to Malaya, Singapore, and Java as key points to be held against any Japanese attack.[40] The list would prove prescient.

But by committing to defend the entire Philippine archipelago, MacArthur created a logistical nightmare as well as an operational "mission impossible" that would soon come back to haunt him. The only thing that would spawn more dire consequences was his unbridled enthusiasm and misplaced confidence. MacArthur's biggest liability was his own unrealistic assessment of the situation. Repeatedly, during the fall of 1941, he advised Marshall and the War Department of his preparations and the effectiveness of his command.

In response, Marshall continued to express satisfaction if not some measure of surprise, given the limited resources available for American defense that Marshall faced daily. "The Secretary of War and I were highly pleased," Marshall cabled MacArthur on November 28, 1941, "to receive your report that your command is ready for any eventuality."[41]

After more than a decade of Washington's lack of interest in the Philippines and its ability to defend itself, MacArthur's exuberance about the capabilities of his staff and the untried Filipino soldiers they led infected the War Department with similar optimism. If MacArthur, in his most pontifical way, said it was so, it must be so, and given the enormous demands cascading on them from around the globe, the Washington establishment momentarily believed him.

CHAPTER FOUR

Lost Hours

In his memoirs, written long after the fact, Douglas MacArthur lamented, "No one will ever know how much could have been done to aid the Philippines if there had been a determined will-to-win."[1] The truth is that a considerable amount *was* done in the fall of 1941, in large part because MacArthur had convinced the War Department of his ability to hold the islands against any attack. Largely on his assessment, American strategy — rapidly reversed from the prior decade — called for a firm stand in the Philippines as a general deterrent to Japanese expansion and an impediment to any attack they might launch.

During the few short months between creating the USAFFE command in July and that December, the War Department made what, given other needs around the world, can only be termed supreme commitments of men, aircraft, arms, and ammunition. Secretary of war Henry Stimson, chief of staff George Marshall, and the war planners would not have done so had they not believed MacArthur's assertion that he could successfully defend the islands.

On July 31, 1941, US Army forces in the Philippines, including the Army Air Corps, totaled 22,532 troops, of which 11,937 were Philippine Scouts. The scouts were elite units of Filipinos generally serving under American officers, and they had been part of the American army in the Philippines since the days of Arthur MacArthur. Just four months later, on November 30, these force totals had grown to 31,095 troops. The biggest jump—indicative of the response to MacArthur's pleas to strengthen his air defenses—had been in the air corps. It had more than doubled, to 5,609, and included 669 officers and 4,940 enlisted men.[2]

Records for US Army aircraft operating in the Philippines by the first week of December in 1941 vary. By one account, there were thirty-five B-17 heavy bombers, fifteen B-18 medium bombers, ninety-one P-40 fighters, twenty-six P-35 fighters, and fourteen assorted observation and utility aircraft, for a total of 181 planes. Other sources report a higher number of P-40s and P-35s and apparently count some aging B-10 bombers and P-26 fighters for a total of 277 planes.[3]

What is certain, however, is the number of B-17s and that MacArthur counted on their presence to form the backbone of his offshore defenses as well as provide an offensive punch against Japanese shipping and land bases in Formosa and Indochina. And more B-17s were on the way. Washington had decided to send additional B-17s to the islands, and the B-17s that so famously arrived over Pearl Harbor from the mainland during the Japanese attack had in fact been scheduled to continue on to the Philippines. Incredibly, and in rebuttal to any claim—MacArthur's or otherwise—that the War Department abandoned MacArthur *before* Pearl Harbor, the thirty-five B-17s in the Philippines on December 8, 1941, were three times the number in operation throughout the entire Hawaiian Islands. The cream of the new P-40E fighters had also gone to the Philippines in a similar ratio.[4]

In contrast to this direct American buildup, Philippine defense forces numbered far below the levels MacArthur had anticipated in 1935. In some measure, this was attributable to vacillation within the Philippine government regarding the overall importance of national defense. There was a belief in certain quarters, among them Quezon himself, that the Philippines could remain neutral and untouched in the face of Japanese aggression in Southeast Asia. That hope—misplaced though it almost certainly was—may have been behind Quezon's push for independence earlier than the 1946 mandate. As part of the United States' sphere of influence, the islands were sure to become embroiled

in any American-Japanese conflict; as an independent backwater, they might just fade into the periphery and remain untouched. It was a rather unrealistic view, but it was what some Filipinos hoped would happen.[5]

By 1940, the regulars of the Philippine army—projected to number eleven thousand under MacArthur's original National Defense Plan—totaled only 468 officers and 3,697 enlisted men. The real foundation of MacArthur's defense scheme, however, had been a citizen army, for which his goal was to train forty thousand new reserve troops a year. This target had not been realized, either. When MacArthur assumed the USAFFE command, Philippine reservists spread throughout the archipelago totaled only 76,000 men—on paper. Those who were properly equipped and retained an effective measure of their training were far fewer in number.[6]

The neophyte Philippine air corps and navy had not fared any better. By the end of 1940, the air force had only forty antiquated planes, one hundred pilots, and around three hundred ground personnel against MacArthur's target of 250 planes. His charge to build fifty torpedo boats had resulted in the purchase of two lightly armed models from the British in 1939 and five additional vessels that were then under construction in a Manila shipyard. It was no wonder that when MacArthur received his orders as USAFFE commander, his chief of staff, Colonel Richard Sutherland, remarked, "You know, General, it adds up to an almost insurmountable task."[7] Nothing, however, had dampened MacArthur's blind enthusiasm and resolve.

On December 3, 1941, MacArthur issued an order to his field commanders that any Japanese invasion was to be repulsed on the beaches and that the territory was to be "held at all costs." But theirs was an impossible task. With thousands of miles of suitable landing sites scattered among the archipelago's seven-thousand-plus islands, there was simply no way that the meager forces of the Philippine army, even augmented by US Army units, could defend the country. On northern Luzon, where Major General Jonathan Wainwright commanded four infantry divisions and one cavalry regiment—all understrength—there were six hundred miles of coastline to protect. MacArthur had indeed been successful in amending Rainbow 5 so that he could defend the entire archipelago, but his forces were spread far too thin to do it.[8]

*   *   *

Meanwhile, Douglas MacArthur had a partner in the United States Navy. The American Asiatic Fleet was hardly a powerhouse, but given the exigencies then requiring attention in an undeclared war in the North Atlantic against German U-boats and the consolidation of the Pacific Fleet in and around Pearl Harbor, the fleet was nonetheless a welcome addition to Philippine defenses. Its commander was Admiral Thomas C. Hart, an 1897 graduate of the Naval Academy and an accomplished hand in Far Eastern waters. Hart's ships included his flagship, the heavy cruiser *Houston,* the light cruisers *Marblehead* and *Boise* (the latter borrowed from the Pacific Fleet after it arrived in Manila on December 4, escorting an inbound convoy), thirteen destroyers, twenty-nine submarines of various ages and capabilities, and a number of gunboats, torpedo boats, and auxiliary craft.

Throughout the fall, Hart's angst over the gathering war clouds had been exacerbated by a side duel with Douglas MacArthur. Hart was meticulous by nature and not one to rest until every hatch was doubled and every line secured. Faced with an uncertain situation in the Far East, Hart left his flagship at the end of June, 1941, and moved ashore into an apartment one floor below MacArthur in the Manila Hotel in an attempt to foster better cooperation with the general and address the requirements of defending a huge area with a less-than-modest force.

Hart had been operating under the original dictates of Rainbow 5. It ordered his fleet to disperse to the south in the event of a Japanese attack and link up with British and Dutch units to protect the Malay Peninsula and Java while the army concentrated on the short-term defense of Manila Bay. However, Hart couldn't help but be influenced by MacArthur's contagious optimism. As early as September 2, 1941, MacArthur assured Hart that there was "plenty of time" for defensive preparations. A few weeks later — before he got Rainbow 5 amended to his satisfaction — MacArthur told Hart he was "not going to follow, or be in any way bound by whatever war plans had been evolved, agreed upon and approved."[9]

On October 27, sensing that MacArthur was making progress in building up defenses in the Philippines, Hart informed Admiral Harold Stark, chief of naval operations, that given the apparent wide latitude in his standing orders, he intended to keep his small fleet together and concentrated in Manila Bay, assured of defensive air cover by MacArthur's P-40s and aided in any offensive operations against approaching Japanese ships by the newly arrived B-17s.[10] This decision was not made because Hart and MacArthur were getting along well: their relationship was just the opposite.

While Hart had moved in only one floor below the general, MacArthur made it clear on multiple occasions that he considered Hart and his navy far down the ladder of importance when it came to the defense of the Philippines. Their major substantive disagreement came when Hart tried to clarify lines of responsibility between the navy and the army for offshore air defenses. When he received no response from MacArthur, Hart drafted a plan that gave the navy control of all air operations over water. This got MacArthur's attention. He reacted immediately and quite negatively to what he considered a power grab by Hart and responded with what Hart called a "perfectly rotten" letter "being nasty to the Navy in general and me in particular."[11]

A few weeks later, they settled the matter by agreeing that MacArthur's B-17s would take responsibility for the coastal waters off Luzon and northward toward Formosa, while Hart's amphibious PBY Catalinas would patrol south of Luzon and as far west as the coastal waters of Indochina.[12]

According to Hart, a seemingly innocuous event—what should have been viewed as a minor clerical mix-up—occurred around the same time and showed the extent of MacArthur's wrath toward the navy and the admiral personally. Concerned that shore leaves in the international section of Shanghai might provoke an incident between American and Japanese personnel, Hart issued orders to his fleet about shore leave precautions. But an information copy of the order got mixed up with the action copy, which went to MacArthur by mistake, and "that made it appear," wrote Hart, "that I was giving MacArthur orders!"[13]

The general's wrath was predictable, even in the face of Hart's explanation and subsequent apology. MacArthur telephoned Hart and launched into a full tirade before firing off a letter to Washington castigating Hart over military protocol and the limits of his authority. MacArthur may also have been reacting to Hart's appearance on the cover of the November 24, 1941, issue of *Time* magazine. The article made it seem as though the admiral was the key US representative in the Far East. It certainly grated on MacArthur that because Hart was the commanding admiral of a fleet—no matter how small—his flag flew the four stars of a temporary full admiral. MacArthur, as a temporary lieutenant general, was one star short. This did not, however, keep MacArthur from disparaging Hart's situation as "Small Fleet, big Admiral."[14]

"Get yourself a real fleet, Tommy, then you will belong," Hart recalled MacArthur telling him after MacArthur, clad in his bathrobe, as usual, made one of his frequent visits to Hart's quarters on the floor below. "I listened to such patronizing talk," Hart wrote his wife, "and under the circumstances it was not pleasant." But Hart had an edge on MacArthur that may have contributed to MacArthur's pique. As someone who had attended Annapolis with MacArthur's older brother, Arthur III, and as someone who had been one of Arthur's best friends and pallbearers, Tommy Hart knew the MacArthur family well. He was one of the few people not awed by Douglas MacArthur or cowed by his rants. Consequently Hart did not treat MacArthur with the deference that so many others did, and he was one of the very few who thought nothing of addressing MacArthur as Douglas.[15]

That didn't necessarily make it any more comfortable for Hart to endure MacArthur's magisterial manner, but it did give him a forty-year perspective in observing MacArthur. "Douglas," Hart confided to his diary early in 1940, "knows a lot of things which are not so; he is a very able and convincing talker—a combination which spells danger."[16]

While much of this was petty, MacArthur believed it was not, and it set the tone for his relations with the navy over the next several years. Those critical weeks in Manila were the first time MacArthur had to work closely with the navy, save for the budget battles when he was chief of staff. In his memoirs, MacArthur waxed poetic about his wonderful relationship with the navy, but by the final months of 1941, before a single gun had been fired, the navy had already served as his ready scapegoat. MacArthur would later grouse, "Apparently, [Hart] was certain that the islands were doomed and made no effort to keep open our lines of supply," but the truth was that Hart admired the fighter in MacArthur and was in fact responding as a fighter himself when he proposed concentrating his fleet in Manila Bay.[17]

But Washington was not going to let Hart do it. Admiral Stark disapproved Hart's plan to concentrate in Manila Bay and ordered him to disperse his forces in keeping with the earlier Rainbow 5 plan. Accordingly, the admiral dispatched the cruiser *Marblehead* and four destroyers to Tarakan, in eastern Borneo, and the tender *Black Hawk* and another four destroyers to Balikpapan, a little farther south. The *Houston* left Manila Bay, bound eventually for Surabaya, in Java. For the moment, Hart stayed in Manila at MacArthur's side to command the big picture.[18]

General MacArthur, Admiral Hart, and Francis Bowes Sayre, high commissioner of the Philippines, met on November 27, 1941, in Sayre's office to discuss the latest round of urgent messages each commander had received. For MacArthur, it was an alert from George Marshall to him and his counterpart in Hawaii. "Negotiations with Japan appear to be terminated [for] all practical purposes," Marshall warned. Japan's future strategy was unpredictable, but "hostile action" was "possible at any moment." The message went on to stress that if hostilities could not be avoided, the United States wanted Japan to commit the first overt act, but US forces should not hold back to the extent that it "might jeopardize your defense." Then came rather key words, particularly for MacArthur. "Should hostilities occur," Marshall directed, "you will carry out the tasks assigned in Rainbow 5."[19]

The warning message Hart received from Admiral Stark was worded even more strongly: "Negotiations with Japan...have ceased and an aggressive move by Japan is expected within the next few days." Hart was alerted to the possibility of a Japanese invasion of the Philippines, Thailand, or Malaya and told to take appropriate defensive measures. This was the same warning that was sent to the United States Fleet at Pearl Harbor.[20]

According to Sayre, MacArthur held court at the meeting and assured Hart and Sayre that because of "the existing alignment and movement of Japanese troops...there would be no Japanese attack before the spring." Hart was skeptical and argued otherwise without convincing MacArthur.[21] But the next day MacArthur replied to Marshall: "Within the limitations imposed by present state of development of this theater of operations, everything is in readiness for the conduct of a successful defense."[22]

If MacArthur had left the regal confines of his penthouse suite or his nearby office at 1 Calle Victoria more frequently, he might have felt otherwise. His office log for the critical three months of October, November, and December of 1941 shows only three brief trips, all in October, to military installations near Manila and at Baguio.[23] MacArthur seemed mired in a time and pace that were much slower than that the Japanese were about to visit upon him.

Plans to cooperate with British and Dutch forces received a lift early in December, when Vice Admiral Sir Tom Phillips of the Royal Navy flew to Manila from Singapore to confer with Admiral Hart. Phillips brought encouraging news: the British were strengthening their battle fleet at Singapore with the deployment of the battle cruiser *Repulse* and the battleship *Prince of Wales,* the latter of which had dueled with the *Bismarck* and more recently had carried Winston Churchill to his Atlantic Charter conference with Franklin Roosevelt.

The first order of business was for the two pint-size admirals — neither weighed more than 150 pounds or stood taller than five feet six — to meet with MacArthur. Towering above them and pacing about as usual, the general reiterated his standard refrain about his plans and preparations for the war he expected in the spring. Playing the ever-gracious host and congenial interservice ally, MacArthur assured Phillips that he acted "in the closest cooperation" with Hart and that the two were "the oldest and dearest friends."[24]

Once MacArthur departed, Hart and Phillips wrangled over how quickly the American navy would implement Rainbow 5 and commit destroyers to aid the British in the defense of Singapore. Clearly the fighter in Hart responded well to the fighting spirit that he found in Phillips, and the British admiral went so far as to agree with Hart that Manila made a better base for offensive operations in the South China Sea than Singapore, farther to the south.

But on Saturday, December 6, as these discussions entered a second day, Phillips received an urgent communiqué confirming the presence of a Japanese amphibious force in the Gulf of Siam, bound for somewhere along the Malay Peninsula. Phillips immediately flew back to Singapore, telling Hart that he would gather what ships he could around the *Repulse* and *Prince of Wales* and sail north to meet the threat. Hart was by no means certain that an attack on the Philippines would occur and had only just received indirect word that an attack on British or Dutch possessions would be enough to trigger Rainbow 5. Nonetheless, as Phillips boarded his plane, Hart told him that he was ordering his Balikpapan destroyers to Singapore.[25]

On that same day, MacArthur ordered Wainwright to be ready to deploy his North Luzon Force to its assigned positions for beach defense. According to Wainwright, the tension around his headquarters, at Fort Stotsenburg, around forty miles northwest of Manila, "could be cut with a knife."[26] His troops were not expecting to wait until spring for an attack. Meanwhile, MacArthur assured the Army Air Forces chief, Major General Henry H. "Hap" Arnold, that a full air alert was in effect and that all aircraft were dispersed and under guard to protect against sabotage.[27]

The man in direct command of MacArthur's air force was Major General Lewis H. Brereton, newly arrived in Manila from the States early in November. Brereton had a reputation as a pilot's pilot, although it had not come easily. He had transferred to the army upon graduation from Annapolis in 1911 and weathered two air crashes, a stint in the field artillery, and an overseas tour in the Philippines, flying off Corregidor, before rising to command the Twelfth Aero Squadron during World War I. For a time, his squadron flew above the trenches of France in support of the advance of MacArthur's Rainbow Division.

During the post–World War I period, Brereton's marriage disintegrated, partly as a result of his heavy drinking. He was also involved in another fatal crash, and his mentor, Billy Mitchell, was court-martialed. In the 1930s, Brereton remarried and largely rehabilitated himself, although hard living and partying remained his style. By the summer of 1941, Brereton was a major general in command of the Third Air Force. That was when Arnold summoned him to Washington and told him that MacArthur had personally requested his assignment to the Philippines.[28]

MacArthur immediately dispatched Brereton to Australia to survey ferry routes and bases from Hawaii across northern Australia to the Philippines and Java to accommodate reinforcements of B-17s. This was important, but it was also indicative of the fact that MacArthur did not intend to rush preparations in the Philippines. Brereton and MacArthur both might have been better served if Brereton had stayed on the scene to hurry construction of new facilities at Del Monte, on Mindanao, or the expansion at Clark Field, on Luzon, which was critical to the dispersal of parked aircraft.

On November 26, Brereton flew into Clark Field in a B-17 on his return from Australia and was appalled by what he saw from the air. "Gentlemen," Brereton seethed to the officers who assembled to meet him, "I have just seen this field from the air. Fortunately for you and all who depend on us, I was not leading a hostile bombing fleet. If I had been, I could have blasted the entire heavy bomber strength of the Philippines off the map in one smash. Do you call that dispersal?"[29]

Thirty-four B-17s were neatly parked in various groups, and the twenty-three P-40s of the Twentieth Pursuit Squadron were clustered together even more tightly. Lieutenant Colonel Eugene Eubank, the commander of the Nineteenth Bomb Group, winced under Brereton's tongue-lashing, but he knew that a large part of the problem was that there was simply no room to spread the planes out within the current confines of Clark Field. The airstrip was an island of developed space surrounded by boggy ground that could not support the 35,000-pound empty weight of B-17s without their getting stuck in the mud.

Brereton met with MacArthur the next day, and the general was so pleased with his air chief's report on the Australia trip that he wanted Brereton to depart immediately on a similar mission to Singapore and the Netherlands East Indies. This time, Brereton begged off for a few days in order to address the Clark Field situation and the status of his other units. Once MacArthur received Marshall's alert that same day, the Singapore mission was put on hold indefinitely and Brereton, with MacArthur's approval, issued a twenty-four-hour alert order to his squadrons. They were to be ready for action around the clock.[30]

The alert order included critical instructions for Colonel Eubank and his Nineteenth Bomb Group. Two squadrons of B-17s from Clark, totaling sixteen planes, were to stand ready to fly to Del Monte, in northern Mindanao, on twelve hours' notice. Since the facilities there were primitive at best, the crews would have to take tents, food, ammunition, and other essentials to sustain them for at least a three-day stay. Brereton's plan was to remove them from the danger and congestion of Clark Field and then, in the event of war, rotate them back and forth between Clark and Del Monte.

Given what was to occur at Clark Field on December 8, there would always be considerable finger-pointing over who gave what orders regarding the movement of B-17s to Del Monte. Brereton claimed that his staff had worked on the airfield construction at Del Monte since his arrival in the Philippines and that he was the proponent of basing the bulk of the heavy bombers there. Sutherland maintained that the initiative was his own—or MacArthur's—and that he had given Brereton a direct order, which had not been obeyed, to move all B-17s to Del Monte. There is evidence, however, that Sutherland opposed permanent dispersal to Del Monte because, as he said at the time, "the war plan for the Philippines does not provide for any ground forces for the defense of Mindanao."[31]

On the morning of December 5, Captain Colin Kelly, who would soon become one of the war's first heroes, flew his B-17 northward from Clark Field on the Nineteenth Bomb Group's daily reconnaissance run toward Formosa. Kelly had orders, possibly from Eubank, to overfly the southern tip of the island and photograph the harbor and airfield at Takao. This was a bit of a gamble, and the orders may or may not have originated with Eubank.

After the alert message of November 27, Brereton had asked MacArthur for permission to conduct such overflights, but the general rejected the request on the grounds that they could be considered just the sort of provocation that Marshall had warned against. On the other hand, Eubank knew that he might soon be called upon to lead a full-scale air strike against Takao, and getting intelligence ahead of actual hostilities seemed worth the risk.

Brereton likely agreed and was willing to provide Eubank cover if MacArthur learned of the mission. MacArthur himself was being less than candid with Brereton and evidently did not tell his air commander that two B-24 Liberator bombers, equipped for high-altitude photography, were en route to the Philippines for just that purpose. Within seventy-two hours, the issue of a photo recon mission over Takao would figure heavily in events.[32]

Following the return of Kelly's B-17 to Clark Field—his crew would later give conflicting reports about whether they had taken photographs and/or come under fire from a Japanese floatplane—Eubank ordered two squadrons, totaling sixteen of his bombers, to make the planned move south. They were to take off that night and arrive at Del Monte at first light on December 6. Del Monte wasn't much of a place—only one grassy runway that sloped downhill toward a gaping canyon. The B-17s that arrived there were still painted bright silver, making them visible for miles against the airfield's verdant grass. Ground crews made plans to paint them dark green as soon as possible.

But the operational problem remained one of limited ground space. Clark Field was expecting the arrival of the thirteen B-17s of the Seventh Bomb Group. They were scheduled to depart the West Coast for Hawaii on the evening of December 7, Manila time, and they had to base somewhere. Rather than move the remainder of Eubank's bombers from Clark to Del Monte, Eubank advised Brereton to base the arriving Seventh Bomb Group at Del Monte instead. This would keep them out of the congestion of Clark, but it would also mean that Del Monte would be able to accommodate only two of Eubank's four squadrons.[33]

By Sunday evening, December 7, half the B-17s at Clark Field had been flown to Del Monte. That left nineteen B-17s, twenty-three of the older P-40s, and ten B-18s still at Clark. But while Clark was the only strip in Luzon capable of handling heavy bombers, it was by no means Luzon's only airfield. The other fighters of Brereton's command were based among four other fields roughly surrounding Manila Bay. At Iba Field, on the coast of the South China Sea west of Clark, eighteen P-40s of the Third Pursuit Squadron sat on the flight line in tactical readiness. These planes were the best fighters in the American arsenal, but although each was equipped with six .50-caliber machine guns, none had been test-fired. Iba's fighters and twenty-two older P-35s of the Thirty-Fourth Pursuit Squadron at Del Carmen Field, just south of Clark Field, were charged with intercepting enemy bombers and fighters inbound to the Manila area and with providing air cover to Clark Field.

At Nichols Field, just south of Manila, the Twenty-First Pursuit Squadron had received its first ten P-40s on December 4 and a second ten two days later. None had more than two hours' time on their engines, and the planes were parked in the woods at the edge of the field. Twenty-one P-40s of the Seventeenth Pursuit Squadron and some observation aircraft rounded out the complement at Nichols. At nearby Nielson Field, just east of Manila, the pilots of the Twenty-Seventh Bomb Group were raring to go, but they were without planes. The group was to receive fifty-two A-24 Banshees, the army version of the navy's single-engine Douglas SBD Dauntless dive-bomber, but they had yet to arrive. With no planes, they were not subject to Brereton's 24-7 alert order, so they gathered on Sunday evening at the Manila Hotel to throw a belated welcome party for General Brereton, who had been the group's commander back in the States.[34]

Brereton's party, with MacArthur's chief of staff, Richard Sutherland, and Hart's chief of staff, Rear Admiral William Purnell, in attendance, was just getting into full swing shortly before midnight when the Air Warning Service (AWS) at Brereton's headquarters at Nielson Field reported that radar at Iba had picked up unidentified planes coming in from the north. Brereton hurriedly left the party, called his staff together at Nielson, and notified all airfields to go on combat alert at first light. According to Brereton, this meant that the bombers were to be loaded and ready for takeoff "in a little over an hour" and the fighters ready to roll "in a little under an hour."[35]

At the headquarters of Hart's Asiatic Fleet, in the Marsman Building, around three hundred yards from the Manila Hotel, the duty officer that evening was Marine Lieutenant Colonel William T. Clement. At 2:30 a.m. on December 8, Manila time—which was 8:00 a.m. on December 7 in Hawaii—Clement's radio operator handed him an intercepted message that had been hurriedly tapped out without being encoded. It was not addressed specifically to the Asiatic Fleet, but by the key technique the Manila operator recognized the sender to be a friend from prior service, and he assured Clement that the message was authentic. It read: "Air raid on Pearl Harbor. This is no drill."[36]

Clement telephoned Admiral Hart's apartment in the Manila Hotel and woke him. "Admiral," said Clement, "put some cold water on your face. I'm coming over with a message." A few minutes later, after Clement had delivered the news, Hart sat on the edge of his bed and wrote out a dispatch for immediate transmission to his fleet: "Japan started hostilities. Govern yourselves accordingly." Then Hart called his chief of staff, got dressed, and — assuming correctly that it would be a long day — grabbed a hurried breakfast before heading to his office around 4:00 a.m.[37]

Hart later recalled that Clement was unable to get any response from MacArthur's headquarters and finally passed the news "to one of the staff duty officers at his home."[38] According to Samuel Eliot Morison, Hart's chief of staff, Admiral Purnell, drove to MacArthur's headquarters at 1 Calle Victoria and gave the same message to Sutherland, "who," Morison claimed, "had not yet heard the news."[39] Other reports, including Sutherland's own, are adamant that Sutherland learned the news — not from the navy or a communication from Washington but from a commercial radio broadcast.[40] However he learned of it, at around 3:40 a.m. Sutherland picked up the private telephone that was connected to the penthouse atop the Manila Hotel and woke Douglas MacArthur.

In Washington, it was midafternoon on December 7. Secretary of the navy Frank Knox was finishing a conference with chief of naval operations Harold Stark and Stark's war plans chief, Rear Admiral Richmond Kelly Turner. Reading a message thrust into his hands by an aide, Knox exclaimed, "My God, this can't be true, this must mean the Philippines." Stark gave it a quick perusal and replied, "No, sir, this is Pearl."[41]

Knox immediately called President Roosevelt at the White House, and Roosevelt in turn phoned secretary of war Stimson. Stimson's first reaction was also to think of the Philippines — both because of his past association with the islands and his and Marshall's high degree of pre-occupation with them over the previous few months. Two hours earlier, Marshall had sent his Pacific commanders the ultimate war warning — that Japanese diplomats in Washington were presenting within the hour "what amounts to an ultimatum" and preparing to destroy their code machines. "Just what significance the hour set may have," Marshall concluded, "we do not know but be on alert accordingly."[42]

Stimson ordered Marshall to send a highest-priority message to MacArthur. Reporting the start of hostilities between Japan and the United States and its British and Dutch allies, Marshall reiterated the instructions of his November 27 alert: with hostilities begun, MacArthur was to "carry out tasks assigned in Rainbow Five so far as they pertain to Japan."[43] This second message was transmitted at 3:22 p.m. Washington time, and both Stimson and Marshall waited with growing impatience for some response from MacArthur, which would let them know whether or not the Philippines had been attacked. From Stimson and Marshall's perspective, with the United States at war, MacArthur was to conduct his assignments under Rainbow 5 regardless.

Having been awakened around 3:40 a.m. Manila time by Sutherland, MacArthur dressed and took a telephone call from Admiral Hart. As the general prepared to leave the penthouse for his office, an aide handed him Marshall's first message of the day, warning of the unknown consequences of Japan breaking diplomatic relations. Around an hour later, as MacArthur huddled with members of his staff at his 1 Calle Victoria headquarters, he received Marshall's second message, with the explicit order to execute the Rainbow 5 war plan.[44]

One key member of MacArthur's command was not, however, allowed into the inner sanctum of 1 Calle Victoria. The commander of the USAFFE, Lewis Brereton, was awakened by a call from Sutherland around 4:00 a.m. "I knew," Brereton later wrote in his diary, "we could expect an attack from the Japs any time after daylight."[45] According to Brereton, Sutherland told him that a state of war existed. Whether or not Sutherland asked Brereton to report to MacArthur's headquarters, Brereton decided to do so. Before leaving, he called the commander of his B-17s at Clark Field and asked him to fly to Nielson to receive orders. "Well, boys," said Eugene Eubank to those around him as he put down the phone, "here it is. It's what we've been waiting for." Eubank took his operations chief, Major Birrell "Mike" Walsh, with him and left Major David R. Gibbs in command of the B-17s at Clark.[46]

But when Brereton arrived at MacArthur's headquarters expecting to see the general and discuss the offensive use of Brereton's bombers under Rainbow 5, Sutherland brought the air chief up short. MacArthur was in conference, Brereton was told, and could not be disturbed. In his published diary, Brereton was gracious enough to say that he believed MacArthur was with Admiral Hart, although there is no evidence of that in any records or in the accounts of either man. But even if MacArthur were so occupied, adding his air commander to the mix would have been logical and expedient.

Instead Brereton conferred with Sutherland, who listened to his request that the B-17s at Clark be sent on their previously assigned mission to bomb Formosa and that the B-17s recently deployed to Del Monte be returned to Clark, where they could be refueled and loaded with bombs for subsequent operations. Sutherland agreed to general preparations but made it very clear that only MacArthur could authorize the attacks against Formosa.[47]

Brereton evidently returned to his quarters expecting some summons or directive from MacArthur. In the meantime, Eubank and Walsh flew into Nielson Field at around 6:30 a.m. and joined a planning conference with Brereton's staff while Brereton's chief of staff, Colonel Francis Brady, assured them Brereton was getting direction from MacArthur and would be arriving soon. There was considerable discussion about specific targets on Formosa, and the consensus was that the harbor at Takao would be the best choice.

At 7:15 a.m., having heard nothing from MacArthur, Brereton again presented himself at MacArthur's headquarters and asked Sutherland if the general had made his decision. Exactly what Brereton was doing for the two or so hours in the interim and why he was so patient in awaiting MacArthur's decision are two of the many mysteries of that morning.

When Sutherland informed Brereton that MacArthur had yet to make a decision, Brereton demanded to see MacArthur. But Sutherland was already well along in his role of stony gatekeeper, and while acknowledging that MacArthur was alone, he refused to permit Brereton to enter. Instead Sutherland told Brereton, "I'll ask the general," and slipped into MacArthur's office. According to a staff officer who witnessed this exchange, Sutherland was back all too soon with a firm "no" and the explanation that MacArthur wanted to wait for the Japanese to make the first overt act.

What had Pearl Harbor been, Brereton asked angrily, if not an overt act? Sutherland shook his head and held firm. But Sutherland and MacArthur were being disingenuous, because according to the USAFFE log, they had been made aware at 6:15 that morning—around an hour earlier than Brereton's second visit—that Japanese fighters and bombers from the aircraft carrier *Ryujo* had attacked an unoccupied airfield in Davao, in southeastern Mindanao, destroyed two navy PBYs, and chased the seaplane tender *William B. Preston* out of its anchorage. The Philippines were already under attack.[48]

Brereton left MacArthur's headquarters in a huff and ordered his driver to take him to his own headquarters, at Nielson Field. With "his face pale, his jaw hard," Brereton strode briskly into the room where his staff and Eubank were finishing plans for striking Takao. Brereton heard their recommendation and approved, but was forced to withhold an order to execute. "No," he said, shaking his head in frustration and repeating MacArthur's assertion. "We can't attack until we're fired upon."[49]

Meanwhile, it was early evening in Washington, and Stimson and Marshall were growing increasingly frustrated that they had heard nothing from MacArthur in reply to Marshall's two cables earlier in the day. MacArthur had also not responded to a more recent radiogram that instructed him to confirm the cables' receipt and "reply immediately." He still had not done so when, at 7:55 a.m. Manila time, Marshall's war plans chief, Brigadier General Leonard Gerow, succeeded in reaching MacArthur by telephone. MacArthur acknowledged receipt of Marshall's cables but offered no explanation for his failure to respond.

"Have you been attacked?" Gerow wanted to know. "No attack at all," MacArthur calmly replied, although he did tell Gerow that the Iba radar had tracked unidentified planes—they proved to be four weather reconnaissance bombers—the night before. As with Brereton, however, MacArthur failed to tell Gerow about the Japanese attack on Davao.

Gerow asked MacArthur to keep Washington informed at all times about anything that happened and promised to attempt daily telephone connections. "I wouldn't be surprised," Gerow concluded, "if you got an attack there in the near future." Gerow repeated that line for emphasis, then MacArthur signed off by asking Gerow to "tell General Marshall that our tails are up in the air."[50]

MacArthur no doubt meant that figuratively, but within minutes most of the planes of his air force were to literally have their tails in the air. At Cape Bojeador, at the extreme northwestern tip of Luzon, a detachment of men were hard at work that morning trying to get their new radar unit operational. Suddenly, around the time that MacArthur was in conversation with Gerow, a flight of twin-engine bombers streaked overhead, heading south. The detachment's commander tried to report the sighting to Brereton's headquarters at Nielson, but through a snafu, the Air Warning System there was monitoring a different channel.[51]

Nevertheless, as the intruders flew south, the radar at Iba picked them up and spread the alert. By then it was around 8:30 a.m., and fighters were scrambling to the skies from Clark, Del Carmen, and Nichols Fields. Only the P-40s of the Third Pursuit Squadron at Iba, having searched in vain for the weather reconnaissance flight the night before, were momentarily on the ground. At Clark, the frantic takeoff rolls of the Twentieth Pursuit Squadron's P-40s crisscrossed those of the B-17s as Major Gibbs, acting on his own authority in Eubank's absence, ordered the bombers that were fueled but not loaded with bombs to seek safer haven in the skies.

At that point, either Brereton or Eubank, who were both in touch with Clark from Nielson Field by radio, might have ordered the B-17s to head for refuge in Del Monte—however crowded the field—but there was still a strong offensive bent among the airmen. The bombers were instead ordered to steer clear of the immediate area of Clark Field but stay within range of the control-tower radio.[52]

As this mad scurrying was taking place, Brereton was on the phone to MacArthur's headquarters trying to find out if the Iba radar report was enough indication of an overt attack to change the commanders' minds about bombing Formosa. Brereton didn't get through to Sutherland, but Sutherland called him back and advised him to "hold off bombing Formosa for the present." The log at Brereton's headquarters recorded the gist of the rest of their conversation: "Planes not authorized to carry bombs at this time."[53]

But by then, in addition to the early report of the attack at Davao, MacArthur was also aware that the twin-engine bombers that had been sighted at Cape Bojeador had dropped their bombs on Camp John Hay, in the mountains at Baguio, just east of Lingayen Gulf. Around the same time, another group of bombers struck the unoccupied airfields at Tuguegarao, in northeastern Luzon, and Aparri, at the northern edge of the island.[54]

Around 10:00 a.m., Brereton put in a second telephone call to MacArthur's headquarters. The evidence was mounting on all sides, but Sutherland insisted that MacArthur wanted his forces in the Philippines to remain in a defensive posture. MacArthur did, however, agree to conduct the sort of photoreconnaissance mission over southern Formosa that Brereton had requested days earlier. Eubank departed Nielson for the hop back to Clark to organize this and prepare for a follow-up strike.

As Eubank flew north, the fighters patrolling the skies around Clark Field had yet to spot an approaching enemy plane. It had looked as if the attack at Baguio was as far south as the Japanese were coming. The control tower at Clark gave the all clear, and the B-17s straggled in by ones and twos to land and refuel. Brereton had initially told Eubank to load them with bombs upon landing, but Eubank, anticipating that it would be some hours before they departed for Formosa, persuaded Brereton to delay arming them in case the recon mission showed the need for different ordnance. Besides, Eubank advised, it would be dangerous to have fully loaded bombers on the field in the event an errant Japanese plane or two appeared.

As the B-17s began their return to Clark, the telephone in Brereton's office rang, and Brereton was surprised to hear MacArthur on the line. Brereton reported that despite the earlier alert, Clark had not been bombed and his B-17s were being readied for the Formosa strike. This time, MacArthur approved and gave Brereton the green light for offensive operations. Almost seven hours had passed since Sutherland's wake-up call about Pearl Harbor.[55]

During these long hours, MacArthur seemed frozen in time. It was only prudent that he take reasonable time to evaluate the intelligence, but by 6:15 a.m., after the report of the attack at Davao, and certainly by around 8:00 a.m., after bombs fell at Baguio, on northern Luzon, it was clear that the Japanese were attacking the Philippines in force. Whom was MacArthur serving by delaying a response?

If MacArthur, too, harbored illusions of the islands being able to remain neutral in the face of a conflagration — as Manuel Quezon suggested to Dwight Eisenhower several months later[56] — he was naively mistaken. Given his dual roles as the commanding general of USAFFE and a field marshal in the Philippine army, he may also have been conflicted by those illusions. The United States had ordered him to implement Rainbow 5 and attack, but what would that do to his beloved Philippines? Was MacArthur trying to spare Manila? Why did he wait so long to order an offensive response? Admittedly it might not have mattered, given the meager force of B-17s at Clark, but at the very least one expects that he should have more readily conferred with Brereton. The best strategic view in the face of considerable tactical uncertainty may well have been to order the remaining bombers south to Del Monte.

Perhaps the most simplistic explanation, but one as convincing as any, for the general's hours of apparent stupor was that Douglas MacArthur, who was always one to operate on his own schedule, could not believe that the Japanese were disrupting his assumed timetable for a war in the spring and consequently failed for some seven hours to react. His earlier comments to Marshall and Stimson on that point aside, MacArthur knew very well — or certainly should have known — that even the thirty-five B-17s in which he placed so much value were but a pittance against the assembled Japanese might.

As the returning B-17s settled into Clark, they taxied to their assigned horseshoe-shaped revetments of dirt piled fifteen feet high, and gas trucks came out to refuel them as their crews went to the mess hall for lunch. The fighter squadrons also returned to their respective bases, although the pilots of the Seventeenth Pursuit, rather than flying seventy miles south to their home base, at Nichols Field, also put down at Clark to be closer to any action. Without assigned dispersal locations, the visitors' twenty-one P-40s parked wingtip to wingtip in front of the hangars while the planes of the Twentieth Pursuit Squadron took up their usual parking locations along the field's perimeter.

Eubank and Walsh, meanwhile, had landed at Clark and were busy briefing the three B-17 pilots assigned to the photoreconnaissance. There were no suitable cameras at Clark — a situation indicative of the limited amount of equipment available — and one of the B-18s at Nielson Field was quickly ordered to fly north with a supply of them. In addition, Brereton's staff had decided that the harbor at Takao, which Eubank's staff had agreed in his absence would make the most suitable target, was no longer the best choice for an attack. Eubank then briefed his approximately forty senior flying officers about a mission to hit Japanese airfields instead. But of the nineteen B-17s at Clark, one was out of commission, two were flying a patrol, and three were to fly the photoreconnaissance mission. That left Eubank with only thirteen bombers for the mission and had many wondering about both the timing and advisability of the photo exercise. As one of the operations staff put it, "What do they want to know that they don't already know?"[57]

There then began a fast cascade of unfortunate events for MacArthur's air force. At around 11:20 a.m., the radar at Iba came to life with what appeared to be large formations of aircraft coming toward Iba from the sea and streaming across Luzon toward Clark. Telephone reports from civilian observers throughout northern Luzon added to the torrent of data. Amid the flurry of back-and-forth reports, the AWS reported that the flight west of Iba was headed for Manila and that because of the mountains, contact had been lost with the flight inbound to Clark over the Lingayen Valley.

At Clark, the Clark-based Twentieth Pursuit and the visiting Seventeenth Pursuit — a total of forty-four P-40s — had been refueled but were still on the ground. But the aging P-35 fighters at Del Carmen and the brand-new P-40s of the Twenty-First Pursuit still at Nichols took to the air, as did the long-suffering P-40 pilots of the Third Pursuit, who had been waiting all morning at Iba. But faulty communications, flickering radar images, and conflicting orders about covering Manila versus heading toward Clark bred chaos.[58]

At Clark Field, Eubank was still briefing his B-17 pilots for the Formosa bomb run, apparently unconcerned about the fighter alerts. The fighter group commander, Major Orrin Grover, ordered the visiting Seventeenth Pursuit Squadron into the air but sent its planes south to cover Manila. Grover kept the Clark-based Twentieth Pursuit on the ground, with the pilots in their planes, while he tried to figure out in which direction the greatest threat lay. Baking in their cockpits, the pilots munched sandwiches and guzzled Cokes under the Southern Hemisphere's blazing December sun while their ground crews huddled in the shade of their planes' wings. More than one pair of eyes nervously scanned the cloudless skies for any sign of intruders.[59]

Meanwhile, Brereton's men were not the only pilots nervously scanning the skies that morning. Five hundred miles to the north, on Formosa, hundreds of Japanese army and navy pilots had been waiting anxiously all morning. Their planes were gassed, armed, and ready to fly to Luzon, but a dense fog had rolled in and dropped visibility almost to zero. Only a handful of army bombers assigned to attack Tuguegarao and Baguio had managed to take off and elude the fog. What fate awaited their small numbers their delayed comrades could only imagine, but as it turned out, their light attacks at northern outposts lulled defenders in the Philippines into thinking that those were the limits of the Japanese forces.

No word had been received in Formosa from the four bombers that had been dispatched the night before to report on weather conditions and any sign of changes in the enemy's preparedness. Given the priority assigned to radio silence, no news was good news, and there was no way of knowing that the bombers' appearance on radar had caused Brereton to depart his party early or that the P-40s scrambled from Iba to intercept them had failed to do so.[60]

News of the successful attack on Pearl Harbor raised a cheer, but then the sobering truth hit: but for the fog, they would have been on their way to their own targets. It seemed only logical that once American commanders received word of the Pearl Harbor attack, their air forces in the Philippines would either be well prepared or, worse, winging their way north to attack Formosa. At Tainan Naval Air Base, Flight Petty Officer Saburo Sakai, who piloted a Mitsubishi A6M Zero fighter, found it incredible that the Americans "would not be waiting for us in strength in the Philippines."[61]

But the fog persisted, and the hours crawled by. Finally, at 10:00 a.m. Formosa time, the sky lightened; no enemy bombers appeared. The signal was given to launch planes, and Sakai's Zero, encumbered with extra fuel tanks for the long flight, lumbered down the runway and formed up with thirty-five other Zero fighters and twenty-seven Mitsubishi G3M "Nell" bombers heading south. They would be joined by upwards of eighty-one Mitsubishi G4M "Betty" bombers and forty-five Zero fighters from the Japanese naval base at Takao, plus dozens more planes from army units throughout Formosa.[62]

Barely had Sakai's advance flight of Zeros cleared the southernmost tip of Formosa when he sighted a nine-plane bomber formation headed straight north toward the island. Even if a B-17 raid had been launched from Clark Field as late as Brereton's second attempt to see MacArthur, Eubank's bombers would have had the good fortune to arrive over Takao and Tainan just as the fog lifted, unveiling rows of heavily armed aircraft lined up for takeoff. Given the numerical odds against them, such serendipity might have been the only chance of success for Eubank's B-17s.

Sakai and his fighter comrades dropped out of the main formation and dove toward the approaching bombers. Just as he started to squeeze the trigger, Sakai realized his mistake. The bombers belonged to the Japanese army. The United States was not the only military to have coordination issues between its service branches. "Those fools in the bombers!" Sakai later wrote of his army comrades. "No one in the Army command area had taken the trouble to coordinate with the Navy, and these idiots were out on a routine training flight."

Some three hours later, Sakai's wave of Japanese fighters "flashed in from the China Sea and headed for Clark Field" to secure the airspace in advance of the bombers. But instead of encountering a swarm of fighters there, Sakai looked down and saw bombers and fighters neatly parked along the runways. "They squatted there," Saburo Sakai recalled, "like sitting ducks."[63]

CHAPTER FIVE

Blame and Bataan

By the time Japanese bombs stopped falling on Clark Field and the strafing Zeros departed from Clark and nearby Iba, MacArthur's already meager air force had been cut in half. Of the nineteen Clark-based B-17s (the other sixteen were at Del Monte), twelve were destroyed and four damaged. At least half the ninety-some P-40s — the only fighter remotely capable of taking on the Zero — were burning piles of rubble, and two of the five pursuit squadrons in the Philippines, the Third at Iba and the Twentieth at Clark, were no longer fighting units. Several dozen other planes, including aging B-18s, were also destroyed. By MacArthur's count, seventy-seven officers and enlisted men were killed and 148 wounded in the attacks.[1]

While MacArthur reported his own air losses as "heavy," he termed the Japanese losses "medium," characteristically skewing the numbers to cast the best possible light on his command.[2] With only seven Japanese planes downed out of some two hundred bombers and fighters, Japanese losses could only be called negligible — not "medium" — although a number of their aircraft returned to Formosa with the scars of antiaircraft fire and .50-caliber slugs from American P-40s. The destruction of MacArthur's air force and the subsequent recriminations would be overshadowed by far more numerous losses and much more frenzied scapegoat-hunting at Pearl Harbor — but that has not stopped three generations from assessing blame for the debacle at Clark Field.

To begin with, Douglas MacArthur continued to take his time

communicating with his superiors in Washington. As George Marshall's patience wore thin, he once again prodded MacArthur with a terse one-liner: "Request report on operations and results."[3] In the meantime, MacArthur had received a message from Army Air Forces chief of staff Hap Arnold noting that "reports of Japanese attacks [in Hawaii] show that numbers of our planes have been destroyed on the ground" and admonishing MacArthur to "take all possible steps at once to avoid such losses in your area."[4] Given what had just occurred at Clark Field, Arnold's words stung more than a little.

At least partly in consequence, it was not until very late on the evening of December 8 — at least eight and perhaps as many as ten or eleven hours after the Japanese attackers departed Clark — that MacArthur sent Marshall his communiqué reporting "our air losses heavy and enemy losses medium." Significantly, MacArthur went on to tell Marshall that he was "launching a heavy bombardment counter attack tomorrow morning on enemy airdromes in southern Formosa."[5] Of the seventeen surviving B-17s MacArthur planned to commit, sixteen were still to the south, at Del Monte.

Despite this assertion of a planned strike against Formosa, the issue of *any* contemplated B-17 counterattack became central to finger-pointing for the surprise at Clark Field. MacArthur would later claim that he had ordered all B-17s removed from Clark days before the attack, and supporting testimony from Sutherland made it seem as if Brereton had been derelict in carrying out those orders. Later, in a postwar interview with historian Louis Morton, MacArthur softened this somewhat and recalled that he had "for safety reasons ordered the bombers to withdraw from Luzon to Mindanao" and that "this was in process of accomplishment when the enemy's air attacked."[6]

But MacArthur always remained adamant that Brereton "never recommended an attack on Formosa" and that he knew "nothing of such a recommendation having been made." The general claimed that if such a proposal had been intended seriously, Brereton should have made it "to me in person."[7] Someone, of course, was being disingenuous. Either Brereton was not as forceful as he claimed in his visits to MacArthur's headquarters that morning or Sutherland did not convey the gist of Brereton's message to MacArthur. It is also possible that

MacArthur chose to selectively forget any reason for the bombers remaining at Clark despite his assertion to Marshall that he intended to use them in a counterattack. In reality, of course, there was little tactical value to be had in bombing Formosa with such a limited force—unless the timing of the fog lifting had been serendipitous—other than perhaps to prove to the Japanese that the Americans were not about to go quietly. Even if thirteen, sixteen, or eighteen B-17s had departed Clark and flown to Formosa, it is likely that many would not have returned.

But many airmen would have derived satisfaction from the fact that those losses would have been sustained in the air. Believing "our airmen would fight it out" and aghast that they had been "caught flat-footed on the ground," Hap Arnold reached Brereton by telephone two days later, demanding to know what had happened. "How in the hell could an experienced airman like you get caught with your planes on the ground?" Arnold fumed. Brereton tried to explain the circumstances, but was interrupted by another Japanese air attack. According to Brereton, when he reported his conversation with Arnold to MacArthur, the general told him "to go back and fight the war and not to worry."[8]

Only then did MacArthur reply to Arnold's warning cable of December 8. As was his custom in such circumstances, MacArthur took the high ground with almost Churchill-like praise of others to divert attention from the magnitude of the defeat and his own culpabilities. "Every possible precaution within the limited means and the time available was taken here by the Far East Air Force," MacArthur assured Arnold. "Their losses were due entirely to the overwhelming superiority of enemy force. They have been hopelessly outnumbered from the start but no unit could have done better. Their gallantry has been conspicuous; their efficiency good. No item of loss can properly be attributed to neglect or lack of care. They fought from fields not yet developed and under improvised conditions of every sort which placed them under the severest handicap as regards to an enemy fully prepared in every way. You may take pride in their conduct."[9]

Arnold took little solace from MacArthur's words and diplomatically concluded in his memoirs, "I never have been able to get the real story of what happened in the Philippines." And as historian William

H. Bartsch succinctly noted in his thorough analysis of the Clark Field attack, "Nothing in MacArthur's defense of his airmen addressed the basic question of how it was possible that an air force on full alert, notified of the attack on Pearl Harbor, and forewarned of a force of enemy aircraft approaching could have been caught with its planes on the ground when the attack began."[10]

But whose fault was it?

After the war, Major General Claire L. Chennault, of Flying Tigers fame, criticized the War Department for its failure to reprimand those in command on December 8, 1941 — including, by implication, MacArthur. "If I had been caught with my planes on the ground," Chennault wrote in his memoirs, "as were the Air Corps commanders in the Philippines and in Hawaii, I could never again have looked my fellow officers squarely in the eye. The lightness with which this cardinal military sin was excused by the American high command when committed by Regular Army officers has always seemed to me one of the more shocking aspects of the war."[11]

Junior officers were no less critical. Lieutenant Edgar D. Whitcomb, a B-17 navigator at Clark who would go on to perform some harrowing exploits while eluding the Japanese invaders, wrote harshly after the war that "our generals and leaders committed one of the greatest errors possible to military men — that of letting themselves be taken by surprise. That error can be exceeded only by treason."[12]

"It's all clear to me now except one thing," George Marshall told Robert Sherrod of *Time* two weeks later: "I just don't know how MacArthur happened to let his planes get caught on the ground."[13]

Was it truly MacArthur's fault? Certainly MacArthur was not expecting an immediate Japanese attack, despite Marshall's warnings to the contrary. Likewise, MacArthur must shoulder the blame for failing to react more quickly to news of the Pearl Harbor attack and the direct attacks on the Philippines at Baguio and Davao — no matter how misguided his and Quezon's thoughts of Philippine neutrality might have been. At a minimum, he should have consulted quickly and directly with his air commander, Brereton.

But given the limitations of a neophyte early warning system and the cramped ground space at Clark Field, MacArthur's air forces had actually acquitted themselves rather well. The B-17s were put in the air on Major Gibbs's initiative, and fighters were scrambled at the early reports of enemy aircraft above northern Luzon. Had these initial aircraft been the subsequent attack wave instead of the few Japanese bombers that had eluded the Formosa fog to fly on schedule against Baguio, the result at Clark Field likely would have been quite different—the airborne B-17s would probably have been ordered to disperse to Del Monte while the P-40s did what they could against the attackers. Indeed, the great luck of the day lay with the Japanese and the fog that grounded the bulk of their attacking force, turning the Baguio strike into a deceptive feint.

The bad luck was with the Americans, who initially thought they had weathered the worst, bravely planned a counterattack, and then were jolted into the reality of both the speed and ferocity with which the Japanese war machine could operate. In the days after December 8, Philippine defenses would crumble like a house of cards, and Japanese landing forces would come ashore at multiple points throughout the archipelago.

Nonetheless, as every military commander throughout history has known, the officer in command is ultimately accountable for the victory or defeat of his forces. The surprise attack on Clark Field must be judged a black mark on the MacArthur record. Still, as controversial and egregious as MacArthur's actions remain, they pale beside the decisions he would soon make—decisions that ultimately resulted in one hundred thousand starving troops caught in a box on Bataan.

Heavy rain grounded Japanese planes on Formosa on December 9, but they were back over the Philippines with a vengeance the following day. This time, with only a marginal number of P-40s and ineffective P-35s to challenge them, they rained destruction on the navy yard at Cavite. Admiral Hart watched the attack from the roof of his Marsman Building headquarters and, noting the impunity with which Japanese aircraft were operating, ordered most of his remaining ships south. Many of Hart's ships had already sortied on orders from Admiral Stark in Washington, but that did not stop MacArthur from protesting to General Marshall the "inactivity" of the Asiatic Fleet and the Japanese navy's "complete freedom of action."[14]

MacArthur's frustration did nothing to improve the MacArthur-Hart relationship. A major point of contention was a convoy of seven supply ships shepherded by the heavy cruiser *Pensacola*. Formed at Pearl Harbor on November 29, the convoy contained a treasure trove of reinforcements for MacArthur—if it could reach him. Among its cargo were a field artillery brigade consisting of twenty 75mm guns, eighteen P-40s, fifty-two A-24 dive-bombers (destined for the planeless pilots of the Twenty-Seventh Bomb Group), five hundred thousand rounds of .50-caliber armor-piercing ammunition, and some 4,600 men, around half of whom were National Guard troops in the artillery brigade. The other half were ground elements destined for the air corps.[15]

On December 10, in the wake of Pearl Harbor and with the *Pensacola* convoy at sea, the Joint Board met in Washington. Navy representatives demanded the recall of the convoy to Hawaii to stiffen defenses there. Marshall swallowed hard and initially agreed, but then had second thoughts about appearing to abandon MacArthur. Marshall prevailed upon Secretary Stimson, and the following day they found an ally in President Roosevelt, who countermanded the recall. The situation in Manila was changing by the hour, and the convoy was diverted to Brisbane, Australia, with the hope that a way could be found for it to avoid Japanese attacks and reach the Philippines.[16]

MacArthur's protestations of lack of support to the contrary, Marshall and Stimson worked feverishly to reinforce him before the Japanese could tighten a naval blockade. Their efforts indeed ran into opposition from the American navy, "particularly," wrote Stimson in his diary, "because the Navy has been rather shaken and panic-stricken after the catastrophe at Hawaii and the complete upset of their naval strategy which depended upon that fortress."[17]

But there was also an element of stark reality to be faced. Rushing westward with its aircraft carriers and surviving cruisers, the Pacific Fleet would likely have been doomed by Japan's land-based air en route to the Philippines. There was no more grievous an indication of this than the news on December 10 that feisty admiral Sir Tom Phillips and the Royal Navy's mighty *Repulse* and *Prince of Wales* now rested on the bottom of the South China Sea.

Still, Marshall tried desperately to send MacArthur any hint of good news. With the *Pensacola* convoy not recalled but nonetheless detoured to Australia, Marshall fretted about having to inform MacArthur "in the midst of a very trying situation that his convoy had to be turned back." He told his staff that he needed to send some news that "would buck General MacArthur up."[18]

The man to whom George Marshall turned for advice was no stranger to Douglas MacArthur or to the Philippines. MacArthur's patient and long-suffering aide Dwight Eisenhower was by then fifty-one and a brigadier general who had been hastily summoned to work in Marshall's War Plans Division. Eisenhower was so new to the job that he arrived in Washington by train one week after Pearl Harbor and within hours found himself seated before Marshall. Describing the chaos in the Pacific, Marshall bluntly asked Eisenhower for his assessment of a general line of action. "Give me a few hours," Eisenhower replied.

When Eisenhower returned, his assessment was bleak but realistic, and it cemented Marshall's faith in him. "General," Eisenhower began, "it will be a long time before major reinforcements can go to the Philippines, longer than the garrison can hold out...but we must do everything for them that is humanly possible." The people of China, the Philippines, and the Netherlands East Indies would be watching, Eisenhower stressed: "they may excuse failure but they will not excuse abandonment."

"I agree with you," Marshall replied. According to Eisenhower, Marshall's tone implied that he "had been given the problem as a check to an answer he had already reached." As Eisenhower took his leave, Marshall gravely exhorted him, "Do your best to save them."[19]

It was a gargantuan task, made all the more difficult by the tempo of events in the Philippines. On December 10, the same day Japanese bombers rained destruction on Nichols Field and the Cavite naval station, initial Japanese amphibious landings were made at Vigan and Aparri, on the northern coast of Luzon. Two days later, a similar invasion force came ashore at Legaspi, near the extreme southeastern tip of Luzon.

Luzon
December 1941

120°E

Japanese
Landings

Cape
Bojeador

Cape
Engaño

Dec 10

Aparri

Dec 10

Vigan

Tuguegarao

*Philippine
Sea*

Luzon

Dec 22

Lingayen Gulf

Baguio

Agno River

PHILIPPINES

15°N

Pampanga R.

Tarlac

Zaragoza

Cabanatuan

Iba Field

Clark
Field

San Fernando

Del Carmen
Field

Calumpit

Olongapo

Bataan

Manila

Nielson
Field

Nichols
Field

Dec 24

Lamon Bay

Japanese
Landings

Corregidor

Cavite
Naval
Base

*Laguna
de Bay*

Dec 12

*South
China
Sea*

Mindoro

*Sibuyan
Sea*

Legaspi

Zambales Mts.

0   50 Miles

These operations had been planned to provide Japanese planes with advance bases encircling the Manila area, from which they could fight a protracted battle for control of the skies and support the main landings to follow. The success of the Clark Field raid made air duels less of an issue and rapidly compressed the Japanese invasion timetable. But the Japanese also looked to the base at Legaspi to give them air control over the San Bernardino Strait, between Luzon and Samar, and prevent American reinforcements from slipping through and reaching Manila from the south. It would not be the last time the strait would attract such attention.[20]

To MacArthur's credit, these ancillary landings did not unduly distract him, and his sense of geography correctly predicted that the main Japanese invasion would come at Lingayen Gulf, in northwestern Luzon. But given MacArthur's edict to defend the beaches anywhere Japanese troops came ashore, Wainwright's North Luzon Force was spread thin against the Vigan and Aparri beachheads. At the same time, American resistance in the air dwindled.

On December 15, MacArthur approved Brereton's request to move his remaining fourteen B-17s to Batchelor Field, near Darwin, Australia. The day before, after an extensive air reconnaissance of the entire southern Philippines, the Japanese had finally located the American bomber base at Del Monte. The B-17s had been shuttling between there and Clark—sometimes remaining in the air during daylight hours to avoid detection on the ground—in what Brereton called "a game of hide-and-seek that wore out men as well as planes."

Attempts at offensive operations met with little success—only three of six B-17s dispatched to bomb transports at the Legaspi landings made it to the target—and their failure was compounded by the fact that there was not a single spare part, engine, or propeller in the islands. "Our Air Force," Brereton bemoaned, "was gradually fading away."[21]

Brereton professed his willingness to stay in Manila and serve MacArthur in any capacity, but MacArthur told him, "No, Lewis. You go on south. You can do me more good [there,] with the bombers you have left and those you should be receiving soon, than you can here." So on Christmas Eve, Brereton took his leave of MacArthur with the general's expression of gratitude.[22] In retrospect, it seems more than a little strange that MacArthur, who had personally requested Brereton's assignment to the Philippines and greeted him so warmly upon his arrival and who then bade him farewell with nothing but sincere thanks, could not bring himself to talk directly with Brereton or acknowledge his presence during those tense hours on the morning of December 8.

Brereton, his chief of staff, Colonel Francis Brady, and Colonel Eugene Eubank, without his bombers, all departed Manila together late on Christmas Eve. They drove amid yet another Japanese air attack to Cavite—or, as Brereton put it, "what was left of it"—and boarded a twin-engine navy PBY Catalina for the flight south. Even then, air operations didn't go as planned. On its takeoff run, the Catalina hit a fishing boat and damaged a wing float. The plane taxied back to the dock, and Brereton and his party looked around for other transport. Only after driving fifty miles to the south and wading in the dark another three miles through rice paddies did they reach another Catalina that was cached on Laguna de Bay, the large inland lake south of Manila. A dicey takeoff in waning moonlight followed, but MacArthur's air force commander was soon safely out of the Philippines.[23] And Hart's navy was, too.

Douglas MacArthur was certain, and remained so his entire life, that Tommy Hart and his Asiatic Fleet abandoned him. But in the big picture of a two-ocean global war, what choice was there? Learning that the *Pensacola* convoy had been diverted to Brisbane and that its planes, as well as others promised, were to be flown to the Philippines if a way could be found around the tightening Japanese chokehold, MacArthur still did not give up hope that aircraft reinforcements could be brought directly into the Philippines by ship. On December 14, oblivious to their vulnerability to land-based air attacks, he suggested to Marshall that aircraft carriers deliver planes directly, thus eliminating the need to build or expand bases on a transport line between Australia and Luzon.

A week later, even as he prepared to say good-bye to Brereton, MacArthur told Marshall that the encirclement the Japanese had long planned was threatening to cut his lines of communication southward, and he pleaded for some major demonstration of power by the American navy to limit or at least retard the enemy's freedom of movement. Pointedly, he demanded to receive "any inkling" as to strategic plans for the Pacific Fleet and again urged Marshall to use carriers to bring fighter planes within operating radius of the Philippines. "Can I expect anything along that line?" he queried.[24]

To Marshall's continuing angst and regret, the answer was no. Stark, chief of naval operations, decreed that risking valuable carriers as transports was "impractical in the existing strategic situation," and Admiral Ernest J. King, whom Roosevelt and secretary of the navy Frank Knox had just lifted from preretirement obscurity to the reestablished post of commander in chief, United States Fleet, concurred. What aircraft and supporting supplies could be gotten to MacArthur would have to come via cargo ships and flights by way of Australia.[25]

All this led to additional acrimony between MacArthur and Hart as they had what proved to be their last conversations. On December 18, MacArthur went to see Hart about getting the *Pensacola* convoy closer than Brisbane, but rather than inspecting the charts Hart had prepared, MacArthur launched into one of his lectures — Hart called them speeches — "about his own side of the war." According to Hart, MacArthur "asked no questions whatsoever, evinced no curiosity and, as has too often been the case, the interview was quite futile as far as furthering any meeting of minds between us."[26]

Four days later, it was Hart's turn to call on MacArthur, who had just been told by Marshall that he was being brevetted to the four stars of a full general he had worn as chief of staff. Hart offered congratulations, and MacArthur responded by remarking that he finally had his "rightful rank back."[27] Having deployed his larger ships south prior to December 8, as commanded, Hart was under orders from Stark to depart Manila whenever he determined that he could effectively direct his fleet from another location. Stark also instructed him to place any remaining naval and marine personnel under MacArthur's command.[28]

Hart hoped to discuss final evacuation plans with MacArthur, but he failed to engage MacArthur in what Hart called any "useful channels."[29] Instead MacArthur took Hart to task for the abysmal failure of his submarines against the Japanese landing forces. "What in the world is the matter with your submarines?" MacArthur demanded. Hart had no ready answer, because on paper his fleet of submarines appeared to be a powerful deterrent against Japanese convoys in the South China

97

Sea, particularly those that were landing troops in the Philippines. The reality was quite different.

During one two-week period in mid-December of 1941, ten different submarines operating off the Philippines fired twenty-eight torpedoes against Japanese targets and scored zero hits. Green skippers and crews were not nearly as much of a problem as were defective torpedoes, which would frustrate the American submarine force for the better part of two years.[30]

But at the time, MacArthur's criticism stung, and Hart was well aware that he and the navy were likely scapegoats for whatever befell MacArthur and the Philippines. "He [MacArthur] is inclined to cut my throat and perhaps of the Navy in general," Hart recorded in his diary on December 19. "So I have to watch the record and keep it straight lest I wait up some morning and read that T. Hart lost a war or something."[31]

Indicative of their lack of cooperation, MacArthur gave Hart only twenty-four hours' notice that he planned to declare Manila an open city on Christmas Day. Hart was not opposed to the concept, which under international law would demilitarize Manila and supposedly leave it immune from attack, but the scant notice sent him scurrying to close his headquarters and arrange the departure of his staff. Some flew out in a PBY on the evening of December 24, while Hart and two aides boarded the submarine *Shark* and finally sailed in the wee hours of December 26. Notwithstanding the intent of MacArthur's open-city proclamation, the Manila waterfront was soon ablaze with Japanese bombs, and the docks that held so many navy munitions and other supplies added jarring explosions to the inferno. Tommy Hart was the last high-ranking officer to leave Manila.[32]

Barely were Hart and Brereton out of Manila when MacArthur leveled his guns upon them as scapegoats. "Enemy penetration in the Philippines resulted from our weakness on the sea and in the air," MacArthur cabled Marshall two days after Christmas. "Surface elements of the Asiatic Fleet were withdrawn and the effect of submarines has been negligible. I wish to emphasize the necessity for naval action and for rapid execution by land, sea and air."[33]

The withdrawal of Hart's Asiatic Fleet southward pending reinforcements had long been a part of Plan Orange. As recently as his December 6 conference with Hart and the now-deceased British admiral Phillips, MacArthur was fully aware of the navy's orders in the event of war to cooperate with allies far south of the Philippines. Hart's flirtation with changing that in the fall of 1941, and his asking Stark's permission to mass his fleet in Manila, had been encouraged by MacArthur's assurances of adequate air cover. Now, dismally stripped of airpower, MacArthur blamed Hart for doing what had long been planned.

Whatever the shortcomings of Brereton's air force and Hart's navy, the truth was that MacArthur had his hands full with consequences of decisions of his own making. Having strenuously lobbied the War Department throughout 1941 to embrace his plan for a widespread beachhead defense of the Philippines, MacArthur faced the reality of retreating to the confines of two decades of Orange plans and awaiting some measure of reinforcements.

While history would show that the Japanese attack on Pearl Harbor was far from the decisive strike that the Japanese admiral Isoroku Yamamoto had intended—the American carriers had escaped unharmed, the oil storage tanks and dry docks were largely intact, and the submarine force, albeit with impotent torpedoes, remained generally unscathed—it did have the effect of steering the most recent Rainbow 5 version of Plan Orange onto the sidelines. While the plan's general strategy would be employed over a period of years, there would be no immediate rush to aid the Philippines. It was simply impractical operationally and, in most minds in the wake of Pearl Harbor, unthinkable psychologically. In truth, a limited effort aside, MacArthur was on his own.

After the initial Japanese landings on Luzon at Vigan, Aparri, and Legaspi, the major Japanese thrust in the Philippines came at dawn on December 22, when elements of Lieutenant General Masaharu Homma's Fourteenth Army splashed ashore in Lingayen Gulf. These forces were hardly the cream of Japan's military. The landings, hampered by high seas, heavy rainsqualls, and inexperience in moving men and equipment ashore, ended up on the wrong beaches and proved a comedy of errors. But it really didn't matter.

Resistance from a few American planes and submarines was ineffective, and even though a Philippine Scouts regiment and three infantry divisions of Wainwright's North Luzon Force were close by, the fighting on the beaches, except for a flurry from the Scouts, was short-lived. By noon, three Japanese regiments, supported by tanks and artillery, were safely on the beach and moving inland. Within a few days, Homma would have forty-three thousand troops in position and be poised to move south against Manila. So much for MacArthur's plan to defend the beaches and stop any invasion cold.[34]

MacArthur would take credit for predicting Lingayen Gulf as the primary invasion site, but decades of war-gaming in the islands had anticipated it. From the Lingayen beaches a network of roads through relatively gentle terrain across the Central Luzon Plain led toward Manila, one hundred miles away. What MacArthur had not anticipated was that the Japanese would also land at Lamon Bay, east of Manila. The American consensus was that seasonally high tides and prevailing winds blowing in from the Philippine Sea, along with the defensive barrier of the mountains near Tayabas, would discourage such an assault. But two days after the Lingayen landings, Homma did just that, putting ashore some seven thousand troops of his Sixteenth Division. The Philippine army's Fifty-First Division crumpled. By the following morning, Japanese forces had crossed the narrow isthmus to Tayabas Bay, effectively cutting off southern Luzon from Manila.[35]

Given the mountainous defenses between Manila and Lamon Bay and the small number of enemy troops on that front, MacArthur remained convinced that the far greater threat lay to the north. The Philippine army's Seventy-First Division, led by Brigadier General Clyde A. Selleck, was supposed to bottleneck the Japanese thrust toward Manila, but Selleck's regiments were quickly outflanked, and they disintegrated. Selleck was demoted to the rank of colonel because of the defeat, but that was the least of his concerns.

"The division was never organized," Selleck recalled, "was never adequately equipped, and the training was so meager that when attacked by veteran troops, and bombed and confronted by tanks, it had a minimum of stability." Another American officer characterized the Filipino recruits facing the attacking Japanese as "a mob."[36]

This was the result of MacArthur's vaunted citizen army. More planes, additional dispersed airfields, and better fighter coordination may have been well served by four or five additional months of preparation — MacArthur's war-in-the-spring scenario — but it is difficult to see what difference that amount of time would have made on the army side of things.

There is some evidence that even as the smoke cleared from Clark Field, MacArthur recognized that his plan to defend the beaches throughout the archipelago was doomed. It was much more than the invader's expedited time schedule that had thrown off his notions of war in the spring. The magnitude and effectiveness of the initial Japanese onslaught was strong evidence that this was not to be a leisurely affair. MacArthur, who considered himself a military historian, must have been aware of the blinding speed of the German blitzkrieg of May 1940. He had also been espousing the importance of airpower. But MacArthur's core experience was still intuitively anchored in a more ponderous military era, when the regular army had considerable time to deploy.

Just as he did for seven hours on the morning of December 8, MacArthur spent the better part of two weeks refusing to act on the changed circumstances. He seems to have understood early on that he would have to revert to Plan Orange and marshal forces on Bataan. Why then didn't he use those two weeks to stockpile supplies that were essential to its long-term defense? Once again, the rapid flow of events sailed past him.

Sutherland remembered that MacArthur had told him privately on December 8 that they would have to "remove immediately to Bataan." Four days later, MacArthur had told Quezon much the same thing and had brought up the option of declaring Manila an open city. For his part, Quezon, who had spent more time in the field witnessing training exercises than had MacArthur, was not surprised. Given the apparent inevitability of a retreat to Bataan, an inevitability that was recognized by most of his staff, MacArthur, however, still refused to give the orders. When a proposal was floated at one staff meeting for the need to stock Bataan with provisions as a safety measure, MacArthur wouldn't hear of it. That was defeatist talk, he said, and he "didn't want any divided thought on it." This was a classic example of the way MacArthur frequently characterized any reality that conflicted with his own views as defeatism.

After the main Japanese force came ashore at Lingayen and moved south with lightning speed, evidence that the Philippine army of which MacArthur had boasted for years was but a hollow shell still did not prompt him to change his position for another two days. In the words of historian D. Clayton James, "why [MacArthur] hesitated until the [evening of the] 23rd to renounce his cherished beach defense plan, especially after the ruin of his air and naval defense plans, continues to be a mystery."[37]

Even in the face of enormous evidence from all front lines that the Philippine troops simply had no fighting skill or resolve, MacArthur could not admit that he had been wrong. His reason for reverting to Plan Orange and abandoning the beach defense that he had so strenuously persuaded Marshall to adopt was, he said, "the imminent menace of encirclement by greatly superior numbers [that] forced me to act instantly."[38]

But neither "superior numbers" nor "act instantly" is an accurate term. Given the number of reliable troops MacArthur had in the field, he was more than evenly matched numerically with Homma's invaders, and he had not acted "instantly" until a total rout into Manila seemed likely. Calling the Japanese pincer movements upon Manila from Lingayen and Lamon Bay "a perfect strategic conception," MacArthur rationalized in his memoirs that by retreating — *retiring* was his word — to the Bataan peninsula as envisioned in Plan Orange, he "could pit my own intimate knowledge of the terrain against the Japanese superiority in air power, tanks, artillery, and men."[39]

The Bataan peninsula sticks out from Luzon across the western reaches of Manila Bay like a big thumb. It's around thirty miles long from Olongapo, in the north, to its southern tip, near Mariveles, and fifteen to twenty miles wide between Subic Bay and the South China Sea on the west and Manila Bay on the east. It is not gentle country. Mount Natib, at 4,111 feet, sits astride the northern half, while the Mariveles Mountains, rising to 4,554 feet, dominate the southern half. Around one-third of the way across the mouth of Manila Bay from the southern tip of Bataan sits the island of Corregidor.

That island, too, is a mountainous jumble, one and a half miles north to south at its widest point and three and a half miles long. It has a high point more than five hundred feet above sea level at what was called Topside and a long hooked spit that stabs like a bony finger eastward into Manila Bay. On either side of the narrow isthmus where this spit joins the island's main body there were docks. Into four-hundred-foot Malinta Hill, which rises just east of the docks, the Army Corps of Engineers had blasted an eight-hundred-foot-long main tunnel and a honeycomb of lateral tunnels during the 1920s.

With the decision belatedly made to revert to concentrating on Bataan, MacArthur faced three enormous challenges. First, stockpiles of food and ammunition had to be moved from Manila and other points throughout Luzon to the peninsula. Second, the remaining part of the South Luzon Force north of Lamon Bay had to be evacuated around Manila to Bataan via strategic bridges at Calumpit. Finally, Wainwright's North Luzon Force had to delay Homma's advance across the Central Luzon Plain via a series of defensive lines, each of which would have to hold long enough to force the Japanese to deploy out of column for a frontal assault. In the first of these challenges, MacArthur was to fail miserably, a failure that would ultimately generate defeat no matter how successfully the other challenges were met.

On Christmas Eve, having told Admiral Hart that he was declaring Manila an open city, MacArthur cabled Marshall to tell him that another Japanese landing force stood off the South Channel entrance to Manila Bay and that he intended "to disengage my forces under cover of darkness" that evening. "For the present," MacArthur continued, "I am remaining in Manila, establishing an advanced headquarters on Corregidor."[40]

That same afternoon, however, MacArthur, along with his wife, Jean, their son, Arthur, and Arthur's nanny, Ah Cheu, moved from their penthouse apartment, festooned with Christmas decorations, to Corregidor. Jean packed but one suitcase, stuffing it with food and clothes for soon-to-be-four-year-old Arthur. For herself, she rummaged to the back of her closet to grab only the brown coat with a fur collar she had worn on her wedding trip, almost five years earlier. But at the last moment, two other things caught her eye.

One was a glass case containing her husband's medals. The other was a small bronze vase inscribed to General Arthur MacArthur from the emperor of Japan for his service as an observer during the

Russo-Japanese War. Jean crammed the medals into her suitcase and delicately placed the vase on a small table in the entryway, where it would be noticed by Japanese invaders. "Maybe when the Japanese see it," she said with her usual optimism, "they will respect our home."[41]

Manuel and Aurora Quezon and high commissioner Francis Sayre and his wife, Jessie (a daughter of Woodrow Wilson), sailed from Manila to Corregidor midafternoon on the interisland steamer *Mayon*. MacArthur's family and staff boarded the steamer *Don Esteban* around 6:00 p.m. They waited two hours, until MacArthur and Sutherland strode up the gangplank and directed its crew to cast off. Upon arriving on Corregidor, the three families were all housed together, along with Sutherland, MacArthur's close aide Lieutenant Colonel Sid Huff, and other staff in two of the lateral tunnels off the main Malinta Tunnel—the males in one and the females in the other. Each tunnel had but one shower, one toilet, and one washbasin.[42]

Personal belongings among both parties were limited, but the heavy boxes that were loaded onto the *Don Esteban* contained, according to Huff, "all of the American money in the Manila banks and the gold reserve of the Philippine Government."[43] Under the headline MACARTHUR IN THE FIELD, the *New York Times* reported the move as: "United States Army forces with General Douglas MacArthur personally in the field staved off Japanese advances toward Manila from both the north and south this Christmas Day."[44]

While MacArthur and most of his staff were making the move to Corregidor, it was Brigadier General Richard Marshall, as deputy chief of staff, who was given the unenviable task of shepherding any remaining troops and as much food and supplies as possible out of Manila. Here was the real Achilles' heel of MacArthur's reversal. Under MacArthur's "fight on the beaches" plan, many of the supplies formerly earmarked for a last stand on Bataan had been shipped to various advance quartermaster depots on the Central Luzon Plain. With Homma's tanks bearing down on these forward locations, and with Japanese control of the skies hampering large-scale movements by truck and rail, it would prove difficult to retrieve these supplies and revert to the Plan Orange disposition on Bataan.[45]

As will be seen, Richard Marshall was the wheelhorse among MacArthur's close subordinates, the steady hand on the inside of the turn, the one who balanced MacArthur's and Sutherland's mercurial moments. Marshall and supply chief Colonel Lewis Beebe did what they could to spirit as much out of Manila as possible, moving thirty thousand tons of supplies across the bay via barges and other vessels to both Bataan and Corregidor in the week following MacArthur's decision to revert to Plan Orange. But it was not nearly enough for Bataan, particularly after an inordinate amount of the material was stored on Corregidor.[46]

Among the war-crimes charges filed against General Homma after the war was the complaint that he failed to recognize MacArthur's declaration of Manila as an open city and that his planes continued to bomb and strafe it with a vengeance. Part of this may have been justified, because for at least four or five days after MacArthur's December 26 proclamation, Marshall and Beebe continued to evacuate all manner of supplies and destroy others that might fall into Japanese hands. American troops set almost ten million gallons of gasoline in commercial tanks ablaze, while thousands of panic-stricken Filipinos stormed the docks and raided food caches that had been prepared for Bataan. Marshall and his rear echelon finally departed Manila for Corregidor on New Year's Eve. Two days later, Japanese troops marched into Manila.[47]

The challenge of supplying Bataan from the Central Luzon Plain was even more problematic. In the rush to withdraw to Bataan, huge stockpiles of fresh beef, dried rations, clothing, ammunition, gasoline, and assorted military hardware were simply abandoned at Fort Stotsenburg, near Clark Field. The Manila Railroad north of Tarlac, near Clark Field, had recently hauled supplies north to quartermaster depots near Lingayen Gulf to support beachhead defenses, but with the withdrawal to Bataan, attacks by Japanese planes rendered attempts to reverse the flow exceedingly difficult. By Christmas Day, not one locomotive on the line was operational.

Even more tragic was Philippine president Manuel Quezon's objection to American troops confiscating food stocks in commercial warehouses, even those of Japanese firms. Acting on orders from MacArthur, Sutherland told the officer in charge of the Tarlac supply depot that he would be court-martialed if he removed two thousand cases of canned fish and corned beef from Japanese-owned warehouses. When quartermasters tried to purchase rice from local sources outright, Quezon again pressured MacArthur to forbid it, claiming the rice was only for the use of people in the province in which it was grown and could not be transported elsewhere.[48] Apparently Quezon did not grasp the dire straits facing his country, and MacArthur, still evidencing some measure of divided loyalty, was inclined to support him.

But by far the worst supply snafu occurred at the rice storage warehouses at Cabanatuan, on another branch of the Manila Railroad, east of Tarlac. Some ten million bushels of rice were stored there, and, according to the US Army official history, they would have been "enough to have fed the troops on Bataan for almost a year." An American tank commander on the scene later claimed that local trucks could have supplemented available military vehicles to facilitate nighttime transfers and elude marauding Japanese planes, but because of MacArthur's adherence to Quezon's prohibition of rice transfers outside the province, "not one grain of the rice at Cabanatuan was touched!"[49]

Harold K. Johnson, then a young first lieutenant with the 57th Infantry Regiment who would go on to become US Army chief of staff, later called MacArthur's defend-the-beaches plan "a tragic error" that should never have occurred. But, said Johnson, the most crippling blow to American forces was that it took MacArthur so long to recognize it. Those two or three weeks were critical to stocking Bataan with food. "It wasn't the enemy that licked us," Johnson maintained. "It was disease and absence of food that really licked us."[50]

The Clark-Iba air raid disaster had many fathers — among them bad luck. But the failure to stock Bataan adequately and prepare for the defense at the core of two decades of Orange plans had only one. Douglas MacArthur was determined to fight it out on Bataan, but his vacillation, inaction, and poor decisions prior to that had already tied the hands of his troops. In his memoirs, MacArthur agreed with young Lieutenant Johnson. "The slow starvation," MacArthur acknowledged without admitting a shred of blame, "was ultimately to produce an exhaustion which became the most potent factor in the destruction of the garrison."[51]

CHAPTER SIX

Dugout Doug

With the battle of getting supplies to Bataan lost, it remained for the remnants of the South Luzon Force north of Lamon Bay to fight their way north to the Calumpit bridges and for Wainwright's North Luzon Force to delay Homma's advance across the Central Luzon Plain as long as possible. Wainwright's five projected defense lines were labeled D-1 through D-5. The *D* stood for "defense," but the numbers could have stood for the approximate number of days it took the Japanese to overrun them.

D-1 was little more than a line of wishful thinking along which, Wainwright's chief of staff observed, his forces "hoped to be able to reorganize the badly disorganized forces north of the Agno River." That didn't happen, and on Christmas Day, three days after the Japanese landings, D-2 stiffened along the river twenty miles inland from the Lingayen beachheads. It held for a day before troops withdrew to D-3, stretching from Santa Ignacia on the west to San Jose on the east. On December 27, this line was relatively quiet as the Japanese consolidated their gains and brought up more troops. By the following day, American and Filipino units fell back and dug in along D-4, a line approximately twenty-five miles long between the key points of Tarlac on the west and Cabanatuan, on the Pampanga River to the east.[1]

The halt at D-4 was supposed to be brief, with a final stand at D-5, but late on December 27, Wainwright issued new orders — it is uncertain whether they originated from him in the field or came from

MacArthur—to hold D-4 at all costs and effect maximum delay. He did so to give the South Luzon troops retreating to Bataan over the Calumpit bridges more time to effect their withdrawal.

As this was happening, MacArthur signaled Washington from Corregidor that he was attempting to stand firm in the north until the South Luzon Force could link up with Wainwright, then he would "pivot on my left into Bataan." MacArthur reported that he was facing three Japanese divisions who were well trained and well equipped. Homma was, MacArthur warned Washington, "undoubtedly setting up a powerful attack both north and south simultaneously designed to pin me down in place and crush me."[2]

It would have bruised MacArthur's ego to know that Homma's forces were far short of three divisions—mostly he had only the Forty-Eighth Division and the 9th Infantry Regiment from the Sixteenth Division, which had landed at Lamon Bay—and that Homma was focused not on MacArthur and Bataan but on his orders to secure Manila. Some Japanese officers later claimed that the American-Filipino withdrawal to Bataan even expedited their drive to the capital.[3]

Toward this goal, Japanese forces fell strongly against the right flank of the D-4 line at Cabanatuan, on the east side of the Pampanga River, the most direct route to Manila. This rapid pressure shortened the intended right flank of the final D-5 line and put most of it west of the river, between Fort Stotsenburg and 3,366-foot Mount Arayat. The result was that the Calumpit bridges awaiting the retreating South Luzon Force were all the more exposed.

The South Luzon Force, commanded by Brigadier General Albert M. Jones, had engaged in a similar series of delaying tactics as it retreated from Lamon Bay around the southern and western reaches of Laguna de Bay. By the evening of December 29, part of the Fifty-First Division of the Philippine army was already evacuating to Bataan, while the remainder of the South Luzon Force prepared to follow the next day. At midmorning on December 30, however, Jones received orders from Richard Marshall telling him to hold firm in his current position and withdraw only if forced to do so. This order may have been given to buy more time for Marshall to extract supplies from

Manila despite MacArthur's open-city declaration. Jones promptly dug in just thirty-six hours after he had been issued orders for a top-speed withdrawal.

But before the advancing Japanese could pound Jones's lines, MacArthur recognized that if the Calumpit bridges fell, Jones would be cut off. Consequently, by the evening of the thirtieth, another order was given for Jones once again to expedite his withdrawal. This situation left Homma's main body advancing south from Cabanatuan and Jones's South Luzon Force retiring northward past Manila, both racing toward the Calumpit bridges. Jones won, but barely.

Throughout the day on New Year's Eve, 1941, elements of the Fifty-First Division streamed across the bridges toward Bataan. Despite the momentary change of orders, in just seven days Jones had accomplished the impressive feat of withdrawing the bulk of his command across 140 miles and leaving the enemy grappling with blown bridges and destroyed roads in its wake. Had it not been for the threat of getting cut off at Calumpit, Jones long maintained, his forces "could have effectively delayed the enemy's advance on Manila [from the south] for a considerably longer period."[4]

MacArthur's staff on Corregidor tensely monitored the Calumpit race and, according to MacArthur's headquarters diary, only "when it became evident that the two forces would be able to join in Bataan" did the officers relax a little and take "a few nips in honor of New Year's Eve."[5]

With Jones linked up with Wainwright, the only thing left to do had been to destroy the Calumpit bridges and deny Homma that easy route toward Bataan. While Japanese ground forces were attacking the eastern approaches to the bridges, there had been divided opinion in Homma's headquarters over the merits of destroying them from the air to cut off Jones or leaving them intact. For whatever reason—perhaps Homma's continued fixation on Manila—only limited air action occurred, and early on January 1, 1942, Wainwright gave the order on the American side to "blow the bridges."

The next bottleneck was the key road and rail junction of San Fernando. Jones's southern troops had to pass that way before completing a left turn into Bataan, and the bulk of Wainwright's forces along the surviving D-5 line also had to retreat through San Fernando. Civilians fleeing in all directions, some to the imagined safety of Bataan, others simply away from the advancing Japanese, further affected military traffic.

Part of the reason for the successful withdrawal to the D-5 line was that a major portion of Homma's Forty-Eighth Division continued to advance east of the destroyed Calumpit bridges toward Manila. Those units that turned west to pursue the retreating Americans and Filipinos were delayed in ferrying troops across the river. By the time the Japanese reached San Fernando, on the evening of January 2, the D-5 line defenders and Jones's rear guard at Calumpit had all successfully moved beyond the town toward Bataan.[6]

At many levels, it had been a complicated but highly successful withdrawal against surging forces. The lines had held when necessary and saved not only Wainwright's troops but also those of the South Luzon Force. MacArthur then had an estimated eighty thousand troops marshaled on Bataan, just as Plan Orange had envisioned. Whether they would soon have anything to eat was another matter.

As his troops poured into Bataan and MacArthur contemplated their fate and his own, important strategy discussions were being held in Washington. Three days before Christmas, British prime minister Winston Churchill arrived in the capital, made himself at home on the second floor of the White House, and showed no inclination of leaving until he and his new ally had developed a framework of global strategy for the Anglo-American coalition. From MacArthur's viewpoint, their focus had to be on checking Japan's rapid advance.

MacArthur sent chief of staff Marshall repeated exhortations to take immediate and aggressive countermeasures in the Pacific. "Enemy appears to have tendency to become overconfident," he cabled Marshall on January 7, "and time is ripe for brilliant thrust with air carriers."[7] Neither statement was true. Far from overconfidence, Homma was showing the first signs of concern that the sixty-day timetable his superiors had given him to subdue the Philippines might have to be extended because of MacArthur's concentration on Bataan. As for American carriers, they would soon be sent on limited raids against

Japanese positions in the Gilbert and Marshall Islands. These locations were 3,500 miles east of Corregidor, however, and Admirals Stark and King remained adamant that ordering the precious ships any closer would only lead to their destruction by Japan's land-based aircraft.

With Great Britain and the Netherlands his firm allies in the war against Japan, MacArthur saw the Philippines as "the locus of victory or defeat." If the Philippines fell, he lectured Marshall, the entire sweep of Southeast Asia, from India across the Malay Barrier to Australia, would be vulnerable. Consequently, MacArthur urged that British and Dutch resources be placed at his disposal, along with American reinforcements.

MacArthur's pleas reached President Roosevelt, Prime Minister Churchill, and their military chiefs of staff as they convened in Washington. Officially called the First Washington Conference, this three-week series of meetings was code-named Arcadia and was the first wartime gathering of what came to be called the Combined Chiefs of Staff.

Throughout the deliberations, Marshall tried to keep MacArthur's spirits up with optimism, but outright promises to provide him with anything beyond the men and materiel already en route to Australia could not be made. Despite MacArthur's naive suggestion that the winter months in England afforded it protection from an invasion across the English Channel and should be used as an occasion to release forces to aid the Philippines, Churchill could not agree to that. Not only were British forces spread thin, but shipping them halfway around the world and back again in time for a spring offensive was also highly impracticable. The best hope the conferees could extend MacArthur, Marshall wrote him on January 2, "is that the rapid development of an overwhelming air power on the Malay Barrier will cut the Japanese communications south of Borneo and permit an [Allied] assault on the southern Philippines."[8]

It was painfully obvious to MacArthur that this strategy promoted only a holding action along roughly the line to which Admiral Hart's handful of ships had already been dispatched. It hardly allowed for Allied reinforcements to counterattack and support his position. Any short-term hope of changing that was foreclosed when, much to

111

Churchill's relief, Roosevelt reassured the British leader that the United States remained committed — MacArthur's entreaties notwithstanding — to the strategy of Germany First. This meant that Germany's defeat was the primary Allied objective and that its downfall was assumed to be the ultimate key to victory over Italy and Japan.

Not only did the Combined Chiefs of Staff fail to embrace MacArthur's call for a concerted counterattack, but when they created a combined Allied military command, MacArthur was also only one of five regional commanders — for Burma, Malaysia, the Netherlands East Indies, the Philippines, and northwestern Australia — ostensibly reporting to a Dutch general in charge of land forces. In retrospect, ABDACOM, for American, British, Dutch, and Australian command, was a last-ditch military effort to save territory between Rangoon and Darwin, but it was also the first attempt at unity of command among Allied forces anywhere around the globe. The learning curve would be steep, as witnessed by on-again, off-again decisions regarding the Philippines.

On January 15, British lieutenant general Sir Archibald Wavell became supreme commander of ABDACOM. Among Wavell's instructions from the Combined Chiefs of Staff were orders to strengthen lines of communication with MacArthur and support the Philippine garrison. Wavell objected and proposed that the Philippines be excluded from the ABDA area — the equivalent of abandonment. Roosevelt was also facing a steep learning curve as a wartime commander in chief, and, hearing from Churchill of Wavell's exclusion proposal, he agreed to it without consulting his own chiefs of staff.

When General Marshall learned of Roosevelt's decision, he strongly objected, both because it would likely have an adverse effect on morale among MacArthur's command and because the United States was allocating most of the aircraft originally destined for MacArthur — but now unable to reach him — to the ABDA effort. The same was true of America's limited naval resources, and Admiral King concurred with Marshall's rationale: ABDA was MacArthur's best hope, slim though that might be. Together they persuaded Roosevelt to rescind his approval of the exclusion, and the day after Wavell assumed command, he was told that the Philippines would remain in his area of operations, even if in reality there was little he could do for the islands.

These machinations had little operational effect on MacArthur, holed up as he was on Corregidor, but he nonetheless technically had his command reduced. He had already lost the remnants of his air force when he ordered Brereton south. These planes were now operating under Brereton in support of ABDACOM and were part of the recently created United States Army Forces in Australia (USAFIA), a post carved out of MacArthur's broader United States Army Forces in the Far East (USAFFE), with Brereton momentarily in command of it as well. This step was taken because of the difficulty of MacArthur's exercising command from the Philippines. Marshall nonetheless assured MacArthur, "When satisfactory communications with the Philippines have once been reestablished your resumption of actual command of all American Army forces in the Far East will be easily accomplished."[9]

But as Wavell and others had feared, reestablishing any link to the Philippines was next to impossible. Unknown to MacArthur, even as Marshall continued to offer encouragement, War Plans Division chief Leonard Gerow drafted a report coming to the same conclusion: the Philippines could not be reinforced, and MacArthur's pleas for an offensive northward from Australia would be "an entirely unjustifiable diversion of forces from the principal theater—the Atlantic." No one, however, was willing to sign off on this as policy. Both secretary of war Stimson and chief of staff Marshall read Gerow's report but made no comment and extended no approval.[10] For the moment, they would continue to operate under Dwight Eisenhower's original analysis: the situation was hopeless, but they had to try.

Part of Stimson's and Marshall's efforts to save MacArthur's command included dispatching former secretary of war Patrick J. Hurley to Australia on a special mission. Hurley was an ardent admirer of MacArthur from the Hoover administration, and as he met with Marshall to prepare for his post as ambassador to New Zealand, he saw one of MacArthur's desperate pleas for assistance. "If I can just help Doug," Hurley pleaded with Marshall, and Marshall agreed to appoint him a temporary brigadier general.[11]

Marshall ordered Hurley to Australia to organize disparate attempts to run the Japanese blockade. As Eisenhower told the story, the army had already "sent officers to Australia with money to hire, at no matter what fantastic prices, the men and ships needed to carry supplies into the islands and to smuggle them into the beleaguered garrison." These efforts seemed stalled, and what was needed was "a man of [Hurley's] known energy and fearlessness."

"When can you be ready to report for duty?" Eisenhower asked him after Hurley left Marshall's office.

"Now," Hurley replied.

"Be back here at midnight," Eisenhower instructed him, "prepared for extended field service."

According to Eisenhower, Hurley "seemed to change color slightly" but never batted an eye. Instead, he replied evenly, "That will give me time to see my lawyers and change my will."[12]

Delayed en route by bad weather, Hurley finally arrived in Australia early in February of 1942, determined to recruit soldiers of fortune willing to risk life and limb to run the Japanese blockade for mega-cash. Ships and willing crews proved in short supply, however, and tales of vessels that had sailed north never to be heard from again didn't help Hurley's effort. Only three vessels made successful supply runs north from Australia. Two ended up on Cebu and the other on Mindanao, all far from Bataan. Of the ten thousand tons of rations and munitions they delivered, barely one-tenth made it by interisland steamer the remainder of the way to MacArthur's garrison.[13]

Hurley worked feverishly to force more supplies through the Japanese stranglehold, but in the end he reluctantly admitted, "We did not have the ships, the air force or ground forces necessary to make the operation successful. We were out-shipped, out-planed, out-manned, and out-gunned by the Japanese from the beginning."[14]

While the strategic decisions being made in Washington were largely beyond his control, Douglas MacArthur faced other situations that were his alone to confront and resolve. One of his actions — like his ouster of the Bonus Marchers and his reversals of Plan Orange defenses — would come under severe criticism and be judged by many as a dark mark on his reputation.

Throughout the trenches of World War I — and in other arenas, from his first tour in the Philippines to his spy mission at Veracruz—no one had ever questioned MacArthur's personal courage. His reputation was one of a leader who led from the turmoil of the front, not the quiet of a rear-echelon command post. Yet as his beleaguered troops hunkered down only a short PT boat ride from his headquarters on Corregidor, MacArthur's frontline behavior was the antithesis of this reputation.

To be sure, MacArthur was twenty-five years older than he had been during those days of World War I. The dashing brigadier in command of a regiment was now a full general commanding a theater. An inordinate amount of his time was directed to pleading with Washington for reinforcements and monitoring the rapidly changing circumstances throughout Southeast Asia. These tasks could be done most effectively from his communications center on Corregidor. But during three months of fighting, MacArthur made only one documented visit (there are vague reports of a second) to Bataan. The general, who theretofore had always been conspicuous near the front, was inexplicably absent from the field.[15]

The documented trip occurred on January 10, 1942. The latest round of supportive messages from Marshall had momentarily buoyed MacArthur, and he decided to cross over to Bataan and personally give his top commanders encouragement: significant help was on the way.

With the retreat to Bataan, MacArthur had reorganized the North Luzon Force and the South Luzon Force into I Philippine Corps under Wainwright, holding the line from Mount Natib west to the coast, and II Philippine Corps, under Major General George M. Parker Jr., running from that massif east to Manila Bay. Each corps had around twenty-five thousand troops. Parts of two other divisions, along with supporting tank and artillery units and various coastal defenses, totaled another twenty-five thousand troops. In opposition, Homma had roughly one-third that number, because on January 2, thinking they had Manila won and that the occupation of the Philippines was largely complete, Tokyo had ordered Homma's best division, the Forty-Eighth, to disengage from the Philippines and deploy farther south. Homma did not object, because, unlike MacArthur, who routinely overestimated the numbers engaged against him, Homma calculated that only twenty-five thousand troops remained in opposition.[16]

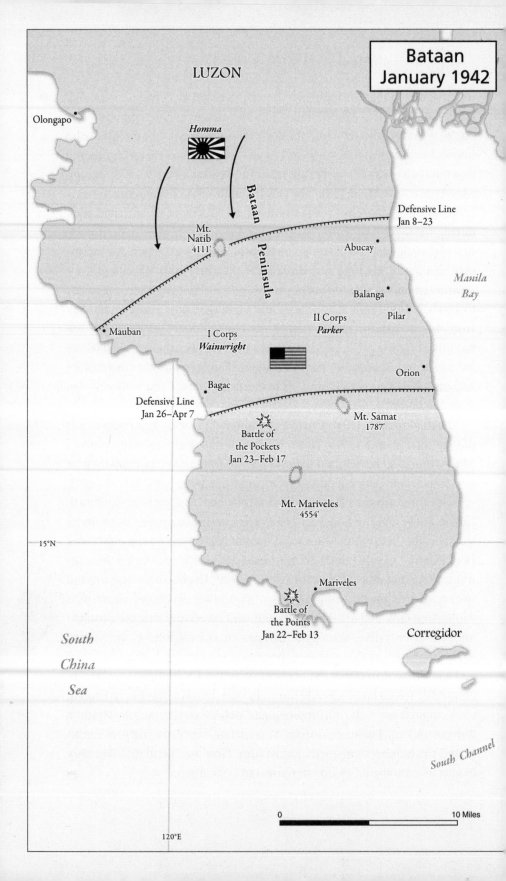

MacArthur left Corregidor's North Dock with Sutherland shortly after sunrise on the tenth and crossed to Mariveles, a distance of around ten miles. There they commandeered a beat-up Ford sedan and drove the dusty one-lane road along the eastern side of Bataan to the front near Balanga, stopping briefly along the way at field hospitals and rear command posts. At Balanga, MacArthur met with Parker and his senior field commanders and spread the word that help from the United States was on the way. A few miles to the north, at Abucay, soon to be the scene of fierce fighting, the churchyard had already come under heavy Japanese artillery fire.

Then MacArthur backtracked south of Balanga to Pilar and took the main east-west road across the peninsula to Bagac to repeat his message to the division and regimental commanders of Wainwright's I Corps. Brigadier General Clifford Bluemel, commanding the Thirty-First Division, remembered MacArthur's message as: "Help is definitely on the way. We must hold out until it arrives."

MacArthur clapped Wainwright on the back and told him with the usual MacArthur superlatives that his fighting withdrawal from Lingayen had been as fine an operation "as anything in history." Then, employing another familiar technique, one that assumed others valued rank as much as he did, MacArthur promised to recommend to the War Department that Wainwright's temporary rank of major general be made permanent.[17]

Sutherland warned Wainwright that his right flank, pressing against Mount Natib, was exposed and that he should effect a strong linkup with Parker's II Corps. Then, proceeding south from Bagac along the west coast of Bataan, MacArthur and Sutherland reached Mariveles and returned to Corregidor after around nine hours in the field. According to Harold K. Johnson, a ditty spread through the troops: "Crafty Mac, he'll never be back."[18]

Caught up in his own enthusiasm, MacArthur reported to Quezon that the morale of the troops was high and he "felt confident that he could hold Bataan and Corregidor for several months without outside help." Quezon, who by then was dying of tuberculosis, beamed when MacArthur praised the Filipino reservists, who, the general said, had become "veterans in less than one month [of] actual fighting against a determined and superior force." He made no mention of the thousands who had never reported for duty or deserted, however, and the glow did not last long for either MacArthur or Quezon. Barely had MacArthur settled back on Corregidor when Japanese planes dropped leaflets throughout Bataan demanding an immediate surrender.[19]

The question that was asked repeatedly on Bataan during the weeks after MacArthur's visit and that has baffled historians ever since is: Why didn't MacArthur ever return to Bataan? It certainly was not that he lacked personal courage. There are many accounts of MacArthur being out in the open as Japanese planes rained bombs on Corregidor. "There was nothing of bravado in this," he claimed in his memoirs. "It was simply my duty." But was it?

He went on to note a far more compelling reason: "The gunners at the batteries, the men in the foxholes, they too were in the open. They liked to see me with them at such moments." This was one of the intangibles he understood so well. "Leadership," MacArthur professed, "is often crystallized in some sort of public gesture."[20]

MacArthur usually excelled at this aspect of leadership, so why did he not apply it to Bataan? In his memoirs, MacArthur made no mention of his lone visit, nor did he offer any explanation, casual or otherwise, for why he did not make more appearances there. Where the visit to Bataan would have been chronologically in the narrative, he quotes what he calls a deeply moving letter from Quezon. The Philippine president told his field marshal to be careful in exposing himself, because his death would have a negative impact on both Americans and Filipinos. "And may I add," Quezon concluded, "that you have personal obligations to your wife and your boy which require you to be careful of your safety when duty does not compel you to do otherwise."[21]

These were comforting and prudent words, but they were not enough for MacArthur to change his habits on Corregidor. They alone were not enough to keep him from Bataan. He was a very proud man. It grieved him considerably to see his troops in dismal conditions on Bataan. Why, then, short of one brief appearance, didn't he comfort them? Rally them? Lead them?

In the years ahead, he would instruct his staff to answer his headquarters phone with the words "This is Bataan." Not "This is Corregidor," but "This

is Bataan." Part of it was the usual MacArthur theatrics. Part of it was soli-
darity and an ingrained resolve that had been in his genes since his father's
dash up Missionary Ridge. But another part of it may have been guilt.

No one will ever know for certain what went through MacArthur's
mind during those weeks following his sole visit to his troops on Bataan,
but deep down he had to have known two realities about the condition of
his men: the possibility of any significant relief from the United States
in time to save them was minuscule, and a large part of their gnawing
hunger was attributable to his own vacillations and intransigence.

The huge contradiction between MacArthur's usual leadership style
and his actions regarding Bataan encouraged a host of generally derog-
atory grumbling by the rank and file. He became "Dugout Doug." Part
of it was the usual ridicule subordinates traditionally heap on superiors
as relief when things get tough. But as conditions worsened and food
became ever scarcer and of dubious quality, these criticisms became
more pointed and personal.

In and of itself, the term "Dugout Doug" was not necessarily derog-
atory. A dugout is a trench or shelter excavated into the ground or a
hillside, and MacArthur was certainly no stranger to dugouts during
his time in France. Had he joined his troops in a few more foxholes in
the Philippines, though, what was a handy alliteration might have been
repeated with admiration. But he didn't, and the nickname, particularly as it was repeated in verse and song, proved damning.

While there were many ditties and poems composed around the
name, the most famous and oft-repeated version was sung to the tune
of "The Battle Hymn of the Republic":

Dugout Doug MacArthur lies a-shaking on the Rock
Safe from all the bombers and from any sudden shock
Dugout Doug is eating of the best food on Bataan
And his troops go starving on.

Such lyrics were decidedly inaccurate. MacArthur routinely stood
impassively out in the open with his hands in his rear pockets watching
wave after wave of Japanese bombers pound Corregidor. He lost

twenty-five pounds from his always lean frame during his first month on the Rock. And he and his family shared the same rations as his men, even if Corregidor was better stocked. But none of this mattered on Bataan. The verses rolled on:

Dugout Doug's not timid, he's just cautious, not afraid
He's protecting carefully the stars that Franklin made
Four-star generals are rare as good food on Bataan
And his troops go starving on.

Dugout Doug is ready in his Kris Craft for the flee
Over bounding billows and the wildly raging sea
For the Japs are pounding on the gates of Old Bataan
And his troops go starving on.

We've fought the war the hard way since they said the fight was on
All the way from Lingayen to the hills of Old Bataan
And we'll continue fighting after Dugout Doug is gone
And still go starving on.

Between the verses there was a grating chorus:

Dugout Doug, come out from hiding
Dugout Doug, come out from hiding
Send to Franklin the glad tidings
That his troops go starving on.[22]

With these songs in the air and recent developments in the fight, it was no wonder that the patrician tone of MacArthur's orders from Corregidor struck increasingly raw nerves. The Japanese attacked the initial line of resistance on Bataan in force on January 11. The coastal areas north of Abucay, on the east, and Mauban, on the west, were particularly hard hit. Then Japanese troops pushed through the jungle on either side of Mount Natib, which many American officers had considered impenetrable. Sutherland had been right, and these attacks drove a wedge between I Corps and II Corps.

MacArthur issued a lofty proclamation exhorting the rank and file, "If we fight we will win; if we retreat we will be destroyed," and he called upon his officers to remember the "demeanor of confidence, self-reliance and assurance which is the birthright of all cultured gentlemen and the special trademark of the Army Officer."[23] Already on half rations, bombed from the sky, and harried on every front by advancing infantry, "cultured" gentlemen were hard to find.

On January 22, as MacArthur stayed on Corregidor, Sutherland returned to Bataan for another firsthand look. Wainwright and Parker urged a withdrawal to a second major defense line halfway down the peninsula, between Bagac and Orion. As this retreat began, MacArthur beseeched Marshall—in an almost Alamo-like way—to be certain that the courage of his troops ("their fame and glory," he wrote) would "be duly recorded by their countrymen." In the event of his own death, MacArthur continued, he recommended Sutherland as his replacement, because "of all my general officers he has the most comprehensive grasp of the situation."[24]

What Marshall thought of this communication is not readily apparent, as no record of a response exists. Eisenhower's personal take, however, recorded in the privacy of his diary, was neither laudatory nor high-minded and was no doubt colored by his prewar association with Sutherland in Manila. "Today, in a most flamboyant radio[gram]," wrote Eisenhower, "MacArthur recommends successor in case of 'my death.' He picked Sutherland, showing that he still likes his boot lickers."[25]

For his part, Sutherland, for the moment, was optimistic. Between late January and the middle of February, the Bagac-Orion line stiffened and held. In addition to stemming sustained pressure along the II Corps front, Wainwright's and Parker's forces mopped up pockets of the Japanese troops that had driven the wedge south of Mount Natib and repelled battalion-strength landings on several promontories (or "points") on the west coast that attempted to turn MacArthur's left flank and threaten rear service areas. Respectively called the Battle of the Pockets and the Battle of the Points, these actions were fierce and bloody but checked the Japanese advance.

"We have stopped the Japs cold on Bataan, inflicting very heavy casualties," Sutherland wrote Brigadier General Bradford Chynoweth, commanding on Cebu, in the southern Philippines. "The Jap is going to have to put a lot more troops up here to push us around any."[26]

Among those agreeing with Sutherland was General Masaharu Homma. Tokyo's recall of the Forty-Eighth Division—earlier than planned because successes expedited the timetable for the second wave of assaults along the Malay Barrier—left Homma relying on the Sixteenth Division and the Sixty-Fifth Brigade, the latter an untried garrison unit newly arrived from Takao. Homma later claimed that if MacArthur's forces had counterattacked early in February, "I thought they could walk to Manila without encountering much resistance on our part."[27]

Rear Admiral Matome Ugaki, Admiral Yamamoto's chief of staff, also sensed the danger of what he termed "the poorest strategy—to surround the most important center"—and the impact it would have on MacArthur personally. "The army offensive on Bataan Peninsula has stalemated," Ugaki wrote in his diary as Japanese troops occupied other islands in the archipelago. "In this way," Ugaki continued presciently, "the peninsula and Corregidor will remain until the last and it will only make MacArthur a hero."[28]

Yet the Japanese continued to have an increasingly deadly ally— the Americans' and Filipinos' own hunger. One wonders what might have happened had the defenders been better provisioned and supplied. Even as the front stabilized, American and Filipino morale sank as starvation, malnutrition, and disease took their toll. It was obvious from activity behind the Japanese lines that Homma was slowly rebuilding his strength with reinforcements and stockpiles of food and munitions, but no such relief appeared on the American side.

Lieutenant Edgar D. Whitcomb of the Nineteenth Bomb Group had escaped the destruction at Clark Field and fled with remnants of his unit to Bataan, where they made an attempt to hack a rudimentary airstrip out of rice paddies for the replacement aircraft thought to be en route. One night Whitcomb found his tent mate—apparently quite deranged—standing stark naked in the middle of a nearby stream and singing "When Johnny Comes Marching Home" at the top of his lungs.

"Christ, Whit, haven't you heard the news?" the singer proclaimed. "A big convoy is coming through the San Bernardino Straits right this minute. Aircraft carriers, battle wagons, the whole works. It's only a matter of hours until..." His voice trailed off, and he launched back into song.[29]

A few weeks later, Whitcomb saw the relief column for himself — or thought he did. Along with hundreds of others, he climbed a hill overlooking Manila Bay and watched what appeared through the haze to be a large convoy round the eastern tip of Corregidor and head straight for Bataan. "Each time another big ship appeared around the point," Whitcomb recalled, "another wild cheer rang out over the hillside and into the valley below." Sadly, the ships were only empty merchantmen being moved beyond the range of Japanese artillery at Cavite.[30]

But one night, reinforcements appeared overhead. Whitcomb and his comrades scrambled to their makeshift strip to the sound of friendly aircraft. Three P-40s from a nearby field landed and sputtered to a halt. A fourth came in too high over the short strip, and as it circled for another try, its engine coughed and died and the plane went down in a loud explosion. "We had received our reinforcements," Whitcomb noted glumly. "Three beat-up P-40s from Bataan Field, three kilometers away!"[31]

Despite the shortage of everything but courage across Bataan, during the first two months of a very grim 1942, the American public became captivated by the image of Douglas MacArthur almost single-handedly leading the fight against Japanese aggression. With almost uncanny timing, Clare Boothe Luce had focused the spotlight on MacArthur in a complimentary cover story that appeared in *Life* on December 8, 1941. "I do hope, most sincerely," Luce wrote MacArthur when she sent him an advance copy the day before Pearl Harbor, "that as it stands there is nothing which will displease you. To do so was, and is, and will always be the farthest thing from my mind — or pen."[32] This article became a bedrock source for characterizations of MacArthur's military persona, his career to that point, and his commitment to the Philippines.

Life's sister publication, *Time,* also run by Luce's husband, Henry R. Luce, reciprocated by putting MacArthur on the cover of its December 29, 1941, issue. Before television, these two weekly magazines reached an estimated four million households out of a total population of 133 million and were the chief source of information for middle America beyond radio and local newspapers.[33]

This sweeping introduction to the rank and file of America was augmented by MacArthur's press machinery. By one count, out of 142 press releases issued by MacArthur's headquarters between December 8, 1941, and March 11, 1942—an average of eleven a week—109 mentioned only MacArthur by name.[34] These reports referred to "MacArthur's front line" or "MacArthur's men" without giving credit to or mention of the officers and men engaged in the hardships.

At the same time, MacArthur clamped a tight lid of censorship around Corregidor and Bataan that made certain his were the only reports to get out to the public. Some reports were plainly false, such as the claim that Captain Colin P. Kelly's B-17—Kelly's personal heroism in saving his crew aside—had sunk a Japanese battleship and the unbelievable story that Homma had committed suicide in MacArthur's former penthouse atop the Manila Hotel.[35] Exaggeration was a hallmark of these releases, particularly the repeated characterization that MacArthur's troops were vastly outnumbered when in fact they outnumbered their attackers after Tokyo withdrew the Forty-Eighth Division in January.

The draftsman behind these releases was frequently MacArthur himself. Lieutenant Colonel LeGrande A. "Pick" Diller, who was the general's public relations officer, admitted as much and was quite accustomed to MacArthur's editorial pen revising anything Diller wrote himself.[36] Major Carlos P. Romulo dutifully served as Diller's assistant and went to great lengths to catalog the positive reports of MacArthur's activities published in the American press. These frequently not only repeated MacArthur's own misleading assessments but also characterized him as America's supreme hero.

A sampling from Romulo's list includes:

Washington Post, January 27, 1942, quoting Senator Elbert Thomas, Democrat of Utah: "Never has a commander of his troops met such a situation with greater and cooler courage, never with more resourcefulness of brilliant action."

Philadelphia Record, January 27, 1942: "He is one of the greatest
fighting generals of this war or [any] other war. This is the kind
of history which your children will tell your grandchildren."
Baltimore Sun, February 1, 1942: "He is something in the nature
of a military genius with the capacity to foresee contingents
and take the best use of resources at his disposal."

The syndicates and wire services spread the stories farther afield.
The Associated Press, on February 2, 1942, reported, "Almost every
day jolts Japanese with unpleasant new reminder of strength [of] General
MacArthur's Gibraltar." And the Scripps Howard News Service,
run by Roy Howard, one of the general's adoring supporters, found
him "every inch a soldier equally flamboyant he has always been able
to instill army spirit into younger generations."[37]

Those nonmilitary reporters whom MacArthur allowed close were
effusive in their praise. Bob Considine, a correspondent for William
Randolph Hearst's International News Service, jumped to tell MacArthur's
story in syndication and then published a book, the title of which
left no doubt about his position: *MacArthur the Magnificent.*

Even Drew Pearson, arguably one of MacArthur's shrillest critics
during the 1930s and the target of MacArthur's ill-fated libel action,
joined the MacArthur bandwagon. Writing with just a hint of wry sarcasm,
Pearson nonetheless pinpointed the reason MacArthur "is the
hero of his country today. He has dash, swagger, dramatic flair, plus
great courage, brains, and a tremendous capacity for hard work."

Pearson even took back some of his Bonus March criticism by labeling
MacArthur "an unfortunate scapegoat" in that affair and asserting,
"Dynamic and dramatic, MacArthur has made good press copy wherever
he has gone." Certainly no stranger to having his name in print,
Pearson acknowledged that "every day since [Pearl Harbor] the name
MacArthur has appeared on the front page of every paper in the land."[38]

Thus, in a fragile period of the American psyche, when the general
American public, still stunned by the shock of Pearl Harbor and uncertain
what lay ahead in Europe, desperately needed a hero, they wholeheartedly
embraced Douglas MacArthur. There simply were not any

other choices that came close to matching his mystique and allure, not to mention his lone-wolf stand — something that has always resonated with Americans.

Those in the know in Washington reacted differently. Festooned as MacArthur's communiqués were with grandiose claims and Alamo-like statements, they were a large part of the reason Eisenhower was so negative about MacArthur in the privacy of his diary.[39] Marshall was more circumspect, as was his nature, but he, too, recognized that he was dealing with a prima donna. Roosevelt, of course, had known that for at least a decade. The key result of these communiqués was that MacArthur's credibility was compromised and he was subject to disdain and measured criticism in Washington.

Among his beleaguered troops, there was little reason for measure. The preponderance of MacArthur's name in the headlines — frequently to the exclusion of all others — was no secret to the embattled men on Bataan. Before the Japanese jammed radio reception, some units were able to pick up the shortwave station KGEI out of San Francisco. Edgar Whitcomb recounted that one night one of the men did an impromptu routine mimicking the broadcasts.

"Ladies and Gents," intoned the would-be announcer, "KGEI now brings you fifteen minutes of the latest war news from the Pacific. MacArthur, MacArthur, MacArthur, MacArthur, etc. And now to repeat the headline news — MacArthur, MacArthur, MacArthur. Ladies and Gentlemen, for the past fifteen minutes you have been listening to news from the war in the Pacific. KGEI now signs off!"[40] It was good for a laugh, but once the laughter died, the sobering reality returned, and it furthered their bitterness toward Dugout Doug. MacArthur appeared bathed in glory while any bath they took was in mud and blood.

CHAPTER SEVEN

Ordered Out

As food supplies dwindled on Bataan and MacArthur's personal popularity rose in the American press, the people of the Philippines were caught between surviving under their new Japanese landlords and fighting for Quezon's government, in exile on Corregidor. Most chose survival. In an effort to solidify their control of the islands, the Japanese unleashed widespread propaganda heralding their arrival as liberators from American imperialism and vaguely promising independence within Japan's "Greater East Asia Co-Prosperity Sphere" sooner than the American target of 1946. General Homma established a puppet government nominally headed by Jorge Vargas, Quezon's former secretary, and many members of the Philippine legislature and Manila's upper class collaborated with the Japanese.

President Quezon, who was inaugurated for his second term above the rocky cliffs of Corregidor days after arriving on the island, and General MacArthur were not pleased. But then things got worse. Messages signed by Vargas fluttered down behind the lines on Bataan, calling on Filipino solders to surrender and "shake off the yoke of white domination forever." Aging Emilio Aguinaldo, the nationalist leader who had fought both the Spaniards and the Americans at the turn of the century, took to the airwaves to broadcast a similar surrender appeal to MacArthur.[1]

Racked with high fevers as his tubercular condition worsened, Quezon began to doubt his own loyalty to the United States, and he shared

127

with MacArthur a deep sense of frustration over their apparent abandonment. "It is remarkable," Quezon cabled President Roosevelt, "that no assistance by sea or by air has been afforded the Philippines since the beginning of the war."[2] Hearing nothing from Roosevelt in reply, Quezon directed his frustration toward MacArthur, reminding him that "this war is not of our making" and asking whether the sacrifices he and his countrymen were making had any value.

MacArthur had a long habit of drafting letters for others to send that reinforced his positions — including Quezon's letter requesting MacArthur's appointment to the Philippines in 1935 — and he may well have had a hand in this one, particularly as it asked that publicity be given to "the determination of the Filipino people to continue fighting side by side with the United States."[3] MacArthur passed it on to Roosevelt and got a reply just two days later for Quezon. Roosevelt assured Quezon that "the magnificent resistance of the defenders of Bataan is contributing definitely toward assuring the completeness of our final victory in the Far East."

But that was part of the problem from Quezon's perspective: he was concerned for the Philippines and the Philippines alone — not for the broader requirements of a global war, be they in Europe or other parts of the Pacific. Even as Roosevelt cataloged for Quezon the men and materiel that "every ship at our disposal is bringing to the southwest Pacific," he professed he could not "indicate the time at which succor and assistance can reach the Philippines."[4]

This exchange turned Roosevelt and Marshall to thinking about what might happen to President Quezon and his family, as well as the families of Commissioner Sayre and MacArthur himself, as the situation in the Philippines continued to deteriorate. Marshall advised MacArthur on February 3 that if any of them wanted to leave the Philippines it would be "your decision in the light of the military situation, the feasibility and hazard of operation of evacuation and wishes of individuals concerned," but speculated that at some point such evacuation would become "desirable."[5]

The key man in Marshall's office drafting these communications was Brigadier General Dwight Eisenhower, then still the deputy for the Pacific theater in War Plans but about to become chief of the entire division. "MacArthur," Eisenhower confided in his diary, "has started a flood of communications that seem to indicate a refusal on his part to look facts in the face, an old trait of his. . . . He's jittery!"[6]

MacArthur did momentarily choose to ignore Marshall's query about evacuations and instead sent him, as Marshall had diplomatically requested he do from time to time, a strategic assessment of the situation. Characterizing the official strategy of building up defensive forces along the Malay Barrier as a fatal blunder, MacArthur again called for a major naval thrust on Japan's flank to cut its lines of communication. "Combat must not be avoided," MacArthur lectured, "but must be sought so that the ultimate policy of attrition can at once become effective." Acknowledging that in offering such advice he might be exceeding the proper limits of his authority, MacArthur professed he nonetheless was giving it because "from my present point of vantage I can see the whole strategy of the Pacific perhaps clearer than anyone else."[7]

Marshall, through Eisenhower, replied graciously—assuring MacArthur that he "invariably" submitted his ideas to the president—and with considerable detail as to Allied efforts around the globe. The naval thrust MacArthur wanted remained impractical for two reasons, Marshall wrote: Japan had established security on its central Pacific flank by seizing Guam and Wake Island and had land-based air in the Marshall and Gilbert Islands, and the US Navy was still reeling from the attack on Pearl Harbor as well from as recent torpedo damage to the carrier *Saratoga*. Yet the navy had just carried out a daring hit-and-run raid, even if it was not the major effort MacArthur advocated. Led by Vice Admiral William F. Halsey Jr., a determined fighter whom MacArthur would soon have reason to know well, a task force built around the carrier *Enterprise* made a surprise attack against Japanese bases in the Marshall Islands.[8]

This news did little to cheer MacArthur, and in the course of four days he turned from grand strategist to worried pessimist. Much of the reason could be found in his close relationship with Manuel Quezon. The Philippine president was grasping for any hope of saving his country, and he reached again for the concept of a neutral Philippines, which he had advocated years before. MacArthur, in another show of conflicted loyalties between the United States and the Philippines, also briefly flirted with neutrality both in support of Quezon and as a solution to his own military situation.

On February 8 Quezon's position solidified, and, citing the futility of further armed resistance, he cabled Roosevelt about his plan for the United States to grant the Philippines immediate independence. The islands would then be declared neutral, the Philippine army disbanded, and the military forces of both the United States and Japan withdrawn. However unlikely the latter was, Quezon claimed that this solution would "save my country from further devastation as the battleground of two great powers."[9]

MacArthur might simply have transmitted Quezon's message without comment, but he chose to include his own lengthy observations, which he addressed to Marshall in the second part of the message. For the first time in his communications with Washington, MacArthur assessed his military situation as grim. Referring to casualty rates as high as 50 percent, the "badly battle worn" state of his troops, and the scarcity of supplies on Bataan, MacArthur predicted that any addition to the enemy's strength would "insure the destruction of our mobile force."

"Since I have no air or sea protection," MacArthur continued, "you must be prepared at any time to figure on the complete destruction of this command." He described the attitude of Filipinos toward the United States—because reinforcements had not been forthcoming—as one of "almost violent resentment" and claimed that "they believe they have been betrayed in favor of others." MacArthur was likely reporting some Filipino views, but mostly he was allowing his own frustrations to show through.

"So far as the military angle is concerned," MacArthur concluded, "the problem presents itself as to whether the plan of President Quezon might offer the best possible solution of what is about to be a disastrous debacle." Neutralizing the Philippines, MacArthur maintained, would neither affect the struggle throughout the rest of Southeast Asia and Europe nor result in the loss of any military advantage. Then, quite uncharacteristically, MacArthur signed off with three words he usually did not use: "Please instruct me."[10]

In Washington, Franklin Roosevelt, secretary of war Stimson, and George Marshall could not believe what they read. Declaring neutrality was akin to surrender. "We can't do this at all," the president exclaimed. Stimson termed the Quezon-MacArthur missives "most disappointing" and "wholly unreal." Stimson greatly appreciated Roosevelt's resolve, though the situation was "ghastly in its responsibility and significance" and though it essentially meant they were consigning "a brave garrison to a fight to the finish."

But it was Marshall who was the most impressed, and the chief of staff seems to have taken this moment to bond with FDR in his conduct of the war. When Roosevelt made that firm stand and rejected neutralization, Marshall later recalled, "I immediately discarded everything in my mind I had held to his discredit... and decided this was a great man."[11]

Eisenhower spent the entire day on February 9 preparing drafts of Roosevelt's replies to MacArthur and Quezon. Privately, he called the process "long, difficult, and irritating" and characterized both men as "babies." At 6:45 p.m., Eisenhower met with the president and received his approval for sending the messages.[12]

Roosevelt's letter to Quezon evoked some measure of sympathy for the Philippine president's position and that of his country, but it was emphatic that the United States would never accept even the slightest hint of neutrality. "Whatever happens to the present American garrison," Roosevelt assured Quezon, "we shall not relax our efforts until the forces which are now marshaling outside the Philippine Islands return to the Philippines and drive the last remnant of the invaders from your soil."[13]

MacArthur read this portion of the communiqué before it was passed on to Quezon, and he may well have filed the phrase "return to the Philippines" away in the vast storehouse of his brain. But at that moment MacArthur had to consider what Roosevelt's letter meant for him. Suddenly it appeared as if their political philosophies of the 1930s were reversed so that Roosevelt was the hawk and MacArthur the dove.

"The duty and the necessity of resisting Japanese aggression to the last," as Roosevelt in turn lectured MacArthur, "transcends in importance any other obligation now facing us in the Philippines." The president understood MacArthur's military assessment, but the Allied cause was beginning to stiffen around the globe, Roosevelt told him, and "as the most powerful member of this coalition we cannot display weakness in fact or in spirit anywhere."

MacArthur was free to permit Filipino capitulation of the commonwealth's defense forces if he determined it necessary and if he first placed those troops under independent Filipino command, but as to American troops, Roosevelt ordered him "to keep our flag flying in the Philippines so long as there remains any possibility of resistance." Lest there be any doubt among friend or foe, Roosevelt drew a line in the sand and declared it "mandatory that there be established once and for all in the minds of all peoples complete evidence that the American determination and indomitable will to win carries on down to the last unit."

MacArthur had asked that his men be remembered in "fame and glory," and Roosevelt appeared to be giving them that chance. "I particularly request," the president directed MacArthur, "that you proceed rapidly to the organization of your forces and your defenses so as to make your resistance as effective as circumstances will permit and as prolonged as humanly possible."[14]

This response brought MacArthur up short, and the pendulum of his mood immediately swung back the other way. His father's legacy and the shadow of Missionary Ridge loomed large. "I have not the slightest intention in the world of surrendering or capitulating the Filipino elements of my command," MacArthur replied to Roosevelt. He counted "upon them equally with the Americans to hold steadfast to the end" and reaffirmed his previously announced intent to defend Bataan "to destruction" and hold Corregidor "in a similar manner."[15]

But in the meantime, MacArthur had transmitted to Roosevelt from Quezon a draft of Quezon's neutrality plea, which Quezon proposed to send to both Roosevelt and the emperor of Japan. It was couched in terms that suggested it would only be sent if Quezon's plan met with Roosevelt's approval, but it nonetheless further raised the ire of those in Washington. Telling Quezon that his most recent message had "evidently crossed" with Roosevelt's initial answer, FDR was far more blunt in response this time. When it came to the Philippines, which was still an American territory regardless of its track toward independence, Quezon had "no authority to communicate with the Japanese Government without the express permission of the United States Government."[16]

To make absolutely certain that MacArthur understood the situation, Marshall separately radioed MacArthur and ordered him not to permit Quezon to make any public statements on neutrality from any radio station or other source under his control unless Roosevelt gave prior approval. MacArthur was back in the fold, and he assured Marshall in reply that Quezon had "no intention whatsoever so far as I know to do anything which does not meet with President Roosevelt's complete acquiescence."[17]

MacArthur transmitted a similar message from Quezon, but their initial two-part letter had shown just how far both were willing to go on the subject of neutrality. For Quezon, it was a grasp at his own political survival and the national survival of the Philippines. For MacArthur, it was military survival and a way to leave the Philippines with his American forces intact. But given its actions throughout Southeast Asia, it is highly unlikely that Japan would have accepted and abided by such a plan. And despite his support for neutrality at the time, MacArthur remembered his own role differently. "I remonstrated with Quezon as best I could against the proposals involved," MacArthur wrote in his memoirs, "and said bluntly I would not endorse them [and] that there was not the slightest chance of approval by either the United States or Japan."[18]

With the issue of a military solution brokered through a neutrality agreement put to rest, MacArthur returned to Marshall's query of February 3. What would happen to his family? The general and his wife, Jean, discussed it at length. Her feeling was that they had "drunk from the same cup" and would continue to do so. MacArthur communicated this decision to Roosevelt and Marshall after being chastised over Quezon's neutrality gambit: his family would "share the fate of the garrison."[19]

As it became clearer what that fate would be, Roosevelt and Marshall questioned MacArthur's thinking. It certainly would not do for MacArthur's wife and his young son to be killed or, worse, captured and paraded around for propaganda purposes. MacArthur asked Sid Huff to find bullets for a small pistol that MacArthur's father had once carried in the Philippines and swore to Huff that he would not be taken alive. It is not entirely clear whether he was preparing for a frontline encounter or contemplating suicide. But how did he expect it to end for his family?

On February 14, 1942, after the dust had settled from the frenzied neutrality exchanges, Marshall sent MacArthur a "his eyes only" message diplomatically suggesting that he rethink his decision not to evacuate his family. Hinting that there might be duty for MacArthur other than remaining on Corregidor that might "compel separation from them under circumstances of greatly increased peril," Marshall told MacArthur that while he did not intend to interfere with MacArthur's own decision in the matter, he was "anxious that you do not overlook this particular possibility of poignant embarrassment to you personally."[20]

The "poignant embarrassment" Marshall referred to was, of course, MacArthur's family's capture and public humiliation. Marshall's gentle expression of concern may have made MacArthur reconsider his decision, or his reconsideration may have come from other events weighing heavily on all concerned. The Japanese were still running across Southeast Asia unchecked. Great Britain surrendered Singapore with the loss of eighty thousand British, Indian, and Australian troops on February 15 after only a seven-day siege. If Churchill's "Gibraltar of the East" could suffer such a fate, it did not look good for Corregidor. The Philippines became increasingly isolated as the Japanese drove south through the Netherlands East Indies, captured what would become a key base at Rabaul, and eyed Java and Timor.

"Loss of Singapore and Southern Sumatra has created dangerous situation here and enemy invasion of Java in the near future possible," ABDACOM commander in chief Archibald Wavell, who had initially wanted the Philippines excluded from his responsibility, radioed MacArthur on February 19. The British field marshal professed to agree with MacArthur that the "Japanese air force is their weak point"—however misinformed each was in his calculation. Wavell nonetheless admitted that "things may worsen here," and he could only "wish we could do something to relieve you."[21]

Tommy Hart and the ABDACOM navy were not faring any better. MacArthur had neither said nor done anything to support Hart personally, and Hart's combined command of ships from four navies — American, British, Dutch, and Australian — proved problematic for him from the start. Hart survived barely a month as commander of ABDACOM naval forces before being replaced on February 15 by Dutch Admiral Conrad Helfrich, a move politically motivated on the part of the new allies but also encouraged by Hart's own protestations of being too old for the command.

A few weeks later, while countering the Japanese invasion of Java, the bulk of what remained of ABDACOM naval forces was destroyed in the Battle of the Java Sea. The surviving American heavy cruiser *Houston,* a prewar favorite of FDR, and the Australian light cruiser *Perth* went down a few days later trying to escape through Sunda Strait into the Indian Ocean. Dive-bombers off the southern coast of Java also sank the *Langley* — originally a collier, then America's first aircraft carrier, then a seaplane tender — as it ferried forty P-40s to airfields on Java.[22] MacArthur could expect no aid from those quarters.

While MacArthur pondered his personal decision about evacuating Corregidor, including the fate of "the two human beings dearest to me," President Quezon and High Commissioner Sayre took the opportunity to leave. Under the command of Lieutenant Commander Chester C. Smith, the submarine *Swordfish* was patrolling off Davao, on Mindanao, when it received orders to proceed to Corregidor and take the president's and high commissioner's parties aboard. Other submarine commanders tried to get out of what they considered errand duties to the Rock — taking in meager loads of ammunition or foodstuffs and evacuating key personnel, such as members of the navy's code breaking unit — but Smith didn't seem to mind. With confirmed sinkings of two merchantmen and one transport to its credit, *Swordfish* was one of the few exceptions to the navy's dismal record of faulty torpedoes.

Swordfish arrived at the Mariveles harbor, opposite Corregidor, on February 19, took on additional torpedoes, and refueled. The next evening President Quezon, his wife, Aurora, their three children, Vice President Sergio Osmeña, Chief Justice José Abad Santos, and three

135

Philippine army officers came aboard via a launch after MacArthur bid them farewell at Corregidor's North Dock. *Swordfish* slipped through the minefields surrounding Corregidor and took Quezon's party south around three hundred miles to San Jose de Buenavista, on the island of Panay. Quezon hoped to rally local resistance there, but his final destination was still uncertain. Roosevelt offered a warm welcome in the United States, in part because, after Quezon's flirtation with neutrality, Roosevelt judged that it would be more difficult for Quezon to negotiate surreptitiously with Japan if he were out of the islands.

On February 24, *Swordfish* returned to Corregidor for a second load and took on High Commissioner Sayre, his wife and son, and seven members of his staff. Sayre also took along a trunk belonging to MacArthur. It was addressed to the Riggs National Bank in Washington, and, according to MacArthur, it contained "valuable records and documents from my personal files." It was to be placed in the bank's safe deposit vault and withdrawn only by MacArthur or Sutherland.[23]

It says something about MacArthur's "carry on" attitude that even as he said good-bye to Quezon, he exchanged radio messages with General Pershing about having Pershing's son, Warren, then thirty-two and a Yale graduate, join him as his aide-de-camp. He would "deem it a great honor," MacArthur professed, to have Pershing's son "serve under me as I served under his father." Pershing replied with nothing but affection and noted, "Your courageous stand is daily becoming a source of increasing pride to the American people."

Warren had only just enlisted as a private and was still engaged in basic training.[24] But another name from MacArthur's past was to play a role in determining the general's fate in the Philippines. MacArthur's friend and admirer, former secretary of war Patrick Hurley, had been unsuccessful in getting more than a pittance of supplies into MacArthur's beleaguered garrison, but as the evacuations proceeded he gave Marshall advice on how to get MacArthur out. Hurley well knew that MacArthur was a very proud man, unaccustomed to defeat. Even when confronted by it, he frequently failed to acknowledge it. Yet upon learning of Hurley's arrival in Melbourne, MacArthur had cabled him: "Delighted you are there. I need you badly."[25]

On February 21, Hurley dispatched to Marshall his assessment of MacArthur's situation. MacArthur would not leave the Philippines, Hurley told Marshall, unless he could do so in a way that assured both the public and his troops that command had passed to competent leadership and that his cherished honor and record as a soldier would not be compromised. Even then, Hurley thought it would take a direct order from the president to get MacArthur "to relinquish command and proceed elsewhere."[26]

But where? There was an increasing crescendo of calls in certain quarters, including the US House of Representatives, for MacArthur to return to the United States and assume supreme command of all its armed forces. He had been chief of staff, and after his recall to active duty he was the army's senior general by date of grade. Franklin Roosevelt and George Marshall were hardly keen on that idea.

Roosevelt had dealt with MacArthur as chief of staff once before. Roosevelt was his own favorite actor. Marshall was just coming into his own in the role to which he had devoted thirty years of being understudy. But political and personal feelings aside, both Roosevelt and Marshall realized that MacArthur's preoccupation would be the Philippines and the Pacific. That did not square well with their affirmation of Germany First during their meetings with Churchill.

The world struggle was so complex that even someone of MacArthur's grandiosity might expect only a piece of it. It was only natural, given all his years of experience and expertise there, that his piece would be Southeast Asia. As for whether or not Roosevelt and Marshall had to try to save him, that question had been made largely moot by the outpouring of media support MacArthur had been receiving.

Besides the continuing flurry of press releases emanating from "MacArthur headquarters," the general's command in the Philippines was the only domino not falling under the Japanese onslaught. The French had collapsed in French Indochina months before Pearl Harbor. The mighty British in Singapore and the proud Dutch in Java had surrendered, or were about to surrender, armies larger than MacArthur's with barely a whimper. Battered and bruised though they were, MacArthur's troops on Bataan and on Corregidor were still standing.

*   *   *

On Sunday, February 22, Roosevelt met at the White House with Marshall, Admiral Ernest J. King, and adviser Harry Hopkins to decide MacArthur's fate. Dwight Eisenhower recorded the result in his diary: "We have concocted a message to MacArthur directing him to start south to take command of Australian area, etc." Afterward, Eisenhower joined the Marshalls for Sunday dinner at their quarters at Fort Myer. It was, Eisenhower recalled, the "longest I've been out of the office in daytime since coming here ten weeks ago."[27]

The following day, Roosevelt approved the message to MacArthur, and it was sent over Marshall's signature. But Eisenhower was not convinced. "I cannot help believing," he wrote privately, "that we are disturbed by editorials and reacting to 'public opinion' rather than military logic." Expressing doubt that his longtime boss would "do so well in more complicated situations," Eisenhower claimed, "Bataan is made to order for him. It's in the public eye; it has made him a public hero; it has all the essentials of drama; and he is the acknowledged king on the spot. If brought out, public opinion will force him into a position where his love of the limelight may ruin him."[28]

Eisenhower's personal thoughts notwithstanding, his draft was crafted to give MacArthur's ego plenty of room. Trying to identify the positives in an otherwise gloomy situation, Eisenhower had Marshall mentioning the reorganization of the disintegrating ABDA area, a momentary lull in the fighting on Bataan, and the buildup of resources on Mindanao as reasons Roosevelt ordered him to leave Corregidor. The message added that MacArthur was to proceed to Mindanao as quickly as possible so that he could see to the defense of that region, particularly as President Quezon had made his way there from Panay.

But MacArthur was to stay no longer than a week on Mindanao before continuing to Australia, where he was to assume command of all United States troops there. While no promise was made, Marshall implied that Roosevelt was also arranging with his Australian and British allies for MacArthur to become supreme commander of a reconstituted ABDA command.

Submarines and planes would be made available for his travel to Mindanao and Australia. No mention was made of Jean and little

Arthur, no doubt because it was assumed they would accompany him. As to others, Marshall noted only, "You are authorized to take with you your chief of staff General Sutherland."[29]

There is an oft-told story in MacArthur's memoirs and many biographies that he seriously considered disobeying the order to leave Corregidor and in fact drafted a refusal to do so before being persuaded otherwise by his staff. It makes a great story, particularly in light of later travesties inflicted upon the troops left behind on Bataan, but it is more in keeping with the MacArthur legend than fact. The record simply doesn't support it. Notably, Sutherland, who was privy to just about every conversation and was frequently the only person MacArthur consulted — even when he used the term "my staff" — did not recall any such discussion, let alone a heated one, about MacArthur's departure.[30]

To be sure, MacArthur was chagrined, disheartened, and perhaps even embarrassed, but he replied promptly to Marshall, asking only for some discretion in deciding when to leave — what he termed the proper "psychological time." He expressed his appreciation for the confidence implied in the president's orders and couldn't help but once again lament the lack of support for the Philippines, which had "created a very difficult situation which I have been able to meet only through the peculiar confidence placed in me by the Filipino people and Army." They were depending on him, he told Marshall, and any idea "that I was being withdrawn for any other purpose than to bring them immediate relief could not be explained."[31]

A collective sigh of relief passed through the White House and the War Department when MacArthur's answer arrived. They still had to get him out, but critics could not then say that they hadn't tried. His request regarding the timing, Marshall told MacArthur the next day, "has been carefully considered by the President. He has directed that full decision as to timing of your departure and details of method be left in your hands." Since his date of departure was undetermined, MacArthur was given full authority to call on the army and navy commands in Australia for submarine and aircraft transportation as he saw fit.[32]

As MacArthur prepared to depart Corregidor, there was one particular transaction that he was very careful not to mention in his ubiquitous press releases or his mainstream communications with Washington. His old friend Manuel Quezon had arranged a parting gift before he left Corregidor. If its details had become known, it is likely they would have lessened the heroic image of MacArthur being trumpeted in the American press.

Despite the secrecy surrounding it at the time—the details would not become widely known until long after the general's death—it was one of those transactions that on its face was technically legal but in context had the appearance of impropriety.

The gift was related to MacArthur's 1935 deal with Quezon to build the Philippines a first-rate army over a ten-year period. Despite the fact that at the time, and again after his recall to active duty, MacArthur was receiving a US paycheck, President Roosevelt and the War Department approved his receiving additional compensation from the Philippines—not a foreign government but still an American territory—for services rendered. In addition to his Philippines salary of $18,000 per year and an annual expense allowance of $15,000, MacArthur was to receive, as a bonus, .46 percent of the total ten-year defense budget of the Philippines.[33]

Despite the rather dismal performance of the Philippine military, Quezon chose to bestow this bonus, calculated at $360,000 for the ten-year period and $33,000 in salary and expenses for each of the remaining four years (1942–45) of the contract, upon MacArthur immediately. These amounts totaled $492,000, and it is possible that in their discussions of the matter prior to Quezon's departure from Corregidor, the Philippine president and MacArthur simply agreed to a round figure of $500,000.

Whether Quezon raised the issue himself or MacArthur broached the matter, as he had with his field marshal appointment, is unknown. Equally unknown are any quid pro quos attached to it. Some historians in the years since this transaction became widely known have suggested that the money was an outright bribe—either Quezon was encouraging MacArthur to evacuate or he was exacting MacArthur's promise to use everything in his power to expedite an American return to the Philippines.

Underlying any theory, however, must be the close affinity that

MacArthur felt for the Philippines. There is no question that the bonus — $7 million in 2014 dollars — made longtime public servant Douglas MacArthur an independently wealthy man, but that seems to have been more of a benefit of his longtime relationship with Quezon and the Philippines than an inducement for any particular future action.

But there were others who would also benefit financially. The copy in Sutherland's file of what was called "Executive Order No. 1 by the President of the Philippines" is dated January 3, 1942. There is considerable evidence, however — primarily the testimony of Sutherland's clerk, Paul Rogers — that Sutherland prepared it and Rogers typed it on February 13. (The backdating might possibly have been intended to provide MacArthur with four full years of lost salary and expenses.)

After a lengthy recitation of the invaluable services that General MacArthur and certain other officers had rendered to the Commonwealth of the Philippines between November 15, 1935 — the date of Quezon's first presidential inauguration — and December 30, 1941, the following payments were to be made in US currency:

General Douglas MacArthur	$500,000
Major General Richard K. Sutherland	$75,000
Brigadier General Richard J. Marshall	$45,000
Lieutenant Colonel Sidney L. Huff	$20,000[34]

Sutherland, Marshall, and Huff had not been party to MacArthur's 1935 agreement, although they were members of the American military mission to the Philippines prior to the creation of the USAFFE. Not much attention was paid to this distinction at the time. How the American public would have reacted if, instead of blaring his reported military triumphs, newspapers had written a headline along the lines of MACARTHUR TO LEAVE PHILIPPINES WITH A HALF-MILLION-DOLLAR BONUS is another matter.

Two days after Sutherland drafted the executive order and Quezon signed it, MacArthur wired Chase National Bank, where commonwealth funds were on deposit, to execute the transfers to himself and the three other officers. MacArthur also wired the War Department, asking the adjutant general to confirm with Chase that the transfers had the approval of the president and secretary of war and should be made. Since the Philippines was still technically administrated as a territory under the Department of the Interior, that department transmitted approval to Chase to make the transfers. On February 18, Chase wired the department that the transfers were complete, and the War Department informed Quezon of that fact hours before he boarded the *Swordfish* and left Corregidor.[35]

There is circumstantial evidence that these transactions did not sit well with the people asked to approve them in Washington. For once, George Marshall does not appear to have been in the loop. Secretary of the interior Harold Ickes, never a MacArthur fan, was so unclear about the matter that he believed Jonathan Wainwright was one of the recipients. Secretary of war Stimson, previously a MacArthur supporter, remained mum, but Stimson became increasingly critical of MacArthur around this time, which may or may not have been related to the transactions.[36]

Several months later, when Manuel Quezon arrived in Washington, he went to see the head of the army's Operations Division, formerly the War Plans Division, who was about to depart for an assignment in London. For services rendered during his prewar assignment in the Philippines, Quezon offered this officer a payment of sixty thousand dollars. Dwight Eisenhower, not that far removed from being a poor farm boy in Kansas, politely but firmly declined.[37]

On March 1, 1942, the Japanese began landings in Java; eight days later the Dutch army surrendered. By the time Rangoon fell, a week later, the Japanese controlled the land, air, and sea lanes from Rangoon eastward along the Malay Barrier to New Guinea and Rabaul and threatened northwestern Australia. On Bataan, there was a momentary lull as Homma stockpiled men and munitions for a final assault. On the American-Filipino side, the loudest noises came from the bellies of troops reduced to quarter rations or less.

Once MacArthur agreed to leave Corregidor on his own schedule, Marshall did not push him, except to make a gentle observation on March 6: "Australian situation developments indicate desirability of your early arrival there."[38] MacArthur assumed, per his understanding of Roosevelt's order, that these "developments" were related to a military buildup that foreshadowed a prompt return to Luzon, or at the very least Mindanao, from which Bataan and Corregidor might be supported.

Meanwhile, MacArthur saw to his travel arrangements, telling Lieutenant General George H. Brett, the commander of US forces in Australia pending MacArthur's arrival, that Brett should detail his best pilots and best available planes—"B-24's if available otherwise B-17s"—and put them in top condition for an on-call ferry mission to Mindanao around March 15. He requested the initial landing on the return flight to be south of the combat zone. "You have probably surmised," MacArthur noted slyly, "purpose of mission."[39]

MacArthur also requested the arrival at Corregidor of the submarine *Permit*. Under the command of Lieutenant Commander Wreford Goss "Moon" Chapple, *Permit* was patrolling off Surabaya, Java, when Chapple received orders to proceed to the Rock. But before *Permit* could arrive, MacArthur decided it was time to go.

Initially, his orders from Roosevelt had specifically given him permission to take along only his chief of staff. Later, Marshall added Brigadier General Harold H. George of the Army Air Corps to the list because air commanders in Australia were eager to profit from his experience fighting Japanese planes over Luzon. MacArthur appears to have been given—or taken—the same liberties in compiling his final list of passengers as Marshall accorded him in regard to the timetable. Still, some observers were surprised by the large number of people MacArthur wanted to take along. This was indeed to be an evacuation of the king and his court, and its magnitude would not sit well with increasingly embittered field commanders left behind on Bataan.

No one questioned that MacArthur would be accompanied by his wife and four-year-old Arthur. For almost three long months on Corregidor, Jean had been one of his bravest soldiers. While she never visited Bataan—unthinkable under the circumstances—Jean seemed to be everywhere throughout the tunnels and fortifications of Corregidor. As for young Arthur, by all accounts—almost to the point of Jean's exasperation—he was doted upon by his father, just as Douglas had revered his own father. The fourth member of the immediate MacArthur family was Arthur's Cantonese amah, or nanny, Ah Cheu. Given her relationship with the family since Arthur's birth, MacArthur believed that "her death would have been certain had she been left behind."[40]

The remainder of the evacuation list numbered seventeen. They ranged from the chief and deputy chief of staff—Sutherland and Brigadier General Richard J. Marshall—to a medical officer pulled from Bataan, Major C. H. Morhouse, and Sutherland's chief clerk and the only enlisted man in the group, Paul Rogers, newly promoted from private to master sergeant. Also included in the seventeen were two naval officers, Rear Admiral Francis W. Rockwell and Captain Harold G. Ray, and the requested General George of the air corps.

And they would go by PT boats. Rockwell, the commandant of what was left of the Sixteenth Naval District, gave the naval orders. Motor Torpedo Boat Squadron Three, then comprising four serviceable boats under the command of Lieutenant John D. Bulkeley, would carry the general's party six hundred miles south to Cagayan, on Mindanao, adjacent to Del Monte Field. From there, the summoned B-17s would fly the group the rest of the way to Australia.[41]

But why risk travel by PT boat? Seventy-seven feet in length with a twenty-foot beam, these boats were meant for high-speed coastal patrols with seasoned crews, not long-distance voyages carrying passengers. The odds of an escape by submarine seemed better, as *Swordfish* had proved when it evacuated Quezon and Sayre, although the Japanese continued to tighten their noose around Manila Bay. Many years later, after books and movies propelled MacArthur's voyage into legend, Bulkeley would call MacArthur "a sheer genius...because no one in the whole world would expect him to go out on a PT boat."[42]

But was it a matter of fooling the Japanese, or was there more to it? Sid Huff, certainly among the general's most loyal supporters, later suggested that MacArthur definitely favored the PT boats over a submarine. "I'm not sure why," wrote Huff, "but it was almost as if he suffered a touch of claustrophobia." Ever the pacer who couldn't sit still for long, MacArthur may well have resisted the idea of being cooped up in a submarine, just as he resisted sleeping in the confines of the Corregidor tunnels if quarters topside were an option. "As always, he was willing to take plenty of risks," Huff concluded, "but he wanted room to move about."[43]

Then, too, there may have been an element of the theatrical in his decision. Once again, images of his father's dash up Missionary Ridge crossed his mind. If he were to fail in his escape and be killed, which image spoke of greater glory—MacArthur entombed in a steel coffin below the ocean depths or MacArthur meeting his fate head-on, flags flying, atop the waves? If he could make good his escape in such a fashion on the surface, he would have the added satisfaction of showing both the American and Japanese navies that the blockade of the Philippines was not impenetrable.

Bulkeley's orders instructed PT-41, with Bulkeley as the squadron commander, to pick up the MacArthur foursome as well as Sutherland, Huff, army doctor Morhouse, and navy captain Ray at Corregidor's North Dock at 7:30 p.m. on March 11. Sutherland made the boat assignments and divided the remainder of the party among Lieutenant Robert Kelly's PT-34, Ensign Anthony Akers's PT-35, and Lieutenant Junior Grade Vincent Schumacher's PT-32. To avoid raising suspicion, the passengers for PT-34 and PT-35 were shuttled from Corregidor by launch to meet their boats in Sisiman Cove, on Bataan. PT-32 met its passengers at the dock in Mariveles. Once loaded, the four boats were to rendezvous in the North Channel, between Corregidor and Bataan.

Sid Huff and Jean MacArthur scrounged the Corregidor tunnels for enough canned goods to last ten days and divided them into four duffels, one for each boat. Personal items were few and far between, but MacArthur had Huff remove the four-star license plates from his vehicle because, the general told him, "We may not be able to replace them in Australia." Then, after "a tense and unhappy and uncomfortable few minutes" of saying good-bye to those left behind, the little caravan of vehicles drove the short distance from the mouth of the Malinta Tunnel to the North Dock.[44]

The MacArthur party boarded PT-41, and MacArthur told Bulkeley to cast off whenever he was ready. A flood of emotions coursed through MacArthur as he looked back at the dark hulk of Corregidor, but Jean MacArthur may have captured them best when she recalled years later, "He was just heartbroken, you know, just heartbroken."[45]

Bulkeley's boat made its way into the North Channel and rendezvoused with the other three boats of his squadron. Together they picked their way through the channel minefield, then roared westward into the open sea. In blackness illuminated only by starlight, Bulkeley navigated seaward of Cabra Island, then streaked south toward Mindanao. The tiny boats bucked like broncos as they rose and fell across the waves. Rare was the passenger who wasn't affected. Somehow Douglas MacArthur's battered cap with gold braid, which would become so famous, found a momentary safe haven inside the boat as the general retched his guts into the choppy seas.

PART II

EXILE

1942

*The order to leave the Philippines had come as
a complete surprise to [MacArthur]...and, if the
choice had been left to him, he would have remained
in the Philippines.*

— MINUTES OF ADVISORY WAR COUNCIL
MEETING, CANBERRA, MARCH 26, 1942,
QUOTING MACARTHUR

*A foul trick of deception has been played on a large
group of Americans by a Commander in Chief and
small staff who are now eating steak and eggs in
Australia. God damn them!*

— BRIGADIER GENERAL W. E. BROUGHER,
DIARY WRITTEN AT POW CAMP O'DONNELL,
APRIL 1, 1942

Dressed in a bush jacket but with his braided cap intact, Mac-Arthur arrives at the Melbourne railway station with chief of staff Richard K. Sutherland (left) after his escape from the Philippines, March 21, 1942. *Courtesy of the MacArthur Memorial, Norfolk, VA*

CHAPTER EIGHT

Waltzing Matilda

Throughout the night of March 11, 1942, the four boats of Motor Torpedo Boat Squadron Three roared southward as rapidly as the rolling waves would permit. A strong easterly wind blowing at right angles to their course pushed swells fifteen to twenty feet high and made for a wild ride. According to MacArthur, PT-41 "would toss crazily back and forth, seeming to hang free in space as though about to breach, and then would break away and go forward with a rush." Afterward, he described the voyage as akin to "what it must be like to take a trip in a concrete mixer."[1]

By midnight, the high seas were taking a toll on the boats as well as their passengers. Saltwater foamed everywhere and fouled spark plugs and carburetors, necessitating frequent stops to clean them. Given these sporadic delays and lack of radar, the four boats became separated. Each was forced to make its own way by dead reckoning toward a prearranged rendezvous at Tagauayan, in the Cuyo Islands, around 250 miles south of Corregidor.

The next morning, Lieutenant Robert Kelly's PT-34 pulled into what he thought was Tagauayan an hour or so after the specified rendezvous time of 7:30. The cove on the lee side of the island was empty, and Kelly and his passengers and crew settled down for an uncomfortable wait, not entirely sure they were in the correct location. Admiral Rockwell was on board Kelly's boat, and his earlier orders to the squadron called for the boats to remain at Tagauayan until 5:00 p.m. before making another nighttime run the remainder of the way to Cagayan, on Mindanao.

149

Meanwhile, Lieutenant (JG) Vincent Schumacher's PT-32 was limping along on only one of three engines, trying to find the rendezvous point. Suddenly lookouts reported what appeared to be a Japanese destroyer bearing down on their stern. Schumacher, a 1938 graduate of Annapolis and only twenty-six years old, had already seen plenty of action cruising around Bataan with Bulkeley's squadron, but having four of MacArthur's brigadier generals on board made him all the more nervous.

Assuming that his slow speed had made his PT-32 the rear boat, Schumacher ordered his crew to man the .50-caliber machine guns and prepare to launch torpedoes at the onrushing ship. But then caution got the better of him and he decided to jettison the twenty fifty-five-gallon barrels of extra fuel that were lashed to the deck and make a run for it. Barely had the fuel drums hit the water when the pursuing ship took on a clearer form in the early morning light. It wasn't a Japanese destroyer but Bulkeley's PT-41. The US Navy had almost fired upon the US Navy.

Bulkeley pulled alongside Schumacher's boat and ordered him to retrieve the fuel drums, both because the fuel was needed and because the floating barrels were an obvious marker for Japanese aircraft and surface vessels. For the most part, that proved a slippery impossibility in the rolling seas, and the remaining barrels were finally sunk by gunfire. Then PT-32 followed Bulkeley's PT-41 into the lee of a very small island. It wasn't Tagauayan, but it would do as a hideout for the day.[2]

Jean, Arthur, and Ah Cheu sat on deck in wicker chairs and tried to recover somewhat from the storm-tossed terror of the previous night. MacArthur had been as sick as anyone, although most remembrances delicately skirt that point. But he once again could not sit still, and he paced the deck like a caged animal. Indeed he was.

At sixty-two, despite his reputation for robust health, he was, by the standards of the day, an old man. The trip was physically grueling, but much more so emotionally. Cut off from communications, beastly hot under the South Pacific sun, MacArthur found no solace in the white beaches and dotted palms of this deserted speck of land. This was not the way he had envisioned that his tenure in the Philippines would end.

His career had not been perfect. He had made some mistakes. He would make more. But no one will ever know the depths of despair that Douglas MacArthur reached and then turned into steely resolve as he prowled the wooden deck of a seventy-seven-foot PT boat. For all the criticism heaped on MacArthur, his critics would be well advised to ponder this moment. He was being tested by fire, and he emerged from it with his best qualities— as well as his exasperating weaknesses—accentuated.

As the day of waiting wore on, MacArthur became more and more agitated—antsy to be on the move. Bulkeley figured they were at the northern end of the Cuyo Islands, still thirty-some miles from the rendezvous point on Tagauayan. If they pressed on, they could arrive there on schedule, at 5:00 p.m., before any other boats departed for Cagayan. Tagauayan was also important because the submarine *Permit,* which MacArthur had not deigned to await on Corregidor, had been ordered to arrive there early the following morning, March 13, as a backup should the PT boats encounter difficulty along the way.

Upon coming into the cove on the western side of Tagauayan, Bulkeley and Schumacher were relieved to find Kelly and his PT-34 waiting for them. There was, however, no word about Ensign Anthony Akers and PT-35. MacArthur and Admiral Rockwell held a hurried conference on board PT-41 and weighed the odds of casting off for Cagayan or waiting for the *Permit,* although its arrival was in no way guaranteed. The trip south through the Sulu Sea and then eastward into the passage between Panay and Mindanao was sure to be every bit as rough as what they had experienced thus far. In fact, Bulkeley predicted it would be rougher. MacArthur nodded. They would proceed as planned.

Having dumped its fuel reserve overboard, Schumacher and PT-32 drew the short straw and were ordered to remain at Tagauayan to await the *Permit.* Schumacher's army passengers were divided between the other two boats. After meeting the *Permit,* Schumacher was to cross eastward to Panay for repairs and fuel before heading south to Mindanao on his own.

It proved another miserable night for MacArthur and his party. Scarcely an hour out of Tagauayan, the dark silhouette of a Japanese cruiser appeared to the south on a course that would intersect the two-ship flotilla. Bulkeley ordered a course change due west and made a wide loop around the vessel's stern. There was no way of telling for certain, but Bulkeley and Kelly both thought the roller-coaster waves kept their boats in the troughs long enough to keep them from being spotted.

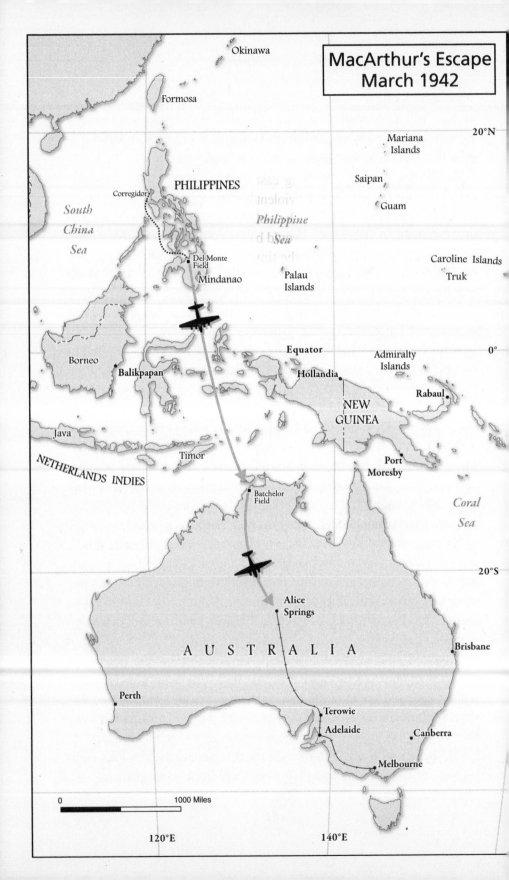

MacArthur's Escape
March 1942

Okinawa

Formosa

20°N

Mariana
Islands

Saipan

Guam

PHILIPPINES

Corregidor

*South
China
Sea*

*violent

Philippine

Sea*

Del Monte
Field

Mindanao

Palau
Islands

Caroline Islands

Truk

Borneo

Balikpapan

Equator

Hollandia

Admiralty
Islands

0°

Rabaul

NEW
GUINEA

Java

Timor

NETHERLANDS INDIES

Port
Moresby

*Coral
Sea*

Batchelor
Field

20°S

Alice
Springs

A U S T R A L I A

Brisbane

Perth

Terowie

Adelaide

Canberra

Melbourne

0   1000 Miles

120°E   140°E

Memories of that night blurred with those of the previous night. MacArthur and his little family were all seasick once again, as were all but the heartiest of sailors. Bulkeley made for the coast of Negros in hopes of finding calmer seas, but protection from the easterly winds was minimal, and upon turning eastward into the Panay-Mindanao passage shortly after midnight, violent thunderstorms and lashing rain-squalls added to the misery. The only good news was that the wild weather made it unlikely they would be spotted by Japanese patrols.

As lightning flashed about, the tiny dot of Silino Island provided a navigation reference toward Cagayan, and the two boats surged onward. Bulkeley and Kelly had never been in this part of the Philippines, and in the pitch-black night they were running blind. Admiral Rockwell, who had sailed just about every ship in the navy over the course of a thirty-year career, shouted to Kelly above the roar of the storm that this was the worst bridge he'd ever been on and he "wouldn't do duty on one of these for anything in the world."[3] To his credit, Rockwell stayed topside and shivered alongside Kelly for the entire trip.

On Bulkeley's boat, MacArthur appeared in a state of semiparalysis. As the general lay sprawled on a thin straw mattress beside Arthur, Jean sat at his side, rubbing his hands to stimulate circulation. Incredibly, just as some worried that he was dying, the general sat up and told a haggard Sid Huff that he wanted to talk. Huff remembered it as "a couple of the strangest hours of my life." But it was good catharsis for MacArthur. When he was finished ruminating on everything from his early years in the Philippines to the men he had left behind on Corregidor, MacArthur showed a spark of his old self. "Sid," he told Huff characteristically, "if we ever get to Australia, the first thing I'm going to do is to make you and [LeGrande] Diller full colonels. Good night."[4]

By then the wind was dying down and the sky lightening in the east. They had come through the worst, but dawn would leave them vulnerable to Japanese planes unless they reached their destination quickly. "Good navigation, Kelly," Admiral Rockwell grunted as the point west of Cagayan harbor came into view. Bulkeley, who had the harbor charts, took over the lead in PT-41 and led the way into Cagayan harbor.

Unshaved and likely as disheveled as he had ever been in his life, Douglas MacArthur, with Jean at his side, gamely climbed on deck and

153

went to stand in the prow as Bulkeley steered the boat toward the dock. One army officer waiting on the dock to greet him recalled that he stood there "looking very much like Washington crossing the Delaware."[5] Stepping ashore, MacArthur shook Bulkeley's hand. "You have taken me out of the jaws of death," MacArthur told him, "and I shall not forget it."[6]

But the jaws of death were still snapping. Brigadier General William F. Sharp, commander of American-Filipino forces on Mindanao, greeted MacArthur on the dock at Cagayan with bad news. Four B-17s had been dispatched from Australia to meet MacArthur's party at nearby Del Monte Field. These bombers were among the remnants of the Ninety-Third Squadron of the Nineteenth Bomb Group that had flown south from Clark Field just before the December 8 attack. They had been operating out of Darwin and were showing the strain of rigorous combat missions without proper maintenance. Two had turned back with engine trouble, and another ran out of fuel and crashed into the sea just short of Del Monte. The fourth, piloted by twenty-four-year-old second lieutenant Harl Pease Jr., had arrived with faulty brakes, non-working superchargers, and a maze of bullet holes that had been patched with pieces of ration cans.

When MacArthur got a close-up look at Pease's B-17 after the five-mile drive to Del Monte Field, he went apoplectic. The bomber didn't look as though it could take off, let alone fly 1,500 miles to Australia. The general was also skeptical of the youthful appearance of its pilot. He fired off a radio message to General Marshall in Washington demanding that "the best three planes in the United States or Hawaii should be made available with completely adequate and experienced crews." To attempt to continue what he termed "such a desperate and important trip" with inadequate equipment would be tantamount "to consigning the whole party to death," and he refused to accept such a responsibility.[7]

Lieutenant General George H. Brett, the commander of US Army forces in Australia, had tried to provide MacArthur with better transport by borrowing four B-17s from the navy. Brett's naval counterpart in Australia, Vice Admiral Herbert Leary, had just taken delivery of a dozen newer B-17s, but the admiral claimed that none could be spared for what he deemed "ferry service" no matter how important the cargo.

Upon receipt of MacArthur's message, Marshall conferred with Admiral Ernest J. King, recently appointed chief of naval operations as well as commander in chief of the United States Fleet. The result was that when Brett again asked Leary for a loan of the bombers, three were hastily dispatched northward to Del Monte.

Meanwhile, the PT boat passengers savored a breakfast of fresh fruit at the Del Monte plantation house. No one had eaten fresh fruit since leaving Manila almost three months before, and enjoying it was one of those memories that remains crystal clear. "I can remember that pineapple as long as I live," Jean MacArthur reminisced forty years later—"that fresh pineapple."[8]

Several hours later, MacArthur breathed a sigh of relief for the rest of his staff as Ensign Akers's PT-35 glided into the harbor at Cagayan. The boat had rendezvoused with Schumacher and his PT-32 at Tagauayan just hours after MacArthur's departure. The PT-35 had continued on, but Schumacher claimed that PT-32 was a wreck, still operating on only one engine and badly leaking. The next morning, when the *Permit* appeared off Tagauayan on schedule, Captain Chapple took Schumacher and his crew on board the submarine and sank the PT-32 with his deck gun.[9]

Two tense days followed as MacArthur and his party waited for the replacement B-17s. The Japanese troops who had landed at Davao were driving north toward Cagayan, and some reports had them within thirty miles. Daylight brought air attacks by Japanese bombers. Finally, after sunset on March 16, two B-17s landed on the dirt airstrip, which was marked only with a solitary flare at each end. A third plane had experienced engine trouble and had been forced to turn back to Australia.

Thirty-four-year-old first lieutenant Frank P. Bostrom of Maine piloted the lead plane. Bostrom had been at the controls of one of the B-17s that flew into Honolulu amid the action of December 7. That morning, he had ended up setting his aircraft down on a golf course, so a nighttime landing on a dirt strip marked by two flares was just part of the job.

It would be tight, but Bostrom calculated that by leaving behind most of what little personal baggage they had and taking only the straw mattress for Arthur, the twenty-one passengers could squeeze into the two B-17s. Sid Huff and Dick Marshall drew the seats normally occupied by the bombardier, in the Plexiglas nose of Bostrom's plane. Having just flown 1,500 miles, Bostrom reportedly gulped eight cups of coffee to fortify himself before babying one of the four engines through a spasm of sputtering. Ahead there was nothing but darkness, except for a tiny red glow at the far end of the field. "At this moment," Huff shouted to Marshall above the roar, "our lives are worth something less than a nickel."[10]

The two tightly packed bombers lifted off from Del Monte in the darkness and droned south. Airsickness among the passengers replaced seasickness as Bostrom flew over the occupied Netherlands East Indies and gave wide berth to Japanese forces around Timor. Eight hours into the flight, with dawn lighting the eastern horizon, the coast of Australia appeared as a dim line up ahead. But they weren't home free quite yet.

Approaching Darwin, Bostrom received a report that the airfield was under attack from Japanese planes, so he diverted fifty miles to the south and landed at Batchelor Field, a small auxiliary strip, around 9:00 a.m. on March 17. It was Saint Patrick's Day, 1942. What MacArthur's Scottish ancestors might have said is unknown, but MacArthur likely would not have agreed with his clerk, Paul Rogers, who, remembering that the replacement B-17s were sent with Admiral Leary's belated assistance, later wrote, "So we were saved by the navy in both segments of the journey."[11]

Once the two B-17s were on the ground, Jean MacArthur, who had been such a stalwart sailor on board PT-41, rebelled at the thought of flying farther. "Never, never again will anybody get me into an airplane!" she exclaimed to Huff before commanding the majordomo, "Sid, please find some way that we can get to Melbourne without getting off the ground."[12]

Ever attentive to his wife's concerns, and feeling much the same way about the next leg, MacArthur ordered Sutherland to organize a car caravan to the narrow-gauge railhead at Alice Springs, around 750 miles south across the Tanami Desert. General Brett had dispatched two twin-engine Australian National Airways DC-3s to carry them on to Melbourne, and Sutherland assured MacArthur that the remainder of the journey would be less rigorous. But the general was adamant. They would not fly.

Finally, Sutherland and Huff played young Arthur as their trump card. Arthur had continued to be very sick on the flight, and they enlisted Dr. Morhouse to advise MacArthur that the boy might not survive the long, hot drive. What Sutherland didn't tell MacArthur was that there were also reports of Japanese bombers en route from Timor to Batchelor Field, necessitating the immediate departure of the DC-3s. Faced with concern for Arthur, both Jean and the general relented. MacArthur's party—what would soon be called the Bataan Gang— was hurriedly herded aboard the two planes as they sat on the tarmac with their engines running.

The passengers were still in the aisle and not buckled in their seats when the pilot of MacArthur's plane pushed the throttles forward and started toward the runway. Everyone was thrown toward the rear of the plane. MacArthur recovered his balance and shouted to Huff in a cold rage, "Sid, get that pilot's name!" But there was good reason for the haste. Moments after the DC-3s took off and headed south toward Alice Springs, Japanese planes appeared over Batchelor Field.[13]

The flight to Alice Springs, which lay astride the hot confines of the MacDonnell Ranges, went without incident or apparent discomfort for the passengers. When they landed, even Jean seemed relieved by the choice of faster transport. But then, safe from enemy attack, MacArthur decreed that he and his family would go no farther by air. While the remainder of his staff flew on to Melbourne, MacArthur, Jean, Arthur, Ah Cheu, Sutherland, Huff, and Dr. Morhouse settled down in the town's lone, ramshackle hotel to await the arrival of a special train. It wasn't a case of privilege but necessity. They had just missed the weekly service, and a belching steam engine and two aging coaches were dispatched northward on the narrow-gauge line from Terowie, near Adelaide, to fetch them.

As they waited for the train on the morning of March 18, Patrick Hurley, about to give up his blockade-running attempts and assume his duties as ambassador to New Zealand, flew into Alice Springs in a C-47 transport plane (the military version of the DC-3). If MacArthur had any doubts about how his reputation was faring in the United States, Hurley put his concerns to rest. The general's reputation as a national hero, Hurley assured him, was right up there with Admiral

Dewey's, General Pershing's, and Charles Lindbergh's. Hurley assumed that the MacArthurs would return to Melbourne with him in his plane, but they held firm in their decision to wait for the train.[14]

That afternoon it arrived, and they departed Alice Springs. There was no speed to this leg of their journey, and that was for the best. As the train chugged its way south on the rickety three-foot-wide rails, the slow rocking motion lulled the general to sleep on Jean's shoulder. It was, she recalled, the first time he had really slept since Pearl Harbor.[15]

It took almost two days at this leisurely pace to cover the nine hundred miles between Alice Springs and Terowie. The "MacArthur special" chugged into the station there early on Friday morning, March 20, but MacArthur's optimistic determination soon hit a brick wall of reality. Terowie was the junction and transfer point between the narrow-gauge tracks that ran into the interior and the broad, or standard-gauge, line running south another 137 miles to Adelaide on the coast. On a siding at the end of the broad-gauge line stood a well-appointed private car. Having flown from Alice Springs to Melbourne, Dick Marshall had commandeered the car and returned from Melbourne to meet his chief.

Marshall brought devastating news. Despite MacArthur's understanding, based on repeated assurances from Roosevelt and George Marshall, that all possible reinforcements were on the way to Australia and that MacArthur's presence was required in anticipation of leading them back to the Philippines, Dick Marshall reported that there were fewer than twenty-five thousand American army and air personnel in Australia. MacArthur had left three times that number trapped on Bataan.[16]

MacArthur swallowed hard but momentarily brushed aside his despair to address a small knot of reporters with what would come to rank among his most quoted words. "The President of the United States ordered me to break through the Japanese lines," he told them, "and proceed from Corregidor to Australia for the purpose, as I understand it, of organizing the American offensive against Japan, a primary object of which is the relief of the Philippines. I came through and I shall return."[17]

MacArthur's private car was pulled the remaining miles to Adelaide, where he repeated a shortened version of his statement and introduced Jean as "the best soldier I have." Totally without a wardrobe,

Jean was wearing the fur-collared coat that had managed to make its way from Manila to Corregidor to Australia. In due course, MacArthur's coach was hooked to the rear of the Adelaide express train, and, around 7:30 p.m. on Friday, it departed Adelaide for Melbourne, some five hundred miles to the east.[18] Alone again with his closest confidants, MacArthur slipped into a gloomy trance and spent a restless night pacing the confines of his car.

Meanwhile, the American public was regaled with news of his escape, and MacArthur was hailed as a victorious conqueror. President Roosevelt himself started the momentum on March 17, Washington time, when the War Department announced MacArthur's appointment as supreme commander of Allied forces in the southwestern Pacific. The news essentially heralded the planned resurrection of ABDACOM and was the result of an agreement with Great Britain that the British would take the lead west of Singapore, in defense of India, while the Americans did the same to the east, in defense of Australia.

A few hours later, Roosevelt told a press conference that he knew "every man and woman in the United States admires with me General MacArthur's determination to fight to the finish with his men in the Philippines" but that every American "could come to only one answer" if asked where MacArthur could best serve his country. Axis propaganda would characterize the move as an abandonment of the Philippines, the president said, but he assured reporters that this was not the case. MacArthur would be "more useful in Supreme Command of the whole Southwest Pacific than if he had stayed in Bataan Peninsula."[19]

The *New York Times* called the move a "dramatic shift of command and [a] promotion" and referred to MacArthur as "the dashing officer who has held the Japanese at bay on the Island of Luzon for three months and ten days."[20] This view of events was repeated in newspapers throughout the country. The need to find and embrace a hero was so intense, and the ignorance of Philippine geography so widespread, that few realized that Bataan was but a tiny fragment of Luzon and that MacArthur's retreat there had come within inches of being a rout.

But this wasn't just about reporting. The *Times* editorial sounded as if it had been lifted from a MacArthur press release. The general's appointment as supreme commander "will be applauded by an overwhelming majority of Americans, and will certainly bring enormous heart to the endangered people of Australia," the editorial began. Noting that the practical difficulties of his evacuation had been "brilliantly surmounted," the *Times* assured its readers that MacArthur "consented to leave his men at Bataan with the greatest reluctance, and only in response to a direct command from his superior."

That much was generally true, but then the facts were not allowed to stand in the way of the legend. "By the sheer force of his personality," the *Times* continued, "General MacArthur knit together into a fighting team a heterogeneous collection of troops in the Philippines [and] showed an amazing ability to hold his own against vastly superior forces." The *Times* repeated the erroneous assertion, contained in a MacArthur press release, that General Homma "was driven to commit suicide because of the disgrace of his failure to crush [MacArthur's] smaller forces."

The *Times* also noted the danger of "placing our expectations too high" and the "limit to the miracles that one general can achieve." Echoing MacArthur's furtive pleas for assistance, the *Times* appealed on his behalf for trained men and equipment and acknowledged the race against time: "At Australia we want no desperate last stand as at Bataan. We must be able not only to defend that base but to strike back offensively from it. Whether or not we are able to do this depends upon our efforts at home."[21]

In a move indicative of the way MacArthur had quickly come to personify early war efforts in the Pacific, the same issue carried a page of photos showing men on board ships. They were not identified as US Army personnel but as "M'Arthurmen: On the alert en route to Australia."[22]

Not everyone was impressed. "MacArthur is out of Philippine Islands," Dwight Eisenhower recorded in his diary. "The newspapers acclaim the move — the public has built itself a hero out of its own imagination. I hope he can do the miracles expected and predicted; we could use a few now."[23]

The Adelaide express train pulled into Spencer Street Station in Melbourne at 9:30 a.m. on Saturday, March 21, 1942. The demands of the war aside, this was to be a highly choreographed event. Detailed orders issued the day before from Brigadier General Stephen J. Chamberlin, the chief of staff of United States Army Forces in Australia, spelled out the particulars. A battalion from the Forty-Third Engineers lined the tracks as a guard of honor. Three Australian officers, along with Admiral Leary and General Brett, composed a five-man welcoming committee. Four cars made up MacArthur's motorcade: one seven-passenger Wolseley, with a four-star flag and license plate, one seven-passenger Packard, and two five-passenger Packards. A detailed map accompanied Chamberlin's orders and showed the route to the Menzies Hotel, where the MacArthurs and their immediate party would take over the entire sixth floor. From the station to the hotel was a grand total of three blocks.[24]

As the train came to a stop, Brett boarded MacArthur's coach and immediately felt an icy wind of rebuke. MacArthur largely ignored Brett and stepped onto the platform to acknowledge the other members of the welcoming committee, leaning on his habitual walking stick as he did so. The words he had uttered in Terowie were being flashed around the world, and "I shall return" was already taking on an almost magical aura. Seeing the press corps being held back by a cordon of soldiers, MacArthur directed that they be allowed forward, telling them, "Some of my best friends in the world are pressmen and I hope in the near future to meet you individually."[25]

He wore his gold-braided cap, which had survived the PT-boat ride and B-17 flight only slightly worse for wear. Instead of a uniform tunic, he had on a rumpled khaki bush jacket, complete with belt but void of any insignia. He wore neatly pressed khaki trousers, black-and-white checked socks, and tan civilian shoes with little decorative holes in them. One of the reporters in attendance was John Hersey (later acclaimed as the author of *Hiroshima* and *A Bell for Adano*), who wrote, "Among the braid-horses and stovepipes, he looked like business."[26]

With the press corps gathered around him, MacArthur began to read a prepared statement. Given the news that Dick Marshall had delivered about Allied strength in Australia, most of MacArthur's words were directed to military and political leaders on other continents. Noting that he knew the Australian soldier "from World War days, and admire him greatly," MacArthur cautioned that "success in modern war requires something more than courage and willingness to die; it requires careful preparation."

This meant, he continued, "the furnishing of sufficient troops and sufficient material to meet the known strength of a potential enemy. No general can make something out of nothing. My success or failure will depend primarily upon the resources which the respective Governments place at my disposal. My faith in them is complete. In any event, I shall do my best. I shall keep the soldier faith."[27]

Learning of these remarks, Japanese rear admiral Matome Ugaki recorded in his diary that MacArthur, "the hero of Bataan Peninsula," had escaped to Australia and become "the anti-Axis nations' idol." Then Ugaki asked himself the question many would ponder in the years ahead: "Is he a great general or a crazy one?"[28]

After the honor guard of the Forty-Third Engineers presented arms, MacArthur strode purposefully toward the waiting caravan and climbed into the star-adorned Wolseley. But it had only gone a few yards when the general ordered it stopped, and he got out to allow photographers to take more pictures. This attention to publicity complete, MacArthur once again entered the Wolseley, and his motorcade, with Jean and Arthur in a separate car, moved through loudly cheering crowds that lined the short route to his hotel. At its front steps, he turned and waved stoically to yet another group of well-wishers.[29]

Never one to understate the historic nature of his actions, MacArthur, the following morning, sent chief of staff George Marshall a short recap of his weeklong journey from Corregidor, unabashedly opining, "This hazardous trip by a commanding general and key members of his staff through enemy controlled territory undoubtedly is unique in military annals."[30]

Surprisingly, MacArthur supporter Patrick Hurley was one of the few observers who sensed that Australia might develop an early case of MacArthur overload. Australians largely embraced MacArthur as a highly visible symbol of American support at a time when Japanese landings on Australia's north coast seemed likely. Nonetheless, there was friction when hordes of red-blooded Yanks began making themselves at home among women whose menfolk had been serving abroad for the better part of two years. And that was just Hurley's point: there were thousands of Australian soldiers who had been fighting for the British Empire from North Africa to Singapore and Java, and they didn't view men who had escaped from the Philippines as "supermen."

To hear MacArthur's staff tell the story, Hurley warned, "they're the greatest heroes and finest soldiers the world ever saw. That might be all right in the States, where the people don't know anything more about war than what they read in the papers," Hurley continued, but it was different in Australia, and "too much publicity about General MacArthur...won't sit well with a lot of people."[31]

Their public statements notwithstanding, Franklin Roosevelt and the Joint Chiefs felt much the same way. If MacArthur had said, "*We* shall return," they might have been more inclined to overlook the sweeping strategic implications of his Terowie remarks. In a global, two-ocean war, the relief of the Philippines might or might not become a primary objective of the American offensive against Japan. It certainly didn't square with Admiral King's and the navy's view of a direct cross-Pacific advance, and there would be much discussion about the importance of the islands in the effort to defeat Japan over the next three years.

But for the time being, Roosevelt, shrewd political observer that he was, recognized that he needed Douglas MacArthur. The general might not be worth "five army corps," as FDR's military aide, Brigadier General Edwin "Pa" Watson, had professed during the debate about ordering him out of Corregidor, but MacArthur certainly had a galvanizing effect on American opinion.[32] Those "M'Arthurmen" who rushed to enlist may well have made up five corps.

Thus it was all the more important that something be done to underscore the president's point that MacArthur had come out of the Philippines as a hero destined for a bigger role. What better exclamation point to the spreading tales of his harrowing PT-boat ride than to give him the one thing his father had achieved but he had not? That achievement was the Medal of Honor. The idea of awarding it to MacArthur appears to have originated with George Marshall.

Critics later scoffed that America's highest military decoration had been bestowed for nothing more than MacArthur's seasick escape from the Philippines. But Marshall had been planning this for a long time and would make certain that the citation acknowledged MacArthur's greater role. As early as January 31, the War Department had advised Sutherland that the secretary of war was "extremely anxious [that] no opportunity be overlooked" to recognize MacArthur's "gallant and conspicuous leadership by award[ing the] Medal of Honor." Sutherland was ordered to select the proper time to submit his recommendation and supporting statement "with appropriate description" of "any act believed sufficient [to] warrant this award."[33]

Marshall prodded Sutherland again after MacArthur's arrival in Australia, and on the day that MacArthur's headquarters got up and running in Melbourne, Sutherland sent a priority message marked SECRET to Marshall: "Earnestly recommend the immediate award of the medal of honor to General MacArthur because such recognition of his services at this time would be peculiarly appropriate in view of his assumption of an international command and would certainly have a most beneficial effect here."[34]

Sutherland's message contained no supporting documentation, but having a recommendation from the field, Marshall wasted no time in taking it from there, writing the citation himself with input from Eisenhower. In submitting the recommendation to secretary of war Stimson, Marshall told him that he was doing so "not only because I am certain that General MacArthur is deserving of the honor but also because I am certain that this action will meet with popular approval, both within and without the armed forces, and will have a constructive morale value."[35]

Marshall sent Sutherland a telegram instructing that he was to arrange for the United States ambassador to Australia, Nelson T. Johnson, to present the award at the earliest practicable date. That proved to be March 26, when Australian prime minister John Curtin was to give an elaborate dinner in Canberra in MacArthur's honor to welcome him to the capital city.

Johnson read the citation, which said that MacArthur was receiving the medal "for conspicuous leadership in preparing the Philippine islands to resist conquest, for gallantry and intrepidity above and beyond the call of duty in action against invading Japanese forces, and for the heroic conduct of defensive and offensive operations on the Bataan Peninsula. He mobilized, trained, and led an army which has received world acclaim for its gallant defense against a tremendous superiority of enemy forces in men and arms. His utter disregard of personal danger under heavy fire and aerial bombardment, his calm judgment in each crisis, inspired his troops, galvanized the spirit of resistance of the Filipino people, and confirmed the faith of the American people in their armed forces."[36]

To MacArthur's credit, even if he did it with one eye on public opinion, he acknowledged the congratulations sent from beleaguered Corregidor by Jonathan Wainwright, whom he had left in overall command on Luzon, and told him, "It was not I but the gallant army which I commanded."[37]

The Medal of Honor, a warm Australian welcome, and adulation galore in the American press all smoothed Douglas MacArthur's bruised ego. But it was not nearly enough to reduce his anxiety. Always readily at home in the Philippines, MacArthur momentarily found himself to be a fish out of water in Australia. The title of supreme commander aside, he had few troops and fewer resources under his immediate command. Those he had left behind on Bataan became more and more dispirited as food supplies evaporated and the Japanese prepared for a final assault. Soldiers heading to the latrine made light of the situation and declared, "I shall return." Dugout Doug became one of MacArthur's kind nicknames. He was called a deserter, a coward, and worse.

At that point there was no specific demarcation of boundaries marking the geographic extent of MacArthur's command area. He continued to find little comfort in the efforts of the United States Navy — John Bulkeley's recent exploits excepted. He felt strongly that his own air force had failed him, and he took out his frustrations on George Brett. Everywhere he turned there was uncertainty. He wasn't even sure where he would establish his permanent headquarters. So for a time, Douglas MacArthur became akin to the main character in Australia's most popular ballad, "Waltzing Matilda" — a swagman whose fate it was to roam the country with little more than a bundle on his back.

CHAPTER NINE

CINCSWPA

If Douglas MacArthur was momentarily adrift and disgruntled, he would have been more so had he not had the continuing support of his senior staff. Whatever criticisms he faced about removing his inner circle from Corregidor, he would have had difficulty getting his feet on the ground in Australia without them. MacArthur did not suffer staff change easily—witness his long-term reliance on Eisenhower—and, if he had left the Philippines with only his family and perhaps Sutherland, starting over with a largely unknown and untried staff would have further compounded his adjustment difficulties and disrupted his equilibrium. Not only did the Bataan Gang rally around him and bring with them an established routine performed by known entities, they also possessed an unwavering loyalty and commitment to their leader. Of those who left Corregidor with him, most would serve him throughout the war. Three of them would be omnipresent, if not indispensable.

Richard Kerens Sutherland, MacArthur's chief of staff since 1938, was the unquestioned senior member. He was born on November 27, 1893, during a stopover in Hancock, Maryland, while his parents were moving from Washington, DC, to Elkins, West Virginia. His father, Howard, parlayed coal, railroad, and timber interests into a seat as a Republican in the West Virginia Senate in 1908 and an election to Congress in 1912.

While certainly not averse to politics, young Sutherland wanted to go to West Point. His father likely could have arranged it, but he was adamantly opposed, thinking a military career beneath his son. He insisted he go to Yale instead. By the time Sutherland graduated, in 1916, his ROTC training nonetheless got him a National Guard commission in the field artillery. Within a year, he had transferred to the infantry of the regular army and was serving in the trenches of France.

By then, Howard Sutherland was a United States senator eyeing a presidential run in 1920, but Richard—Sutherland's contemporaries and MacArthur called him Dick—remained set on an army career. He taught at the United States Army Infantry School, at Fort Benning, for three years, attended the Army War College, and served on the General Staff. He was still a long-suffering captain, posted as the executive officer of a battalion in Tientsin, China, when MacArthur tapped him to replace Eisenhower's friend James Ord after Ord was killed in a plane crash early in 1938.

Suave, sophisticated, and unabashedly sure of himself, Sutherland was MacArthur's alter ego. This meant, however, according to the editor of Australia's official World War II history, "Sutherland was the wrong kind of chief of staff for MacArthur, whose foibles he would not offset but nourish."[1] He was also the general's self-appointed hatchet man. Historian D. Clayton James noted that Sutherland "was contemptuous of mediocrity and inefficiency and ruthlessly denounced subordinates found guilty of such cardinal sins." Taking pleasure in his role, Sutherland once explained to deputy chief of staff Richard Marshall, "Well, Dick, somebody around here has got to be the S. O. B. General MacArthur is not going to be, and you certainly aren't going to be, so I guess I'm it."[2]

Nonetheless both MacArthur and Sutherland were greatly aided and offset by the steady calm of Richard Jaquelin Marshall. If there was sometimes confusion between the two "Dicks" on the senior staff, one could always remember that Dick Marshall was the antithesis of Dick Sutherland: soft-spoken, methodical, a dedicated team player. He lacked the flair of MacArthur and Sutherland, but that was a definite plus when it came to getting work done. Dick Marshall was born on June 16, 1895, in Markham, Virginia. Graduating from Virginia Military Institute in 1915, with a degree in electrical engineering, he joined the chase for Pancho Villa along the Mexican border before obtaining a commission in the field artillery and serving in France.

After the war he was assigned to the Quartermaster Corps and spent a tour as quartermaster at Fort Benning shortly after Sutherland served there. Beginning in 1929, Marshall did a three-year stint in the Philippines, where he worked on harbor defenses around Manila Bay and Subic Bay as well as on the Malinta Tunnel. His assignments during the 1930s included attending the Command and General Staff School at Fort Leavenworth, the Army Industrial College, and the Army War College.

In 1939 he was serving in the water transportation branch of the Quartermaster Corps when MacArthur chose him to replace Eisenhower, who was returning to the United States. Marshall's training made him MacArthur's resident logistics and supply expert, and he made the best of the changes in strategic direction mandated by MacArthur both before and after Pearl Harbor. Before the war was over, Dick Marshall would lose both a son and a stepson in combat.

The third member of the inner trio was Charles Andrew Willoughby, who fancied himself the consummate intelligence officer but whose own résumé contained plenty of uncertainty if not outright intrigue. Willoughby was reportedly born Adolph Karl Weidenbach in Heidelberg, Germany, on March 8, 1892, although his name, birth date, and parentage are open to question. In 1910, he immigrated to the United States and enlisted in the army as Adolph Charles Weidenbach. After a three-year hitch and promotion to sergeant, he was discharged and enrolled at Gettysburg College as a senior based upon prior coursework, reportedly completed at the Heidelberg University and the Sorbonne. Graduating in 1914, he was commissioned a second lieutenant in the reserves and transferred to the regular army in 1916. Deploying to France soon afterward, he initially served in the infantry but wrangled an assignment with the air service, where he learned to fly before returning to the infantry.

During the 1920s, Willoughby's fluency in multiple languages earned him tours as military attaché to Venezuela, Colombia, and Ecuador. He taught at staff schools in the States and earned a reputation as the stereotypical spit-and-polish Prussian officer: immaculate in manners, natty in custom-tailored uniforms, and authoritarian in demeanor. At some point he changed his name to Charles Andrew Willoughby, the surname a rough translation of Weidenbach, meaning "willow brook."

MacArthur met Willoughby when he was chief of staff and Willoughby was an instructor at Fort Leavenworth. As with Sutherland, MacArthur might have been looking in the mirror when he was looking at Willoughby, and he was suitably impressed. Willoughby responded with a steady stream of letters requesting assignment to MacArthur's command. Finally, in 1940, MacArthur sent for him and appointed him assistant chief of staff for intelligence.

Willoughby's ego frequently put him at odds with Sutherland, particularly on those occasions when MacArthur accorded Sutherland wide latitude in operational decisions. Because he was regal and restrained at times, headquarters staff dubbed him Sir Charles behind his back, but he could also be mercurial. He was calm one moment, brooding the next, and offensive to anyone he thought was meddling in his supposed specialty, intelligence.

He was also well read in military history and, like many who hold that interest, Willoughby assumed himself an authority on strategy and tactics. More than anything else, his background in military history, as well as his very conservative political views, gained him ready access to MacArthur for endless discussions. Indeed Willoughby was one of the few people who could challenge MacArthur in historical knowledge and personal self-importance. In a clique of MacArthur devotees, Willoughby may have been the most devoted of all.[3]

As closely tied to West Point as MacArthur was, it is interesting that no one in this trio of key aides was a West Point graduate. All, however, were models of efficiency, competence, and commitment — West Point values to be sure. MacArthur had a talent for recognizing and following skilled young officers with potential and then requesting their assignment to his command. Along with their other strengths, they were expected to bring unquestioned loyalty, not just to the army but also to MacArthur personally. In addition to doing their chief's bidding, the Bataan Gang thus served as a shield against the conspiracy that MacArthur was certain raged against him in Washington.

Douglas MacArthur was no stranger to seeing conspirators hovering in the wings and foiling his best-laid plans. This was a mind-set that gripped MacArthur his entire career. The paranoia may have had its genesis in the way his father was pushed aside instead of promoted to chief of staff. It may have been an inborn trait in his personality. In retrospect, it is difficult to imagine MacArthur in any role — even president of the United States — in which he would have failed to see a host of conspirators out to get him.

MacArthur was particularly certain that sinister plotters were at work against him in Pershing's headquarters at Chaumont, while he was trying to reform West Point, and during his tenure as chief of staff, especially after Roosevelt expedited Malin Craig's promotion. Given the deteriorating situation on Bataan and Corregidor and the meager — in MacArthur's eyes — amount of men and materiel making their way to Australia, it was easy for such fears to escalate in the spring of 1942. The record, however, simply does not justify MacArthur's extreme paranoia.

The three "usual suspects" that MacArthur and his staff, particularly Sutherland, routinely castigated for being anti-MacArthur — Franklin Roosevelt, George Marshall, and Dwight Eisenhower — were in fact supporting him publicly with both words and actions. None of them, including Eisenhower by this point in his career, could be called MacArthur fans or admirers, but this did not deter them from extraordinary wartime efforts on MacArthur's behalf.

Franklin Roosevelt would always be at odds with MacArthur politically, and the president certainly preferred Marshall to MacArthur as chief of staff. But Roosevelt gave the order for the *Pensacola* convoy to continue and later reversed his own hasty decision about ABDACOM boundaries. Given the opportunity in a press conference just before MacArthur left Corregidor to criticize MacArthur's assessments of the Philippine situation, Roosevelt took it on the chin and mumbled a disjointed answer rather than hold MacArthur up to ridicule. Indeed, the first question that Roosevelt routinely asked at his morning intelligence briefings during these months was what was happening on MacArthur's front.[4]

George Marshall was no less supportive. He embraced MacArthur's pleas to change Plan Orange defenses — ill-advisedly, in retrospect — but he did so out of respect for MacArthur's on-the-ground assessment and because he shared MacArthur's premature infatuation with the power of the B-17. From expediting the delivery of more planes to encouraging Patrick Hurley's blockade-running efforts, Marshall backed MacArthur to the full extent of the limited resources at hand. And when it came to discussions of unity of command among allies or with the United States Navy, Marshall was on record as saying, "If one commander were designated out there, it couldn't be anybody but MacArthur, on the basis of pure competence alone."[5]

And while Dwight Eisenhower vented his frustrations while working eighteen-hour days — frequently on MacArthur's behalf — by ranting about the general's pompous style, he, too, tried every reasonable measure to support him. "For many weeks — it seems years," Eisenhower wrote in his diary shortly after MacArthur arrived in Australia, "I've been searching everywhere to find any feasible way of giving more help to the Philippine Islands. We've literally squandered money; we wrestled with the navy, we've tried to think of anything that might promise even a modicum of help."[6]

Asked point-blank after MacArthur's death if there had been "an actual 'anti-MacArthur' faction in the War Department," Eisenhower responded with an emphatic no. "This was an illusion," Eisenhower said, "either of General MacArthur or of his staff. I never heard General Marshall disparage MacArthur." Eisenhower reminded his interviewer that it was Marshall who initiated the awarding of the Medal of Honor to MacArthur despite Eisenhower's opinion that MacArthur's actions had not placed him at the extreme combat risk for which the medal was intended.

According to Eisenhower, "Marshall went ahead in the belief that we should do something and that MacArthur already had all the other medals the Army could give." Eisenhower concluded, "Hostility between us has been exaggerated. After all, there must be a strong tie for two men to work so closely for seven years."[7]

None of these facts altered MacArthur's perception of the situation as he prowled the corridors of his new headquarters in the commandeered offices of a stately insurance building at 401 Collins Street in Melbourne, several blocks from the Menzies Hotel. Part of the delay in sending specific orders to MacArthur was that the American high command was still in its infancy when it came to the execution of a two-ocean war. Overall strategy — except the understood commitment to Germany First — was still evolving, and Roosevelt and the chiefs of staff were as yet unsure as to how MacArthur would fit into that big picture. There was, however, no lack of ideas.

MacArthur was still on Corregidor when Congressman Knute Hill, a Democrat from Washington State, introduced a bill authorizing the president not only to create the office of Supreme War Command but also to designate MacArthur supreme war commander, with authority over the War and Navy Departments, the air corps, and all other armed forces. If the bill had passed, it would have made MacArthur a veritable assistant president to Roosevelt for all military matters.[8]

This, of course, was not acceptable to Roosevelt, Stimson, or Marshall. But where was MacArthur to fit? Returning him to the States in some role under Marshall seemed out of the question. Giving him too much control over operations in the Pacific was also out of the question, because the mere prospect put him on a collision course with Admiral King and the American navy. Appointed commander in chief of the United States Fleet shortly after Pearl Harbor, King assumed the additional title and duties of chief of naval operations on March 12, when Roosevelt signed an executive order to that effect. It left no doubt that King was America's top sailor and the commander of US Navy and Marine Corps forces throughout the world.[9]

King and Marshall approached each other warily as the Joint Chiefs began to function as a team, but they quickly agreed that they could and would work together. This was attributable far more to Marshall's calm demeanor and self-control—even if it was forced at times—than to King's bombastic and frequently abrasive personality. Nonetheless, there would be limits to their cooperation.

When Eisenhower, in his role as War Plans chief, initially drew up an overview of army operations in the Pacific, far from diminishing MacArthur's role, he tentatively assigned the entire Pacific—from the Philippines all the way eastward to longitude 170° west (decidedly *east* of New Zealand)—to the army. This implied that MacArthur would command navy and marine forces deployed there and, predictably, it brought King up short. Marshall found King immovable when it came to naval units operating under army command. Admittedly, Marshall found it difficult to argue with King's point that if an army commander should have unified command of air, land, and sea forces in Europe, where the preponderance of fighting would occur over, on, or near land, then the navy should be accorded that role throughout the watery expanses of the Pacific.

Not only did King refuse to place naval units under army command, he also stood firm that while there would be unity of command in the Pacific at the operational level in each theater, strategic decisions would be made only at the Joint Chiefs level. Marshall agreed, and this made the Joint Chiefs the supreme American military authority and Marshall and King the undisputed heads of their services, subject only to the president.[10]

On March 18, 1942, Franklin Roosevelt and Winston Churchill agreed in principle to the division of strategic decisions between Great Britain and the United States, giving the British chief responsibility west of Singapore and leaving the Pacific to the Americans. Thus, Marshall, King, and Army Air Forces chief of staff Hap Arnold subsequently set about dividing the Pacific into four areas of operational command, with the understanding that as commander in chief of the Pacific Fleet (CINCPAC), Admiral Chester W. Nimitz would retain command of the principal American fleet regardless of where its ships operated.

Eisenhower's initial draft aside, the bulk of the Pacific north of the equator and east of longitude 160° east was placed in the Pacific Ocean Area, with Nimitz as commander in chief (CINCPOA). This area was further divided into the North Pacific Area, north of latitude 42° north, including Alaskan waters; the core Central Pacific Area; and the South Pacific Area, south of the equator and east of longitude 160° east, including New Caledonia, Fiji, and Samoa.

The fourth command was to be MacArthur's. As initially drawn, its lines delineated an area south of the equator and west of longitude 160° east and included Australia, New Guinea, and most of the Malay Barrier. This was designated the Southwest Pacific Area. Significantly, it did not include the Philippines, which lie north of the equator. As the lines were finalized, Marshall requested one change for what he termed "psychological reasons," and MacArthur's area was expanded northward from Borneo to encompass the Philippines. Marshall's "psychological reasons" meant MacArthur's ego, and at that early stage in the war, King agreed to the concession.[11]

The directives to Nimitz and MacArthur officially implementing these commands were issued on March 30, subject to the approvals of President Roosevelt and the Allied governments whose forces would be under MacArthur's command: Great Britain, the Netherlands, Australia,

173

Pacific Commands 1942

U.S.S.R.

Sea of Okhotsk

Bering Sea

Aleutian Islands

NORTH PACIFIC AREA *Nimitz*

International Date Line

42°N

Kuril Islands

Hokkaido

KOREA

Sea of Japan

JAPAN

Tokyo

Kyushu

CHINA

East China Sea

Okinawa

Iwo Jima

PACIFIC

OCEAN

Midway

To Hawaiian Islands

CENTRAL PACIFIC AREA *Nimitz*

20°N

Formosa

Mariana Islands

PHILIPPINES

Saipan

Guam

Wake Island

Manila

South China Sea

Philippine Sea

Eniwetok

Marshall Islands

Mindanao

Caroline Islands

Truk

Kwajalein

Palau Islands

Makin

Gilbert Islands

Borneo

Balikpapan

Admiralty Islands

Equator

Tarawa

0°

Hollandia

Java

Rabaul

Solomon Islands

Extent of Japanese Expansion

NEW GUINEA

Timor

Port Moresby

Guadalcanal

SOUTH PACIFIC AREA *Ghormley / Halsey*

NETHERLANDS INDIES

Darwin

Coral Sea

New Hebrides

Fiji

Townsville

20°S

SOUTHWEST PACIFIC AREA *MacArthur*

Nouméa

New Caledonia

A U S T R A L I A

Brisbane

Perth

Canberra

Melbourne

NEW ZEALAND

0   1000 Miles

Wellington

40°S

120°E   140°E   159°E   160°E   180°

and New Zealand. While waiting for these approvals, MacArthur compared his orders to those Nimitz received and did not like what he read.

While both men were designated the top commander of all armed forces that the governments concerned might assign to their respective areas, MacArthur's orders viewed him more as a supreme coordinator of international forces. As such, he was declared ineligible "to command directly any national force." The orders he issued, however, were to be received by his subordinates—American or otherwise—as if they had come directly from their respective governments. Nimitz, on the other hand, was to "exercise direct command of the combined armed forces in the North and Central Pacific areas" as well as the command of forces in the South Pacific Area through a subordinate to be appointed.

This may appear to be a splitting of hairs, but King and Marshall not only understood the distinction, they also underscored it when they designated MacArthur supreme commander of the Southwest Pacific Area (COMSWPA) and Nimitz commander in chief of the Pacific Ocean Area (CINCPOA). MacArthur was to have significant numbers of Australian forces under his command as well as British and Dutch units. Denying him direct command was the Joint Chiefs' way of attempting to ensure that he would give equal attention to all forces, work to promote Allied harmony, and avoid any complications that might arise from his issuing direct orders to the forces of other nations. In the remainder of the Pacific, most of the forces were US Navy and Marine Corps units supported by the United States Pacific Fleet. King argued, and Marshall agreed, that given the geographic expanse of the area and the dearth, or absence, of international structure, Nimitz could logically and efficiently exercise direct command over whatever forces were engaged.[12]

Because they would be the foundation on which MacArthur would base his future actions—as well as his frustrations—for the following three years, it is instructive to look at his first orders from the Joint Chiefs. As the supreme commander of the Southwest Pacific Area, MacArthur was directed to:

A. Hold the key military regions of Australia as bases for future offensive action against Japan, and in order to check the Japanese conquest of the Southwest Pacific Area.

B. Check the enemy advance toward Australia and its essential lines of communication by the destruction of enemy combatant, troop, and supply ships, aircraft, and bases in Eastern Malaysia and the New Guinea–Bismarck–Solomon Islands Region.

C. Exert economic pressure on the enemy by destroying vessels transporting raw materials from the recently conquered territories to Japan.

D. Maintain our position in the Philippine Islands.

E. Protect land, sea, and air communications within the Southwest Pacific Area, and its close approaches.

F. Route shipping in the Southwest Pacific Area.

G. Support the operations of friendly forces in the Pacific Ocean Area and in the Indian Theater.

H. Prepare to take the offensive.[13]

While the ever-present issue of available resources loomed large over each task, the directives nevertheless appeared straightforward— that is, until MacArthur compared them with Nimitz's. King had made it quite clear to Nimitz upon his assignment to the Pacific Fleet within days of Pearl Harbor that his two primary missions were to hold Hawaii and maintain a West-Coast-to-Australia lifeline through New Caledonia, Samoa, and Fiji. Nimitz's orders as CINCPOA built on these but included a decidedly offensive overtone. Nimitz's orders read:

A. Hold the island positions between the United States and the Southwest Pacific Area necessary for the security of the line of communications between those regions; and for supporting naval, air and amphibious operations against Japanese forces.

B. Support the operations of the forces in the Southwest Pacific Area.

C. Contain Japanese forces within the Pacific Theater.

D. Support the defense of the continent of North America.

E. Protect the essential sea and air communications.

F. Prepare for the execution of major amphibious offensives against positions held by Japan, the initial offensives to be launched from the South Pacific Area and Southwest Pacific Area.[14]

MacArthur's displeasure came from comparing his paragraph H, which merely directed him to "prepare to take the offensive," with Nimitz's paragraph F, which used the word *execution,* named a method of attack, cited "major amphibious offensives," and listed the two areas from which they would be launched, implicitly under Nimitz's command. Accordingly, MacArthur judged his directive to be more defensive than Nimitz's and was certain that the army was being slighted. Again, this may seem like a splitting of hairs, but MacArthur was a master of it when he suspected the most minor of slights, even if it was unintended.

It is possible that navy planners drafting these directives simply displayed the long-standing Plan Orange mentality of a drive across the central Pacific and in doing so assumed that MacArthur's Southwest Pacific Area would take a defensive role. Other prejudices may have existed. For example, Rear Admiral Richmond Kelly Turner, director of the navy's War Plans Division before Pearl Harbor and later King's assistant chief of staff for the United States Fleet, was on record as questioning MacArthur's fitness for unity of command because he felt MacArthur had limited familiarity with proper naval and air functions.

In the absence of any overt evidence, however, it is more likely that the specifics of these offensive operations had yet to be determined. Indeed, when MacArthur asked Marshall for specifics of the operations contemplated in Nimitz's paragraph F, Marshall took the course he occasionally employed with MacArthur when he either had no news or did not want to go on record in response to MacArthur's questions: he ignored them.[15]

MacArthur's reaction in the short term was to unilaterally change his own title from supreme commander of the Southwest Pacific Area to commander in chief of the Southwest Pacific Area (CINCSWPA). He did so, he told the Australian defense minister, because he could "find no precedent anywhere for the actual title of Supreme Commander ... [and] the general acceptance of the term Commander-in-Chief throughout the years as designating the senior officer commanding."[16] The broader issues between MacArthur and Nimitz would last throughout the war, but when it came to their titles, MacArthur wanted parity. Meanwhile, there was bad news from Bataan.

*   *   *

On Good Friday, April 3, after six weeks spent revitalizing his forces, General Homma launched a full-blown attack against the starving defenders of Bataan. It began with a five-hour artillery barrage punctuated by wave after wave of bombers and strafing fighters. Many of the defenses so meticulously constructed during the preceding lull were, according to the US Army official history, "churned into a worthless and useless mess."[17] As the smoke cleared, Japanese infantry and armor moved forward to concentrate on the left end of the II Corps line around Mount Samat, which was held by two Philippine army divisions. Dazed by artillery and aerial attacks, these divisions disintegrated and fled south.

II Corps commander Major General George Parker tried to plug this growing gap, but the success of the Japanese attack persuaded Homma to alter his original plan to advance only within striking distance of Mount Samat and instead press on and assault the mountain. Tanks spearheaded the attack without fear of Allied air intervention. At dawn on Easter Sunday, as many Americans and Filipinos tried to pause for a moment of worship, the Japanese unleashed another devastating artillery and air bombardment. By nightfall Sunday evening, Homma's troops had broken the American-Filipino line wide open, seized Mount Samat, and stood poised to drive the II Corps into Manila Bay.

Monday, April 6, proved the day of decision. American and Philippine troops attempted desperate counterattacks in the hope of stabilizing their line and reforming another defensive position, but by nightfall continuing Japanese pressure had foiled these efforts. Jonathan Wainwright, left by MacArthur in overall command of all troops on Luzon, reported the situation to MacArthur from his headquarters on Corregidor, and MacArthur relayed the news to Marshall that "the enemy has driven a wedge between I and II Corps and is still advancing."[18]

By the evening of April 8, II Corps was in shambles. I Corps was intact, barely, but beginning to withdraw to positions that might stabilize its crumbling right flank and the link to what remained of II Corps. Near midnight, Wainwright, on Corregidor, passed MacArthur's latest orders to Major General Edward P. King Jr., who was in direct command on Bataan. MacArthur wanted a Hail Mary assault along the western side of the peninsula to capture Olongapo, some twenty miles behind Japanese lines. If successful, MacArthur claimed it would seize much-needed supplies and permit further operations into Luzon. On a map in Melbourne it made strategic sense, but in the field on Bataan, among starving, decimated troops, the mere suggestion of such a plan showed how out of touch MacArthur was with the reality facing his command.[19]

Wainwright issued the orders with little expectation they would be executed, having already told MacArthur, "It is with deep regret that I am forced to report that the troops on Bataan are fast folding up."[20] That same evening, General King had already made the decision that he had no choice but to surrender. Disease and starvation had eliminated any hope of stopping the Japanese advance. Despite MacArthur's standing orders that there be no surrender and his determination that if the force were to be destroyed "it should be upon the actual field of battle taking full toll from the enemy," King felt he had "to surrender or have his people killed piecemeal."[21] According to the recollection of one staff officer, King took full responsibility and said simply, "In my opinion, if I do not surrender to the Japanese, Bataan will be known as the greatest slaughter in history."[22]

With supply areas in imminent danger of being overrun and field hospitals holding more than ten thousand patients coming under light artillery fire, King sent two officers forward under a white flag early on April 9. Knowing the situation King faced, Wainwright did not disagree, but because of MacArthur's "no surrender" orders, he could hardly approve. For his part, Wainwright advised MacArthur: "At 6 o'clock this morning General King commanding Luzon force without my knowledge or approval sent a flag of truce to Japanese commander. The minute I heard of it I disapproved his action and directed that there would be no surrender. I was informed it was too late to make any change that the action had already been taken.... Physical exhaustion and sickness due to a long period of insufficient food is the real cause of this terrible disaster."[23]

If MacArthur harbored doubts about his decision to defend the beaches and the resulting food and supply shortages, he kept them to himself. Instead he would never forgive Jonathan Wainwright for failing to prevent King from taking the action MacArthur had sworn he never would. Further complicating matters was the command structure that MacArthur's departure had left throughout the Philippines. General

King told the Japanese that he had authority to surrender only those troops on Bataan. Others, including the Japanese, weren't so sure. This confusion would persist as Wainwright hunkered down on Corregidor and other American forces in the southern Philippines continued to resist. On Bataan, 78,000 American and Filipino troops became prisoners of war and were left to endure a humiliating march of death.

As Louis Morton wrote in his history of the fall of the Philippines: "Denied food and water, robbed of their personal possessions and equipment, forced to march under the hot sun and halt in areas where even the most primitive sanitary facilities were lacking, clubbed, beaten, and bayoneted by their Japanese conquerors, General King's men made their way into captivity." During the horrific sixty-five-mile "death march" from Mariveles to San Fernando, the Japanese visited upon them "even greater privations and deeper humiliation than any they had yet suffered on Bataan."[24]

The question that will never be answered definitively is what might have happened had MacArthur remained in the Philippines and not been evacuated. Would he have insisted upon a fight to the death? Would he have ventured to Bataan for the final stand? If he had died in 1942, how might his death have affected the strategic vision of the war in the Pacific over the following three years? To the latter question we will return multiple times, but perhaps the most telling detail of this most horrific of American defeats is that Douglas MacArthur never allowed even a hint of his own personal responsibility to creep into his discussions of it.

If anything, as the years went by, he became more and more adamant that the blame lay elsewhere. More than a year after Bataan surrendered, MacArthur told Brigadier General Bonner F. Fellers, an OSS operative who was to become MacArthur's chief of psychological warfare, "It has been a desperate time for me ever since the war started, always the underdog, and always fighting with destruction just around the corner. I could have held Bataan if I had not been so completely deserted."[25] In MacArthur's view, the proverbial "they" had let him down.

To MacArthur's point, one thing seems clear: if he had been able to field one hundred thousand trained and equipped citizen soldiers—as he had planned since 1935—and adequately supply them with food and munitions, Bataan might have held out much longer or at least slowed the Japanese invasion schedule through Southeast Asia by requiring a larger commitment of forces to the Philippines. That the Japanese didn't make such a commitment in their early planning was based in part on reports from Japanese spies long at large in the islands who had gotten a good look at the results of MacArthur's vaunted Philippine army.

Yet from the side of MacArthur's allies, the Bataan campaign was always cast in a heroic light. "The epic operation in Bataan and Corregidor," said Willoughby, who wrote one of the many laudatory MacArthur biographies, "became a decisive factor in the winning of the war" because it disrupted the Japanese invasion schedule in the East Indies and prevented them from detaching "enough men, planes, ships, and material to nail down Guadalcanal."

Such wild assertions, responded Australian historian Gavin Long, "are contradicted by simple facts of history, geography and arithmetic."[26] Far from permitting operations on Bataan to impede their timetable, the Japanese withdrew troops from Homma's command to stay on schedule elsewhere—one might even argue that they employed an early version of island-hopping. By no measure, however, except that of the triumph of the human spirit and will to survive, can Bataan be considered anything but a major military defeat.

MacArthur's unwillingness—perhaps even his inability—to recognize his role in this, particularly when it came to his failure to stockpile supplies, did nothing to tarnish his image in the American press and with the American public. If anything, the specter of a beleaguered garrison fighting against what the public was told were vastly superior numbers—not raw hunger—appealed to Americans. They responded by pushing MacArthur ever higher on the pyramid of adoration.

At some level the public's infatuation with MacArthur defies common sense. Within the space of a few short months in the spring of 1942, he went from being the commander of troops who had been caught with their planes on the ground despite the warning of Pearl Harbor through a hasty withdrawal to a dead-end peninsula inadequately stocked for a protracted siege—where the largest surrender in American history took place—to being the most esteemed military hero in the eyes of the American public. At least three things help explain how this phenomenon occurred.

First, MacArthur's staff, especially his publicity chief, Lieutenant Colonel LeGrande "Pick" Diller, tightly controlled the news emanating from his headquarters, not only casting it in the singular terms of "MacArthur" but also playing up the reported miracles he achieved in the face of supposedly enormous odds. And when MacArthur spoke, be it to intone "I shall return" or otherwise, his rhetoric was perfectly suited to the grave tenor of the times. In addition, the Philippines was then the only theater of operations where Americans were readily—and publicly—engaging the enemy. Bill Halsey's carrier raids against Japanese islands and the Doolittle mission were still very hush-hush for fear of betraying Allied strength and capabilities. In the Atlantic, the first months of 1942 brought staggering merchant losses from German U-boats, but news of these, too, was largely censored, and on the fluid waters of the North Atlantic, what progress there was could not easily be drawn as a line on a map. By contrast, Americans could keep their eyes on the Philippines. Finally, an uneasy public, suddenly faced with a two-ocean war for which it was less than prepared, desperately needed heroes. Good press copy that he was— even if he had provided it himself—MacArthur filled the bill.

In the early months of a grim 1942, still reeling from Pearl Harbor and not yet learning of counterattacks, the American public indulged in the hero worship of Douglas MacArthur. Roosevelt and his chiefs of staff did not share this view, but it hardly mattered. They understood powerful propaganda when they saw it and recognized the need for it. Even if they did not do so as enthusiastically as the American public, they, too, embraced it. MacArthur would always be difficult to work with, but when it came to rallying the home front, maybe Pa Watson was right: MacArthur might be worth five army corps.

In the first three months of 1942, *Time* magazine made mention of Admiral King seven times, General Marshall five times, Admiral Nimitz twice, and General Eisenhower not at all, while news of MacArthur's exploits appeared thirty-two times. Once his arrival in Australia was secure, his image, complete with jutting chin and gold-braided cap, appeared on the March 30 cover. The caption read: "Australia's MacArthur: Of Destiny he could ask no more."[27]

After Bataan fell, in one week in New York City alone, *Time*'s Milestones column reported the births of Douglas MacArthur Brotherson, Douglas MacArthur Bryant, Douglas MacArthur Francis, Douglas MacArthur Miller, Douglas MacArthur Gunner, Douglas MacArthur Salavec, Douglas MacArthur Thompson, and Douglas Harold MacArthur.[28] *The Neighbors,* a popular cartoon by George Clark, portrayed two nurses in a maternity ward, one reaching for a baby and the other holding a checklist. The caption read: "MacArthur Jones has already had his bath. Now we're ready for MacArthur Smith and MacArthur Murphy."[29]

Bob Considine, a war correspondent and later the perennial coauthor of such staples as *Thirty Seconds over Tokyo,* rushed a book version of his MacArthur dispatches into print. Among the tales Considine ingrained into the MacArthur legend in *MacArthur the Magnificent* were Pinky arranging for Douglas to meet Jean en route to Manila (not true), a far more chummy relationship with Franklin Roosevelt than existed, and the false reports of Homma committing suicide in MacArthur's penthouse. Bombs were said to have fallen on Manila at the first attack; no mention was made of Clark Field.

Considine's adjectives told the story. MacArthur was "the amazing man," an "utterly sensational speaker," and even had a "virile masculine thigh"—a phrase used to describe a ripped-trousers incident in World War I. Hyperbole was rampant. MacArthur's reaction to the Manila attack was "the first of a series of dramatic moves that were to give the world one of the great fighting under-dog stories," and one of the struggling B-17 forays against Japanese-occupied Davao became an attack "so unexpected that the Japanese hardly had a plane in the air."[30] However exaggerated those accounts were, the American public relished them, and they played a huge role in boosting morale as America geared up its war machine.

What is clear is that those who served under him, particularly those left behind on Bataan, did not participate in this adoration of MacArthur. Whatever devotion those embattled soldiers chose to give would be reserved for Wainwright and others who had shared their agony. Their stories were not yet known, but had they been, they would likely have tempered the image MacArthur worked so hard to cultivate. In the tenuous days of the spring of 1942, it also remained to be seen if MacArthur, having been unable to save Bataan, could save Australia.

CHAPTER TEN

Saving Australia

On April 18, 1942, with the concurrence of the Allied governments in hand, MacArthur formally incorporated the land, naval, and air forces in the Southwest Pacific Area into his CINCSWPA command structure. Command of land forces went to Lieutenant General Thomas Blamey, the commander of the Australian army, who had just returned from service in the Middle East. Since most SWPA troops, save around two divisions of Americans, were Australians, the War Department had instructed MacArthur to designate an Australian, and Blamey's appointment was well received. Commander of Allied naval forces was to be Vice Admiral Herbert F. Leary, a 1905 classmate of Nimitz's at Annapolis and the commander of a force of American, Australian, and New Zealand cruisers and destroyers charged with enforcing King's mandate of a West-Coast-to-Australia lifeline.

The Allied Air Forces were under the command of Lieutenant General George H. Brett, who had been the commander of United States Army Forces in Australia (USAFIA). This was a curious choice in that Brett, whether by his own fault or not, already had two strikes against him from MacArthur's point of view — the lack of air support in the Philippines in general and the dilapidated state of the B-17s that rescued him in particular.

Barely had MacArthur landed in Australia and given Brett the cold shoulder when he told Marshall, "I have found the Air Corps in a most disorganized condition and it is most essential as a fundamental and primary step that General Brett be relieved of his other duties [as USAFIA commander] in order properly to command and direct our air effort."[1]

Major General Julian F. Barnes, who had been the commander of the forces on the *Pensacola* convoy, was left to command American forces in Australia, which were largely to function as the logistics and services command. Barnes's job, short of a Japanese invasion of the Australian mainland, may have been the most important in the short term: get as many men and as much materiel to Australia as possible and put both in a position to fight.

In the spirit of Allied harmony, Marshall advised MacArthur to include a representative sample of Australian and Dutch officers among the key staff positions in his headquarters. Not only did MacArthur not do so, he also looked no further than his Bataan Gang to fill eight of the eleven top spots. It was so exclusive a fraternity that one is almost tempted to list them by the numbers of their PT boats: Dick Sutherland became chief of staff, Dick Marshall became deputy chief of staff, Charles Stivers was put in charge of G-1 (personnel), Charles Willoughby was put in charge of G-2 (intelligence), Spencer Akin was made signal officer, Hugh Casey was made engineering officer, William Marquat became the antiaircraft officer, and LeGrande Diller became the public relations officer.

Six other members of the Bataan Gang remained close: Sid Huff, as MacArthur's personal aide, was charged in particular with taking care of Jean and little Arthur; C. H. Morhouse was on call as the general's aide, personal physician, and sounding board regarding the health of his subordinates; Francis Wilson became Sutherland's aide; Joseph McMicking became assistant G-2; Joe Sherr, assistant signal officer, was increasingly involved with code breaking; and youthful master sergeant Paul Rogers was Sutherland's clerk.

The three newcomers to MacArthur's staff were Brigadier General Stephen J. Chamberlin, Brett's former chief of staff at USAFIA, now in charge of G-3 (operations); Colonel Lester J. Whitlock, head of G-4 (supply); and Colonel Burdette M. Fitch, adjutant general. Whitlock and Fitch had been in Australia with the USAFIA command.

As for the Australians and the Dutch, MacArthur told Marshall that he had found no qualified Dutch officers available in Australia and that the mushrooming size of the Australian army left him "no prospect of obtaining senior staff officers from the Australians." There is, however, no record of MacArthur requesting that Blamey provide such staff members, even though there were many Australians equal to the Americans in military training who had the added advantage of wartime experience in recent operations in Africa, Europe, and Asia. As time went by, this cliquishness of MacArthur's staff made it an American enclave and led to the subsequent disgruntlement of Australians, particularly after large numbers of Australian troops were committed to operations in New Guinea.[2]

A final member of the Bataan Gang, Brigadier General Harold H. George, was deployed in the field to help Brett revitalize the Allied air effort. Known as "Pursuit" George to differentiate him from Brigadier General Harold L. "Bomber" George, who was about to head the new Air Transport Command in Washington, Pursuit George flew north toward Darwin, where he had just been given command of air defenses for the Northern Territory. Upon landing at Batchelor Field to drop off an Australian major who was bumming a ride north, George and his entourage, which included veteran war correspondent Melville Jacoby, suffered tragedy. They were standing just off the runway alongside their Lockheed C-40 transport plane when two P-40s roared down the strip, taking off. The rear plane got caught in the other's prop wash and careened out of control into George's group. Jacoby and a lieutenant were killed instantly; George died of head and chest injuries the next morning. By some accounts, George's death affected MacArthur more than any other during the war. Had George lived, MacArthur may well have opted to elevate him to Brett's position.[3]

The choice of an Australian ground commander for MacArthur's Allied forces also made sense because many in Australia anticipated an imminent Japanese invasion. "Experts believe that the Australian campaign will prove to be one of manoeuvre," the *Chronicle,* based in Adelaide, reported within a week of MacArthur's arrival in Melbourne. "It is considered doubtful whether General MacArthur will be able to prevent the establishment of enemy beachheads on Australia's long, exposed coastline, since a static cordon of defence would require an astronomical number of men."[4] If the *Chronicle* knew of MacArthur's ill-conceived beachhead defense plan for the Philippines, it made no mention of it.

But what were the Japanese planning? Their drive through Southeast Asia had taken most of the Philippines, save Corregidor and increasingly isolated areas throughout the southern islands, routed the Dutch from Java, and occupied the extent of the Malay Barrier from Timor west to Rangoon. Would they next look west to India or southeast to Australia? Sensing the rapid completion of Japan's first-stage operations, Matome Ugaki, Yamamoto's chief of staff, had posed that very question three months earlier. "What are we going to do after that?" Ugaki queried his diary. "Advance to Australia, to India, attack Hawaii, or destroy the Soviet Union at an opportune moment?"[5]

In mid-March, Prime Minister Hideki Tojo and his army and navy chiefs of staff tried to provide an answer by agreeing on a "General Outline of Policy of Future War Guidance." Hopes for an early negotiated settlement with the United States had been dashed by American reaction to the Pearl Harbor attack, and as Tojo and his chiefs recognized, "It will not only be most difficult to defeat the United States and Britain in a short period, but, the war cannot be brought to an end through compromise."

With repeated references to the need to build up the nation's war machinery, the conclusion of the Japanese leaders was to remain on the offensive and take all measures possible to force the United States and Britain to remain on the defensive. That said, the report warned that any "invasion of India and Australia" should be decided upon only after careful study.[6]

Australia at the time had a population of a little more than seven million people, the majority of them clustered in the southeast, between Brisbane and Melbourne. As a member of the British Commonwealth, the country had been loyally fighting on Great Britain's side for more than two years. Nine squadrons of the Royal Australian Air Force were scattered across the United Kingdom, the Middle East, and Malaya. Some 8,800 additional Australians were serving in the Royal Air Force. The principal ships of the Royal Australian Navy, two heavy and three light cruisers, had only recently returned to home waters after long service with the Royal Navy. The four trained and equipped divisions of the overseas Australian Imperial Force (AIF) were mostly in the Middle East, although after Pearl Harbor, British prime minister Winston Churchill slowly and reluctantly agreed to their return.[7]

Exposed though it appeared militarily, what Australia had going for it was scale. Sprawling over approximately three million square miles, it is roughly the size of the continental United States. Any enemy landing on the expanse of Australia's northwestern coast would face several thousand miles of sparsely populated desert terrain before approaching the farming and industrial centers in the southeast. Just prior to MacArthur's arrival in Australia, however, General Brett told Marshall that he was convinced that the Japanese would push forward the concentrations of ships, planes, and troops that they had used to capture Java and land them on the northwestern coast, probably at Darwin.

The Australian chiefs of staff weren't so sure. The Japanese might indeed take Darwin, but the chiefs surmised that if they did, it would be to prevent its use as a "springboard" from which Allied troops could counterattack in the East Indies rather than as their own "stepping stone" to an invasion of Australia. Even if the latter occurred, the Japanese would find themselves relatively isolated and not that much closer to Brisbane or Melbourne than they already were at Timor.

Instead, the Australian chiefs looked at the bigger map and became convinced that the ultimate Japanese objective had to be cutting the air and shipping lanes between the United States and Australia in order to prevent Australia from becoming a major base for just the offensive operations the Japanese Imperial General Headquarters already feared. This meant that the northeastern coast of Australia, including nearby Papua, in New Guinea, might be in far more danger than Darwin and the northwestern coast were. As it turned out, the enemy agreed with them.

On March 15, army and navy representatives of the Imperial General Headquarters met to begin the careful study Tojo had assured the emperor would be undertaken with regard to an Australian strategy. Navy officers emphasized the increase in air and sea traffic between the United States and Australia and urged an invasion of the continent before it could be turned into a platform for offensive operations. But the army calculated that it would take ten or more divisions to invade and hold Australia, even if the navy could find the ships for such an attack. Such a major maneuver was likely to hamstring operations throughout the Pacific and significantly reduce mobility. With that the Imperial Japanese Navy could hardly disagree.

Thus the Japanese plan became to encircle and isolate Australia from its American allies by driving eastward through the Solomon Islands to capture New Caledonia, Fiji, and Samoa and cut the West-Coast-to-Australia lifeline. Doing so would isolate Australia, which in due course would drop from the Allied tree without a costly invasion.[8]

The foundation for this plan was already in place as, concurrent with its drives throughout the Malay Barrier, Japan had been expanding toward New Guinea from its naval bastion of Truk, in the Caroline Islands. The huge island of New Guinea, the second largest in the world (after Greenland) and approximately twice the size of California, guarded the northern approaches to Australia. It was divided into three political units: Netherlands New Guinea, occupying the western half of the island; Northeast New Guinea and the adjacent Bismarck Archipelago, which were Australian mandates from German spoils at the end of World War I; and Papua, an Australian territory roughly separated from Northeast New Guinea by the rugged Owen Stanley Range. Papua extended eastward to Port Moresby and the Louisiade Archipelago, in the northern reaches of the Coral Sea. The sprawling harbor at Rabaul, on the island of New Britain, in the Bismarck Archipelago, was a particularly inviting prize, a place from which to move into the Solomon Islands.

The Imperial General Headquarters of the Japanese army ordered a force of around five thousand men drawn from the Fifty-Fifth Infantry Division, called the South Seas Detachment, to embark from Guam, capture Rabaul, then move south from there. These forces had captured Guam just days after Pearl Harbor, and among the ships that escorted its transports south were the aircraft carriers *Kaga* and *Akagi*. This invasion convoy stood off Rabaul on the night of January 22–23, 1942, and commenced landing operations shortly after midnight.

Resisting mostly with mortars and machine guns, the 1,400-man

Australian garrison was overwhelmed within hours. As on Bataan, many of the defenders were captured and massacred, although around four hundred of them made their way to the coast and were evacuated by small boats from New Guinea. The resulting Japanese occupation of Rabaul posed a looming threat to northeastern Australia, given Rabaul's harbor, central location, and two developed airfields within easy range of the northern coast of New Guinea and the western Solomons.[9]

The next stops for the South Seas Detachment were Lae and Salamaua, opposite New Britain, on the northern coast of New Guinea. Although Lae was born as a gold-rush town in the 1920s, its main claim to fame was that it served as a refueling stop in 1937 for Amelia Earhart on one of the final legs of her ill-fated around-the-world attempt. It was her last stop prior to her disappearance, en route to Howland Island. Proving that the United States was not the only country with interservice rivalries, Japanese forces reached an agreement that navy troops would assault Lae while army troops took Salamaua.

The landings were delayed when the US aircraft carrier *Lexington* and an accompanying task force of four heavy cruisers and ten destroyers made a threatening foray northeast of Rabaul. Finally, in the wee hours of March 8, a battalion of the Japanese 144th Infantry Regiment landed unopposed at Salamaua. A few hours later, naval troops did the same at Lae. What few locals were there to oppose the landings melted into the jungle.

The *Lexington* soon returned, this time from the southeast in concert with the carrier *Yorktown*. The carriers sailed west of Port Moresby and — beyond the range of Japanese land-based air from Rabaul — dispatched air attacks from the Gulf of Papua directly over the Owen Stanley Range against the new beachheads on the northern coast. Damage reports varied, but in the end three transports and one converted minesweeper were sunk, and a transport, seaplane tender, minelayer, and two destroyers sustained medium damage.

These results were easily the greatest loss of ships yet suffered by the Japanese. But only one attacking aircraft out of 104 failed to return to the American carriers. MacArthur routinely groused about a do-nothing American navy, but here was strong evidence that Nimitz was using his carriers carefully but aggressively — a strategy that King termed "calculated risk."

If nothing else, this carrier raid seasoned American airmen and sailors in battle and prepared them for bigger things to come, but in retrospect, there was much more to it than that. The foray by the *Lexington* and *Yorktown* is largely unremembered, being overshadowed by the Coral Sea battle sixty days later. But the loss of transports and the evident need for carriers to cover future landings caused the Japanese to postpone their thrusts into the Solomons and against Port Moresby until carriers could be returned from operations in the Indian Ocean. At a time when mere days meant a great deal in terms of increasing Allied preparedness, a month's delay was significant.[10]

Despite the showing of the *Lexington* and *Yorktown* off New Guinea, MacArthur pressed for carriers under his own command to augment Admiral Leary's meager naval forces. Told on April 27 that "all available carriers are now being employed on indispensable tasks,"[11] MacArthur continued his demands for more troops and resources. Dissatisfied with Marshall's responses, delivered through the established chain of command, MacArthur turned to Australian prime minister John Curtin and attempted to apply political pressure, a frequent MacArthur tactic.

MacArthur's relationship with Curtin was an interesting one. Politically, they were polar opposites. While conservative MacArthur was leading troops with the Rainbow Division during World War I, liberal Curtin had been the editor of the *Westralian Worker* in Perth and an outspoken opponent of conscription. Five years MacArthur's junior, Curtin became prime minister of a coalition government with a narrow Labor plurality on October 7, 1941. Without military training, he had nonetheless spent years arguing for stronger Australian defenses and less reliance on the British fleet.[12]

Curtin's skepticism proved well placed after Pearl Harbor and the loss of the *Prince of Wales* and *Repulse*. In his New Year's message, a few weeks later, Curtin told his countrymen: "Without any inhibitions of any kind, I make it quite clear that Australia looks to America, free of any pangs as to our traditional links or kinship with the United

Kingdom." Great Britain was preoccupied and could hold on without Australia, Curtin continued, so Australians must "exert all our energies towards the shaping of a plan, with the United States as its keystone, which will give our country some confidence of being able to hold out until the tide of battle swings against the enemy."[13]

Perhaps the critical moment when that swing began, politically if not militarily, had been MacArthur's arrival in Australia. While bookish Curtin would rouse his fellow Australians with his own brand of Churchill-like speeches, MacArthur's display of assurance and resolve from the moment he stepped from his railcar in Melbourne helped bolster the same in Curtin. How much MacArthur allowed his ego to cast him in the role of Australia's savior differs with the telling.

Lieutenant Colonel Gerald Wilkinson, MacArthur's first British liaison officer in Australia, quoted MacArthur as saying that "Curtin and Co. more or less offered him the country on a platter when he arrived from the Philippines."[14] MacArthur readily told Curtin, however, that "though the American people were animated by a warm friendship for Australia, their purpose in building up forces in the Commonwealth was not so much from interest in Australia but from its utility as a base from which to hit Japan."[15]

Meeting with Curtin late in April, MacArthur professed his bitter disappointment with the "utterly inadequate" assistance he was receiving from Washington and suggested that Curtin plead with Churchill for an aircraft carrier, two British divisions then en route to India, and an increase in British shipping assigned to the West Coast–Australia lifeline. Curtin took up the reins and immediately passed these requests on to Churchill, saying he was doing so at MacArthur's request.

Upon the receipt of Curtin's letter, Churchill did what most leaders do when a subordinate of someone with whom they have an equal and trusted working relationship appears to be "out of channels": he promptly passed the Curtin/MacArthur letter on to Roosevelt, saying, "I should be glad to know whether these requirements have been approved by you ... and whether General MacArthur has any authority from the United States for taking such a line."[16]

The answer, of course, was a firm no. Marshall immediately told MacArthur that such indirect tactics on his part served only to create confusion, and he "requested that all communications to which you are a party and which relate to strategy and major reinforcements be addressed only to the war department."[17]

"I am embarrassed by your [letter]," MacArthur disingenuously began his reply, "which seems to imply some breach of frankness on my part. I can assure you that nothing is further from my thoughts." But then MacArthur launched into a four-page missive that left no doubt about the way he really felt—that Marshall and Roosevelt were the ones who should be embarrassed by their lack of support. Professing to "know nothing of the communications between the prime ministers of Great Britain and Australia," MacArthur pointedly told Marshall that he had explained fully to Curtin "the limitations placed upon me by my directive to the effect that I am responsible neither for grand strategy nor for the allocation of resources from the British Empire or from the United States."

Noting that Curtin had asked his advice and that he deemed open communications with the Australian prime minister to be part of his charge, MacArthur claimed to have the confidence of both the Australian government and people "due largely to the lack of any attempt on my part at intrigue or reservation." They were rallying to him, and whatever he did was only in response to the overarching exigency of defending Australia. "It is hard to conceive the unanimity and intense feeling which animates every element of Australian society in its belief that proper protective measures for the safety of this continent are not being taken," MacArthur concluded. "It represents an avalanche of public opinion that nothing can suppress."[18]

When Marshall received this communiqué, it was clear that it was time for another personal letter from Roosevelt. "I fully appreciate the difficulties of your position," FDR began. "They are the same kind of difficulties which I am having with the Russians, British, Canadians, Mexicans, Indians, Persians and others at different points of the compass." No one was "wholly satisfied," but the president noted he had managed to keep all of them "reasonably satisfied" and avoid "any real rows."

What Roosevelt did not say to MacArthur in so many words is that Marshall had just returned from England and agreed with the British that top priority would be given to Operation Bolero, the buildup of

American troops and materiel in England in anticipation of an invasion of France in 1943. This "second front" in the war with Germany was deemed critical, as was the continued supply of munitions to the ally who was then bearing the brunt of the "first front."

On that issue, Roosevelt was quite candid with MacArthur: "In the matter of Grand Strategy," FDR wrote, "I find it difficult this spring and summer to get away from the simple fact that the Russian armies are killing more Axis personnel and destroying more Axis material than all the other 25 United Nations put together. Therefore, it has seemed wholly logical to support the great Russian effort in 1942 by seeking to get all munitions to them that we possibly can, and also to develop plans aimed at diverting German land and air forces from the Russian front."

MacArthur would feel this effect, Roosevelt acknowledged, but he also reaffirmed that "we will continue to send you all the air strength we possibly can" and work to secure the line of communication between the United States and Australia. "I see no reason why you should not continue discussion of military matters with Australian Prime Minister," Roosevelt concluded, "but I hope you will try to have him treat them as confidential matters and not use them for public messages or for appeals to Churchill and me." MacArthur had to be "an ambassador as well as supreme commander."[19]

Despite Roosevelt's words and those of others, MacArthur would never accept the reality that his command was only a *secondary* front—not even "the second front." In a global war, MacArthur presided over a relatively small piece. Nonetheless, his Southwest Pacific Area stretched 3,700 miles from the Indian Ocean to longitude 160° east, in the Solomon Islands, and 4,700 miles from Tasmania north to Luzon, an area almost twice the size of Europe. Regardless of the emphasis of the central Pacific in the vestiges of Plan Orange, Japan's rapid dominance throughout the Southwest Pacific Area and the importance of the natural resources of the East Indies to Japan's war economy made the Southwest Pacific heavily contested. Pragmatists did not question the commitment to Germany First, but MacArthur had an unlikely ally in his emphasis on the Pacific, even if he never fully recognized it.

The chief champion of pouring resources into the Pacific — even as he managed a two-ocean war and fought the battle against German U-boats in the North Atlantic — was Admiral Ernest J. King. While King went out of his way to avoid the wartime publicity that MacArthur courted — fearing such attention could not help but telegraph future operations to the enemy — the admiral and the general were far more alike than either would have admitted.

Both men were supreme egotists, each certain that his way was the right way. Both were avid readers of military history, biography, and strategy and took from that an exceptionally high opinion of their own military acumen. Both rubbed a good many subordinates the wrong way with a grating manner, a practiced sense of entitlement, and strict expectations, yet each also had his inner circles of devoted followers. Both were said to have a soft underside — particularly toward their children. But first and foremost, both men were determined fighters.

A 1901 graduate of Annapolis, King served his first tour in the Far East in time to observe the Russo-Japanese War. Staff positions during World War I gave him a close look at emerging developments in submarines and aviation as well as a lesson or two in working with allies. Between the wars, King pioneered submarine rescue operations, learned to fly, and embraced the emergence of the aircraft carrier. He pushed night carrier operations, introduced combat air patrols (CAP) circling overhead, and war-gamed surprise carrier attacks against the Hawaiian Islands.

When William D. Leahy retired as chief of naval operations in 1939, King desperately wanted the job, but his abrasive style and advocacy of naval aviation in the face of the still-dominant battleship crowd cost him the position. Relegated to the navy's General Board as the final step before retirement, King found a champion in Roosevelt's secretary of the navy, Frank Knox. At Knox's urging, Roosevelt gave King command of the North Atlantic fleet as it struggled to shepherd lend-lease convoys to Great Britain in an icy, undeclared war with German U-boats. After Pearl Harbor, Roosevelt and Knox immediately summoned King to Washington to command the United States Fleet. Among King's first actions was to dispatch Chester W. Nimitz to command the Pacific Fleet.[20]

Nimitz was the polar opposite of MacArthur and King in both personality and command style. Born in the sand hills of Texas west of Austin, Nimitz went to Annapolis only after there were no openings at West Point; otherwise, he would have been two years behind MacArthur there. Nimitz did not, however, enjoy the meteoric rise that family connections and World War I afforded MacArthur, and, while given the four stars of a full admiral when he assumed command of the Pacific Fleet, Nimitz was far below MacArthur in seniority.

His early specialty had been converting the neophyte American submarine force from gasoline to diesel. He supervised the construction of the submarine base at Pearl Harbor in the early 1920s, anticipated aircraft carriers as the center of the fleet while studying at the Naval War College, and taught Naval ROTC at the University of California, Berkeley. His sea commands included the heavy cruiser *Augusta,* then the flagship of the Asiatic Fleet.

Whether in the classroom or on the bridge, Nimitz taught by example, not tirade; he led men rather than drove them. He had a razor-sharp mind for details as well as an adroit sense of overall strategy. In a trio of keen intellects, Nimitz may have been smarter than either MacArthur or King. He certainly was far more humble, self-effacing, and diplomatic, a dedicated team player. Never afraid to argue his points, Nimitz nonetheless accepted the command decisions of his superiors and gave his all to execute them. He expected the same from his subordinates: discussion but full commitment to his final decisions.[21]

Having been chief of the navy's Bureau of Navigation—despite its name, essentially the personnel branch—when tapped to be CINCPAC, Nimitz had an in-depth understanding of the strengths and weakness of the officers who were flooding into the Pacific. What he shared most with MacArthur and King, however, was that he, too, was a fighter. He hated to lose, and he fully embraced King's plans for offensive operations as early as was practical.

King instructed Nimitz that his two primary missions were to hold Hawaii and maintain the West-Coast-to-Australia lifeline, but King had also made it clear to Roosevelt and Marshall that he viewed the best defense to be a strong offense. To his instructions to Nimitz, King proposed adding a third task. "The general scheme or concept of operations," King wrote, "is not only to protect the lines of communications with Australia but, in so doing, to set up 'strong points' from which a step-by-step general advance can be made through the New Hebrides, Solomons, and the Bismarck Archipelago."

Marshall immediately seized on the words "general advance" and questioned how, with the priorities of Germany First, King could even consider a general advance in the Pacific. But King maintained that an offensive rather than passive line of operations would "draw the Japanese forces there to oppose it, thus relieving pressure elsewhere, whether in Hawaii, [the Southwest Pacific], Alaska, or even India."[22] Marshall warmed to the plan; Roosevelt embraced it, providing it did not disrupt Bolero; and King's strategy for offensive operations in the Pacific—as opposed to defensive containment—was adopted.

To be sure, there would always be friction between the US Navy's South Pacific command and MacArthur's SWPA over allocation of resources, but had not King aggressively pushed for offensive operations *and* done his best to increase resources throughout the general Pacific theater, MacArthur might have spent the war simply ensuring that the Japanese did not invade Australia. MacArthur was to push the limits of his initial operational orders and, rather than simply "*prepare to take the offensive*" (emphasis added), plan and execute offensive operations: King's aggressive stance gave him the cover to do so. MacArthur would never have admitted that, and King was not particularly thinking of aiding MacArthur when he crafted his strategy, but it had that effect.

MacArthur's PR machine needed no cover: it was already on the offensive. In fact, under the auspices of Pick Diller, with heavy contributions from MacArthur himself, it had continued its Manila and Corregidor practice of cranking out ubiquitous press releases from the moment the Bataan Gang landed at Batchelor Field. On the one hand, Japanese propaganda boasted verbosely about the triumphs—real and imagined—of the Japanese army and navy, and MacArthur appears to have felt that part of his charge was to counter this stream with propaganda of his own. But on the other hand, his communications were released so quickly that they frequently did not have all the facts straight. In addition, they sometimes reported results for operations over which MacArthur had no direct command, and their revelations threatened to undercut the top-secret code-breaking operations being performed not only by the US Navy but also by his own intelligence unit.

Marshall called MacArthur to task for just those reasons after a press release datelined "Allied Headquarters, Australia, April 27," reported in great detail on the buildup of Japanese forces at Rabaul. The Japanese had to suspect, Marshall told MacArthur, that reconnaissance alone could not have gathered such information and that their codes were compromised, if not broken. "This together with previous incidents," Marshall admonished, "indicates that censorship of news emanating from Australia including your headquarters is in need of complete revision."[23]

MacArthur replied that after what he termed had been "a careful check," the material in question had not been announced "by direct communiqué" from his headquarters. He professed to have Marshall believe that the term "Allied Headquarters, Australia," had been loosely appropriated by reporters—despite MacArthur being so particular about such things—and that its use did not imply his control or approval. MacArthur blamed an Australian censor for the release, then pointedly noted, "As I have explained previously, it is utterly impossible for me under the authority I possess to impose total censorship in this foreign country."[24] But then the stakes got higher.

The US Navy's code-breaking unit in the Philippines, code-named Cast, had been a high-priority evacuation from Corregidor early in February. A similar army unit, Station 6, delayed leaving until after MacArthur's departure but was partially evacuated late in March. Both units reassembled in Melbourne and continued deciphering signal intelligence. The center of Pacific intelligence against the Japanese, however, was Station Hypo, located at Pearl Harbor under the leadership of Lieutenant Commander Joseph J. Rochefort.

Based on Rochefort's intercepts, Commander Edwin T. Layton, Nimitz's chief intelligence officer, sent a message through channels that advised Sutherland that the Japanese appeared to be preparing to extend their reach from Rabaul and that Port Moresby might be attacked by sea as early as April 21. MacArthur ordered an aerial reconnaissance of Simpson Harbor at Rabaul, but General Brett's pilots found no concentration of ships that would suggest a major amphibious operation.

On April 22 in Hawaii, Layton reaffirmed his suspicions to Nimitz: despite the reconnaissance results, he still anticipated an imminent Japanese offensive from Rabaul, either against southern New Guinea or eastward into the Solomons. Given the predilection of the Japanese navy to advance under the protection of land-based air—the Battle of Midway was soon to be a major exception—Layton suggested that the target was Port Moresby.

Willoughby read the same decoded message and came to a different conclusion. Noting the reported presence of four Japanese carriers, Willoughby predicted an attack beyond the cover of land-based air, either against the northeastern coast of Australia or on New Caledonia, the critical link in the West-Coast-to-Australia lifeline. When Port Moresby remained quiet, additional naval intelligence convinced Sutherland that the attack had only been delayed a week or two. Willoughby backed off his appraisal and revised it: thereafter he expected a landing in division strength at Port Moresby between May 5 and May 10.[25]

In response to Layton's intelligence, Nimitz ordered the carriers *Lexington* and *Yorktown,* under the command of Rear Admiral Frank Jack Fletcher, to rendezvous and venture into the Coral Sea. Convinced by Layton that the Japanese were making a major offensive thrust, Nimitz also ordered the carriers *Enterprise* and *Hornet,* which were returning from the Doolittle Raid under Bill Halsey's command, to join Fletcher. Bunching the only four American carriers in the Pacific into one force marked a major shift in the way the US Navy deployed its carriers—even though *Enterprise* and *Hornet* would arrive too late to engage—and, to Nimitz's credit, it signaled his emergence as an aggressive theater commander. Nonetheless, it took Nimitz's muscular lobbying with King to persuade him to do the bundling—and to do it without the millstone of lumbering battleships slowing him down.[26]

The Japanese sortied three main groups: a battle, or "striking," force from Truk under Rear Admiral Takeo Takagi, including the carriers

Shokaku and *Zuikaku;* an invasion force from Rabaul bound for Port Moresby containing seven destroyers, five transports, and several seaplane tenders; and an escort, or "covering," force that shadowed the invasion force and included the light carrier *Shoho* along with four heavy cruisers, two light cruisers, and a squadron of submarines.[27]

The architect of the Japanese attack was Admiral Shigeyoshi Inoue, the commander of the Imperial Japanese Navy's Fourth Fleet, based at Truk. In addition to Port Moresby, Inoue had his eye on a seaplane facility at tiny Gavutu, near the island of Tulagi, at the far eastern end of the Solomons. Capturing Gavutu and Tulagi would allow Japanese seaplanes to patrol the eastern reaches of the Coral Sea while an airfield for land-based air was constructed nearby on the larger island of Guadalcanal.

As a small force wove its way through the Solomons from Rabaul and made the Tulagi landings, Takagi's striking force would sweep around the eastern end of the islands, sprint westward across the Coral Sea, and launch a surprise attack against the Allied airfields at Townsville, on the Australian mainland, crippling a chunk of MacArthur's air force prior to the Port Moresby landing. Inoue did not expect that Takagi would encounter American carriers until Takagi moved northward after the Townsville raid to cover the Port Moresby landings.[28] At least that was the plan.

On May 2, the small Royal Australian Air Force detachment at Tulagi learned of the advance of the Japanese landing force and escaped to the New Hebrides after demolishing some facilities. The following day, the Japanese force, landing unopposed, was observed by SWPA reconnaissance planes. MacArthur passed the report to Admiral Fletcher, who, unbeknownst to Inoue, was cruising on the *Yorktown* in the Coral Sea south of the Solomons. Fletcher ordered *Yorktown* north and launched a raid against Tulagi that returned with high boasts but did little actual damage to the invasion force. The result, however, was to warn Takagi of the presence of an American carrier and expedite his approach with the *Shokaku* and *Zuikaku* around the eastern end of the Solomons and into the Coral Sea by midday on May 5.

General Brett's bombers, flying out of Townsville and Port Moresby, caught glimpses of the Port Moresby invasion force slowly making for

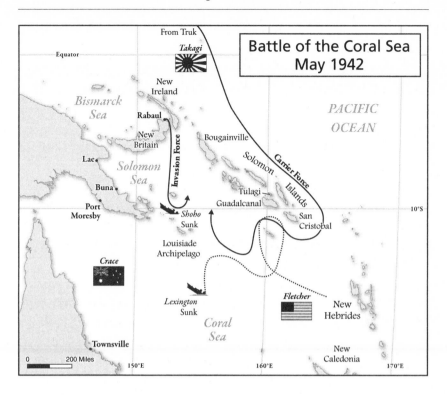

Jomard Passage, between the New Guinea mainland and the Louisiade Archipelago. Repeated air attacks over the course of three days ended with little damage to the Japanese ships, but inexplicably, Brett, or perhaps it was MacArthur, did not relay any of these sightings or actions to Fletcher—just one consequence of a less-than-unified command.[29]

Elements of what would come to be called MacArthur's Navy were, however, on the scene. Admiral Leary had sent the bulk of his SWPA naval forces—two Australian and one American cruiser and three destroyers—to assist Fletcher, but on the morning of May 7, Fletcher detached them westward to protect Port Moresby from any force steaming out of Jomard Passage. Successive waves of Japanese medium and heavy bombers found the ships and pressed attacks dangerously close, at one point straddling Rear Admiral John G. Crace's Australian flagship with a spread of bombs. Barely had these planes departed when three more medium bombers dropped bombs from twenty-five thousand feet on one of the destroyers.

"It was subsequently discovered," Crace later reported, "that these aircraft were U.S. Army B-26 from Townsville." Photographs taken as the bombs were released left little doubt that they had attacked their own ships. "Fortunately," Crace concluded, "their bombing, in comparison with that of the Japanese formation a few moments earlier, was disgraceful."[30]

Records showed only eight Allied B-17s then engaged anywhere in the vicinity. General Brett flatly denied that his planes — B-26s, B-25s, or otherwise — had attacked Crace's command and rejected an offer from Leary to work on improving the air forces' recognition of naval vessels. MacArthur seems to have stayed above this fray, but he held conferences with both Brett and Leary the next day, and the affair likely did not improve his regard for either man.[31]

Meanwhile, both Fletcher and Takagi launched search planes to find each other's carriers. They found targets, but not the ones they were looking for. The first strike from the Japanese carriers mistook the destroyer *Sims* and oiler *Neosho,* idling by themselves waiting for a refueling rendezvous, for a carrier and cruiser and sank them after a furious onslaught. The Americans fell victim to a similar problem of misidentification and launched full complements of aircraft from *Yorktown* and *Lexington* against reports of "two carriers and four heavy cruisers" 175 miles to the northwest. The nervous pilot had meant to encode "two heavy cruisers and two destroyers," but dive-bombers from the *Lexington* stumbled upon the light carrier *Shoho* in the covering force, sinking it to one pilot's cry of "Scratch one flattop."[32]

Finally, on the morning of May 8, planes from the two principal carriers on each side found their targets, leaving the *Lexington* and the *Shokaku* the most heavily damaged of the four and proving that carrier aircraft could fight major encounters without surface ships ever coming into direct contact with each other. The Americans made headway to save the *Lexington,* but gasoline vapors from ruptured fuel lines ignited and started a series of chain explosions. Sailors lined the flight deck in a calm evacuation, and Fletcher had the grim duty of ordering a destroyer to sink the flaming wreck to avoid any chance of its salvage by the Japanese.

Having already been instructed by Admiral Inoue to abandon the raid against Townsville, Takagi turned northward with the *Zuikaku* to follow the wounded *Shokaku*. The loss of the *Shoho* prompted a similar recall as both the Port Moresby invasion fleet and the remnants of its covering force turned around and sailed back to Rabaul. Tactically, the Americans had sustained heavier losses, but strategically, they had dealt the first major setback to Japan's unchecked post–Pearl Harbor romp and managed to blunt the Japanese drive to cut Australia's lifeline. King would never forgive Fletcher for the loss of the *Lexington,* but five months after Pearl Harbor, Fletcher had taken on a slightly superior force and, at worst, emerged with a draw. At best, he had saved Australia.[33]

But the Battle of the Coral Sea was not quite over. There was to be a secondary fight of press releases between MacArthur and the American navy. During the course of the running naval battle, the Australian Advisory War Council had taken the unprecedented step of granting MacArthur just the sort of supreme censorship over SWPA operations that MacArthur had just told Marshall was "utterly impossible" to enforce. News was to come only from Diller's SWPA communiqués. The first two dispatches of May 8 reported ten enemy ships sunk and five badly damaged in the Coral Sea action, with MacArthur's bombers playing a leading role and without any mention of specific American losses, including the *Lexington*. It was an egocentric way for MacArthur to show he was "in the know," but it had just the opposite effect. Such shabby reporting sparked criticism from the Australians and outrage from the American navy.[34]

The *Lexington* had barely settled beneath the warm waters of the Coral Sea when Marshall told MacArthur that King and Nimitz were quite disturbed by his "premature release of information" concerning forces under Nimitz's command because it imposed "definite risks upon participating forces and jeopardize[d] the successful continuation of fleet task force operations." King decreed that thenceforth, news of Nimitz's forces would be "released through the Navy Department only."[35]

Predictably, MacArthur took affront and immediately dispatched a characteristically lengthy reply: "Absolutely no information has been released from my headquarters with reference to action taking place in the northeastern sector of this area except the official communiqués. By no stretch of possible imagination do they contain anything of value to the enemy nor anything not fully known to him." The forces so engaged, MacArthur noted, included a large part of his air force, a major portion of the Australian navy, and his heavily Australian ground forces at Port Moresby and elsewhere. The battle involved "the very fate of the Australian people and continent," MacArthur maintained, "and it is manifestly absurd that some technicality of administrative process should attempt to force them to await the pleasure of the United States Navy Department for news of action."[36]

In response to this tirade, Marshall took his usual calm approach — he did not reply. It is difficult to imagine that Marshall would have brooked such insolence from another subordinate. Far from being cowed by MacArthur, Marshall was simply following the party line. The president had decided that MacArthur's worth as an asset outweighed his liabilities, and Marshall would do his best to follow suit. That did not mean, of course, that Roosevelt did not share Marshall's frequent exasperation.

"As you have seen by the press," Roosevelt wrote Canadian prime minister Mackenzie King on May 18, "Curtin and MacArthur are obtaining most of the publicity. The fact remains, however, that the naval operations were conducted solely through the Hawaii command!"[37]

Far from shying away from Nimitz, MacArthur complimented the admiral on the manner in which his forces were handled and announced he was eager to cooperate. "Call upon me freely," MacArthur wrote. "You can count upon my most complete and active cooperation."[38] Meanwhile, MacArthur regaled his staff with stories of how his planes had discovered the Japanese invasion fleet. "He told it all in the most wonderfully theatrical fashion," Brigadier General Robert H. Van Volkenburgh, his antiaircraft chief, remembered years later. "I enjoyed every second of it."[39]

CHAPTER ELEVEN

Kokoda Trail

No matter how the Battle of the Coral Sea would come to be characterized from a military viewpoint, it gave Allied morale a significant uplift. This was particularly true because it came on the heels of the gloomy though hardly unexpected news that Corregidor had surrendered. "Poor Wainwright!" Eisenhower wrote in his diary. "He did the fighting in the Philippine Islands, [and] another got such glory as the public could find in the operation... General MacArthur's tirades, to which TJ [Davis, one of MacArthur's prewar aides] and I so often listened in Manila, would now sound as silly to the public as they then did to us. But he's a hero! Yah."[1]

Jonathan Wainwright had been left with an impossible task. Compounding the problem of the meager food and munitions, there was considerable confusion as to the chain of command in the wake of MacArthur's departure. MacArthur assumed that he remained in overall command. Prior to leaving Corregidor, he created four separate subcommands: Wainwright was in charge of what was called the Luzon Force; Major General George F. Moore commanded the Manila Bay harbor defenses; Brigadier General William F. Sharp was in charge of the island of Mindanao; and Brigadier General Bradford G. Chynoweth commanded the Visayan Islands, including Cebu and Panay. It was shrewd of MacArthur to create these subcommands, because if any one of the commanders surrendered his own force, he would not have authority to surrender the others.

MacArthur, however, neglected to inform Marshall and the War Department of his plans to continue in overall command from Australia. Indeed, he may simply have presumed in the absence of orders to the contrary that he would. Washington presumed otherwise and considered Wainwright to be the senior officer in the islands and the successor to MacArthur. When MacArthur protested this arrangement, Marshall overruled him and gave as reasons the great distance between Melbourne and Manila and MacArthur's assignment as supreme commander of an Allied force. It is also possible that, recognizing the seemingly inevitable fate of the Philippines, both Roosevelt and Marshall did not want MacArthur in command when they fell in order to preserve his hero image.[2]

When Major General Edward P. King assumed responsibility for surrendering the troops on Bataan, General Homma initially demanded the surrender of all troops in the Philippines. King managed to sidestep this issue, albeit with some confusion, but Homma was not about to have a repeat when Wainwright struck his colors on Corregidor. Despite Wainwright's attempts to dissociate himself from the southern commands, Homma forced him, over the threat of continued loss of life, to broadcast surrender orders to both Sharp and Chynoweth. These were received and begrudgingly followed despite MacArthur's belated message to Sharp: "Orders emanating from General Wainwright have no validity."[3]

If the War Department had adopted MacArthur's recommended command structure—even with someone besides MacArthur in overall command from Australia—it would have permitted continued resistance in the southern islands. Given the scattered geography and relatively well-stocked supplies in the region, that resistance might have lasted for some time, although it should be noted that by the time Wainwright surrendered Corregidor on May 6, the Japanese had already overrun Cebu and Panay and were closing in on Mindanao.

MacArthur remained aggrieved over the fall of the Philippines, but he took the brunt of it out on Wainwright. "His animosity toward Wainwright," George Marshall later told his own biographer, "was tremendous."[4] Marshall wanted to recognize Wainwright's efforts by awarding him the Medal of Honor, which MacArthur had received only weeks before. Having been asked by Marshall for his recommendation, MacArthur replied that the affidavits gathered in Wainwright's behalf were submitted by officers without knowledge of the pertinent circumstances, that Wainwright's actions fell short of the requirements, and that awarding Wainwright the medal would be an injustice to other general officers who had distinguished themselves "to a degree greatly superior to that of General Wainwright."[5] Unwilling to spark an army feud that might become public, Marshall put the issue on the back burner.

The Battle of the Coral Sea may have momentarily disrupted Japan's plans to seize Port Moresby, but the Japanese quickly resumed the offensive. They held Tulagi and consolidated their positions throughout the northern Solomons, including Bougainville Island and New Georgia Island. And they certainly did not lose interest in Port Moresby. As long as there was an Australian garrison and a small but determined group of airmen based there, it was a threat to Japan's new posts at Lae and Salamaua and a thorn in the side of any naval operations in the Bismarck and Solomon Seas.

In hindsight, the Japanese should have moved to capture Port Moresby immediately after the Lae and Salamaua operations in March, but the Imperial Japanese Navy general staff decreed that the bulk of Japan's fleet should make a raid into the Indian Ocean in the hope of destroying the British Eastern Fleet and raiding Ceylon. The Japanese sank two heavy cruisers and the British aircraft carrier *Hermes* but achieved no permanent strategic results. The delay in capturing Port Moresby would have lasting ramifications.

The Australian chiefs of staff had long recognized the importance of Port Moresby, but in view of the paucity of their air and naval resources and the audacity of Japan's early offensive thrusts, they focused first on the defense of the continental mainland rather than its approaches and offshore territories. A month before MacArthur's arrival in Australia, the chiefs determined that a major reinforcement of Port Moresby was out of the question—because it would strip forces from the vulnerable eastern coast—but they still decided to hold it as long as possible and "exact heavy toll from the enemy should he attack it."[6]

On the other hand, continental defense, given the twelve thousand

miles of Australian coastline, was also problematic. The chiefs estimated that without adequate air and naval forces it would require a minimum of twenty-five divisions to hold Australia against a determined
attack. This would have required the Allies to supplement the Australian army with ten fully equipped divisions, something judged impossible given British and American commitments around the globe.[7]

What the Australian chiefs did not know at the time was that the
Japanese general staff had made similar calculations and determined
that *they* could not mount the manpower and logistics for such an operation.[8] The result was the Japanese incursions into northern New Guinea
and the thrust eastward into the Solomons in an attempt to isolate rather
than conquer Australia. By the Battle of the Coral Sea, Japan's strangu-
lation strategy—as opposed to a continental invasion strategy—was
not yet fully recognized by the Allies, but reinforcements of men,
planes, and munitions from the United States, as well as the pending
return of two Australian divisions from the Middle East, had hardened
Australian resolve not only to hold Port Moresby but also to defend key
points well north of what came to be called the Brisbane Line.

The concept of a Brisbane Line was relatively short-lived and never
implemented. Frederick Shedden, Prime Minister Curtin's key civilian
adviser on defense matters, asserted that MacArthur's reference to it
"was a flamboyant utterance" and that "no such plan existed." By the
time MacArthur arrived in Australia, far from hunkering down in the
southeast behind an imaginary line stretching southwestward from
Brisbane, the Australian chiefs had begun to increase troops at Darwin
from two brigades to a full division, at Perth and points along the western coast from one brigade to a division, and in and around Townsville,
in Queensland, from one brigade to a division. Nothing was done for
Port Moresby at that point, but the general movement was definitely
northward.[9]

Far from disagreeing with this general strategy, MacArthur embraced
it. He reportedly told Prime Minister Curtin that he doubted even
twenty-five divisions would be sufficient to hold the mainland without
adequate air and naval support.[10] Nonetheless, MacArthur's directive
after formalizing his SWPA headquarters called for General Blamey
to "perfect plans for the coordination of all defensive forces" and pre-

vent "any landing in the north-east of Australia and on the south-west coast of New Guinea." This communiqué was issued partially in response to intelligence warnings predicting just the sort of carrier strike that Admiral Inoue had been planning against Townsville.[11]

The Australian official history of the war notes this defensive preoccupation: "So hesitant had General MacArthur and General Blamey been to send reinforcements to New Guinea that on 10th May, the day on which the Japanese planned to land round Port Moresby, the defending garrison was not materially stronger than the one...established there early in January." Four days after the end of the Coral Sea battle, MacArthur gave Curtin a gloomy report claiming that Japan could strike "a new blow of the most dangerous potentialities against the S.W.P.A. or against India" and urged the development of "the Australian 'defensive bastion.'"[12] Curtin shared this view, having just warned his nation, "Invasion is a menace capable hourly of becoming an actuality."[13]

This defensive posture, arrived at over time and calculated to secure the Australian mainland before moving too far afield, appeared to make eminent political and military sense and to have been arrived at in concert between MacArthur and the Australians—until, that is, MacArthur began to rewrite history. Six months later, he told Curtin that his strategy had always been to defend Australia on the "outer perimeter territories rather than within the territory to be defended."[14] In other words, the defense of Australia would be waged in the jungles of New Guinea and not on the Australian mainland. Given the battles then raging on New Guinea, that, too, made sense.

But on the one-year anniversary of his appointment as supreme commander, MacArthur's headquarters released a communiqué stating, "When General MacArthur came to Australia, the defence plan... involved north Australia being taken by the enemy." It went on to claim, "It was General MacArthur who abandoned the 'Brisbane Line' concept and decided that the battle for Australia should be fought in New Guinea."[15]

Curtin, Blamey, and those Australians in the know took exception to this version. Six months after that, in November of 1943, MacArthur was still pressing his case on Curtin: "It was never my intention to defend Australia on the mainland of Australia," MacArthur lectured the prime minister. "That was the plan when I arrived, but to which I never subscribed, and which I immediately changed to a plan to defend Australia in New Guinea."[16] As Curtin told the story to Blamey, MacArthur characterized the decision to fight in New Guinea as his alone and, in his view, as "one of the most decisive as well as one of the most radical and difficult decisions of the war."[17]

After the war, MacArthur's recollection got even more pointed on the subject when he told US army historians that the Australian concept of a Brisbane Line—holding the southeast part of the continent while outposting the remainder—was "passive and defeatist, strategically unsound and 'fatal to every possibility of ever assuming the offensive.'"[18]

This theme, saving a defeated Australia by choosing to fight in New Guinea, was sounded loudly by MacArthur in his memoirs and echoed by two glowing biographies written by members of his staff. It became part of the MacArthur legend. Courtney Whitney, writing in *MacArthur: His Rendezvous with History,* termed it "bold almost to the point of desperation" and claimed history to have shown it to be "one of the world's greatest decisions of military strategy." Willoughby called it "one of [MacArthur's] greatest decisions; in ultimate effect one of the greatest in world strategy."[19]

The truth is that MacArthur was a fighter and all too glad to take the fight to the enemy. Like Ernest King and Chester Nimitz, he believed that the best defense was a good offense. He came to take the offensive in New Guinea in full concert with his Australian comrades in arms, after they had together beefed up Australia's continental defenses. This story is worth telling as a prelude to the New Guinea campaign because it makes the point that Douglas MacArthur was frequently his own worst enemy.

Making Port Moresby the fulcrum both of the defense of northern Australia and the anticipated offensive maneuvers northward from there—the start of a long return march to the Philippines—made eminent sense. No one doubted MacArthur's role in it; it was militarily sound; it was inspired. It is to the detriment of his reputation, however, that MacArthur couldn't have shared a bit of the credit for it with his Australian allies, particularly because much of the blood initially to be spilled north of Port Moresby was to be Australian.

*　　*　　*

Work began at Port Moresby late in April to improve the port and two existing airfields and build three additional airfields. To facilitate this construction, US engineering troops arrived, including the largely African American Ninety-Sixth Engineer Battalion. These were quickly followed by a US antiaircraft unit and augmented in mid-May by the Australian Fourteenth Infantry Brigade, some 3,400 strong, along with seven hundred Australian antiaircraft troops. Their deployment to Port Moresby was made possible by the arrival in Adelaide of the US Thirty-Second Infantry Division, under the command of Major General Edwin F. Harding, sent for the purpose of bulking up the defenses of mainland Australia.[20] The Thirty-Second was the first complete American division—consisting of around twelve thousand men and equipment—to be transported en masse in one convoy. Its arrival in Adelaide after a nine-thousand-mile, twenty-three-day voyage proved that the flow of men and munitions from the West Coast to Australia was increasing—MacArthur's criticisms notwithstanding.

As these deployments were under way, MacArthur looked east of Port Moresby toward the tip of New Guinea for areas where he could build more frontline bases. An airstrip was planned at Abau but never built, because a more suitable location was soon discovered on an old Lever Brothers coconut plantation at the head of Milne Bay. On June 8, Lieutenant Colonel Leverett G. Yoder, commanding officer of the Ninety-Sixth Engineers, made a reconnaissance of the Lever site and found a small landing field and several small jetties. Milne Bay's initial garrison—two companies and a machine-gun platoon from the Fourteenth Brigade at Port Moresby—disembarked on June 25 from a Dutch merchantman and secured the site for the arrival of the engineers. Although the Dutch are frequently given short shrift for the rapid loss of the Netherlands East Indies, Dutch merchant vessels of the KPM line, totaling twenty-nine ships, played a critical transport and supply role throughout the Southwest Pacific Area.[21]

In an Allied group effort, the Milne Bay airfield was expanded. Dispersal strips were constructed, and the field was made operational for fighter aircraft. An advantage of Milne Bay over Port Moresby was that aircraft flying against Rabaul or Lae did not have to climb over the

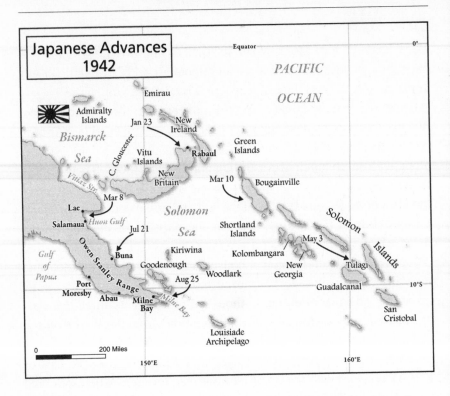

Japanese Advances
1942

thirteen-thousand-foot peaks of the Owen Stanley Range en route. A similar air base was constructed at Merauke, west of Port Moresby in Netherlands New Guinea, to protect Port Moresby's western flank as well as to safeguard Torres Strait, between New Guinea and Australia.[22]

These Allied efforts to strengthen the defenses of Port Moresby did not go unnoticed by the Japanese. Although the Battle of the Coral Sea stymied a seaborne assault against Port Moresby, and although the airfields at Milne Bay and Merauke would soon protect its flanks, Port Moresby had a little-used back door that offered a direct line of attack.

The jungle-clad Owen Stanley Range divided the long, slender tail of Papua and isolated Port Moresby, on the southwest coast, from Lae and Huon Gulf, on the northeast coast. Named for a Royal Navy captain who charted them in 1849, the steep, rugged mountains rise quickly from sea level to thirteen thousand feet and form an impenetrable barrier—almost. From Port Moresby a single trail, historically called the overland mail route or Buna road, crossed the range via a seven-thousand-foot pass near Kokoda, a small village on one of the few flat spots, then descended to the village of Buna, on the northeast coast.

MacArthur always surrounded himself with maps. They were an integral part of his ability to see the big picture, even if his reactions — witness his beachhead defense strategy throughout the Philippines — were sometimes ill-advised. Looking at Papua and the approaches to Port Moresby, MacArthur stabbed a finger at Buna and drew a line along the Kokoda Trail to Port Moresby. Discovering that Major General Basil Morris, the Australian ground commander in the Port Moresby area, had made no effort to secure the trail or even the critical pass near Kokoda, MacArthur urged action.

"There is increasing evidence," MacArthur wrote General Blamey on June 9, "that the Japanese are displaying interest in the development of a route from Buna...through Kokoda to Port Moresby. From studies made in this headquarters it appears that minor forces may attempt to utilize this route for either attack on Port Moresby or for supply of forces [attacking] by the sea route through the Louisiade Archipelago. Whatever the Japanese plan may be, it is of vital importance that the route from Kokoda westward be controlled by Allied Forces."[23]

The reply MacArthur received several days later was hardly reassuring. Noting the presence on the trail of several provincial officers with radios and two platoons of the Papuan Infantry Battalion, essentially a reconnaissance force made up mostly of natives, Morris reported that a company of regular infantry was being readied for deployment from Port Moresby to Kokoda on short notice should any situation require it. Morris considered it "most unlikely," however, that "any untoward incident" could occur without his knowledge.

Agreeing with MacArthur's concern, Blamey ordered Morris to "take all necessary steps to prevent a Japanese surprise landing along the coast, north and south of Buna, to deny the enemy the grasslands in that area for an airdrome, and to assure that we command the pass at Kokoda." In response, Morris established a new unit, the Maroubra Force, staffed it with around six hundred Australian infantry and the full complement of the Papuan Infantry Battalion — another three hundred or so men — and gave it the task of holding Kokoda.[24]

*   *   *

Meanwhile, June of 1942 had become a decisive month for the Pacific theater. Acting on intelligence gathered by Joe Rochefort and Ed Layton, Nimitz again chose to marshal his remaining carriers—*Hornet, Enterprise,* and Coral Sea survivor *Yorktown*—and defend Midway Atoll against the full force of Admiral Chuichi Nagumo's First Mobile Striking Force. When the sun set on June 4, the *Yorktown* was mortally wounded, but four Japanese carriers, 257 of their planes, and 121 of Japan's most skilled combat pilots along with thousands of men were lost. Had the carriers *Shokaku* and *Zuikaku* not been bloodied at Coral Sea and been present at Midway, as Nagumo originally intended—instead of undergoing repairs in Japan—the outcome might have been different.[25]

Whatever his usual thoughts about the US Navy, MacArthur was quick to praise Nimitz. "The splendid victory at Midway," MacArthur radioed Nimitz on June 8, "has aroused the greatest enthusiasm throughout this area....My own pride and satisfaction is boundless. We will not fail."[26]

What MacArthur surely understood, however, was that the defeat of the main Japanese fleet in the central Pacific was a page straight out of the decades-old Plan Orange. How fast and how far west the American navy might choose to advance in Midway's aftermath, and whether the general axis of that advance would be aimed due west across the central Pacific or southwest toward the Philippines, was another matter. For the moment, the entire American military structure greeted the victory at Midway with an enormous sigh of relief. While America's industries mobilized to crank out aircraft carriers, airplanes, tanks, and trucks in unprecedented numbers, Admiral King determined that the time was right to implement the third piece of his "hold Hawaii, support Australia, strike westward" plan.

The most obvious point against which to do this was the long finger of Japanese expansion that had thrust through the Solomon Islands to Tulagi and was poking at the West-Coast-to-Australia lifeline. Even before the Battle of Midway, Nimitz had suggested using a marine raider battalion—around nine hundred men with Special Forces–like training—to roust the Japanese from Tulagi. While supportive of the strategy, King, Marshall, and MacArthur were all in agreement that one battalion was much too small of a landing force.[27]

MacArthur proposed to Marshall that rather than nibbling at Tulagi, a major effort should be made directly against Rabaul. This was definitely striking at the strongest Japanese advance base in the South Pacific, but doing so, MacArthur noted, would force the Japanese backwards some seven hundred miles to Truk. In addition to the three divisions he had in Australia, MacArthur asked for one amphibious division—it would likely be the First Marine Division, then assembling at Wellington, New Zealand—and at least two carriers to augment his land-based air. "With such a force I could retake that important area," MacArthur assured Marshall, while cautioning him, "Speed is vital."[28]

As the Joint Chiefs pondered MacArthur's proposal, they also considered an offensive utilizing the British Eastern Fleet, either in relief of a beleaguered Australian and Dutch garrison isolated on Timor or as a feint against the recently occupied Andaman Islands, in the Bay of Bengal. King would remain fixated on the Andaman Islands for much of the war, but at that early date he saw either or both operations as a way to divert Japanese attention from his proposed offensive into the Solomons.

There is some speculation that King dangled the bait of British aircraft carriers possibly becoming available—something MacArthur had long wanted under his command—to encourage MacArthur to look northwest from Australia and embark on the relief of Timor. If MacArthur got occupied there, King and the US Navy would presumably have a freer hand in operations in the South Pacific.

To MacArthur's credit, he refused the bait. King had done a good job of arguing the strategic importance of the West-Coast-to-Australia lifeline, and the strategist in MacArthur shrewdly recognized that he had to concentrate his forces on New Guinea and throughout northeast Australia to defend his end of it. D. Clayton James termed MacArthur resisting the Timor temptation "one of the most important decisions [he] made in 1942, as well as one of the least known."[29] When Blamey pressed for a decision on reinforcing Timor, MacArthur told him the Southwest Pacific Area lacked the naval forces required for such a move and instead ordered regular supply missions by air and sea to the troops fighting there. They were finally withdrawn in 1943.

* * *

Thus MacArthur remained focused on a major assault on Rabaul as well as on the entire island of New Britain and neighboring New Ireland. MacArthur's planners, headed by Brigadier General Stephen J. Chamberlin, one of the few higher-ups in MacArthur's headquarters not part of the Bataan Gang, devised strike plans code-named Tulsa I. By one insider's characterization, Chamberlin was "quiet, unassuming, [and] methodical" but also "determined [and] aggressive in defending his position when challenged." He had, Paul Rogers recalled, "a fine sense of timing and integration."[30]

But at MacArthur's directive Tulsa I called for the capture of Rabaul in just two weeks, during which time bases were to be seized — and in some cases constructed from scratch — both on New Guinea and throughout the Solomons. Chamberlin considered the plan and thought the schedule unrealistic, so he reworked it into Tulsa II, which grandly provided for Rabaul's capture in eighteen days instead of fourteen but still had little detail about how the intermediate sites would be seized and readied to support the assault.[31]

On its face, the plan was an example of MacArthur's strategic audacity. *If* he had been able to bring the requisite pieces together and capture Rabaul at that early point, it would have shaved months off the Pacific war, shortcutting the bloody campaigns still to come on Guadalcanal and New Guinea and allowing Nimitz to expedite his timetable for attacking the Gilbert and Marshall Islands. On the other hand, the plan was also an example of MacArthur's tendency to formulate strategic concepts without adequate regard for operational considerations. In this case, an advance that far into enemy-held territory could become a disaster if Japanese naval strength and airpower were to counterattack and tighten a noose around his forces, particularly if he were unable to control intermediate bases en route.

Although a legion of adoring biographers later called MacArthur one of the great strategists of the Pacific war, his role was usually one of implementing strategic directives from the Joint Chiefs rather than devising them himself. Marshall routinely asked his advice — and MacArthur regularly provided it, even when he hadn't been asked — but the major strategic moves in the Pacific came out of a planning system closely managed by the Joint Chiefs and dominated by group thinking and compromise among global priorities.[32]

At the Joint Chiefs level, there was general consensus, even from Admiral King, that the First Marine Division was ready for action and could be deployed in numbers sufficient to overrun Rabaul. The two sticking points, however—MacArthur's timetable notwithstanding— were the adequacy of land-based air to cover the assault and MacArthur's proposed command of American carriers. The first was problematic; the second would occur only over King's dead body.

On the air-cover issue, King and his war plans chief preferred a methodical, step-by-step approach to Rabaul that relied on additional air bases to be built on New Guinea and in the Solomons to neutralize Japanese airpower. It would take longer, but the risks of being cut off and dominated from the air—a circumstance MacArthur should have remembered all too well from the skies above Luzon—would be greatly reduced.

Hearing from Marshall of King's reservations, MacArthur quickly backpedaled on that aspect and assured Marshall that his proposal merely described "the ultimate objective [Rabaul] of the attack and did not contain the details of the progressive steps of the plan that must be executed in order to attain it." He, too, advocated a longer, phased approach and told Marshall, "It would be manifestly impracticable to attempt the capture of Rabaul by direct assault supported by the limited amount of land-based aviation which can be employed from the presently held bases."

As to the issue of command, however, MacArthur remained adamant. In almost daily communiqués to Marshall, MacArthur argued for unity of command over all forces engaged in any South Pacific operation. Anything less, he claimed, would "result in nothing but confusion."[33]

At many levels, MacArthur was right, but instead of striving to develop a compromise command structure wherein he directed the strategic decisions and King and Nimitz retained operational command of major fleet components, MacArthur became his own worst enemy and vented his nearly paranoid frustrations to Marshall. Inferring from dispatches King was sending directly to Leary that the navy was going to conduct a Tulagi campaign with or without him,

MacArthur charged that "the navy contemplates assuming general command control of all operations in the Pacific theatre," thus relegating the army to a "subsidiary" role. He might have stopped there, but in characteristic fashion, MacArthur charged onward.

He told Marshall that during his own tenure as chief of staff, he had "accidentally" stumbled upon a navy conspiracy to assume full control of the entire national defense organization and reduce the army to a mere training and logistics command. "Based on my own experiences as chief of staff," MacArthur warned Marshall, "I would anticipate the possibility of unilateral presentation by the navy of their plan in an endeavor to secure presidential approval without your prior knowledge."[34]

Marshall responded succinctly, ignoring MacArthur's assertions of a grand antiarmy conspiracy, and calmly told him: "I am engaged in negotiations as to command in the proposed operation and will keep you informed."[35]

The result was an agreement among the Joint Chiefs dated July 2, 1942, that identified the ultimate objective as the seizure and occupation of New Britain and its key anchorage at Rabaul, nearby New Ireland, and a significant portion of New Guinea. To accomplish this, three main tasks were identified and assigned between Nimitz and MacArthur. Task 1, the occupation of the Santa Cruz Islands and the expulsion of the Japanese from Tulagi, was assigned to Nimitz, to be executed by his commander of the South Pacific Area, Vice Admiral Robert L. Ghormley.

Tasks 2 and 3 belonged to MacArthur. Under task 2, his forces would capture the remainder of the Solomon Islands and expel the Japanese from Lae, Salamaua, and the northeastern coast of New Guinea. That accomplished, his final task would be to reduce Rabaul and occupy New Britain and most of the adjacent Bismarck Archipelago.[36]

Technically, Tulagi was several miles east of the longitude 160° east dividing line between Nimitz's South Pacific Area and MacArthur's Southwest Pacific Area, but to lessen objections MacArthur held to Nimitz commanding task 1 within what MacArthur broadly viewed as his theater of operations, the Joint Chiefs moved the dividing line one degree of longitude—around sixty-nine miles—west, to longitude

159° east. This gave Nimitz and Ghormley room to operate without MacArthur looking over their shoulders.

"I wish you to make every conceivable effort to promote a complete accord throughout this affair," Marshall advised MacArthur in reporting the July 2 directive to him. "There will be difficulties and irritations inevitably," Marshall acknowledged, "but the end in view demands a determination to suppress these manifestations."[37]

Barely was the ink dry on this directive when the Joint Chiefs learned disturbing news. Australian coast watchers reported that Japanese troops from Tulagi had crossed to the larger island of Guadalcanal, some twenty miles away, and were busy building a new airstrip near the mouth of the Lunga River, on the island's northern coast.[38] King's offensive against the Solomons suddenly took on increased urgency, and he sought to expedite the deployment of the First Marine Division before Japanese construction troops could make the Guadalcanal airstrip operational.

Charged with tasks 2 and 3 of the July 2 directive, MacArthur also looked to compress the timeline. He ordered Chamberlin to fine-tune Tulsa II and, as a first step, immediately construct an airstrip on the grassy plain just inland from Buna, on New Guinea's north coast. This location, across the Owen Stanley Range from Port Moresby, at the other end of the Kokoda Trail, would be used in support of the next phase of operations, particularly the recapture of Lae and Salamaua. On July 15, still confident that he could launch task 2 — the occupation of New Guinea and the remainder of the Solomon Islands — shortly after King's marines landed at Guadalcanal, MacArthur had Chamberlin draft Operation Providence to secure the Buna site.

Brigadier General Robert H. Van Volkenburgh, previously MacArthur's antiaircraft chief, took command of the Buna force and prepared to send four Australian infantry companies and a handful of American engineers by foot over the sixty-mile Kokoda Trail, expecting them to have the Buna site secure by mid-August. But MacArthur was not the only commander with his eyes on Buna. On July 18, long before this advance unit marched out of Port Moresby, Van Volkenburgh received intelligence that large numbers of ships, including troop transports, were gathering at Rabaul and off Talasea, on the northern coast of New Britain. Unless they were headed toward Guadalcanal, their most likely destination was Buna.

Van Volkenburgh radioed an alarm to Sutherland and Chamberlin and urged that Operation Providence be launched immediately. "We may be able to hold Buna," Van Volkenburgh's deputy told Sutherland, "if we get there first."[39] MacArthur's headquarters was in chaos at that moment because the general was preparing to move from Melbourne to Brisbane, nine hundred miles closer to the front. When Willoughby confidently gave assurances that there was no intelligence suggesting that the ships were bound for Buna, Sutherland and Chamberlin discounted the immediacy of the threat.

Van Volkenburgh nonetheless pleaded for flying boats to ferry the advance force to Buna by air instead of having them slog over the mountains, but Sutherland and Chamberlin declined, saying that a small force appearing at Buna would only serve to attract the enemy's attention and provoke a counterattack before Van Volkenburgh could assemble adequate troops for its defense. As for any help from MacArthur's naval units, Admiral Leary seemed wary of coral reefs along the northern New Guinea coast as well as Japanese land-based air and made no promises.

MacArthur's headquarters alerted his own air force of the enemy ship concentrations, but, stretched thin, General Brett picked July 18 and 19, of all days, to suspend bombing missions and give his crews some rest. By the time his planes were flying again, poor weather hampered visibility. Finally one lone B-17 and six B-26s found a convoy steaming south off Salamaua. Without air cover, the ships should have been sitting ducks, but Brett's bombers attacked without scoring any hits.

Early the next morning, July 22, an RAAF twin-engine Hudson patrol bomber radioed the obvious: Japanese transports were unloading troops and equipment just west of Buna. Within hours, three thousand assault troops of Major General Tomitaro Horii's South Seas Detachment had moved under the cover of the dense jungle canopy and deployed an array of antiaircraft guns. Thirteen thousand additional troops soon disembarked and turned once-unoccupied Buna into a formidable forward base.[40]

The loss of Buna, which could have been occupied by MacArthur's command without opposition as late as July 21, was a significant Allied defeat. It frequently gets overlooked as such in the glow of Coral Sea and MacArthur's characterizations of the subsequent fighting to recapture it. But the loss of Buna cost the Allies six months, during which they struggled back and forth along the Kokoda Trail fighting for Papua. Had they been positioned at Buna instead, they would have been better able to interdict supplies flowing from Rabaul to Guadalcanal.

There was plenty of blame to go around on the Allied side for this failure. MacArthur might have reacted earlier and pushed for an occupation of Buna, as he did for Milne Bay in June. The Joint Chiefs themselves might have done less interservice arguing over commands and pushed MacArthur in the direction of Rabaul sooner. When faced with the imminent threat, Sutherland and Chamberlin might have postponed the headquarters move to Brisbane and urged MacArthur to spur Leary into action.

The end result was that, far from beginning task 2 and racing toward Rabaul, MacArthur was backpedaling. Indeed, far from defending Australia by taking the offensive in New Guinea, MacArthur found that his air force remained largely ineffective, his navy was a no-show, and those advance troops positioned on the north end of the Kokoda Trail were in full retreat toward Port Moresby.

The question that must be asked at this point is how much MacArthur had come to understand and appreciate airpower. His professed faith in the thirty-five B-17s in the Philippines prior to December 8, 1941, notwithstanding, was he merely giving lip service to it or did he embrace it as both a strategic and tactical weapon? And what was Sutherland's influence in the matter, both with his chief and down the chain of command as he gave orders in the field to implement MacArthur's operations?

Sutherland regularly issued orders in MacArthur's name and frequently assumed he knew what the general intended, even if MacArthur had made no comment on the matter. Sutherland had some flying experience, and, coupled with the usual arrogance of his personality, it made for a classic case of a little knowledge being a bad thing: it suddenly made him an aviation expert. By the account of one observer who had his share of run-ins with Sutherland, MacArthur's chief of staff had effectively cowed Lewis Brereton, especially during those critical hours on the morning of December 8.[41]

Regardless, MacArthur considered the dismal overall results of the Philippine air campaign—no matter how undermanned and ill-equipped the American air force quickly became—to be Brereton's fault. By many accounts, George Brett, Brereton's successor, was competent by peacetime standards, but MacArthur found him lacking in initiative and never gave him much of a chance as a wartime commander. Sutherland, to his credit, spent considerable time among the air units after arriving in Australia but found no reason to persuade MacArthur to alter his opinion of Brett.

Working with limited resources, Brett was simply unable to get enough planes in the air to bring MacArthur any hint of victory. Replacement parts were scarce, regular maintenance was hit-and-miss, and pilots were worn to a frazzle. What made matters worse was that Brett, having been given the cold shoulder by MacArthur, reacted negatively when Sutherland came calling with operational orders. Brett's response was to ignore Sutherland—always a bad thing—take his time fulfilling MacArthur's directives, and write lengthy memos complaining about "pilot fatigue" and "unserviceable equipment."

The final straw came when Brett wrote a wordy memo objecting to the move of MacArthur's headquarters from Melbourne to Brisbane on the grounds that Brisbane lacked sufficient communications and suitable accommodations for his headquarters personnel. According to Paul Rogers, this was just another indication that Brett "was not really trying and that he was obdurately resisting legitimate authority."[42]

What Army Air Forces units in the Southwest Pacific Area badly needed was a top commander who was one of those rare individuals able to make something out of nothing and inspire his subordinates to do the same. One man who might have fit that description—and carried added credibility with MacArthur as a member of the Bataan Gang—was Hal George, but he had been senselessly killed in the runway accident at Batchelor Field.

When it came to MacArthur and Brett, the friction between them rivaled MacArthur's most strident rants against the US Navy. "From the first," recalled Hap Arnold, "it became evident that [MacArthur] and General Brett could not get along. Brett should have done the 'getting along,' as he was the junior," but he was clearly not inclined to do so.[43] What MacArthur needed was an airpower guru who, in addition to having a can-do attitude, was not afraid to speak his mind, would not be cowed by Sutherland, and who at the same time understood the importance of being MacArthur's loyal and trusted subordinate. Enter George C. Kenney — all five and one-half feet of him.

Almost ten years MacArthur's junior, George Kenney was born on August 6, 1889, in Yarmouth, Nova Scotia. His family traced its American roots to the *Mayflower* but had moved to Nova Scotia in 1761, when Great Britain recruited New Englanders to settle the recently won province toward the end of the French and Indian War. By 1900, his parents were living in Brookline, Massachusetts, and Kenney always claimed that he was born of American parents who happened to be vacationing in Nova Scotia. This seems to be stretching the truth, but Kenney remained quite adamant — and quite touchy — about the subject his entire life.

At twenty-one, Kenney wrangled his first airplane flight while helping out at a Boston air show. "From then on," he recounted, "I knew that was what I was going to do."[44] But he didn't do it right away. He left MIT one year short of graduating with an engineering degree — tight family finances seems the most likely reason — and worked a variety of surveying and construction jobs before enlisting in the US Army's fledgling air program as America entered World War I.

By the summer of 1918, he was flying with the Ninety-First Aero Squadron over the trenches of France. He scored two kills, had his aircraft shot to pieces multiple times, and earned a reputation as someone who quickly assessed any situation and displayed great cool and courage in the cockpit. Awarded the Distinguished Service Cross and the Silver Star for his exploits, Kenney came to believe that the high casualty rates of his squadron called for realistic training under combat conditions. Having been jumped by fifty German planes and escaped with only the sleeve of his coat shot away and a bullet-riddled instrument panel, he was skeptical of any boasts that did not consider air superiority. "I stick to one basic principle," Kenney told Hap Arnold years later: "get control of the air before you try anything else."[45]

Kenney spent the years between the wars on a variety of assignments that provided him with experience in all aspects of airpower. His engineering background stood him in good stead on the technical side as he worked on the research and development of new aircraft and weapons. He spent time as both a student and an instructor at staff schools studying combat tactics, and he held staff and command positions in Washington and around the country. He was a relatively new brigadier general commanding the Air Corps Experimental Depot and Engineering School when Hap Arnold gave him a second star and command of the Fourth Air Force in March of 1942. Based in San Francisco, Kenney was responsible for the air defenses on the West Coast and combat training for fighter pilots and bomber crews about to deploy.[46]

On Tuesday morning, July 7, the direct line on Kenney's desk in San Francisco flashed. It was Hap Arnold summoning Kenney to Washington. By then, Kenney was fifty-two years old, with close-cropped gray hair surrounding probing blue eyes. A scar slashed across his chin — the souvenir of an airplane crash — which, coupled with his stature and usual demeanor, gave him the appearance of a feisty bulldog. When Arnold's staff first floated Kenney's name as a replacement for Brett, Arnold wondered aloud how MacArthur would "get along with sharp, gruff, and forceful George Kenney if he couldn't take smooth and capable George Brett."[47]

But Arnold decided that Kenney was the man for the job, and Marshall gave MacArthur his choice between Kenney and newly minted Brigadier General James H. Doolittle, then basking in the glow of his Tokyo raid. MacArthur picked Kenney and told Marshall that he "would much prefer Kenney to Doolittle not so much because of natural attainments and ability but because it would be difficult to convince the Australians of Doolittle's acceptability." MacArthur thought Doolittle's "long absence in civil life" would be unfavorably received by the Australian air force.[48] In fact, that may have been MacArthur's bias.

Kenney recalled that Arnold's deputy "wished me luck and remarked that, from the reports coming out of [MacArthur's] theater, I was going to need it." Arnold and Marshall confirmed that and told Kenney that personality clashes there went well beyond those between MacArthur and Brett.[49] Confident to his core—and no doubt just a bit cocky—Kenney took these warnings in stride and landed in Brisbane just before sundown on July 28, 1942. His first stop after the billeting officer got him settled into flat 13 in Lennons Hotel, where MacArthur and his family along with other top officers were quartered, was to meet with Dick Sutherland.

Kenney had known Sutherland since their days together at the Army War College in 1933. Kenney had recognized Sutherland's work ethic and brains without being put off by either his ego or his arrogance. He had gotten along with Sutherland then, and Kenney decided "that I'd get along with him here, too, although I might have to remind him once in a while that I was the one that had the answers on questions dealing with the Air Force." As Kenney delicately put it, "Sometimes, it seemed to me, Sutherland was inclined to overemphasize his smattering of knowledge of aviation."[50]

Kenney listened politely as Sutherland spent two hours castigating everyone involved with the American and Australian air forces. Kenney "heard just about everyone hauled over the coals except Douglas MacArthur and Richard K. Sutherland." The next morning, Kenney reported to MacArthur's office in Allied headquarters, two blocks away from Lennons in the Australian Mutual Provident Society building, at the corner of Edward and Queen Streets.

Brett need not have fretted about a lack of facilities. In moving from Melbourne to Brisbane, assistant chief of staff Dick Marshall chose the AMP's nine-story office building for MacArthur's headquarters because it was in the center of town and it was among Brisbane's largest and most modern structures. Built of light-colored sandstone between 1931 and 1934, the AMP building was also the most prominent in the city and had a battery of three elevators—"lifts," as MacArthur's Aussie hosts said. His office and those of Sutherland and their principal aides occupied the eighth floor.

Ushered into MacArthur's office in what had been the insurance company's boardroom, Kenney found MacArthur pacing the spacious room and picking up where Sutherland had left off. He readily denounced the contributions of the air force as "practically nil" and expressed the opinion that "air personnel had gone beyond just being antagonistic to his headquarters to the point of disloyalty."[51]

At that point, Kenney decided that he had had enough and that it was as good a time as any "to sell my stuff," as Kenney put it, or be on "the next plane back to the United States." Kenney rose to his feet and did some pacing of his own. By Kenney's account, he told MacArthur that he "knew how to run an air force as well or better than anyone else." He realized there were a lot of things wrong with MacArthur's air force, but he "intended to correct them and do a real job." And as for loyalty, he had never had his loyalty questioned and would not only be loyal to MacArthur himself but would also "demand of everyone under me that they be loyal, too." If ever he found that loyalty couldn't be maintained, Kenney promised he would tell MacArthur so and report packed and ready for orders home.

MacArthur listened and took Kenney's measure. "George," MacArthur finally said, putting his arm around Kenney's shoulder, "I think we are going to get along together all right."[52] That night, Kenney flew to Port Moresby to begin to bring order out of the chaos of MacArthur's air force. He arrived not a moment too soon. The Japanese had captured Kokoda and were preparing to move farther south along the Kokoda Trail.

CHAPTER TWELVE

"*Take Buna, Bob . . .*"

Unbeknownst to MacArthur's intelligence, elements of General Horii's South Seas Detachment had begun to move south from Buna within hours of their initial landing, early on July 22. Lieutenant Colonel Hatsuo Tsukamoto, the commander of an infantry battalion, received orders "to push on night and day to the line of the mountain range." By that evening, Tsukamoto's nine hundred men were already seven miles inland and making for the crossing of the Kumusi River at Wairopi, which means "wire rope bridge" in Tok Pisin, a language of New Guinea. A company of the Australian Thirty-Ninth Infantry Battalion and troops from the Papuan Infantry Battalion, the only Allied forces on the Kokoda Trail north of the Owen Stanley crest, managed to destroy the bridge before falling back to Kokoda and its primitive airfield.

Tsukamoto's troops crossed the Kumusi in makeshift boats, pressed on to Kokoda, and momentarily routed the Australians from the airstrip. The Australians counterattacked around midday on July 28, recaptured the field, and desperately hoped to be reinforced by a full infantry company to be flown in by four transports capable of landing on the tiny strip. However, in the confusion, it never became clear to commanders in Port Moresby that Kokoda had been recaptured, and the reinforcements never took off. The next day, Tsukamoto's troops again drove the Australians out of Kokoda.[1]

This frenzied fighting, albeit in less than battalion-strength numbers,

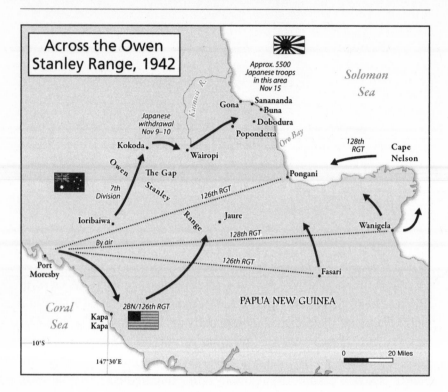

Across the Owen
Stanley Range, 1942

Approx. 5500
Japanese troops
in this area
Nov 15

Solomon
Sea

Gona • Sanananda
• Buna

Japanese
withdrawal
Nov 9–10

• Dobodura

Popondetta

Oro Bay

Kokoda •

Wairopi

128th
RGT

Cape
Nelson

Owen
7th
Division

Stanley

The Gap

• Pongani

126th RGT

Range

Ioribaiwa •

Jaure

128th RGT

Wanigela

By air

126th RGT

Port
Moresby

• Fasari

Coral
Sea

2BN/126th RGT

PAPUA NEW GUINEA

Kapa
Kapa

10°S

0   20 Miles

147°30'E

did not particularly alarm Willoughby. He believed their main objective was to secure airfields on the grassy plains at Dobodura, near
Buna, menacing Port Moresby via an air duel across the mountains but
not advancing directly against it. According to the US Army official
history, Willoughby "conceded that the Japanese might go as far as the
Gap [near the crest of the Owen Stanley Range] in order to establish a
forward outpost there, but held it extremely unlikely that they would go
further in view of the fantastically difficult terrain beyond."[2]

One of those not wanting to take any chances on that score was
Admiral King. With Japanese troops in control of Kokoda, King pointedly asked Marshall for MacArthur's plans "to deny further advance to
the Japanese, pending the execution of Task Two."[3] King was concerned
because if MacArthur's task 2 charge—occupying New Guinea and
the western Solomon Islands—faltered, the US Navy's task 1 mission
against Tulagi and Guadalcanal might be outflanked or overrun.

King was particularly annoyed with MacArthur at that moment

because MacArthur had met with South Pacific Area commander Ghormley in Melbourne on July 8, and together they recommended delaying the Tulagi and Guadalcanal landings. King insisted these had to occur by August 1 in order to halt Japanese airfield construction, but MacArthur and Ghormley feared they did not have enough strength in their areas, particularly land-based air coverage, to guarantee success. They advised that the operation be deferred pending the further deployment of forces.[4]

For King, this was the first strike against Ghormley. As for MacArthur, King snidely reminded Marshall that, only weeks before, MacArthur had been eager to take a couple of carriers and charge into Rabaul. Now, said King, when "confronted with the concrete aspects of the task, he ... feels he not only cannot undertake this extended operation [Rabaul] but not even the Tulagi operation."[5] King's only concession was to grant Ghormley a one-week reprieve.

Thus on August 7, 1942, the first of sixteen thousand US Marines went ashore to confront moderate resistance on Tulagi and nearby Gavutu and initial light resistance on Guadalcanal. They captured the uncompleted airfield there — soon renamed Henderson Field — the next day. But then the bottom fell out. The Japanese counterattacked, and all hell broke loose.

MacArthur and Ghormley, while accused by King of getting "the slows," had been right in their lengthy communiqué, warning, in part, that "a partial attack leaving Rabaul in the hands of the enemy ... would expose the initial attacking elements to the danger of destruction by overwhelming force."[6]

Put simply, land-based air from Rabaul and surrounding bases could cover Japanese convoys steaming through the Solomons to pummel Guadalcanal. The First Marine Division and the US Navy now faced that overwhelming force. There was little MacArthur could do — short of limited air operations and a few ships — to interdict the flow of men and supplies from Rabaul, because he had his hands full north of Port Moresby.

The day after the initial American landings at Guadalcanal, Australian troops yet again recaptured the Kokoda airfield. This success, too, was short-lived, and they were soon forced to yield to a concentrated Japanese force three times their number. These Japanese troops secured Kokoda and probed toward the Gap, a rocky five-mile-wide saddle 7,500 feet in elevation at the crest of the Owen Stanley Range. The Gap was around twenty miles south of Kokoda on terrain so broken that there was no space to pitch a tent and barely room enough for one man to pass another. From the Gap southward, the steep jungle slopes — almost perpetually wet from receiving between two hundred and three hundred inches of rain a year — became a slippery slide as the Kokoda Trail dropped six thousand feet to the foothills north of Port Moresby. As late as August 18, Willoughby still thought a strong Japanese overland movement beyond the Gap was unlikely given the terrain.[7]

Unbeknownst to MacArthur and Willoughby, however, Horii had planned a pincer movement on Port Moresby, sending the Kawaguchi Detachment to capture tiny Samarai, an island on the extreme southeastern tip of New Guinea, and then attack Port Moresby from the sea while the full complement of the South Seas Detachment moved against it overland from Kokoda. But the sudden need to reinforce Guadalcanal caused the Japanese to divert a large portion of the Kawaguchi Detachment there, while only one battalion continued toward Samarai.

But MacArthur had his own surprise. Somehow, amid the far-ranging geography and frequently cloud-shrouded coastal mountains, the Japanese had failed to detect the Allied airfield under construction at Milne Bay. George Kenney was in command of Allied air operations by then and just as determined as MacArthur to reinforce it. One landing strip was operational for P-40s and twin-engine Hudson bombers, and two other runways were under construction. To bolster defenses, MacArthur ordered one brigade of the Australian Seventh Infantry Division to Milne Bay and the other two brigades to Port Moresby.[8]

Finally discovering this Allied threat, the Japanese rerouted the Samarai-bound battalion and additional troops to Rabi, near Milne Bay. P-40s strafed one fleet of landing craft and marooned them on nearby Goodenough Island while Kenney sent all available B-25s, B-26s, and nine B-17s in search of the main invasion force and its escorting cruisers and destroyers. Turbulent rainsqualls and a heavy overcast shielded most of the convoy, forcing it to land on a densely covered alcove flanked by the sea and steep mountains several miles farther east of Rabi than planned.[9]

With much of MacArthur's navy on loan to Ghormley for the Guadalcanal operations, the Japanese held clear naval superiority in Milne Bay; however, when weather permitted, Kenney's air forces played a major role as opposing ground troops engaged in seesaw battles for control of the airfields. The Japanese were clearly surprised by the ferocity of the defenses. While Allied troops faced similar deprivations, Commander Minoru Yano reported that his troops were "hungry, riddled with tropical fevers, suffering from trench foot and jungle rot, and with many wounded in their midst." His superiors ordered an evacuation on the night of September 5 — the first repulse of an amphibious force that Japan had suffered up to that point in the Pacific.[10]

Following fighting there, the airstrips at Milne Bay were rushed to completion and went on to play a critical role in offensives on the northern side of the Owen Stanley Range. In a September 10 communiqué, MacArthur reported that the Japanese thrust against Milne Bay had been anticipated and the position occupied and strengthened with great care so that "the enemy fell into the trap with disastrous results to him."[11] In truth, the victory was more of a testament to a dogged Allied defense and MacArthur's determination not to retreat from New Guinea than it was to a shrewdly planned entrapment.

Meanwhile, despite the stout defense at Milne Bay, the Allies faced a juggernaut rolling along the Kokoda Trail. General Horii took personal command in the field and ordered a full-scale assault south from Kokoda on August 26. The Australians fought bitterly during their retreat, but were swept from the Gap and forced back to Ioribaiwa Ridge, dangerously close to Port Moresby.

In part swayed by Willoughby's continuing reassurances, MacArthur remained convinced that Japanese strength on the trail was light and that there was little prospect of their advancing on Port Moresby. He could not understand the repeated Australian withdrawals. In fact,

Horii had pushed the maximum number of troops he could reasonably supply over the harsh ground along the trail, and it was not until one of the Australian brigades hurriedly disembarked at Port Moresby on September 9 and the other joined it that the Allies achieved some measure of parity.[12]

Finally realizing the magnitude of the Japanese attack, MacArthur looked at his maps and proposed what he called "a wide turning movement," typical of his strategy. He proposed to deploy an American regimental command team, almost four thousand men, around Horii's left flank and into his rear, crossing the Owen Stanley crest east of the Gap and threatening or cutting Horii's tenuous supply line near Wairopi. The plan on paper looked shrewd, but MacArthur, Sutherland, and much of his general headquarters staff had still not come to appreciate the extreme topography of New Guinea. Lines on a map did not readily translate into the reality of the almost impenetrable jungle. MacArthur gave the assignment to Major General Robert L. Eichelberger, newly arrived from the states to command the US Army's I Corps.[13]

Born in 1886, Eichelberger was six years MacArthur's junior. Among his 1909 West Point classmates were George S. Patton, Jacob L. Devers, Edwin F. Harding, and Horace H. Fuller, the latter two by then subordinate to him as division commanders in Australia. Like MacArthur's, Eichelberger's personality could be both engaging and intimidating, with mood swings and his own share of paranoia. No one, however, ever questioned his personal courage. He had his own Distinguished Service Cross for bravery with the American Expeditionary Force in Siberia during World War I and knew George Kenney from the time when they were both assigned to Fort Leavenworth in the mid-1920s. Eichelberger, as post adjutant — for reasons not entirely clear — once tore up charges against Kenney for violating the strict ban on alcohol at the post.

Eichelberger was also well acquainted with Douglas MacArthur from his duty as secretary of the War Department's General Staff when MacArthur was chief of staff. Readily acknowledged as an innovator and rising talent, he became superintendent of West Point in 1940 and quickly cut back on activities associated with an outdated gentleman's army — training on horseback among them.

Instead Eichelberger promoted modernized combat training and optional flight instruction, the latter allowing cadets to receive pilots' licenses. In March of 1942, Marshall determined that Eichelberger was needed in the field, and he took command of the Seventy-Seventh Infantry Division. When MacArthur asked Marshall to send him a corps commander to preside over the two American divisions then in Australia, Marshall dispatched Eichelberger to the Pacific.[14]

Eichelberger was none too pleased by the assignment. He was on the short list for a role in Operation Torch, the Allied landings in North Africa scheduled for November, and knew MacArthur well enough to recognize that he would be difficult to serve under. Marshall had scrapped his initial choice, Major General Robert C. Richardson Jr., after concluding, "Richardson's intense feelings regarding service under Australian command made his assignment appear unwise."[15] Eichelberger's corps headquarters was staffed and ready, had been trained in amphibious operations, and, whatever the potential for friction, Eichelberger had previously worked for MacArthur. He got the orders.

Eichelberger arrived in Australia on August 25. Technically, his immediate superior was Australian general Thomas Blamey, the commander of Allied ground forces in the Southwest Pacific Area. Eichelberger, however, understood MacArthur well enough to know who his real boss was, particularly after MacArthur and his headquarters staff made it a point to instruct him "never to become closely involved with the Australians."[16]

Eichelberger's I Corps contained the Thirty-Second Infantry Division, the core of which were National Guard units from Wisconsin and Michigan, under the command of Edwin Harding, and the Forty-First Infantry Division, largely National Guard units from the Pacific Northwest, under the command of Horace Fuller, both major generals. Their divisions had been called to active duty in the fall of 1940 and — by prewar standards — had undergone rigorous training. The bulk of the Forty-First arrived in Australia in April, followed by its remaining units and the Thirty-Second Division in May.

When Eichelberger inspected both divisions upon arriving in Australia, however, he found the Thirty-Second's training "barely satisfactory" and particularly deficient in jungle warfare, even though it had spent much of the preceding year on maneuvers in the swamps of

233

Louisiana. Nonetheless, on Harding's recommendation that the 126th Infantry was the best trained and best led of the Thirty-Second's three regiments, Eichelberger chose it to make MacArthur's flanking attack against the Kokoda Trail. The 128th Infantry would follow to bolster the Australians outside Port Moresby.[17]

To facilitate the mission, Eichelberger found a willing and creative ally in feisty George Kenney. Within days of his arrival in Australia, Kenney had had a predictable run-in with Sutherland over air operations. Sutherland sent Kenney detailed orders for an air strike, prescribing takeoff times, bomb sizes, numbers and types of aircraft, and all manner of other things best left to the air force. Kenney stormed into Sutherland's office and told him that when he was given a mission he expected that the best way to execute it would be left to his professional judgment. When Sutherland protested, Kenney stood firm. Fine, he said: "Let's go in the next room, see General MacArthur, and get this thing straight. I want to find out who is supposed to run this Air Force."[18] Sutherland backed down, and Kenney's stock with MacArthur— who was listening from his adjoining office—went up another notch.

The movement of anything—men, equipment, munitions, and supplies—between Australia and New Guinea was problematic because of the extended distances—1,300 miles between Brisbane and Port Moresby—and a shortage of ships. Kenney's initial inspection visit to New Guinea had convinced him that time was of the essence in holding Port Moresby, and he urged MacArthur to let him fly a full regiment to New Guinea by air and save the two weeks required to load and transport it by ship.

Sutherland and most of MacArthur's staff were skeptical, but MacArthur asked how many men Kenney might lose that way. Kenney replied that his planes had been ferrying freight to Port Moresby without losing a pound, and he figured he could do the same with troops. MacArthur agreed to a test, and on the morning of September 15, Eichelberger and Kenney arranged to move one company from the 126th Infantry—230 men with small arms and packs—from Amberley Field, near Brisbane, to Port Moresby in a collection of Douglas DC-3s and Lockheed Lodestars.

The flight went off without a hitch—the first American infantry to arrive in New Guinea—and Kenney asked to move the remainder of the regiment. Told that it was already embarking by ship, Kenney said, "All right, give me the next regiment to go." With Sutherland looking askance, MacArthur agreed and ordered Kenney to get together with Eichelberger and make the arrangements. This move, too, of the 128th Regiment, went off without incident, becoming the largest deployment of ground troops by air up to that point and giving Eichelberger and Kenney ideas for future operations.[19]

At the same time these transport operations were under way, Kenney's combat aircraft from Port Moresby and Milne Bay pounded Japanese positions along the length of the Kokoda Trail. A-20 twin-engine light bombers, modified to carry eight forward machine guns and drop parachute fragmentation bombs, which Kenney himself had had a hand in developing, made low-level attacks against Japanese supply trains, ammo dumps, and landing barges as well as the airstrip at Buna and the river crossing at Wairopi. These operations dramatically disrupted the Japanese supply chain, and by mid-September there was not a grain of rice to issue to troops in the front lines at Ioribaiwa.

At that point the Japanese faced a reality check. While MacArthur believed the Joint Chiefs continually subordinated his efforts to Allied priorities elsewhere, particularly the battle raging on Guadalcanal, Horii may well have felt the same way about his superiors. On September 18, under pressure from air attacks and out of rice, Horii received orders to abandon his forward position at Ioribaiwa and effect a fighting withdrawal back across the Owen Stanley Range, past Kokoda and Wairopi, to a stronghold at the Buna beachhead.

Japanese strategy then called for the bulk of its army and naval forces in the Rabaul region to destroy the US Marines on Guadalcanal as their first priority. When this was accomplished, the force would turn its attention to New Guinea, moving back across the mountains against Port Moresby and seizing Milne Bay with much greater numbers than those just repulsed. Consequently, Horii began his withdrawal from Ioribaiwa, and by September 28, the Australian Twenty-Fifth Infantry Brigade had moved from defense to offense, retaken Ioribaiwa, and was proceeding northward on the Kokoda Trail.[20]

MacArthur grumbled about the effectiveness of the Australian troops and found similar fault with Harding's Thirty-Second Division, but Kenney's air force became a newfound source of pride. Kenney's can-do attitude rapidly filtered down to his pilots and crews. He cleaned out what he considered dead wood, particularly among the colonels and brigadier generals serving in Australia, and made Brigadier General Ennis C. Whitehead his deputy and point man in New Guinea and Brigadier General Kenneth N. Walker his bomber command chief at Townsville. Both men were newcomers. "I had known them both for over twenty years," Kenney recalled. "They had brains, leadership, loyalty, and liked to work. If Brett had had them about three months earlier his luck might have been a lot better."[21]

That may well have been true, but it was Kenney's own personality, no doubt helped by the success of his airmen, that quickly earned MacArthur's trust and confidence. MacArthur interacted the most with Dick Sutherland and discussed military strategy and history at length with Charles Willoughby, but gruff George Kenney quickly made it into MacArthur's inner circle. Kenney became one of the very few officers permitted to saunter from his offices on the fifth floor of the AMP building to MacArthur's office on the eighth floor or from his quarters to MacArthur's suite in Lennons Hotel, uninvited and unannounced, and receive a warm welcome.[22]

In a military hierarchy where a commanding general with MacArthur's aloof and distancing personality might be said to not have any friends, Kenney came as close as anyone to filling that role. MacArthur would not have described Kenney as a friend, but he was glowing in his praise—always reciprocated by Kenney—and certainly considered him a close confidant.

A little more than a month after Kenney assumed command of his air forces, MacArthur told Kenney, "The improvement in its performance has been marked and is directly attributable to your splendid and effective leadership."[23] Ten days later, MacArthur boasted to Marshall: "General Kenney with splendid efficiency has vitalized the air force and with the energetic support of his two fine field commanders, Whitehead and Walker, is making remarkable progress. From unsatisfactory, the air force has already progressed to very good and will soon be excellent."[24]

By the end of September, Kenney had made an airpower believer out of MacArthur, and MacArthur recommended Kenney for promotion to lieutenant general, citing his "superior qualities of leadership and professional ability." In the same letter, MacArthur also recommended Robert Eichelberger for promotion to lieutenant general, but Eichelberger was momentarily to take a backseat in operations in New Guinea.[25]

Delighted in Kenney and satisfied for the moment just to have Eichelberger on his team, MacArthur scrutinized his naval commander, Herbert F. Leary. A classmate of Nimitz's at Annapolis, Leary had spent most of his sea duty in cruisers. Handicapped by limited combat ships—Southwest Pacific Area naval forces then floated only five cruisers, eight destroyers, twenty submarines, and seven auxiliary vessels—Leary had nonetheless supported the Coral Sea fight and the initial Guadalcanal campaign until MacArthur begged Marshall to order the ships returned to his area to augment the Milne Bay defenses.

Leary proved reluctant, however, to dispatch his cruisers and destroyers into what he viewed as dangerous, reef-strewn waters. Tentativeness was never a good thing with MacArthur, and it didn't help Leary's standing with him that regardless of the SWPA unity of command—Leary was supposed to report to and receive his orders from MacArthur on operational matters—Admiral King routinely communicated directly with Leary, and Leary responded directly to King, on *all* naval matters. MacArthur pushed for a change, and Vice Admiral Arthur S. Carpender took over from Leary on September 11 as commander of the US Navy's Southwest Pacific Force as well as Allied Naval Forces in the Southwest Pacific Area. To MacArthur's frustration, Carpender would prove equally timid in the waters between Milne Bay and Buna.[26]

Meanwhile, the crisis continued on Guadalcanal. King and Nimitz shared MacArthur's view that subordinate commanders should be fighters. Alarmed that there had been neither determination nor daring in Ghormley's brief command of the South Pacific Area, Nimitz flew four thousand miles from Hawaii to Ghormley's headquarters at Nouméa, New Caledonia, in late September to confer. With MacArthur's

Brisbane headquarters only nine hundred miles farther west, Nimitz suggested through King and Marshall that MacArthur attend the conference "as a means to reach a common understanding of each other[']s problems and future plans."[27]

MacArthur was on record, only days before, as once again asking what assistance he could expect from the US Pacific Fleet should the Japanese launch a seaborne attack on New Guinea.[28] Such a conference would have been highly beneficial in answering these operational questions as well as in building a personal rapport. Marshall had already encouraged MacArthur to communicate directly with Ghormley and/or Nimitz in critical situations as long as MacArthur kept him informed of any action taken.[29] This was an exception to the formal protocol — MacArthur reporting to Marshall and Nimitz reporting to King, with communications and decisions passed via the Joint Chiefs.

MacArthur, however, claimed that it was inadvisable for him to leave his command and declined to travel less than a quarter of the distance that Nimitz had traveled. MacArthur went on to tell Marshall that he and Ghormley had already conferred — albeit back in early July — "so extensively that we understand thoroughly our mutual situations." Not only did this raise the question of why MacArthur had just queried the navy's intentions, it also kept MacArthur firmly in Ghormley's corner.

Instead of going to Nouméa, MacArthur invited Nimitz to extend his trip to Brisbane so that he "could see at first hand the problems of this area." Stressing the importance of his personal presence in Brisbane, and overlooking Nimitz's far more sweeping geographic responsibilities, MacArthur said he doubted that he could leave his command at any time and concluded, "The emergencies of command make it impossible for me to attend a conference outside of this area."[30]

Marshall did not try to persuade MacArthur otherwise, but he instructed him that it was very important that a member of his staff attend. Sutherland and Kenney went in MacArthur's place, making their first of many trips together to represent MacArthur's interests. While Sutherland, as MacArthur's chief of staff, was clearly the senior officer, Kenney gave observers some insight into his own ego and interaction with Sutherland when he later wrote that he flew to the conference "taking Sutherland along."[31]

What Marshall knew but could not yet say was that King and Nimitz had strong doubts about Ghormley's suitability for the South Pacific command. In the nearly two months since the invasion, Ghormley had never visited Guadalcanal. More disconcerting was the fact that twice during the conference at Ghormley's headquarters a staff officer delivered high-priority radio dispatches to Ghormley only to have him mutter, "My God, what are we going to do about this?"

Rather than visiting MacArthur, Nimitz decided to see the Guadalcanal situation for himself, and after the conference—which included planning air operations, conducted by Kenney, against Rabaul and Guadalcanal-bound convoys—he flew there in a B-17 to confer with the commander of the embattled First Marine Division, Major General Alexander Vandegrift. After a good deal of candid discussion, both men resolved that there would be no retreat from Guadalcanal, and Nimitz returned to Pearl Harbor convinced he had to relieve Ghormley.[32]

Had the Guadalcanal campaign failed and ended in an American withdrawal, the Japanese might well have directed far greater force in a much more timely manner against New Guinea. Viewed in that light, it is not too great a leap to say that what saved Port Moresby and kept MacArthur from a defeat in New Guinea may well have been the First Marine Division slugging it out on Guadalcanal. With the Japanese firmly committed there, MacArthur had the opportunity to turn the tide on New Guinea and move forward toward Buna.

With the Japanese retreating over the Kokoda Trail, MacArthur issued offensive plans on October 1 to recapture Buna. These were based in part on a memo Eichelberger had prepared at MacArthur's request two days before. Eichelberger pleaded that he and his I Corps headquarters staff be deployed to New Guinea to direct Harding's Thirty-Second Division staff and gain combat experience with it. Otherwise, Eichelberger asserted, there would be nothing for him and his staff to do but cool their heels in Australia and watch the training of the Forty-First Division.[33] MacArthur refused the request—apparently with substantial input from Sutherland.

Consequently, Eichelberger and his corps staff remained in Australia while MacArthur expanded his proposed right hook into the Japanese rear at Wairopi. He decided on an even wider sweep to the east in two columns. This would bring three lines of attack to bear on the Japanese strongholds around Buna: the Australian Seventh Division, via the Kokoda Trail; the 126th Infantry, from Kapa Kapa, on the southern coast, over the Owen Stanley Range to Jaure; and the 128th Infantry, via air and sea along the north coast. Obligingly, the Japanese remained committed to falling back to the coastal strongholds after appropriate delaying actions.

As this three-pronged offensive was beginning, MacArthur chose to make his first visit to New Guinea. Since his arrival in Australia some six months before, he had remained largely remote and isolated in his Melbourne and Brisbane headquarters, so much so that "MacArthur sightings" were the talk of the citizens and servicemen alike who happened to catch a glimpse of him. At one level this added to his mystique — the grim-faced warrior beneath his crushed cap ducking into a car or striding through a doorway — but it did little to build esprit de corps among his frontline troops, be they American or Australian.

Save for his early trip to Canberra to address Parliament and a sixty-mile excursion out of Melbourne to inspect the training camp of the Forty-First Infantry Division, MacArthur did not travel out of Melbourne until his move to Brisbane in July. Once there, he hunkered down in similar fashion at Lennons Hotel and his headquarters in the AMP building and insisted that visitors come to him. By Kenney's account, it was he — Kenney — who suggested that the time had come for him to see New Guinea, and MacArthur readily agreed.[34]

On October 2, MacArthur and Kenney flew in a B-17 from Brisbane to Townsville, then continued to Port Moresby. MacArthur spent the next day touring the area with Blamey. According to Kenney, MacArthur "made quite a hit with the Aussies." He fired up Brigadier John E. Lloyd, the commander charged with driving the Japanese back up the Kokoda Trail, with characteristic MacArthur flair: "Lloyd," intoned MacArthur, "by some act of God, your brigade has been chosen for this job. The eyes of the western world are upon you. I have every confidence in you and your men. Good luck and don't stop."[35]

MacArthur also inspected recently arrived American infantry and found them "fresh and full of pep." MacArthur took a dose of that pep with him when he returned to Brisbane early the next day. Indeed, his first trip to New Guinea seems to have wiped away some of the regret he may have felt over his failure to visit Bataan more often. Certainly its success spurred him to undertake more frontline excursions.

Until his next visit to New Guinea, Allied troops doggedly pressed his three lines of attack. On the Kokoda Trail, the Australians pushed the Japanese back through the Gap and, after a bitter fight at Eora Creek, recaptured Kokoda and its airfield for the final time on November 2. The orderly withdrawal General Horii had hoped to execute took the form of a rout. The main Japanese force fled across the Kumusi River at Wairopi on the night of November 12–13. The Australians wiped out the rear guard, took possession of the crossing, and erected a temporary bridge. Horii and his chief of staff drowned farther downstream while trying to cross the swift and swollen river on a raft.

The center prong, from Kapa Kapa to Jaure, quickly became a grueling quagmire. Companies of the 126th Infantry forced their way across the Owen Stanley divide at a pass two thousand feet higher than the Gap. The terrain on both sides was rougher and more precipitous than the tough Kokoda Trail and said to be so narrow that "even a jack rabbit couldn't leave it." The troops marched in single file, and there was usually no place on either side of the trail for a bivouac. Still, by October 28, the Second Battalion of the 126th Infantry, weakened by dysentery and assorted jungle maladies, was marshaled at Jaure and hacking its way toward Buna.

The likelihood of adequate reinforcements and supplies following the battalion, however, was low. Thanks to information provided by a local missionary, it was discovered that suitable landing sites were located north of the range, and transports airlifted the remainder of the 126th directly from Port Moresby to points north on the coast. These hastily constructed dirt strips — created mostly by burning off tall grasses and small trees — put to rest any thoughts of attempting a similar overland route. The men of the Second Battalion thus remained the only American troops to cross the Owen Stanley Range on foot.

For the eastern prong, MacArthur was severely handicapped by a lack of landing craft and small vessels to move west from Milne Bay. Kenney solved this problem by flying a battalion of Australian infantry and American engineer and antiaircraft troops from Milne Bay to Wanigela, on the eastern side of the Cape Nelson peninsula. After they secured and expanded an airfield, Kenney's Fifth Air Force flew the bulk of the 128th Infantry directly to Wanigela from Port Moresby — avoiding the cross-mountain slog. Meanwhile, another Australian battalion from Milne Bay landed on Goodenough Island to roust the Japanese troops marooned there since the Battle of Milne Bay and preclude the Japanese from using the island for flanking operations.[36]

While these three lines of attack developed, MacArthur kept a wary eye on Guadalcanal, fearful that a Japanese victory there would bring increased forces against him on New Guinea. By mid-November, Nimitz's new South Pacific commander replacing Ghormley, Vice Admiral William F. Halsey Jr. — with whom MacArthur was about to have considerable interaction — was far from declaring victory, but he seemed to have gained the upper hand, thanks in part to some fierce naval battles. Buoyed by this news, MacArthur was confident that the ring around Buna and Gona, to the west, which the Australians and Americans had formed by mid-November, could be squeezed tight in a matter of days.

Sensing that victory was close at hand, MacArthur returned to Port Moresby on November 6 along with Kenney. Preceded several days earlier by Sutherland and a small staff, they moved into Government House, the rambling one-story former residence of the Australian territorial governor, which perched on a small rise overlooking the harbor. Shortly afterward, MacArthur's headquarters issued a press release saying that it could "now be revealed" that MacArthur, Kenney, and Allied land forces commander Thomas Blamey were "personally conducting the campaign from the field in Papua."[37]

Assuming he would be back in Brisbane long before Christmas, MacArthur issued his plan of attack on the Gona-Buna stronghold on November 14. It tasked the Australian Seventh Division with taking Gona and Sanananda, west of the point where the Girua River emptied into the sea. East of the river, two regiments of the American Thirty-Second Division were charged with taking the village of Buna (hereinafter referred to as Buna Village) and what was called Buna Mission, the latter not a religious enclave but rather a government station.

An impenetrable swamp of murky waist-deep water, bottomless mud, and a thick tangle of jungle growth split the Buna front in two. Humidity averaged 85 percent, daily temperatures approached one hundred degrees Fahrenheit, and a long list of tropical maladies inflicted debilitating illness. Beyond these natural obstacles and infirmities, Japanese defenders had had ample time to turn even the smallest spots of relatively dry ground into well-concealed foxholes. These guarded every conceivable route around the swamps and were backed up by a string of heavily fortified bunkers.[38]

In the face of these defenses, Blamey suggested to MacArthur a rather daring leapfrog by air. He proposed landing a brigade from Milne Bay two hundred miles to the north of Buna at Nadzab, near Lae, to frustrate Japanese supply lines. MacArthur judged it too big of a gamble, fearing that Japanese control of the waters between Buna and Lae—Admiral Carpender still refused to commit his vessels to the area—might lead to reinforcements at Lae that could isolate the brigade. When Blamey later wanted to move the Milne Bay brigade to bulk up his forces opposite Gona, MacArthur again demurred because he was not convinced that Milne Bay was immune from another attack.[39]

At that point, the major difference between the Australian and American troops was that many of the Australians were battle-tested from combat along the Kokoda Trail. The Americans had as yet faced only the rigors of climate and terrain. These were, of course, significant, and Eichelberger later reported that even before the Thirty-Second Division had its baptism by fire in mid-November, its troops "were riddled with malaria, dengue fever, tropical dysentery, and were covered with jungle ulcers."[40]

A final burden to be faced by the Allied troops was that Willoughby's intelligence estimated that the Japanese had only between fifteen hundred and two thousand troops in the Gona-Buna area. Actual numbers were three to four times this, and not only were they heavily dug in, they were also well supplied with ample stocks of food and ammunition. The Allies, on the other hand, were dependent on sketchy supply lines from Kokoda by land and Milne Bay by sea and the increasingly reliable drone of Kenney's transports, either dropping supplies from the air or landing on jungle airstrips. According to

Eichelberger, "Both Australian and American ground forces would have perished without 'George Kenney's Air.' "[41]

As MacArthur's Allied forces attacked the Gona-Buna area starting in mid-November, they met harsh reality on all fronts. On the evening of November 22, despite a week of little progress, MacArthur ordered Harding to launch another all-out attack regardless of the cost. Meeting tough resistance, Harding halted the attack and pulled back. To MacArthur and those in Port Moresby, this appeared premature, and it particularly did not square with MacArthur's ideas of "going over the top" from World War I. With continuing pressure from MacArthur, Harding ordered another assault on November 30. The Japanese defenders also repulsed this effort with heavy casualties. Harding claimed, with considerable justification, that a major part of the problem was that he lacked tanks and heavy artillery to counter the stout defenses.[42]

Once again, Blamey proposed a creative approach and asked to make an amphibious landing seaward of the line of defenses. This time MacArthur heartily concurred, but Carpender remained adamant about not committing his ships off Buna. The plan was further frustrated by a lack of landing craft in New Guinea. In desperation, MacArthur appealed to Halsey for a loan of naval resources to conduct the operation.

The two had not yet met, and while Halsey appeared on the cover of *Time* magazine that week as the savior of Guadalcanal, he was far from confident. "Until Jap air in New Britain and Northern Solomons has been reduced," Halsey responded to MacArthur, "risk of valuable naval units in Middle and Western reaches [of the] Solomon Sea can only be justified by major enemy seaborne movement against South coast New Guinea or Australia itself."[43]

This was not a matter of some sinister Washington conspiracy, the likes of which MacArthur frequently denounced, and MacArthur was well justified in complaining to Marshall about the response. However grudgingly, MacArthur had supported the Guadalcanal operations with Allied ships until launching his own Milne Bay operation, and Kenney's bombers had pounded Rabaul as much as possible to interdict the flow of aircraft, shipping, and troops toward Guadalcanal. The effectiveness of these air operations varied with the telling — whether the reports came from MacArthur's Southwest Pacific Area or Halsey's South Pacific Area headquarters — but MacArthur had seriously tried to help.

Now MacArthur faced the possibility of a defeat brought on as much by disease as by enemy troops if he did not take Buna quickly. He heatedly told Marshall that despite his support for the South Pacific during its crises, at a moment when he faced similar pressure and appealed for naval assistance, he had "not only been refused but occasion has been taken to enunciate the principles of cooperation from my standpoint alone."[44]

MacArthur was further vexed by reports from Blamey and other Australian commanders, as well as from Sutherland's firsthand impressions, that the American leadership in the Thirty-Second Division, from Harding on down, was unaggressive and that its soldiers lacked the will to fight, disease-ridden though they were. Consequently, in a final measure of desperation, MacArthur turned to the man he and Sutherland had theretofore kept from the action, I Corps commander Bob Eichelberger.

In mid-November, Eichelberger had finally made it to Port Moresby, but his reception by Sutherland had been less than warm. Eichelberger planned to stay a few days and observe the Thirty-Second Division in combat, but before he could get north of the Owen Stanley Range, Sutherland ordered him back to Australia on a courier plane, telling him that his job was to train troops. In Eichelberger's words, despite being the second-ranking American army officer in the Pacific, he "was being given a monumental brush-off."[45]

Two weeks later, Sutherland was forced by MacArthur to do an about-face and cable Chamberlin, MacArthur's operations chief in Brisbane: "Advise Eichelberger immediately to be prepared to proceed [to Port Moresby] . . . to take command of the American troops in the Buna Area. If such an order issues it will come Monday [the following day] and should be executed immediately."[46]

The order came around midnight on November 29, and Eichelberger, his chief of staff, Brigadier General Clovis E. Byers, and others of his staff arrived in Port Moresby on December 1 and made the trip to Government House to get their marching orders from MacArthur. The general paced back and forth from one end of the sweeping veranda to the other in his characteristic pontifical manner. Sutherland, just returned from the Dobodura airfield, near Buna, sat at a desk looking grim-faced and perturbed. Only Kenney, animated as usual, greeted Eichelberger and Byers with any measure of warmth.

According to Eichelberger, there were no preliminaries. "Bob," MacArthur said, "I'm putting you in command at Buna. Relieve Harding. I'm sending you in, Bob, and I want you to remove all officers who won't fight. Relieve regimental and battalion commanders; if necessary, put sergeants in charge of battalions and corporals in charge of companies — anyone who will fight."

He went on to complain about reports of "American soldiers throwing away their weapons and running from the enemy." Then MacArthur stopped his pacing and looked Eichelberger squarely in the face. "Bob," he said pointedly, "I want you to take Buna, or not come back alive." Pausing a moment and not looking at Byers, he added, "And that goes for your chief of staff too."[47]

This exchange, as reported by Eichelberger in his account of the Pacific war, became one of the most quoted of MacArthur's career. Two of his most worshipful biographers, Courtney Whitney and Clark Lee, do not mention it, nor did MacArthur in his own memoirs. Stalwart friend Kenney chose to ignore the "don't come back alive" part and remember MacArthur's orders to Eichelberger as "an inspiring set of instructions" from a real leader who knew how to inspire people. The remark has usually been cited as an example of MacArthur's tough, even callous, leadership, although at least one biographer termed it "the absolute nadir of his generalship."[48]

But whatever was said, it was really just vintage MacArthur hyperbole — the sort MacArthur had employed against himself when he boasted before Châtillon in World War I that his name would head the casualty lists if the place were not taken. In context, it was a typical MacArthur pep talk, and Eichelberger seems to have taken it that way.

At breakfast the following morning, as Eichelberger prepared to fly north, MacArthur showed his other side. He and Eichelberger laughed over stories about their days together in Washington when MacArthur was chief of staff. Kenney remembered MacArthur saying, "Now, Bob, I have no illusions about your personal courage, but remember that you are no use to me — dead."

Eichelberger remembered that MacArthur put his arm around him afterward and promised him the two things that MacArthur always assumed motivated other men as much as they motivated him: a Distinguished Service Cross, second only to the Medal of Honor and the highest award in MacArthur's discretion to bestow, and the ultimate prize, regardless of the anonymity under which he required commanders in his theater to function — a promise to "release your name for newspaper publication."[49]

But just as he had with conditions on Bataan, MacArthur seemed removed from the field conditions and couldn't understand the delays. MacArthur had not visited — nor would he ever visit — the battlefields around Buna, which were only a short flight away from Port Moresby. Eichelberger and his staff landed at Dobodura around 10:00 a.m. on December 1, in Eichelberger's words, "forty minutes from Moresby — but when the stink of the swamp hit our nostrils, we knew that we, like the troops of the 32nd Division, were prisoners of geography."[50]

Eichelberger toured the front and came to the conclusion that while the deck had been stacked against Harding on many counts, inspired leadership was lacking. Harding's relief and that of two regimental commanders were necessary to reinvigorate the division. Harding went quietly, but not without a long letter to MacArthur. "I do not feel I failed you or the men I commanded," Harding told him, adding, "We took chances on a shoestring supply line and maintained it by expedients that aren't in any textbook." He disputed Eichelberger's claim that his men were beaten and told MacArthur: "To the criticism that the men of the division did not fight, my answer is the casualty lists."[51]

Eichelberger himself became appalled as casualties continued to mount, but he pressed forward on all fronts. On December 8, the Australians captured Gona, and the Thirty-Second Division renewed its drive on Buna Village. The night before it finally fell, a week later, Eichelberger wrote Sutherland: "The conditions since the heavy rains are indescribable. For hours I walked through swamps where every step was an effort." Reporting regularly to Sutherland and MacArthur,

Eichelberger once noted, "[I] cannot get this off tonight as it is dark now and the stenographer is getting eaten up by mosquitoes. More tomorrow."[52]

Meanwhile, that same day, MacArthur continued to send his own brand of encouragement Eichelberger's way: "However admirable individual acts of courage may be; however important administrative functions may seem; however splendid and electrical your presence has proven, remember that your mission is to take Buna. All other things are merely subsidiary to this." Hasten your preparations, MacArthur told him, and "strike."[53]

Even the capture of Buna Village had not satisfied MacArthur. Buna Mission remained a Japanese stronghold, and Sanananda, between Gona and Buna Village, promised even tougher fighting. MacArthur had long planned to be celebrating Christmas Day with Jean and Arthur in Brisbane, but he found himself still in Port Moresby and far from certain about ultimate victory. He wrote Eichelberger and thanked him for the gift of a captured Japanese sword, but rather than returning the general's Christmas greetings, he launched into a critique of Eichelberger's campaign to date. It was being done "with much too little concentration of force on your front," MacArthur told him. He wanted an attack in such force as would overwhelm the Japanese lines, reminiscent of the trench warfare of the last war.

Casualties, which MacArthur would later boast were low, were not on his mind at that moment. "It will be an eye for an eye and a tooth for a tooth — and a casualty on your side for a casualty on his," MacArthur wrote. Then, in words that sounded particularly calculating, he added, "Your battle casualties to date compared with your total strength are slight so that you have a big margin to work with."[54]

As a final prod, MacArthur sent Sutherland to the Buna area between Christmas and New Year's with full authority to get Eichelberger moving on MacArthur's timetable or relieve him. According to Paul Rogers, whose desk was in a corner of the sweeping veranda at Government House, MacArthur told Sutherland, "If Eichelberger won't move, you are to relieve him and to take command yourself. I don't want to see you back here alive until Buna is taken."[55]

PART THREE

REDEMPTION

1943

*I am indebted to General MacArthur for the high
statesmanship and breadth of world vision he has
contributed to the discussions. The complete integration of our concepts, which has been a source of such
strength in the past, will continue to the end.*

— WRITTEN BY MACARTHUR AND INSERTED
AT HIS REQUEST INTO A RADIO BROADCAST
DELIVERED BY AUSTRALIAN PRIME MINISTER
JOHN CURTIN, CIRCA DECEMBER 1, 1943

*MacArthur is shrewd, selfish, proud, remote, highly
strung and vastly vain. He has imagination, self-
confidence, physical courage and charm, but no
humor about himself, no regard for truth, and is
unaware of these defects. He mistakes his emotions
and ambitions for principles.*

— LIEUTENANT COLONEL GERALD WILKINSON,
MACARTHUR'S BRITISH LIAISON OFFICER,
IN A MEMORANDUM TO THE BRITISH
FOREIGN OFFICE, OCTOBER 15, 1943

MacArthur looks pensively out the window of his B-17, the *Bataan*, as he flies between Australia and New Guinea, circa 1943. *Courtesy of the MacArthur Memorial, Norfolk, VA*

CHAPTER THIRTEEN

Finishing Buna, Looking Ahead

Ｎew Year's Eve of 1942 was a moment of marked contrast for Douglas MacArthur and for the world. In one year's time, on the many fronts of a global war, the Axis tide had been halted, if not turned. In the South Pacific, Guadalcanal and Buna were not yet free of Japanese troops, but the Allies were advancing. In the Middle East and North Africa, the British had prevailed at El Alamein and were pushing Erwin Rommel's Afrika Korps westward toward the Allied forces landed under Operation Torch. In Russia, the expanse of that country and the sacrifices of Soviet soldiers had worn down the Nazi onslaught and trapped a German army at Stalingrad. Perhaps most important to ultimate victory, the American industrial complex had surged into high gear and was turning out ships, planes, and vehicles in staggering numbers.

The war was far from won, but the Allies perceived that it *would* be won. At MacArthur's forward headquarters at Port Moresby, there was still angst over Buna, but many remembered the despair of the year before as troops hurried to withdraw across the Calumpit bridges to Bataan. Incredibly, the year that had begun with destruction on Bataan and MacArthur's retreat from Corregidor had ended with MacArthur more admired and revered by the general American public than any other American army or navy officer. Asked in a *Fortune* poll in

November of 1942 to "name two or three living Americans you would really call great," ten million high school students ranked MacArthur a close second to Franklin Roosevelt, both of whom received almost ten times the support as the third and fourth names on the list, Jimmy Doolittle and Henry Ford.[1]

Rank-and-file Australians felt the same way. When the US Congress passed a joint resolution designating June 13, 1942, MacArthur Day—so picked to mark the forty-third anniversary of MacArthur's enrollment at West Point—Australia celebrated with equal enthusiasm by flying the American flag from public flagpoles. Two months later, a poll by the *Daily Telegraph* of Sydney found MacArthur to be "the most important public figure" in Australia, well ahead of Prime Minister John Curtin and eclipsing all others.[2] Many of the soldiers, sailors, and airmen under his command—Australians as well as Americans—remained less enthusiastic in their assessment, but this hardly mattered to the general public.

Despite Roosevelt and the Joint Chiefs agreeing to a Germany First strategy, there was considerable public support among Americans for a "Pacific First" effort. During 1942, until the November landings in North Africa, the Pacific was the only theater—save the U-boat war in the North Atlantic—in which American combat troops were directly engaged. Certainly there was an American commitment to defeating Germany, but the war in the Pacific, with its lingering images of American ships lying in smoking ruins as the result of a surprise attack, was at that point far more personal. These images had a profound and continuing impact on the collective American psyche, and Americans readily embraced MacArthur's public swagger and resolve. MacArthur carefully cultivated this hero image with his own stagecraft and publicity efforts, but frequently, they proved to be a double-edged sword, particularly with those under his command.

Responding to General Blamey about inevitable friction between Australian and American troops when they were in Australia, MacArthur suggested that attempts to use mandatory lectures to improve relations might do more harm than good. "The reaction of the American soldier to formal talks and lectures is not particularly favorable," he presciently noted. "He is quick to detect propaganda and inclined to resent it."[3]

This shrewd observation did not, however, stop MacArthur from dispatching his own propaganda. According to Australian war historian Gavin Long, MacArthur's "communiqués could not deceive the forward troops and indeed demonstrated a degree of indifference on the part of the flatterers who surrounded MacArthur towards the feelings of the men who were doing the fighting."[4]

The Dugout Doug songs and parodies took on new life when it came to lampoons of his ubiquitous communiqués. Among the most widely circulated were these lines:

Here, too, is told the saga bold
Of virile, deathless youth
In stories seldom tarnished with
The plain unvarnished truth.
It's quite a rag, it waves the flag,
Its motif is the fray,
And modesty is plain to see in
Doug's communiqué....

"My battleships bombard the Nips from
Maine to Singapore;
My subs have sunk a million tons;
They'll sink a billion more.
My aircraft bombed Berlin last night."
In Italy they say
"Our turn's tonight, because it's right in
Doug's communiqué...."

And while possibly a rumor now,
Someday it will be fact
That the Lord will hear a deep voice say,
"Move over, God—it's Mac."
So bet your shoes that all the news
That last great Judgment Day
Will go to press in nothing less than
Doug's communiqué![5]

Indeed, of all the enemies Douglas MacArthur faced over his long military career, the greatest threat to his playing an even larger role in World War II, and certainly to his long-term legacy, came from self-inflicted wounds — his own self-serving communiqués and public relations efforts being prime examples. MacArthur repeatedly demonstrated that he was not a team player when it came to American and Allied command decisions. He was definitely on a team, but it was his own team, and he was the undisputed captain of it — neither willing nor, perhaps, psychologically able to submit to others.

As US Marines splashed ashore on Guadalcanal and Roosevelt made the decision to land American troops in North Africa before the end of the year, no less a household staple than *Time* magazine reported that, his own headlines aside, MacArthur was presiding over "a secondary, rather than a second, front."[6] MacArthur was enormously sensitive to the indisputable fact that his theater was only a small part of the global Allied strategy.

The *New York World-Telegram* also noted this in an editorial a few weeks later and suggested that Australia could not receive — despite MacArthur's and Curtin's regular entreaties —"a larger share of planes and shipping without jeopardizing global strategy." The editorial was reprinted in Australian papers — perhaps with MacArthur's encouragement.

MacArthur complained to Marshall that the editorial "has caused a tremendous upheaval of bitter resentment throughout this country... [and] tends to destroy the morale of the Australian public." He suggested, "Such an incorrect and damaging statement should not be passed by American censors."[7]

Marshall made his usual patient response, noting that MacArthur had received regular high-level briefings about Allied global strategy and reminding him of "American newspaper practice regarding freedom of the press with particular reference to the editorial pages." But then Marshall got to the heart of the matter.

In the *Washington Post* and other papers, under the dateline "Gen. Douglas MacArthur's Headquarters in Australia, Aug. 6," Lee Van Atta, a wire services reporter, had quoted an unnamed spokesman who enumerated seven specific points that disparaged the American commitment to Australia, including characterizing the American-Australian supply line as "merely a 'big trickle' " and American airpower in the Southwest Pacific Area as "completely insignificant" when compared to the potential.

"Each of the seven points," Marshall scolded MacArthur, "was designed to deprecate the part played by the United States in aiding the war effort in your theater," and he concluded, "This press release originating from your headquarters can only serve to fan the indignation and resentment that has resulted from the editorial of which you complain."

Marshall ended by noting that Van Atta's article created the impression that MacArthur objected to stated policy and that he assumed "this to be an erroneous impression." Then, in case his words were to fall on deaf ears, Marshall succinctly recapped the global situation faced by the Joint Chiefs and stressed that widespread demands "make our problem exceedingly difficult and complex."[8] .

MacArthur responded immediately and denied that his headquarters was resorting to subterfuge to influence strategic control. Much as he had done on other occasions, MacArthur, who so zealously controlled information emanating from his headquarters, also denied that Van Atta had gotten his points from him.[9]

But it was hardly a secret that MacArthur disdained the global strategy of the Combined Chiefs of Staff. When Hap Arnold made his visit to Australia and New Guinea late in September, MacArthur went on at length about his opinion that England could "only be considered as a besieged citadel." No second front could be launched from England; air bases could never be established in sufficient numbers there to provide air cover for a second front, and any move into North Africa was a waste of effort. The one thing that made sense globally, MacArthur told Arnold, was that the Allies should be giving more aid to Russia.[10]

Arnold reported these views back to the Joint Chiefs as well as to the Combined Chiefs. Everyone well understood that it was the prerogative, indeed even the duty, of a theater commander to lobby for additional resources for his theater. MacArthur, however, took this to extremes and employed political and public pressure far outside the normal chain of command. It is difficult to imagine anyone else getting away with this, but ultimately Roosevelt judged that the rewards of MacArthur's image galvanizing American public opinion outweighed the political risks of firing him. It was left to Marshall to manage MacArthur as best he could.

Having contributed to the making of the MacArthur legend by spiriting him off Corregidor and putting up with his press releases and protestations, Roosevelt, Stimson, and Marshall found it difficult if not impossible to rein him in. Exasperated, Stimson tried one more tactic. He summoned the services of the World War I flying ace Eddie Rickenbacker, a man who still enjoyed considerable hero worship in the United States but carried it with a self-effacing humility. Rickenbacker was then president of Eastern Airlines and doing his part for the war effort with an occasional special assignment. Rejecting multiple offers to be commissioned a brigadier general, Rickenbacker turned down the two stars of a major general as well, telling Stimson, "Let me serve as a civilian, where I can do the most good."

So Rickenbacker was still just "Captain Eddie" when he left Hawaii in a B-17 early on October 21, 1942, destined for MacArthur's headquarters in Brisbane and charged with delivering a top-secret verbal message to him. It was "a message of such sensitivity," Rickenbacker recalled, "that it could not be put on paper." Stimson gave it to Rickenbacker verbally, and he memorized it "in order to be able to pass it on to General MacArthur the same way."

En route to Australia, Rickenbacker's B-17 overshot a refueling stop at Canton Island, and he and his crew were forced to ditch at sea. Their twenty-four days adrift in rafts became one of the epic survival stories of World War II, but after recovering, Rickenbacker continued on to see MacArthur, who by that time was at Port Moresby. According to Rickenbacker, they had not crossed paths since Billy Mitchell's court-martial, when they had said some unpleasant things to each other.

Rickenbacker had had plenty of time while drifting and recovering to mull over his message to MacArthur, and he resolved to deliver it without emotion. But MacArthur met him on the runway at Port Moresby—an accommodation he extended to very few—and threw his arms around him, exclaiming, "God, Eddie, I'm glad to see you." Rickenbacker melted briefly but delivered his message nonetheless.

Although Rickenbacker professed to remember every word of it, when it came time to write his autobiography, he refused to divulge it. "Stimson and MacArthur took it with them to the grave," wrote Rickenbacker, "and so shall I."[11]

It is not too far of a leap, however, to speculate that his message to MacArthur was a sharp reprimand, demanding that MacArthur cease his personal publicity campaign, stop complaining about the Joint Chiefs and the resources allocated to his theater, and stop waging war against the United States Navy.[12] If Rickenbacker indeed delivered such a message with the firmness Stimson intended, there is little, if any, evidence that MacArthur moderated his ways, certainly not in the final days at Buna.

Sutherland visited the Buna front twice during the week between Christmas of 1942 and New Year's in 1943, carrying MacArthur's insistent charge that time was of the essence. MacArthur had ordered Sutherland to get Eichelberger moving and finish the campaign or relieve him. Sutherland would have been Eichelberger's only readily available replacement, and there is some evidence that Sutherland had zero interest in taking over Eichelberger's I Corps command, no matter how temporary the assignment would have been. Not only would this have removed him from MacArthur's side and concomitant power, he also feared becoming stuck in the mire of Papuan operations. It was far easier to fly back and forth from Port Moresby as a critic than it was to take Eichelberger's place and be held accountable for results.[13]

MacArthur's perception notwithstanding, Eichelberger and the Thirty-Second Infantry Division had been moving forward despite stout defenses and a tangle of logistics. On January 2, 1943, Buna Mission fell, effectively eliminating Japanese resistance east of the Girua River. The next day, Eichelberger sent a message to his troops praising their efforts. "You are now veterans," he told them, "and the lessons which have been learned in this campaign must serve to reduce our losses in the future and bring further victory."[14]

The next step toward that victory was to face the final concentration of some seven thousand Japanese troops at Sanananda, midway between Buna and Gona. But as the Thirty-Second Division secured

Buna Mission and elements pivoted westward to assist the Australian Seventh Division, MacArthur issued a communiqué that gave the distinct impression that the battle was over. The annihilation of Horii's South Seas Detachment had been "one of the primary objects of the campaign," MacArthur reported on January 8, and "this can now be regarded as accomplished."[15]

That same day, MacArthur wrote Eichelberger in much the same vein, congratulating him on the success achieved and suggesting his return to Australia as soon as the Forty-First Infantry Division could be rotated in to relieve the Thirty-Second. Then, in contrast to his expressed sentiments from a month before, when he sent Eichelberger to the front, MacArthur added, "I am so glad that you were not injured in the fighting. I always feared that your incessant exposure might result fatally."[16]

The next morning, January 9, MacArthur, Sutherland, and Kenney flew out of Port Moresby and relocated their headquarters back to Brisbane. In doing so, MacArthur was anxious to emphasize his declared victory in Papua no matter how premature his field commanders considered it. At least part of his motivation came from Guadalcanal. The tough campaign there had proved MacArthur and Ghormley right in their preinvasion concerns about amphibious operations beyond the range of land-based air. By claiming he had things wrapped up in Papua when he did, MacArthur beat Halsey by a full month in reporting a major victory. Halsey did not acknowledge the final Japanese defeat on Guadalcanal until February 9.[17]

This rush to declare victory overlooked the Japanese troops still ensconced at Sanananda, and it left Eichelberger skeptical of MacArthur's motives. While the world greeted MacArthur's return to Brisbane as that of a conquering hero, Eichelberger sensed that MacArthur's premature actions would serve not only to downplay the final success when it came but also to hold Eichelberger alone accountable should the campaign drag on.[18]

As Eichelberger later put it, "Public-relations officers on General MacArthur's staff chose to call this last phase of the Papua campaign a 'mopping-up operation.' Instead, it was a completely savage and expensive battle." Even as MacArthur issued his "victory" communiqué,

Brisbane's *Courier-Mail,* well aware that Australian troops would bear the brunt of this last phase, acknowledged that "Sanananda...may take a while to master."[19]

It did. As the Allied noose tightened, the Japanese fought to the death. Around two thousand mostly sick and wounded Japanese troops evacuated in small numbers by boat and made their way north along the coast to Salamaua and Lae. Others were trapped as they tried to slip through the lines and flee west of Gona. Increased pressure on the Allied side came from the fresh troops of the 163rd Infantry Regiment of the Forty-First Division, recently landed at the growing airfield at Dobodura.[20]

"I never know which of you two to write to or whether you appreciate my letters," Eichelberger, referring to Sutherland and MacArthur, tellingly told Sutherland on January 16, "but I imagine you are always glad to get a word. Today I begin to see some signs that the Japanese may be clearing out of this altogether." Eichelberger went on to tell Sutherland, "You may assure General MacArthur that I will push things in every possible way, short of swinging a ball bat myself."[21]

Australian Lieutenant General Edmund F. Herring, who had come to work closely with Eichelberger, announced the end on January 22. Marking the real cessation of the fighting in Papua, Herring thanked all involved but paid special tribute to the infantry. "Seldom have Infantry been called on to endure greater hardships or discomfort," Herring wrote, "than those provided by the mountains, the swamps, the floods, of tropical New Guinea."[22]

On the American front, there can be no question that the Thirty-Second Division prevailed under those hardships. Whether the same result would have occurred in the time frame it did had Eichelberger not done MacArthur's bidding and fired Harding remains debatable. Even Eichelberger was not sure. "A great deal has been said and whispered about the 32nd Division," Eichelberger wrote, "and much of it makes no sense. The 32nd which 'failed' at Buna was the same 32nd that won the victory there."[23]

Much as they did in the American and Filipino defeat on Bataan, hunger and disease played a major role in the Japanese defeat. Major Mitsuo Koiwai, the only Japanese field grade officer of the South Seas

Detachment to fight from Buna to Ioribaiwa Ridge and back and live to tell about it, recounted after the war, "We lost at Buna because we could not retain air superiority, because we could not supply our troops, and because our navy and air force could not disrupt the enemy supply line." When asked about the effectiveness of the Allied attack, Koiwai said it had been skillfully conducted but added that the Japanese had "wondered whether the Americans would by-pass us and leave us to starve." Had the Allies not been so determined to take the Buna beach-head by direct attack, starvation would likely have accomplished the same thing in due course.[24]

But time had been of the essence, hadn't it? On January 28, MacArthur issued a communiqué announcing that Allied casualties in the Papua land campaign, including numerous deaths from illness, were less than half those of the Japanese. That much was true. "These figures," MacArthur continued, "reverse the usual results of a ground offensive campaign, especially against prepared positions defended to the last, when losses of the attacker are usually several times that of a defender."

That may have been true in certain historical circumstances, but what angered MacArthur's ground commanders, from Herring and Eichelberger on down, was his attempt at further explanation. "There was no necessity to hurry the attack," MacArthur reported, "because the time element in this case was of little importance; and for this reason no attempt was made to rush the positions by mass and unprepared assault." Eichelberger, who had labored under MacArthur's exhortations of urgency, was incredulous.

The only thing missing up to that point was a superlative appeal to history, and MacArthur took care of that in his final paragraph. "The utmost care was taken for the conservation of our forces," MacArthur concluded, "with the result that probably no campaign in history against a thoroughly prepared and trained army produced such complete and decisive results with a lower expenditure of life and resource."[25]

In future operations, for a variety of reasons, MacArthur's forces would sometimes achieve low casualty rates, but this was not the case in the grueling Papua campaign. Although seemingly detached at times from actual conditions on the Kokoda Trail or beyond Kapa

Kapa, MacArthur nonetheless undoubtedly understood that speed was his best weapon against the debilitating diseases and living conditions facing his troops. Indeed he rushed to announce the victory before it had occurred. Why, then, color the facts?

During the six months of the Papua campaign—from the initial Japanese landings at Buna to their final defeat at Sanananda—the Australians committed almost twenty thousand ground troops to the effort and suffered 2,165 killed and 3,533 wounded. Out of just less than fifteen thousand men engaged, American losses were 930 killed and 1,918 wounded. These numbers do not include countless noncombat cases of malaria, dysentery, and other jungle maladies. The Japanese committed between sixteen thousand and seventeen thousand troops to the campaign, of which some twelve thousand were killed. The remainder, including many wounded, were evacuated to Rabaul and Lae.[26]

On Guadalcanal, US Marine Corps and army ground forces suffered around 1,600 killed in action and 4,245 wounded out of sixty thousand engaged. Japanese losses out of thirty-five thousand army and navy troops fighting on the island were 14,800 killed or missing in combat and nine thousand dead of disease.[27]

Despite MacArthur's boast that "probably" no campaign in history had achieved such decisive results with such a low number of casualties, his command suffered twice the number of dead—3,095 versus 1,600—that the army and marines saw on Guadalcanal. He also had more troops wounded than they did—5,451 on Papua versus 4,245 on Guadalcanal. Considering that twice as many Allied troops were engaged on Guadalcanal as on Papua, one out of eleven Allied combat soldiers lost his life in Papua compared to one out of thirty-seven at Guadalcanal.

These losses were tragic. MacArthur may even have sincerely believed it was his duty to minimize them for morale purposes, but rather than stopping there, he went well beyond the facts to paint the results of his command in the best possible light, not only against contemporary commanders but also against the entire sweep of history. "The conclusion is inescapable," the official US Army history of the campaign acknowledged, "that the fighting in Papua...proportionate to the forces engaged, had been one of the costliest of the Pacific war."[28]

Despite this disregard for the facts in some of his Papua communiqués, MacArthur was right on the mark in others. "The outstanding military lesson of this campaign," MacArthur announced as Sanananda fell, "was the continuous calculated application of airpower... employed in the most intimate tactical and logistical union with ground troops." For months on end, MacArthur noted, "air transport with constant fighter coverage moved complete Infantry regiments and Artillery battalions across the almost impenetrable mountains and jungles of Papua, and the reaches of the sea; transported field hospitals and other base installations to the front; supplied the troops and evacuated casualties."

Having evolved a long way from his prewar attempts to downplay airpower, and by then readily seeing it as a radical change in warfare, MacArthur also presciently noted that it would "permit the application of offensive power in swift, massive strokes, rather than the dilatory and costly island-to-island advance that some have assumed to be necessary in a theatre where the enemy's far-flung strongholds are dispersed throughout a vast expanse of archipelagos."[29] Put simply, MacArthur was talking about island-hopping, about which much more will be said. But in the meantime, anyone doubting that MacArthur wrote—or, at the very least, heavily edited—his own press releases should read that last sentence again. MacArthur never said anything in one phrase that could be made to flow for three or four.

There were two final barrages to come out of the Buna campaign. One was personal and rather petty; the other went to the core of MacArthur's professional reputation and had global ramifications.

In dispatching Eichelberger to Buna, MacArthur had promised him glory and fame—and indeed, as he said he would, MacArthur released Eichelberger's name to the press. But after the American press focused on Eichelberger as the fighting general of the Southwest Pacific Area, MacArthur had second thoughts. He recommended Eichelberger for an oak-leaf cluster to go with his Distinguished Service Cross, but he made the award with a citation identical to the one he used for a dozen other officers, many of whom had not been in the front lines.[30]

Colonel Gordon Rogers, who was Eichelberger's I Corps intelligence chief, gathered recommendations for the Medal of Honor for Eichel-berger and submitted them to MacArthur's headquarters. Inexplicably, these were "lost," but when Rogers was reassigned to Washington some weeks later, he took another set with him. The War Department was in favor of the award, but protocol required MacArthur's approval. As in the case of Jonathan Wainwright the year before, MacArthur replied that he "didn't think a Medal of Honor was warranted."[31]

MacArthur was generous in awarding medals, including the second highest available to army personnel — the Distinguished Service Cross, of which he had two of his own from World War I. It seemed an unwritten rule, however, that awards for general officers were never to equal or outshine his own. Eichelberger came to learn that MacAr-thur's Medal of Honor slight — for the man who indeed had repeatedly risked his life to take Buna — was the least of his problems.

As Eichelberger recalled, he discovered that to steal "any publicity from MacArthur was like driving a dagger into his heart."[32] The trou-ble began when *Life* ran an article on the battle at Buna that included photographs of Eichelberger looking every bit a muddied and engaged hands-on battlefield commander. A week later, a *Saturday Evening Post* series, "These Are the Generals," featured Eichelberger after resistance came to an end at Sanananda.[33] According to Eichelberger, MacArthur sent for him shortly afterward. "Do you realize I could reduce you to the grade of colonel tomorrow and send you home?" MacArthur demanded. "Of course you could," Eichelberger responded. "Well," replied MacArthur, "I won't do it."[34]

What Eichelberger took from this strange encounter was a veiled threat: Eichelberger should minimize his personal publicity — in spite of MacArthur's earlier promises — or else. "I would rather have you slip a rattlesnake in my pocket than to have you give me any publicity," Eichelberger told an old friend in the War Department. Later, he went on at some length and professed to his brother: "I went through many unhappy months because of the publicity that came out about me after Buna. I paid through the nose for every line of it."[35]

It wasn't that MacArthur didn't hold Eichelberger in high regard. MacArthur wrote in his memoirs that Eichelberger "proved himself a commander of the first order, fearless in battle, and especially popular with Australians." Eichelberger himself acknowledged that MacArthur spoke highly of him. It wasn't a question of his abilities, Eichelberger concluded, but rather that MacArthur "didn't intend to have any figures rise up between him and his place in history."[36]

While there is probably considerable truth to Eichelberger's rendition of these events, it is likely that Eichelberger, who had his own measure of ego and bouts with paranoia, judged MacArthur a little too harshly. Although MacArthur did not choose Eichelberger when he needed a general to command the first American army in the Southwest Pacific theater—that story to come—MacArthur and Eichelberger would continue to work together all the way to Tokyo.

The other post-Buna barrage was a good deal more complicated. During the final days of the Buna campaign, Franklin Roosevelt, Winston Churchill, and the Combined Chiefs of Staff (except Leahy, who was sidelined with bronchitis) met for a major planning conference in Casablanca, Morocco. Churchill initially suggested Iceland in hopes that Stalin might attend, but Roosevelt decreed it too cold, and in any event Stalin declined to leave the Soviet Union while the situation on the German front remained volatile. As the location of the first wartime conference outside the United States, Casablanca suited Roosevelt perfectly. He could avoid going to London and, with it, any hint of subservience to Great Britain while highlighting the American combat effort in North Africa.

Three major strategic decisions affecting the Allied war effort came out of the Casablanca Conference. First, the offensive drive begun in North Africa would continue with the July 1943 invasion of Sicily. Second, there would be no invasion across the English Channel in 1943; instead, operations against Germany would focus on antisubmarine efforts in the North Atlantic and on round-the-clock bombing campaigns over the continent. Finally, while Germany First remained the overall Allied strategy, Admiral King successfully increased the resource allocation for the Pacific—for both Nimitz and MacArthur—from around 15 percent to 30 percent of the total war effort.[37]

This latter situation was somewhat forced upon the Joint Chiefs by Japan's ferocious reaction not only against Guadalcanal, where a modest American counterattack turned into an epic six-month campaign, but also against MacArthur in New Guinea, where it had taken the Allies six months to get back to ground zero at Buna.

At the time of the Casablanca Conference, strategic direction throughout the Pacific was still based on the "three tasks" directive of July 2, 1942. The Guadalcanal campaign, essentially task 1, had proved far costlier and lengthier than anticipated. MacArthur had encountered similar cost and time overruns simply by getting into a position where he could begin to execute task 2—seizing the remainder of the Solomons and New Guinea as far north as Lae. Task 3, the capture of Rabaul, looked increasingly difficult and far off.

Considering who was to command task 2 brought the Joint Chiefs back to the shadowy issue of unity of command. Any operations along the coast of New Guinea were well within MacArthur's Southwest Pacific Area. At the time, the remainder of the Solomon Islands was, too, although King and Nimitz, having witnessed the frenzied naval action around Guadalcanal, anticipated more of the same as the advance moved forward. They were as loath as ever to place major naval forces under MacArthur's command.

When Hap Arnold returned to Washington from his September 1942 inspection trip to the Pacific, he wrote Marshall a blunt memo urging unity of command in the entire Pacific. His reasons for wanting an army officer at the top were rather harsh on the navy. Arnold felt "the Navy has not demonstrated its ability to properly conduct air operations, particularly land-based air operations," and further claimed that it had no appreciation for logistics. This, Arnold said, had consequently hamstrung operations with a shortage of supplies and installations. (Evidently, Arnold did not give the navy credit for delivering the fighters Kenney's ground crews were uncrating and getting into the air.)

Knowing King would howl in protest, Arnold told Marshall that Roosevelt would have to order unity of command in the entire Pacific by presidential decree. Then Arnold recommended three army officers whom he judged qualified for such a command: MacArthur; Lieutenant General Joseph T. McNarney, an Army Air Forces officer serving as Marshall's deputy chief of staff; and Lieutenant General Lesley J. McNair, commanding general of the Army Ground Forces, who was responsible to Marshall for the training and logistics of combat troops deploying overseas.[38]

Just as he occasionally did with those of MacArthur's missives he judged likely to create a firestorm, Marshall did not respond directly. Instead he passed Arnold's memo to his war plans staff. Brigadier General St. Clair Streett, an airman and the head of the Pacific Theater Group, thought unity of command in the Pacific expressed a "Utopian view," but he suggested it might be made palatable to the navy if the right commander were chosen. Major General Albert C. Wedemeyer, chief of the war plans staff, agreed and advised that the top commander should come from the service branch that would carry the chief operational burden. At that point, Wedemeyer judged the Pacific to be largely an air operation, and he recommended Arnold himself.[39]

After reconsidering, Streett concluded that the chief obstacles to "a sane military" solution were the political ramifications involving Douglas MacArthur as a media star. To ease the situation, Streett suggested making MacArthur ambassador to the Soviet Union, replacing him in the Southwest Pacific Area with Eichelberger, then combining the South Pacific and Southwest Pacific Areas under either Nimitz or McNarney as supreme commander—"depending on whether air or Navy was considered to have the dominant role."[40]

MacArthur as ambassador to the Soviet Union was not as far-fetched as it now sounds. He would have been going to Stalin's proletariat and not the court of the Romanovs, but Russia nonetheless held a measure of intrigue for MacArthur. He was always one to recognize Russia's pivotal importance to Allied global victory, even if he skewed that importance toward the Pacific instead of Europe. MacArthur initially complained about aircraft and munitions going to Russia instead of to the Southwest Pacific Area, but he understood the same fundamental truth that Churchill and Roosevelt did: the Soviet Union was the essential key to victory and must be kept in the war.

Despite his prior hard-line positions—he had seen Communists behind every bush at the Bonus March—MacArthur issued a greeting to the Red Army while still on Corregidor, calling the defense of Moscow the "greatest military achievement in all history" and saying that the "hopes of civilization rest on the worthy banners of the courageous Russian Army." He was thinking far more militarily than politically at that point, but the fact that MacArthur could get away with releasing such a politically charged statement shows how difficult it was for Washington to control his press releases. MacArthur repeatedly called for early Soviet entry into the war in the Pacific and advocated that the much-touted second front be one that waged war directly against Japan.[41]

All Streett's recommendations came to naught, however. In a memo to Roosevelt, Marshall included a rather bland recommendation for further unity of command in the Pacific, at least between the South Pacific and Southwest Pacific Areas, but no action was taken. The truth of the matter was that as compelling as unity of command sounded from army and navy perspectives when each assumed it would hold the lead role, unity of command, even in Europe, was limited to a specific theater of operations and not given hemispheric or even continental scope. There were supreme commanders in the Mediterranean, Europe, and the waters of the North Atlantic as well as Southeast Asia. This got dicey in the South Pacific, where a theater dividing line bisected a tiny island, but the Joint Chiefs had managed that situation — on Guadalcanal — by moving the line a degree of longitude westward, then instructing MacArthur and Ghormley, and later MacArthur and Halsey, to work together.[42]

All this raises the question: Would Douglas MacArthur have been given supreme command of a unified Southwest Pacific and South Pacific Area if it weren't for the enmity he displayed toward the United States Navy (which, it should be noted, was readily reciprocated)? Secretary of war Stimson, who slowly but surely seems to have gotten his fill of MacArthur, confessed that MacArthur was "a constant bone of contention" between the War and Navy Departments and that his "extraordinary brilliance...was not always matched by his tact." Nonetheless, Stimson felt "the Navy's astonishing bitterness against him seemed childish."[43] Clearly, both service branches had to reach some measure of accommodation.

Prior to the Casablanca Conference, King had asked Nimitz to propose scenarios in which either Halsey or MacArthur would be in command of flanking maneuvers against the remainder of the Solomons that would avoid costly and time-consuming frontal attacks like those at Guadalcanal. Nimitz urged that task 2 of the original directive be changed to provide for Halsey to command in the Solomons instead of MacArthur. "I estimate that the bulk of the Pacific Fleet," Nimitz told King, "will continue to be required and I consider that any change of command of these forces which Halsey has welded into a working organization would be most unwise."[44]

While the Joint Chiefs were at Casablanca, navy planners concurred with Nimitz that the time had not yet come to turn over the Solomons campaign to MacArthur. They suggested, however, that MacArthur might be given direction over task 2, but only if his Southwest Pacific Area was responsible to Nimitz's Pacific Ocean Area command. That possibility sent shock waves through the army. While Marshall agreed in principle to unity of command in the entire Pacific, he chose to sidestep the lightning-rod matter of overall Pacific command and instead took King and the navy up on the suggestion that MacArthur be given strategic command of task 2 as an initial step.

Fine-tuning this notion, Marshall suggested—and King generally agreed—that the dividing line between the South Pacific and Southwest Pacific Areas should be kept as it was. MacArthur would have strategic direction of all forces involved in operations in the Solomons, New Guinea, and the Bismarck Archipelago with the ultimate objective of Rabaul, but Nimitz would retain control of the Pacific Fleet in any actions required to accomplish tasks 2 and 3 so as to be able to meet other exigencies around the Pacific. Further, Halsey, as commander of the South Pacific Area (COMSOPAC), responsible to Nimitz, would exercise direct command of all naval forces in the campaign against Rabaul. While subject to MacArthur's strategic directives about when and where to attack, Halsey would be answerable to Nimitz for just about everything else.[45]

King was not yet fully committed to MacArthur's assuming strategic control, but he nonetheless agreed when the Joint Chiefs asked MacArthur to submit his plans for carrying out tasks 2 and 3. Thus, as 1943 progressed, MacArthur was to have the immediate task of pressing operations in New Guinea from Buna toward Lae as well as working with Halsey in the Solomons. How well he could satisfy the Joints Chiefs with his strategic plans, and how well he could work with Halsey to implement them, remained to be seen.

CHAPTER FOURTEEN

"Skipping" the Bismarck Sea

During the six months since the Japanese beat MacArthur to the punch and seized the Buna beachhead, MacArthur's forces had fought a tenacious and costly campaign, first retreating and then advancing across Papua. Strategically, however, they were right where they would have been had they gotten to Buna before the Japanese. This weighed particularly heavily on Admiral King as the Joint Chiefs awaited MacArthur's plans for executing tasks 2 and 3 of their July 2, 1942, directive. MacArthur's initial response did nothing to alleviate King's apprehensions.

MacArthur merely dusted off the memo he and Admiral Ghormley had crafted before Guadalcanal and reiterated a five-step plan to capture (1) Lae and Salamaua, on New Guinea; (2) Gasmata and other toeholds on the opposite end of New Britain from Rabaul; (3) Lorengau, on Manus Island, in the Admiralty Islands, and Buka, at the western end of the Solomons; (4) Kavieng, on the northern tip of New Ireland; and (5) Rabaul itself.[1] MacArthur believed these phases were necessary, making possible the orderly advance of airfields to provide land-based air protection for naval movements and to bring bombers with fighter escorts over the ultimate objective, Rabaul. However, MacArthur asserted that he was not yet prepared to undertake *any* of these phases because he lacked sufficient ground and air forces.[2]

King retorted that MacArthur's reply was more of a "concept" than a "plan" and told Marshall, "It does not give us any concrete idea of what he intends to do or how he expects to do it or what the command setup is to be." Given the expanse of the Japanese-occupied Solomons between American-held Guadalcanal and MacArthur's target of Buka, King was especially concerned that MacArthur did not appear to have given much thought to Halsey's operations. King recommended that, unless MacArthur provided specific plans soon, Halsey should develop his own operations for the Solomons and the Joint Chiefs should withhold MacArthur's authority over the South Pacific Area.[3]

Complicating the planning for these operations was the fact that, at King's urging, navy planners were studying a westward advance across the central Pacific. Initially, this thrust would be against the Gilbert and Marshall Islands, the former a British protectorate captured by the Japanese within a week of Pearl Harbor and the latter a Japanese mandate since World War I. Striking directly westward across the central Pacific was the manifestation of the time-honored Plan Orange, and King saw this axis as the most direct route to Japan. His goal of stopping any Japanese threat to the West-Coast-to-Australia lifeline had been met at Guadalcanal, and he had little enthusiasm for conducting similar island-by-island fights across the expanse of the southwestern Pacific.

The ultimate planning challenge for the army and navy thenceforward would be to make operations on these two separate axes — west across the central Pacific under Nimitz, largely a navy and marines operation, and northwest from the Solomons and New Guinea under MacArthur, primarily an army action — complement, rather than complicate, one another.

In order to flesh out the details of his strategic plan, MacArthur suggested that he send representatives to meet with army and navy planners in Washington. Marshall concurred, and, although King himself was on the West Coast conferring with Nimitz, the Joint Chiefs directed MacArthur, Nimitz, and Halsey to dispatch officers from their theater staffs to meet and map out future operations in the Pacific. Before the conference could convene, however, MacArthur and his team had to contend with a counterattack against New Guinea.[4]

In early February of 1943, senior Japanese commanders at Rabaul held a strategy session of their own to discuss options on the northern coast

of New Guinea after the loss of Buna. Having also abandoned Guadalcanal, Imperial General Headquarters called for an "active defense" in
the Solomons while pursuing an "aggressive offensive" in New Guinea,
just as MacArthur had long feared. With the loss of Lieutenant General
Tomitaro Horii, the responsibility fell to General Hitoshi Imamura and
the recently created Eighth Area Army. Headquartered at Rabaul, the
Eighth Area Army comprised Lieutenant General Hatazo Adachi's
Eighteenth Army in New Guinea and Lieutenant General Haruyoshi
Hyakutake's Seventeenth Army spread throughout the Solomons.[5]

Adachi was a hard-drinking, stone-faced veteran from campaigns in
China who exemplified the Japanese warrior values of patience, perse-
verance, and endurance. He also wrote tanka—a structured form of
Japanese poetry—on the side. Imamura directed Adachi to fortify Lae
and prevent MacArthur from advancing westward along the New
Guinea coast. Well aware that Kenney's air forces were taking a toll on
shipping in the Huon Gulf between Buna and Lae, Adachi faced a

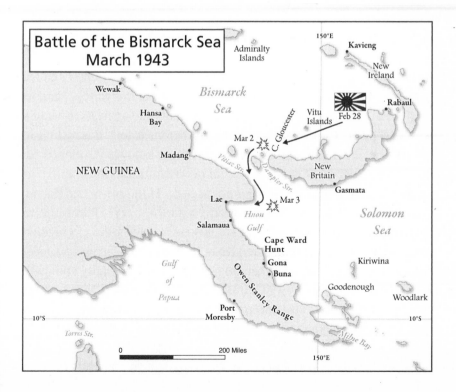

dilemma. He could land reinforcements at Madang— 140 air miles to the west of Lae and beyond the reach of most Allied air— and attempt to march to Lae via a roadless tangle of swamps, or he could transport reinforcements directly to Lae by ship and confront the full fury of Allied bombers and fighters.

The gritty Kanga Force, a small detachment of Australian troops, had been holding Wau and the Bulolo Valley since May of 1942 and receiving supplies and reinforcements mostly by air. When this force repulsed a Japanese offensive aimed at Wau and pushed toward Sala-maua, only twenty-five miles from Lae, Imamura and Adachi decided to reinforce Lae directly. The odds were not good.

Eighth Area Army staff war-gamed a ten-ship convoy inbound to Lae and estimated losses as high as 40 percent of the ships and 50 percent of their aerial escorts. Nevertheless, the urgent need to reverse the setback at Wau left no alternative, and on February 14, Imamura ordered Adachi to lead his Fifty-First Division to Lae by sea. Imamura and Adachi didn't know that the odds against them were worse than they thought.[6]

MacArthur's secret weapon was Ultra, the broad name for the special intelligence obtained by monitoring and decoding enemy radio traffic. Distinct from the US Navy's efforts to crack the Imperial Japanese Navy codes that gave warning of the Coral Sea encounter and led to victory at Midway, MacArthur's Ultra unit, Central Bureau, had its origins in a prewar group of army code breakers and analysts in Manila who evacuated from Corregidor shortly before it fell. Based first in Melbourne and then in Brisbane, Central Bureau slowly developed the capability to decipher Japanese military communications.

Directed by Brigadier General Spencer B. Akin, one of the Bataan Gang, Central Bureau worked closely with the navy's Ultra unit in Australia, the core staff of which had also evacuated from Corregidor. As a theater commander, MacArthur received both army and navy Ultra. These intercepts and their analyses varied in quantity and quality over the years, but by 1943, traffic analysis permitted MacArthur's subordinates to ascertain and plot detailed unit deployments, convoy schedules, and major aircraft movements with considerable certainty.

Like nearly everything surrounding MacArthur, the relationship between the Ultra operators of the War Department and US Navy and

MacArthur's Central Bureau code breakers was characterized by a degree of friction. But Edward J. Drea, the leading authority on MacArthur's use of Ultra, asserts that "overemphasizing this aspect diminishes an appreciation of the remarkable accomplishment of MacArthur's people, of the degree of cooperation, and of the exchange of Ultra intelligence among the three parties."[7]

The results were significant and consequential. Kenney utilized Ultra intercepts in planning air attacks, and they proved key to his aircrafts' ability to find Japanese ships. The key to sinking them was a tactic that Kenney and his deputy Ennis Whitehead perfected. Both men had experienced significant exposure during their careers to Hap Arnold's most cherished technique: high-level daylight precision bombing. But bomb drops from fifteen thousand or twenty thousand feet had not proved very effective in the southwestern Pacific, particularly against moving targets at sea. Having already worked with the legendary Paul "Pappy" Gunn to modify B-25s for strafing attacks by installing .50-caliber machine guns in the noses, Kenney—always the innovative engineer—ordered the relatively agile medium bombers to make low-level attacks and skip their bombs to the target.

Skip bombing was similar in concept to the favorite pastime of skipping flat stones across a pond. Twin-engine B-25s and A-20s came in at full throttle, flying 250 miles per hour at three hundred feet or less above the sea. Mere yards from the target, sticks of between two and four bombs equipped with four- or five-second delay fuses were dropped. With the proper angle of release, these skipped across the waves and either struck the side of the target and detonated or submerged and exploded below the waterline. Meanwhile, the bombers' machine guns and those of the escort aircraft raked the decks of the target ship and thereby suppressed its antiaircraft fire.

As General Adachi and most of the Fifty-First Division—some seven thousand men on eight transports escorted by eight destroyers— sailed out of Rabaul around midnight on February 28 and steamed west through the Bismarck Sea, MacArthur and Kenney fully expected a major Japanese effort to reinforce New Guinea. Kenney's overflights of Rabaul harbor in the preceding days had disclosed a large concentration of shipping reminiscent of the July 1942 buildup just before the landings at Buna. The question was, where would Adachi land—Lae, Madang, or even Wewak, farther west? Based on Ultra traffic analysis, US Navy cryptanalysts in the Melbourne unit handed MacArthur the answer and predicted that Adachi's convoy would land at Lae sometime in early March.[8]

This information, welcome though it was, posed the usual quandary in the use of Ultra intelligence: it had to be made to appear that the enemy movement had been stumbled upon in the execution of routine operations. Too specific a targeting of forces would be a tipoff to the Japanese that their codes or other communications had been compromised. Even with Ultra information in hand, actual intercept operations could still be chancy.

A reconnaissance aircraft spotted the Lae-bound convoy, designated Operation 81 by the Japanese, off the northern coast of New Britain on March 1 but lost it in the evening darkness. Shortly after dawn, contact was reestablished off Cape Gloucester, and by midmorning, long-range B-17s and B-24s from Port Moresby made their usual high-altitude attack, sinking one transport and damaging two other ships, an especially good score for high-altitude bombing. Hoping this might be the worst of it, the convoy churned on at a plodding seven knots and during the night passed from the Bismarck Sea into the Solomon Sea via Vitiaz Strait, the westernmost of the two passages between the Huon Peninsula and New Britain and its last chance to make a dash toward Madang.

As its ships moved through Huon Gulf in clear daylight, Operation 81 had some protective air cover, but these planes flew at seven thousand feet in anticipation of another high-altitude attack. That's when Kenney's medium bombers roared in just above sea level and skipped their bombs against the targets. "We went in so low we could have caught fish with our props," one pilot reported.

As the bombers skipped their payloads and fired their machine guns, P-38 and P-40 fighters, along with Australian twin-engine Bristol Beaufighters, strafed the decks of the transports as troops rushed topside to abandon ship when the bombs found their marks. The convoy was turned into chaos, and one after the other, the transports slowly began to sink. When the escorting destroyers moved to rescue survivors, they received a similar dose of bombs and machine-gun fire. It was a grisly business as bombers and fighters returned again and again throughout the day on March 3. Finally, PT boats from Buna moved in to finish off any crippled transports still afloat.

Over the running battle, eight Japanese transports and four destroyers sank. Only a handful of Allied planes and pilots were lost. Although records vary, of 6,900 troops in the convoy, an estimated three thousand died. Only one thousand reached their destination: the remaining survivors were rescued and returned to Rabaul on destroyers. General Adachi himself had to be pulled from the water. This loss of the Fifty-First Division as a fighting force marked the end of large-scale convoys to Lae and halted Japan's efforts at an "aggressive offensive" in New Guinea. Adachi turned his efforts to road construction from Wewak through Madang to Lae and reluctantly assumed an "active defense."[9]

By all accounts, the three-day action, which MacArthur immediately called the Battle of the Bismarck Sea—even though it was primarily fought in the waters of Huon Gulf, in the Solomon Sea—was a smashing Allied victory. MacArthur, Kenney, and Whitehead—not to mention their pilots and crews—might well have basked in unquestioned glory. But Douglas MacArthur had repeatedly shown that he was not often satisfied with the raw facts, no matter how exceptional and complimentary they might be to him. He had to reach for superlatives, even if that meant embellishing the truth.

In a March 4, 1943, press communiqué, MacArthur grandly announced, "The battle of the Bismarck Sea is now decided. We have achieved a victory of such completeness as to assume the proportions of a major disaster to the enemy. His entire force was practically destroyed." This was absolutely true. But MacArthur went on to describe the Japanese naval component as "22 vessels, comprising 12 transports and 10 warships—cruisers or destroyers," and claimed, "All are sunk or sinking." Additionally, he reported fifty-five Japanese aircraft destroyed and a staggering fifteen thousand troops "killed almost to a man."[10]

This tally of enemy ship and aircraft losses probably came from individual battle reports, which frequently duplicated sightings and sinkings as one air unit after another reported in. Even MacArthur's public relations chief, LeGrande "Pick" Diller, cautioned MacArthur to wait for a final accounting. MacArthur, however, simply responded, "I trust George Kenney." As Diller later remarked, "It wasn't up to me to verify the communiqués."[11]

Two days later, with Kenney's concurrence, MacArthur issued another communiqué affirming the ship and personnel losses but raising to 102 the number of aircraft shot down. This was essentially the accounting submitted to Washington by both MacArthur and Kenney in their official reports.[12]

Such high enemy losses, particularly when they were considerably more than Ultra estimates of vessels en route in the first place, were met with skepticism in Washington. Yet in the euphoria of victory, especially one so sweeping, this might have been the end of the matter. MacArthur, however, could not refrain from trumpeting the Bismarck Sea victory in a way guaranteed to incur the supreme wrath of the US Navy.

Around a month after the victory, secretary of the navy Frank Knox responded to Australia's latest expression of anxiety over fears of a Japanese invasion. MacArthur had frequently orchestrated such Aussie angst in order to apply political pressure to increase aid to his theater. And these expressions had become routine and continued despite Allied successes in New Guinea and the Solomons. In this particular case, Knox issued a reassuring statement noting that an invasion of Australia would require "a tremendous sea force" and there was "no indication of a concentration pointing to that."[13]

There was no reason for MacArthur to weigh in on the matter, but still basking in the Bismarck Sea victory, he couldn't resist. "The Allied naval forces can be counted upon to play their own magnificent part," he began patronizingly, "but the battle of the western Pacific will be won or lost by the proper application of the air-ground team." Despite his having just proved the opposite in the seas off Lae, MacArthur nonetheless maintained that "the Japanese, barring our submarine activities, which are not to be discounted, have complete control of the sea lanes in the western Pacific and of the outer approaches toward Australia."

But Australians should not fear. According to MacArthur, control of those sea lanes no longer depended primarily upon naval power but rather on airpower operating from land bases held by ground forces. Apparently forgetting the final days in Manila, when he had boasted that his thirty-five B-17s made the Philippines a fortress, MacArthur concluded, "The first line of Australian defense is our bomber line."

But then MacArthur twisted the knife. "A primary threat to Australia," he lectured, "does not therefore require a great initial local concentration of naval striking power. It requires rather a sufficient concentration of land-based aviation."[14] If MacArthur had made his point any stronger, he might as well have said that there was not much reason for the US Navy to be in the South Pacific. It was little wonder that General Marshall was told by his planning chief to expect a visit from Admiral King, who reportedly was more disgruntled than usual.[15]

Truth be told, MacArthur had a point—at least as far as the ever-increasing role of Kenney's air force is concerned—but this was hardly a very politic way to put it with the US Navy. Having knocked down the hornets' nest, MacArthur had to deal with the consequences.

Whether the navy's pique over this incident played any role in what happened next is uncertain, but Hap Arnold's staff in Washington decided to take a second look at MacArthur's and Kenney's claims of sinking twenty-two ships, downing 102 planes, and killing fifteen thousand soldiers in the Bismarck Sea. Considering it was wartime, they conducted a rather exhaustive review that included captured Japanese documents and Ultra intercepts. The inquiry concluded that there were never more than sixteen ships in the Japanese convoy and that, except for one rescue destroyer dispatched from Kavieng, no other ships joined it, as Kenney had claimed in trying to explain the discrepancy. Of this number, investigators confirmed that all eight transports and four destroyers were sunk, with a loss of around three thousand men.[16]

The results of this investigation were relayed to MacArthur and Kenney in August of 1943 with a request to file an amended action report. This was relatively routine and frequently occurred following the analysis of all after-action reports. But this time, there was no response from either MacArthur or Kenney. Three weeks later, Marshall wrote to MacArthur noting that his biennial report to the secretary of war was due. In the interest of incorporating "only uncontested factual material," Marshall said, "if the facts are as stated in [the] Air Force letter, I [should] be advised immediately and a corrected communiqué be issued."[17]

Wrong though he almost certainly was, MacArthur would not simply submit a revised report. Instead he fired off an angry response, which, coming from any other subordinate's pen, would likely have had him relieved. His original communiqué was factual as issued, MacArthur claimed, and subsequent data gathered confirmed every essential fact. Then he got personal, as only he could. "Operations reports and communiqués issued in this area," MacArthur wrote, "are meticulously based upon official reports of operating commanders concerned, and I am prepared to defend both of them officially or publicly."

If Marshall was not going to include his report as originally issued, MacArthur demanded that any report "challenging the integrity of my operations reports of which the Chief of Staff is taking cognizance, be referred to me officially in order that I may take appropriate steps, including action against those responsible if circumstances warrant."[18]

Given far more important ongoing matters, Marshall chose not to pick up MacArthur's gauntlet. He printed MacArthur's version in his biennial report to the secretary of war and was inclined to let the matter drop. Kenney, however, contested the findings of the inquiry in a point-by-point refutation to Arnold, who assured him that had he not been in Europe and ignorant of the air force investigation, he would have put a stop to it.[19]

This should have been the end of the matter, but MacArthur could not stop fighting. Two years later, in an interview held the day after accepting the final Japanese surrender, MacArthur brought up the Battle of the Bismarck Sea, calling it "the decisive aerial engagement in his theater of war" as he reflected on the course of the Pacific campaigns. "Some people have doubted the figures in that battle," he then noted, "but we have the names of every ship sunk."[20]

A few days after this interview, Kenney's headquarters created a committee to reexamine all records in the hope, according to one of the investigators, "that Japanese sources would bear out the Kenney-MacArthur position." When this didn't happen, the new report was never sent to Washington, and, according to one account, "MacArthur's headquarters ordered that the report be destroyed." Far from naming twenty-two ships, it had concluded that "the number of Japanese personnel lost was 2890, not 15,000, the number of vessels sunk twelve, not twenty-two," thus affirming the findings of the 1943 inquiry.[21]

Nonetheless, MacArthur and Kenney never wavered in their stated version. In the years that followed, they stood by it in interviews and their respective memoirs. Somewhat tellingly, two of MacArthur's most ardent supporters did not. Writing in *MacArthur: His Rendezvous with History,* Courtney Whitney gave the convoy total as sixteen ships and seven thousand troops, but instead of giving losses, he merely noted that there had been "some slighting comments" made about MacArthur's characterization of the battle as "a major disaster to the enemy." Intelligence chief Charles Willoughby, writing in *MacArthur 1941–1951,* correctly excused the higher numbers as early estimates that "included duplication of eyewitness accounts that was inevitable in haze and rain" and reported that Japanese records "definitely established that Kenney's raids got a minimum of eight transports and four of the eight destroyers."[22]

Much of this story is decidedly petty. But it must be recounted because it strikes to the core of the dark side of Douglas MacArthur. Kenney, writing in *The MacArthur I Know,* maintained that "the actual number [of losses] is unimportant and the whole controversy is ridiculous." The important fact, he continued, "remains that the Jap attempt to reinforce and resupply their key position at Lae resulted in complete failure and disaster."[23] Kenney was correct all around. But why couldn't MacArthur see that?

Samuel Eliot Morison, chronicler of the navy's official history of the war, was generous in his appraisal, even if MacArthur grumbled to Kenney that "he thought the Navy was trying to belittle the whole thing because they weren't in on it." It was understandable that MacArthur would base his official communiqué on early aviator reports, Morison wrote, "but such mistakes are common in war and inevitable in air war. It would be more credible to acknowledge the truth, which is glorious enough for anyone, than to persist in the error."[24]

D. Clayton James, MacArthur's most balanced and definitive biographer, agreed. "It is amazing," James wrote, "that MacArthur would have accepted their challenge to make the affair a cause célèbre, particularly since he could have quietly excused his erroneous statements on the grounds of incomplete battle reports." But as was evidenced by his intense and inflexible reactions in similar situations throughout his career—the Veracruz Medal of Honor recommendation and later

279

censorship exchanges with Marshall among them—whenever Douglas MacArthur perceived an affront to his honor, pride, or public image, no matter how incontrovertible the evidence against him, he did not retreat from his position.[25]

All of which gets back to Ultra. When Ultra intercepts confirmed the sinking of the lower total of ships within days of the battle, MacArthur and Kenney might have amended their reports then and there, particularly as these same intercepts were read in Washington and contributed to the skepticism over MacArthur's and Kenney's claims. But as Edward Drea observes, "Both commanders ignored ULTRA confirmations of results not to their liking. In other words, they exploited ULTRA when it supported their operational preference, but this did not necessarily mean that they regarded this intelligence as definitive, particularly when the ULTRA version of events conflicted with their own perceptions."[26]

For all his exaggerations and defiant intransigence, the Battle of the Bismarck Sea was unquestionably a defining moment for Douglas MacArthur, both in terms of his embrace of airpower as well as his professional and personal regard for George Kenney. MacArthur had already seen airpower applied to the jungles along the Kokoda Trail and had seen it used as a tactical weapon to move full regiments of men and supplies quickly and stealthily, but after the Bismarck Sea battle he saw it as an increasingly strategic weapon. "We never could have moved out of Australia," he told reporters after the war, "if General Kenney hadn't taken the air away from the Jap."[27]

Allied land-based air was proving itself in New Guinea and making a believer out of MacArthur. According to Eddie Rickenbacker's account of his visit with MacArthur a few months before the Bismarck Sea fight, MacArthur told him, "You know, Eddie, I probably did the American Air Force more harm than any man living when I was chief of staff by refusing to believe in the future of the airplane as a weapon of war. I am now doing everything I can to make amends for that great mistake."[28] MacArthur was learning. The question was, would the MacArthur of fact be able to catch the MacArthur of legend?

Fresh from the Bismarck Sea triumph, Kenney joined Sutherland and flew to Washington to represent MacArthur in what came to be called the Pacific Military Conference. They were indeed an odd couple, the proverbial Mutt and Jeff: tall, spit-and-polish Sutherland, who greeted everyone with a curt, commanding nod, and short, rumpled Kenney, who took his down-home, "How's it going, boys" attitude with him, whether on the flight line or in the staff room.

For both men, the conference marked a transition in their careers. Sutherland stepped out of MacArthur's shadow and into his own as a strategic planner. Having seen to theater operations as MacArthur's chief of staff, he increasingly focused on intertheater relationships and took on a quasi-ambassadorial role as a liaison between MacArthur's headquarters and the Joint Chiefs.

Kenney was hailed as the architect of the Bismarck Sea battle — no matter what the number of enemy losses might be — and he emerged as the champion of using the full spectrum of airpower. Hap Arnold and his British counterparts might promote heavy bombing to wear down German industry, but Kenney had proved airpower's value at all levels, from fighter support for ground troops to medium and heavy bomber strikes to transport operations for troop and supply movements.

Both men were well aware, of course, that they owed their positions and increasing prominence to Douglas MacArthur. In their own ways, they were both fiercely loyal to him, Sutherland as the by-the-book martinet, Kenney as the irreverent buccaneer, as MacArthur called him. In both instances, it was obvious that the more MacArthur believed in someone, the more power that person could assume and the more he could get away with. Unlike Sutherland, who eventually became a little too quick to decide what MacArthur wanted done, Kenney seems never to have taken advantage of the relationship and remained genuinely loyal to MacArthur, warts and all.

The Pacific Military Conference, convened in Washington on March 12, 1943, was a who's who of the supporting cast in the Pacific. In addition to Sutherland and Kenney, MacArthur also sent Brigadier General Stephen J. Chamberlin, his operations (G-3) officer. Halsey's South Pacific Area headquarters was represented by Lieutenant General Millard F. Harmon, commanding the army and air forces under Halsey; Major General Nathan F. Twining, commanding the Thirteenth Air Force; Captain Miles R. Browning, Halsey's mercurial chief of staff;

and Brigadier General DeWitt Peck, the chief Marine Corps planner on Halsey's staff. From the Central Pacific Area, Nimitz dispatched Lieutenant General Delos C. Emmons, commanding the Hawaiian Department; Rear Admiral Raymond A. Spruance, Nimitz's chief of staff; and Captain Forrest P. Sherman, of Nimitz's staff. Admiral King and General McNarney, the latter representing Marshall, welcomed the group but left Rear Admiral Charles M. "Savvy" Cooke Jr. and Major General Albert Wedemeyer to orchestrate the discussion.[29]

The first order of business was for Sutherland to present MacArthur's detailed strategy for carrying out tasks 2 and 3 of the July 2, 1942, directive. Code-named Operation Elkton, the plan fleshed out the five phases MacArthur had proposed and called for a two-pronged advance along the northeastern coast of New Guinea and northwest through the Solomons, culminating in the capture of Rabaul. The first step on the western prong would be to capture Lae to advance Kenney's line of operational airfields. Halsey had already made a small step in the Solomons beyond Guadalcanal by seizing the Russell Islands en route to New Georgia and Bougainville.[30]

A major bone of contention between the Pacific representatives and the Washington planners became the number of troops and aircraft available. MacArthur proposed — to which Halsey agreed — a total of twenty-three divisions for the Southwest Pacific Area and the South Pacific Area. But the planners foresaw only twenty-seven divisions in the entire Pacific by the end of September, 1943. That included US Army, US Marines, and Australian divisions, six of the latter being mostly militia units assigned to Australian defense.

If two of the remaining twenty-one divisions were assigned to the Central Pacific Area for operations against the Gilbert and Marshall Islands, this left nineteen divisions to be divided between the Southwest Pacific and South Pacific Areas. MacArthur was projected to get eleven divisions and Halsey eight divisions, in each case two divisions — or around twenty-five thousand troops — shy of what they judged Elkton required.

An even greater shortage of aircraft existed, with fifteen air groups in the two areas and forty-five requested. Even if there had not been an overriding concern about shipments of aircraft to the European theater, the planners judged a shortage of shipping problematic in deliveries to the Pacific. On the other hand, as for manpower, at the end of February in 1943, despite the Pacific being judged a secondary front, the US Army alone had 374,000 men in the Pacific, exclusive of Alaska, compared to 298,000 in the Mediterranean and 107,000 in the British Isles.[31]

Nonetheless, the scramble for resources led to the usual jockeying for position between the army and the navy as well as among the three Pacific areas. As Kenney put it, "Representatives of both the South and Central Pacific Areas were watching the situation very closely to see that, if anything was passed out, they would get their share of it before MacArthur's crowd from the Southwest Pacific grabbed it off."[32]

Wedemeyer finally reminded the group that the Combined Chiefs of Staff had committed to capture Rabaul. The Pacific commanders either had to find a way to execute the operation with the resources available or request a change in directive from the chiefs. Sutherland relented and agreed that the next step — moving on Lae and through the Solomons — might be accomplished with the resources available. Even then, however, Kenney warned that the operations could not occur until additional aircraft were received in September. With similar reservations, Halsey's South Pacific representatives agreed to proceed through the Solomons, leaving specific operations against Rabaul to be decided later.[33]

The Joint Chiefs directed the principal representatives to put that plan in writing. Without committing their respective commanders, Sutherland, Spruance, and Browning proposed that the available forces execute task 2, including Madang and the southeast portion of Bougainville Island, and extend the line forward to include Cape Gloucester and the islands called Kiriwina and Woodlark.[34]

The addition of Kiriwina and Woodlark was a major change to MacArthur's original Elkton plan, but it made sense, as these would provide Kenney with forward air bases both to support operations in the northern Solomons with medium bombers and to serve as a stepping stone for operational interchanges of air units between the South Pacific and Southwest Pacific Areas. (The latter was evidence that, reports of intertheater friction aside, there was considerable cooperation between MacArthur's and Halsey's commands.) The revised

Elkton plan still called for mostly a mile-by-mile, island-by-island advance, but an important change for Halsey was the decision to bypass New Georgia, in the midst of the Solomons, and capture Bougainville directly, thanks in part to the anticipated air cover from Woodlark.[35]

The end result of this sixteen-day conference was that the Joint Chiefs issued a directive on March 28 canceling their charge of July 2 of the prior year and outlining specific offensive operations in the South Pacific and Southwest Pacific Areas for the remainder of 1943. As Marshall and King had already tentatively agreed, the Joint Chiefs confirmed MacArthur's supreme command of his Southwest Pacific Area with no change in boundaries. They put Halsey under MacArthur's command for matters involving general strategy to facilitate intertheater cooperation and left the United States Fleet, other than the units the Joint Chiefs assigned to task forces in those areas, under Nimitz's control as CINCPAC.

Together, MacArthur and Halsey were charged with establishing airfields on Kiriwina and Woodlark, seizing the Huon Peninsula from Lae west to Madang, occupying Cape Gloucester, on the western end of New Britain, and moving through the Solomons as far as the southern portion of Bougainville. MacArthur was ordered to submit specific plans to the Joint Chiefs for the composition of task forces and the sequence and timing of major operations.[36]

No matter how MacArthur chose to sequence the actions, it was clear that there would be a pause in offensive operations throughout the South Pacific and Southwest Pacific Areas. King argued that during this self-imposed lull, the bulk of Halsey's South Pacific naval strength should be used to move against the Gilbert and Marshall Islands. But many of the same reasons for delay also existed there: a shortage of men, planes, and ships and the need to maintain the initiative and continue an aggressive advance beyond those points once they were captured. Instead, Admiral Spruance advocated moving part of the fleet back to Hawaiian waters as a safety measure—Ultra was thin during that period because of a change in codes, and there was some uncertainty as to Japanese whereabouts—and he recommended using other elements of the fleet to oust the Japanese from two tiny islands in the Aleutians in Alaska.

As part of the Midway operations the year before, Japanese troops had taken possession of the islands of Attu and Kiska, at the far western end of the Aleutians. The American response was to build the Alaska Highway, safeguard the Northwest Staging Route, via which airplanes were ferried to Russia, and pour men and materiel into a series of airfields and army bases. Now, with the rest of their Pacific operations idling, the Joint Chiefs agreed to the Alaskan operation. In May, a bloody battle ensued for Attu after the Allies skipped over Kiska, which planners thought to be more heavily defended. Later, the largest battle fleet ever to assemble in Alaskan waters, including three battleships and five cruisers, pounded Kiska before an invasion found that the Japanese had abandoned the island.

For MacArthur and Halsey, this meant that during the summer of 1943, the Alaskan theater and various on again, off again Japanese attempts to reinforce the Aleutians diverted Japanese naval forces to the northern Pacific and left the Solomons relatively quiet. Perhaps most significant to MacArthur, out of this northern campaign would come a new naval commander much to his liking.

And for all of Ernie King's impatience during 1943, as well as MacArthur's and Halsey's cries for more resources, America's industrial might was reaching a fever pitch in the summer of 1943. The United States had gone from having a total of eight aircraft carriers, including the seaplane tender *Langley,* on December 7, 1941, to having seven new *Essex*-class aircraft carriers and nine smaller *Independence*-class light aircraft carriers commissioned in 1943 alone. More were on the slipways, readying to be launched and commissioned during 1944. They would speed the drive westward across the Pacific, and no matter what his thoughts about the United States Navy were, Douglas MacArthur would be a prime beneficiary of their power. As Sutherland, Kenney, and Chamberlin returned to Brisbane and got to work on the revised Elkton plans, MacArthur decided it was time to meet with a man reputed to be almost as tough and opinionated as he was. It was time for him to meet Bill Halsey.

CHAPTER FIFTEEN

Meeting Halsey

William F. Halsey Jr. was always something of a brawler. Not quite three years MacArthur's junior, Halsey was born in Elizabeth, New Jersey, on October 30, 1882, while his father, an 1873 graduate of the United States Naval Academy, was away at sea. His mother, Anne Brewster, traced her roots to the Brewsters of Plymouth Colony, and her son, like MacArthur, grew up proud of his family lineage. William senior, both a strict disciplinarian and a keen academic, soon became an instructor at Annapolis, and "Willie" grew up in his shadow.

Wanting to attend Annapolis came naturally enough, but young Halsey wasn't one to excel academically. Even with family connections and a year at the University of Virginia, it took repeated efforts before he won a presidential appointment. The cadet battalion commander during Halsey's first year was Ernest J. King; among those cadets entering the academy the following year was Chester W. Nimitz.

Applying himself just enough to make respectable marks, Halsey put his passion into social and athletic pursuits. Nicknamed Pudge, he was short and stocky but had the rugged good looks of a solidly built sailor. He looked, the Academy yearbook maintained, "like a figurehead of Neptune." Like MacArthur, Halsey made up for what he lacked in athletic skill with unrelenting determination. When an injury sidelined the Academy's varsity fullback, Halsey moved into his slot. Halsey later claimed he was the worst fullback ever to play for Annapolis, but he earned a varsity *N* and the coveted Thompson Trophy Cup, awarded to the midshipman who has done the most to promote athletics.

After graduating in 1904, Halsey reported to the aging battleship *Missouri* for a two-year tour, sailed around the world on board the brand-new battleship *Kansas* as part of Theodore Roosevelt's Great White Fleet, then became a destroyer man. From 1910 until 1932 — except for one year as executive officer of the battleship *Wyoming* — all Halsey's sea duty was on destroyers, including a stint chasing U-boats during World War I. Much as MacArthur did in the trenches, Halsey had no trouble asserting command. When his seniority put him in charge of two US destroyers and two British sloops, Halsey confessed that he "had the time of my life bossing them around."[1]

In 1933, while MacArthur was serving as chief of staff, Halsey, by then a seasoned captain, spent a year at the Naval War College. The following year, he attended an exchange program at the Army War College and rubbed shoulders with Lieutenant Colonel Jonathan Wainwright. But then Ernie King, who had just gotten his first stars as a rear admiral and taken command of the navy's Bureau of Aeronautics, made Halsey an offer he couldn't refuse. If Halsey would take the aviation observers' course at the navy's flight school at Pensacola, King promised him command of the aircraft carrier *Saratoga*.

Many army officers, particularly MacArthur, disparaged the navy in the 1930s for not embracing the potential of aviation, although when it did so, they criticized it for infringing on the army's turf. In many respects, this sparring was a long and undeserved hangover from the Billy Mitchell era. Certainly King and others did their part for naval aviation during the 1930s, and King was about to push the limits of aircraft carrier operations much further. He needed commanders who got things done and weren't afraid to make waves, and he recognized those qualities in Bill Halsey.[2]

On the morning of December 7, 1941, Halsey was a vice admiral on board the *Enterprise* in command of a task force that had just delivered a marine fighter squadron to Wake Island. During the six months that followed, MacArthur dramatically occupied the headlines and the public's imagination, but Halsey came in a close second. With relatively little fanfare, he took the *Enterprise* on daring raids against Japanese positions in the Marshall Islands. Although these were largely nuisance raids, Halsey's efforts were the first counterattacks in the Pacific, and they provided a huge morale boost to the American public. Halsey got some press for these efforts, but unlike MacArthur, whose office cranked out daily press communiqués from wherever he happened to be, the navy, at King's insistence, kept a much tighter lid on publicity. King was adamant about not offering the enemy any hints of the whereabouts of his ships or where they might strike next.

Halsey's success sparked the confidence to launch the Doolittle Raid, and in April of 1942, he took Doolittle's raiders within 650 miles of Tokyo, the particulars of which King guarded even more closely. Afterward Halsey would have assumed overall command at Coral Sea had the *Enterprise* and *Hornet* returned from the Doolittle Raid a couple of days sooner. He missed Midway because of a debilitating illness, but when it was time for his return, in September of 1942, it didn't take King and Nimitz long to decide that Bill Halsey was the strong tonic they needed to salvage operations on Guadalcanal.

In their initial exchange of messages during the fall of 1942, MacArthur and Halsey were formal, cautious, and highly protective of their own resources. Each had his hands full wrapping up Buna and Guadalcanal, respectively, and was in no position to offer more than limited assistance to the other. One of their exchanges had been particularly edgy. Fearing a renewed Japanese assault in the Solomons, Halsey appealed to MacArthur for the loan of a few heavy bombers. MacArthur declined, noting in a "boy-that-cried-wolf" reprimand that the "emergency anticipated by you in your previous dispatches has failed to materialize" and that "my own operations envisage the maximum use of my air forces." MacArthur added, however, that he might consider some support in the future if Halsey submitted "some knowledge" of his intentions. At present, MacArthur said, "I am in complete ignorance of what you contemplate."[3]

Halsey thought he was being treated like a schoolboy asking to use the restroom and forwarded MacArthur's reply to Nimitz. Nimitz counseled calm, and Halsey ultimately agreed, but not without referring to MacArthur as Little Doug and telling Nimitz, "I refuse to get into a controversy with him or any other self-advertising Son of a Bitch."[4]

But once the Joint Chiefs issued their directive of March 28, 1943, for what would become Operation Cartwheel against Rabaul, it became essential that MacArthur and Halsey work closely together and coordinate their plans — otherwise Halsey would be the proverbial man caught in the middle. As Halsey recalled, "My original hat was under Nimitz, who controlled my troops, ships, and supplies; now I had another hat under MacArthur, who controlled my strategy."[5] Halsey felt that he had no option but to insist on a face-to-face meeting with MacArthur. How well Mars and Neptune would get along remained to be seen.

After almost a year in Australia, Douglas MacArthur had not earned a reputation as a welcoming host. Several months before, he had done his best to discourage Nimitz and secretary of the navy Frank Knox from stopping in Brisbane while on an inspection tour of the South Pacific. After offering a long memo on strategy, MacArthur concluded, "An exchange of views may preclude the necessity for an immediate conference that requires long journeys and prolonged absence of higher commanders." As to his coming to meet them at Nouméa, MacArthur professed, "Present circumstances here involving current operations and the question of passage of command to an officer of another nationality prevent my leaving the area at this time."[6]

Nimitz and Knox took the hint and did not stop in Brisbane. Marshall queried MacArthur about the particulars, telling him, "Indirectly I gather that the visit to Brisbane was cancelled primarily due to receiving no...word of acknowledgement from you. I also gather indirectly that a message was received from you pointing out that no useful purpose might be served by such a conference." To this MacArthur made no reply, and Knox told Marshall that he wished the matter dropped.[7]

With Halsey, however, it was different. For one thing, the Joint Chiefs had just made it clear that, at least at a strategic level, Halsey would be answerable to MacArthur. It also no doubt helped Halsey's cause that MacArthur recognized and responded well to Halsey's growing reputation as a no-nonsense, rough-and-tumble fighter. Having earned the four stars of a full admiral for his tenacity around Guadalcanal, Halsey had recently appeared on the cover of *Time* looking every bit the fighting sailor. His was arguably the second most recognized name in the

Pacific, after only MacArthur himself. While MacArthur usually bristled when one of his subordinates threatened to outshine him—as was the case with Eichelberger—he looked upon Halsey as almost an equal and certainly the best thing he had seen come out of the navy.

Somewhat to Halsey's surprise, MacArthur responded graciously to his request for a meeting and extended a warm invitation to arrive in Brisbane on April 15, 1943. MacArthur never did anything halfway, so having determined to meet with Halsey, he greeted him in person as Halsey's amphibious PB2Y Coronado taxied to a stop at the Brisbane wharf. When Halsey alighted, MacArthur shook his hand with all the enthusiasm of a long-lost friend.

But as the group walked from the wharf to the waiting cars, one innocuous comment almost ruined the mood. Brigadier General Julian Brown and Commander H. Douglass Moulton, two of Halsey's senior staff, were walking together when Brown started a causal conversation. "Say, Doug," Brown began with a gesture to Moulton. MacArthur stopped short, spun on his heel, and fixed an icy stare on Brown, who nervously motioned that he had been speaking to Moulton and not the general. Without comment, MacArthur wheeled back around and resumed his friendly conversation with Halsey as he led the way to the cars.[8]

Although the two four-star officers had never met, Halsey remembered a tenuous connection. Their fathers had served together during their respective army and navy tours in the Philippines. "Five minutes after I reported," Halsey later wrote in his memoirs, "I felt as if we were lifelong friends. I have seldom seen a man who makes a quicker, stronger, more favorable impression. He was then sixty-three years old, but he could have passed for fifty. His hair was jet black; his eyes were clear; his carriage was erect. If he had been wearing civilian clothes, I still would have known at once that he was a soldier.

"The respect that I conceived for him that afternoon grew steadily during the war," Halsey continued, and "I can recall no flaw in our relationship." To be sure, they had their arguments, Halsey acknowledged, but he claimed, "They always ended pleasantly. Not once did he, my superior officer, ever force his decisions upon me."[9]

For his part, MacArthur professed to remember Halsey from his days on the gridiron against Army. He characterized Halsey as "blunt, outspoken, [and] dynamic," and noted, "He had already proven himself to be a battle commander of the highest order." Indeed, it was Halsey's devil-may-care, bulldog tenacity that seemed to appeal to MacArthur the most. "His one thought," MacArthur recalled, "was to close with the enemy and fight him to the death."

Perhaps remembering his frustration with a long line of naval commanders, MacArthur wrote, "The bugaboo of many sailors, the fear of losing ships, was completely alien to his conception of sea action. I liked him from the moment we met, and my respect and admiration increased with time. His loyalty was undeviating, and I placed the greatest confidence in his judgment. No name rates higher in the annals of our country's naval history."[10]

Far from being like oil and water, MacArthur and Halsey proved to be of much the same ilk, and they responded extraordinarily well to one another. The two immediately formed a mutual admiration society, much to the surprise of their staffs and perhaps to their own surprise. A month after their visit, Nimitz couldn't help but tweak Halsey just a little by starting a routine communication with "Dear Bill, I enclose a clipping from this morning's Honolulu Advertiser which you may find of interest. I note that 'General MacArthur and Admiral Halsey are kindred souls.' "[11]

So the two "kindred souls" got down to work. Halsey was particularly eager to convince MacArthur of the need to seize New Georgia, in the central Solomons, and the principal Japanese airfield at Munda. He felt strongly that this was the next logical step toward Bougainville, because New Georgia would provide forward airfields to support that assault. While specifying that the occupation of the Solomon Islands would include the southern portion of Bougainville in its directive of March 28, the Joint Chiefs had omitted New Georgia, intending to bypass it, and Halsey was not certain where he stood with MacArthur in that regard.

He need not have worried. MacArthur had become the apostle for forward air bases in his theater—both to harry Rabaul and its environs and to protect his advance—and he readily agreed with Halsey about the need for the same in the Solomons. Their first lockstep together would be for Halsey to seize New Georgia while MacArthur took unoccupied Kiriwina and Woodlark, east of Buna in the Solomon Sea.

The end result of their three-day series of meetings was a plan code-named Elkton III, which MacArthur issued on April 26. It was an evolution of the previous Elkton plans to capture Rabaul that MacArthur's staff had been working on since the end of the Buna campaign. It was also the first phase of Operation Cartwheel, the continuing strategy to capture Rabaul by early 1944. Cartwheel initially called for thirteen amphibious landings between the Southwest Pacific and South Pacific theaters over an eight-month period.[12]

Halsey was happy, but for unknown reasons MacArthur stalled sending the Elkton III plan to the Joint Chiefs. This delay gave Admiral King room to grumble to Marshall that MacArthur's forces had been idle since Buna and should be prodded into action. Marshall asked MacArthur for a status report, and MacArthur promptly forwarded the Elkton details along with proposals for the other pieces of Operation Cartwheel. He anticipated that the Kiriwina–Woodlark–New Georgia phase with Halsey would kick off around June 1. Barely had MacArthur reported this to Marshall, however, when he was forced to postpone the initial assaults by two weeks and then by a full month, to June 30, because of shipping delays and landing-craft shortages.[13]

This "inactivity," as King termed it, gave rise to another request from King to Marshall that MacArthur be required to set precise dates for each of the subsequent Cartwheel landings. MacArthur replied with a tentative date of September 1 for operations against Lae in New Guinea, but refused to provide dates for the subsequent pieces, noting that the start of each phase was "so dependent on the degree of success attained and probable enemy reaction that an estimate of dates is pure guess work."[14]

King's request for specific dates wasn't just a matter of being difficult. As chief of naval operations and commander in chief of the United States Fleet, King had to know the what, where, and when of the navy's amphibious commitments. King also had to plan for the navy's long-awaited push across the central Pacific. Much to the navy's satisfaction,

Roosevelt, Churchill, and the Combined Chiefs of Staff approved the central Pacific offensive at their post-Casablanca conference, which was held in Washington in May and code-named Trident. Consequently, the Joint Chiefs ordered Nimitz to seize the Marshall and Caroline Islands, including the major Japanese base at Truk, which was in fact more important than Rabaul as a linchpin of Japanese naval operations, by early 1944.[15]

This was the epitome of Plan Orange. When MacArthur learned of it from Marshall in mid-June, he howled in protest, particularly upon realizing that it anticipated taking the battle-hardened First Marine Division from his theater and the Second Marine Division from Halsey's as well as considerable naval forces and two bomber groups. "Air supremacy is essential to success," MacArthur responded, and "the withdrawal of two groups of bombers would, in my opinion, collapse the offensive effort in the Southwest Pacific Area." He went on to tell Marshall, "In my judgment the offensive against Rabaul should be considered the main effort and it should not repeat not be nullified or weakened by withdrawals to implement a secondary attack" in the central Pacific.[16]

Once again MacArthur championed his view that the best offensive in the Pacific was a movement from Australia through New Guinea to Mindanao. These operations could be supported by land-based air, whereas any operations in the central Pacific required amphibious assaults against enemy troops who were themselves supported by established land-based aviation. "Moreover," MacArthur pointed out, on the central Pacific axis "no vital strategic objective is reached until the series of amphibious frontal attacks succeed in reaching Mindanao." He could get to the same objective more quickly and with less risk via New Guinea.[17]

Marshall was in no way swayed by MacArthur's arguments against the central Pacific operations, nor was he convinced that the southwestern Pacific axis was the most feasible line to Mindanao, particularly since the entire issue of needing to return to the Philippines in order to defeat Japan was still simmering in the background. But Marshall did come to MacArthur's defense over the planned diversion of resources. He agreed that reducing the trained amphibious forces planned for MacArthur's and Halsey's commands would jeopardize the prosecution of Operation Cartwheel.

After some back-and-forth between King and Marshall, the Joint Chiefs agreed that MacArthur could keep the First Marine Division, revitalized in Australia following Guadalcanal, and Halsey could rely on the Third Marine Division, newly arrived in the Solomons for training after organizing in New Zealand, for the Bougainville offensive. Only the Second Marine Division would be diverted to help Nimitz. In return, MacArthur agreed to support the Joint Chiefs' overall planning by providing anticipated invasion dates beyond Lae, including Halsey's push to Bougainville by mid-October and his own jump to Cape Gloucester, on New Britain, by December 1.[18]

Meanwhile, the Japanese response in anticipation of these plans had begun.

After his visit with MacArthur, Halsey spent a few days making a goodwill tour through Canberra, Melbourne, and Sydney. At that point, with Nimitz having gotten no closer to Australia than Nouméa and MacArthur's naval commanders rating barely a mention, Halsey quickly became the face of the upper echelon of the American navy in Australia and an Aussie favorite, in part for his straight-talking manner. When asked why Halsey had waited so long to meet MacArthur, a spokesman told the *Sydney Morning Herald,* "The only reason Admiral Halsey had not visited General MacArthur sooner was because the Admiral was too busy fighting the war."[19]

Halsey arrived back in Nouméa on April 25, but his extended tour in Australia kept him away from his headquarters for one of the most dramatic events of the war. Ultra information in Nimitz's headquarters uncovered the travel itinerary of Admiral Yamamoto in minute detail. The architect of the attack on Pearl Harbor would be flying from Rabaul to Bougainville in the Solomons to encourage a massive aerial counteroffensive that he had planned against both MacArthur's and Halsey's forces.

On April 7, Yamamoto had sent several hundred planes against Guadalcanal, and he dispatched similar numbers against Port Moresby and Milne Bay several days later. The attackers suffered severe losses without inflicting significant damage to Allied air bases or shipping, but grossly optimistic reports of the results by Japanese aviators encouraged Yamamoto to take a victory lap at forward bases on Bougainville.

When the decision was made to target Yamamoto, Rear Admiral Marc Mitscher, commander of air operations in the Solomons, assigned the mission to army twin-engine P-38 Lightnings equipped with long-range drop tanks. To preserve the secrecy of Ultra, Mitscher ordered other long-range patrols so that the key intercept flight would not stand out as specifically targeting Yamamoto. The result was that early on Sunday morning, April 18, the P-38s made an almost perfect rendezvous with two Japanese G4M "Betty" bombers carrying Yamamoto and his party. Outdueling an escort of Zero fighters, the P-38s sent Yamamoto's bomber crashing into the jungle and the other bomber into the sea. Admiral Yamamoto was among the casualties, and his absence from the Japanese high command would be keenly felt as the war ground on.[20]

Other than entertaining Halsey at the time, MacArthur had nothing to do with the intelligence or the mission, but that did not stop him from writing a dramatic account in his memoirs that managed to convey a sense that his command had been responsible for the results. In one of the few instances where he employed the plural rather than the singular, MacArthur cited "our Air Force" and noted that "we made one of the most significant strikes of the war." With patented MacArthur hyperbole, he concluded, "One could almost hear the rising crescendo of sound from the thousands of glistening white skeletons at the bottom of Pearl Harbor."[21]

Even without Yamamoto, the Japanese high command was determined to press its strategy of an "active defense." MacArthur's unopposed landings on Kiriwina and Woodlark on the night of June 29–30 became a training exercise for amphibious operations, but Halsey's troops, landing on Rendova Island and other points in the New Georgia Islands, fought bitter opposition for the better part of two months. On June 30, MacArthur also put elements of the 162nd Infantry Regiment of the Forty-First Division ashore against little opposition at Nassau

Bay, northwest of Buna. This landing was in support of the Australians fighting around Wau and in anticipation of the drive against Lae. These actions in MacArthur's theater brought two new faces to the forefront.

The first was Rear Admiral Daniel E. Barbey. Born in Portland, Oregon, in 1889, Barbey graduated from Annapolis in 1912 and saw service mostly on destroyers as an engineering officer prior to and during World War I. Likable and easygoing, Barbey had an engineer's brain for solving problems. Between the wars, his sea duties included tours on the battleship *Oklahoma* and command of a destroyer division in the Pacific. His shore assignments found him at Annapolis as an aide to the superintendent and in Washington working on war plans and studying Japan's military operations in China. In the latter assignment, Barbey became interested in Japan's use of landing craft with hinged bows for amphibious operations. By 1940, this led to his updating Fleet Training Publication 167 — the Landing Operations Doctrine — which became the bible of the US Navy's amphibious operations.

By then a captain, Barbey spent time with the Atlantic Fleet and supervised amphibious training along the North Carolina coast for both the First Marine and First Infantry Divisions. In May of 1942, King tapped him to organize the navy's new amphibious warfare section, which in addition to amphibious training included supervision of what would become a gargantuan landing craft construction program. This got Barbey his first stars, and in December of 1942, King ordered him to Australia in response to MacArthur's amphibious needs.

He didn't have much to work with. Establishing his headquarters on the aging attack transport *Henry T. Allen* — Barbey claimed that it trailed a telltale oil slick wherever it went — he initially had only three Australian transports and a handful of beach landing craft: LSTs (landing ship, tank), LCIs (landing craft, infantry), and LCTs (landing craft, tank). This shortage of shipping, particularly ship-to-shore craft, was one reason MacArthur and Kenney had come to rely so heavily — and ingeniously — upon airpower to advance the Papuan campaign. When King turned MacArthur's Southwest Pacific Force into the Seventh Fleet, Barbey became the commander of the VII Amphibious Force and slowly began to receive more resources.[22]

The Kiriwina and Woodlark landings were the VII Amphibious

Force's first operational test. It proved a good thing that the landings were unopposed. Seasickness among the disembarking troops was the least of the problems as Barbey, who quickly became "Uncle Dan, the Amphibious Man," chose to make a night landing and withdraw before dawn to avoid interference from Japanese aircraft. At one level this made great sense, but sailing around in the dark spotlighted the inexperience of his crews and the amount of time it took to reach the right landing zone and unload. When geography intervened, as it did on a sandbar on Woodlark and a necklace of coral reefs encircling Kiriwina, it took even longer. The Kiriwina landings dragged on for almost two weeks. It was a lesson in what became Barbey's mantra for such operations: get on and off the beach as quickly as possible and hope for plenty of air cover.[23]

Barbey was initially taken aback when MacArthur, displaying his long-held bias against the navy, told him early on, "Since you were on Admiral King's staff, I assume you will write to him from time to time as well as to other friends in the Navy Department; but it is well to remember that echoes of what you say will come back to me." But Barbey slowly warmed to MacArthur's leadership and later claimed, "General MacArthur proved to be the finest commander I have ever worked for...He gave his subordinates a job and then left to them the details of how it was to be done."[24]

That said, "MacArthur was never able to develop a feeling of warmth and comradeship with those about him," Barbey wrote in his memoirs. "He could not inspire the electrifying leadership Halsey had. He was too aloof and too correct in manner, speech, and dress. He had no small talk, but," Barbey admitted, "when discussing military matters he was superb."[25]

It would take MacArthur some time to come to trust Dan Barbey, but as with George Kenney and his air operations, the key to earning that trust would be operational success in delivering MacArthur's troops where he wanted them. With the possible exception of unabashed patriotism, there was nothing MacArthur admired more or responded more positively to than operational success — getting the job done.

Another MacArthur subordinate whom the general would come to trust and value highly also made his debut during the operations against

Kiriwina and Woodlark. Walter Krueger was born in Flatow, West Prussia, then part of the German Empire (now Zlotow, Poland), on January 26, 1881 — one year to the day after Douglas MacArthur. Krueger's career rise, however, was almost exactly the opposite of MacArthur's. His father, an officer in the German army during the Franco-Prussian War, died when Krueger was four, and his mother immigrated with her three children to Saint Louis, Missouri, to be near her uncle.

In the summer of 1898, during the excitement of the Spanish-American War, Krueger and some of his high school buddies enlisted in the army. Short-lived though the war was, Krueger spent eight months on occupation duty in Santiago, Cuba, before reenlisting and getting his first look at the Philippines while fighting Aguinaldo's resistance. During this service he rose through the ranks from private to second lieutenant. Staff schools and a second tour in the Philippines followed, along with postings on the Mexican border against Pancho Villa and in France during World War I.

Between the wars, Krueger was posted to the United States Army Infantry School, at Fort Benning; the Army War College; and the War Plans Division, where he worked on the color-coded plans, particularly Plan Green (which prepared for a hypothetical war with Mexico) and Plan Orange. He requested assignment to an exchange program at the Naval War College because of his interest in the study of command, particularly the dynamics of interservice cooperation. "Doctrine," he wrote for one of his courses, "knits all the parts of the military force together in intellectual bonds, and assures that each part will work intelligently for the interests of the others and of the whole."

In June of 1932, after the better part of a decade in staff and command colleges as both student and instructor, Krueger returned to command of troops as a colonel leading an infantry regiment at Jefferson Barracks, in Missouri. Like many regular officers between the wars, Krueger resigned himself to serving out his career short of his goal of generals' stars. But two years later, he returned to the War Plans Division in Washington, becoming its chief and receiving his first star in 1936, shortly after MacArthur left as chief of staff to return to the Philippines.

More field commands followed: the Second Infantry Division, two corps appointments, and, in May of 1941, a promotion to lieutenant general, in which capacity he was given command of the Third Army. A shrewd judge of talent, Krueger asked for and temporarily received Colonel Dwight Eisenhower as his chief of staff before Marshall gathered Ike into his own fold. By the time Eisenhower was off to command the invasion of North Africa, late in 1942, Krueger told an old friend that while he would "love to try to rommel Rommel," he did not delude himself, because younger men were receiving those commands, and he would be sixty-two the following January.[26]

But before his birthday arrived in 1943, Krueger received word that MacArthur had requested his services in Australia. MacArthur wanted an American army command structure—usually comprising at least two corps—between his supreme headquarters and I Corps. "I am especially anxious to have Krueger," MacArthur told Marshall in making the request, "because of my long and intimate association with him."[27]

MacArthur phrased his request in such a way that he seemed to be asking for Krueger *and* the entire Third Army headquarters staff en masse. Instead, the War Department created a new Sixth Army, and Krueger was given wide latitude in recruiting officers from Third Army headquarters to staff it.

As for MacArthur's "long and intimate association" with him, Krueger later confessed to being flattered that MacArthur had remembered him favorably enough from his War Plans days to ask for his services, but MacArthur seems to have overstated their closeness. More likely, MacArthur was well aware of Krueger's growing reputation and his success in shaping the Third Army. MacArthur was always keen to bring talented officers into his command, even if few rose to the level of the Bataan Gang in acceptance.

Although he wore an American uniform, Krueger was the consummate example of the stereotypical Prussian officer: stern, precise, and demanding—of himself as well as his subordinates. He shunned publicity—always a plus when one worked for MacArthur—and executed his orders with steely resolve. As Dan Barbey observed, "What [Krueger's] seniors wanted done, he wanted done—and well." Since Krueger's immediate senior was MacArthur, there was never any question about whose wishes he was following.[28]

The creation of Sixth Army put a command level between

MacArthur and Eichelberger, who was still commanding I Corps. Eichelberger had done MacArthur's bidding at Buna, but MacArthur's gratitude was lukewarm, in part because Eichelberger rather naively embraced the publicity he received from it without anticipating MacArthur's response. Eichelberger was qualified for an army command— particularly as it was then still largely I Corps and several associated regiments—but Krueger's appointment to the Sixth Army instead of Eichelberger was MacArthur's way of keeping Eichelberger in his place. Although Eichelberger described Krueger's friendship toward him as "very real" and avowed that "perhaps I will be better off now with a buffer," this arrangement set up friction among the three that would continue as MacArthur pressed his return to the Philippines.[29]

In creating the Sixth Army, MacArthur also bypassed the Allied chain of command that ran to General Thomas Blamey as commander of the Allied Land Forces. MacArthur established a task force, known as Alamo Force, which was essentially the Sixth Army, and placed it directly under his general headquarters at the same level as Kenney's Allied Air Forces, Blamey's Allied Land Forces, and Carpender's Allied Naval Forces. This had the effect of removing most American combat troops from Blamey's chain of command and left him directly commanding mostly Australian troops, who would be increasingly relegated to garrison and rear-echelon duties after the fall campaigns around Lae.[30]

According to Samuel Eliot Morison, when it came time to step out together for the Kiriwina and Woodlark landings, "The newly organized Alamo Force of General Krueger's Sixth Army and web-footed boys of Admiral Carpender's Seventh Fleet [specifically, Barbey's amphibious forces] drank from the same coffeepot and drafted plans at the same table."[31] The planning became a model for future amphibious operations throughout the Southwest Pacific Area and—the usual interservice grumbling aside—showed MacArthur's land and sea forces to be working as a balanced team.

Barbey's working relationship with Kenney wasn't so easygoing. Barbey wanted Kenney to provide an around-the-clock air umbrella over his amphibious forces, while Kenney, recognizing the huge amount of resources this would require and the limitations it would place on other operations, instead chose to continue pounding Japanese air bases and keep his fighters ready to repulse any attack against the landings. Barbey later confessed that he was "skeptical" of Kenney's plan and that he envied Halsey's operations against New Georgia, "where carrier planes would provide continuous daylight cover."[32]

According to one navy captain, Kenney earned a reputation as the "biggest anti-Navy agitator" in MacArthur's headquarters, but it was hard to argue with his success in the air. This was particularly true in the run-up to the landings at Lae, when Ultra intercepts showed the Japanese to be massing aircraft at Wewak, three hundred miles to the west and beyond the range of Kenney's fighters. Kenney quickly ordered an airfield secretly built at Tsili Tsili, north of Wau, to bring them closer.[33]

Shortly after midnight on August 17, twelve B-17s and thirty-eight B-24s from Port Moresby dropped bombs on four airdromes at Wewak in the opening round of a massive attack. Five squadrons of B-25 medium bombers followed, accompanied by a fighter escort from all six P-38 squadrons. Thanks to the new base at Tsili Tsili, this effort was a fighter deployment on a scale never before seen in the Southwest Pacific Area.[34]

The Wewak raids, which found large numbers of Japanese planes on the ground, tightly parked in anticipation of major offensive operations, dealt Japanese airpower another major blow just as Barbey was moving beyond the dress rehearsals of Kiriwina and Woodlark and preparing a full-blown amphibious assault against Lae. MacArthur's press communiqué of August 18 described the Wewak attack as "a crippling blow at an opportune moment." Then, perhaps taking some satisfaction for partially avenging Clark Field, MacArthur went on to report, "Numerically, the opposing forces were about equal in strength, but one was in the air and the other was not. Nothing is so helpless as a plane on the ground."[35]

Contemplating the next round against Lae, MacArthur wrote his newfound buddy, "my dear Halsey," and asked him to consider a deceptive movement by elements of his fleet that would distract the enemy's air strength away from Lae. Assuring Halsey that "the decision is yours as to the practical feasibility of execution of this plan," MacArthur took on the unfamiliar role of grateful supplicant. Halsey replied immediately to "my dear General" and proposed three deployments in and around the Solomons that he hoped would focus Japanese attention on his South Pacific Area and away from MacArthur's landings.[36]

On September 1, with the threat of an aerial onslaught greatly reduced because of the Wewak raid, Barbey's Task Force 76 took the Australian Ninth Division on board at Milne Bay, sailed to Buna, where they were joined by the American Second Engineer Special Brigade, then landed the combined force on beaches around twenty miles east of Lae at sunrise on September 4. Somewhat to Barbey's surprise, these landings, too, were largely unopposed, although two Japanese bombers accompanied by a fighter escort damaged two LCIs before Kenney's planes could appear.

General Imamura immediately dispatched a follow-up force of eighty planes from Rabaul to attack Barbey's assault ships and the beachhead, but P-38s and P-47s intercepted the formation and broke it up. Some planes got through nonetheless and damaged two LSTs off Cape Ward Hunt, killing more than one hundred Australian soldiers and American sailors. That evening, another Japanese air attack against the beachhead destroyed an ammunition dump and damaged two beached LCIs. Notwithstanding these limited results—and proving that exaggeration occurred on all sides—the Japanese "claimed to have sunk 14 transports, 2 barges, 1 PT boat, 3 destroyers, and to have shot down 38 planes."[37]

As the Australian troops and American engineers moved inland from the beachhead, MacArthur looked to the capture of Lae and contemplated his next moves. By then, however, the Combined Chiefs of Staff had met again, this time for the First Quebec Conference, code-named Quadrant. When Roosevelt and Churchill ratified their deliberations, MacArthur's long-held goal to capture Rabaul was turned on end.

CHAPTER SIXTEEN

Bypassing Rabaul

The World War II strategy of island-hopping—isolating and bypassing enemy strong points—had many fathers. The Japanese, consciously or not, employed a version of it when they left MacArthur and some eighty thousand troops on Corregidor and Bataan. They rushed past to attack the East Indies and reach their goal of an unfettered supply of natural resources. When the North Pacific Force directed its assault against Japanese-occupied Attu, in the Aleutians, in May of 1943 after bypassing what was thought to be more heavily defended Kiska, they made the first American use of the strategy in the Pacific. The fact that Attu proved a buzz saw of opposition, and the fact that the Japanese later abandoned Kiska without a ground fight, in no way dissuaded planners from looking for similar opportunities to employ island-hopping as a strategic concept.

The idea of recapturing Rabaul, on New Britain, had been ingrained in Allied thinking since the Japanese wrestled it away from Australian forces early in 1942. MacArthur was a vocal proponent of the absolute necessity of doing so. He was clearly headed in that direction before the Japanese disrupted his plans by occupying Buna and forcing him to fight for Papua.

By the early summer of 1943, in the broad context of Aleutians operations and the debate between a central Pacific and southwestern Pacific advance, Washington planners began to ponder the economies that might result if Rabaul were neutralized rather than taken in a direct and likely prolonged assault. Doing so would benefit both Nimitz and MacArthur by permitting those resources to be allocated elsewhere in their respective theaters. The Joint Strategic Survey Committee came to favor the proposed central Pacific operations over Rabaul-bound Operation Cartwheel. Not only did the committee worry that the drive against Rabaul was, strategically speaking, merely a pushback against Japanese thrusts into the Solomons and at Buna, they also worried that it held "small promise of reasonable success in the near future."[1]

By July 21, these staff discussions about isolating Rabaul had set George Marshall to thinking. He suggested to MacArthur that the ultimate objective of the Cartwheel operations be modified. Instead of assaulting Rabaul directly, why not encircle it and render it useless by capturing Kavieng, on the northern tip of New Ireland, and Manus, one of the Admiralty Islands? Marshall also suggested capturing Wewak, northwest of Lae, to spur the drive westward along the coast of New Guinea. This meant that MacArthur had to seize Lae, continue operations westward along the New Guinea coast, and bypass Rabaul rather than meet Halsey there.[2]

MacArthur was not convinced. He argued that a direct assault against Wewak would involve "hazards rendering success doubtful." Interestingly enough, however, in rejecting the attack against Wewak, MacArthur did not propose to advance steadily toward it from Lae but rather to jump over it and seize a base farther west from which to isolate Wewak—exactly the sort of strategy Marshall was proposing against Rabaul. As for Rabaul itself, MacArthur remained of the mind that it would have to be captured—rather than merely neutralized—sooner or later, in part because he thought Simpson Harbor would make an excellent naval base from which to support his westward advance.[3]

On this latter point, Bill Halsey disagreed. At that moment, Halsey had his hands full with stiff enemy resistance on New Georgia, but he had long recognized that Rabaul would, in his words, "be a hard nut to crack." Not only would the fighting be difficult—an estimated one hundred thousand ground troops waited in opposition—but also, once Rabaul was won, "we would not have anything worthwhile" that could not have been had elsewhere.[4]

The "elsewhere" decisions were several months off, but in the meantime, Marshall and King also opposed MacArthur's fixation with Rabaul. The result at the First Quebec Conference in August of 1943

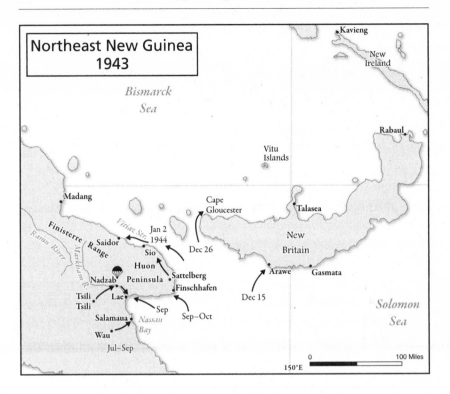

Northeast New Guinea 1943

Kavieng

New Ireland

Bismarck Sea

Rabaul

Vitu Islands

Madang

Cape Gloucester

Talasea

New Britain

Finisterre Range

Vitiaz Str. Jan 2 1944

Saidor

Sio

Dec 26

Huon Peninsula

Sattelberg

Finschhafen

Arawe

Gasmata

Ramu River

Markham R.

Nadzab

Tsili Tsili

Lae

Salamaua

Wau

Nassau Bay

Sep

Sep–Oct

Dec 15

Solomon Sea

Jul–Sep

0   100 Miles

150°E

was that the Combined Chiefs of Staff, and ultimately Roosevelt and Churchill, approved the Joints Chiefs' recommendation that Rabaul be neutralized, not captured. Momentarily, Kavieng was substituted for Rabaul as the primary target in the vicinity.[5]

Marshall dispatched a staff officer to MacArthur's headquarters to brief the general on this decision, and MacArthur seems to have acquiesced to it rather than argue his position. He was in the midst of the Lae operation, and there is at least some speculation that he had begun to lean toward a similar decision regarding Rabaul. This may have been the result of interaction between his staff and the Washington planners as well as his own conversations with Halsey. Perhaps more to the point, Marshall reassured MacArthur that progress along the northern coast of New Guinea toward the oil fields of the Vogelkop Peninsula remained a priority. From there, the next logical objective was MacArthur's cherished goal of Mindanao, although, Marshall warned him, "It may be found practicable to make this effort from the Central Pacific."[6]

*   *   *

Meanwhile, Allied operations against Lae continued. Indeed, MacArthur had already employed a mini leapfrog maneuver to gain ground in his pursuit of it. Repeated air attacks and feints by Australian ground troops near Salamaua convinced General Adachi and his Eighteenth Army staff that MacArthur's next major move would be directly against it. Accordingly, they steadily reinforced their frontline positions there. Instead, the Allied landings had occurred east of Lae, on Huon Gulf, decidedly *behind* the Japanese lines at Salamaua. The result was to isolate Salamaua's defenders and eventually cause the death of two thousand Japanese troops and the loss of large quantities of materiel, provisions, and barges.[7]

Aside from the Salamaua deception, the Allied attack against Lae was a variation on a plan prematurely conceived by General Blamey and the Australians during the Buna campaign. The amphibious forces just landed would move westward toward Lae and join up with troops descending the Markham River valley from Nadzab, squeezing Lae between them. Since the rugged Markham Valley acted as a barrier between the Huon Peninsula and the rest of New Guinea, the hope was that this maneuver would not only trap the Lae garrison but also cut off Japanese forces on the peninsula from Madang, their next base to the west.[8]

The key to success was to get a large number of troops to Nadzab as quickly as possible. The solution was to drop 1,700 men from the American 503rd Parachute Infantry Regiment on Nadzab and seize a prewar Australian airstrip so that brigades of the Australian Seventh Division could be flown in from a staging area at nearby Tsili Tsili and directly from Port Moresby shortly thereafter. Although the First Marine Parachute Battalion had fought at Guadalcanal and Tulagi on foot, this was to be the first use of airborne troops as such by Allied forces in the Pacific.[9]

As George Kenney briefed MacArthur on this airborne operation, he casually mentioned that he would be flying in one of the accompanying B-17s to observe what he called "the show." MacArthur took exception to this and reminded his air commander that he had been ordered to stay out of combat. Kenney protested and told MacArthur that given the recent success of raids against Wewak and the fact that a weather front was expected to keep planes grounded in Rabaul, he didn't expect any trouble from Japanese aircraft. "They were my kids," Kenney told MacArthur, "and I [am] going to see them do their stuff."

According to Kenney, MacArthur "listened to my tirade" and pondered this last comment before finally replying, "You're right, George, we'll both go. They're my kids, too." That caused Kenney to regret he had ever brought up the topic, but MacArthur was adamant, saying that he wasn't afraid of getting shot, only a little worried that he might get airsick crossing the mountains and "disgrace myself in front of the kids."[10]

MacArthur remembered the story a little differently. When he inspected the paratroopers, he said he found, "as was only natural, a sense of nervousness among the ranks." He continued, "I decided that it would be advisable for me to fly in with them. I did not want them to go through their first baptism of fire without such comfort as my presence might bring to them."[11]

Kenney arranged what he called a brass-hat flight of three B-17s to shadow the C-47 transports as they made their Nadzab run. He put MacArthur in the lead bomber, named *Talisman,* climbed aboard the number two plane himself, and had "the third handy for mutual protection, in case we got hopped." MacArthur suggested they ride together, but Kenney convinced him that was tempting fate just a little too much.[12]

At 8:25 a.m. on September 5, 1943, the first C-47s rolled down the runway at Port Moresby. By the time the airborne flotilla assembled southwest of Nadzab, it numbered 302 aircraft from eight different fields. Six squadrons of B-25s led the attack, strafing Nadzab with their .50-caliber nose guns and dropping bombs. Six A-20s followed, to lay a smoke screen for the paratroopers jumping from ninety-six C-47s. Bevies of P-38s and other fighters circled at various altitudes, while the heavy bombers— twenty-four B-24s and four B-17s—pounded a Japanese position halfway between Nadzab and Lae to disrupt ground reinforcements. Five other B-17s, their bomb racks loaded with three-hundred-pound packages of supplies, circled the drop zone and disgorged their loads as needed in response to markers on the ground. High above the transport columns, MacArthur and Kenney flew in their brass-hat flight of B-17s.[13]

Kenney reported to Hap Arnold that MacArthur watched the whole assault "jumping up and down like a kid." That seems out of character and a decided exaggeration, but it was nonetheless an impressive array of Allied airpower, and MacArthur was elated. The timing of the bomb runs, the fighter cover, and the air drops were near perfect, causing MacArthur, despite his thoughts of providing moral support, to admit, "They did not need me."[14]

But Kenney had a surprise for MacArthur. "To my astonishment," MacArthur wrote in his memoirs, "I was awarded the Air Medal." The citation, which Kenney recommended, noted that MacArthur "personally led the American paratroopers on the very successful and important jump against the Nadzab airstrip" and "flew through enemy infested airlanes and skillfully directed this historic operation." That, too, was a bit of Kenney exaggeration, and even MacArthur, while saying "this exceptionally pleased me," graciously admitted, "I felt it did me too much credit."[15]

Medals aside, MacArthur's presence in a B-17 over Nadzab was a transformative event in his personal conduct in combat zones. The flight was certainly not without risk, and it was a long way from characterizations of Dugout Doug. It marked a return to the MacArthur of the trenches of World War I and stood in sharp contrast to his lone visit to Bataan and his failure to visit Eichelberger at Buna. It emboldened MacArthur to get out in the field more often.

By nightfall on September 5, the troopers had burned the tall kunai grass off the abandoned Nadzab airstrip, and the following afternoon the first transports, carrying elements of the Australian Seventh Division, landed. Within a week, engineers had constructed two parallel runways of six thousand feet each with a dispersal area capable of simultaneously handling thirty-six transports. This allowed the Seventh Division to hasten down the Markham Valley toward Lae. Salamaua fell on September 14 to Australian and American units that had linked up after the landings at Nassau Bay, and the Australian Seventh and Ninth Divisions entered Lae from opposite directions on September 16.[16]

The rapid collapse of Salamaua and Lae caused the Japanese considerable angst. Rather than wage a last-ditch defense, as they had at Buna and Gona, they conducted a withdrawal designed to save as many of their troops as possible. The result was a harrowing jungle march that nonetheless saw the bulk of nine thousand soldiers and sailors reach the north coast of the Huon Peninsula. This move became a small piece of a broad strategy to tighten Japan's defensive perimeter throughout the entire Pacific.

Major General Jonathan Wainwright (left), the senior American field commander in the Philippines, and MacArthur observe maneuvers in October 1941. MacArthur expected war with Japan but not until the spring of 1942. *Courtesy of the MacArthur Memorial, Norfolk, VA*

Philippine president Manuel Quezon stands with MacArthur during prewar days in Manila. *Courtesy of the MacArthur Memorial, Norfolk, VA*

By the time they retreated to Corregidor, their mood was grim and Quezon was dying of tuberculosis. *Courtesy of the MacArthur Memorial, Norfolk, VA*

Exuding public confidence, MacArthur and Major General Richard K. Sutherland, his chief of staff, stride out of the Malinta Tunnel on Corregidor for his daily walk and inspection tour. *Courtesy of the MacArthur Memorial, Norfolk, VA*

There wasn't much to smile about in private, however, as MacArthur and Sutherland ponder the fate of the troops at their desks in a lateral of the Malinta Tunnel. *Courtesy of the MacArthur Memorial, Norfolk, VA*

This view looks generally northwest across the mouth of Manila Bay. Corregidor with its flat Topside area and sweeping long tail extending east from Malinta Hill are in the foreground. On Bataan in the background, 4,554-foot Mount Mariveles dominates the tip of the peninsula. *Courtesy of the MacArthur Memorial, Norfolk, VA*

Seventy-seven feet in length with a twenty-foot beam, PT-41 under the command of Lieutenant John D. Bulkeley spirited MacArthur and his family off Corregidor. *Courtesy of the MacArthur Memorial, Norfolk, VA*

Jean MacArthur with her effervescent smile and four-year-old Arthur with his stuffed toy, "Old Friend," do not look as if they have just survived a harrowing, two-day, PT-boat ride. Del Monte Plantation, Mindanao, March 1942. *Courtesy of the MacArthur Memorial, Norfolk, VA*

Shortly after his arrival in Australia, MacArthur and Australian prime minister John Curtin subscribe to war bonds at Commonwealth Bank in Melbourne as part of Australia's Second Liberty Loan. *Courtesy of the MacArthur Memorial, Norfolk, VA*

MacArthur appointed Australian general Sir Thomas Blamey commander of Allied Land Forces in the Southwest Pacific Area (SWPA) and held his first meetings with him in Melbourne in April 1942. *Courtesy of the MacArthur Memorial, Norfolk, VA*

(Left to right) Frank Forde, Australian minister for the army; MacArthur; Blamey; Major General George Kenney, Allied Air Forces commander, SWPA (soon to be promoted to lieutenant general); Australian lieutenant general Edmund Herring, New Guinea Force commander; and Brigadier General Kenneth Walker, V Bomber Command commander on MacArthur's first trip to New Guinea in early October 1942. Walker was shot down leading an attack against Rabaul several months later. *Courtesy of the MacArthur Memorial, Norfolk, VA*

General Sir Thomas Blamey greets MacArthur at Seven Mile Airdrome near Port Moresby upon MacArthur's first visit to New Guinea, October 2, 1942. *Courtesy of the MacArthur Memorial, Norfolk, VA*

On his first visit to New Guinea, MacArthur reviews Australian troops with Major General Arthur "Tubby" Allen (rear left). *Courtesy of the MacArthur Memorial, Norfolk, VA*

Lieutenant General George Kenney (left) and his right-hand man, Major General Ennis Whitehead, discuss air operations in Kenney's office in the AMP Building in Brisbane. *Courtesy of the Mac-Arthur Memorial, Norfolk, VA*

Admiral William F. Halsey Jr. arrives in Brisbane to consult with MacArthur. *Courtesy of the MacArthur Memorial, Norfolk, VA*

Brigadier General Charles A. Willoughby, MacArthur's intelligence chief, Lieutenant General Robert L. Eichelberger, and Eichelberger's chief of staff, Brigadier General Clovis Byers (left to right), confer in Eichelberger's headquarters in Brisbane. *Courtesy of the MacArthur Memorial, Norfolk, VA*

The long screened porch of Government House on a hill above Port Moresby gave MacArthur plenty of room to pace. *Courtesy of the MacArthur Memorial, Norfolk, VA*

After the heavy toll at Buna, Eichelberger and General Sir Thomas Blamey tour the battlefield. MacArthur never did. *Courtesy of the MacArthur Memorial, Norfolk, VA*

MacArthur and Kenney (right) wish Lieutenant Colonel John Jarvis Tolson III, of the 503rd Parachute Infantry Regiment good luck before the daring jump on Nadzab, September 5, 1943. "They're my kids, too," MacArthur told Kenney, when he decided to fly along. *Courtesy of the MacArthur Memorial, Norfolk, VA*

When it came to major strategic decisions, MacArthur received his orders from the Joint Chiefs of Staff. In addition to regular meetings, they met informally weekly for lunch: (left to right) Lieutenant General Henry H. "Hap" Arnold, commanding general US Army Air Forces (promoted to full general, March 19, 1943); Admiral William D. Leahy, chief of staff to the commander in chief and de facto JCS chairman; Admiral Ernest J. King, commander in chief US Fleet and chief of naval operations; and General George C. Marshall, chief of staff US Army. *National Archives, 80-G-K-14010*

General George C. Marshall, Army chief of staff (left), made a major show of support for Southwest Pacific operations by circling the globe after the Teheran Conference and visiting MacArthur on Goodenough Island, December 1943. *Courtesy of the MacArthur Memorial, Norfolk, VA*

Lieutenant General Walter Krueger, commanding general Sixth Army (left), MacArthur, and Marshall at the airfield on Goodenough Island, December 1943. *Courtesy of the MacArthur Memorial, Norfolk, VA*

The Alamo Force high command gathers on Goodenough Island prior to the landings on New Britain at Arawe and Cape Gloucester: (left to right) Major General Stephen J. Chamberlin, MacArthur's operations chief (G-3); Lieutenant General Walter Krueger, commanding general, Sixth Army; MacArthur; Brigadier General Clyde Eddleman, Krueger's assistant chief of staff for operations (over Kinkaid's shoulder); Vice Admiral Thomas C. Kinkaid, commander, US Seventh Fleet; Major General Ennis Whitehead, commanding general, Fifth Air Force; and Major General William H. Rupertus, commanding general, First Marine Division. *Courtesy of the MacArthur Memorial, Norfolk, VA*

MacArthur and Kinkaid hold an earnest conversation on the *Bataan* while flying to Milne Bay to board the cruiser *Phoenix* for the Admiralties invasion. *Courtesy of the MacArthur Memorial, Norfolk, VA*

A gamble in the making, Colonel Lloyd Lehrbas, Kinkaid, and MacArthur (left to right) watch the landings at Los Negros in the Admiralties, February 29, 1944. *Courtesy of the MacArthur Memorial, Norfolk, VA*

Krueger visits with troopers of the First Cavalry Division who went ashore with the first wave on Los Negros in the Admiralties. *Courtesy of the MacArthur Memorial, Norfolk, VA*

On board the cruiser *Nashville,* MacArthur, with Lieutenant Colonel Roger Egeberg staring intently at his side, points out the bombardment off the Tanahmerah beachhead during the Hollandia landings, April 22, 1944. *Courtesy of the MacArthur Memorial, Norfolk, VA*

MacArthur shakes hands with Major General Frederick A. Irving, Twenty-Fourth Infantry Division commander, on the beach at Tanahmerah Bay, Hollandia, April 22, 1944. Eichelberger is over MacArthur's right shoulder with bloused fatigues and natty gaiters; immediately to Eichelberger's left, Egeberg keeps his eyes focused on his general. *Courtesy of the MacArthur Memorial, Norfolk, VA*

While Egeberg and Lehrbas look on (second and third from left), Major General Horace H. Fuller, Forty-First Infantry Division commander, escorts MacArthur through the sand on the beach at Humboldt Bay, Hollandia, April 22, 1944. MacArthur would later find fault with Fuller and relieve him when the Forty-First Division ran into tough fighting at Biak a month later. *Courtesy of the MacArthur Memorial, Norfolk, VA*

On the deck of the heavy cruiser *Baltimore* in Pearl Harbor, MacArthur, Franklin D. Roosevelt, Admiral Chester W. Nimitz, and Admiral William D. Leahy (left to right) take part in the requisite photo op, July 26, 1944. *Courtesy of the MacArthur Memorial, Norfolk, VA*

The epitome of combined operations: (left to right) amphibious guru Dan Barbey, MacArthur, air boss George Kenney, and Sixth Army commander Walter Krueger. Likely photographed on Goodenough Island in December 1943, this quartet was about to launch an incredible year of offensives. *Courtesy of the MacArthur Memorial, Norfolk, VA*

MacArthur consults with Rear Admiral Daniel E. "Uncle Dan, the Amphibious Man" Barbey after boarding a landing craft to head for the beach at Morotai, September 15, 1944. The cruiser *Nashville* is in the background. *Courtesy of the MacArthur Memorial, Norfolk, VA*

Whatever the Army-Navy rivalries, Sutherland (right) manages a tight-lipped smile in greeting Halsey and his chief of staff, Rear Admiral Robert B. "Mick" Carney, on one of Halsey's visits to Brisbane. *Courtesy of the MacArthur Memorial, Norfolk, VA*

Admiral William F. Halsey Jr. bids an emotional farewell to his South Pacific command and prepares to take command of the Third Fleet for the final campaigns against Japan. *Courtesy of the MacArthur Memorial, Norfolk, VA*

Having disembarked from the *Nashville* in the background and heading for the Leyte beaches, MacArthur talks to Sutherland, with Lehrbas (left) and Egeberg standing behind them. *Courtesy of the MacArthur Memorial, Norfolk, VA*

Philippine president Sergio Osmeña, Kenney (almost completely hidden), Colonel Courtney Whitney, Philippine Army brigadier general Carlos Romulo, MacArthur, Sutherland, CBS correspondent Bill Dunn, and Staff Sergeant Francisco Salveron (left to right) wade ashore just south of Tacloban at Palo, Leyte, October 20, 1944. *Courtesy of the MacArthur Memorial, Norfolk, VA*

MacArthur established his headquarters in the Price House, easily Tacloban's most impressive structure, within a week of the initial landings at Leyte. *Courtesy of the MacArthur Memorial, Norfolk, VA*

Despite his frustration with the speed of Krueger's advance on Luzon, MacArthur recommended him for promotion to full general in March 1945. *Courtesy of the MacArthur Memorial, Norfolk, VA*

After crossing to Corregidor by PT boat, MacArthur strides down the dock with Colonel George M. Jones, commander of the 503rd Parachute Regimental Combat Team that parachuted onto the island. Krueger and Kenney (mostly hidden) follow close behind, March 2, 1945. *Courtesy of the MacArthur Memorial, Norfolk, VA*

Despite the waves made by Sutherland with the Navy in wanting immediate unit transfers to MacArthur's AFPAC command, MacArthur and Nimitz greeted each other like old friends when Nimitz flew from Guam to Manila on May 15, 1945, to work out the details. *Courtesy of the MacArthur Memorial, Norfolk, VA*

Aboard the cruiser *Boise* with cotton in their ears, Brigadier General Courtney Whitney, General George Kenney, and MacArthur (left to right) watch the bombardment before Australian troops land at Brunei Bay, June 10, 1945. Recently promoted, Kenney wears the four stars of a full general. *Courtesy of the MacArthur Memorial, Norfolk, VA*

A group of American servicemen and Filipinos look on as the Japanese surrender delegation arrives at MacArthur's headquarters in Manila's bullet-marked city hall, August 19, 1945. Some are more interested in watching MacArthur stare from the balcony. *Courtesy of the MacArthur Memorial, Norfolk, VA*

With pilot Weldon "Dusty" Rhoades partially hidden behind his left ear and Suther-
land, Eichelberger, and Eleventh Airborne Division commander Major General
Joseph M. Swing to his immediate left, MacArthur walks away from his C-54,
Bataan II, after landing at Atsugi airfield, Japan. August 30, 1945. *Courtesy of the
MacArthur Memorial, Norfolk, VA*

When Japanese foreign minister Mamoru Shigemitsu appeared uncertain where to
sign the articles of surrender, MacArthur growled, "Sutherland, show him where to
sign." USS *Missouri,* Tokyo Bay, September 2, 1945. *Courtesy of the MacArthur
Memorial, Norfolk, VA*

One look at the map in Imperial General Headquarters told the rest of the story. In the South Pacific, Halsey gnawed away at the central Solomons and had just done his own island-hopping—bypassing Kolombangara in favor of a landing on Vella Lavella. To the north, the Gilbert and Marshall Islands lay exposed to any American advance through the central Pacific. In the northern Pacific, withdrawals from Attu and Kiska, in the Aleutians, had cost Japan its toehold in Alaska. It was time for Imperial General Headquarters to mandate a defensive line to be held at all costs.

The line drawn ran from western New Guinea in the face of MacArthur's advance through Truk and the Carolines to Saipan and Guam, in the Mariana Islands. Rabaul, once considered an important hub by both sides, took on the character of a strong outpost, as did Kwajalein, in the Marshall Islands. This did not mean, however, that the Japanese would not aggressively defend them. In September, as Lae fell, Imperial General Headquarters dispatched the Seventeenth Division from Shanghai to Rabaul "to reinforce the troops manning the forward wall."[17]

In organizing his Eighteenth Army for its new defensive role, General Adachi confronted a dilemma not unlike that which MacArthur had faced in defending the Philippines. From the Vogelkop Peninsula east to the Admiralty Islands and New Britain, there were thousands of miles of shoreline and hundreds of islands and inland locations that attackers might seize for airfield sites. Kenney had already proved he was adept at that, and Barbey's budding amphibious forces promised to become an equal partner. If Adachi dispersed his troops too widely, he exposed them to selective attacks by larger forces, but if he concentrated them in certain strongholds, they risked being cut off by the type of leapfrog maneuvers both MacArthur and Halsey were beginning to employ.

The fall of Lae had also caused the Allies to reevaluate their own strategic plans. MacArthur's original timetable for the following round of Operation Cartwheel called for an assault against Finschhafen six weeks after the landings at Lae. Finschhafen, seventy miles east of Lae, near the tip of the Huon Peninsula, and Cape Gloucester, on New Britain, were considered essential to controlling the intervening Vitiaz and Dampier Straits. This would permit Allied naval vessels to pass from the Solomon Sea into the Bismarck Sea and effect landings to encircle Rabaul as well as advance along the coast of New Guinea.

MacArthur assigned the assault against Finschhafen to George Wooten's Australian Ninth Division and against Cape Gloucester to Walter Krueger's Alamo Force.

Before embarking from Milne Bay for Lae, Wootten had gotten a hint that he might be required to dispatch one of his brigades to Finschhafen on short notice. Given the rapid demise of Lae, that came sooner than even he anticipated, when MacArthur decided on September 17 to invade Finschhafen immediately. Dan Barbey showed that he was getting the knack of amphibious operations by assembling four transports, eight LSTs, sixteen LCIs, and ten destroyers and landing Wootten's Twentieth Brigade infantry group six miles north of Finschhafen just before dawn on September 22, almost a month ahead of the proposed schedule. As Commander Charles Adair, who had responsibility for scouting the landing site, reminisced years later, Finschhafen "was not too bad when you consider that we landed, in about four hours, the following: 5,300 troops, 180 vehicles, 32 guns, and 850 tons of bulk stores."[18]

Part of MacArthur's decision to expedite the Finschhafen landing was based on the rapid progress at Lae, but Willoughby had fueled his decision by estimating that Japanese defenders there numbered only 350. In fact, there were almost five thousand Japanese troops in and around Finschhafen. Adachi had also relieved his Twentieth Division of its Madang-Lae road-building project and ordered it to reinforce Finschhafen and nearby Sattelberg. This was not the first time Willoughby had made a major blunder in numbers, and it would not be the last. The Australians faced heavy resistance before reinforcements moving along the coast from Lae joined up with the landing force and secured the town on October 2.[19]

The quick thrust at Finschhafen — Willoughby's faulty intelligence aside — initially looked to be inspired, but as elements of the Japanese Twentieth Division counterattacked, the Allied positions there and along the tip of the Huon Peninsula became very exposed. This did not keep MacArthur from prematurely announcing on October 4 that all enemy forces between Finschhafen and Madang had been "outflanked and contained."[20]

Among those most disgruntled by this misplaced optimism was Wootten's Ninth Division, whose troops were fighting fiercely between Finschhafen and Sattelberg to keep themselves from being outflanked and contained. Barbey landed a major reinforcement on the Finsch-hafen beach on October 20, but the official Australian war history groused, "MacArthur's planners felt that Finschhafen would be a 'pushover' and that the operation could be considered as finished" even before the town was secured.[21]

At MacArthur's strategic level, the next question became whether to order the Australians to push around the Huon Peninsula and capture intermediary points toward Madang or have Krueger strike at Cape Gloucester and secure the opposite side of the Vitiaz and Dampier Straits. Simultaneous blows might have been advisable, but Barbey lacked the ships to conduct both operations at the same time. Which to undertake first was a tricky decision.

Against this backdrop, the plans for Cape Gloucester caused dissension at MacArthur's headquarters. Code-named Operation Dexterity, these plans called for Krueger's Alamo Force to seize airfield locations at Cape Gloucester, on the western tip of New Britain, with a combined airborne and amphibious operation as well as to assault a forward Japanese base at Gasmata, on the southern coast. The invasion force at Gasmata would drive north to Talasea, on the northern coast, effectively lopping off Cape Gloucester and the western third of the island from Japanese control. For good measure, they would also capture the tiny islands of Long and Vitu, in the Bismarck Sea.

These were significant steps toward Rabaul, and they seem to have been premised on tightening the noose in preparation for an invasion of Rabaul rather than isolating and bypassing it. Indeed, the official US Army history notes—the decision to bypass Rabaul at the Quebec conference notwithstanding—that there seemed to be "a strategic lag" before that decision was reflected in the operational orders emanating from MacArthur's headquarters. This was not necessarily out of any disregard on the part of MacArthur or his staff for the bypass decision but more likely a case of long-held inertia that took some time to reverse.[22]

George Kenney was the first to protest the Cape Gloucester plan. Operation Cartwheel's original concept had been to encircle Rabaul with a ring of air bases, but Kenney told MacArthur that the bypass decision rendered this moot. Now that faster action was contemplated, it would

311

take too long to develop Cape Gloucester into a viable base. By then, it would no longer be essential because the existing bases at Dobodura, Nadzab, and Kiriwina, as well as the one under construction at Finschhafen and whatever might be developed en route to Madang, could support further advances in the Admiralties and against Kavieng. Rabaul would wither on the vine while the thrust of MacArthur's advance continued toward the Philippines instead of diverting back toward Rabaul.[23]

Stephen Chamberlin, MacArthur's operations chief, took exception to Kenney's view and asserted that airdromes at Cape Gloucester could be taken and upgraded in a timely manner and that they would ensure both tighter control of the Vitiaz Strait and closer support for future attacks. Even with Cape Gloucester, Chamberlin argued that Gasmata or another point on the southern coast of New Britain would be needed to control the straits and provide an emergency airfield for planes attacking Rabaul.

Admiral Arthur Carpender, for the moment still MacArthur's senior naval commander, and Dan Barbey supported Chamberlin in the need to hold both sides of the straits. General Krueger agreed. But the admirals were far from keen on the operation against Gasmata, fearing that it would needlessly expose ships to Rabaul-based aircraft.[24]

With Chamberlin determined to seize Cape Gloucester, Kenney joined forces with Carpender and Barbey against the Gasmata operation. The proposed landing site, just east of Gasmata at Lindenhafen, was swampy even by New Guinea standards; the coral runway was located on an island and limited to 3,200 feet in length; and the Japanese were reinforcing the area with the recently arrived Seventeenth Division. Kenney's deputy, Ennis Whitehead, who remained the tactical maestro behind Kenney's air successes, offered his own analysis when he told Kenney, "Any effort used up to capture any place on the south coast of New Britain is wasted unless an airdrome suitable for combat airplanes can be constructed there." Both air bosses, although confident of their growing air superiority, also thought Gasmata a little too close to Rabaul for adequate warning of incoming attacks.[25]

The matter was finally resolved on November 21 in a conference that included MacArthur, Chamberlin, Kenney, Carpender, and Barbey. While the navy continued to oppose Gasmata, they nonetheless wanted a PT boat base somewhere on the southern coast of New Britain from which to patrol the straits. Kenney claimed in his memoirs that it was his idea to substitute Arawe, a lightly defended harbor halfway between Gasmata and the straits. Conversely, Barbey remembered poring over charts with Carpender to find the solution. When they presented Arawe as an option, Barbey said that Kenney appeared relieved and promised better air cover to Arawe than he could provide to Gasmata.[26]

This plan was approved, but the dates initially selected for the Operation Dexterity landings—November 14 for Gasmata-Lindenhafen and November 20 for Cape Gloucester—had already been postponed once, in part because heavy fighting around Finschhafen had slowed construction of its supporting airfield. This had a ripple effect—because of the lack of nearby air cover, Barbey's VII Amphibious Force was disrupted in stockpiling supplies, a task that had to be completed before Barbey could turn his ships loose from Finschhafen for the New Britain landings.

Given that amphibious invasions usually occurred during the new moon to avoid silhouetting the landing force, this meant that the New Britain landings would have to be made either prior to December 4 or after the full moon on December 11. MacArthur wanted to make the Cape Gloucester landing on December 4, but Krueger protested that because Barbey's amphibious force would have to finish at Finschhafen, return to Milne Bay for assault troops, land the Arawe force, and reload for Cape Gloucester, there would not be time for rehearsals and that any ship losses at Arawe would hamper the main Gloucester force. MacArthur reluctantly agreed. The regiment-size landings at Arawe were set for December 15 and the full-blown assault on Cape Gloucester for December 26.[27]

In the midst of these operations, there was a new face on the US Navy side. Vice Admiral Thomas C. Kinkaid was the last senior officer to join one of MacArthur's two inner circles: the tight-knit circle reserved for the Bataan Gang and, for lack of a better word, the "fighting" circle, made up of those commanders who were to earn MacArthur's respect for their military accomplishments, including Kenney, Barbey, Krueger, and, somewhat begrudgingly, Eichelberger.

Born into a navy family in 1888, Kinkaid graduated from Annapolis in 1908. He served tours on battleships, including the *Nebraska* as part of the Great White Fleet, and developed a specialty in ordnance and gunnery. World War I found Kinkaid doing special assignments in between postings on the battleships *Pennsylvania* and *Arizona*. Afterward, he commanded a destroyer, attended the Naval War College, served as a naval adviser to the Conference for the Reduction and Limitation of Armaments in Geneva, and returned to battleships as executive officer of the *Colorado*. After Kinkaid's stint in the Bureau of Navigation, Rear Admiral William D. Leahy supported his promotion to captain, and Kinkaid took command of the cruiser *Indianapolis* in 1937.

Kinkaid was interested in the plum diplomatic post of naval attaché in London, but when the job went to someone else, he accepted the post in Rome instead. This put him on the front lines of wartime diplomacy after Italy declared war on Great Britain and France. He returned to the United States in March of 1941 looking for a promotion to rear admiral, but he lacked a few months of required sea command because he had left the *Indianapolis* early for his Rome assignment. An Annapolis classmate then in the Bureau of Navigation came to his rescue and arranged a few months in command of a destroyer squadron based in Philadelphia to make up the time. The classmate, Arthur Carpender, was himself a newly minted rear admiral, and the irony of his favor would not become apparent for several years.

With his new flag rank, Kinkaid replaced Rear Admiral Frank Jack Fletcher as commander of a cruiser division several weeks after the attack on Pearl Harbor. Kinkaid led cruiser forces at the Battles of the Coral Sea and Midway and afterward became commander of Task Force 16, which was built around the carrier *Enterprise*. Task Force 16 sailed near the Solomons as one of three task forces under Fletcher's overall command, and *Enterprise* took a mauling in the Battle of the Eastern Solomons.[28]

By the fall of 1942, Halsey was in charge of the South Pacific Area, and Kinkaid and *Enterprise* were back on station there. This time, however, Kinkaid was the overall commander of two carrier task forces as a major Japanese force of carriers, battleships, and cruisers attempted another end run around the eastern Solomons. Halsey exhorted Kinkaid, "Strike—repeat—strike," but a mix-up in radio communications gave the Japanese a head start in attacking the Americans.

Kinkaid saved Guadalcanal, but the *Enterprise* came away damaged once again and the *Hornet* had to be scuttled—a decision for which Halsey and a host of naval aviators never forgave Kinkaid. The Battle of the Santa Cruz Islands was the last time a nonaviator commanded a carrier task force, and, more important for their future relations, it put Halsey and Kinkaid on less-than-friendly terms.[29]

Having weathered the major engagements of 1942 in the Pacific, Kinkaid returned to the United States for leave shortly thereafter and early in 1943 was sent to Alaska to command the North Pacific Force. Interservice rivalry was not limited to the South Pacific, and Kinkaid's first job was to promote harmony among army, navy, and air force commands and cut through the tangled chain of command that had developed there. The result was success in the Aleutians campaign.

After MacArthur twice requested Arthur Carpender's relief as his naval commander—among Carpender's sins, from MacArthur's view-point, were his less-than-aggressive use of ships off the New Guinea beachheads and his direct communications with the Navy Department— King and Nimitz determined that Kinkaid's reputation in working with the army in Alaska and his combat experience in major Pacific engagements made him the most appropriate choice.[30]

MacArthur was finally to get his own fighting admiral, but Secretary of the navy Frank Knox prematurely announced the appointment at a press conference before either MacArthur or the Australian government had been consulted. The latter was required under the Allied agreement covering MacArthur's appointment as supreme commander. MacArthur noted this lack of proper process to Marshall but made no objection to Kinkaid personally.

Marshall forwarded a kindly worded explanation from Admiral King that noted that Kinkaid's orders had not yet been cut and asked whether Kinkaid would be acceptable to MacArthur. To King's conciliatory message, Marshall added praise of Kinkaid's work in the northern Pacific and noted: "His relations have been particularly efficient and happy with Army commanders, and...I think you will find him energetic, loyal, and filled with desires to get ahead with your operations. I think he is the best naval bet for your purpose."[31]

MacArthur and Australian prime minister John Curtin concurred, and Kinkaid arrived in Brisbane as commander of Allied Naval Forces in the Southwest Pacific Area and commander of the Seventh Fleet. As such, he wore two hats, just as Halsey did. Kinkaid was responsible to MacArthur as the Allied naval commander and to King for the Seventh Fleet. (Kinkaid's chain of command ran directly to King and not through Nimitz because Nimitz controlled only those units of the United States Fleet that ventured into the Southwest Pacific Area and not those permanently assigned there.) But one thing was certain: no matter how much MacArthur and his staff might rant and rave against the US Navy, it would have been difficult for King to have found an officer better suited in temperament, experience, and self-confidence to serve MacArthur than Thomas C. Kinkaid.

Kinkaid met at length with MacArthur on November 26, the day after Kinkaid formally relieved his old classmate Carpender, who had helped him get his first stars. Despite receiving a warm welcome from MacArthur, Kinkaid was not shy about delivering a dose of reality. Barbey's amphibious forces, Kinkaid told MacArthur, would continue to make do with what they had or could beg on a ship-by-ship basis, but MacArthur's dreams of receiving carriers, cruisers, and even some battleships would not be realized in the near future.

If Kinkaid's oral history tapes are to be believed, the new Seventh Fleet commander went so far as to tell MacArthur that he didn't think these larger ships should be assigned to the Seventh Fleet at that point because they would likely be held in Australian waters beyond the reach of Japanese air attack and thus be ineffective in directly engaging the Japanese fleet. It was a better use of limited resources, Kinkaid said, if they sailed with Halsey in the South Pacific or Nimitz in the central Pacific.[32]

Kinkaid was correct in this analysis, but within a few months, the tremendous surge of America's industrial production would dramatically change the picture. In fact, Halsey had already received several of the new *Essex*-class carriers, and their planes were raining destruction in and around Rabaul in conjunction with Kenney's bombers.

As Kinkaid engaged in his new assignment, there was more controversy over the Cape Gloucester operation. Instead of overall strategic importance and invasion dates, the discussion centered over tactics. No doubt influenced by the successful airborne assault on Nadzab, MacArthur's planners called for a lone regiment of the by-then-veteran First Marine Division to land by sea at Cape Gloucester, while the Nadzab veterans, the 503rd Parachute Infantry Regiment, jumped behind the beachhead and linked up with the marines at two Japanese airfields.

Alamo Force commander Krueger was never keen on this arrangement, and the First Marine Division's commander, Major General William H. Rupertus, even less so, fearing that the assault logistics as well as Japanese defenses were far more complex than they had been at Nadzab. Add in uncertain weather, and there were just too many things that could go wrong with the proposed linkup.

According to the official history of the First Marine Division, MacArthur and Krueger visited division headquarters on Goodenough Island late in November and stumbled onto the division's internal debate. When MacArthur casually asked how the Cape Gloucester plan was coming, the division operations officer, Lieutenant Colonel Edwin A. Pollock, boldly replied, "We don't like it." Asked by MacArthur what it was that he didn't like, Pollock replied, "Sir, we don't like anything about it."

MacArthur raised an eyebrow in Krueger's direction while Krueger glared at Pollock. MacArthur and Krueger left, but shortly afterward, general headquarters planners and the division's staff held a joint planning session, undoubtedly at MacArthur's directive. The airborne assault was scrapped and the entire First Marine Division ordered in at full strength to take the beaches with plenty of support. It was an instance of MacArthur listening to his troops in the field and not just to the planners in his headquarters. It was also a case of MacArthur listening to the navy's Marine Corps and not his army planners.[33]

The other piece of the Cape Gloucester operation that concerned the navy was air cover for Barbey's landing forces. According to Barbey, Kenney had beefed up the air cover over the Finschhafen beaches only "after a bit of nudging by MacArthur."[34] Barbey was determined to get that much or more for Cape Gloucester.

With Barbey occupied with the landing at Arawe, it fell to Kinkaid to emphasize Barbey's concerns to MacArthur. Still in his first few weeks on the job, Kinkaid once again did not mince words. He told a conference at MacArthur's headquarters — where Kenney was present —

that while the navy maintained combat air patrols over an objective, army planes sat on the ground until an attack was imminent. The problem with that approach, Kinkaid said, was that "bomb holes on an airfield could be filled in, but a bombed ship might be lost." MacArthur listened intently, then responded, "You can tell Barbey, you can assure him that he will have adequate air cover to go into Gloucester, and he'll have better cover than he has ever had."[35] Kenney got the point, and it turned out to be true.

On December 15, the 112th Cavalry Regiment and a field artillery battalion landed at Arawe to light resistance after Kenney's air forces had pounded Gasmata and Cape Gloucester as a diversion. On Christmas Day in 1943, the First Division marines embarked from Oro Bay, Goodenough Island, and Milne Bay for Cape Gloucester and went ashore there the next day. Initial light resistance led to heavier fighting around the airfields until they were secured on December 30. Heavy fighting continued, but medium and light tanks landed by Barbey's LSTs finally won the day. It also helped that Allied air attacks pounded the defenders and generally cut them off from support from Rabaul.[36]

The landings at Arawe and Cape Gloucester proved successful, but in hindsight they renewed Kenney's initial question about whether *any* attack on New Britain was essential to the strategy of bypassing Rabaul. Willoughby waxed poetic about the result and claimed after Gloucester, "The approach to the Admiralties lay miraculously open, with a Japanese Army on each flank rendered powerless to hinder the projected breakthrough." Willoughby went on to say that in context, " 'miraculous' is a superficial word. To immobilize with a relatively small force the Japanese Eighth Army on the Rabaul flank represents a professional utilization not only of astute staff intelligence but of time and space factors cannily converted into tactical advantage."[37]

Others weren't so sure. While these landings pushed Japanese forces back toward Rabaul, naval chronicler Samuel Eliot Morison claimed, "Arawe was of small value. The harbor was never used by us; the occupation served only to pin down some of our forces that could have been used elsewhere." As for the capture of Cape Gloucester, Morison found it "an even greater waste of time and effort than Arawe." His main point was that the bypass of Rabaul should have been made to include *all* of New Britain. "With the Huon Peninsula in our possession," he concluded, "a big hole had been breached in the Bismarcks Barrier and there was nothing on Cape Gloucester to prevent General MacArthur from roaring through Vitiaz Strait to the Admiralties, Hollandia and Leyte."[38]

Indeed, MacArthur chomped at the bit to get on with the drive westward from the Huon Peninsula toward Madang. He had found the intermediary point between Finschhafen and Madang from which to impede the Japanese retreat and put Kenney's planes that much closer to the Admiralties and Wewak. The location was Saidor, on the coast of the Vitiaz Strait, around two-thirds of the way from Finschhafen to Madang. MacArthur assigned the task to the Thirty-Second Division of Krueger's Alamo Force, which had been held in reserve for the New Britain operations.

Krueger protested. Conservative plodder that he was, Krueger pointed out that his command was already engaged in two landings on New Britain and that MacArthur's January 2, 1944, timetable for Saidor left no reserve and stretched the limits of Barbey's amphibious force yet again. "I am most anxious," MacArthur replied, "that if humanly possible this operation take place as scheduled. Its capture will have a vital strategic effect which will be lost if materially postponed."[39]

The strategic effect MacArthur wanted—cutting off retreating Japanese troops and extending his forward air reach—showed that, the diversion of resources to New Britain notwithstanding, he was embracing the leapfrog concept of bypassing, or island-hopping.

The question of whose idea it was to bypass Rabaul would be forever debated. Pro-MacArthur accounts during the postwar years gave rise to the legend that not only had MacArthur originated the plan to bypass Rabaul, he had also conceived the entire strategy of island-hopping. In reality it was much more of a team effort and gradual evolution. Indeed, MacArthur initially opposed bypassing Rabaul, but when it served his purposes, no commander embraced island-hopping more readily than MacArthur.[40]

CHAPTER SEVENTEEN

One General to Another

In the wake of the Quadrant conference at Quebec, in August of 1943, there was a great deal of speculation about Douglas MacArthur's ultimate fate. Speculation was nothing new when it came to MacArthur. There had been those who were certain he was doomed on Corregidor early in 1942 even as others advocated his appointment as supreme commander of all American forces, perhaps even all Allied forces.

The post-Quadrant speculation centered on the strategy to be employed in the American drive across the Pacific. Would the primary axis be through the central Pacific or from MacArthur's front in the southwestern Pacific? Sensing the momentum shifting to the central Pacific, Brisbane's *Courier-Mail* asked in a headline, 'GARRISON' POST FOR MACARTHUR? Quoting a *New York Herald Tribune* correspondent, the Australian newspaper noted the probability that MacArthur's SWPA command "will be reduced within six months to the status of a garrison holding recaptured territories while drives from other directions aim at the East Indies and the Philippines." MacArthur's old friend John C. O'Laughlin, publisher of the *Army and Navy Journal*, offered a different viewpoint. He claimed that MacArthur's "recent victories justify the expectation that he is destined for the direction of a far greater sphere of operations in the Pacific than he now commands."[1]

Which it would be was in large measure a decision for the Joint Chiefs of Staff, a decision that would require ratification by the Combined Chiefs of Staff and, ultimately, by Roosevelt and Churchill. Col-

320

lectively, they held MacArthur's fate in their hands, and in the late fall of 1943, the Allies once again convened wartime conferences to ponder it among their long list of global priorities and exigencies.

Franklin Roosevelt left Washington on November 11, 1943, to meet his Allied partners in Cairo and then Tehran. His immediate party included his increasingly indispensable chief of staff, Admiral William D. Leahy; presidential confidant, Harry Hopkins; and physician, Ross McIntire. They cruised down the Potomac to Chesapeake Bay on the presidential yacht and boarded one of America's newest battleships, the *Iowa*. Marshall, King, and Arnold were already on board, and the battleship immediately steamed to the naval base at Hampton Roads to top off its fuel before racing eastward across the Atlantic.

Dwight Eisenhower met the presidential party as it disembarked at Oran, Algeria, and flew east to Allied headquarters at Tunis. That night, Leahy was obliged to accompany Roosevelt, but Eisenhower invited Marshall and King to spend a quiet evening at his little getaway cottage in nearby Carthage. Inevitably, perhaps, the casual conversation turned to the question of who would command Operation Overlord, the cross-channel invasion of mainland Europe set for the late spring of 1944.

Never one to fail to speak his mind, King opined that Roosevelt had tentatively decided to give the Overlord command to Marshall, despite King's strenuous objections. It wasn't that King didn't like Marshall. They had in fact been working well together—albeit warily—to forge an army-navy partnership. King believed that "Marshall always wanted that command," but King felt Marshall couldn't be spared from the work of the Joint Chiefs and particularly that of the Combined Chiefs. The only mitigating circumstance with Marshall commanding Overlord, King went on to say, was that Eisenhower was the likely heir to Marshall as chief of staff. King had become friendly with Eisenhower early in the war when Ike stood up to King's usual bluster. King would have been very glad to work with him, but he nonetheless "believed it was a mistake to shift the key members of a winning team."[2]

Marshall listened in silence to King's discourse, as always keeping close counsel of his own emotions. King's opinions aside, the decision was Roosevelt's and Roosevelt's alone, but it is interesting to speculate how Marshall's command of Overlord and Eisenhower's appointment as chief of staff might have affected MacArthur had Eisenhower become the direct superior of the man he had long served as an aide.

The next morning, the entire American delegation flew to Cairo to join Churchill and his military chiefs and rehearse a united front before flying on to Tehran to meet their third major ally, Joseph Stalin. Instead of proceeding in harmony, however, the Cairo meetings proved more combative than most, with arguments over the date of Overlord, Churchill's preoccupation with Allied exploits in the eastern Mediterranean, and the viability of an amphibious assault against the Andaman Islands, in the Bay of Bengal, intended to pressure Japan in Burma and French Indochina. It didn't seem to help Anglo-American relations that Generalissimo and Madame Chiang Kai-shek, of China, were present.

Like the Soviet Union, China was sometimes a forgotten ally in the war. The British were more interested in India, but Roosevelt and the American Joint Chiefs recognized that as barely manageable as China was as a country — not to mention as an ally — it had several million men under arms who ostensibly kept a like number of Japanese troops occupied there instead of allowing them to oppose MacArthur and Nimitz elsewhere in the Pacific. At the time, MacArthur's cherished thrust through the Philippines notwithstanding, Leahy and King generally assumed that Japan would ultimately be attacked from land bases in China.[3]

With less collegiality than originally planned, the key American and British representatives flew east to Tehran on the morning of November 27 after waiting three hours for a clingy fog to dissipate. Despite the American and British debates about strategy in the Mediterranean and Southeast Asia, Stalin had only one thing on his mind: in essence, he would not consider his allies irrevocably committed to a second front in Europe until American and British boots came ashore in France. Assured by Roosevelt that that would happen, Stalin put the president on the spot by asking who the commander of the effort was to be. Roosevelt couldn't tell him because, as he whispered to Leahy, "I have not yet made up my mind."[4]

In a subsequent meeting of the Combined Chiefs, the British representatives—their prime minister's fixation with the Mediterranean aside—"fell into line," in Leahy's words, and agreed to launch Overlord's cross-channel attack in May of 1944 and support a follow-up invasion of southern France from the Mediterranean. While European plans continued to dominate the remainder of the conference in Tehran, Stalin made one pronouncement that was to reverberate through future American planning in the Pacific when he announced the Soviet Union's commitment to join in the war against Japan after Germany's defeat. Carrying the brunt of the Pacific effort as they were, the American Joint Chiefs viewed this as an essential ingredient in Japan's unconditional surrender and a helpful clarification of long-range Pacific strategy.[5]

The most significant portion of the Cairo-Tehran conferences for MacArthur and the Pacific occurred when the British and American delegations returned to Cairo after Tehran for a portmortem. Given the sacrosanct commitment to Stalin for Overlord, American plans for both MacArthur's and Nimitz's areas in the Pacific, and Roosevelt's wish to aid China by invading the Andaman Islands, Allied amphibious requirements for 1944—particularly landing craft—were stretched beyond the breaking point. Something had to give.

The weak link proved to be Operation Buccaneer, the Andaman Island invasion. Despite Roosevelt's longtime support for China as an ally, Chiang Kai-shek had generally failed to reciprocate. While Marshall and King were initially as reluctant as Roosevelt to relegate China to a secondary theater, MacArthur's and Halsey's drives across the South Pacific, Nimitz following suit in the Central Pacific Area, and Stalin's vow to join in the Pacific effort all lessened the military importance of China in defeating Japan. Whatever long-range political goals Roosevelt had sought in aiding China were sidetracked in the interests of accomplishing the overriding objective: the timely unconditional surrender of both Germany and Japan.[6]

With Buccaneer off the table, the Joint Chiefs focused on the question that had hung over Pacific operations since MacArthur's presence in Australia and King's counterattack at Guadalcanal challenged the long-held Plan Orange concept of one drive through the central Pacific. Embracing what had evolved almost by default in the two years since Pearl Harbor, the post-Tehran "Overall Plan for the Defeat of Japan" proposed advances by both MacArthur and Nimitz and envisioned mutual support and the ready transfer of forces and resources from one area to another as needed.

The overall objective was to seize positions from which a bombing campaign and a sea and air blockade could be conducted and from which an invasion of Japan proper could be mounted if that was to prove necessary. As to priorities between the two fronts, the plan held: "When conflicts in timing and allocation of means exist, due weight should be accorded to the fact that operations in the Central Pacific promise at this time a more rapid advance toward Japan and her vital lines of communications; the earlier acquisition of strategic air bases closer to the Japanese homeland; and, of greatest importance, are more likely to precipitate a decisive engagement with the Japanese Fleet."[7]

While planners presented this statement in a Combined Chiefs of Staff memorandum, CCS 417, the Americans and the British both understood that the Pacific remained largely an American effort — the Australians fighting in New Guinea notwithstanding. CCS 417 as drafted reinforced two ingrained perceptions: first, that MacArthur would still look over his shoulder, convinced he was not getting the priority he demanded, and, second, that the US Navy still anticipated meeting the Japanese fleet in one grand battle as opposed to chipping away at it by attacks of attrition.

Before the Combined Chiefs approved CCS 417, MacArthur's representative at the Cairo conferences was given a chance to convince the Joint Chiefs that the top priority for operations in the Pacific should be given to MacArthur's Southwest Pacific Area. It was no surprise that his representative was Major General Richard K. Sutherland, but the evolution of Sutherland's role since he had represented MacArthur at the Pacific Military Conference the preceding March requires some scrutiny.

For starters, might MacArthur have attended the Cairo conferences himself? There is no record of his having been invited, and there is in fact ample evidence of his eschewing opportunities to leave Australia for strategic conferences in Nouméa and Honolulu. MacArthur routinely cited command responsibilities that precluded his absence from Brisbane. Yet similar command issues did not keep Nimitz from leaving Honolulu for the West Coast to confer repeatedly with King, nor did they keep Lord Louis Mountbatten, recently appointed supreme allied commander for the South East Asia Command (SEAC), from attending the Cairo conferences.

Did MacArthur really not trust Blamey to act in his absence? He had already removed Krueger's Alamo Force from Allied control, making the point largely moot. Or did he wish to preserve his kingpin status and a certain amount of aloofness? In Brisbane, MacArthur had no equal. Even the Australian prime minister bowed—almost literally—before him. At Cairo, Tehran, or even in Honolulu, MacArthur would have been but one of many wearing four stars and clearly subservient to Franklin Roosevelt. Whatever the reason, MacArthur generally stayed in Brisbane—with occasional visits to Port Moresby—while Sutherland carried MacArthur's banner around the globe.

Having represented MacArthur in Operation Cartwheel planning earlier in the year, Sutherland again left Brisbane for Washington to present MacArthur's Reno plans, the next phases of the return to the Philippines. Sutherland's charge from MacArthur seemed sweeping in scope. As MacArthur explained in a message to Marshall, "Plans revised in accordance with Quadrant decisions [principally, bypassing Rabaul] are being taken to Washington by Sutherland who will present also my summary of the present situation and my recommendations for future actions in the Pacific. He is scheduled to arrive in Washington about November fourth. Sutherland is completely familiar with my tactical and strategical views and is authorized to speak with my full authority. I urgently recommend that he be given an opportunity to present them fully before the Joint and Combined Chiefs of Staff."[8]

What was extraordinary about this message is that, according to Sutherland's clerk, Paul Rogers, Sutherland dictated it and then, without MacArthur having seen it, had Rogers initial it on Sutherland's behalf and send it. Had MacArthur seen it, Rogers was certain MacArthur would have approved it, so in sync were the two men. Nonetheless, this message and Sutherland's subsequent journey to Washington and on to Cairo marked Sutherland's stepping out of MacArthur's shadow and acting as though he belonged on the stage of global strategic planning in his own right.[9]

Sutherland would not have dared to take this step but for his years of tutelage under MacArthur and MacArthur's confidence in him. The dynamic between the two, however, had become increasingly complex. The master-student relationship begun in Manila in the late 1930s slowly evolved to the point where Sutherland became MacArthur's alter ego—it will be remembered that on the chaotic morning of December 8, 1941, Sutherland may have held air boss Brereton at bay on his own and kept him from seeing MacArthur.

In those years, particularly after their escape from Corregidor together, MacArthur trusted Sutherland implicitly. In return, Sutherland, a definite control freak and workaholic, saw to every detail and anticipated every MacArthur need, even as he went to extremes in mirroring some of MacArthur's harsh feelings—most obviously, his strident hostility to the navy.

If MacArthur sometimes appeared brooding, distant, and moody, his demeanor was in part enabled by Sutherland's management of his headquarters, which gave MacArthur time to wax reflective. How many of those hours MacArthur spent pondering the strategy of the southwestern Pacific versus rehashing his paranoia over the Washington cartel he was certain was out to get him—or perhaps even daydreaming of his father's charge up Missionary Ridge—only he knew. In retrospect, it seems likely that at least some of that time was spent rehearsing in his mind, if not out loud, the pronouncements he made so seemingly effortlessly on major occasions.[10]

As the loyal and efficient chief of staff, Sutherland had seen his star rise as MacArthur's had. There was no question that Sutherland had power and could issue almost any order in MacArthur's name with impunity from his chief. That power belonged to MacArthur; it was only on loan to Sutherland. But during the six months between Sutherland's representation of MacArthur at the Pacific Military Conference and his mission to Washington—whether in a case of vaulting ambition or wanting to be judged on his own merits—Sutherland increasingly assumed more of the MacArthur mantle as his own.[11]

Once in Washington with the Reno plans, Sutherland met with the Joint Staff planners and confronted their proposed schedule for Pacific operations in 1944. While central Pacific operations extended as far as the Mariana and Palau islands, the southwestern Pacific advance stopped with an August 1944 invasion of the Vogelkop Peninsula. This schedule embraced the first three Reno phases, advancing along the New Guinea coast and through the Admiralties, but omitted any reference to the final two phases, which called for landings in Mindanao and the recapture of the southern Philippines. If Sutherland wanted to assume MacArthur's mantle by keeping the Philippines a priority, he had his work cut out for him.

Repeating MacArthur's familiar arguments for returning to the islands, Sutherland made the case that an invasion of Mindanao might force the Japanese into a decisive fleet engagement, provide a favorable position from which to strangle Japanese shipping, and permit the Allies' land-based air strength to apply maximum pressure. "We thereby attack the enemy," Sutherland argued, "in each of his four major points of weakness: oil, naval and merchant shipping, and the air." Discounting the evolving dual drives across the Pacific, Sutherland termed the central Pacific offensive "most hazardous" and claimed that it captured only island outposts rather than severing Japan's East Indies lifeline.

"To attempt a major effort along each axis," Sutherland concluded, "would result in weakness everywhere in violation of cardinal principles of war, and . . . in failure to reach the vital strategic objective at the earliest possible date, thus prolonging the war." His solution — and MacArthur's, of course — was one concerted drive through the Southwest Pacific Area.[12]

The Joint Staff planners were not swayed by Sutherland's arguments, and the next order of business was to pack for Cairo. En route via Tunis, Sutherland met Eisenhower and renewed their acquaintance from prewar Manila. Seeing Ike with two more stars on his shoulder than Sutherland wore as a major general, Sutherland would have found it difficult not to reflect on their different career paths. Sutherland had remained a staff officer, while Eisenhower left Manila seeking a field command. Although Marshall kept pulling Eisenhower back into staff circles—much to Eisenhower's eventual benefit—Ike was about to become either chief of staff or commander of the largest amphibious invasion in history. Sutherland was far too ambitious not to feel some measure of jealousy, and it further spurred his growing independence from MacArthur.

After the initial round of British-American talks in Cairo, Sutherland waited less than patiently as only Roosevelt, the Joint Chiefs, and a few key aides flew on to Tehran with their British counterparts. When they returned to Cairo for the portmortem, Sutherland finally had the opportunity to address the Joint Chiefs on Pacific strategy, just as MacArthur had requested a month earlier. He went to great lengths to characterize the activities along the central Pacific axis as a slow process of attrition that in and of itself did not achieve any vital strategic results. It was also a course of action, he claimed, that did not employ what MacArthur, with help from Kenney and Barbey, had begun to demonstrate in the southwestern Pacific, namely, in Sutherland's words, the "effective combination of the three essentials of modern combat: land, sea and air power."

Sutherland's "enthusiasm," the Joint Chiefs' official history reports, had no more effect on the Joint Chiefs than it had had earlier with the planning staff. Admiral King's mind appeared made up before Sutherland spoke, and his colleagues leaned the same way. They simply were still not ready to designate one axis of advance in the Pacific to the exclusion of the other. Instead they approved the basic language of CCS 417 and sanctioned twin drives of mutually supporting operations with due weight being given to the central Pacific in the event of conflict.[13] What was to happen as MacArthur and Nimitz converged on the Philippines from two different angles would be dealt with down the road.

As the second round of Cairo talks adjourned, the Allied leadership headed home. Sometime on his return flight west from Cairo to Tunis, Roosevelt told Leahy that he had made his decision about who would be the supreme commander for Operation Overlord. "Well, Ike," Roosevelt told Eisenhower upon landing in Tunis, "you are going to command Overlord." George Marshall, Roosevelt had decided, simply could not be spared in Washington.[14]

Sutherland, meanwhile, prepared to fly east. Sometime before leaving Washington, perhaps even before departing Australia, he hatched a plan to return from the Cairo conference across the Middle East, India, and the Indian Ocean, thereby circumnavigating the globe. Admittedly, it was shorter than retracing his path, but the route was also more dangerous, given Japanese forces around Java.

To pilot his C-54, a four-engine transport akin to the civilian DC-4, Sutherland tapped Weldon E. "Dusty" Rhoades, a veteran United Airlines pilot about to be inducted into the Army Air Forces mostly because MacArthur and Sutherland wanted him to be their personal pilot. Rhoades was one of those rare people to whom MacArthur and Sutherland took an instant liking. Rhoades, in turn, was among the few who idolized both men.[15]

On the evening of December 7, 1943, Rhoades prepared to take off from Cairo bound for Karachi with Sutherland on board when he learned he was to have additional passengers. Chief of staff Marshall wanted to hop a ride to the Pacific and had been planning the trip for some time. As early as November 22, Marshall advised an aide to have a courier bring him a summer cap and uniform.

"I have aboard more brass than I've ever hauled on one trip before," Rhoades recorded in his diary. In addition to Marshall, the nine general officers included Major General Thomas Handy, assistant chief of staff for operations; Lieutenant General Albert Wedemeyer, slated to be Mountbatten's chief of staff; and Rear Admiral Charles "Savvy" Cooke, King's top planner.[16]

The trip got off to a nearly fatal start. With his regular copilot sprawled in the cabin, sick, Rhoades had Sutherland in the copilot's seat as they battled turbulence over the Persian Gulf and headed directly toward Karachi. The best map available was in French and of dubious quality. Suddenly, a lightning flash revealed a towering wall of mountains dead ahead. Rhoades did a quick 180-degree turn and took a closer look at the map. The elevations were in meters instead of feet. Rhoades decided not to tell his crew and passengers about the near miss but later conceded it was "the nearest I have ever come to killing myself in an airplane."[17] Certainly Marshall's loss would have been almost incalculable.

After Marshall and Sutherland conferred with Mountbatten in New Delhi, where Wedemeyer deplaned, Rhoades flew the party on to Colombo, Ceylon, and then prepared to fly the 3,200 miles to Exmouth Gulf, on the northwestern tip of Australia. Navigating mostly by the stars, Rhoades arrived right on the spot just before sunrise and ended up sharing a room with Marshall as they all tried to get some sleep. Broiling heat soon foiled those plans, and the generals decided that if Rhoades weren't too tired to continue, they might just as well find cooler air in the sky and press on for Brisbane. By then, Rhoades called the 2,600-mile flight across Australia "almost trivial," and they landed at Amberley Field, outside Brisbane, on the morning of December 13.[18]

According to biographer Forrest Pogue, Marshall had planned trips to MacArthur's theater twice before, only to have them thwarted by pressing business elsewhere. He thought it "highly important that he see the Pacific situation for himself...and show MacArthur that he had not been forgotten." MacArthur, however, was not on hand in Brisbane to greet him.[19]

The day before, MacArthur flew to his forward headquarters at Port Moresby in anticipation of the Arawe and Cape Gloucester landings. He had received word that Marshall was flying to Australia, but he chose to stick to his plans to visit Goodenough Island for a preinvasion conference with Krueger rather than remain in Brisbane and meet Marshall. So instead, Marshall, Cooke, and Handy followed MacArthur from Brisbane to Port Moresby, where Kenney met them and proceeded to give them a flying tour of the New Guinea front.

This circumstance was quite logical and happened to provide Marshall with a much better picture of the theater than he would have gotten from a hotel suite in Brisbane, but as with everything MacArthur, these events stoked controversy. Despite countless assertions to the contrary in secondary sources, Marshall had not been part of the Chaumont clique supposedly out to get MacArthur during World War I, and MacArthur had held Marshall in nothing but esteem when as chief of staff he delegated him to train National Guard troops. Their history together since Marshall's appointment as chief of staff had had its moments of friction, but Marshall generally recognized MacArthur's military and political worth. Marshall had managed MacArthur's mercurial traits even as he served as the lightning rod for MacArthur's aggressive and occasionally manipulative advocacy of his Southwest Pacific Area operations.

These basic facts did not, however, keep storytellers from spinning a more pointed version of the relationship between the two generals. Chief among them was Frazier Hunt, who wrote in *The Untold Story of Douglas MacArthur* that MacArthur "was of the opinion that as a result of both the present and the past differences between himself and Marshall, their meeting might be somewhat embarrassing to his distinguished visitor. MacArthur seriously considered conducting the Gloucester operations in person, thus relieving Marshall of his presence." Whether that would have been gracious or the ultimate snub is debatable. Then MacArthur supposedly remarked, "No, I'll stay, but I'll make the prophecy that he'll never see me alone. He'll always find a way to have someone else present."[20]

On the afternoon of December 15—after Kenney's flying tour of Nadzab, Lae, and Buna—Marshall and his party landed on Goodenough Island and met MacArthur and members of his staff, including operations chief Stephen Chamberlin and Admiral Kinkaid, for lunch. Paul Rogers remembered Marshall as an imposing and dignified figure who called MacArthur Douglas, something Rogers had never heard anyone else do. While "their demeanor was formal and restrained" with no signs of "intimacy or close friendship"—which, after all, was not characteristic of either man—"there did not appear to be any particular strain." Rogers reported that the sixty-two-year-old Marshall showed the effects of his many hours in the air and "seemed fatigued."[21]

Marshall nonetheless briefed MacArthur, Chamberlin, Kenney, Kinkaid, and Krueger on the situation in Europe, and MacArthur responded with a review of operations in the southwestern Pacific. Admiral Cooke added a report on central Pacific operations, which included the landings at Tarawa, in the Gilbert Islands, although Kenney showed the SWPA bias by later writing that he "didn't see any reason for fooling with the Central Pacific." By all accounts, it was a frank but nonetheless harmonious exchange of news and ideas. As General Handy remembered years later, "I didn't see any evidence of any conflict between Marshall and MacArthur."

The following morning, Marshall inspected troops with Krueger, then flew back to Port Moresby with MacArthur. After a few hours on the ground, Marshall and his party were back in the air before midnight on December 16, headed for Guadalcanal to meet Halsey and take similar stock of the situation in the South Pacific Area.[22]

Whether MacArthur and Marshall met alone during their less than thirty-six hours together is unclear. Marshall left no record, and MacArthur in his memoirs seemed to contradict Hunt's version of antipathy and the assertion that Marshall "never saw him alone." MacArthur claimed they had "a long and frank discussion," but then went on to give a decidedly MacArthur-like spin to it. Marshall, according to MacArthur, "called attention to the paucity of men and materiel I was receiving as compared with all other theaters of war. He said he realized the imbalance and regretted it, but could do little to alter the low priority accorded the area."

According to MacArthur, Marshall blamed this on King, who supposedly "resented the prominent part I had in the Pacific War" and was "vehement in his personal criticism of me and encouraged Navy propaganda to that end." By MacArthur's version, King "had the complete support of the Secretary of the Navy, Knox, the support in general principle of President Roosevelt and his Chief of Staff, Admiral Leahy, and in many cases of General Arnold, the head of the Air Force."[23]

This seems disingenuous at best and indicative of MacArthur's repeated failure to acknowledge the support he received. Knox was definitely pro-navy and a King fan, but Roosevelt had supported MacArthur at critical strategic moments, Arnold had kept Kenney supplied with planes, and Leahy, far from teaming with King in a navy-versus-army tug-of-war, had long since proved that his one and only role on the Joint Chiefs was to represent Roosevelt and not add another navy voice.

Marshall's potentially dangerous globe-girdling visit to Goodenough Island was the ultimate show of personal support for MacArthur and his Southwest Pacific Area. The very first thing Marshall did upon arriving back at his desk in Washington was to cable MacArthur his "appreciation for the reception you gave me in the Southwest Pacific."[24] Far from being one of the "they" out to get MacArthur, Marshall continually advanced MacArthur's agenda within the constraints of a global war. In the year ahead, MacArthur would be the beneficiary of both Marshall's dominance of the Joint Chiefs and Leahy's growing closeness with Franklin Roosevelt.

In perpetuating the MacArthur myth of having been abandoned and persecuted, however, Frazier Hunt quoted MacArthur as telling an officer after Marshall's visit: "No theatre commander has ever been kept in such abysmal ignorance by his government as I have been."[25] Those who agree with that assertion would do well, as D. Clayton James so succinctly phrased it, "to ponder the probable fate of MacArthur's Southwest Pacific offensive if King had been foremost among the Joint Chiefs."[26] MacArthur came away citing Marshall's visit as evidence that all he thought and held about the navy and Washington was true, but it is really evidence of the support Marshall showed for MacArthur and the Pacific war effort.

Marshall's visit to MacArthur was one indication of support, but as 1943 ground toward a close, there were many tangible signs that resources of men, ships, planes, and materiel were, and had been, flowing toward the Southwest Pacific Area in staggering numbers. Indeed, despite an Allied policy of Germany First, the entire Pacific theater had more than kept pace with the European theater. Among the reasons were (1) King's championing of general Pacific operations; (2) Marshall's specific support of MacArthur; (3) procrastination by the British on a cross-channel invasion commitment; (4) the recognition by the Joint Chiefs that America would not politically tolerate a long war in the Pacific; and (5) a less than enthusiastic British response to sending resources to the China-Burma-India theater. Pacific allocations would fall behind only as deployments to Europe escalated in the buildup for Overlord. As the War Department official history noted, "MacArthur and Nimitz were far from being forced to fight on a shoestring when compared with the European commanders. After two years of war, the balance of U.S. forces between the European and Pacific theaters was fairly even."[27]

During the course of 1943, operations in the Pacific — exclusive of activities in Alaska and the China-Burma-India theater but including the invasion of the Gilbert Islands — US Army forces almost doubled, from 350,720 in December of 1942 to 696,847 at the end of 1943. This included thirteen army divisions and one hundred thousand more personnel than planners had estimated would be committed. As evidence of the enormous logistical requirements of delivering and supplying troops across the expanse of the Pacific, for every combat division deployed, twice as many service troops were required for transport and supply.

During the same period, the number of air groups increased from seventeen to thirty-two, and the number of aircraft in the Pacific more than doubled. The largest increase was in medium and light bombers, which Kenney and Whitehead in New Guinea and Halsey's air commanders in the Solomons used so effectively. These numbers almost quadrupled. Out of the army deployments in the Pacific, Army Air Forces personnel amounted to 162,376, or approximately 23 percent of the total.[28]

When Alaska and the China-Burma-India theater numbers were added to these, there were 912,942 US Army and Army Air Forces personnel in the Pacific, compared to 1,416,485 in the European, Mediterranean, and Middle Eastern theaters. US Navy and Marine Corps figures tipped the other way and totaled 965,210 personnel in the Pacific and 393,882 in Europe. Thus total US overseas deployments on December 31, 1943, were 1,878,152 personnel fighting against Japan and 1,810,367 fighting against Germany. By comparison, there were 7,857 aircraft and 713 combat ships in the Pacific and 8,807 aircraft and 515 combat ships in Europe.[29]

Despite these facts, MacArthur's standard line remained, as he wrote John O'Laughlin near the close of 1943, that "probably no commander in American history has been so poorly supported....At times it has looked as though it was intended that I should be defeated." The only thing more disingenuous was MacArthur's assertion that he had "absolutely no contacts in the United States" and, despite almost daily messages with Marshall and the War Department, that his "opinions are rarely sought and my advice on important matters given little consideration. My isolation, indeed, is complete."[30]

Notwithstanding MacArthur's chronic complaints, his Southwest

Pacific Area's share of these totals was far from the tail end of a shoe-string. Of the approximately seven hundred thousand US Army personnel among SWPA, the South Pacific Area, and the Central Pacific Area, three hundred thousand were in MacArthur's command—as well as four hundred thousand Australian personnel. US Navy and Marine Corps personnel on shore and on ships in these three areas totaled almost 370,000, with 57,000 assigned to SWPA.[31]

MacArthur's aircraft in SWPA totaled 429 bombers, 474 fighters, 234 transports, and 160 reconnaissance and patrol planes from among SWPA, the South Pacific Area, and the Central Pacific Area totals of 1,009 bombers, 1,245 fighters, 359 transports, and 596 reconnaissance and patrol planes.[32]

All these numbers did not mean that there were not critical shortages of certain resources in any given theater. The shortage of landing craft plagued all amphibious operations well into 1944 and played a key role in the abandonment of Operation Buccaneer. However, even recognizing late in 1943 that a chronic shortage of ships would continue to affect planning, Marshall and the Joint Chiefs were responsive to MacArthur's needs within the limits of available resources.

When MacArthur asked the War Department for seventy-one Liberty ships and ten freighters to move 150,000 men and their equipment and supplies as part of Operation Cartwheel, Washington responded with a sixty-day loan of a number of Liberty ships and scraped together various cargo ships to accommodate the bulk of MacArthur's needs. Sometimes, however, this rapid influx of materiel created other problems because of the lack of adequate port and unloading facilities in the forward areas. In just one example of this, 140 cargo ships clogged Milne Bay in January of 1944 waiting to be unloaded; some of them had been at anchor more than a month.[33]

Adequate numbers of landing craft for lighter duty would have been helpful in alleviating these jams as well as stockpiling beachheads, but there never seemed to be enough of them. "It is difficult to state with any certainty," the War Department official history opined, "why the landing craft deficiency was allowed to develop and grow for so long without interference." Priorities in producing cargo and antisubmarine vessels, failure to anticipate the amphibious demands of multiple global operations, and an initial flurry of construction that was momentarily deemed adequate all played a role. What is certain is that the shortage affected amphibious operations globally and was not skewed to the detriment of the Southwest Pacific Area.[34]

The same War Department aide who brought official word to MacArthur of the decision to bypass Rabaul reported back to the Operations Division—likely with MacArthur's encouragement—that MacArthur could have pressed simultaneous attacks against Saidor and Cape Gloucester shortly after the Finschhafen landing were it not for a lack of adequate shipping in Barbey's amphibious forces. This discounts the sharp Japanese counterattack against Finschhafen, but it is true that Barbey's limited number of ships could not be in three or four places—Finschhafen, Saidor, Arawe, and Cape Gloucester—at once. Washington planners took this issue seriously, and Lieutenant General Brehon B. Somervell, the head of Army Service Forces and the top man in logistical planning, spent five days in SWPA in October of 1943 reviewing requirements.[35]

Nonetheless MacArthur was certain that powers in Washington begrudged the deployment of landing craft to the Southwest Pacific Area and took it personally. According to Dan Barbey, during the debate over the Cape Gloucester invasion date and the concomitant need for shipping and landing craft, MacArthur growled, "There are some people in Washington, who would rather see MacArthur lose a battle than America win a war."[36]

The snag in landing-craft production aside, 1943 proved a record-breaking year for American shipyards. They poured out 19.2 million deadweight tons of oceangoing shipping vessels, more than 2.3 times as much as they produced in 1942. Incredibly, this output might have been even greater had it not been for a steel shortage. In oceangoing merchant shipping, this resulted in a net gain of 15.2 million tons for the year. At the year's end, the US oceangoing merchant fleet was almost 2.5 times as large as it had been at the start of the European war, in 1939.[37]

Of the 1,949 ships built in 1943, most were cargo vessels constructed in response to the demands of a two-ocean global war. But 156 of them were combat ships, the most important of which were seven *Essex-*

class aircraft carriers (CVs), nine smaller *Independence*-class light aircraft carriers (CVLs), and sixteen escort, or "jeep," carriers (CVEs). Many more were under construction, to be launched in 1944. MacArthur had long pleaded for carriers, and, while none had yet to be placed under Kinkaid's command, MacArthur and the Southwest Pacific Area would soon be the beneficiaries of this outpouring of American industrial might.[38]

None of this, however, kept Douglas MacArthur from consistently repeating his refrain of neglect and abandonment. Even as he made inroads in New Guinea and marshaled his forces for leaps toward the Philippines, MacArthur told an old friend from World War I: "No resources and no supplies made the situation precarious from the start. I have done the best I could with what I had, but no commander in American history has so failed of support as here. We have come through, but it has been shoestring stuff."[39]

As dramatic as the change was between the end of 1941 and the close of 1942 for the general Allied war effort and for MacArthur personally, the transformation during 1943 was even more so. From the stalemate at Buna, MacArthur's forces had advanced well beyond Lae and—although it was not his idea—almost completed the bypass of Rabaul. MacArthur was not the only commander to do so, but he had come to embrace wholeheartedly and execute adroitly the combined use of air, sea, and land forces, which was the best argument for unity of command that he could put forth.

With Dan Barbey and Walter Krueger—and soon, Thomas Kinkaid—gaining his confidence and joining George Kenney in his inner circle of field commanders, MacArthur had developed a competent general staff committed to doing his bidding. Only time would tell how well Dick Sutherland continued to fit into that picture and whether Bob Eichelberger would return to MacArthur's good graces.

Beyond competent personnel and an increase in resources, much of the year's success could be traced to Ultra. The controversy of its after-action reports aside, the Battle of the Bismarck Sea decisively stopped major Japanese reinforcements from reaching New Guinea. Other Ultra intercepts helped Kenney beat down Japanese airpower over

New Guinea and permitted American submarines to prey on Japanese resupply convoys. Growing amphibious resources would soon allow Kinkaid and Barbey to take advantage of Ultra-identified weaknesses in Japan's widespread defenses for further advances.[40]

To the north, the central Pacific drive championed by Ernest King and Chester Nimitz had come up against reality on the heavily defended beaches of Tarawa, but the Gilbert Islands were secure and served as a springboard to the Marshall Islands, some 2,500 miles beyond Hawaii. Halsey had yet to complete the capture of Bougainville, in the Solomons, but he was eyeing more island-hopping and had proved both his tenacity and his ability to work with MacArthur.

On the global scale, the Russians had reversed the tide on Germany's eastern front, Sicily and part of Italy were in Allied hands, and Allied bombers rained destruction on German infrastructure. Tapped to command Overlord, Dwight Eisenhower was quoted as saying that the war in Europe would be over in 1944. Seeking the person who had had the biggest impact on the world in 1943, *Time* chose chief of staff George C. Marshall as its Man of the Year.

Meanwhile, Douglas MacArthur was as determined as ever to return to the Philippines.

PART FOUR

RETURN

1944

I think I know at firsthand something about what the next Presidency will require. I believe that General MacArthur has what it takes in full measure.
— SENATOR ARTHUR H. VANDENBERG,
"WHY I AM FOR MACARTHUR,"
FEBRUARY 12, 1944

He ended our talk with the sarcastic remark that MacArthur seemed more interested in making good his promise to return to the Philippines than in winning the war.
— VICE ADMIRAL DANIEL E. BARBEY,
RECOUNTING A MEETING WITH
ADMIRAL ERNEST J. KING, JUNE 1944

MacArthur poses in front of the tail of the *Bataan* as he prepares to depart Brisbane for the last time, en route to Port Moresby, Hollandia, and the Philippines, October 14, 1944. *Courtesy of the MacArthur Memorial, Norfolk, VA*

CHAPTER EIGHTEEN

Gambling in the Admiralties

Douglas MacArthur didn't waste any time committing his forces to new action in 1944. On January 2, 6,800 men of the Thirty-Second Infantry Division of Krueger's Alamo Force landed at Saidor, on the northeastern coast of New Guinea. Given the ongoing operations at Arawe and Cape Gloucester, on New Britain, Krueger protested the leap as stretching his forces too thin, but MacArthur wanted to cut the Japanese Eighteenth Army in half and trap its eastern units on the Huon Peninsula.

Dan Barbey's amphibious forces were also stretched thin by the Saidor assault, but Barbey later claimed, "The Saidor landing was an excellent example of MacArthur's concept of 'hit them where they ain't' and 'bypass the strongpoints.'" Barbey said both phrases translated into "big gains with little losses." Saidor had "good beaches, a good airstrip, and was weakly defended."[1] Kenney especially welcomed the airstrip. Lying 125 miles west of Finschhafen and two-thirds of the way to Madang, Saidor was a key pivot point from which his planes could support both an advance farther west along the New Guinea coast and a move northward against the Admiralty Islands, the latter being the final step in the isolation of Rabaul.

The immediate priority, however, was to effect MacArthur's contemplated entrapment of the Japanese forces east of Saidor. They were under pressure from the Australian Ninth Division, moving northward from Finschhafen. Despite encountering minimal enemy resistance at the Saidor beachhead and soon having fifteen thousand men ashore, Brigadier General Clarence Martin's task force delayed moving inland to cut the Japanese escape route. This was the result of garbled communications and multiple warnings from Krueger that they should prepare the Saidor area defensively in anticipation of a counterattack rather than link up with the Australians and pinch the Japanese between them.

Meanwhile, Japanese Eighteenth Army commander Adachi visited divisional headquarters at Kiari and Sio, between Finschhafen and Saidor. After evaluating the situation, he received orders from General Imamura in Rabaul to move these troops westward and concentrate on defending Madang and Wewak rather than force an action at Saidor. Consequently, the Japanese undertook their own form of leapfrogging, and the Twentieth and Fifty-First Divisions surreptitiously retreated from Kiari and Sio via an inland route that avoided the Americans recently landed at Saidor. Adachi left Sio by submarine deeply depressed because the two divisions would be forced to go through an arduous retreat reminiscent of the withdrawal from Lae.

Their departure left the way open for the Australian Ninth Division to march into Sio on January 15. Not until February 6, however, when American advance patrols in the steep, jungle-clad mountains beyond Saidor reported large numbers of Japanese troops struggling along the inland trail, did Martin know for certain that Saidor would not be attacked. An estimated ten thousand Japanese troops—only half the strength of those divisions two months before—survived the grueling two-hundred-mile withdrawal to Madang.[2]

Through operational delays and unwillingness on the part of the Japanese to engage, MacArthur had failed to close the trap he intended on the Huon Peninsula. But the concentration of these survivors and other reinforcements that Adachi rushed to Madang and Wewak set MacArthur and his planners to thinking about a much grander leap in the future. Until then, aside from the Saidor airfield, the biggest prize had come at Sio.

As the headquarters' radio platoon of the Japanese Twentieth Division broke down their equipment for the torturous retreat on foot, they deemed the division's codebooks, substitution tables, and key registers too heavy to haul along. They merely tore off the covers as proof of destruction, put the bulk of the material in a steel trunk, and buried the trunk near a streambed, hoping that rising water would obliterate the remainder.

As Australian troops leery of booby traps moved into the abandoned Japanese headquarters area, they detected what they first took to be a buried land mine. Demolition experts soon found otherwise and unearthed the trunk. An intelligence officer quickly recognized the treasure trove. The soggy mess was transported to MacArthur's Central Bureau, in Melbourne, and it gave his Ultra efforts a huge boost. With the Sio documents in hand, US Army cryptologists decrypted more than thirty-six thousand Japanese army messages in March of 1944 alone. The result was that code breakers could monitor Japanese army signals with the same speed and precision as they did Japanese naval traffic.[3]

With the advance to Saidor secure, the Joint Chiefs directed MacArthur to close the ring around Rabaul by invading the Admiralty Islands. Centered on the main island of Manus and nearby Los Negros, this island cluster forms the northwestern boundary of the Bismarck Sea. The Japanese had occupied the islands in 1942 and developed two airfields, but they generally ignored the fine anchorage of Seeadler Harbor. Formed by the horseshoe-shaped curvature of Los Negros against the eastern end of Manus, its protected waters are six miles wide, twenty miles long, and 120 feet deep — the perfect assembly, provisioning, and repair point for fleet operations against the Philippines. The chiefs set April 1 as the target date for the invasion.

Meanwhile, Halsey's parallel thrust through the Solomons had resulted in the invasion of Bougainville in November of 1943. Fighting was tough and would continue for months, but in the interim, Halsey looked ahead for another opportunity to bypass heavy opposition. His next stop was supposed to be Kavieng, on New Ireland, though Halsey had other ideas. Complicating both his plans and MacArthur's were Nimitz's activities in the central Pacific and the requirement for the main United States Fleet to support amphibious operations anywhere in the South or Southwest Pacific Areas.

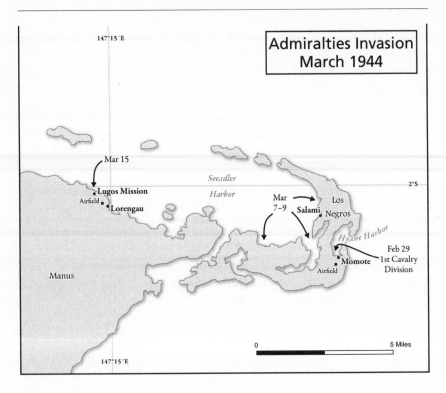

The central Pacific campaign began in earnest on November 20, 1943, with the invasion of Makin and Tarawa, in the Gilbert Islands. Code-named Operation Galvanic, the campaign provided a steep learning curve and demonstrated that naval firepower alone could not eliminate deeply dug-in fortifications, particularly on volcanic atolls. Nimitz came under harsh criticism from all sides — including from his marine commander, MacArthur, and the public at large — for the resultant casualties as well as for his decision to attack the Gilberts in the first place instead of bypassing them and attacking the Marshalls directly. But as in the Aleutians and MacArthur's own experiences in Papua, certain lessons of amphibious warfare and specific geography (cold-weather operations, jungle warfare, coral-fringed landing sites) had to be learned somewhere.

Nimitz applied the lessons of Tarawa to the Marshalls invasion and, against the advice of his top commanders, chose to strike directly for the main Japanese base at Kwajalein rather than nibble away at the outer islands. Supported by the main Pacific Fleet, whose growing collection of fast carriers was given the task of blocking reinforcements from Truk and the Marianas, this assault began on February 1, 1944. Within a week, Kwajalein was secure. Vice Admiral Raymond Spruance urged Nimitz, King, and the Joint Chiefs to keep the drive rolling and seize the atoll of Eniwetok, four hundred miles west of Kwajalein, before it could be reinforced. With a circumference of fifty-some miles, the Eniwetok lagoon provided the largest natural harbor in the Pacific. By mid-February, this, too, had been accomplished.[4]

Douglas MacArthur was probably the only American military officer celebrating these successes with less than unqualified enthusiasm. Despite the dictates of Combined Chiefs of Staff memorandum 417, agreed upon at the Cairo conference for twin offensives via both the Central and Southwest Pacific Areas, MacArthur remained adamant that his New Guinea–Vogelkop–Mindanao axis provided the key to defeating Japan. Having convinced himself that he was to be given "a big piece of the fleet" and that the British were likewise going to contribute ships, MacArthur decided he needed a veteran, high-profile naval commander all his own.

When Halsey made a brief visit to Brisbane in December of 1943 to confer with MacArthur before heading to the States for conferences with Nimitz and King, he was taken aback by the unexpected offer. "How about *you*, Bill?" MacArthur pointedly asked Halsey. "If you come with me, I'll make you a greater man than Nelson ever dreamed of being!" Halsey responded graciously but said he would have to take the matter up with Nimitz and King. He did—and that's the last he ever heard of it, either from MacArthur or the US Navy.[5]

Halsey and MacArthur also discussed their coordinated next moves— MacArthur against the Admiralties and Halsey against Kavieng. Yet when Halsey got to his conference with King, the admiral asked him, "When are you going to be ready to take Rabaul or Kavieng?" Halsey, in what he recalled was a flippant manner, replied, "Why take either one?" Then, as Halsey told the story, "in a most delightful sarcastic tone, which you know as well as I do, [King] said 'and what have you to suggest in lieu thereof.'" Halsey replied with one word, "Emirau."[6]

Emirau is a tiny island eight miles long and two miles wide located ninety miles north of Kavieng. It was unoccupied and offered a location for an airfield, which Halsey thought would make an assault against Kavieng unnecessary. King appeared noncommittal, and Halsey went east on leave. By the time the schedule for the Southwest Pacific and South Pacific operations was next discussed in depth, at a planning conference in Honolulu at the end of January, Halsey's plane was grounded by bad weather in the States and he was unable to attend.

In his absence, Sutherland, representing MacArthur and the original plan, argued convincingly that MacArthur deemed an assault by Halsey's South Pacific forces on Kavieng, not Emirau, to be essential. Nimitz, for his part, agreed to provide long-range carrier support by making a major strike against Truk around March 26 in anticipation of the coordinated Admiralty and Kavieng landings on April 1.[7]

Momentarily stymied in his bid to take Emirau, Halsey invaded the Green Islands. This tiny group of four coral atolls lies north of Bougainville and east of Rabaul and offered yet another potential airfield from which to attack Kavieng or Rabaul. Troops from the New Zealand Third Division, previously in the Solomons, landed there on February 15 to only minimal ground resistance and a last-ditch air assault from Rabaul. Within two days, a PT base was operational, and by March 4, navy Seabees had constructed a five-thousand-foot fighter airstrip, to be followed shortly thereafter by a longer bomber strip.[8]

Against this backdrop, MacArthur pondered his directive to wait until April 1 to invade the Admiralties, particularly in light of Nimitz's successful jump from Kwajalein to Eniwetok at least two months ahead of schedule. MacArthur's fixation on Kavieng notwithstanding, he was well aware from Kenney's air-operations reports that Rabaul had been rendered largely ineffective. Continuous bombardments had reduced its strength so much that, after February 19, there were no warships in its harbor, and no fighters rose to challenge Allied bombers.

An estimated one hundred thousand well-supplied Japanese ground troops remained in Rabaul, but they were to prove that in the war of island-hopping, ground forces without coordinated naval and air strength were largely impotent—unless the enemy decided to attack them directly in a ground assault. Japanese naval aircraft effectively abandoned the skies over eastern New Guinea, the Bismarck Archipelago, and the Solomon Islands while army planes concentrated at Wewak to block MacArthur's advance along the New Guinea coast. The door to the Admiralties appeared to be wide open.[9]

George Kenney and his trusted deputy, Ennis Whitehead, were determined to keep it that way. Whitehead in particular wanted to get the planned Admiralties invasion out of the way and have his flank covered so he could concentrate operations against the Japanese air buildup around Wewak. Kenney was always looking for an opportunity to seize an airfield in a quick strike, as he had done at Nadzab and other locations in New Guinea. By February 6, their attacks had rendered the airfields at Lorengau, on Manus and Momote, on Los Negros, unserviceable, with no sign of enemy aircraft. Antiaircraft fire had stopped, but unbeknownst to them, this was because the Japanese commander had ordered his defenders to conceal their positions for the time being.

Consequently, on February 23, Whitehead showed Kenney a reconnaissance report attesting that three B-25s had lazed for ninety minutes at low altitudes over the Admiralties without drawing any opposition and without detecting any ground movement. According to Whitehead, the whole archipelago looked "completely washed out," and he recommended that a reconnaissance party be landed at once to take a look.[10]

Kenney, who had been with Sutherland in Honolulu and had been part of those discussions, was back in Brisbane when he received Whitehead's report. Judging, in his words, that "Los Negros was ripe for the plucking," Kenney hurried upstairs to MacArthur's office. He proposed to seize the Momote airfield immediately with a few hundred troops and some engineers and then use it to control the islands rather than making the full-scale assault directly into Seeadler Harbor as planned on April 1. According to Kenney, MacArthur paced back and forth as Kenney expounded on the idea, then stopped suddenly and said, "That will put the cork in the bottle. Let's get Chamberlin and Kinkaid up here."[11]

MacArthur's operations officer and naval commander quickly

bought into the plan and coordinated it with Krueger's Alamo Force. One thousand men from the First Cavalry Division would board two destroyer transports (APDs) at Oro Bay and sail north to Los Negros in just five days' time. It was a huge gamble. As the US Army official history points out: "MacArthur was sending a thousand men against an enemy island group approximately one month ahead of the time that his schedule had originally called for a whole division to make the invasion."

What's more, there was a wide difference of opinion as to how many Japanese troops — if any — remained on Los Negros and nearby Manus. Whitehead told Kenney that there were no more than three hundred Japanese defending the islands, although how he arrived at that number is unclear. Willoughby, who had badly underestimated the Finschhafen defenders, gave an estimate of 4,050. The First Cavalry Division's own intelligence estimates pushed that figure to 4,900, although in its field order it noted that air reconnaissance had shown no signs of enemy occupation.

In fact, Willoughby's use of Ultra had correctly identified the Japanese units present, and this time his estimate of strength was about right. The men from "the First Team," with the emblem of a horse's head on their shoulder patches, might be sailing into a buzz saw. Aware that Whitehead's estimate did not jibe with Willoughby's, MacArthur ordered the First Cavalry Division to field a second force of 1,500 combat troops and 428 Seabees to land two days after the initial landings if the decision was made to keep the reconnaissance force on Los Negros. The remainder of the division was to follow as necessary.[12]

An issue that would become more pertinent six months later was that the Admiralties operation involved three separate naval forces under three separate chains of command: Halsey's naval forces, reporting to him as SOPAC commander; Kinkaid's Seventh Fleet, reporting to him and then MacArthur as CINCSWPA; and any Pacific Fleet units that might play supporting or diversionary roles, including Spruance's Fifth Fleet, reporting to Nimitz as CINCPAC. Chamberlin suggested that in the event of a major naval engagement, the command of those three forces should reside with Halsey as the senior admiral. "This suggestion was accepted," according to the US Army official history, "although for some reason it was not followed in similar situations at Hollandia and Leyte."[13]

Then MacArthur made a brash decision. Just as he had done with Kenney in the air attack on Nadzab, he decided to accompany the troops on their reconnaissance-in-force, claiming that he would thus be on the scene to decide whether to evacuate the beachhead or hold it. When MacArthur invited Kinkaid along, the admiral could hardly decline, and the invasion force suddenly swelled from two APDs and four destroyers to include two cruisers and another four destroyers. Years later, Kinkaid claimed that the cruisers were necessary because a destroyer "had neither accommodations nor communications suitable for a man of MacArthur's position" and that it was "poor practice to send but one ship of any type on a tactical mission."[14]

Before MacArthur sailed into the fray at Los Negros, however, he fired a heavy barrage against Chester Nimitz and the US Navy in a lengthy memo addressed to the chief of staff. MacArthur's song had a familiar refrain: the navy wanted to usurp his command and fold his Southwest Pacific Area into the broader Pacific Ocean Area, the command of which Nimitz held as one of his two hats.

This latest exchange had started with a cable MacArthur had sent Marshall earlier in February in which he once again urged the New Guinea–Vogelkop–Mindanao axis as the best route to the Philippines. He criticized the central Pacific offensive as lacking a "major strategic objective" and being ineffective as an approach to the Philippines because of the distances involved and the lack of major airfields and fleet bases. MacArthur strongly recommended that after the operations in the Marshalls, "the maximum force from all sources in the Pacific [should] be concentrated in my drive up the New Guinea coast."[15]

Admiral King took exception, of course, and remarked that MacArthur must not have "accepted the decisions of the Combined Chiefs of Staff at Sextant [Cairo]" about dual offensives. Nimitz's response had been action-oriented, as Spruance rapidly pushed beyond the Marshalls and seized Eniwetok, admittedly nine hundred miles farther from Mindanao than MacArthur's position at the time but also four hundred miles closer to Japan.[16]

But Nimitz was also interested in using Seeadler Harbor, in the Admiralties, after its capture by MacArthur as a base for the Pacific Fleet. He consequently recommended that, after its capture, Manus Island be assigned to Halsey's South Pacific Area for development and control. This seemed logical in many quarters, particularly because Halsey's staff — not MacArthur's — had already been working on harbor plans and because the island was near the dividing line between the Southwest Pacific and Central Pacific Areas. MacArthur saw the matter quite differently.

MacArthur claimed that by wanting to control Manus Nimitz was projecting his own command "into the Southwest Pacific by the artificiality of advancing South Pacific Forces into the area." Harking back to earlier proposals to put the entire Pacific under Nimitz's supreme command, MacArthur found this relatively minor boundary change to be a step toward that goal and predicted that it would "be followed by others until the desired result is effected."

Such a move, MacArthur asserted, would disrupt relations with the Australians, demoralize soldiers and the general public, and reflect poorly upon his capacity to command. If Manus and Seeadler Harbor were assigned to the South Pacific Area, it was evidence that the ultimate issue was the command of the campaign to retake the Philippines. If he were denied that command, MacArthur was convinced that "my professional integrity, indeed my personal honor would be so involved that, if otherwise, I request that I be given early opportunity personally to present the case to the Secretary of War and to the President before finally determining my own personal action in the matter."[17]

George Marshall must have sighed upon reading this. As he usually did, the chief of staff patiently worked to defuse the matter. MacArthur should indeed retain command of bases in his area, Marshall told him, but it was essential to the war effort that naval facilities be developed "as desired by the fleet and that the fleet will have unrestricted use of them." There was no grand conspiracy, and Marshall had heard nothing about boundary changes or "any idea that control of the campaign for recapture of the Philippines should be taken from you."

If "a real military reason" arose for any changes, they would be made, Marshall said, but he did not "see them in prospect." As for the oft-used gauntlet of MacArthur's "professional integrity and personal honor," Marshall assured him they were "in no way questioned or, so far as I can see, involved." But should MacArthur still desire to do so, Marshall said he would willingly "arrange for you to see the secretary of war and the president at any time on this or any other matter."[18] Meanwhile, MacArthur was out the door and on his way to attack the harbor that had just caused him so much anguish.

Early on the morning of February 27, with Dusty Rhoades at the controls, MacArthur's B-17, the *Bataan,* lifted off from the Archerfield airport, outside Brisbane, with MacArthur and Kinkaid on board and headed north. At the usual refueling stop at Townsville, the trip almost came to a premature end when the bomber's brakes failed to hold after landing on a short runway, and Rhoades "narrowly averted a crack-up." They flew on to Milne Bay, where MacArthur and his party boarded the cruiser *Phoenix* late that afternoon.[19]

That same day, a stealthy reconnaissance conducted by a six-man scouting party that had landed from a PBY Catalina floatplane paddled a rubber raft off Momote and Hyane Harbor and reported that the wooded area between Momote and the coast was "lousy with Japs." Whitehead worried that Kenney had gotten himself and MacArthur "out on a limb," but Kenney discounted this report, claiming that "twenty-five Japs in those woods at night" might well make it appear that the place was "lousy with Japs."[20]

Among MacArthur's small entourage on the *Phoenix* was Roger O. Egeberg, a medical doctor from Cleveland, Ohio, who had spent a year at Milne Bay as a surgeon with a field hospital. Shortly after being reassigned to Brisbane, Egeberg was summoned for an interview with MacArthur. The general was looking for a personal physician to replace Charles Morhouse, who was returning to the States after having been with him since Corregidor. Egeberg was at first leery of the assignment, but he quickly became a MacArthur admirer, and MacArthur in turn took to him, even though on one of his first visits Egeberg casually suggested that little Arthur be given nothing more than a day or two of rest to get over a fever.

Barely had Egeberg settled into his quarters at Lennons Hotel when Lloyd "Larry" Lehrbas, the general's assistant public relations officer, warned him to be ready for a trip. Egeberg was in his cabin on the *Phoenix* the night before the Los Negros landing when a marine guard knocked on his door and told him that MacArthur wanted to see him. Egeberg found the general in an excited state, restlessly circling his little stateroom. Egeberg quickly took his pulse and found it "strong, slow and regular." MacArthur brushed off any further examination but launched into a long discourse on his youth, West Point athletics, and early assignments in the Philippines. After an hour or so, he calmed down and said he would like to go back to sleep.

The next morning, as they assembled in the predawn darkness to watch preparations for the landing, MacArthur grinned and told Egeberg, "Doc, you missed that diagnosis last night. I went back to bed after you left and pretty soon I began to feel excited again." MacArthur claimed he discovered that, at the speed the cruiser was moving, the foot of his bed was several inches above his head, and when he made up the bed the other way, he finally got a restful sleep.[21]

Egeberg's story aside, it is likely that MacArthur was more than a little keyed up by the prospect of his first close encounter with the enemy since his days in the trenches with the Rainbow Division. No doubt he also pondered the prospects of success for the gamble he was about to make as he watched the first wave of troops climb down cargo nets into the waiting landing craft.

Sporadic fire from coastal guns dogged the troops as they made for the beach, but well-placed shells from the cruisers and an accompanying destroyer quickly silenced them. This wave hit the beach at 8:17 a.m. on February 29, and by 9:50 a.m., a portion of the Momote airfield was in American hands. Three hours later, the entire landing force was ashore. Two soldiers were killed and three wounded, and a like number of sailors was lost on one of the landing craft.

Five Japanese were reported slain, but there was an uneasy air about the apparent success. To many troops moving forward, it appeared as if the Japanese defenders had melted inland. The landing force commander, Brigadier General William C. Chase, reported to Krueger, "Enemy situation undetermined." In part this was because Colonel

Yoshio Ezaki's garrison had expected a concerted landing via Seeadler Harbor. By coming in the back door of Los Negros, at tiny Hyane Harbor, the First Cavalry Division troops caused an initial surprise and avoided the bulk of Ezaki's defenses, reports of the area being "lousy with Japs" notwithstanding.[22]

MacArthur, Kinkaid, Lehrbas, and Egeberg came ashore at 4:00 p.m. MacArthur's mind was on the decision to withdraw or stay, but he took time to award a Distinguished Service Cross to the first man ashore. Immediately afterward, as Lehrbas reported in his press release, MacArthur "walked through the muck and blasted palms to inspect the extent and condition of the Momote Airfield disregarding possible Jap snipers." He was reported to have admonished Chase, "You have all performed magnificently. Hold what you have taken no matter against what odds. You have your teeth in him now. Don't let go."[23]

Had Colonel Ezaki chosen that moment to launch a concerted counterattack, MacArthur and the entire beachhead might have been overwhelmed. But Japanese forces were still spread thin and reacting slowly to both the surprise of the landing and its location at Hyane Harbor. Nonetheless, the obvious uncertainty and danger raises the questions of why MacArthur accompanied the expedition and why he went ashore. By his own account, MacArthur did not mention that he had gone ashore, saying only, "I was relying almost entirely upon surprise for success and, because of the delicate nature of the operation and the immediate decision required, I accompanied the force aboard Admiral Kinkaid's flagship."[24]

Roger Egeberg offered a less direct version of the story. Walking along the Momote runway, MacArthur stopped to look at two dead Japanese soldiers. Egeberg heard the voices of other Japanese in the nearby woods. While they were walking, Egeberg positioned himself on the general's left, between MacArthur and the woods on the far side of the strip. When they turned around to come back, Egeberg took up a similar position, even though he was then on the general's right, a clear violation of protocol. One martinet called Egeberg out on it and demanded rather loudly, "Shouldn't you be on the other side of the General?" MacArthur heard him, looked around, and said, "I think I know why Doc is there. This is not a parade ground."[25]

After they were back on board the *Phoenix,* MacArthur had one more comment for Egeberg. "Doc," he said, according to Egeberg, "I noticed you were wearing an officer's cap while we were ashore. You probably took a look at me and put it on. Well, I wear this cap with all the braid. I feel in a way that I have to. It's my trademark... a trademark that many of our soldiers know by now, so I'll keep on wearing it, but with the risk we take in a landing I would suggest that you wear a helmet from now on." That same evening, MacArthur took one of his few drinks of the war when he had Egeberg "prescribe" a shot of bourbon as "a little medicine in celebration of this successful reconnaissance in force."[26]

That evening, the *Phoenix,* an accompanying cruiser (the *Nashville*), and six destroyers departed the Los Negros beachhead for New Guinea, leaving two destroyers on station. Lehrbas released a second press release, noting that "the assault on the Admiralty Islands was carried out under the immediate observation of General MacArthur" because the operation was "one of the most important of the entire campaign and as is his practice, [he] wished to be present at the crisis."[27]

But there was a major difference between this communiqué and those issued earlier in the war. Instead of begrudging his subordinates their publicity, MacArthur named three ground commanders, four naval commanders, and air-operations chiefs Kenney and Whitehead as having led the operation. It was a far cry from his bristling over Eichelberger's press after Buna.

Arriving at Finschhafen the next morning, March 1, MacArthur and his group found Rhoades and the *Bataan* waiting for them, and they made the hop back to Port Moresby for the night. Rhoades described MacArthur as "in rare humor" and "most pleased over the success of the landings." Even so, Rhoades wondered about MacArthur's reported stroll along the Momote runway. "I hate to see him take these chances," Rhoades confessed to his diary, "but he wants to do it and it instills respect in his troops, I guess."

The next day, Rhoades delivered MacArthur and Kinkaid back to Brisbane in time for dinner.[28] But on Los Negros, things were not yet fully calm. As MacArthur sailed away, Colonel Ezaki's defenders counterattacked with a vengeance but without concentrating their forces. The First Cavalry troops dug in, and by daylight on March 1, most of the attackers had withdrawn three to four hundred yards. A tense standoff followed, but by the morning of March 2, the supporting force of ground troops and Seabees unloaded and joined the action.[29]

The Seabees' Fortieth Naval Construction Battalion played a critical role in capturing the remaining portion of the Momote airstrip, and MacArthur later recommended it for a Presidential Unit Citation. Landing during a critical situation, they went to work clearing and repairing the airstrip and bulldozing fire lanes into the surrounding jungle. But, MacArthur boasted, they "still found time during their few hours of leisure off duty to rout out small bands of the enemy, locate and report pillboxes, and otherwise carry the offensive to the enemy's positions."[30]

Japanese resistance throughout the Admiralties continued for weeks, but Los Negros was largely cleared within ten days of the invasion. The Momote airstrip was made operational for fighters in short order, and the second airfield — at Lorengau, on Manus — was captured after a landing at Lugos Mission. MacArthur's communiqué of March 10 reported, "Our naval and supply ships entered Seeadler Harbor without interference." Nonetheless, it was not until May 18 that Krueger officially declared the Admiralties operation complete. Only seventy-five of Ezaki's defenders — a number that did not include Ezaki himself — survived to surrender. The Japanese dead amounted to 3,280, and Krueger estimated that another 1,100 had already been buried, coming close to Willoughby's intelligence estimate. The cost to the First Cavalry Division totaled 326 men killed, 1,189 wounded, and four missing.[31] There was, however, to be one more fight over the Admiralties.

Barely had MacArthur returned to Brisbane on the evening of March 2 when he revisited the issue of who would control the facilities soon to be under construction in Seeadler Harbor. Halsey's representative on MacArthur's staff alerted Halsey, in Nouméa, that a crisis was at hand and requested that he come to Brisbane at once. Halsey did so with his chief aides in tow and went immediately to MacArthur's office to meet with the general, Admiral Kinkaid, and key members of their respective staffs.

As Halsey recalled, "Even before a word of greeting was spoken, I saw that MacArthur was fighting to keep his temper." Having not yet received Marshall's quieting response to MacArthur's pre-Admiralties rant over shifting boundaries and concomitant control, MacArthur had his sights set on Halsey as a coconspirator with Nimitz. "I had had no hand in originating the dispatch," Halsey recalled. "I did not even hear of it until after it had been sent; but MacArthur lumped me, Nimitz, King, and the whole Navy in a vicious conspiracy to pare away his authority."

Angry as MacArthur was, Halsey's recollection offers an insight into the general's temperament. Confessing that, when he got angry himself, strong emotion made him profane, Halsey said that MacArthur did not need that crutch because "profanity would have merely discolored his eloquence." And eloquent but forceful the general was for around fifteen minutes — by MacArthur standards, a short presentation.

He had no intention of submitting to such interference, MacArthur thundered, and, according to Halsey, "he had given orders that, until the jurisdiction of Manus was established, work should be restricted to facilities for ships under his direct command." When he had finished this diatribe, MacArthur jabbed his pipe stem in Halsey's direction and demanded, "Am I not right, Bill?"

Halsey responded with an emphatic, "No, sir!" which was promptly seconded by Kinkaid. What was more, Halsey told MacArthur, if he stuck to those orders, he would be "hampering the war effort!"

MacArthur's staff squirmed under this rebuke to their chief, and the argument lasted around an hour. Finally MacArthur seemed to acquiesce to Halsey's plea, and the session adjourned, only to reconvene at MacArthur's summons the following morning. "We went through the same argument as the afternoon before, almost word for word," Halsey recalled, "and at the end of an hour we reached the same conclusion: the work would proceed."

Halsey thought that ended the matter and prepared to return to Nouméa, but he was asked to return to MacArthur's office again. "I'll be damned," wrote Halsey, "if we didn't run the course a third time!" Finally MacArthur gave Halsey "a charming smile" and told him, "You win, Bill!"[32]

When Admiral Leahy published his memoirs in 1950, he opined in his characteristically understated and diplomatic way that, when it came to general Pacific strategy, "it appeared that MacArthur's ideas might conflict with those of Nimitz, and the difference in the personalities of these two able commanders was going to require delicate handling."[33]

Going on to recount the particulars of the Seeadler Harbor battle, Leahy wrote, drawing upon his diary: "MacArthur was reported to have said he would not stand for the Nimitz proposal, that the American people would not stand for it, that the Australians would not stand for it, and furthermore that nothing was going to be allowed to interfere with his march back to the Philippines." This was pretty much a paraphrase of MacArthur's points in his February 29 letter to Marshall.

As for Halsey, Leahy recounted, "Halsey, no shrinking violet himself, in turn charged that MacArthur was suffering from illusions of grandeur and that his staff officers were afraid to oppose any of their General's plans whether or not they believed in them." This generally squared with Halsey's account in his memoirs.[34]

Nonetheless, when MacArthur received a galley proof of Leahy's *I Was There*, he took exception to Leahy's account, writing, "Dear Bill...the quoted statement is so lacking in factuality that I very much doubt its insertion was with your own personal knowledge." MacArthur asked Leahy to eliminate the quoted passages from his book. "There has been much rumor mongering concerning my differences with Nimitz and Halsey," MacArthur maintained, "and yet my relations with both have always been on the warmest plane of cordiality."[35]

"Dear Douglas," Leahy assured him in response, "nobody is better qualified than you are to comment on my notes insofar as they refer to the war in the Pacific." However, Leahy claimed that his account was "taken from notes made by me at the time" and passed on to the Joint Chiefs, as was his custom, "in order that they might have all the information that came to us for use in their consideration of the problem and in reaching their decision." Citing a publishing deadline, Leahy concluded, "I believe it would be practically impossible to eliminate that part of the text to which you offer objection."[36]

Leahy termed MacArthur-navy relations and the Seeadler Harbor ruckus "the most controversial single problem before the JCS during

March, 1944."[37] Considering that the chiefs were occupied with deciding how far and how rapidly Nimitz should push westward after seizing Eniwetok, whether to assault or bypass Truk, in the Carolines,[38] and what role, if any, Formosa should play in an attack on Japan—not to mention planning the upcoming Normandy invasion—that was a significant assessment.

There was also an about-face. The chiefs reversed themselves and came to an overdue decision on Kavieng. Halsey had been right. There was no reason to force another bloody assault when Kavieng could be bypassed in the general envelopment of Rabaul. The Joint Chiefs told Halsey to take Emirau instead. He dusted off his plans, and South Pacific troops landed there without opposition on March 20. The only casualty was a broken leg when a Seabee fell off a bulldozer.

The Joint Chiefs also affirmed Marshall's earlier caution to MacArthur. Manus and Seeadler Harbor would remain under MacArthur's control in the Southwest Pacific Area, but he had best roll out the red carpet for the harbor's use by *all* units of the US Navy, be they assigned to his Seventh Fleet, Halsey's South Pacific Area, or the Pacific Fleet in general.

Just to be certain there was no misunderstanding, Admiral King circulated a memo that quoted from a JCS directive of almost two years before, when the chiefs had initially carved up the Pacific: "Boundary lines of ocean areas...give a general definition to usual fields of operations; they are not designed to restrict or prevent responsible commanders from extending operations outside their assigned areas when such action will assist or support friendly forces, when it is necessary to accomplish the task in hand, or when it will promote the common cause."[39]

King's reminder was perhaps a needless stab in MacArthur's direction, but in a broader operational sense, it highlighted an area where MacArthur was still evolving. As much as MacArthur had come to embrace coordinated air and naval operations, he still showed the bias of his army roots by fixating on lines on a map, stationary fortifications, and rigidly defined areas of control rather than adopting the more fluid operational views traditionally espoused by the navy—out of necessity—on the seas. In short, whereas MacArthur's pins tended to stay in place on the map, the navy's were constantly moving. Although this was dictated to a large extent by geography, neither approach was necessarily correct, exclusive, or an assurance of victory. Rather, the differences between the two approaches begged for coordination and mutual support rather than routine avoidance.

Interservice bickering and MacArthur's usual pontificating aside, his success in the Admiralties had an important effect on the Joint Chiefs and their view of him. He had gambled and won. Had he delayed the landings a month, until the projected April 1 date, it is probable that his forces would have faced reinforced defenses. That likely would have delayed operations against or beyond Wewak and/or Nimitz's move to the Marianas rather than, as will be seen, expediting them.

The Joint Chiefs were far from easing up on their supervision of MacArthur, but his success in the Admiralties was the first step toward the virtual carte blanche his operations were to receive the following spring. Had his reconnaissance-in-force been repelled — or had he been captured or killed during his beachhead stroll — it would have had just the opposite effect.

The success in the Admiralties also emboldened MacArthur and his staff to draw lines on their maps ever farther afield, particularly if carrier aviation was available to support a leap beyond the range of Kenney's land-based fighters. "Please accept my admiration for the manner in which the entire affair has been handled," Marshall cabled MacArthur, speaking only to field operations, "and pass it on to Krueger, Kenney [and] Kinkaid."[40] The four men made a good team, and they were about to get ever bolder.

CHAPTER NINETEEN

Hollandia —
Greatest Triumph?

Douglas MacArthur's gamble in the Admiralties was barely won when he turned his attention to the next operation. It was to be a longer leap, an even bigger gamble, but if successful it might result in what was arguably his greatest strategic triumph of World War II.

However MacArthur chose to portray the advances of his Allied command, the basic math of the previous two years—from his arrival in Australia in March of 1942 until the seizure of the Admiralties in March of 1944—showed that the New Guinea front of his Southwest Pacific Area had progressed from the outskirts of Port Moresby to Buna and then westward to Saidor, a distance of approximately four hundred miles. At that rate, it would take another four years to advance the remaining 1,600 miles to Mindanao, let alone reach Luzon or Japan.

Admittedly, the pace was quickening and would continue to do so as more men and materiel, as well as increased amphibious capabilities, were brought to bear. But at that point, MacArthur's goals—to trap major portions of Adachi's Eighteenth Army at Lae and east of Saidor—had not been realized, in part because he attempted encircle-ments over small distances well within the range of George Kenney's land-based air. As MacArthur pondered the map of New Guinea in the wake of the Admiralty landings, he would focus on two weapons in his arsenal that were gaining in both reliability and strength.

The first was Ultra. Kenney had long been relying on navy Ultra to orchestrate his air operations. Ultra was at the core of his two greatest air victories to date — the destruction of the Bismarck Sea convoy, in March of 1943, and the Wewak airdrome assault, in August of 1943. Without either or both of those victories, MacArthur's advance to Lae would have been far more problematic.

The capture of Japanese codebooks at Saidor provided Ultra on Japanese army movements in similar detail. Willoughby would never be considered brilliantly insightful, but Ultra analyzed by MacArthur's chief signal officer, Spencer Akin, had allowed Willoughby to make an accurate estimate of Japanese troop strength in the Admiralties. This success dispelled doubts about Ultra's credibility and firmly cemented Ultra information as an essential component of future operations.[1]

The aircraft carriers of the United States Navy comprised MacArthur's second new weapon. Having witnessed Kenney's air successes, MacArthur repeatedly lobbied for land-based air to cover his advances and charged that a lack of it was the Achilles' heel of Nimitz's thrust through the central Pacific. Yet in just six months' time, Nimitz had advanced the central Pacific front several thousand miles, from Hawaii to the Gilbert and Marshall Islands, and stood poised to leap another thousand miles to the Marianas by relying on an outpouring of new aircraft carriers. It would take some coordination with Nimitz — and a solid plan to follow up rapidly with bases for land-based air — but if carrier aircraft could support amphibious landings during initial assaults, the radius of MacArthur's potential reach could be greatly expanded.

Asserting that the seizure of the Admiralties presented "an immediate opportunity for rapid exploitation along the north coast of New Guinea," MacArthur told Marshall on March 5 that he proposed to make the Hollandia area, not Hansa Bay, his next objective.

One hundred and forty miles west of Saidor but still one hundred miles short of Wewak, Hansa Bay was the next logical assault point if MacArthur were to make another jump of approximately the same distance as he had from Finschhafen to Saidor. General Adachi expected as much and planned a warm reception. MacArthur knew this from

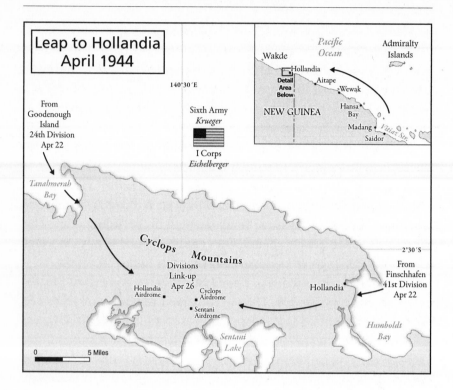

Leap to Hollandia
April 1944

From
Goodenough
Island
24th Division
Apr 22

Sixth Army
Krueger

I Corps
Eichelberger

*Tanahmerah
Bay*

Cyclops Mountains

Divisions
Link-up
Apr 26

Hollandia
Airdrome

Cyclops
Airdrome

Sentani
Airdrome

*Sentani
Lake*

Hollandia

From
Finschhafen
41st Division
Apr 22

*Humboldt
Bay*

140°30′E
2°30′S

0   5 Miles

Wakde

*Pacific
Ocean*

Admiralty
Islands

Hollandia

Detail
Area
Below

Aitape
Wewak

NEW GUINEA

Hansa
Bay

Madang

Saidor

Ultra intercepts and reported to the Joint Chiefs that the Japanese had concentrated ground forces east of Hollandia in the Madang-Wewak area on either side of Hansa Bay while also concentrating air defenses west of Hollandia.

MacArthur didn't phrase it quite this way, but relatively weak Japanese forces in the Hollandia Bay area were like the hole in a doughnut. From three airfields in that vicinity, MacArthur could isolate the remainder of Adachi's Eighteenth Army to the east at Madang-Wewak while stopping further development of airfields that might block his advance westward. To do this, MacArthur told the chiefs, it would be necessary to retain naval reinforcements borrowed from the Central Pacific Area for the Emirau operation.

More significant, MacArthur said it was necessary — despite talk that Halsey's South Pacific forces would soon be out of a job — "to continue the operation of the South Pacific Force in the theatre of the Southwest Pacific area until Hollandia is secured." In other words, with the bulk of Halsey's opposition in the Solomons bypassed or defeated, MacArthur wanted to keep control of those forces and not see them transferred to Nimitz for Central Pacific Area operations. Noting that Halsey concurred with his plan, MacArthur asked for the Joint Chiefs' prompt approval.[2]

Much like the plan to bypass Rabaul, this leap to Hollandia had many fathers. Kenney claimed that upon MacArthur's return from Los Negros, the two men discussed "bypassing Hansa Bay and jumping all the way to Hollandia." The evidence suggests, however, that Kenney was focused on advancing his fighter operations to an intermediate base and was not terribly keen about relying on air cover from carriers.[3]

As Bill Halsey recalled, success in establishing airfields to cover advances throughout the South Pacific "made me feel that the same thing could be accomplished at Hollandia by bypassing all strong points in between." Halsey didn't take full credit for the idea but reminisced that he had been "aided and abetted in this presentation to MacArthur by a Brigadier General, whose name I unfortunately have forgotten."[4]

The brigadier general in question worked for Chamberlin as the head of the G-3's planning section and was not one to be forgotten. His name was Bonner Fellers, and, although he was not one of the Bataan Gang, he had served under MacArthur in the prewar Philippines and had carried on a correspondence with him afterward. An unabashed MacArthur admirer, Fellers held posts as military attaché in Egypt and with the OSS in Washington before again landing a spot on MacArthur's staff in 1943.

In postwar correspondence, Fellers did not deny that Halsey may have championed the idea of taking Hollandia to MacArthur at a conference in Brisbane on March 3, but "by that time," Fellers recalled, "the Hollandia operation had already been planned in our planning section and MacArthur knew all about it." Fellers claimed that during the Finschhafen campaign, he had looked at the map of New Guinea and "then and there I decided that if ever we were to liberate Manila, which was some 2500 miles away, we had better start taking longer hops."

Fellers talked the Hollandia idea over with his navy and air force counterparts and found that "both were enthusiastic." But when Fellers disclosed the concept to his immediate supervisor, Chamberlin "hit the ceiling," according to Fellers, "and ordered me to drop the wild scheme." Nevertheless, Fellers and his group continued to work on the plan and found a way to pass the concept on to MacArthur.

Because Fellers was, in his words, "on evil terms with C/S Sutherland" — not an unusual occurrence — he went to MacArthur's aide-de-camp and asked him to relay it to MacArthur. According to Fellers, MacArthur "sent word immediately to continue the plan."[5]

By one account, on the day the operational plans for landings at Hansa Bay were being mimeographed in preparation for the "dry-run" planning conference that MacArthur always held before operations, MacArthur announced that he had reconsidered the options and decided that the next objective would be Hollandia instead of Hansa Bay. He directed Chamberlin to "take the staff to your office and spell out the details."

According to Fellers, Chamberlin was "livid." Outside in the hall Chamberlin told Fellers, "You have double-crossed me. You'll have to hold the critique as I have never seen your plan." Then Chamberlin went on to tell Fellers that "for the first time MacArthur's staff had failed its Chief and that [Fellers] was to blame. He said the operation would fail."[6]

Years later, Dan Barbey told Fellers that he "was always under the impression that this leap frog along the New Guinea coast and into Hollandia was your idea."[7] Perhaps. But having crossed Chamberlin and ignored Sutherland — a dangerous tightrope to walk — Fellers was fired as chief of the G-3's planning section. MacArthur saved him, however, by making Fellers his military secretary and chief of psychological operations. Fellers continued to work for MacArthur, and he played a major role in the administration of postwar Japan.

His banishment notwithstanding, Fellers assured Chamberlin that the optimistic schedule of a rapid advance to Hollandia was justified by the enemy's increasingly difficult position. "In actual ground combat," Fellers concluded, "the enemy west of Wewak will be as formidable as ever but his air force is on the wane, his fleet out of balance, his supply unsatisfactory."[8]

More than just providing a glimpse of the occasional friction among MacArthur's staff, the Hollandia planning process shows that, as in the case of bypassing Rabaul, operational ideas evolved through discussions among many parties rather than originating with one person—contrary to the image-burnishing descriptions of MacArthur or any other individual being struck by a lightning bolt of strategic genius. Ultimately, of course, the decision to implement any strategic idea rested with the Joint Chiefs of Staff—Leahy, Marshall, King, and Arnold.

The Joint Chiefs responded to MacArthur's proposal to bypass Hansa Bay and strike at Hollandia via a wide-ranging joint directive to MacArthur and Nimitz. Among the thorny issues in their discussions had been whether to assault Truk directly or bypass it à la Rabaul. Issued on March 12, 1944, the directive's principal author was Admiral King, and it left no doubt that Pacific strategy was pointed toward "the Formosa-Luzon-China area" by way of "the Marianas-Carolines-Palau-Mindanao area"—but it continued to envision twin drives across the Pacific by MacArthur and Nimitz.

Specifically, the Joint Chiefs charged MacArthur and Nimitz with six tasks:

1. Halsey's consolidation on Emirau as the final step in the encirclement of Rabaul;
2. prompt completion of the Manus airfields and Seeadler Harbor facilities for the benefit of *all* naval forces;
3. occupation of the Hollandia area, as proposed by MacArthur, with a target date of April 15, the primary objective of which would be the establishment of air bases for heavy bombers from which to strike the Palau islands and neutralize western New Guinea and the island of Halmahera—essentially protecting the left flank of the twin attack;
4. Nimitz seizing the Marianas-Carolines-Palaus triangle by invading the southern Marianas on June 15, then bypassing Truk and landing in the Palaus by September 15, the primary objective being to establish forward staging areas for operations against Mindanao, Formosa, and China;
5. Occupation of Mindanao by MacArthur's SWPA forces, supported by the Pacific Fleet, with a target date of November 15,

1944, further extending left-flank protection into the Philippines but still leaving unanswered the perennial question of whether to attack Formosa directly or via Luzon; and

6. Occupation of Formosa by Nimitz with a target date of February 15, 1945, and, on the same target date, occupation of Luzon by MacArthur, "should such operations prove necessary prior to the move on Formosa."[9]

Joint Chiefs chairman Leahy felt that this directive for operations against Japan "greatly clarified the situation" in the Pacific for the following twelve months. MacArthur and Nimitz were directed to confer with each other to ensure ample coordination and mutual support. "It appeared, for the time being at least," Leahy recalled, "that MacArthur and the Navy would be working in harmony in the far-flung areas that constituted our Pacific battlefront."[10]

From MacArthur's viewpoint, the directive certainly did not pour the bulk of Pacific resources into his Mindanao axis, which Sutherland had been lobbying for, but neither did it preclude MacArthur from attaining his long-stated goal of returning to the Philippines. Having lost the battle of Seeadler Harbor and desperately needing Nimitz's carriers to make the leap to Hollandia, MacArthur did what he usually did in such situations: he made an abrupt about-face.

"I have long had it in mind to extend to you the hospitality of this area," MacArthur cordially wrote Nimitz. With assurances of "a warm welcome," he invited the admiral to Brisbane for a personal conference so that "the close coordination of our respective commands would be greatly furthered."[11]

Nimitz received MacArthur's invitation upon returning to Pearl Harbor from a Washington conference with King. "It will give me much pleasure to avail myself of your hospitality in the near future," he immediately cabled MacArthur. "I am certain that our personal conference will insure closest coordination in the coming campaign."[12]

And generally it did. Nimitz and his planning staff arrived in Brisbane by PB2Y Coronado on March 25. As the four-engine flying boat taxied to the dock, MacArthur, as was his custom when receiving important visitors, was waiting to greet the admiral. Seeking to break the ice in their first meeting, Nimitz came bearing gifts: orchids for Jean, playsuits for Arthur, and several boxes of Hawaiian candy for the entire family. Naturally, MacArthur put Nimitz up at Lennons, then hosted a rather grand banquet in his honor in the hotel's ballroom that evening.[13]

When MacArthur, Nimitz, and their respective staffs got down to business the following morning, MacArthur seemed pleased that the JCS had laid out a schedule of objectives for the entire 1944 calendar year, including MacArthur's return to the Philippines via Mindanao — a plan, Nimitz acknowledged to King, that was "very dear to [MacArthur's] heart."

More immediately, in support of the Hollandia landings, Nimitz agreed that the fast carriers of Task Force 58, part of Raymond Spruance's Fifth Fleet, would pound Truk and other bases in the Carolines, then raid the Palau islands within a matter of days. Afterward they would stand off New Guinea to provide two days of air cover for the Hollandia landings. Should the Japanese navy sortie in strength to oppose any of these operations, Nimitz prepared to deploy a battle line of six battleships, thirteen cruisers, and twenty-six destroyers from forces screening the carriers to engage them.

More than the Japanese fleet, however, Nimitz was nervous about the Japanese aircraft — between two hundred and three hundred of them — reportedly massed at the three airfields near Hollandia. Confident that they were safely beyond the reach of Kenney's P-38 fighters, the Japanese had distributed aircraft across the fields in a way that was almost reminiscent of the atmosphere at Clark Field on December 8, 1941. George Kenney, however, was determined not to be constrained when it came to the operational range of P-38s. He assured Nimitz that he would find a way to eliminate the threat from Hollandia by April 5. Most in attendance at the meeting looked skeptical, but MacArthur merely accepted Kenney's statement at face value.[14]

Thus, in Nimitz's words, "everything was lovely and harmonious until the last day of our conference when I called attention to the last part of the JCS directive." This was the paragraph ordering Nimitz to prepare Formosa assault plans and MacArthur to do the same for Luzon, but only should those "operations prove necessary." Those were the wrong three words to focus upon, as Nimitz quickly learned.

367

As Nimitz reported to King, MacArthur "blew up and made an oration of some length on the impossibility of bypassing the Philippines—his sacred obligations there—redemption of the 17 million people—blood on his soul—deserted by American people—etc. etc.—and then a criticism of those gentlemen in Washington who—far from the scene and having heard the whistle of bullets, etc.—endeavor to set the strategy of the Pacific War."[15]

Marshall, King, and others had heard MacArthur's mantra before, of course, but it also became clear to Nimitz that by returning to the Philippines, MacArthur meant a liberation of Manila and Luzon, not merely a flank holding action on Mindanao. Nimitz nonetheless responded diplomatically to MacArthur's rant and salvaged the unity of the conference. When he next met with King face-to-face in May, Nimitz characterized his relations with MacArthur as "excellent."

The Hollandia operation was divided into three pieces. The little town of Hollandia itself sat on Humboldt Bay, reportedly the best anchorage between Wewak and Geelvink Bay, some five hundred miles farther west. The place names told the story: just east of Hollandia, one passed from Australian-administered North-East New Guinea into Netherlands New Guinea, the eastern end of the Netherlands Indies that extended west to Sumatra.

Inland a dozen miles from Hollandia, behind a jungle-clad uplift seven thousand feet in elevation called the Cyclops Mountains, three Japanese airfields sprawled on a level plain between the mountains and the northern shore of tropical blue Lake Sentani. As Admiral Dan Barbey put it, "MacArthur wanted those airfields,"[16] and to take them, Walter Krueger's Alamo Force planners devised a two-pronged movement: inland and west from Humboldt Bay and inland and east from Tanahmerah Bay, twenty miles distant, at the other end of the Cyclops Mountains.

The third piece called for a landing at Aitape, around 120 miles east of Humboldt Bay. Ground forces there could protect MacArthur's eastern flank and block Eighteenth Army reinforcements from Wewak. More significant, however, was another airfield complex at Tadji Plantation, around eight miles inland and southeast from the landing zone, which appeared lightly defended. Allied engineers estimated they could repair any bomb damage to at least one runway within forty-eight hours of its capture. An airstrip at Tadji was the final piece Kenney needed to fulfill his promise to eliminate Japanese airpower from Hollandia and assume the burden for landing-zone air cover from the navy.[17]

Years later, Barbey reminisced to Bonner Fellers: "I always thought [Kenney] was a pompous, unimaginative little runt, but if one were to believe what he says about himself in his book the conclusion might be reached that MacArthur won the war because of Kenney and his B-17s—and that even MacArthur might not have been necessary in the final showdown."[18] Kenney's cocksure attitude may well have deserved such a critique, but it is hard to argue with the plan Kenney, Whitehead, and their operations staff devised to subdue Hollandia.

Recognizing the importance of stretching the range of its P-38s, but not wanting the Japanese to know the full extent of its capabilities too soon, the Fifth Air Force took delivery of fifty-eight new long-range P-38s and outfitted another seventy-five older models with extra wing tanks. Kenney limited his strikes against Hollandia to occasional nighttime attacks by solitary bombers without fighter cover and forbade any fighters to fly beyond Tadji, even if they were equipped to do so. This had the effect of further lulling the Japanese into a false sense of security. As part of their big defensive buildup, they parked airplanes wingtip-to-wingtip, even in double lines alongside the runways.

Originally, Kenney and Whitehead planned a massive low-level assault similar to the surprise strike against Wewak in August of 1943. Then reconnaissance photos disclosed a concentration of antiaircraft batteries at both ends of the broad Lake Sentani plain. Kenney decided to concentrate on the antiaircraft batteries as part of the first strike. On the morning of March 30, eighty-two B-24s appeared in the skies over the Hollandia airfields. Forty Japanese fighters confidently rose to meet them but were quickly jumped by twice that number of P-38s suddenly showing off their long-range capabilities. The B-24s dropped a carpet of fragmentation bombs, destroying twenty-five planes on the ground and badly damaging another sixty-seven while knocking out antiaircraft batteries and setting fuel tanks ablaze. As one squadron of B-24s reported, "Hollandia had really been 'Wewaked.' "

The next day, the Fifth Air Force struck again in similar strength with similar results. By the third attack, on April 3, after-strike photographs showed the fields littered with almost three hundred wrecked and burned-out aircraft and the installations riddled and pockmarked from repeated strafing by B-25s and A-20s. The escorting P-38s took out most of the remaining Japanese fighters, and the survivors sought refuge at fields well to the west of Hollandia. As one disgruntled Japanese seaman put it, "We received from the enemy greetings, which amount to the annihilation of our Army Air Forces in New Guinea." Kenney had made good on his promise to MacArthur and Nimitz.[19]

The brunt of the Hollandia landings was to be borne by Krueger's Alamo Force, but the corps commander assigned by MacArthur to direct the Twenty-Fourth and Forty-First Infantry Divisions as they went ashore at Tanahmerah and Humboldt Bays was a name that had not been heard much during the previous year. Lieutenant General Robert Eichelberger, who had indeed taken Buna and come back alive, was returning to combat after his year in semiexile in Australia.

Charged with training troops, Eichelberger's duties had included squiring Eleanor Roosevelt around the South Pacific on an inspection tour in September of 1943, an event MacArthur chose to ignore. Three times during that year, the War Department requested that MacArthur release Eichelberger for duty in Europe, but according to Eichelberger, "General MacArthur disapproved all three requests."

Eichelberger soon learned, however, that at Hollandia he would command the largest army operation in the Pacific up to that point. As Eichelberger recalled, "It was obvious that surprise would be our strongest ally." MacArthur chose the code name Reckless for the assault.[20]

After his personal appearance in the Admiralties, there was never much doubt that MacArthur would accompany the landing force to Hollandia. On April 18, Dusty Rhoades was scheduled to fly MacArthur and his party from Brisbane to Port Moresby in the *Bataan,* but an oil leak grounded the general's B-17. MacArthur flew north in Kenney's borrowed B-17 instead and, after stopping to pick up a photographer and several correspondents in Port Morseby, arrived at Finschhafen and went aboard the cruiser *Nashville.*[21]

Until the beachheads were secured and Eichelberger moved his headquarters ashore, overall control of the landing operations was vested in Dan Barbey as attack force commander.[22] For the sake of mobility among the three beachheads, Barbey flew his flag from the destroyer *Swanson*. Eichelberger joined Barbey on board the *Swanson* as it sailed from the embarkation point of the Twenty-Fourth Division at Goodenough Island.

"I had not seen much of Eichelberger since the wind-up of the Buna campaign more than a year previously," Barbey recalled, noting that "because of his outspoken, critical, and sometimes belligerent manner, [Eichelberger] had not endeared himself to the top command in the Southwest Pacific." "Top command" was a polite way of saying "MacArthur," but Barbey claimed to enjoy his "close association" with Eichelberger.[23]

Krueger, as overall commander of Alamo Force, sailed on board the destroyer *Wilkes* from the embarkation point of the Forty-First Division just south of Finschhafen. With so much brass at sea, Admiral Kinkaid, SWPA's top naval commander, chose to stay at Port Moresby, where he had the communications equipment to effectively coordinate Nimitz's loan of attack carriers for air cover over the landings. Kinkaid didn't say so at the time, but a few weeks later, he professed to see "no earthly reason" why Barbey "should be saddled with the additional hazard" of having Krueger—and, by inference, MacArthur—afloat and taking up "a badly needed destroyer" and light cruiser that would have been better used for other duties.[24]

But the brass sailed in force, and warships, transports, freighters, and a bevy of plodding LCIs, LSTs, and other amphibious vessels converged on the Admiralty Islands. This was indeed the circuitous route to Hollandia, but the islands provided a protected rendezvous point and, more important, disguised the true destination from snooping Japanese planes and submarines along the New Guinea coast. Even after a search plane spotted some of the ships, their location seems to have fooled Japanese commanders into believing that their destination might be Rabaul, Kavieng, or Truk, which had just been raided again by Nimitz's carriers. As for New Guinea itself, General Adachi still expected the next Allied assault to come near Hansa Bay or Wewak, and deceptive Allied air attacks and PT boat activity in the area had been calculated to do nothing to dissuade him.

Shortly after sunrise on the morning of April 20, an assault convoy of 164 ships formed northwest of the Admiralties and headed west at nine knots. Eichelberger marveled at the difference between this force and the thirty landing craft and two PT boats that had put part of a regiment ashore at Nassau Bay prior to the Lae campaign only ten months before. Staging the three-pronged Hollandia invasion was an immensely complicated job, but Eichelberger said it proved "that both the American Army and Navy had come of age."[25]

Still, there were some anxious moments. On the second night out, radar picked up a large number of vessels lurking in the convoy's path. All ships went to general quarters, including the *Nashville,* with MacArthur on board. Radio silence precluded any inquiries to Kinkaid at Port Moresby, and only later did Barbey learn that what the radar had picked up was the attack carriers shepherding them along.

Then it was time to turn south and strike quickly toward the New Guinea coast.

Shortly before sunset on the evening before D-day, the eastern attack prong peeled off from the main convoy and headed southeast for Aitape. In the darkness that followed, the central prong soon did the same, bound for Humboldt Bay. The *Swanson*—with Barbey and Eichelberger on board—the *Wilkes,* and the *Nashville* continued toward the westernmost landing zone, at Tanahmerah Bay. Both groups arrived off their respective beaches at 5:00 a.m. on April 22.[26]

Eichelberger had been up since 3:00 a.m., and after dressing slowly and reluctantly, he ambled into the *Swanson*'s mess room to find hot coffee and the table piled with mountains of paper-wrapped sandwiches made the night before. Given the day ahead, you could eat them or put them in your pocket for future emergencies. "Some sensible men," Eichelberger recalled, "did both."[27]

The day dawned overcast, and aircraft from Nimitz's carriers swept over the landing zones and what remained of the airstrips at Lake Sentani and Tadji, but they encountered little if any resistance, and subsequent missions were canceled. Brief naval bombardments followed just before the first wave of landing craft came ashore. The surprise appeared to be complete. As one Japanese commander later admitted, "The morning that we found out that the Allies were going to come to Hollandia, they were already in the harbor."[28]

The only major snag proved to be the narrow confines of the Tanahmerah beaches. Two landing zones were long and thin, one backing up to an impenetrable swamp, the other at the end of an almost impassable jungle trail that was supposed to lead directly to Lake Sentani but in fact was a dead end. Eichelberger quickly shifted the bulk of his reinforcements and arranged to land them at Humboldt Bay instead.[29]

Shortly after noon, the *Nashville* anchored in the outer harbor of Tanahmerah Bay, and MacArthur signaled for Eichelberger and Barbey — along with Krueger, who was offshore on the *Wilkes* as the destroyer did antisubmarine duty — to report on board his flagship. The next order of business was a visit to the beach.

With Barbey a little nervous about the responsibility, MacArthur, Krueger, and Eichelberger climbed into a landing craft and, under Barbey's direction, headed toward shore. Halfway there, a report of a lone Japanese plane prompted Barbey to order the coxswain to steer toward the safety of a nearby destroyer, but MacArthur countermanded the order and directed that they continue toward the beach. The plane swooped over without firing and headed inland. Barbey claimed, "There was never the feeling that it was an act of bravado on MacArthur's part, but rather that he was a man of destiny and there was no need to take precautions."[30]

Barbey's concern had not been misplaced. Two nights later, a lone Japanese plane dropped a stick of bombs on the fringe of an old Japanese ammunition dump at the Humboldt landing zone, and the resulting fire spread to an American gas dump and other supplies and equipment. The fire raged for several days, destroying the equivalent of eleven loads of LST cargo and killing twenty-four men — more casualties than were suffered on all three beaches in the initial landings.[31]

But MacArthur's beach walk had gone off without incident — so well, in fact, that when his party returned to the *Nashville,* MacArthur proposed a bold idea. Perhaps they should have made an even grander leap. Why not expedite the capture of Wakde Island, 120 miles farther west? Barbey termed the idea "another of his startling proposals" but professed to be ready to carry out the navy's part of the operation. Alamo Force commander Krueger was noncommittal, possibly letting Eichelberger take the lead in challenging MacArthur's optimism. Eichelberger indeed came out strongly against the plan, arguing that it was far too soon to declare the Hollandia landings unqualified successes and that the full extent of Wakde's defenses was as yet unknown.[32]

MacArthur mulled over the advice and decided to stick with the original plans, although Eichelberger's relative caution may have been just one more reason for MacArthur to be less than satisfied with him. After MacArthur ordered the *Nashville* to stop by the Humboldt and Aitape beachheads for similar inspection tours ashore, it then returned him to Finschhafen. There, early on April 24, Dusty Rhoades and the repaired *Bataan* were waiting for the return flight to Port Moresby, even as the SWPA's press release reported: "General MacArthur is at the front supervising activities of the landing. He reached the scene on one of our light cruisers engaged in the initial bombardment."[33]

The coordinated air cover over the beachheads from Nimitz's carriers had worked smoothly, even if it was limited in duration, because Kenney's land-based planes had already decimated most of the Japanese airpower around Hollandia. Eichelberger wanted the carriers to remain and strike farther west as a precautionary move, but Barbey felt the situation was in hand and stuck to the agreed-upon release schedule for them to return to operations in the central Pacific. According to Barbey, it was the only time he and Eichelberger "disagreed on any matter of importance."[34]

The real significance of the Hollandia operation was its overall success, even if MacArthur was uncharacteristically understated about it in his memoirs. Not mentioning his beach walks, he merely noted, "The Hollandia invasion initiated a marked change in the tempo of my advance westward."[35]

Much more detail and hyperbole—as well as a warm and widespread regard for the contributions of all of the services involved—appeared in his pronouncements at the time. "We have seized the Humboldt Bay area on the northern coast of Dutch New Guinea," SWPA's April 24 communiqué reported. "The landings were made under cover of naval and air bombardment and followed neutralizing attacks by our air forces, and planes from carriers of the Pacific Fleet. Complete surprise and effective support, both surface and air, secured our initial landings with slight losses."

Remembering MacArthur's closest allies as well, the communiqué went on: "To the east are the Australians and Americans; to the west the Americans; to the north the sea controlled by our Allied naval forces; to the south untraversed jungle mountain ranges; and over all our Allied air mastery." Together, they had thrown "a loop of envelopment" over Adachi's Eighteenth Army, and, if anyone needed to be reminded of the parallel, "their situation reverses Bataan."[36]

At the time, it was premature to assess whether the Hollandia operation was, as William Manchester called it in retrospect, MacArthur's "greatest triumph."[37] For one thing, thanks to Ultra intelligence, MacArthur was well aware that Japanese ground strength was concentrated at Hansa and Wewak, not Hollandia. Well executed though the operation was at many levels — including that of a growing logistical capability, which inundated the beachheads with supplies — the assault was less of a daring gamble than has historically been presented.

Nonetheless, in a bold leap that took advantage of Ultra as well as naval air cover, MacArthur moved the Allied front in New Guinea forward almost five hundred miles. The one-two punch of the Admiralties and Hollandia further impressed the Joint Chiefs — even Admiral King. Pontifical though MacArthur could be, it was hard to argue with success.

And Hollandia must not be judged alone but rather as part of a four-month campaign stretching from the Admiralties to Hollandia and farther west to Wakde Island and Biak. Although Eichelberger in particular reined in MacArthur's enthusiasm for expediting the assault on Wakde, that operation nonetheless took place on May 17–18. It was probably a good thing — as Eichelberger always maintained — that Wakde was given separate attention, as it proved more heavily defended than Willoughby's intelligence indicated, proving that Ultra was not always an open book. In short order, however, Wakde's airfields provided a needed base from which to protect the Hollandia airfields and project Kenney's land-based air farther west.

Tiny, coral-ringed Wakde Island soon became even more valuable after engineers working on reconstructing the Hollandia airstrips found that the thick jungle soil above Lake Sentani wouldn't support the weight of heavy bombers. Operations were expedited on the coral-based runways at Wakde instead so it could support the Forty-First Division landings at Biak on May 27. Biak Island sat astride the wide mouth of Geelvink Bay as the bay separated the bulk of Netherlands New Guinea from the dragon's head of the Vogelkop Peninsula. Riddled with caves throughout a maze of coral, Biak proved to be a tough nut of Japanese defense before it was finally secured in mid-August.

MacArthur would become a vocal critic of the bloody battles that Nimitz waged at Peleliu and Iwo Jima, but at Biak MacArthur's own casualty rates exceeded 25 percent, with 471 killed, 2,443 wounded, and thousands more temporarily incapacitated by some measure of jungle diseases. It was harder to argue with the number of Japanese killed in the action—few surrendered, and the total topped six thousand.[38]

In terms of overall Allied military effort, what makes MacArthur's Admiralties-to-Biak campaigns particularly impressive is that they occurred in rapid fire not only as Nimitz's massive central Pacific assault against the Marianas was getting under way but also as the supreme Allied effort was being directed against Europe with the invasion of Normandy on June 6, 1944. This in itself was proof that the United States and its allies were successfully prosecuting a two-ocean global war and that, contrary to his fears, MacArthur had hardly been relegated to a backwater.

On June 8, as the Biak campaign still raged, George Marshall sent MacArthur his congratulations on the campaigns that took him from Hollandia to Biak, which, Marshall said, had "completely disorganized the enemy plans for the security of eastern Malaysia." Marshall's subsequent characterization was just the sort of tonic MacArthur craved, but Marshall was on solid ground when he told his former boss: "The succession of surprises effected and the small losses suffered, the great extent of territory conquered and the casualties inflicted on the enemy, together with the large Japanese forces which have been isolated, all combine to make your operations of the past one and a half months models of strategical and tactical maneuvers."

Advising MacArthur that he was off that morning for England to inspect the Normandy landings, Marshall added, "We are now engaged in heavy battles all over the world which bid fair to bring the roof down on these international desperadoes."[39]

What Marshall did not say in so many words is that by the time of the Hollandia operation, MacArthur had become a master in combined air, land, and sea offensives. He had apprenticed in an army whose doctrine featured the deployment of infantry, cavalry, and horse-drawn artillery, but the far-flung reaches and varying geography of the Pacific demanded more flexibility and fluidity. And he rose to the challenge. Initially skeptical of airpower as chief of staff, MacArthur was forced by lack of troops and shipping to embrace it by 1942.

"As much as I respected MacArthur and liked him as a person," George Kenney told D. Clayton James in a 1971 interview, "I've got to admit that he knew practically nothing at first about aviation. When I got out there, he didn't even want to fly." But Kenney readily admitted that MacArthur learned, adapted, and became an advocate.[40]

The same can be said for MacArthur's embrace of sea power. MacArthur saw that Kenney's inroads in the skies in turn gave him command of the seas and opened up a wide range of possible lines of attack. The result was that while the Japanese were increasingly forced to deploy along marginal jungle roads supported by strained and eventually nonexistent supply lines, MacArthur used his growing amphibious forces to make bold leaps, including those into the Admiralties and against Hollandia.

Aside from his evolution as a commander who utilized combined air, land, and sea operations fully to accomplish an objective, MacArthur's greatest strength was that he kept up the pressure on his subordinates to maintain the advances and surprises necessary to progress the nine hundred miles from Finschhafen to Biak in just four months. He looked ahead with similar resolve toward targets in the Philippines. MacArthur's great distraction, however—if not his most time-consuming weakness—was that he could not abide the threat he saw to his Philippine dreams should Nimitz oversee a direct assault on Formosa.

"It is my most earnest conviction," MacArthur wrote Marshall on June 18, "that the proposal to bypass the Philippines and launch an attack across the Pacific directly against Formosa is unsound." The only thing worse, MacArthur maintained, would be "the proposal to bypass all other objectives and launch an attack directly on the mainland of Japan [which] is in my opinion utterly unsound."

Then MacArthur returned to his favored theme of the political ramifications of such an action. Should the United States deliberately bypass the Philippines and delay the liberation of the Bataan survivors and loyal Filipinos imprisoned by Japan, there would be a grave psychological reaction. "We would admit the truth of Japanese propaganda," MacArthur told Marshall, "to the effect that we had abandoned the Filipinos and would not shed American blood to redeem them...[and] we would probably suffer such loss of prestige among all the people of the Far East that it would adversely affect the United States for many years."

If serious consideration were being given to the direct assault against Formosa to the exclusion of Luzon, MacArthur requested that he "be accorded the opportunity of personally proceeding to Washington to present fully my views."[41]

Marshall received this latest plea for the Philippines upon returning from his Normandy tour. Although the JCS had yet to consider MacArthur's views, Marshall nevertheless responded with a four-page letter, because, as Marshall put it, "I think it important that you should have my comments without delay." Marshall's analysis shows his depth as a global strategist and suggests that the Joint Chiefs routinely exercised a far greater understanding of and ability to balance worldwide military priorities than MacArthur appeared to appreciate.

In the face of MacArthur's leaps to Hollandia and Biak, Marshall told MacArthur that Ultra information suggested a steady buildup of Japanese strength in the wide swath of territory encompassing Mindanao, Celebes, Vogelkop, and Palau: "In other words further advances in this particular region will encounter greatly increased Japanese strength in most localities. There will be less opportunity to move against [the enemy's] weakness and to his surprise, as has been the case in your recent series of moves."

Despite the lessening value of China's role in the Allied war effort, as recognized at the Tehran conference, Marshall nonetheless reiterated the chiefs' "pressing problem" should China collapse and permit Japan to redeploy some of its troops to Formosa or elsewhere. That scenario might result in both Formosa and the Japanese island of Kyushu being more heavily defended in 1945. "Whether or not the Formosa or the Kyushu operation can be mounted remains a matter to be studied," Marshall acknowledged, "but neither operation in my opinion is unsound in the measure you indicate."

There was also, of course, the matter of the still-powerful Japanese fleet. Marshall told MacArthur that he had been insisting that their own Pacific fleet, particularly its burgeoning carrier force, should be employed across a wide front looking for an opportunity to engage. Once the Japanese fleet was destroyed, Marshall advocated going "as close to Japan as quickly as possible in order to shorten the war, which means the reconquest of the Philippines."

Only after making these points did Marshall turn personal. In regard to the reconquest of the Philippines, Marshall noted, "We must be careful not to allow our personal feeling and Philippine political considerations to override our great objective, which is the early conclusion of the war with Japan. In my view, 'by-passing' is in no way synonymous with 'abandonment.' On the contrary, by the defeat of Japan at the earliest practicable moment the liberation of the Philippines will be effected in the most expeditious and complete manner possible."

And should MacArthur seem to see Admiral King and other supposedly sinister forces within the US Navy at work behind a naval lunge directly toward Formosa or Kyushu, Marshall tried to forestall MacArthur's predictable response. "That is not the fact," Marshall told him. "I have been pressing for the full use of the fleet to expedite matters in the Pacific and also pressing specifically for a carrier assault on Japan."

Then Marshall did what he had done on other occasions when MacArthur appeared to threaten to go over his head — he graciously offered to facilitate it. "As to your expressed desire to be accorded the opportunity for personally proceeding to Washington to present fully your views," Marshall concluded, "I see no difficulty about that and if the issue arises will speak to the President who I am quite certain would be agreeable to your being ordered home for the purpose."[42]

This was the second time in only a few months that MacArthur had requested a presidential audience as a way to press his point with Marshall. This time, he was going to get what he asked for.

CHAPTER TWENTY

Presidential Ambitions, Presidential Summons

Douglas MacArthur made a point of publicly denying his presidential ambitions just strongly enough to prove with near certainty that he harbored them his entire life. MacArthur's ingratiating references in early letters to Leonard Wood and General Pershing about their presidential prospects, the 1929 speculation by the *New York Times* about the possibility that MacArthur's long-range plans in the Philippines might stoke his own presidential bid, and MacArthur's surreptitious discussions with Hugh Drum about the 1940 election all stand as circumstantial evidence that the dream was always alive.[1]

More directly, when presented with the prospect of occupying the White House, MacArthur never unequivocally said no. On the contrary, his professed denials sometimes left the door wide open. A case in point was his response early in 1938 to Nelson H. Carver, a Republican activist and former US attorney for the Western District of Tennessee.

"The possibility of my consideration by the Republican Party in 1940 has never entered my mind," MacArthur told Carver. Whatever Carver may have heard on that subject could only be regarded "as amicable expressions of friendship" from which MacArthur could not believe "anything serious could eventuate." Then came the "however" line: "If the state of the country be such that there might be any spontaneous

380

demand for me," MacArthur nonetheless advised Carver, "I would, of course, hold myself entirely at its disposal." In closing, MacArthur professed his gratitude and assured Carver that if "conditions warrant" he would be "glad indeed to have further word from you."[2]

MacArthur's only solace in the 1940 election was that the Republican Party turned to someone who, like MacArthur himself, was not a veteran of electoral politics. Wendell Willkie was a corporate lawyer and businessman at odds with the domestic policies of the New Deal but far more in tune with Roosevelt on international matters than he was with his own party's isolationist wing. Willkie won the Republican nomination on the sixth ballot, besting Robert Taft and Thomas Dewey, but Roosevelt handily carried thirty-eight states to Willkie's ten.

Fifteen months later, in February of 1942, Willkie, still the nominal head of the Republican Party, inadvertently fanned MacArthur's 1944 hopes in a widely quoted Lincoln Day speech in Boston. As MacArthur hunkered down on Corregidor, Willkie beseeched Roosevelt to "bring Douglas MacArthur home. Place him at the very top. Keep bureaucratic and political hands off him. Give him the responsibility and the power of coordinating all the armed forces of the nation to their most effective use."[3]

Indeed, the spillover from efforts to appoint MacArthur supreme commander of all American forces directly under Roosevelt and over the Joint Chiefs became one of the twin pillars of the 1944 MacArthur-for-president movement. The other would be an incessant "anyone but Roosevelt" mantra put forth by fringe elements of the Republican Party. Simply put, MacArthur became an early rallying point for anti-Roosevelt forces because there was no one else of his stature and national renown readily available.

In May of 1942, at the height of MacArthur's popularity after his escape from Corregidor, a Gallup poll placed MacArthur at the top of a list of eighteen men, excluding Roosevelt, considered to be presidential material in 1944. But even as he reported these results, George Gallup shrewdly noted, "War has a way of pushing to the top almost overnight new leaders who but for the stress of national emergency might have continued their work in relative obscurity."[4]

Throughout 1942, conservative newspapers, led by Robert

McCormick's *Chicago Tribune,* New York's *Daily News* (owned by McCormick's first cousin Joseph Medill Patterson), and the Washington *Times-Herald* (owned by another of McCormick's first cousins, Eleanor "Cissy" Patterson), beat the drum against FDR and endlessly replayed MacArthur's protestations about his perceived lack of support from Washington. For his part, MacArthur was always quick—no matter the exigencies of his day—to respond to letters, send congratulations, and provide statements for a variety of organizations and events.

Although MacArthur's forces had yet to retake Buna, the presidential pace quickened just before the 1942 midterm elections when Joseph C. Harsch, the Washington correspondent for the *Christian Science Monitor,* returned to Washington from a visit to Australia. As *Time* reported in early November, "The political fires which burned briefly last spring for General Douglas MacArthur had all but flickered out" when Harsch "repeated a charge often made but never documented: 'Political Washington was largely responsible for setting up two separate commands in the Far Pacific, and it did this partly because of jealousy of MacArthur's great popularity and partly because the conservative opposition press launched a MacArthur-for-President campaign.'"[5]

Harsch's quote was, in *Time*'s words, "buried in the 17th paragraph of a Pacific roundup story, but it made big reading by the time it reached Australian headlines," and its subsequent widespread publication provided MacArthur with a national platform from which to hone his non-candidate rhetoric. In a statement in which MacArthur first praised Australian war efforts—"No nation in the world is making a more supreme war effort"—the general professed "no political ambitions whatsoever." Any suggestion to the contrary, MacArthur again claimed, "must be regarded as merely amiable gestures of good will dictated by friendship."

"I started as a soldier, and I shall finish as one," he concluded. "The only hope and ambition I have in the world are for victory for our cause in the war. If I survive the campaign I shall return to that retirement from which this great struggle called me."[6]

Even as Secretary of war Stimson worried about Eddie Rickenbacker, who was then missing en route to admonish to MacArthur to rein in his personal publicity and moderate his criticisms of just about everything else, the secretary was keenly aware of MacArthur's political dalliances. "MacArthur, who is not an unselfish being and is a good deal of a prima donna," Stimson wrote in his diary, "has himself lent a little aid to the story by sending people here who carry a message from him that he was not a Presidential candidate, thereby playing into the hands of the people who would really like to make him a candidate." Stimson professed that MacArthur should treat the entire political matter "as soldier-like Marshall would treat it" and never say a word on the subject, "assuming that all talk of one's candidacy is nonsense." But MacArthur's statements only "served to keep the story going."[7]

Of course, nothing about MacArthur—from MacArthur's viewpoint—was nonsense. Everything was carefully choreographed; no detail was too minor to overlook if it might be seized upon by others, and no opportunity for gaining intelligence too small to pass up.

When MacArthur sent majordomo Sid Huff with Sutherland and Kenney to attend the Pacific Military Conference in Washington in March of 1943 as a reward for loyal service, MacArthur told Huff to "keep your ear to the ground" for any political news.

MacArthur admirer Clare Boothe Luce, then a Republican congresswoman from Connecticut, arranged for Sutherland and Kenney to sing their boss's praises for mainstream Republican senator Arthur H. Vandenberg of Michigan as part of their visit, but Huff reported back with grittier news. Some people wanted to know why MacArthur carried "that cane around all the time" and wondered if the general were "feeble."

MacArthur bristled. The cane in question had belonged to his mother, and MacArthur had a sentimental attachment to it. But it definitely wasn't a cane for support as much as a swagger stick for effect, and he had been carrying something similar as part of his ensemble since the days of World War I. It was meant to add to his military air. MacArthur took the question to heart, however, and, according to Huff, "the General never carried the stick again."[8]

Perhaps ill-advisedly—because it only shone more light on the issue—Stimson opted that same spring to reiterate long-standing army regulations that banned political activities by regular army officers. Senator Vandenberg and others saw the secretary's actions as singling out MacArthur, and they came to his defense.

"I am most grateful to you for your complete attitude of friendship," MacArthur responded to Vandenberg. "I only hope that I can some day reciprocate. There is much that I would like to say to you which circumstances prevent. In the meantime I want you to know the absolute confidence I would feel in your experienced and wise mentorship."[9] Vandenberg took that as a sign that he could move cautiously ahead with MacArthur's blessing in promoting a MacArthur candidacy.

MacArthur was far more candid in his conversations with his British liaison officer, Lieutenant Colonel Gerald Wilkinson, who reported directly to Winston Churchill. Perhaps because Wilkinson was not in an American uniform, or possibly because MacArthur wanted to impress Churchill with his intentions, he felt less constrained in his remarks. Telling Wilkinson that he never weighed the political consequences of his SWPA actions, MacArthur nonetheless avowed that he would respond to an appeal from the American people and "lead them as president in this time of trouble." His was the "voice from the fighting services" that would one day have to be heard in the White House. Despite having already been reprimanded for attempting to influence Churchill outside the chain of command, MacArthur asked Wilkinson to invite Churchill to Australia so that he might confer directly with him on Pacific strategy.[10]

Sir Campbell Stuart, a Canadian newspaperman, came away from a conversation with MacArthur after hearing similar rhetoric. Stuart passed on to Wilkinson his impressions of MacArthur's "extreme independence, outspokenness to the point of extraordinary indiscretion... about the President," and "close knowledge of *political* matters."[11]

Even as he appeared to be politically adroit, however, MacArthur gloomily and incorrectly predicted to Wilkinson that the Democrats would sweep the 1942 midterm elections. In fact, Republicans picked up nine seats in the Senate and forty-six seats in the House of Representatives as well as a new majority of governorships, which included Thomas E. Dewey in New York.

These electoral results were not so much objections to Roosevelt's conduct of the war as they were a determination to oppose or, if possible, repeal some or all of the liberal New Deal, but the topic of MacArthur as a more capable military leader than Roosevelt and as a possible presidential candidate in 1944 was one that wouldn't die. MacArthur distanced himself from Eleanor Roosevelt's visit to Australia in September of 1943 — Jean hosted one dinner for the First Lady in his absence — but at around the same time, MacArthur had no qualms about spending the better part of three days at Port Moresby discussing presidential politics and global strategy with five visiting United States senators: Republican R. Owen Brewster, of Maine; Democrat Albert B. Chandler, of Kentucky; Republican Henry Cabot Lodge Jr., of Massachusetts; Democrat James M. Mead, of New York; and Democrat Richard B. Russell of Georgia.[12]

Senator Chandler returned to Washington so enamored with MacArthur that he promoted a bill to make MacArthur supreme commander for all Allied forces operating against Japan, apparently forgetting that the Constitution gave this prerogative to the executive branch. MacArthur's ally John O'Laughlin at the *Army and Navy Journal* and his usual supporters at the McCormick-Patterson papers repeated MacArthur's concerns, initially uttered in the wake of the First Quebec Conference, that his Southwest Pacific Area was reportedly to be shrunk for the benefit of Lord Louis Mountbatten's operations in the China-Burma-India theater.

Even the London *Daily Mirror* got into the act, reporting that things got a little personal when pro-MacArthur elements in the American press contrasted MacArthur's "sincere attitude" with "the somewhat flamboyant air of Mountbatten." The *Daily Mirror* went on to quote the *Ohio State Journal,* which said that "it would be a tragic thing if MacArthur were to be shorn of his authority while a London glamour boy is elevated."

This was far more about politics than military priorities, and both Roosevelt and Churchill weighed in on the matter. As Roosevelt put it during an October 5, 1943, press conference in which he read from the *Daily Mirror* story, such reports of command conflicts were not only disseminated with deliberate malice, they also showed "carelessness on the part of some people in this country" and "an extraordinary ignorance of geography — my old hobby." Across the Atlantic, Churchill looked at his globe, found MacArthur's and Mountbatten's headquarters separated by 6,600 miles, and sarcastically asked an American guest, "Do you think that's far enough apart?"[13]

* * *

MacArthur alter ego Charles Willoughby, with help from Clare Boothe Luce, became the clandestine knight errant between MacArthur on the one hand and Senator Vandenberg and the moderate, mainstream Republican forces he quietly hoped to coalesce around MacArthur on the other. If MacArthur were to have a shot at the nomination, a solid foundation would have to be laid among the party faithful based on substance, not on the overexcited machinations of a few right-wing extremists.

But as Vandenberg moved forward, he found himself "disturbed about one thing which to me is quite inexplicable. I am constantly hearing reports," Vandenberg told MacArthur backer General Robert E. Wood, chairman of Sears, Roebuck, "that veterans returning from the South Pacific are not enthusiastic about our friend. One skeptical correspondent has gone so far as to suggest that there is some sort of diabolical arrangement to see to it that only anti-MacArthur veterans are furloughed home."[14]

That last point was hyperbolic, of course, but given MacArthur's rigid censorship and the personally positive communiqués emanating from his headquarters, individual soldiers returning to the States were some of the only sources who could possibly shine a different light on the glowing MacArthur image. A major exception to this was an article by John McCarten entitled "General MacArthur: Fact and Legend," which appeared in the January 1944 issue of *The American Mercury.*

Vowing to take apart the MacArthur legend "to separate fact from fancy," McCarten wrote: "Even if MacArthur were the paragon he is claimed to be by his more passionate promoters, a military man without a trace of other experience seems scarcely an appropriate leader for civilian America in a decisive period of our history." There was indeed a good deal of hero worship at play, McCarten noted: "It is a strange and wonderful thing to watch a hero being created. A man who only yesterday was as fallible and sometimes as foolish as everybody else is suddenly luminous with virtue, prophetic in judgment, incredible in action, profound in thought."

McCarten further opined, "So well has the legend of MacArthur been nurtured that it is now difficult to recall that in December 1941 . . . it was not preposterous at that time to imagine him on the griddle alongside [Pearl Harbor commanders] Admiral Kimmel and General Short." But MacArthur's "share in the tragedy was soon forgotten," McCarten concluded, because "America needed a hero to take the edge off humiliation and MacArthur filled the bill with a margin to spare."

Cataloging MacArthur's Philippine missteps, the extraordinary McCormick-Patterson publicity efforts on his behalf, and the rush of "hasty books by eager literary *entrepreneurs*," McCarten concluded that "few men are able to resist the temptation of trying to live up to the myths that are spun about them. To a man like General MacArthur, who has a very real consciousness of his own greatness, the temptation is doubly severe."

McCarten wrote that MacArthur, since his arrival in Australia, "has cultivated an aloofness so impregnable that both American and Australian soldiers boast of having seen him, as though he were a phenomenon on par with Halley's Comet." McCarten went on to note, "It is difficult to understand MacArthur's motives in neglecting to mingle with his men."[15]

How much this criticism, particularly of his failure to visit the front lines, may have influenced MacArthur's decision a few months later to sail for the Admiralties and go ashore on Los Negros is unknown. Vandenberg countered McCarten's piece with a "Why I Am for MacArthur" article in *Collier's*, saying that MacArthur would bring "a great mind, a great heart, a great capacity and a great devotion to the proud leadership of a great nation," but then another article harshly critical of MacArthur appeared before the censors in the War Department's Bureau of Public Relations.[16]

Walter Lucas, a correspondent for the London *Daily Express*, who had been accredited to MacArthur's Southwest Pacific Area, was then in the United States and writing for *Harper's Magazine*. He submitted an article entitled "MacArthur and His Command" for review. Because it involved MacArthur, the piece was passed up the chain of command until it was Marshall's assistant, Colonel Frank McCarthy, whose duty it was to prepare a memo for his boss explaining the quandary.

McCarthy reported that Lucas was "highly critical of General MacArthur on grounds of vanity, aloofness, conceit, selfishness, histrionics, etc." All that was true to at least some degree, even if it was not well-known at the time, and in any event it was not particularly germane to MacArthur's conduct of military operations. But the article also concluded that MacArthur had lost the confidence of the Australians, that he would accept the vice presidency under either Willkie or Dewey—provided they would "let MacArthur handle the job of winning the war"—and quoted Willoughby comparing MacArthur to Napoleon, the Duke of Wellington, and Robert E. Lee.

"On the other hand," McCarthy continued, "it credits him with being a man of high intellect, great military ability, and thorough military knowledge. But the scales are so heavily weighted towards the sarcastic that one forgets any good before he has finished reading the article." The Bureau of Public Relations had already struck out as much of the text as could be eliminated on security grounds, but McCarthy claimed that "the picture is still a gross one."

Marshall's options, McCarthy said, were to clear the article, send it to SWPA for action there, or kill it on the dubious grounds that it was a security issue because it would undermine "the confidence of General MacArthur's troops in him."[17]

McCarthy recommended that the article be killed. Marshall, no doubt knowing that he would take some heat from a free press over the matter, concurred. Admittedly, in hindsight, it is questionable how much Lucas's piece, even when added to John McCarten's scrutiny, would have deflated either MacArthur's stellar military image or his budding presidential campaign. Two years of nonstop propaganda at home and abroad had conditioned a broad swath of the American public to be starstruck.

Marshall's actions prove at a very basic level, however, that he—with Roosevelt's concurrence—was focused on the priority of winning the war, even if it meant saving MacArthur. Marshall and the president had already saved the general, literally and figuratively, many times since the Corregidor evacuation. Had there truly been a sinister Washington plot to "get MacArthur," the article would have been an easy incoming salvo to let fall through the cracks. But Marshall held it back and took the resulting heat.

The salvos that were fired came from the editors of *Harper's Magazine*. In an editorial in the May 1944 issue, they concluded:

One may write what one pleases about the other candidates; about General MacArthur no opinions based on recent direct observations may apparently be given publicity unless they are flattering.

This situation is intolerable in a free country. It may be that General MacArthur's apparent grievances against the Administration are justified. It may be that the many unfavorable criticisms of him which we have heard—even those which we sought to publish—have been misjudged. But that a man who stands protected by censorship should permit his name to be considered for the Presidency mocks a central principle of democracy—the right of the people to see their political candidates in the light of free discussion.

Before this page reaches print the General may have unequivocally withdrawn his name. Or the censorship may have been relaxed. Otherwise let the public stand warned. The accounts of this candidate which have been appearing are incomplete, biased by censorship, and therefore politically unreliable.[18]

In reporting *Harper's* stance, the *New York Times* challenged the War Department's assertion that release of the article would "undermine the confidence of this country, Australia, and particularly the troops in that theatre." Roosevelt himself was about to be subjected to criticism in a political campaign, and a possible presidential candidate such as MacArthur was "entitled to no more immunity than an incumbent President." Remembering a central tenet of what the war was about, the *Times* concluded, "Nothing should discourage our enemies more than our ability to maintain free public discussions of vital issues and important personalities in the midst of war."[19]

Even more to the point, however, is why a regular army officer on active duty in a combat zone would allow if not outright encourage his supporters to promote his name—against long-standing regulations and past precedent—in an electoral challenge to his commander in chief.[20] The answer is simple: MacArthur wanted the presidency and was convinced he could do the job better than anyone else.

Vandenberg and Republican moderates rationalized MacArthur's unorthodox military opposition to a sitting president in part because they were conducting a stealth campaign that assumed a deadlocked convention between front-runners Willkie and Dewey. What made their task all the more difficult, however, was the fact that MacArthur's most vocal supporters included some of the most venomous Roosevelt haters. Indeed, as John McCarten pointed out in his *American Mercury* article, "It may not be [MacArthur's] fault but it surely is his misfortune that the worst elements on the political Right, including its most blatant lunatic fringe, are whooping it up for MacArthur."[21]

But then MacArthur dealt himself an equally destructive blow. As early as 1939, while in the service of the Philippines and not on active duty, MacArthur had given Bonner Fellers this assessment of the 1940 election: "The greatest disaster that could possibly visit the world today," MacArthur wrote, "is the continuation of Roosevelt as President of the United States."[22] And long after his own name began to be bandied about in connection with the 1944 election, MacArthur did not refrain from indulging in similar sentiments in what he may have presumed to be private communications. Congressman Arthur L. Miller, a Nebraska conservative, encouraged MacArthur in September of 1943 to accept a proffered Republican nomination and urged, "Unless this New Deal can be stopped this time [1944] our American way of life is forever doomed." In response, MacArthur declined to "anticipate in any way your flattering predictions, but I unreservedly agree with the complete wisdom and statesmanship of your comments."[23]

Miller wrote MacArthur again in late January of 1944 and claimed, "If this system of left wingers and New Dealism is continued another four years, I am certain that this monarch[y] which is being established in America will destroy the rights of the common people." Miller urged MacArthur to lead the charge and "destroy this monstrosity."

Calling Miller's characterizations of conditions in America "sobering" and "calculated to arouse the thoughtful consideration of every true patriot," MacArthur asserted, "We must not inadvertently slip into the same condition internally as the one which we fight externally." Summoning the ghost of Lincoln, he concluded, "Like Abraham Lincoln, I am a firm believer in the people, and, if given the truth, they can be depended upon to meet any national crises."[24] It wasn't a declaration of his candidacy, but it came close, particularly when Miller later made these two letters public in what he maintained was a well-intentioned attempt to jump-start the MacArthur campaign.

If MacArthur were to have any real chance for the nomination, he needed a jump-start. Twelve months of polling offered some telling points about his potential candidacy against Roosevelt as well as about the internal fight for the Republican nomination. From April of 1943 to April of 1944, MacArthur's support among Republican contenders remained relatively constant, starting at 17 percent and fluctuating between 15 percent and 20 percent, reaching the latter in April of 1944, after the Admiralties operation. During that year, New York governor Thomas E. Dewey's support rose from 38 percent to 55 percent at the expense of Wendell Willkie, who declined from 28 percent to 7 percent. Governor John Bricker of Ohio and former Minnesota governor Harold Stassen, who had resigned to go on active duty on Halsey's staff and would go on to become a perennial favorite-son candidate during Republican conventions, rounded out the field.[25]

But the more telling polling came when MacArthur's popularity was measured against Roosevelt's. Asked in a *Fortune* poll in March of 1944 who would do "the best job, as President, of running the war," 52 percent of respondents chose Roosevelt, 22 percent chose MacArthur, 7 percent chose Dewey, and 5 percent chose Willkie. The fact that MacArthur was admired when it came to military matters, however, did not necessarily mean that he was politically astute or favored when it came to domestic matters. When the same respondents were asked who could "do the best job, as President, of preventing unemployment after the war," 41 percent chose Roosevelt, 5 percent chose MacArthur, 16 percent chose Dewey, and 12 percent chose Willkie. As for managing foreign affairs after the war, Roosevelt was favored by 43 percent, MacArthur by 9 percent, Dewey by 10 percent, and internationalist Willkie by 14 percent of respondents.[26]

None of this showed a groundswell for MacArthur. Vandenberg had his work cut out for him. A convention deadlocked between Dewey and Willkie remained the general's only hope, even if a potential

MacArthur breakout came in the April 4 Wisconsin primary. MacArthur had as many roots there as anywhere, and he did not campaign. Willkie did and barnstormed the state for seventeen days. Dewey sensed an ambush and tried to get his name removed from the ballot. His efforts proved too late, and it was just as well.

Of twenty-four delegates, Dewey won fifteen, with two more leaning his way. Minnesota neighbor Harold Stassen won four, and MacArthur captured three. Willkie received none, and a few days later he withdrew from the race. Willkie's departure all but quashed Vandenberg's hopes for a deadlocked convention, and he glumly noted, "If people [in Wisconsin] were flocking to Dewey on Dewey's own account then it is all over but the shouting. But if they were flocking to Dewey because he looked like their best chance to 'stop Willkie' then...we should wait until at least the first of May before we take any active step toward joining the Dewey parade. I have written Australia and frankly presented this picture."[27]

It was during this period of wishful thinking that Congressman Miller attempted to breathe new life into the MacArthur-for-president movement by releasing his exchange of letters with MacArthur to the press. They were widely published, including in the *New York Times* and *Washington Post,* on April 14. The general's pronouncements on politics and criticisms of Roosevelt, no matter how veiled, showed him to be disingenuous at best in his assertions that he was not a candidate. Still, MacArthur tried to have it both ways.

On April 17, his SWPA headquarters issued a communiqué noting the publication of what was termed "a personal correspondence" between the general and Congressman Miller that was "neither politically inspired nor intended to convey blanket approval of the Congressman's views." As if his feelings for the New Deal were not readily understood from those letters, MacArthur claimed, "I entirely repudiate the sinister interpretation that they were intended as criticism of any political philosophy or of any personages in high office." Once again professing his dedication to the prosecution of the war, he concluded, "I can only say as I have said before, I am not a candidate for the office nor do I seek it."[28]

But would he accept it? He had yet to make a Shermanesque refusal to run if nominated or a refusal to serve if elected. On April 11, just before Miller released the letters, MacArthur won a beauty contest in the Illinois presidential primary, where his only opposition was an unknown Chicago real estate developer. If not a political charge, it was still a vote of admiration. But then, by the end of April, the censorship fight over Walter Lucas's banned article was front-page news, and some began to consider that where there was so much smoke, there had to be a little fire.

If MacArthur stayed in the race, casually or otherwise, he faced a humiliating loss at the June convention to Dewey, who showed no sign of anointing MacArthur his vice president and wartime consigliore. MacArthur weighed the facts, and on April 30, 1944, issued yet another press release on the subject.

"Since my return from the Hollandia operations," MacArthur began, "I have had brought to my attention a number of newspaper articles professing in strongest terms a widespread public opinion that it is detrimental to our war effort to have an officer in high position on active service at the front considered for nomination for the office of President." Noting that on several occasions he had announced that he was not a candidate, MacArthur finally took a Sherman-like stance and concluded, "Nevertheless, in view of these circumstances, in order to make my position entirely unequivocal, I request that no action be taken that would link my name in any way with the nomination. I do not covet it nor would I accept it."[29]

Say what you will about Douglas MacArthur as a man or a general, this foray into presidential politics — and there would be others to come — was nurtured by MacArthur's lesser qualities. It was not his finest hour. His vanity, conceit, and selfishness — Walter Lucas's unpublished article had been correct in those characterizations — were on graphic display, and they motivated his actions.

Senator Vandenberg was left to thank MacArthur for sending him an autographed photograph, which Vandenberg said he would deeply cherish as "a precious reminder of our recent presidential 'adventure.'" Vandenberg still considered MacArthur "by far the most eligible American" to assume the presidency and lamented that their efforts in that direction had "rather well succeeded right up to that last moment the 'Nebraska accident' occurred."[30]

As MacArthur occupied himself with the Biak landings and looked ahead to Luzon, the Republicans met in Chicago and nominated Thomas Dewey for president and John Bricker for vice president. It was bittersweet. And having dispatched his lengthy missive to Marshall on the need to return to the Philippines, and having included a request to meet with the commander in chief, whose place he had hoped to take, Douglas MacArthur momentarily turned from his presidential ambitions to a presidential summons.

On July 6, 1944, Marshall sent MacArthur a message for his eyes only ordering him to arrive in Honolulu on July 26 and stressing that it was of the "utmost importance that the fewest possible number of individuals know of your expected departure or of your destination."[31] MacArthur had not been to the mainland United States or Hawaii since his 1937 trip stateside to marry Jean. His bluster on the several occasions when he demanded to see the president gave no indication that he really wanted to make such a journey, and he had always seemed content to dispatch the likes of Sutherland, Kenney, and Willoughby to do his bidding.

MacArthur stewed a little over this summons, telling Marshall, "I know nothing of the purpose of my orders," but he undoubtedly expected that it would include Formosa-or-Luzon discussions. Asked by MacArthur for further clarification, Marshall replied, "No further orders are necessary," and told him Nimitz would be notified of his visit by courier three days in advance. The purpose, Marshall said, was "general strategical discussion," and while Marshall himself would be in Washington, MacArthur could expect to see "Leahy, etcetera."[32]

The "etcetera" part should have been very clear. Save for the Casablanca Conference, in January of 1943, when presidential chief of staff Leahy was sidelined with bronchitis, the admiral had been at President Roosevelt's side for all his wartime conferences and travels. Leahy routinely occupied the compartment next to the president's on the presidential railcar, took his yellow pad filled with notes in to see the president every morning, and, with the decline of trusted adviser Harry Hopkins's health, had increasingly become Roosevelt's key adviser on all matters, not just military ones. It was a safe bet that Leahy would not be coming to Honolulu alone.

Shortly after noon on July 15, the presidential train with Roosevelt and Leahy on board pulled into Chicago, where the Democratic Party faithful were gathering for their upcoming convention. At a press conference only four days earlier, Roosevelt had finally acknowledged that he would accept their nomination for a fourth term. The president's train departed Chicago before the convention convened, and as it sped westward toward San Diego, Roosevelt announced his recommendation of Senator Harry Truman for the vice presidential nomination. Leahy confessed that except for Truman's work investigating national defense issues, "he knew almost nothing about him."[33]

Arriving in San Diego, Roosevelt and Leahy spent two days observing amphibious landing exercises. Once Roosevelt's own nomination and that of Truman were in place, the president and Leahy boarded the heavy cruiser *Baltimore* and, shortly after midnight on July 22, sailed for Hawaii. Midvoyage, somewhere above the watery expanse of the Pacific, a BP2Y Coronado carrying Admiral King flew east in the opposite direction. King had been at Pearl Harbor conferring with Nimitz and making an inspection tour of operations in the Marianas. The fact that King had already conducted his business with Nimitz, as well as the fact that Marshall was remaining in Washington, were hints that Roosevelt's conference with MacArthur leaned more toward the political than the military.

Meanwhile, despite the "MacArthur's eyes only" invitation, a good number in the general's Brisbane headquarters were aware of the impending trip. Sutherland informed Dusty Rhoades on July 10 that he would be flying MacArthur to "a world-important conference a long way from here before the end of this month." Five days later, MacArthur confided to Rhoades that their destination would be Honolulu and asked about the aircraft arrangements.

According to Rhoades, "our beloved B-17, *Bataan I,* although ideal for operation in New Guinea, had a crowded passenger compartment and insufficient headroom to permit the general to do his methodical pacing." The twenty-six hours of flying time would require something better suited. Rhoades got authority from Sutherland to requisition a passenger-equipped C-54 that Pan American Airways was operating under military contract. Three rows of seats were moved to make room for a cot for the general's use should he choose to stop pacing.[34]

On the morning of July 26 — it was still only July 25 in Hawaii — MacArthur arrived at Amberley Field fifteen minutes late. Rhoades had the requisitioned C-54 ready to go, and with MacArthur, Bonner Fellers, Larry Lehrbas, Dr. David Chambers (a stand-in for Roger Egeberg), and the Pan American flight crew on board, the plane took off at 8:15 a.m., bound for a refueling stop on New Caledonia after an initial four-and-a-half-hour flight. From New Caledonia, it was another ten hours to Canton Island before the final long leg to Hawaii. According to Rhoades, MacArthur did not sleep for the entire flight and appeared more preoccupied and withdrawn than usual, at one point telling Rhoades that "he was trying to prepare himself mentally for any development that might result from his meeting with Mr. Roosevelt."[35]

As they neared Pearl Harbor early on the afternoon of what was still July 26, Rhoades found the skies filled with aircraft forming a massive review off Diamond Head as the *Baltimore* approached. Rhoades landed at Hickam Field, and MacArthur went to Fort Shafter, where he would be staying to freshen up after his long flight. Some sources, including Rhoades's diary, say that Nimitz was on hand to greet him, but this seems unlikely, as Nimitz and several other officials rode the pilot tug out to greet the *Baltimore* and boarded the cruiser at 2:25 p.m.

With the presidential flag flying and sailors in whites lining the rails of the ships on either side, the *Baltimore* made its way up the channel into the inner harbor and docked at pier 22-B, just astern of the *Enterprise*. More flag officers and general officers came aboard to greet the president, but Roosevelt soon began to look around for MacArthur.[36]

At 3:45 p.m., according to the president's official log, MacArthur made his entrance, by some accounts in the usual ostentatious MacArthur fashion. As the wail of a siren filled the air, a long open car accompanied by a motorcycle escort came into view, circled the dock, and came to a halt at the foot of the *Baltimore*'s gangplank. Its only occupants were a chauffeur in khakis at the wheel and, in the backseat, a lone figure wearing a battered cap encrusted with gold braid and, despite the summer heat, a leather flying jacket. There was no mistaking Douglas MacArthur.

To hearty applause, MacArthur alighted from the car and strode purposefully up the *Baltimore*'s gangplank. Roosevelt greeted him warmly,
and MacArthur acknowledged that their last meeting had been when
MacArthur was his chief of staff. Leahy, whose relationship with
MacArthur went back nearly forty years and who was never one to stand
on too much ceremony, cut to the quick and remarked drily, "Douglas,
why don't you wear the right kind of clothes when you come up here to
see us?" MacArthur gestured to the heavens and replied, "Well, you
haven't been where I came from, and it's cold up there in the sky."[37]

Shortly afterward, Roosevelt posed between MacArthur and Nimitz —
the general in his leather jacket and Nimitz in his immaculate whites —
for a series of photographs. For MacArthur, this session confirmed the
trip's thinly disguised political agenda. The dashing of his own presidential hopes aside, MacArthur still carried considerable influence in
certain Republican circles and remained wildly popular with the
American public at large. Political maestro Roosevelt had weighed the
benefits of either appearing before a partisan crowd at his nominating
convention or showcasing his commander-in-chief role in the company
of two of the country's most popular military heroes.

Political cartoonist Jim Berryman of the Washington *Evening Star*
captured the mood when he depicted MacArthur, Nimitz, and a
vibrant-looking FDR, wearing COMMANDER-IN-CHIEF on his sleeve,
seated at a table labeled PACIFIC WAR COUNCIL. MacArthur and Nimitz
are looking over their shoulders at another figure of FDR leaning jaun-
tily against a palm tree, cigarette holder in hand and lei around his
neck, while his hat reads DEMOCRATIC NOMINEE. "Oh, don't mind him,
gentlemen," FDR's commander-in-chief character tells MacArthur and
Nimitz. "He just came along to get away from politics!"[38]

As for the president, MacArthur was "shocked at his personal
appearance. I had not seen him for a number of years," MacArthur
recalled in his memoirs, "and physically he was just a shell of the man
I had known. It was clearly evident that his days were numbered."[39]
After returning to Australia, MacArthur was more emphatic with
Roger Egeberg. "Doc," MacArthur lectured his physician with a
pointed stab of his forefinger, "the mark of death is on him. In six
months he'll be in his grave."[40]

One would not have known that, however, from the busy schedule Roosevelt maintained the following day. After a night's rest, at mid-morning on July 27, Roosevelt squeezed MacArthur and Nimitz into the backseat of the same car MacArthur had used, and with Leahy in front the driver set off on a whirlwind tour of Oahu military installations. MacArthur handled it all good-naturedly, no matter what pique he may have harbored over Roosevelt's grandiose public displays.

During the evening, there was a break of several hours while Roosevelt signed letters, then he reconvened the principal group of MacArthur, Nimitz, and Leahy, along with Bill Halsey, who had just arrived from the States, for dinner in the Waikiki residence where the president was staying. Only afterward, following what had already been a twelve-hour day, did the foursome, absent Halsey, adjourn to the map-bedecked living room. As MacArthur chose to remember it, he felt decidedly alone and outnumbered, having realized, in his words, "I was to go it alone."[41]

Truth be told, of course, this was exactly the sort of situation in which MacArthur reveled and excelled. After Nimitz laid out what was essentially Admiral King's continuing plan to invade Formosa directly and sever the flow of natural resources from the East Indies to Japan, it was MacArthur's turn. Taking as his text his latest missive to Marshall, MacArthur proclaimed the moral and political importance of returning to the Philippines as quickly and directly as possible. The ensuing discussion went on until midnight and was resumed for several hours the following morning.

"These two meetings were much more peaceful than I had expected after what I had been hearing in Washington," Leahy recorded afterward. "Here in Honolulu we were working with facts, not the emotional reactions of politicians." Noting that there were some parties in Washington who disliked MacArthur and that interservice rivalry frequently attended matters on both sides, Leahy nonetheless professed that he "was personally convinced that MacArthur and Nimitz were, together, the two best qualified officers in our service for this tremendous task" — concluding the Pacific war.[42]

While Leahy correctly decided that MacArthur seemed to be "chiefly interested in retaking the Philippines," he also came away from the conference convinced that both MacArthur and Nimitz were "in agreement with me...that Japan can be forced to accept our terms of surrender by the use of sea and air power without an invasion of the Japanese homeland."[43]

Despite what the parties may have thought—each, save perhaps Nimitz, seemed convinced that he had persuaded the others to accept his position—the issue of Formosa versus Luzon would not be settled for at least another month or two, and then only after the Joint Chiefs thoroughly vetted it yet again. But Leahy was correct in recognizing that in the broad strategic picture, the issue of an attack route via Formosa or Luzon was secondary in importance to the decision of whether or not to invade Japan's home islands.

The planning staffs had been working on those plans "regardless of loss of life," and the topic would be regularly debated for another year. But Leahy was decidedly opposed to a ground invasion. As he put it, "Their agreement on the fundamental strategy that should be employed in bringing defeat to Japan and the President's familiarity therewith acquired at this conference, will be of the greatest value to me in preventing an unnecessary invasion of Japan."

The other thing that impressed Leahy from the conference was that while MacArthur wanted continued naval support from Nimitz's carriers for his future amphibious landings, he professed to have all the other resources he needed—except, perhaps, some additional landing craft. Nimitz claimed that he, too, had sufficient forces, whether to occupy the Philippines or Formosa. In an indication of just how far American military resources had come in two and a half years, Leahy noted, "It was highly pleasing and unusual to find two commanders who were not demanding reinforcements."[44]

As for the much-ballyhooed friction between MacArthur and Nimitz, it appeared to all that both men were permitting Roosevelt to exercise his commander-in-chief persona. "After so much loose talk in Washington," Leahy concluded, "where the mention of the name of MacArthur seemed to generate more heat than light, it was both very pleasant and very informative to have these two men who had been pictured as antagonists calmly present their differing views to the Commander-in-Chief."[45]

After lunch on July 28, having been in Hawaii for almost forty-eight hours, MacArthur took his leave of the president and once again climbed aboard Rhoades's C-54 at Hickam Field. While time would tell whether MacArthur had gotten all that he thought he had from the presidential visit, Rhoades reported the general to be "in a rare good mood... in stark contrast to the depressed mood he had been unable to conceal on our way to Honolulu." Making only one refueling stop at Tarawa, they arrived in Brisbane twenty-three and a half hours later, which Rhoades judged to be something of a record.[46]

Back in Hawaii, after another afternoon and morning of tours, including an extended inspection of the Aiea Naval Hospital, Roosevelt held a press conference and made it clear that whenever and however the invasion of the Philippines would come about, "We are going to get the Philippines back, and without question General MacArthur will take a part in it." Whether he would go to the Philippines directly or not, the president couldn't say.[47] Then Roosevelt and Leahy reboarded the *Baltimore* and cleared Pearl Harbor on the evening of July 29, bound northward for Alaska as part of FDR's continuing efforts to display his commander-in-chief role.

By the time they returned to Washington, DC, it was mid-August. In a special closed-door session, Leahy briefed the Joint Chiefs on the journey and the most important aspect of it. "They may have been somewhat surprised to learn," Leahy recalled, "that Nimitz and MacArthur said they had no disagreements at the moment and that they could work out their joint plans in harmony."[48] Time would tell.

CHAPTER TWENTY-ONE

Toward the Philippines

Despite Douglas MacArthur's professed satisfaction after meeting with Franklin Roosevelt in Honolulu, the debate over returning to Luzon and *all* the Philippines was far from resolved. Admiral King remained the chief proponent of the Luzon-bypass, leap-to-Formosa strategy, but he also found himself temporarily allied with MacArthur on another matter. Having largely abandoned Pacific operations to American control in the spring of 1942, Great Britain was subsequently sniffing the fruits of victory.

MacArthur had warned Roosevelt in Honolulu that British interest in taking over a portion of his Southwest Pacific Area and attacking the Netherlands Indies from bases in eastern Australia was premised far less on military necessity and opportunity than on Churchill's political agenda for the British Empire. The Dutch, Australians, and Americans were all decidedly opposed to such a plan, MacArthur claimed, because "after two and a half years of struggle when American and Australian forces had defeated the Japanese, the British wanted to come in and claim rich territorial prizes."[1]

The primary vehicle for this planned reassertion of British imperialism was to be the time-tested deployment of a sizable portion of the British fleet. As commander in chief of the United States Fleet, King adamantly opposed British naval participation in the Pacific, seeing it as too small to make a real impact, incapable of being self-sufficient, and disruptive to existing chains of command and supply. To that end, before departing Hawaii prior to MacArthur's arrival, King wrote MacArthur with what he termed "some forewarning" about British proposals for just such an encroachment into his area.

King's letter was a not-so-subtle effort to recruit MacArthur's opposition. And it was effective. The admiral's mere mention of the prospect of the British utilizing bases in Australia, sucking supplies out of the American logistics pipeline, and conducting offensive operations near MacArthur's front in western New Guinea (the Banda Sea area around Ambon, for example) was enough to bring MacArthur immediately to King's side.[2]

"I am completely opposed to this proposition," MacArthur responded after returning to Brisbane. "The British have contributed nothing to this campaign and, in fact, opposed the [1942] Australian proposal to make available Australian troops for the defense of their own country." MacArthur waxed eloquent for two full pages about the successes of his existing command structure and his future plans for the Philippines and ended up concluding that he could "see no reason why the American command should be superseded by a British command at the moment of victory in order to reap the benefits of the peace."[3] King had himself an ally, but persuading Roosevelt to stand up to Churchill would be another matter.

As the *Baltimore* arrived at Auke Bay, near Juneau, on the last leg of the president's swing through Alaskan waters, Roosevelt wrote MacArthur a "Dear Douglas" letter, saying it had been "a particular happiness" to see him again. The president made no reference to the British situation, but promised, "As soon as I get back I will push on that [Luzon] plan for I am convinced that as a whole it is logical and can be done."[4]

MacArthur responded with apparent equal warmth, telling Roosevelt, "Nothing in the course of the war has given me quite as much pleasure as seeing you again. I think you know without my saying," he continued, "how deep is my personal affection for you and how great my admiration for your unrivalled accomplishments over the years."

Both these masters of political theater were undoubtedly laying it on a little thick, particularly given MacArthur's own presidential aspirations. But in the midst of the campaign, they undoubtedly chose their words carefully in anticipation that they might become public. Despite his shocked private reaction to Roosevelt's health, MacArthur professed his "fervent hope" that the president would be in Manila to raise the American flag once that city was retaken—a subtle form of continued lobbying for Luzon operations.[5]

By the time Roosevelt replied to MacArthur's message, on September 15, the president was at the Second Quebec Conference—codenamed Octagon—with Churchill, and the prime minister put Roosevelt squarely in a box when it came to the British fleet. Grandly offering Roosevelt assistance for Pacific operations, Churchill bluntly asked if his offer was accepted. There was little Roosevelt could say in response but yes, of course. One wry British observer noted that the official minutes should have read: "At this point Admiral King was carried out."[6]

Marshall explained the outcome more diplomatically when he cabled MacArthur: "For our government to put itself on record as having refused agreement to the use of additional British and Dominion resources in the Pacific or Southwest Pacific was unthinkable." The saving grace to both King and MacArthur was that no additional ground or air resources were to be deployed in the Central Pacific or Southwest Pacific Areas until the spring or early summer of 1945, and even then only in the event of Germany's defeat.[7] Thus there would be no ground or air newcomers to MacArthur's drive toward the Philippines. As for the British fleet, its appearance in the Pacific would also take some time, and managing it would be left to Nimitz's collegial discretion.

Roosevelt told MacArthur much the same thing in his September 15 reply and said he wished MacArthur "could be here [in Quebec] because you know so much of what we are talking about in regard to the plans of the British for the Southwest Pacific." As for American forces, Roosevelt told MacArthur, "The situation is just as we left it at Hawaii though there seem to be efforts to do a little by-passing [of Luzon] which you would not like." Nonetheless, Roosevelt assured MacArthur, "I still have the situation in hand."[8]

This phrasing suggests that, commander in chief though he was, Roosevelt was not one to second-guess his Joint Chiefs militarily—certainly not at that point in the war. He continued to profess to MacArthur that he understood and leaned toward, if not supported, a rapid return to Luzon, but Roosevelt was perfectly content to allow the Luzon-versus-Formosa

403

debate to run its course among the Joint Chiefs and their planners. Meanwhile, MacArthur had his own issues with allies.

Australia—and, to a lesser degree, New Zealand—had readily looked to MacArthur and the United States for help in the bleak spring of 1942 and as a result stretched, if not loosened, their Commonwealth ties to Great Britain. In May of 1944, Australian prime minister John Curtin offered his Commonwealth colleagues no apologies "for asking for American assistance in the days when Australia was seriously threatened," and he insisted that Australia's "acceptance of American help had in no way affected the Australians' deep sense of oneness with the United Kingdom." Curtin expressed his strong desire "to see the British flag flying in the Far East as dominantly and as early as possible."[9]

Curtin was still most grateful to MacArthur for bulwarking Australia during 1942 and 1943, but as the front line moved farther and farther from Australia, there were limits to that gratitude. There was a growing frustration among many Australians over the utilization—or, in some instances, the perceived underutilization—of their air, land, and sea forces. The governments of Australia and New Zealand—the latter had deployed troops in the Solomons—both frequently felt like second-class allies who were informed of major diplomatic and military decisions only in an after-the-fact way, most recently with the decisions at the Teheran-Cairo conferences, which impacted both the China-Burma-India theater and the twin drives across the Pacific.

Early in 1944, Australia and New Zealand took matters into their own hands by convening a conference to urge (1) their representation at the highest levels in matters related to the final campaigns of the war; (2) the establishment of a regional defense zone; and (3) the creation of an international commission to shepherd dependent territories in the Pacific toward self-government. Curtin and New Zealand prime minister Peter Fraser also put their allies on notice that the use of wartime bases in their respective countries implied no postwar rights and that future ownership of Japanese territories in the Pacific should be resolved only as part of an overall Pacific settlement in which Australia and New Zealand participated.[10]

It was not entirely clear whether this spurt of Aussie-Kiwi independence was directed more toward the United States or Great Britain, but MacArthur's political machinations over the deployment of the British fleet certainly didn't foster the sort of cooperation Australia and New Zealand sought. After his return from Honolulu, MacArthur whispered to the Dutch that Australia, either directly or as a surrogate for Great Britain, had designs on the Netherlands East Indies and appealed to them to oppose any expansion of the British-led Southeast Asian theater. MacArthur assured them he was "the guardian of unimpaired Dutch sovereignty in this area."[11]

Even as MacArthur courted the Dutch, however, he professed solid friendship to the British officials with whom he spoke, including the British high commissioner in Australia, Sir Ronald Cross. Quite disingenuously, MacArthur told Cross how much he looked forward to British naval units operating in his area and reportedly went so far as to remark how wonderful it would be if "an American general should sail into Manila under a British flag."[12]

At around the same time, Curtin gave impetus to Churchill's efforts to insert the British fleet into the Pacific by telling him, "There is developing in America a hope that they will be able to say they won the Pacific war by themselves."[13] Curtin's message came mere days before Churchill pressed Roosevelt at Quebec to accept the British fleet's involvement in the Pacific, but his sentiment had been building in Australian circles for some time.

The central issue was MacArthur's use of Australian troops as the Allies advanced farther and farther along the coast of New Guinea. Because of the tenor of MacArthur's communiqués, what most Americans did not know—or remember in hindsight—was that Australian troops had borne the brunt of the early fighting along the Kokoda Trail as well as at Gona, Wau, and Lae. It wasn't until early 1944 that American army units in the Southwest Pacific Area outnumbered Australian forces.

There was little question that Australians had been in the vanguard, but in anticipation of this shift in numbers, MacArthur made it clear to Blamey that once the encirclement of Rabaul was complete, Blamey's New Guinea Force would be reduced to mopping-up operations and garrison duties in increasingly rear areas. The last major Australian-led offensive in New Guinea occurred in late April of 1944, when the New Guinea Force captured Madang, west of Finschhafen, as

MacArthur made the leap to Hollandia. Thenceforth, replacing the New Guinea Force as the spearhead would be Krueger's Alamo Force, essentially the US Sixth Army.[14]

By August of 1944, Marshall questioned not so much the status of Australian units but rather the continuing viability of bypassed Japanese strongholds. "Indications are," the chief of staff wrote MacArthur, "that the large Jap garrisons in the Solomons and New Guinea which have been by-passed possibly are not weakening as fast as we had hoped." Marshall asked about using the newly arrived American Ninety-Third Infantry Division and some "available Australian units" to reduce these remaining strongholds, although he added that it might not be practical because "no additional assault shipping can be made available to you for this purpose."[15]

MacArthur responded that the Ninety-Third Division was not yet combat ready, and in any event, "The enemy garrisons which have been bypassed...represent no repeat no menace to current or future operations." MacArthur claimed that they had no offensive capabilities and would eventually succumb to attrition. "The actual time of their destruction," MacArthur continued, "is of little or no repeat no importance and their influence as a contributing factor to the war is already negligible." To try to take them out immediately would "unquestionably involve heavy loss of life" without gaining any strategic advantage.[16]

That made the mopping-up operations to which MacArthur soon relegated Australian forces sound rather benign, but, as will be seen, that is not what the Australians encountered in the field as MacArthur left them behind in New Guinea and pushed on toward the Philippines.

Meanwhile, the Luzon-Formosa debate was slowly moving toward a resolution. At a conference in Brisbane with War Department representatives shortly after returning from Honolulu, MacArthur argued that he could conduct the Luzon campaign in six weeks, probably even in less than thirty days, after landing in Lingayen Gulf, just as the Japanese had done in December of 1941. By comparison, he termed an assault on Formosa a "massive undertaking." Japanese air left on Luzon might be difficult to neutralize beforehand, and shortages in service troops could make the longer leap problematic.

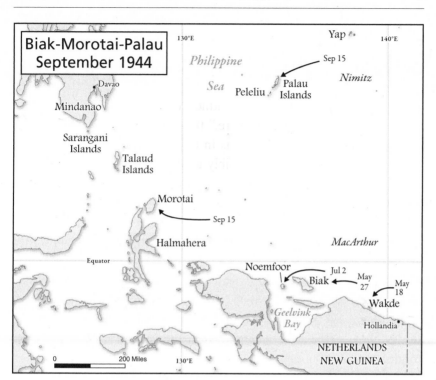

Borrowing a page from the compact schedule of amphibious operations conducted since the strike against Cape Gloucester nine months before, MacArthur proposed to Marshall that his forces invade the island of Morotai, five hundred miles beyond Biak, on September 15; the Talaud Islands, halfway between Morotai and Mindanao, on October 15; the tiny Sarangani Islands, just off the coast of Mindanao, on November 15; Bonifacio, on southwestern Mindanao, on December 7; Leyte on December 20; Aparri, on the northern tip of Luzon, on January 31; southern Mindanao on February 15; and finally Lingayen Gulf, off Luzon, on February 20.[17] Had the stakes not been so high in terms of the human lives at risk, one would be tempted to call it a whirlwind tour de force of the Philippines.

King remained the chief champion of the Formosa plan. Many planners in Washington liked it as well, but almost all field commanders agreed with MacArthur that Luzon was the safer alternative. This was in part because of the proximity of land-based air once Leyte was taken as well as the shorter distances involved for carrier operations from Nimitz's rapidly advancing forward bases, including the soon-to-be-captured anchorage at Ulithi. There was also the uneasy feeling in some quarters that leaping all the way to Formosa — however weakly defended King judged it to be — might arouse Japanese divisions based in China. At that late point in the war, those divisions remained a huge resource should Japan choose to redeploy them and commit the logistics necessary to move them to Formosa or the Philippines.

The fact that Japan didn't divert enough troops from China to oppose the American-Australian advance throughout 1943 and 1944 appears, in hindsight, to be one of the greatest missteps of its military strategy. It is perhaps best explained by a combination of the historic animosity between China and Japan, China's threat to Japan's natural-resource needs in Southeast Asia, the Japanese army's fixation with its seesaw campaigns against China, which had been going on since 1937, and — just as there was in the United States — a fair amount of interservice rivalry between the army and navy regarding overall strategy and concomitant responsibilities.[18]

MacArthur's air and naval commanders, George Kenney and Thomas Kinkaid, strongly opposed the Formosa option as a leap too far. Perhaps that was no surprise given their boss's position, but Bill Halsey also argued against it, advocating taking Luzon and then bypassing Formosa in favor of a direct strike against Okinawa or the Japanese island of Kyushu. Even Nimitz, who played the loyal King subordinate by arguing the Formosa option in front of Roosevelt at Honolulu, seemed increasingly lukewarm to the idea. He quietly instructed his Pacific Ocean Area planners to craft options against Okinawa rather than Formosa after an expected Luzon invasion.

King had previously done a good job of pushing Formosa with Marshall, who liked the basic idea of getting closer to Japan more quickly. But Marshall also recognized the limitations of amphibious capabilities and the numbers of available service troops. As the weeks went by, he pondered a more direct strike against Japan — Okinawa or Kyushu — as an alternative if Formosa were bypassed, regardless of what happened with operations on Luzon.

Then when Leahy weighed in as favoring Luzon instead of Formosa, the Joint Chiefs' pendulum swung away from Formosa and toward the commitment MacArthur thought he had received from both Roosevelt and Leahy in Honolulu: Luzon would not be bypassed. But neither did the Joint Chiefs set a firm target date — yet.[19]

Given the pressing need to issue MacArthur orders beyond Biak and to give Nimitz similar directives in the western Carolines, Leahy suggested, and Marshall readily agreed, that MacArthur's operations in the southern and central Philippines be approved through the contemplated December 20 landing at Leyte. But even the phrasing of these orders caused another round of debate among the Joint Chiefs. King grumbled about specifying the purpose of the Leyte landings — establishing air superiority in the Philippines or preparing for an assault against Formosa — and Marshall reprised his objection to the assumption that Formosa absolutely had to be taken regardless of what happened on Luzon.

Finally, on September 9, 1944, the Joint Chiefs again kicked the Luzon-Formosa can a little farther down the road. They ordered MacArthur to occupy Leyte with a target date of December 20. His objective was to concentrate whatever bases and forces in the central Philippines were necessary to support a further advance to Formosa by Nimitz's forces or his own seizure of Luzon early in 1945.

While going ahead with his Central Pacific Area operations against the Palau islands, including tiny Peleliu, Nimitz was to provide MacArthur with fleet support, including air cover and assault shipping for the Leyte operations, and develop his own plans for either occupying Formosa or once again supporting MacArthur if he were directed to attack Luzon after Leyte.[20] Thus the twin drives across the Pacific that many cheered and MacArthur routinely begrudged continued to converge on the Philippines from slightly different axes.

Part of the reluctance of the Joint Chiefs to resolve the Luzon-Formosa debate once and for all was the uncertainty of the war in Europe and the impact its end might have on the resources available to the Pacific. Unaware of Germany's last gasp, yet to come at the Battle of the Bulge that December, there were many who thought Germany might surrender in the fall of 1944. In fact, at one point in September, news of Germany's reputed surrender delayed the *Bataan*'s takeoff with MacArthur aboard until he could confirm that it was only a rumor.[21]

Amid this European uncertainty, the Joint Chiefs packed up to follow Roosevelt to the Second Quebec Conference with Churchill, Nimitz embarked his troops for the Palau invasion, MacArthur boarded the *Nashville* and sailed for the invasion of Morotai, and Bill Halsey, commanding the US Third Fleet, unleashed his attack carriers in raids against the Philippines. As it turned out, Halsey was about to rock the Luzon-Formosa debate in a big way.

Shortly after the squabble over the use of Seeadler Harbor, in the Admiralties, Bill Halsey worked himself out of a job in the South Pacific. The cleanup of bypassed pockets of Japanese resistance in the Solomons would take some time — as those assigned to the task would learn — but Nimitz wanted Halsey on the first string as the American fleet moved westward across the central Pacific.

Nimitz devised a rather ingenious rotating command structure between Halsey and Admiral Raymond Spruance, previously Nimitz's chief of staff. While one admiral and his staff commanded operations at sea, the other hunkered down with his team at Pearl Harbor and planned the next phase of operations. They would then go to sea and take a turn at operational command. This system had the added advantage of confusing the Japanese somewhat, because when Spruance was at sea, the principal American fleet was designated the Fifth Fleet. When Halsey assumed command of essentially the same force, it was designated the Third Fleet. Task forces, such as those made up of fast carriers, were either Task Force 58 or Task Force 38, depending on the fleet designation.

Spruance drew the first assignment at sea and commanded the fleet for the landings in the Marianas in mid-June of 1944. The Japanese fleet had not sortied in a single combined force since Midway, but most thinking held that sooner or later, it would make one concerted do-or-die attempt to stem the American advance.

When two major Japanese naval forces converged on the Marianas and threatened to either attack the beachheads or engage the Fifth Fleet — or both — Spruance stood by his primary charge and arrayed his ships to defend the landings. Against the ensuing air attacks from enemy carriers, antiaircraft fire from Spruance's battle line and pilots flying from his fifteen carriers shot down 383 Japanese aircraft, as opposed to twenty-five American losses, in what came to be called the Marianas Turkey Shoot.

The next day, Spruance sent his carriers west to engage the combined Japanese fleet. Despite the loss of three Japanese carriers — two from submarine torpedoes and one from air attack — the bulk of the Japanese force escaped, including at least six carriers. Although their air wings had been riddled with losses, the carriers that survived would soon figure heavily in Bill Halsey's decisions.[22]

Having spent twenty months in command of the South Pacific Area, Halsey bade his officers and men an emotional farewell in June of 1944. As he did so, MacArthur assured him that it was "with deepest regret we see you and your splendid staff go" and called Halsey "a great sailor, a determined commander, and a loyal comrade. We look forward with eager anticipation to a renewal of our cooperative effort."[23]

In response, Halsey felt compelled to add a personal note to the official dispatches. "You and I have had tough sledding with the enemy," Halsey wrote MacArthur, "and we have had some other complex problems nearly as difficult as our strategic problems; and I have the feeling that in every instance we have licked our difficulties. My own personal dealings with you have been so completely satisfactory that I will always feel a personal regard and warmth over and above my professional admiration."

"I also know and take great pleasure in telling you," Halsey continued, "that the members of my Staff continually express their satisfaction over the way that business can be done by the South Pacific and Southwest Pacific. I sincerely hope, and firmly believe, that I will have further opportunities to join forces with you against our vicious and hated enemy."[24]

On August 24, after a brief leave in the States and planning time in Hawaii, Halsey sailed west from Pearl Harbor on board the battleship *New Jersey,* one of the four mammoth sisters of the new *Iowa* class. Two days later, command of the fleet officially passed from Spruance to Halsey, and the carriers of the Third Fleet's Task Force 38 unleashed ferocious aerial assaults against Yap, in the Carolines, and the Palau islands in anticipation of the landing on Peleliu. On September 9 and

10, the carriers made similar strikes against Mindanao but found, according to Halsey, that Kenney's Fifth Air Force "had already flattened the enemy's installations and that only a feeble few planes rose" in opposition.

Accordingly, Halsey moved northward and launched the remainder of the planned strikes against Leyte, Samar, and southeastern Luzon, in the central Philippines. On September 12 alone, his aircraft flew 1,200 sorties. After two more such days, Halsey claimed 173 enemy planes shot down, 305 more destroyed on the ground, fifty-nine ships sunk, and widespread damage to other ships and land-based installations. In return, only eight American planes fell in combat.

This gave Halsey pause. Having found the central Philippines, in his words, "a hollow shell with weak defenses and skimpy facilities," he sat in the corner of his flag bridge chain-smoking cigarettes and pondering whether this "vulnerable belly of the Imperial dragon" could not be exploited by shifting MacArthur's planned November assault on Mindanao to an earlier strike directly against Leyte. Finally, Halsey turned to his chief of staff and announced, "I'm going to stick my neck out. Send an urgent dispatch to CINCPAC."[25]

Halsey's message to Nimitz audaciously recommended that (1) the central Pacific assaults about to get under way against the Palau islands and Yap, as well as those scheduled in MacArthur's area against Mindanao and the Talaud and Sarangani Islands, be canceled; (2) the ground forces earmarked for those assaults should be assigned to MacArthur for use in the Philippines instead; and (3) the invasion of Leyte should be expedited and rescheduled as far in advance of its planned December 20 date as possible.[26]

Nimitz was intrigued, but he had an immediate problem. The invasion of Peleliu was only forty-eight hours away, and it had been planned to coincide with MacArthur's landing on Morotai. Eighteen thousand men of the veteran First Marine Division and another eleven thousand from the Eighty-First Infantry Division were crammed on transports inbound to the island. At the striking end of an ever-burgeoning trans-Pacific flow of men and materiel, Nimitz faced a dilemma: use these troops at Peleliu or find someplace to park them without clogging the pipeline behind them.

Nimitz decided that, this late in the game, he had no choice but to go forward with the Peleliu landings. It was a command decision that became controversial in hindsight, when large concentrations of Japanese ground troops fought tenaciously throughout a network of limestone caves and caused heavy American casualties. It proved that while Japan's air resources may have been decimated and its naval commands again scattered after the Marianas, the garrisons of ground troops left behind were not about to give up easily.[27]

But the remainder of Halsey's suggestions was another matter. Nimitz immediately passed them on to the Joint Chiefs, who by that time were in Quebec with Roosevelt for the Octagon Conference. Marshall and King received Halsey's original message to Nimitz and Nimitz's subsequent offer to place the army's XXIV Corps, then loading in Hawaii for Yap, at MacArthur's disposal for an expedited Leyte strike. Marshall, reluctant to make such a drastic change in timetable and objectives without input from MacArthur, asked the SWPA commander for his opinion. The reply came back that MacArthur was fully prepared to shift his plans and land on Leyte on October 20.

This message arrived in Quebec as Leahy, Marshall, King, and Arnold were at a formal dinner given by their Canadian hosts. They promptly excused themselves and met in conference to issue new orders. Because the men had "the utmost confidence in General MacArthur, Admiral Nimitz, and Admiral Halsey," Marshall later reported, "it was not a difficult decision to make." Within ninety minutes after MacArthur sent his enthusiastic endorsement, MacArthur and Nimitz received their orders to skip the three intermediary landings and execute the Leyte operation with a target date of October 20.[28]

According to Marshall, "MacArthur's acknowledgment of his new instructions reached me while en route from the dinner to my quarters in Quebec." But how were the Joint Chiefs able to communicate with MacArthur? Early on September 13, MacArthur departed Hollandia on board the cruiser *Nashville,* bound for the invasion of Morotai. Operating under strict radio silence, he was at sea and incommunicado for three days.

On the third day, September 15, he watched the first troops of the Thirty-First Infantry Division go ashore on a slender sand spit at the southern tip of the island. Shortly afterward, "indicative of the importance he attached to the operation," as his press release put it, MacArthur headed ashore with amphibious chief Dan Barbey, physician Roger Egeberg, and press officer Larry Lehrbas and "landed on the beach with his troops."

Enemy resistance in the landing areas was virtually nonexistent, in part because MacArthur had wisely chosen to occupy Morotai instead of more heavily defended Halmahera, just to the south, but unexpected coral reefs, shallow water, and mudflats caused delays and confusion. MacArthur's landing craft grounded some yards from shore, and Egeberg recalled subsequently wading through water up to his armpits.

As the general's party walked the landing zone for around an hour, MacArthur's conversation with a group of officers was reported to the press with Lehrbas's polished sense of drama: "Talking with a group of officers, General MacArthur said, 'We shall shortly have an air and light naval base here within 300 miles of the Philippines.' He gazed out to the northwest almost as though he could already see through the mist the rugged lines of Bataan and Corregidor. 'They are waiting for me there,' he said. 'It has been a long time.' "[29]

By 1:00 p.m., MacArthur was back on board the *Nashville* and soon would be under way for the return trip to Hollandia. At some point, either because the *Nashville* broke radio silence or because it was monitoring messages flowing in and out of SWPA headquarters at Hollandia, MacArthur may have received an inkling of the exchanges among his headquarters, Halsey, Nimitz, and Marshall.

In fact, to add fuel to the ensuing fire, MacArthur dictated a message to Sutherland from the *Nashville* that not only seemed to imply that he heartily approved of the Leyte expedient but also that he was suggesting an even greater leap.

"Magnificent opportunity presents itself now that air resistance over Philippines will be neutralized," MacArthur wrote, "to combine projected initial and final operations." He wanted a simultaneous attack by six divisions against Leyte *and* Lingayen Gulf. "I am completely confident that it can be done and will practically end the Pacific War," MacArthur concluded. "It is our greatest opportunity. The double stroke would be a complete surprise to the enemy and would not fail."[30]

Whether this was simply the result of MacArthur's grandiose musings as he sailed at sea after another successful landing or a cagey attempt to insert himself into the middle of the Leyte decision is uncertain. Either way, not until arriving in Hollandia midmorning on September 17 did MacArthur sit down at his desk and read the complete file of dispatches that had been received and sent in his absence by the one and only individual who dared issue such in his name — his chief of staff, Richard K. Sutherland.

Over the course of the prior eighteen months, Sutherland had increasingly suffered from vaulting ambition. His representation of MacArthur at the Pearl Harbor and Washington strategy sessions as well as his globe-girdling flight with Marshall after the Cairo conference had only increased his sense of importance and, more dangerous, his sense of entitlement. His promotion to lieutenant general — with MacArthur's blessing, of course — had done nothing to weaken his ego.

According to MacArthur apostle Frazier Hunt, when MacArthur returned to Hollandia after Morotai, he was delighted with Sutherland's Leyte decision and the accelerated timetable, but that wasn't the whole story.[31] Perhaps the best evidence that even Sutherland felt he may have overstepped his authority is his summoning of Kenney, Kinkaid, and Chamberlin hours before MacArthur returned to Hollandia to prepare them for a possible collision with their chief.[32]

Sutherland had already involved these three officers in discussions convened at Sutherland's request as he pondered a response in MacArthur's name to Marshall's query about expediting Leyte. As Kenney told the story, "Quite naturally everyone was reluctant to make so important a decision in General MacArthur's name without his knowledge of what was going on, but it had to be done."

Kenney claims — with his usual hindsight, he placed himself at the center of everything — that he argued persuasively that whatever they "had been prepared to do on October 15 could now be switched to Leyte" as long as the navy had their backs with air cover from Halsey's carriers. Kenney wasn't ready to accept Halsey's assertion that the central Philippines was an empty shell — once again, remaining ground forces would prove to be tough — but he agreed that the Japanese air threat was "not great enough to stop us from landing on Leyte."[33]

Given pressure from the Joint Chiefs to accept the expedited schedule and Leyte as the next objective, and in view of their assessment that it was "highly to be desired and would advance the progress of the war in your theater by many months,"[34] there was little else that a competent chief of staff cognizant of his commander's resources and agenda could have done. It was the correct decision. Furthermore, it was a decision that had not been made in isolation or in haste but rather after focused discussion among the pertinent members of MacArthur's immediate staff.

After lunch, MacArthur convened this same group, and Sutherland quickly brought up the key decision he had made with the counsel of those present in MacArthur's absence. Sutherland had worried, according to Kenney, "about what the General would say about using his name and making so important a decision without consulting him, but his worries were wasted. MacArthur not only approved the whole scheme immediately" but also launched into a description of the "magnificent opportunity" of his one-two punch against Leyte and Lingayen Gulf.[35]

Knowing that logistically they would have their hands full with Leyte alone, MacArthur's men slowly throttled back his enthusiasm. Sutherland took the lead and noted the problems of air cover over two widespread beachheads and the amphibious requirements of moving six divisions simultaneously. MacArthur looked to Kenney, who was usually his most vocal can-do cheerleader, but Kenney said little except to nod in agreement with Sutherland's points. "Okay," MacArthur concluded, "we can't do it. But you must have me in Lingayen before Christmas. If Leyte turns out to be an easy show, I want to move fast."[36]

That should have meant business as usual between MacArthur and Sutherland. Given their long history, during which MacArthur had routinely informed officers from George Marshall on down that Sutherland had full authority to speak on his behalf, MacArthur might simply have reveled in the results of Sutherland's communications in his name and blessed them. After all, MacArthur's long-cherished return to the Philippines was being expedited *and* it was to be supported with ships and troops from Nimitz's command.

Such a seemingly commonsense appraisal of the situation, however, ran afoul of two critical influences. One was MacArthur's own ego, and the other was a continuing error of personal judgment on Sutherland's part in open defiance of MacArthur's direct orders.

According to Dusty Rhoades, MacArthur arrived back in Hollandia from Morotai "in very good spirits." Landing complications aside, Morotai was an important step toward the Philippines. But the rapid leap to Leyte, even if it didn't include Lingayen at the same time — *that* was the epitome of bold strategy. Expediting Leyte even made MacArthur's gamble in the Admiralties look like playground hopscotch. MacArthur simply had to be the central player in the decision.

What made it appear otherwise was the common knowledge in both army and navy command circles that MacArthur had been out of touch on the *Nashville* during the crucial exchanges. This was because Sutherland had been straightforward in advising Marshall of this fact in the course of his signed "MacArthur" communications.[37] That didn't seem to bother Marshall, but it ruffled MacArthur's ego.

Rhoades, who was reasonably close to MacArthur and (given their long one-on-one cockpit conversations as they flew around the southwestern Pacific) arguably the person closest to Sutherland, may have put his finger on it. "It is possible," Rhoades opined, "that MacArthur might have accepted the fact that Sutherland had made the strategic decision on his own but for the fact that all high-level commanders, including those in the navy, knew that Sutherland and not MacArthur was the source of the decision. This made it appear that Sutherland was usurping some of the commander in chief's authority."[38] Perhaps. But what raised MacArthur's temper to the boiling point were Sutherland's actions in another matter.

While in Melbourne shortly after arriving in Australia from Corregidor, the married fifty-year-old Sutherland began a long-term affair with Elaine Bessemer Clarke, the thirtysomething socialite daughter of Sir Norman Brookes, who had been a champion Australian tennis player and was subsequently knighted for public service. By all accounts, Clarke was not a great looker, but, like Sutherland, she had a case of vaulting ambition and a desire to be in the thick of things. Reginald Bessemer Clarke, Elaine's husband, was of the same mold as her father, being both an heir to the Bessemer steel fortune and a three-time Wimbledon player. He was then a prisoner of war in Malaysia, having been captured in the fall of Singapore. Together they had a young son, who had been born in early 1940.

When SWPA headquarters moved from Melbourne to Brisbane, Sutherland moved Clarke along with it and installed her as something of a receptionist for MacArthur's headquarters in the lobby of the AMP building. MacArthur seems to have taken this in stride despite the widely known fact that Clarke's presence had little to do with her secretarial skills. To circumvent MacArthur's agreement with Australian prime minister Curtin that women in the Australian military services would not deploy overseas, Sutherland obtained a commission for Clarke as a US Women's Army Corps (WAC) captain. Perhaps as a smoke screen, two other Australian women were commissioned as WAC lieutenants and continued their assignments as secretaries to Kenney and deputy chief of staff Dick Marshall.[39]

MacArthur seems to have assumed that, WAC commissions or not, these women would not be sent to forward areas or at the very least not put right under his nose. Sutherland chose to challenge this assumption almost immediately by having Rhoades fly him and Clarke to Port Moresby on March 30, 1944, in the *Bataan*.[40] While MacArthur was away in Brisbane preparing for the Hollandia invasion, Sutherland gave Clarke free rein of Government House.

MacArthur learned of this arrangement upon returning to Port Moresby after the Hollandia landings. He ambled out of his room at Government House in his underwear after his customary afternoon nap with a strategy he wanted to discuss with Sutherland. As MacArthur began, "Dick, I have an idea," a blond head popped up above the couch, and Elaine Clarke greeted him with a hearty "Good afternoon, General."

MacArthur blushed, returned for his trousers, and later told Sutherland in no uncertain terms that he would not have women in his advance headquarters. Captain Clarke must leave Port Moresby immediately and not return. MacArthur's decision was less about Sutherland and Clarke's private indiscretions than his own need for some semblance of decorum. As Paul Rogers remembered it, "MacArthur might wander around in his underwear... [but] he did not care to be exposed to the view of a very young Australian woman whose husband languished in prison camp, who had direct, intimate connections with a vicious social circle in Melbourne...and, most of all, who was beginning to display independence and even provocative audacity."[41]

Having issued an order, MacArthur considered the matter resolved. A few days later, both MacArthur and Sutherland returned to Brisbane for the better part of the summer, and Clarke resumed her seat in the lobby of the AMP building. One afternoon, shortly before Sutherland made the move to Hollandia to set up advance headquarters, MacArthur directly told Sutherland, "Dick, that woman must not go to the forward areas again." Rogers did not hear Sutherland's reply, but Rogers remembered MacArthur's final words: "I want it understood. Under no circumstances is that woman to be taken to the forward areas." It was a direct and unequivocal order. Rogers claimed that it was the first time he had ever heard MacArthur speak to Sutherland in such a manner.[42]

But the first thing Sutherland did as he set up an advance base of operations in Hollandia a few weeks later was to arrange for Clarke to be given nearby quarters and assume duties as something of a hostess at the newly constructed headquarters above Lake Sentani. Officers reporting fresh from combat were greeted with a cool drink and warm smile—not exactly the image of his front line that MacArthur wanted to convey.

Uniformed or not, Clarke was a distraction—particularly as she readily assumed the role of Cleopatra and went so far as to have Hank Godman, formerly MacArthur's chief pilot, who was still on his staff, transferred to a combat assignment after he got into a quarrel with Clarke over the use of a jeep. MacArthur, having spent no time in Hollandia except for two nights en route to Morotai, was if not ignorant of the situation at least momentarily too preoccupied to address it.[43]

Returning from Morotai, MacArthur found Clarke performing her public duties. She was stark evidence that Sutherland had disobeyed his direct orders about her disposition not once but at least twice. This wasn't about Sutherland keeping his pants zipped; it wasn't even about Elaine Clarke being in Hollandia. This was about the one man in whom MacArthur had placed complete trust and granted full authority to speak and act in his name defying his direct orders.

How could MacArthur swallow the fact that a man who couldn't even follow orders to keep his girlfriend out of MacArthur's headquarters had taken the lead with the Joint Chiefs in initiating his long-planned leap to the Philippines? Publicly, MacArthur went forward with the Leyte decision and embraced it, but he never forgave Sutherland for making it in his name, largely because of his anger over the Elaine Clarke episode.

Their private confrontation apparently came the following day, after MacArthur informed Rhoades that he was remaining in Hollandia for one more night. What began with a reprimand for having made such a momentous decision as Leyte ended with a shouting match over Clarke. Sutherland begged to be transferred, granted sick leave, or given a field command, but that would have been too easy an out for him. MacArthur refused on all counts. Sutherland would stay and do his duty and send Clarke back to Australia immediately. If Sutherland refused to give such an order, MacArthur would do it for him in a final humiliation. According to Rogers, MacArthur's last words to Sutherland as he left Hollandia were that Clarke would never be permitted to go forward to the Philippines.[44]

Back in Washington, the Joint Chiefs faced what had become an increasingly inevitable decision in the Luzon-Formosa debate. At the end of September, Nimitz finally convinced King that a rapid thrust to Formosa was impracticable on a number of levels. With the Leyte timetable moved forward to October 20, Luzon should be next. After that, the debate could be between Formosa and a direct assault of Japan's southern islands early in 1945.

Consequently, on October 3, 1944, the Joint Chiefs ordered MacArthur to follow Leyte with an invasion of Luzon, presumably at Lingayen Gulf, with a target date of December 20. Nimitz was to provide fleet cover and support via Halsey for the landings as well as his promised army divisions.[45] The question of Luzon versus Formosa was finally settled. The questions that remained — reports of the central Philippines being an empty shell aside — were, what sort of fight might MacArthur face on the beaches of Leyte? And how might the Imperial Japanese Navy respond?

CHAPTER TWENTY-TWO

Sixty Minutes from Defeat

As MacArthur flew to Port Moresby and then on to Brisbane after his testy encounter with Sutherland, he was coming off of a grand total of four nights at Hollandia — two en route to Morotai and two upon his return. He would spend an additional night there on October 15 en route to Leyte.[1] Given his schedule, MacArthur barely had time to look around his headquarters building let alone enjoy the view from its veranda. Yet this structure would bring MacArthur's critics considerable glee and provide strong evidence that those out to disparage MacArthur were determined to do so no matter how ridiculous or trumped-up the charges.

In the first place, it was Sutherland, not MacArthur, who ordered the building's construction. There was a need for a headquarters structure that would serve as quarters for MacArthur, Sutherland, and ranking visitors as well as provide the generals with private offices, conference facilities, a dining room, and office space for support staff. In this respect, it was functionally similar to the Port Moresby facilities.

Yet as construction battalions worked nonstop to turn the Hollandia area into a forward base for operations against the Philippines, rumors began to circulate that MacArthur had ensconced himself in a palatial residence overlooking Lake Sentani and was living the life of a tropical sultan. Such rumors were reminiscent of the Dugout Doug characterizations, but they had far less basis in fact. MacArthur's so-called million-dollar mansion was in fact three prefabricated houses joined together and painted a bright white against the tropical heat. Basic sofas, chairs, and some rugs shipped from Brisbane added comfort, but it was a far cry from palatial.[2]

To be sure, many of MacArthur's associates commented favorably on the structure, but this seems to have been largely an echo of the old real estate saw about "location, location, location." Kenney, who described Kinkaid's headquarters, around a half mile away, as "quite a lot better" and his own as smaller but "very livable," admitted that "perhaps the scenery had something to do with our feeling of comfort." Of necessity, because Kenney's airfields took up the flat ground, these structures were built on the slopes of the Cyclops Mountains, from which one could look south to the azure waters of Lake Sentani or north over the sea in the direction of Mindanao. On the slopes above, a tall waterfall cut a swath through the verdant green of the surrounding hills.[3]

Compared to many of the locations around the globe in which Allied servicemen fought and died, Hollandia appeared to be a picture-postcard paradise. Had MacArthur slept in a slit trench he likely would have come under some criticism for just being in such a beautiful locale. There is no doubt that MacArthur's general demeanor and regal bearing routinely set him up for criticism, but he was not guilty of building a palatial retreat at Hollandia.

According to Sid Huff, even Jean MacArthur, who by some reports was also supposed to be living there, couldn't help but chide the general a little. "When I go to Manila," Jean told MacArthur, "I want you to fix it so I can stop off at Hollandia. I want to see that mansion you built there—the one where I am supposed to have been living in luxury!"[4] The greatest irony of this entire story is that MacArthur spent only five nights there, and they were far from happy ones, first because of the friction with Sutherland and then because of his anxiety over the imminent landings at Leyte.

The island of Leyte is a curious tangle of geography. Located on the eastern side of the Philippine archipelago, roughly two-thirds of the way from the northern tip of Luzon to the southernmost point of Mindanao, it is around 120 miles from north to south and between forty and a dozen miles wide at various points. North of its narrow waist, a range of four-thousand-foot mountains divides east from west and complicates transit. On the coast east of those mountains, the waters of wide Leyte Gulf are protected on the north by Samar and to the south by the Dinagat Islands. Key water passages nearby are San Bernardino Strait, past Samar to the north, and Surigao Strait, between southern Leyte and Mindanao to the south.

Even with reports of weak resistance and the expedited time schedule, the Leyte landings promised to be the largest and most complicated undertaken up to that point in the Southwest Pacific Area. "Leyte," MacArthur later wrote in his memoirs, "was to be the anvil against which I hoped to hammer the Japanese into submission in the central Philippines, the springboard from which I could proceed to the conquest of Luzon, for the final assault against Japan itself."[5]

The first order of business was to coordinate air support from Halsey's carriers until Kenney could construct or rehabilitate airfields on Leyte for land-based air. One of Admiral King's final arguments against the Lingayen landings on Luzon had been that a December 20 target date was likely to require the offshore presence of Halsey's fleet, particularly the Task Force 38 carriers, for six weeks in order to control Formosa airfields and oppose any attack on the beachhead by the enemy fleet.[6] The more immediate needs at Leyte presented the same two problems—beating down Japanese air and anticipating the Japanese fleet—except that the airfields of concern to Leyte operations were on Luzon and much closer than Formosa.

Nimitz had been prompt to promise MacArthur support—both in terms of troops and carriers—almost immediately after Halsey suggested expediting the timeline. "Delighted to be able to assist in your return to the Philippines," Nimitz signaled MacArthur. "This is your show and I stand ready to help in any way practicable to make it a complete success."[7] Nonetheless, the deployments and logistics of the army and the navy, as well as their coordination, would be daunting.

On MacArthur's side, there was little question but that Krueger's Sixth Army would conduct the assault. Krueger's team had worked closely with Admirals Kinkaid and Barbey in the frenzied amphibious assaults that had taken place since Cape Gloucester. They were primed and ready to go. Krueger was irritated, however, because MacArthur had kept Eichelberger waiting in the wings for a year prior to his corps command at Hollandia—not only as a reprimand to Eichelberger for his post-Buna publicity but also as a veiled threat to Krueger. The subtext was that Krueger could be replaced at MacArthur's whim if he didn't move as expeditiously as MacArthur decreed.

By the summer of 1944, sufficient numbers of American troops were pouring into the Southwest Pacific Area to warrant the creation of another army under MacArthur's SWPA command. (Generally, two or more divisions operated as a corps; two or more corps comprised an army.) When the Eighth Army was activated on September 9, 1944, Eichelberger assumed command. According to Eichelberger, Krueger was upset not so much by Eichelberger's role but by the fact that another army existed to challenge the importance and operational assignments of Krueger's Sixth Army. It would take some months for the Eighth Army to be ready to deploy, however, and at Leyte, the Sixth Army would have the field to itself.[8]

Code-named Operation King-Two by MacArthur's planners and issued by MacArthur on September 20, the Leyte plan was based on the assumption that Japanese land and air forces in the Philippines had been seriously crippled and that the Imperial Japanese Navy would elect to remain largely in home waters. It was further assumed that Japanese army strength was limited to one division, which, while well supplied, would soon find itself largely cut off from reinforcements and incoming deliveries.[9]

With MacArthur as supreme commander, Admiral Kinkaid would command all amphibious operations and forces ashore until such time as the beachheads were secure and General Krueger took command of the ground troops—a structure that had evolved and worked well during prior operations. Krueger's Sixth Army was composed of Major General Franklin Sibert's X Corps of the First Cavalry Division and Twenty-Fourth Infantry Division and Major General John Hodge's XXIV Corps, on loan from Nimitz and comprising the Seventh and Ninety-Sixth Infantry Divisions. Counting the Thirty-Second and Seventy-Seventh Infantry Divisions, held in reserve, assorted tank and amphibious truck and tractor battalions, and attached service units, around two hundred thousand ground troops were committed to the Leyte operation.

These units were no longer green troops but battle-tested. The First Cavalry and Twenty-Fourth Infantry Divisions had fought for MacArthur in the Admiralties and at Hollandia respectively. The Seventh Division included veterans of Attu, in the Aleutians, and Kwajalein, in the Marshall Islands. The Thirty-Second had been bloodied in New Guinea, and the Seventy-Seventh had taken part in the capture of Guam. Only the Ninety-Sixth Infantry Division lacked combat experience.[10]

Krueger held Sibert in particularly high esteem as a "cool and very aggressive" commander, and he assigned Sibert's X Corps the crucial first-day task of seizing the port facilities and the airfield near Tacloban. Hodge and his XXIV Corps would land twenty miles to the south and seize airfields around Dulag. The plan then called for these two forces to move away from each other—something that caused Krueger some concern—circle the mountains dividing northern Leyte, and finally link up at Ormoc, on the western coast.[11]

On the navy side, there were two key players: Admiral Kinkaid, commander of Allied Naval Forces in the Southwest Pacific Area, essentially the US Seventh Fleet, and Admiral Halsey, commander of the US Third Fleet. There was also a critical supporting cast. Kinkaid gave Dan Barbey's VII Amphibious Force the task of delivering Sibert's X Corps and assigned Rear Admiral Theodore Wilkinson's III Amphibious Force to do the same for Hodge's XXIV Corps. Rear Admiral Jesse Oldendorf commanded a bombardment and fire support group of older battleships that would soften up the landing zones. No one dreamed they would also engage in the last great clash of battleship against battleship.

Halsey had clear instructions from Nimitz to support the Leyte landings with air cover from his carriers, but should an opportunity present itself to destroy major portions of the Japanese fleet, that was to become his primary task. In that event and all others, it was assumed that Halsey and MacArthur would do whatever was necessary to coordinate their operations.[12]

By any measure, the combined naval strength of Kinkaid's and

Halsey's fleets was staggering. Kinkaid's attack force, officially designated Task Force 77, totaled 738 ships, ranging from Oldendorf's battleships to transports and landing craft. Halsey's Third Fleet totaled
105 combat vessels, including the eighteen carriers of Vice Admiral
Marc Mitscher's fast carrier task force, officially Task Force 38. The
combined forces totaled slightly fewer ships than the armada that had
just assembled off Normandy, but considering its battleships and carriers, it packed a stronger punch in terms of firepower. The logistics of
getting men and materiel to the beachheads were no less staggering.
The Leyte invasion force embarked from nine staging bases scattered
across MacArthur's Southwest Pacific and Nimitz's South and Central
Pacific Areas: Oro Bay, Finschhafen, Manus, Hollandia, Biak, the
island of Noemfoor, Morotai, Guam, and Oahu.[13]

In personal preparation for this massive undertaking, MacArthur
spent a few days resting up with his family. As Dusty Rhoades remembered, the pilot had little flying to do because "General Sutherland is not
here to crack the whip, and General MacArthur is doing the unheard-of
thing of taking a rest." MacArthur even indulged in the luxury of taking
several long afternoon drives with Jean and Arthur. They were good
company, and in addition to the relaxation this time provided, MacArthur also seems to have wanted the peace of mind and the experience of
a pleasant and memorable good-bye should the unthinkable happen to
him during his intended walk on the Leyte beaches.[14]

MacArthur also said another good-bye that was almost as poignant.
Australian prime minister John Curtin was dying of heart disease and
likely would not live out the war. Regardless, MacArthur had made it
clear that once he departed Australia for the Philippines, he did not
intend to return. His next stop would be Japan. Accordingly, on September 30, Rhoades flew MacArthur from Brisbane to Canberra so
that he might say good-bye to Curtin. Their relationship had become
wary, particularly on Curtin's side, and it had always been characterized by the perfunctory words of necessary allies more than by any
genuine personal warmth. But together they had nonetheless turned
Australia from tempting target into offensive bastion, and their parting
had a touch of melancholy for both men.[15]

MacArthur returned to Brisbane that same afternoon and spent the next two weeks in final preparations for the big push north. On October 14, Rhoades flew him to Port Moresby for a night and then on to Hollandia the next day. "Dearest Jeannie," MacArthur wrote that evening, "I was glad to leave Moresby—it was like looking at the skeleton of an old friend. I am sending you a blossom from there which I plucked as I left it forever."

Saying they were leaving Hollandia "tomorrow after breakfast," he noted that "Sutherland is going along although I do not know his future plans"—a rather revealing admission regarding one's own chief of staff, indicative of their growing divide. "I miss you both," MacArthur concluded to Jean, "and send you all love and devotion. Each day now that I am gone brings a day nearer our reunion....God bless you both."[16] The next morning, he went aboard the cruiser *Nashville* and was soon embarked on his greatest crusade.[17]

"We came to Leyte just before midnight of a dark and moonless night," MacArthur later wrote in his memoirs. "The stygian waters below and the black sky above seemed to conspire in wrapping us in an invisible cloak, as we lay to and waited for dawn before entering Leyte Gulf."[18] It was the wee hours of October 20, 1944—what MacArthur had chosen to call A-day because the generic designation D-day had quickly come to refer almost exclusively to the Normandy landings.

Three days before, rangers had seized the islands dotting the wide entrance to Leyte Gulf and installed navigation lights on them. At dawn on the twentieth, the *Nashville* joined an array of ships entering the gulf, and as the transports took up positions in preparation for disgorging their cargoes of men and munitions, the battleships and cruisers began a ferocious barrage. The *Nashville* anchored around two miles off the beaches of the X Corps sector, and MacArthur took a front-row seat on its bridge.

It was a decidedly American show. MacArthur seems to have gone out of his way, both politically and operationally, to exclude his Australian allies. "Without Australian political, logistic and military support it is hard to see how MacArthur could have made this grand return," Australian historian John Robertson wrote after the war, "but no Australian land or air-force unit, and no Australian notables, were there to share the glory."[19]

Midmorning, the assault waves of four divisions poured ashore as planned. The heavy naval bombardment had driven most defenders inland, and initial resistance was light. According to Kinkaid, "The execution of the plan was as nearly perfect as any commander could desire." By 1:00 p.m., MacArthur decided that it was time to head for shore himself along with Philippine president Sergio Osmeña, Quezon having finally succumbed to tuberculosis that summer. Mortar and small-arms fire could still be heard coming from the direction of the highway leading to Tacloban and the nearby hills.

MacArthur was dressed in a crisply pressed set of fresh khakis beneath his ever-present field marshal's cap and did not intend to wade through knee-deep water, although he appears to have gone through that and more in the Admiralties and on Morotai. Still, as the Nashville's launch neared the beach south of Tacloban with a contingent that included Sutherland, Kenney, Egeberg, Rhoades, and Lehrbas, the sandy bottom sloped too gently for the launch to get close enough to shore to permit a dry landing.

One of MacArthur's aides radioed the beachmaster, who was preoccupied with the confusion of hundreds of landing craft unloading amid incoming sniper fire, and requested an amphibious craft to take MacArthur's party the remaining distance to dry ground. Supposedly the otherwise occupied beachmaster angrily replied, "Let 'em walk."

They did just that—pressed khakis or not—and MacArthur's grim expression, recorded in photographs, may have been partly attributable to his disgruntlement over the gruff treatment. Subsequently, of course, MacArthur recognized the huge public relations value of the photographs, and splashing ashore became standard operating procedure. Hints of disgruntlement were considered to be determined looks of destiny and the absolute antithesis of Dugout Doug's image.[20]

As MacArthur and his entourage made one of his by-then-patented beachhead strolls, a gentle afternoon rain began to fall. Then signal corps troops drove up in a weapons carrier at an appointed place in a little clearing carrying a portable transmitter. It would relay MacArthur's soon-to-be-historic words to a larger transmitter on the Nashville, which in turn would broadcast them to the world.

"People of the Philippines," MacArthur began, his voice as well as his hands uncharacteristically shaking with emotion, "I have returned. By the grace of Almighty God, our forces stand again on Philippine soil." Rally to me, he went on to admonish. "Let the indomitable spirit of Bataan and Corregidor lead on."[21] Shrewdly recognizing that in such situations shorter was definitely better than longer, he finished in just two minutes. Osmeña then spoke for ten minutes about restoring civil government in the islands, a task that would prove both complicated and controversial.

After the addresses, MacArthur and his party returned to the *Nashville*. By then, the Japanese defenders had recovered from their initial shock and were counterattacking. According to Kenney, shortly after MacArthur departed, Japanese troops broke through to the beach and got within yards of the spot where MacArthur had stood. "It was a good thing we left when we did," Kenney recalled.[22]

As with so many of the dramatic moments of MacArthur's life, much would be written—both approvingly and critically—of MacArthur's splashing ashore and subsequent words at Leyte. Even the indisputable fact that he had landed on A-day would be questioned, in part because he made landings in other sectors in the days that followed, starting with the First Cavalry Division's sector, near Tacloban, on October 21. That same day, Krueger, Sibert, and Hodge established their headquarters ashore, and Kinkaid turned over command of the beachheads to them.[23]

As the troops fought their way forward, MacArthur's press machine unleashed its own salvos. A special communiqué on October 20—released even as the first waves of Americans went ashore—noted the northward leap of six hundred miles from Morotai and 2,500 miles from Milne Bay almost sixteen months before and said that this landing midway between Luzon and Mindanao "at one stroke splits in two [the] Japanese forces in the Philippines." It caused the enemy "to be caught unawares in Leyte" because of the expectation of an attack in Mindanao. MacArthur was said to be "in personal command of the operation."[24]

While MacArthur's press release the next day again noted that he was "in personal command of the invasion of the Philippines," this release was effusive in naming the supporting cast. It mentioned

Krueger and each of his corps and division commanders; Kinkaid and the commander of the Australian naval squadron, John Collins; Halsey and his carrier task force commander, Marc Mitscher; and amphibious commanders Dan Barbey and Theodore Wilkinson. This listing was more strong evidence that MacArthur's public relations efforts had evolved toward the collective rather than the "MacArthur, MacArthur, MacArthur" that was the subject of jokes in 1942.[25]

Of course the accolades that flowed in to the Southwest Pacific Area in return came first and foremost to MacArthur. "The whole American Nation today exults at the news that the gallant men under your command have landed on Philippine soil," President Roosevelt cabled him. "I know well what this means to you. I know what it cost you to obey my order that you leave Corregidor in February 1942, and proceed to Australia. Ever since then you have planned and worked and fought with whole-souled devotion for the day when you would return."[26] That day had come.

Bill Halsey, whose fast carriers of the Third Fleet had pounded Japanese bases from Mindanao to Formosa in anticipation of the Leyte landings, led the cheers from the navy side. "It was a great day for your fleet team-mates when the successful landing of the 6th Army was announced," Halsey signaled MacArthur the day after the initial landings. "It was a beautifully conceived and executed plan — and now that you have a foothold we are all primed to assist in every way in the succeeding steps which will finally wipe out the enemy garrison in the Philippines."[27]

As it turned out, Halsey's words were about to be put to the test. Japan had long ago decided that both its army and navy must make a do-or-die stand in the Philippines. On land, General Tomoyuki Yamashita, Japan's celebrated "Tiger of Malaya," had been recalled from Manchuria to assume command of the Fourteenth Area Army and confront Krueger's advance. But in the short term, MacArthur faced a far more ominous threat from the sea. The Imperial Japanese Navy was finally sortieing in full strength.

Two days after MacArthur landed on Leyte, two American submarines, *Darter* and *Dace,* made contact in the South China Sea with what appeared to be a major Japanese naval force headed for the central Philippines. Most Japanese leaders believed that their only hope of saving the Philippines and ultimately keeping the Allies out of their home islands was to achieve one great and decisive naval victory. That such an encounter between massive fleets would inevitably occur had been premised on both sides for decades. The Japanese hoped to re-create their 1905 triumph over the Russians at Tsushima. For the Americans, destroying the Japanese fleet en masse while crossing the Pacific had been the cornerstone of multiple Orange plans.

Japan had little choice but to make a last stand in the Philippines. According to Admiral Soemu Toyoda, commander in chief of the Combined Fleet, the loss of the Philippines would cut the Japanese lifeline to the East Indies. If Toyoda's fleet stayed in home waters, it could not obtain fuel from refineries in Borneo. If it remained south of Allied air in the Philippines, it could not resupply from Japan. Consequently, Toyoda testified after the war, "There would be no sense in saving the fleet at the expense of the loss of the Philippines." Thus Japan planned to repulse MacArthur's landings at Leyte and hope for a decisive surface engagement with the American fleet.[28]

To attempt to do so, Toyoda and his planners crafted a complicated four-pronged offensive that dwarfed Japan's earlier operations at Pearl Harbor, the Coral Sea, and even Midway. Since the latter battle, the closest thing to a concerted action had been Japan's massing of ships in the Philippine Sea to oppose the Marianas invasion. Partly because Spruance resolutely chose to defend the beachheads, that encounter had taken place largely via aircraft and had not resulted in the surface duel among battleships that some strategists on both sides still anticipated.

MacArthur, Kinkaid, King, Nimitz, and Halsey would soon have to answer questions about divided command on the American side, but from the start, Toyoda's master plan posed complicated command and control issues for the Japanese. With Toyoda exercising overall strategic direction from southern Formosa, four independent task forces converged on Leyte from different points of the compass. Vice Admiral Jisaburo Ozawa's Main Force (which the Americans called the Northern Force) assembled in Japan's Inland Sea and steamed south. It consisted of one large carrier, three light carriers, two cruisers, and a

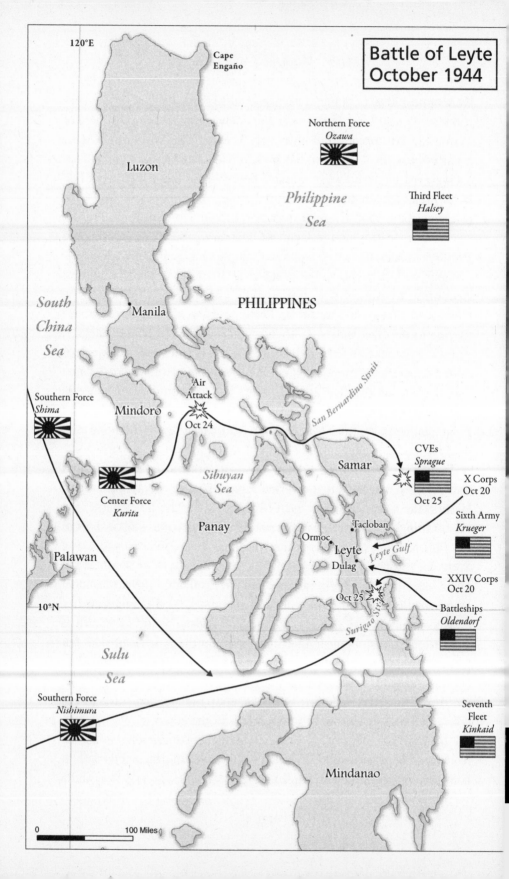

Battle of Leyte
October 1944

120°E

Cape Engaño

Luzon

PHILIPPINES

Philippine Sea

Northern Force
Ozawa

Third Fleet
Halsey

South China Sea

Manila

Mindoro

Air Attack
Oct 24

Southern Force
Shima

Center Force
Kurita

Sibuyan Sea

Panay

Palawan

10°N

San Bernardino Strait

Samar

CVEs
Sprague
Oct 25

X Corps
Oct 20

Sixth Army
Krueger

Tacloban

Ormoc

Leyte

Leyte Gulf

Dulag

XXIV Corps
Oct 20

Oct 25

Surigao Strait

Battleships
Oldendorf

Sulu Sea

Southern Force
Nishimura

Seventh Fleet
Kinkaid

Mindanao

0   100 Miles

dozen destroyers. Lacking full complements of aircraft for his carriers because of the decimation off the Marianas, Ozawa was determined to draw Halsey and the Third Fleet away from the Leyte beachheads, something he had been unable to do against Spruance.

With the beachheads relatively unprotected, it would fall to Vice Admiral Takeo Kurita's First Striking Force (which the Americans called the Center Force), sailing east from Singapore to Brunei Bay, off Borneo, to slip through the central Philippines via the Sibuyan Sea and San Bernardino Strait and pounce on the transports, supply ships, and accompanying escorts off the Leyte beachheads. Relying on surface firepower, Kurita had five battleships, including the 64,000-ton *Yamato,* with its eighteen-inch guns, eleven heavy cruisers, and a bevy of light cruisers and destroyers.

To complete the pincer action against Leyte, two smaller forces — Vice Admiral Kiyohide Shima's Second Striking Force of cruisers and destroyers and Vice Admiral Shoji Nishimura's detachment from Kurita's Center Force of two battleships, a heavy cruiser, and assorted destroyers — would pass north of Mindanao and transit Surigao Strait in time to attack any American ships fleeing Leyte in the face of Kurita's advance or reinforcements steaming to their aid. Together, though they were not closely coordinated on the Japanese side, the Americans would call these two forces the Southern Force.[29]

Hostilities began during the night of October 22–23, when *Darter* and *Dace* worked themselves into firing positions and sank the heavy cruisers *Maya* and *Atago,* the latter being Admiral Kurita's flagship. Kurita then transferred his flag to the battleship *Yamato.* On the morning of October 24, Halsey unleashed air attacks from the carriers of three of his four task groups against Kurita's fleet as it steamed eastward through the Sibuyan Sea. Halsey's fourth task group, under the command of Vice Admiral John S. "Slew" McCain (the senator's grandfather), had been retiring toward Ulithi to rearm and provision, but Halsey ordered McCain to come about, refuel at sea, and return to Philippine waters.

Meanwhile, MacArthur had been going back and forth daily from the *Nashville* to beachhead sectors and Tacloban. On the twenty-fourth, Kinkaid asked him to move his headquarters ashore and free up the

Nashville for combat operations—operations that seemed increasingly likely. MacArthur professed a desire to stay on board and see the action, but the next day Kinkaid insisted, and MacArthur transferred to Barbey's flagship, the amphibious force command ship *Wasatch,* for a night before moving ashore on October 26. Before that occurred, however, there were plenty of fireworks.

Halsey's carrier planes wreaked havoc on Kurita's Center Force in the Sibuyan Sea throughout the day on October 24. Aircraft from Task Group 38.4 also located Shima and Nishimura's converging Southern Force headed toward Surigao Strait. Kinkaid summoned his Seventh Fleet task group commanders on board *Wasatch* around noon on the twenty-fourth and gave Oldendorf and Task Group 77.2 the job of plugging Surigao Strait.

Shima and Nishimura's combined forces were expected to transit the strait around 2:00 a.m. on October 25, and Oldendorf deployed six aging battleships (five of them Pearl Harbor survivors), three heavy cruisers, five light cruisers, twenty-six destroyers, and a bevy of PT boats to stop them. Rear Admiral Thomas Sprague's sixteen escort carriers (CVEs) and destroyer escorts were left to protect the beachheads and Oldendorf's ships from air attack. Kinkaid advised Halsey that his Seventh Fleet would stop the Southern Force but that he expected Halsey's Third Fleet to handle Kurita's Center Force. By late afternoon on the twenty-fourth, Halsey was convinced that he already had done so.

Pilots returning to their carriers reported major losses to Kurita's fleet, including sinking the *Yamato*-class battleship *Musashi*. It appeared to Halsey and the Task Force 38 commander, Marc Mitscher, that they had largely destroyed Kurita's force. A reconnaissance plane from the carrier *Intrepid* seemed to confirm this with the report that Kurita's remaining ships had turned around and were sailing westward. Within an hour, however, Kurita reversed course and was once again bearing down on San Bernardino Strait.[30]

Not knowing this, Halsey turned his ships northward and steamed to engage the third Japanese group, the carriers of Ozawa's Northern Force, which were lurking somewhere off Cape Engaño, on northern Luzon. Before knowing the results of the air attacks in the Sibuyan

Sea, Halsey had issued a battle plan for four battleships, including his own *New Jersey,* two heavy cruisers, and assorted light cruisers and destroyers to form Task Force 34 and block the exit from San Bernardino Strait in a manner similar to what Kinkaid had ordered Oldendorf to do at Surigao. Unlike Kinkaid, however, Halsey never gave the order to execute this plan, and the ships that would have been assigned to Task Force 34 steamed northward instead.[31]

That night, with MacArthur still on board the *Nashville,* anchored near the amphibious force command ships in Leyte Gulf, Oldendorf's battle line conducted textbook battleship maneuvers, including crossing the enemy's *T,* and handily defeated the Southern Force in Surigao Strait. Dawn on October 25 should have brought contented sighs of victory, but instead it brought an urgent summons from Kinkaid: Kurita's Center Force had passed through San Bernardino Strait and was approaching the northern group of escort carriers off Samar, far too close for comfort to the ship-filled waters of Leyte Gulf.

Earlier that morning Kinkaid's operations officer had gotten nervous about San Bernardino Strait. "We've never asked Halsey directly," he told Kinkaid, "if Task Force 34 is guarding San Bernardino Strait." Kinkaid agreed, and he directed that Halsey be queried, "Is TF 34 guarding San Bernardino Strait?" By the time this question worked its way from the Seventh to the Third Fleet and Halsey received it, it was 6:48 a.m., some two and a half hours later. "Negative," Halsey responded. "Task Force Thirty Four is with carrier groups now engaging enemy carrier force."[32]

Nimitz and King, routinely monitoring radio traffic, had also gotten nervous. Nimitz's similar query to Halsey became the source of increased friction when miscellaneous padding at the end of the message seemed to mock Halsey's tactical deployments. The bottom line is that with Halsey's ships about to engage Ozawa's carriers, Kurita's battleship force was inbound to Leyte Gulf opposed only by escort carriers and destroyers. If they continued into Leyte Gulf, the *Nashville,* with MacArthur still on board, was the only large ship available to oppose them.

Kinkaid sent urgent appeals to Halsey for assistance from his fast battleships and carriers. Within reach of Ozawa's decoy carriers,

Halsey agonized over his next move even as he radioed McCain's task group and told it to expedite its return toward Leyte and launch air strikes when within range of Kurita's forces. Finally, at 11:15 a.m. on October 25, Halsey reluctantly ordered his fast battleships to form Task Force 34 and race south to engage Kurita, closely followed by one of his three carrier task groups. Mitscher and the remaining two carrier groups would continue north and finish off Ozawa's force.

Iowa and *New Jersey,* the latter with Halsey on board, charged toward Leyte and arrived shortly after midnight on October 26, but by then the central battle of Leyte Gulf was over. In the face of gritty resistance and selfless sacrifice by Kinkaid's escort carriers and their destroyer escorts, Kurita had hesitated and then turned tail when he was within an hour or so of the Leyte beachheads. Before Halsey arrived, Kurita's fleet slipped back through San Bernardino Strait.

Nonetheless, when the smoke cleared, the combined battles of Leyte Gulf may have been the greatest victory ever won by the United States Navy. As a result of the torpedo attacks by *Darter* and *Dace,* and in the wake of Mitscher's assaults against Ozawa's carriers, Japanese losses totaled twenty-six combatant ships: three battleships, one large carrier, three light carriers, six heavy cruisers, four light cruisers, and nine destroyers—a total of 305,710 tons. American losses included the light carrier *Princeton* and the two escort carriers, two destroyers, and one destroyer escort lost in the last-ditch effort to oppose Kurita; these totaled 36,600 tons.[33]

By any measure, it was a stunning achievement of American naval might—thanks at least in part to Kurita's unexpected early withdrawal, something he never fully explained. After the war Kurita said his decision was predicated on "lack of expected land-based air support and air reconnaissance, fear of further losses from air attack, and worry as to his fuel reserves."[34] Yet the very fact of Kurita's surprising withdrawal despite the closeness he had come to the Leyte beachheads summoned a host of critics.

During the critical hours of October 25, MacArthur appears to have been largely disengaged—not from any sense of personal paralysis, as may have been the case on the morning of December 8, 1941, but rather from a lack of information. This may have resulted from Admiral Kinkaid having his headquarters on the *Wasatch* and a number of MacArthur's key staff being ashore at Tacloban setting up the headquarters he would occupy by the evening of October 26. MacArthur himself was still on the *Nashville* or perhaps in transit to the *Wasatch*.

During the day on October 25, Sutherland dispatched Spencer Akin, MacArthur's signal chief, from Tacloban to the *Wasatch* to request information from Kinkaid on MacArthur's behalf regarding the results of the CVE operations off Samar. Akin reported back that Kinkaid expressed regret at the lack of information MacArthur was receiving and said he would take immediate steps to correct it. Akin duly reported to Sutherland and confirmed the victory in Surigao Strait but optimistically predicted that crippled elements of Kurita's Center Force would "undoubtedly...be sunk by Admiral Halsey tonight" before they could escape through San Bernardino Strait.[35]

As for Halsey, with Kinkaid's emphatic radio pleas for assistance still burning in his brain, he immediately understood that he would face some second-guessing. Even as he sped back toward Leyte on the evening of October 25, he sent Nimitz, MacArthur, Kinkaid, and King a top-secret message attempting to clarify his actions, so that there would be "no misunderstanding concerning recent operations of the Third Fleet."

To "statically guard San Bernardino Strait" and wait for the Japanese "would have been childish," so Halsey struck north for Ozawa's carriers, which had theretofore been "missing from the picture." Saying that he had then been forced "to stand off from my golden opportunity and head south to support Kinkaid although I was convinced that his force was adequate," he went to some lengths to catalog his support over the previous week for MacArthur and Kinkaid. This included the destruction of 1,200 enemy planes, the "crippling" of Kurita's force in the Sibuyan Sea (however premature that assessment was), and the surface movements then under way "to cut off enemy retreat toward San Bernardino," belated though that would prove to be. "The back of the Jap navy has been broken in the course of supporting our landings at Leyte," Halsey concluded.[36]

In response, Nimitz and King seem to have taken their cue from a comment reportedly made by Ulysses S. Grant after he demanded to know who had given the order for the charge up Missionary Ridge. Supposedly Grant grumbled, "Well, it will be all right if it turns out all right."[37]

It had turned out all right, close call though it was, and the US Navy closed ranks around Halsey. MacArthur did much the same thing. He extracted a heavy toll of personal loyalty from his subordinates, but he was usually a loyal supporter in return. Certainly that was true in Bill Halsey's case. The admiral and the general had had their moments of disagreement, but they had generally worked very well together—as, by many reports, had their respective staffs.

Despite the second-guessing that occurred at the time over Halsey's strike against Ozawa—second-guessing that continues today—MacArthur never blamed Halsey or directly questioned his decision. Reports of MacArthur castigating Halsey for having abandoned the beachheads as Kurita bore down on the CVEs seem, in hindsight, to have emanated largely from Sutherland.[38] Not only was MacArthur not with Sutherland that morning, Sutherland was also recognized by no less an authority than George Marshall to be the "chief insulter of the Navy" within MacArthur's headquarters.[39]

The most accurate expression of MacArthur's feelings may have occurred on the first evening MacArthur spent ashore in Tacloban. According to George Kenney, as MacArthur sat down at the dinner table, he heard Halsey's name mentioned with "certain expressions that might be classed as highly uncomplimentary." MacArthur pounded the table and exclaimed, "That's enough. Leave the Bull alone. He's still a fighting Admiral in my book."[40]

Marshall sounded a similar note of interservice cooperation in a meeting of the Joint Chiefs a few weeks later. When Admiral King made sarcastic and disparaging comments about MacArthur, Marshall banged his own table and brought King up short, exclaiming, "I will not have any meetings carried on with this hatred."[41]

MacArthur sent messages of thanks and congratulations to both Nimitz and Halsey. "To you and to all elements of your fine command," MacArthur wrote Nimitz, "[I extend my] deep appreciation of the splendid service they have rendered." To Halsey, MacArthur laid it on especially thick. "We have cooperated with you so long," MacArthur told him, "that we are accustomed and expect your brilliant successes and you have more than sustained our fullest anticipations. Everyone here has a feeling of complete confidence and inspiration when you go into action in our support."[42]

None of this, however, could obscure or eradicate two critical lingering questions. First, why didn't MacArthur, the big-picture strategist in his vaunted map room, either query Kinkaid to confirm that San Bernardino Strait was guarded or go directly to Halsey with the same concern? The usual answer involves some version of the difficulties of Kinkaid's chain of command running to MacArthur while Halsey's command authority for operations at sea ran to Nimitz and ultimately to King and the Joint Chiefs.

Indeed, MacArthur's stock answer to this question was the continuing failure of the Joint Chiefs to give him unity of command throughout the Pacific. "I have never ascribed the unfortunate incidents of this naval battle to faulty judgment on the part of any of the commanders involved," MacArthur wrote in his memoirs. Rather, he found that the blame for the "near disaster can be placed squarely at the door of Washington." This meant, he said, that "two key American commanders were independent of each other, one under me, and the other under Admiral Nimitz 5,000 miles away, both operating in the same waters and in the same battle."[43]

But Halsey and MacArthur had been cooperating on operational matters since the campaigns at Buna and Guadalcanal. Surely MacArthur—who was never shy about dashing off a message to anyone—would not have hesitated to query Halsey on the status of his operations. He had every right and responsibility to do the same with Kinkaid.

The real answer is that MacArthur at that moment lacked a big-picture understanding of Japanese naval movements. This was, at least in part, because he had chosen to be on board the *Nashville* and to take part in the landings and subsequent Philippine government ceremonies in Tacloban. Consequently he was without the communications and intelligence resources more readily available at an established headquarters. Having eschewed Hollandia, he would not find such facilities available in Tacloban until after the sea battles.

But one should not criticize MacArthur too heavily for this. As CINCSWPA, he had by necessity delegated responsibility for air, land, and sea operations to Kenney, Krueger, and Kinkaid. It was up to Kinkaid to supervise Seventh Fleet naval operations, which he did admirably in the immediate waters around Leyte Gulf. Even had MacArthur been in supreme command of both Kinkaid and Halsey, it is highly unlikely that he would have questioned, or even known about, the fluid operational situation that ultimately led to San Bernardino being left unguarded.

The more vexing question is this: Regardless of what Kinkaid's Seventh Fleet was doing, why didn't Bill Halsey leave so much as a picket destroyer guarding the eastern end of San Bernardino Strait? At the very least, why didn't he request that Kinkaid do so? Such an action likely would have provided early warning to both Halsey and Kinkaid hours before Kurita's battleships bore down on the CVEs off Samar. This question has never been satisfactorily answered. One thing, however, became certain: as much as the US Navy was tested at the battles of Leyte Gulf, so, too, would MacArthur and the US Army be tested ashore in the days and weeks that followed.

PART FIVE

RESOLUTION

1945

I am completely under his spell.... He is one of the
most charming and remarkable characters I have
ever met and so sympathetic towards the Southeast
Asia Command.
                    —LORD LOUIS MOUNTBATTEN, WAR DIARY,
                                        JULY 12 AND 14, 1945

To MacArthur everything was subordinate to Mac-
Arthur and his war.
                    —GEORGE H. JOHNSTON, "HOW GOOD
                        WAS MACARTHUR," FEBRUARY 16, 1946

MacArthur signs the Japanese surrender documents for the Allies, September 2, 1945.
Courtesy of the MacArthur Memorial, Norfolk, VA

CHAPTER TWENTY-THREE

Return to Manila

MacArthur had belatedly embraced Bill Halsey's assessment that Japanese defenses in the central Philippines were largely an empty shell — particularly when it came to airpower — at least in part because the resulting timetable expedited his cherished return to the Philippines. Halsey's carrier raids in September of 1944 had indeed found what appeared to be waning resistance, but two days after MacArthur waded ashore, Fourteenth Area Army commander Yamashita received orders to muster all forces and destroy the enemy on Leyte. While Yamashita preferred organizing an all-out defense on Luzon, he nonetheless dispatched major reinforcements to Leyte. On October 24, the day before Kurita's fleet beat a retreat, the Japanese airpower that MacArthur and Halsey had discounted began daily assaults on a scale that MacArthur had not personally experienced since his days on Corregidor.[1]

After establishing his headquarters at the Price House in Tacloban on October 26 — a speedy and almost unprecedented six days after the initial landings — MacArthur witnessed these daily air attacks from its long, covered veranda. The two-story white structure put the controversial "palace" in Hollandia to shame. Built by Walter Scott Price, an American expatriate who had married a Filipina and become a successful Leyte businessman, it was easily the largest and most readily identifiable building in town. The Japanese interned Price as a prisoner of war after they overran the island in 1942 and turned the house into a headquarters. They presumed MacArthur would do the same and consequently made it the target of regular air attacks.

From the second-floor veranda, MacArthur took these raids in stride, calmly smoking his pipe while strolling back and forth. Clearly visible to the rank and file passing in the street below, as well as to those taking shelter in the main headquarters complex across the street, MacArthur displayed the best of his calm Corregidor demeanor and applied it to the front lines, steadily erasing characterizations of Dugout Doug.

His press releases didn't shy away from bolstering this fearless frontline image. "General MacArthur had one of his narrowest escapes during a recent bombing and strafing attack on American positions in Leyte," an SWPA press release reported in early November. "A 50 cal. bullet smashed through a window and gouged a deep hole in the wall of the room in which General MacArthur was working — a foot from his head. When his aides rushed in the General was examining the bullet. Smilingly he observed: 'Not Yet!' "[2]

The threat didn't come only from the skies. Between October 23 and December 11, 1944, at least nine Japanese convoys landed on the western coast of Leyte, principally at Ormoc, bringing ashore fifty thousand troops and ten thousand tons of supplies. Instead of minimal resistance, Walter Krueger's Sixth Army soon faced three divisions, two independent brigades, and elements of two other divisions. Meanwhile, the skies above Leyte were filled with 2,500 planes of the Japanese Fourth Air Army, including the first kamikaze attacks. They frustrated Krueger's ground assaults, disrupted airfield construction, and wreaked havoc with Allied shipping, which was delivering men and equipment to Leyte Gulf.

The key reason for the success of these Japanese efforts was that for the first time in the long history of MacArthur's amphibious landings, Kenney's air force failed to achieve prompt land-based air superiority. Since the early battles on New Guinea, Kenney had quickly provided covering fighter protection from hastily constructed forward airfields, followed closely by bases for medium bombers, in support of every advance MacArthur made. Despite the power of Halsey's carrier strikes before and after the initial Leyte landings, a number of factors conspired to open a window between those operations and Kenney's ability to put up a land-based air umbrella.

The first enemy was the weather. Rain, rain, and more rain fell on Leyte and hampered airfield construction. During the first forty days and nights after the invasion, a biblical thirty-five inches of rain fell at Dulag, turning would-be airstrips into quagmires. Then, too, there was Leyte's geography. Mountainous terrain precluded airfield construction inland, away from the soggy coastal areas. At the same time, the mountains acted as a weather curtain, keeping the rain and the brunt of several typhoons over the Americans, on the eastern coast, while the Japanese, flying from bases in western Leyte and farther away, on Luzon, enjoyed clearer skies en route to their targets.

When two squadrons of P-38s flew north from Morotai and landed at Tacloban on October 27, MacArthur and Kenney greeted them enthusiastically, and MacArthur told Halsey that Kenney's air forces could take over air operations from his carriers. Concerned about increasing kamikaze attacks and in need of resupply, Halsey was only too glad to rotate his task groups back to Ulithi.

But by November 3, the original thirty-four P-38s were down to twenty, and sometimes they found themselves outnumbered fifteen to one by waves of attacking Japanese. The failure to make more airfields operational and get more fighters into Leyte resulted in almost no air support for Krueger's ground troops. On November 10, even as American antiaircraft fire slowly took its toll on the attackers, MacArthur and Kenney were forced to admit that they needed Halsey's fast carriers back on the scene, both to support Krueger's advance and to pound the airdromes on Luzon from which many of these attacks were staged.[3]

Krueger's biggest problem continued to be the influx of Japanese reinforcements landing at Ormoc. In mid-November, he proposed using one of the reserve divisions, the Seventy-Seventh Infantry, to make an amphibious end around so that the troops could land south of Ormoc and close that supply line. Kinkaid's amphibious forces were still on schedule to land troops at Mindoro, the island due south of Luzon, on December 5, and there was some question as to whether they could mount both operations. The main objection, however, came from naval commanders who feared that Japanese planes, particularly with the increase in kamikaze tactics, might inflict heavy losses. MacArthur ordered Krueger to put the Ormoc plan on hold.[4]

Leyte, a Sixth Army report on the campaign later concluded, "brought out very strongly, although in a negative way, the vital relationship of air power to the success of the offensive."[5] The US Army Air Forces official history concurred, although it laid the blame at the army's doorstep. "Not only had the inability of Sixth Army engineers to provide planned air facilities on Leyte cost that army an easy victory," it reported, "but continued constructional delays threatened to jeopardize the whole schedule of future operations."[6]

Leyte proved to be the only major invasion that MacArthur, who had evolved considerably in his perceptions of airpower, launched without the support of adequate land-based air or the ability to develop it within days. As the official history went on to conclude, "the experience at Leyte served to emphasize the soundness of SWPA's traditional pattern of attack: the advancement of ground, naval, and land-based air forces in coordinated moves, with new beachheads always kept within the normal fighter-escorted bomb line. Carrier-based air power had again demonstrated that it was a superior striking force when operating independently and an acceptable supporting force when properly integrated with land-based aviation, but that it was no suitable substitute for land-based bombers and fighters in the support of a beachhead."[7]

As the Leyte operation bogged down, MacArthur chomped at the bit to get to Luzon, but despite his September admonishment to his staff that "you must have me in Lingayen before Christmas," it wasn't going to happen. In fact, as the effects of poor air support over Leyte mounted, Admiral Kinkaid strongly recommended that the planned assault on Mindoro on December 5 be postponed even though that would delay the strike against Luzon.

Noting that five weeks had passed since the Leyte landings and there was still no local control of the air, Kinkaid told MacArthur in a five-page memo that the only way to support the Mindoro landings would be to deploy CVEs into the narrow confines of the Sulu Sea. Perhaps smarting from the CVE losses off Leyte, Kinkaid found the risk unacceptable, fearing heavy air attacks as well as enemy surface forces that could not be successfully interdicted without land-based air. Kinkaid concluded his memo by arguing that any operations into Luzon were "entirely outside the realm of feasibility until control of the air in the Philippines is in our hands." He also suggested, "Even Leyte is far from secure."[8]

MacArthur was not pleased. His confrontation with Kinkaid occurred on the morning of November 30 at the Price House. For two hours the general and his admiral argued the case. MacArthur insisted that Japanese air "would cause very little trouble" and that the Mindoro invasion could not be delayed. When Kinkaid returned to the *Wasatch,* he took the unusual step of drafting an out-of-channels dispatch directly to Admiral King, detailing his reasons for recommending a delay. But before it could be sent—with informational copies to MacArthur and Nimitz, a strategy that might well have resulted in Kinkaid's dismissal—MacArthur summoned Kinkaid back to the Price House for another round.

MacArthur had just received a diplomatically worded message from Nimitz saying that he had discussed the schedule with Halsey and that a short delay in the Mindoro operation would permit Halsey's carriers more time at Ulithi to reprovision. That accomplished, they could return on station with a vengeance to pound Japanese air on Luzon in support of both the Mindoro and Lingayen landings. MacArthur stewed about this even as he paced the floor and engaged in another two-hour argument with Kinkaid. Finally, his pontificating done, MacArthur put his hands on Kinkaid's shoulders. "Tommy, I love you still," MacArthur told him. "Let's go to dinner and then send them a cable."[9]

The result was that MacArthur postponed the Mindoro landings for ten days, until December 15. Initially, the Lingayen landings on Luzon were also delayed a corresponding ten days, from December 20 until December 30. But Kenney, after closer inspection, wanted more time to develop supporting airfields on Mindoro—with less problems than there had been on Leyte, he hoped—and Kinkaid needed more time to redeploy amphibious forces from one operation to the other. Sutherland added the final straw when he pointed out that the full moon at the end of December would illuminate the Lingayen force's night movements. Reluctantly, MacArthur told the Joint Chiefs that the Lingayen landings could not occur until January 9, 1945.[10]

In the long term, these delays in the Philippines had a domino effect on the ships of the Pacific Fleet and on Nimitz's operations in the central Pacific. Because MacArthur needed Halsey's fast carriers for air cover—not only for the initial landings but also for some time afterward, until Kenney could establish air bases on Luzon—Nimitz was forced to recommend corresponding delays in his theater. The planned Iwo Jima invasion was postponed from February 3 until February 19. This in turn pushed the landings on Okinawa back until April 1, 1945, a situation the Joint Chiefs had little choice but to accept.[11] Far from expediting the fall of Japan, as MacArthur had long maintained they would, Philippine operations were in fact delaying it.

In the short term, the added ten days before the Mindoro assault gave a much-needed respite to the ships of Halsey's and Kinkaid's fleets. The biggest beneficiary, however, may have been Walter Krueger's Sixth Army. Amphibious forces were finally available to take the Seventy-Seventh Infantry Division on its end around by sea to attack Ormoc and close the major avenue of Japanese reinforcements into Leyte. This landing occurred on December 7. The naval landing force suffered heavy casualties, including a destroyer and transport sunk by Japanese air attacks, proving that Kinkaid's concerns were well founded. But once ashore, the Seventy-Seventh Division rolled along the coast and captured Ormoc three days later. Even before it did so, MacArthur's daily communiqué grandly announced that the operation had "split the enemy's forces in two."[12]

Before Ormoc fell, General Yamashita had been optimistic about Leyte, even planning an ambitious amphibious counterattack through the shallow waters of Carigara Bay, off Leyte's northern coast. Afterward, with intelligence reports of the impending Mindoro invasion also in hand, he canceled the operation. On December 19, two days before the long arms of the X and XXIV Corps finally completed their planned encirclement of Leyte north of Ormoc, Yamashita informed his local commander that he would receive no more reinforcements or supplies and that his troops would have to become self-supporting.[13]

Meanwhile, the Mindoro task force staged in Leyte Gulf and sailed west through Surigao Strait on the night of December 12–13. MacArthur had originally planned to accompany it, as he has done with every major landing since the Admiralties the previous March. But under some pressure from his staff not to expose himself again, he seems to have concluded that because Mindoro was a secondary show when compared to the effort coming at Lingayen, he would wait for the landings on Luzon.

The cruiser *Nashville* did go, however, as the flagship of Rear Admiral Arthur D. Struble, the attack group commander. Around him were CVEs, old battleships, cruisers, destroyers, and transports laden with twelve thousand combat troops, almost six thousand ground service units, and approximately 9,500 Allied Air Forces personnel. The latter's task was to have one fighter group operational five days after the landing date — this time MacArthur chose U-day as the designation — with another fighter group, a light bomber group, a tactical reconnaissance squadron, and two commando fighter squadrons in place before the Lingayen landings. There would be no repeat of Leyte.

As this force moved westward on the afternoon of December 13, it sailed near the route over which PT-41 had carried MacArthur almost three years before. Suddenly, unseen by lookouts and undetected by radar, a lone kamikaze darted in low over the water and made for the *Nashville*. It slammed into the port-side five-inch gun mount. The resulting explosion and fire killed 130 men, wounded 190 more, and turned the flag bridge and combat information center into an inferno. Among the dead was Struble's chief of staff. Struble transferred his flag to a destroyer, and the *Nashville* limped back toward Leyte. One can only wonder what might have happened to MacArthur had he been on board.[14]

The remainder of the task force sailed on toward Mindoro, although for a time the Japanese were uncertain as to its destination, thinking that Panay, Cebu, or Negros were more likely targets. Mindoro was indeed a longer leap straight toward the belly of Luzon, but the value of its airfields was high. As landing craft made for the beaches on the southern tip of the island on the morning of December 15, Japanese aircraft from Clark Field and Davao, on Mindanao — including ever-increasing numbers of kamikazes—resumed aerial attacks. Aircraft from Kinkaid's CVEs rose to respond and were soon joined by P-38s from Leyte. The CVEs stayed on station a day longer than planned to cover the landing force and beachhead as Halsey's fast carriers struck airfields on Luzon from the northeast.

Then disaster struck Halsey's fleet. Heading for a refueling rendezvous so that Halsey could keep his commitment to MacArthur to unleash another series of raids against Luzon on December 19–21, the Third Fleet sailed into the full fury of a deadly typhoon. By the time it blew through, three destroyers had capsized, incurring the loss of most of their crews. Two light carriers suffered minor damage, but a third almost sank when loose aircraft on the hangar deck ignited a firestorm. The toll for the Third Fleet was 790 dead and 156 aircraft destroyed.

Nevertheless, Halsey tried to keep his commitment to MacArthur by steaming west toward Luzon on December 20 before deciding that the damage to his ships demanded his return to Ulithi to regroup and repair. Just as he had after the battles of Leyte Gulf, Halsey came under heavy criticism for his actions and course changes during the typhoon. A court of inquiry later found Halsey accountable for "errors in judgment under stress of war operations," but in approving the court's opinion, Nimitz defended him by noting that any such errors stemmed "from a commendable desire to meet military commitments"—that is to say, from the promise both of them had made to MacArthur to support the Mindoro and Lingayen landings at full bore.[15]

Despite the typhoon, the Allies managed to destroy 450 Japanese planes in the air and on the ground in the Philippines during the first two weeks of December. Once ground troops were ashore on Mindoro, matters were easier for them. The initial landing was unopposed, in large part because the location came as a surprise but also because Yamashita had poured men and resources into the defense of Leyte and was gearing up to do the same on Luzon. As MacArthur had found out in early 1942, Yamashita and his troops simply could not be everywhere.

Now it was almost Christmas in 1944. MacArthur hunkered down at the Price House in Tacloban, tugged at his battered cap in frustration over the delays on Leyte, and prepared to spend his third Christmas in a row without Jean and little Arthur. Jean had been preparing for months to move out of Lennons in Brisbane and return to their penthouse atop the Manila Hotel, but the Allied advance had been slower than MacArthur had expected. The separation from his family, endured since he had bid them good-bye in mid-October, weighed heavily on a man of almost sixty-five—although it was a sacrifice he shared with every rank-and-file soldier, and for him, the separation was of much shorter duration.

Having mentally left Australia for good and being occupied with the upcoming Lingayen landings, MacArthur decided he could not join Jean and Arthur for Christmas. The powers in Washington nonetheless bestowed an unexpected Christmas present.

For some time, there had been talk in Washington circles about creating a five-star grade senior to that of the four stars of a full general or admiral. Admiral King, as a likely recipient on the navy side, had been among those championing the move, while General Marshall, with his usual reticence, remained concerned with weightier matters. On the practical side, a large number of officers in both services had achieved the four-star grade, and Americans routinely came up one star short in their dealings with the five stars of a British field marshal, air marshal, or admiral of the fleet.

On December 14, 1944, Congress finally passed legislation creating the uniquely American grades of general of the army and fleet admiral and authorized four officers of five-star rank on the active rolls of each service. Significantly, the president's authority to make such appointments, and the grades themselves, terminated six months after the cessation of the current hostilities.[16]

When President Roosevelt began to award the promotions, the dates at which he did so established seniority. Although he was the least known publicly, Admiral William D. Leahy was arguably the most important man in the ailing president's White House. There was no question in Roosevelt's mind that Leahy was the country's ranking military officer. His appointment as fleet admiral was dated December 15, 1944, and the promotion of the other recipients followed, each one day later than the one before it.

Determined to alternate between navy and army, Roosevelt was equally certain that George Marshall should receive the army's first five-star grade. Admiral King received the third slot, then Roosevelt looked to the second army appointment. An argument could be made that Roosevelt had a true choice between Dwight Eisenhower and his former superior, Douglas MacArthur, but in reality, politics and public image, far more than MacArthur's ego, dictated that MacArthur receive his five stars ahead of his one-time aide. Thus, on December 18, 1944, Douglas MacArthur became a general of the army.

The third navy promotion to fleet admiral went to Chester Nimitz, and Eisenhower received his five stars the following day, standing sixth in order of seniority. Roosevelt might have stopped there, but parity with the British on the Combined Chiefs of Staff caused him to award Army Air Forces chief of staff Hap Arnold the seventh set of stars on December 21. The remaining navy slot would not be filled for almost a year. Not without some controversy over his Leyte and typhoon decisions, Bill Halsey was ultimately appointed over Raymond Spruance.

MacArthur immediately sent the president his gratitude. "My grateful thanks for the promotion you have just given me," MacArthur radioed Roosevelt. "My pleasure in receiving it is greatly enhanced because it was made by you."[17] With no readily available insignia for his new rank, MacArthur had a Filipino silversmith at Tacloban craft two circles of five stars each from a collection of American, Australian, Dutch, and Filipino silver coins. These represented the major national forces serving under his Allied command.

The other message MacArthur rushed to send went to his rear-echelon headquarters in Brisbane, marked FOR IMMEDIATE DELIVERY TO MRS. MACARTHUR. Advising Jean that he had just been appointed general of the army, MacArthur told her, "This promotion has been largely due to the comfort, help and devotion you have so loyally and unstintingly given me."[18]

MacArthur's other surprise just before Christmas in 1944 was not nearly so pleasant. The simmering friction between MacArthur and Sutherland was exploding, ignited by Sutherland's continuing insubordination over Elaine Bessemer Clarke. Sometime in November, rumors reached MacArthur's inner circle that Sutherland had ordered engineers to build Clarke a cottage of her own in the maze of offices and barracks under construction south of Tacloban. Roger Egeberg drew the short straw when it came time to tell MacArthur.

The general professed amazement and disbelief, telling Egeberg, "I don't believe it! I can't believe it! I told him not to let her come north of Australia, and he knows that!" When MacArthur summoned deputy chief of staff Dick Marshall to confirm the story — Sutherland himself appears not to have been in Tacloban at the time — Marshall denied the rumor. Afterward, Marshall confirmed it to be true and apologized to Egeberg for making him appear to be a rumormonger. In the meantime, however, no one corrected the facts with MacArthur, and for a few weeks the matter sat as uncomfortably as an uninvited guest.[19]

On November 22, Sutherland told Dusty Rhoades that Clarke would soon be flying with them from Hollandia to Tacloban. Rhoades was aware of the standing agreement that Australian military women would not be deployed in front areas, but he chose not to question Sutherland on the matter. Later, in annotating his diary, Rhoades loyally wrote: "I do not believe Sutherland was informed of the commitment; it is entirely out of character for him to disobey blatantly an order of his commander."[20]

But of course that was just the problem. Not only did Sutherland almost certainly know of the prohibition — regardless of the hairsplitting fact that the Australian Clarke was technically serving as an American WAC — but he had also been specifically ordered by MacArthur to keep Clarke out of the front lines during their earlier confrontation at Hollandia.

Clarke didn't end up joining Sutherland on his flight in a B-24 to Tacloban — perhaps, Rhoades speculated, because Sutherland had straitlaced Stephen Chamberlin, MacArthur's operations chief, along on the flight. Nonetheless, on November 30, Clarke was among the passengers Sutherland ordered Rhoades to fly north on another run between Hollandia and Tacloban. This time, Rhoades was at the controls of MacArthur's personal B-17, the *Bataan*.[21]

The news that Clarke was in the Philippines reached MacArthur's headquarters when Clarke herself telephoned and spoke with Larry Lehrbas. Clarke seemed to be almost baiting MacArthur by announcing her presence. Lehrbas, Bonner Fellers, and Roger Egeberg held a hurried conference, and once again Egeberg was elected to deliver the news to MacArthur.

Egeberg waited until that evening after supper when MacArthur was smoking his pipe as usual on the veranda of the Price House. As Egeberg struggled to find a casual way to bring up the topic, MacArthur suddenly turned to him and asked, "Say, Doc, whatever happened to that woman?"

Egeberg feigned surprised and replied, "Woman? What woman, General?"

"Oh, you know, *that woman,*" MacArthur answered. When Egeberg told him that Clarke was just down the coast in her cottage, MacArthur exploded with a shout loud enough to be heard up and down the street. "Get me Dick!" MacArthur angrily commanded Egeberg.[22]

Egeberg passed that unpleasant assignment to one of the headquarters clerks, and when Sutherland appeared on the veranda, MacArthur launched into a tirade that was both very uncharacteristic and very public. Officers and enlisted men up and down the street and in neighboring buildings saw and heard MacArthur dress down his chief of staff. Sutherland retreated to his office, but MacArthur was not finished with him.

According to chief clerk Paul Rogers, who had been with both men since prewar Manila, MacArthur marched into Sutherland's office and towered over him as Sutherland sat at his desk. "Dick Sutherland," MacArthur raged, "I gave you an order. You disobeyed it. You are relieved of your command. You are under arrest." Rogers, who was standing in the rear doorway to Sutherland's office, quickly backed away as the two generals exchanged more heated words.[23]

Within hours of their stormy confrontation, Sutherland wrote out a five-page letter to Dusty Rhoades, who had arguably been his closest confidant save Elaine Clarke herself. Sutherland instructed Rhoades to return Clarke to Australia and see to her welfare. As for his own future, Sutherland told Rhoades that MacArthur had temporarily relieved him of his duties. He denied that he had known of the prohibition against Australian women at the front, then instructed Rhoades to destroy the letter, which Rhoades did.[24]

MacArthur never put Sutherland's reprimands in writing, but it was clear that Sutherland's days of speaking for MacArthur were over. Assistant chief of staff Dick Marshall assumed more and more responsibility and power. MacArthur again rejected Sutherland's requests for reassignment. MacArthur may well have thought such an exit far too easy on Sutherland and chose to keep him close at hand, still as nominal chief of staff, but with everyone at his headquarters well aware that his power had been shorn. That MacArthur was soon conversing with him again as if nothing had changed—albeit on matters of lesser substance—only increased his sense of exile.[25]

When Rhoades returned to Tacloban on December 29, he gave Sutherland a lengthy account of Clarke's weepy and emotional return to Brisbane. Afterward, Sutherland started into a long conversation with him about MacArthur, blaming MacArthur's actions on the general's frustrations with the pace of the Leyte campaign. "Sutherland said MacArthur's mood was much like it had been in the early days of the New Guinea campaign," Rhoades remembered, "when progress had been slow and disappointing. MacArthur wanted to get on to Luzon and Manila and the delays had been most distressing to him, increasing his impatience."[26] That much of what Sutherland said was probably true.

In MacArthur's mind, his pledge of returning to the Philippines would not be fulfilled until he reentered Manila. First, of course, he had to get out of Leyte. After Ormoc fell, Japanese resistance on Leyte was doomed, but much heavy fighting remained to be done around a handful of fiercely defended pockets, particularly in the hills above the Ormoc Valley, on Leyte's western thumb.

On the day after Christmas in 1944, MacArthur rushed, as usual, to declare victory and move on. "The Leyte-Samar campaign can now be regarded as closed except for minor mopping-up," MacArthur's communiqué announced. "General Yamashita has sustained perhaps the greatest defeat in the military annals of the Japanese Army."[27]

That same day, Eichelberger's Eighth Army assumed command of operations on Leyte, relieving Krueger's Sixth Army and thus permitting it to prepare for the invasion of Luzon. "This closes a campaign that has had few counterparts in the utter destruction of an enemy's forces with a maximum conservation of our own," MacArthur wrote Krueger in congratulation.[28]

Some of that may have been true. The entire Leyte campaign cost the US Army 3,504 men; almost twelve thousand were wounded. Estimates of Japanese strength on Leyte—and the number of men killed—vary: there were very few wounded and captured. Assessments range from 56,263 killed and 389 captured as of December 26 to upwards of eighty thousand killed over the course of the entire campaign.[29]

But the Leyte campaign was far from over when Eichelberger and the Eighth Army took charge. MacArthur's "minor mopping-up" became, as the unit history of the Eleventh Airborne Division reported, "bitter, exhausting, rugged fighting—physically, the most terrible we were ever to know."[30] Eichelberger estimated that the Eighth Army killed more than twenty-seven thousand Japanese troops between December 26, 1944, and the end of hostilities, in May of 1945.

"I never understood the public relations policy that either [MacArthur] or his immediate assistants established," Eichelberger wrote after the war. "It seemed to me, as it did to many of the commanders and correspondents, ill advised to announce victories when a first phase had been accomplished without too many casualties. Too often, as at Buna and Sanananda, as on Leyte, Mindanao, and Luzon, the struggle was to go on for a long time."[31]

But MacArthur was moving forward and headed for Manila. In December of 1941, he had predicted that the invading Japanese would land in Lingayen Gulf and strike south across the Central Luzon Plain. Three years later, as the attacker, MacArthur hoped to surprise Yamashita by coming ashore someplace less obvious. Lingayen's geography, however, was compelling. It had the advantages of wide beaches, protected waters, and, perhaps tellingly, a straight shot toward the Philippine capital.

Despite the unexpected flow of Japanese troops and aircraft into the Leyte campaign, it seemed logical that Ultra information, coupled with reports from Filipino guerrillas, would provide a reliable estimate of enemy forces awaiting MacArthur and Krueger on Luzon. The problem, however, was that calculations made by MacArthur's and

Krueger's staffs based on the intelligence differed widely and made one wonder if they were analyzing the same thing.[32]

Willoughby analyzed Ultra intercepts and reduced his estimate for enemy troops on Luzon from 158,900 in October to barely 137,000 at the end of November. This was in part because he thought the reinforcements sent to Leyte had stripped Luzon of Yamashita's best units. He did not, however, adequately take into account new units arriving undetected in the Philippines from as far away as Manchuria. Non-Ultra sources, principally guerrilla reports, suggested that between 115,000 and 140,000 Japanese soldiers and sailors were on Luzon.

Krueger's Sixth Army G-2 chief, Colonel Horton White, read the same intelligence but concluded that there was a minimum of 234,500 Japanese troops on Luzon at the beginning of December. He theorized that if guerrillas had reported the presence of certain units that had slipped into the Philippines undetected by Ultra, there might well be more of them that both sources had overlooked. As it turned out, the actual number of Japanese was 267,000. As valuable of a tool as Ultra intelligence had become, it was not omniscient, and, ultimately, its utility had much to do with its analysts.[33]

As the Lingayen attack force took to its ships early in January of 1945, Willoughby revised his estimates of opposition upward to 172,000, but by then the number of actual Japanese forces had increased to 287,000. Arrayed against this, Krueger planned to commit 203,000 combat and service troops, which would soon be augmented by reinforcements and organized guerrilla units so that the total would exceed 280,000.

While these American troops did not equal the number of US Army ground forces engaged in western Europe at the time, the Luzon campaign employed the equivalent of fifteen divisions and was by far the largest deployment of the Pacific war. The initial Lingayen assault and those ancillary landings to come near Manila included more US Army ground combat and service forces than earlier operations in North Africa, Italy, and southern France. Luzon was larger than the entire Allied commitment against Sicily. Certainly it far outnumbered the forces used in the Japanese invasion of the Philippines in 1941–1942, when the Japanese landed the equivalent of four divisions.[34]

As for supplies and shipping, MacArthur soon received a reprimand from Marshall saying that cargo vessels arriving in his theater were taking too long to unload and return. The chief of staff's office counted 446 such ships within the Southwest Pacific Area, of which 113 were either loading or discharging, 102 were idle waiting to load or discharge, 62 were servicing or repairing, and 169 were en route. "You have previously been requested to invoke extraordinary measures to improve the shipping turnaround," Marshall reminded MacArthur. "Global commitments cannot sustain this extraordinary tax against shipping effectiveness [and] your future operations and those in other theatres are already being penalized by shipping shortages."[35]

Given those numbers of men, materiel, and ships, it is difficult to see how MacArthur could argue with a straight face and dose of self-righteousness that the Pacific in general and his Southwest Pacific Area in particular were still being habitually shortchanged.

During the first eight days of January in 1945, Halsey's carriers pounded Japanese air bases on Luzon as well as Formosa to prevent an influx of reinforcements and direct attacks from the latter. On January 4, MacArthur and his key personal staff, including Roger Egeberg and Larry Lehrbas, boarded the light cruiser *Boise* with no expectation that they would be returning to Tacloban. MacArthur had every intention of establishing his headquarters ashore on Lingayen Gulf as soon as possible.

"Dearest Jeannie," MacArthur wrote to his wife in longhand from the *Boise* on the night of January 8. "This is my 'ships' letter to tell you about the voyage. To begin with the Boise is the most comfortable cruiser on which I have travelled. The suite I occupy is much larger, has artificial ventilation, and better cooking than the others." MacArthur went on to describe what he termed "the suiciders" who had been harrying the convoy and admitted that he would "be glad to come to battle grips on land [where] I believe I have him but will not know definitely until I test his strength."[36]

Kamikazes had indeed taken a toll on the landing force and on Jesse Oldendorf's supporting group of battleships and CVEs. The escort carrier *Ommaney Bay* sank, and the battleship *New Mexico* took a direct hit on its bridge that killed its commanding officer as well as Winston Churchill's personal representative to MacArthur. The *Boise* itself narrowly dodged two torpedoes fired from midget submarines off Mindoro, yet during the continuing kamikaze attacks MacArthur insisted on staying near the quarterdeck to stare intently at Corregidor and Bataan as they appeared in the distance to starboard. "I could not leave the rail," MacArthur later confessed.[37]

By the morning of January 9, nearly one thousand ships were spread across Lingayen Gulf. Yamashita offered no resistance on the beaches, but kamikaze attacks continued to take their toll on the waters. Lieutenant General Oscar Griswold's XIV Corps of the Thirty-Seventh and Fortieth Infantry Divisions went ashore between Lingayen and Dagupan, and by nightfall they had both towns and the Lingayen airfield under their control. Meanwhile, the Sixth and Forty-Third Infantry Divisions of Major General Innis Swift's I Corps bracketed San Fabian, to the east. The Sixth Division rolled inland for more than three miles, but the Forty-Third began to receive pressure from the adjacent hills. This gave Krueger pause and suggested that Yamashita might launch a massive assault on his left flank. Those concerns would soon put Krueger at odds with MacArthur's timetable.

Four hours after the first assault waves, MacArthur judged it was his turn to go ashore. That MacArthur could even make such landing-zone excursions—as he had done since the Admiralties—spoke volumes about his leadership team. It is to MacArthur's credit as a leader that he generally picked competent subordinates, delegated responsibility, and trusted them to produce results.

This was particularly true of Kenney and Ennis Whitehead in air operations, Dan Barbey in amphibious operations, and Dick Marshall as his deputy chief of staff. MacArthur ranted and railed from time to time against both Krueger and Eichelberger, but they proved competent field commanders. Then, of course, there was Sutherland. MacArthur might have been better off had someone with less of an alter-ego personality been his chief of staff, but theirs had been a mutually sustaining relationship until Sutherland forced MacArthur to reassert himself.

Had MacArthur not had this support group of capable staff and field commanders, he could not have disappeared into radio silence while

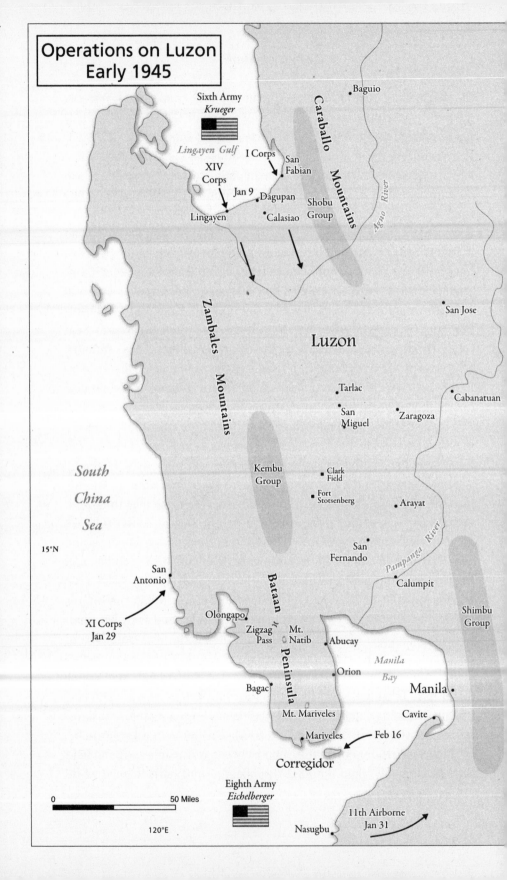

Operations on Luzon
Early 1945

Baguio

Caraballo Mountains

Aguo River

Sixth Army
Krueger

Lingayen Gulf

I Corps
San Fabian

XIV Corps

Jan 9

Dagupan

Calasiao

Shobu Group

San Jose

Lingayen

Luzon

South China Sea

Zambales Mountains

Tarlac

San Miguel

Zaragoza

Cabanatuan

Kembu Group

Clark Field

Fort Stotsenberg

Arayat

Pampanga River

15°N

San Fernando

San Antonio

Calumpit

Shimbu Group

XI Corps
Jan 29

Olongapo

Bataan Peninsula

Zigzag Pass

Mt. Natib

Abucay

Manila Bay

Orion

Bagac

Manila

Mt. Mariveles

Cavite

0   50 Miles

Mariveles

Feb 16

Eighth Army
Eichelberger

Corregidor

120°E

11th Airborne
Jan 31

Nasugbu

aboard ships en route to landing zones. He liked to say that he needed to see the action firsthand to understand what he was up against, but such excursions cost him some measure of command and control. Thanks to his leadership team, he was able to do so without seriously compromising his command's ability to accomplish its mission.

Now off Luzon, MacArthur headed for the beach south of San Fabian along with Sutherland, Fellers, Egeberg, and Lehrbas. This time, the Seabees had already used a bulldozer to construct a little jetty on which he could alight, but instead the general stepped off into the water and waded the remaining yards to shore. As D. Clayton James put it: "His Leyte wading scene was unintentional, but this one seems to have been a deliberate act of showmanship. With the worldwide attention that his Leyte walk through the water received, apparently the Barrymore side of MacArthur's personality could not resist another big splash of publicity and surf."[38]

In his memoirs, MacArthur chose to remember it a little differently. "As was getting to be a habit with me," he wrote self-effacingly, "I picked a boat that took too much draft to reach the beach, and I had to wade in."[39]

MacArthur and his party visited Sixth Infantry Division headquarters and took a jeep toward Dagupan, where he intended to establish his own headquarters. Stopped from entering the town by a blown bridge, they returned to the *Boise* late that afternoon. Early the next day, MacArthur went ashore again and toured the deployments of all four divisions. "The decisive battle for the liberation of the Philippines and the control of the Southwest Pacific is at hand," the SWPA communiqué announced that day. "General MacArthur is in personal command at the front and landed with his assault troops" — not "the" assault troops but "his" assault troops.[40]

MacArthur remained on the *Boise* two more nights, then moved ashore permanently on the afternoon of January 13 to occupy a school building in Dagupan as his headquarters — once again a structure with a wide veranda on which to pace and brood. While kamikaze attacks would wreak havoc on Nimitz's fleet off Okinawa a few months later, for MacArthur's forces, the worst of these attacks off Luzon were over by then. A combination of Halsey's carrier attacks, concentrated antiaircraft fire, and land-based support—initially from Mindoro and Leyte and later from captured airfields on Luzon—destroyed and exhausted the Japanese aerial threat.[41]

Then began a contest of wills—not between MacArthur and Yamashita but between MacArthur and Krueger. According to Krueger's chief of staff, Brigadier General Clyde Eddleman, the opening round took place on the *Boise* just before MacArthur moved ashore. MacArthur wanted a lightning thrust across the Central Luzon Plain toward Manila, recapturing Clark Field along the way to aid Kenney's air efforts. Always the stoic Teutonic plodder, Krueger trusted his own G-2 reports much more than he did Willoughby's and had no intention of allowing Yamashita to sweep down from the mountains east of the plains and cut off an extended advance that wasn't adequately supported on both flanks.

Krueger and Eddleman became convinced that MacArthur, who was always keen about anniversaries—routinely observing others' as well as relishing celebrations of his own—desperately wanted to be in Manila by January 26 for his sixty-fifth birthday. (By coincidence, the date was also Krueger's sixty-fourth birthday.) "Where are your casualties? Where are they?" MacArthur thundered at Krueger during what Eddleman recalled "was not a pleasant scene."[42]

MacArthur repeatedly emphasized that losses up to that point had been minimal. "He expressed the view," Krueger recalled, "that the advance would encounter little opposition and that the Japanese would not attempt to defend Manila but would evacuate it."[43] The latter would prove to be wishful thinking, but MacArthur's fixation on low casualty counts ran counter to his boasts that he had done more with less, including fewer casualties, than any other commander. When push came to shove, MacArthur reverted to his World War I mentality of trench warfare to judge a commander's efforts: if the casualty count was not high enough, the effort to advance had not been great enough. He had used that measure against Eichelberger at Buna, and he employed it again with Krueger on Luzon.

As it turned out, Krueger had ample reason to be cautious. Recognizing that the open Luzon plain was not readily defensible, particularly after Japanese air forces sputtered out, Yamashita chose to deploy his forces among three widespread mountain strongholds, planning to cost the Allies dearly in lives and time. Quite consciously, he ordered that whatever they did, Japanese troops were not to retreat to the cul-de-sac of Bataan and face the same circumstances MacArthur had in early 1942.

Yamashita directly commanded 152,000 troops in the Shobu Group, which concentrated in the Caraballo Mountains, east of the Central Luzon Plain, and threatened Krueger's left flank. The Kembu Group, comprising some thirty thousand troops, occupied the foothills of the Zambales Mountains, north of Bataan and west of Clark Field. Its charge was to deny the attackers the use of Clark Field as long as possible and to threaten Krueger's right flank as he moved south. That left eighty thousand troops in the Shimbu Group east of Manila, not to defend the city street by street but to delay the assault by destroying key bridges and controlling the dams and reservoirs that supplied Manila's water.[44]

Still, MacArthur pushed Krueger onward, sometimes with unconventional tactics. "Walter's pretty stubborn," MacArthur told Egeberg. "Maybe I'll have to try something else."[45] The something else was jumping his advanced general headquarters forward around sixty miles from Dagupan to a large sugar plantation at Hacienda Luisita, near Tarlac. This left Krueger's Sixth Army headquarters well to his rear in Calasiao, almost within sight of Lingayen Gulf. Never mind that Krueger had reasons for the position, mostly its proximity to Yamashita's large Shobu Group, but MacArthur's message was less than subtle: the supreme commander was well out in front of his field commander. Krueger didn't bite. He stuck to his script and methodically pushed forward on all fronts.

On January 28, three days after his move to Hacienda Luisita, MacArthur found himself in the thick of the frontline action while visiting units on Krueger's left flank. Yamashita's Shobu Group put up a fight-to-the-death resistance, then launched a savage counterattack spearheaded by tanks and aimed at the 161st Infantry Regiment of the Twenty-Fifth Division. "Our lines reeled," MacArthur recalled, "and I became so concerned over a possible penetration that I personally hastened to the scene of action" and joined its commander "in steadying the ranks."[46]

That same day, the Fortieth Division, on Krueger's right, engaged in equally fierce fighting to wrest control of Clark Field, which was essential to Kenney's large-scale air operations, from the Japanese. The Kembu Group did not retreat very far, however, and it took another three weeks to roust its troops from the hills just to the west and give the Clark complex, the whole of which extended some fifteen miles from north to south, some breathing room. On January 30, MacArthur toured the field in person even as sporadic enemy artillery shells still rained down.[47]

Beyond Clark Field lay the bridges at Calumpit. MacArthur and his Bataan Gang well remembered the race to cross them en route to Bataan at the end of 1941. Now their troops were driving in the opposite direction. Leaving Clark Field, MacArthur snooped southward and found the Thirty-Seventh Division moving toward Calumpit with what he radioed Krueger was "a noticeable lack of drive and aggressive initiative." In the previous few days, the Japanese had blown the bridges, but it was essential for the Americans to secure the crossing site before the retreating enemy could construct a strong defensive line behind the deep and unfordable Pampanga River.[48]

The US Army official history speculates that Krueger passed MacArthur's caustic comment about a lack of drive down the chain of command and that it spurred the Thirty-Seventh Division to move a regiment across the Pampanga the very next day. That, of course, was exactly what MacArthur wanted, but his characterizations on the battlefield were at odds with what he later wrote in his memoirs. "The rate of progress in this operation was fast and more than fulfilled all hopes and expectations," he remembered before claiming, "No greater danger can confront a field commander than too-close 'back seat driving' and too-rigid 'timetables' of operations from those above."[49]

That may have been a bit of self-protective revisionism, given that MacArthur's frontline tours and continual prodding of Krueger were in evidence (and in sharp contrast to his behavior on Leyte, when he moved into the Price House and followed the action from his veranda). Just why he took to the field so aggressively — and, in the opinion of his staff, sometimes rather carelessly — on Luzon is a question without a definite answer. Among the plausible reasons: he was wiping out any vestiges of Dugout Doug; he had a death wish—unlikely, given his devotion to Jean and Arthur; he had smelled the gunpowder again and in old age was once again the dashing young brigadier of World War I; or, perhaps most likely, after three years (a period that was supposed to have been only three months) he was at last returning to rescue what remained of his companions from Manila, Bataan, and Corregidor. This close, he simply couldn't abide sitting still. Like a horse, he smelled the barn and was determined to push ahead.

Amid this savage ground fighting, MacArthur was waging yet another battle with the US Navy. For some months, Nimitz and Halsey had not only provided MacArthur with fast-carrier raids and air cover for his landing operations but had also loaned him Kinkaid's Seventh Fleet battleships, cruisers, and destroyers. The latter had been done with the understanding that the "loaners" would be returned to Nimitz for the invasion of Iwo Jima, an assault that had already been pushed back two weeks because of the delays on Leyte.

When Nimitz routinely reminded MacArthur in mid-January of the pending departure of these ships for Ulithi so that they could be outfitted for the next operation, MacArthur responded that the Seventh Fleet alone was incapable of defending the Lingayen beachhead and mounting additional amphibious assaults. One senses that he feared a concentration of enemy surface vessels such as the one Admiral Kurita had almost visited upon him at Leyte.

Kinkaid then got himself in the middle between Nimitz and MacArthur when he agreed with MacArthur. Nimitz reassured them both that the best way to protect progress in the Philippines was for Halsey and the Third Fleet to seek out and destroy the remaining units of the Japanese fleet, not to stand statically off Lingayen. But once MacArthur got control of something, he was loath to relinquish it. When pressed again by MacArthur, Nimitz agreed that if the Seventh Fleet returned the two most heavily damaged battleships for repairs, including the *New Mexico,* it could keep four battleships, two cruisers, and twenty-two destroyers— most of the ships that had been loaned—a little while longer.

MacArthur may have been afraid that Kinkaid would go soft when it came to negotiations with Nimitz, and he advised Kinkaid that he would personally handle all communications regarding the battleship loan. On February 7, Nimitz called in his marker on the remaining four battleships and asked for their return to Manus by February 16 for repairs and reprovisioning. By then, Kenney's makeover of Clark Field was well on its way to being able to provide an air umbrella, and MacArthur ordered Kinkaid to return the ships. As for MacArthur's version, written in hindsight, he termed Nimitz's partial enforcement of the long-standing agreement a "new and unexpected situation."[50]

Meanwhile, elements of Eichelberger's Eighth Army joined the fray. On January 29, the Thirty-Eighth Infantry Division and the 34th Regimental Combat Team landed unopposed on the coast northwest of Bataan. Their mission was to take Olongapo and outflank the Kembu Group's defenses near Clark Field. On January 31, the Eleventh Airborne Division, less one regiment, went ashore at Nasugbu, just south of the entrance to Manila Bay. The "missing" regiment, the 511th Parachute Infantry, jumped onto Tagaytay Ridge, twenty miles east of Nasugbu, three days later and led the drive against Manila from the south.

By February 1, the final race for Manila was on. Three divisions—the hard-fighting Thirty-Seventh Infantry; the newly arrived First Cavalry, from the Sixth Army reserve; and the recently landed Eleventh Airborne—converged on the capital city from opposite directions. But this was not all about MacArthur's ego. He was "deeply concerned," as he later wrote, "about the thousands of prisoners who had been interned at the various camps on Luzon since the early days of the war." This concern was fueled by reports of a December 1944 massacre of around 150 detainees in a POW camp on the island of Palawan.

MacArthur ordered the First Cavalry to send two flying columns ahead of the main division. On the evening of February 3, these troops became the first Americans to reenter Manila, and they secured the civilian internment camp at the University of Santo Tomas after a fierce firefight. The next morning, elements of the Thirty-Seventh Division reached the Bilibid prison, in northern Manila, and freed around five hundred civilians and eight hundred POWs.[51]

MacArthur himself pressed close behind these advance elements in his jeep but was prevented by a blown bridge from entering the outskirts of Manila with the main force of the First Cavalry. This did not stop him, however, from once again prematurely declaring victory. From his field headquarters at Hacienda Luisita, MacArthur issued a communiqué on February 6 that claimed, "Our forces are rapidly clearing the enemy from Manila. Our converging columns... entered the city and surrounded the Jap defenders. Their complete destruction is imminent." Many Allied leaders and newspapers around the world took this communiqué literally and announced the fall of Manila, but it would not be so easy.[52]

"MacArthur has visions of saving this beautiful city intact," XIV Corps commander Oscar Griswold wrote. "He does not realize, as I do, that the skies burn red every night as [the Japanese] systematically sack the city."[53]

MacArthur had long expected — perhaps "hoped" would be more accurate — that Yamashita would declare Manila an open city and spare it major destruction, as MacArthur had done, with varying degrees of compliance on both sides, in 1941. Yamashita in fact issued orders to abandon the city and combine its troops and supplies with the Shimbu Group in the mountains to the east. The Imperial Japanese Navy, however, had other ideas.

Proving once again that issues of command unity and interservice discord were not unique to the Americans, Rear Admiral Sanji Iwabuchi chose, after considerable debate over his orders, to defend Manila to the death with around sixteen thousand sailors and four thousand soldiers, the latter of whom had missed their chance to escape from the city to the Shimbu Group. The sailors were hardly battle-tested infantrymen, but within the aging walls of old Manila, they became a potent defensive force that made taking control of the city costly and time-consuming. This was to be inner-city warfare at its most grim, and high on the list of casualties was to be Manila itself. [54]

CHAPTER TWENTY-FOUR

Hail the Conquering Hero

The day after Douglas MacArthur issued his premature capture-of-Manila communiqué, he made an emotional visit to the Bilibid prison, in the northern section of the city. There he found around eight hundred military prisoners who had somehow survived the deprivations of three long years of captivity. "The men who greeted me," MacArthur wrote in his memoirs, "were scarcely more than skeletons." Those who could stand dragged themselves to a semblance of attention and offered a quiet "You're back" or "You made it." Yes, MacArthur acknowledged, "I'm a little late, but we finally came."[1]

These sobering encounters, however, did not stop MacArthur from planning a triumphant victory parade through the streets of Manila. Following directly behind his own jeep were to be those surviving members of his Bataan Gang. Sutherland took exception to this and insisted that the planning staff, which had done the work to effect the return, take precedence instead. It was a trifling point, and Paul Rogers concluded that Sutherland, whose relationship with MacArthur could hardly have sunk lower than it was at that point, pressed it only to goad MacArthur. As it turned out, a confrontation never occurred because the conqueror's parade was postponed indefinitely after it became clear that capturing the remainder of Manila would require grim block-by-block fighting.[2]

As elements of the Thirty-Seventh Infantry Division crossed the Pasig River and advanced toward the center of Manila, MacArthur remained convinced that he could take the city largely intact. Only reluctantly did he permit artillery fire within Manila, and he stead-fastly forbade air attacks. When Krueger pressed him on the air ban in mid-February, particularly against heavily entrenched Japanese troops in the old walled Intramuros district, MacArthur termed air attacks on a city occupied "by a friendly and allied population" as "unthinkable."[3]

But the unthinkable occurred nonetheless when upwards of one hundred thousand Filipinos lost their lives over the course of the battle for the city. Many were raped, murdered, burned, shot, and bayoneted by besieged Japanese troops. Whether early and concerted air opera-tions against an entrenched enemy largely committed to self-destruction would have altered this outcome is debatable. These atrocities remain despicable, however, and the drawn-out battle left Manila an unrecog-nizable ruin of rubble and rotting corpses. "This was not Manila," Paul Rogers recalled. "It was simply hell."[4]

MacArthur visited the front lines of this urban battlefield just as he had throughout the advance from Lingayen. By February 23, the area around the Manila Hotel was secure enough for MacArthur to return to what for six years had been his residence. Following heavily armed troops up the ruins of the stairway leading to the penthouse, he arrived at its doorway with a dark sense of foreboding. The vase presented to Arthur MacArthur by the Japanese emperor in 1905 that Jean MacArthur had so carefully left in the entryway lay smashed on the floor next to the remains of a dead Japanese colonel. Whatever of MacArthur's prized military library had not been looted lay in ashes. His and Jean's personal possessions were missing or in ruins. The visit, MacArthur recalled, left him "tasting to the last acid dregs the bitterness of a devastated and beloved home."[5]

Two weeks later, MacArthur made another poignant return—this time to Corregidor. Given MacArthur's earlier embrace of island-hopping and his repeated protestations that his methods of assault rou-tinely resulted in fewer casualties, one may wonder what the rush was. Corregidor nominally blocked the entrance to Manila Bay, but repeated air attacks against ships and dock facilities in the harbor had left the port almost unusable. The island itself had been under heavy air and naval bombardment since January 22, and its garrison might well have withered on the vine along with others. Corregidor's capture, however, was to be far more symbolic than strategic.

469

On February 16, MacArthur ordered the 503rd Parachute Regimental Combat Team, the same unit that had made the daring jump into Nadzab, in New Guinea, in 1943 — to make a risky drop onto the narrow confines of Corregidor's Topside area while a reinforced battalion of the Twenty-Fourth Infantry Division came ashore near the South Dock. Willoughby's G-2 estimated that there were only nine hundred Japanese defenders on the island to oppose these two thousand paratroopers and another thousand of infantry, but the defenders actually numbered more than 5,200 troops. The 503rd suffered 280 casualties related to the jump — most attributable to causes other than enemy fire. The infantry came ashore to light resistance as most of the defenders took to Corregidor's labyrinthine network of tunnels and caves.[6]

That same day, MacArthur left his field headquarters at Hacienda Luisita and toured the front lines on Bataan. Driving in a jeep with only a small entourage, which included Egeberg, Lehrbas, and a handful of correspondents and armed infantrymen, MacArthur pushed along the eastern coast. This had been the route both of Wainwright's retreat and the subsequent death march, in the opposite direction. Once again, much to the consternation of Egeberg and Lehrbas, MacArthur insisted on proceeding well beyond any semblance of fixed lines, at one point coming upon a hastily abandoned Japanese camp that still had hot rice in the cooking pot.

Part of the reason for the excursion was MacArthur theater at its best — the pensive conqueror in cap and sunglasses pressing forward at the head of his troops. Even from his critics' perspective, there could be no doubt that Dugout Doug was dead. But for all his rigid pomp and choreographed actions, Douglas MacArthur was an intensely emotional private person. He had carried the burden of the defeat on Bataan — however he chose to characterize his own role in it — for three long years. Any responsibility he felt would never be washed away, but he needed to exorcise part of the guilt. Three times that day he confided to Egeberg, "You don't know what a leaden load this lifts from my heart."[7]

Back on Corregidor, the Japanese lost more than 1,500 men in three days of wild banzai charges. Then, on the night of February 21–22, as American infantry closed in around the Malinta Hill complex, an estimated two thousand Japanese committed mass suicide by igniting explosives that literally rocked the island. Nasty tunnel fighting lasted another week before the 503rd's commander, Colonel George M. Jones, reported the island secure on March 1.

The next day, MacArthur embarked the surviving members of his Bataan Gang on a symbolic flotilla of four PT boats and headed for Corregidor. From Topside to the depths of the Malinta Tunnel, MacArthur inspected the ruins where he had endured so much uncertainty, then drew himself up in front of the bent and battered flagpole. Echoing words he had cabled to the aging John J. Pershing a month earlier, MacArthur instructed Jones to "have your troops hoist the colors to its peak, and let no enemy ever haul them down."

Then he paid tribute to the defenders of Bataan and Corregidor and continued to exorcise the ghosts of his past. History would remember, he said, what had happened there "as one of the decisive battles of the world." Had Corregidor not held out, he continued, "Australia would have fallen, with incalculably disastrous results." Given Japanese war plans, the latter was almost certainly not true; however, decisive or not, Bataan and Corregidor would be forever etched in the American memory of World War II.[8]

The images of MacArthur at the front—from the Leyte landings until his return to Corregidor—also permanently etched the name of Douglas MacArthur onto that collective memory. His self-inflated aura had been a welcome and needed crutch in the dark days of 1942, and now, in the light of victory, the American public embraced him even more tightly. The weekly political report from the British embassy in Washington to London offered an outsider's appraisal of the Americans' reaction:

"MacArthur's 'I have returned,' his new cry of 'on to Tokyo' ... and the satisfying reversal of Japanese and American roles in the Philippines ... have touched off in the press one of the greater emotional outpourings of the Japanese war. Unstinted praise is being lavished upon MacArthur as a 'master strategist' and his champions, especially the Hearst-Patterson-McCormick press, have already renewed their campaign for MacArthur as supreme commander of all Allied forces in the Far East."[9] That battle concerning command had been raging since the beginning of the war, and it was about to come to a head.

*   *   *

What role was Douglas MacArthur to play in the Pacific thenceforth? It was a question with which Franklin Roosevelt and George Marshall had long grappled. MacArthur had repeatedly urged his appointment to a unified command of all Allied forces and the primacy of his SWPA line of advance. Roosevelt and Marshall had saved MacArthur from almost certain death in the Philippines and had earnestly provided him with far more men and equipment than MacArthur gave them credit for, even as they juggled the political realities of interservice rivalries and global commitments.

When faced with a decision to designate either Nimitz's Central Pacific Area or MacArthur's Southwest Pacific Area as the primary locus of the thrust against Japan, the Joint Chiefs had regularly delayed a decision, never categorically subordinating one theater to the other. The result was that the two lines of advance had finally met near the Philippines. With the Formosa option largely off the table, a single line of attack led northward from Luzon and the Marianas against the Japanese homeland. The line from the Central Pacific Area was clearly shorter.

In December of 1944, in between Leyte and Lingayen, MacArthur had made another run at Marshall on the issue. That time, however, he seems to have realized that butting heads with Ernie King and the US Navy remained pointless. He no longer recommended a unified command in the Pacific. In a change of direction, MacArthur told Marshall on December 17 that he was "of the firm opinion that the naval forces should serve under naval command and that the army should serve under army command. Neither service willingly fights on a major scale under the command of the other."[10]

That sentiment had been proved generally untrue throughout the Pacific, but what led MacArthur to his change of heart was that he looked ahead to the invasion of Japan itself, saw it as principally land-based, and was determined to be at its head. Were he to remain only CINCSWPA, the 1942 dividing line between the Southwest Pacific Area and Nimitz's Pacific Ocean Area would leave him with nothing to do north of Luzon. What MacArthur wanted was supreme command of all army and air force units throughout the Pacific.

When Marshall assured MacArthur that army planners were working on just such a revision to the 1942 Pacific command structure, MacArthur characteristically doubled down and pushed his point. "My anxiety over the completely faulty organization which now exists increases daily," he told Marshall, "and it is my confirmed belief, based upon recent battle experience, that if it is not repeat not promptly remedied the United States will face one of the greatest military disasters in its history."[11]

MacArthur was more emphatic in a draft of this communication that was never sent. He had considered saying: "It is evident that the emasculation of this command [SWPA] is contemplated despite the fact that it is commanded by the senior and most experienced U.S. Army commander in the Pacific, who has a highly integrated, competent and veteran staff, and under whom there has been an unbroken series of successful operations of the most complicated type ever undertaken." Without naming Nimitz or giving credit to any of the senior army commanders who had served under him in the Marianas, MacArthur asserted, "These great land forces are to be commanded by an Admiral who cannot possibly have the professional background, tactical or logistical, to accomplish such an Army mission."[12]

When the more tactful version was sent instead, MacArthur nonetheless called the command structure "the gravest issue in the Pacific that the country now faces" and strongly recommended that "if necessary the whole issue be placed before the President so that the responsibility for what may happen may not repeat not rest upon the army."[13]

When Secretary of war Stimson questioned Marshall on MacArthur's desire for unified army command in the Pacific, Marshall replied that MacArthur was correct in principle but "failed to recognize the limitations and exceptions" to those principles, including the fact that it would take some time to transfer the chain of command of army units under Nimitz to MacArthur, particularly those forces slated to invade Okinawa. According to Stimson, Marshall then "said what we both knew, that MacArthur is so prone to exaggerate and so influenced by his own desires that it is difficult to trust his judgment on such a matter."[14]

During early 1945, Marshall also faced two external issues when it came to the Pacific command structure and resulting deployments.

First, the anticipated transfer of troops from the European theater to the Pacific had been delayed by Germany's unexpected surge in the Battle of the Bulge. Second, the entry of the Soviet Union into the Pacific war and the ways that might affect Pacific strategy and manpower requirements against Japan's home islands was likely to be a topic at the upcoming Allied summit at Yalta.

Consequently, Marshall did not push the Joint Chiefs to address the change in command structure in the Pacific until February 26—after the Yalta Conference had revealed little that was new about Russia's intentions against Japan. Six weeks of back-and-forth between army and navy planners followed. Differences of opinion included Admiral King's continuing interest in operations against the coast of China north of Formosa and a Nimitz proposal to make Japan's home islands a separate theater of operations.[15]

President Roosevelt, whose health was rapidly failing after Yalta, does not seem to have been directly involved in these discussions, despite MacArthur's suggestion, but Admiral Leahy, who by then, with Roosevelt's encouragement, had assumed supervision of all White House matters, discussed the command structure with secretary of the navy James Forrestal at length. Forrestal had just returned from an extended Pacific trip that included an offshore tour of the fighting on Iwo Jima as well as conferences with Nimitz on Guam and MacArthur in Manila.

MacArthur had expressed the opinion to Forrestal that any help from China "would be negligible"—by then this was widely accepted—but he urged securing a Russian commitment to attack Manchuria and pin down the large numbers of Japanese troops there, preventing them from redeploying to defend the home islands. MacArthur insisted that this Russian pressure had to occur before any American attack on the main islands.

Leahy, who had written MacArthur a "Dear Doug" letter of congratulations for his "splendid progress through the rain and the mud" of Leyte and remained among MacArthur's biggest supporters, asked Forrestal his view of MacArthur.

"I told him," Forrestal recorded in his diary, "that I thought MacArthur had a high degree of professional ability, mortgaged, however, to his sensitivity and vanity. I said I thought if it were possible for him [MacArthur] to have a conversation with Nimitz in the same manner in which Admiral Leahy and I were now talking, these two men could evolve the framework for command on the basis of...the Navy to run the fleet, the Army to conduct the operations when land masses are reached." Forrestal declined to make a recommendation, but Leahy took from this conversation that the navy could be persuaded to accept the army position advocated by Marshall, his planners, and MacArthur.[16]

Finally, on April 3, two days after army troops and marines went ashore on Okinawa, the Joint Chiefs adopted the basic army proposal. MacArthur had gotten what he asked for and would be designated commander in chief of the US Army forces in the Pacific (CINCAF-PAC) and would command all army and most air force units there. (The eight hundred B-29s of the Twentieth Air Force pounding Japan from the Marianas remained a sometimes nebulous third partner, responsible directly to Hap Arnold and the Joint Chiefs.) Nimitz retained his CINCPAC and CINCPOA titles and would command all naval units in the Pacific, including Kinkaid's Seventh Fleet.

MacArthur was charged with responsibility for all land campaigns, while Nimitz was responsible for all fleet and amphibious operations. This directive effectively abolished the operational areas into which the Pacific had been carved in 1942, but it was not immediately as sweeping as it appeared. To secure Admiral King's approval, the chiefs agreed that this change would not disrupt Nimitz's current operations against Okinawa and that Nimitz and MacArthur would continue to command all forces of the other services in their respective theaters until they were transferred to the other command either by mutual agreement or JCS directive.

A JCS operational directive issued that same day tasked Nimitz with completing the occupation of Okinawa, subduing remaining elements of the Japanese fleet, and opening a sea route through La Perouse Strait, between Japan's northern island of Hokkaido and Sakhalin Island. The latter was partly to anticipate Russia's entry into the war but mostly to prevent Japanese troops in Manchuria from reinforcing the home islands, as MacArthur feared. MacArthur's orders were to "complete the occupation of Luzon and conduct such additional operations in the Philippines as required for the accomplishment of the over-all objective in the war against Japan" and to utilize Australian troops for the occupation of North Borneo. Pursuing both these objectives would not be without controversy.

MacArthur and Nimitz were also charged with supporting each other's operations in the Philippines and the Ryukyu Islands, principally Okinawa, and with cooperating with one another in planning and preparing for the land and sea campaign against Japan's home islands. That, too, would not prove to be as easy as Forrestal had hoped.[17]

MacArthur, however, was quite pleased. "My heartiest congratulations on your great success in reorganizing the Pacific Command," he cabled Marshall from Manila on April 5. "To have accomplished as much as you did amicably is a masterly performance. This represents an outstanding contribution not only to the Army, but to the country." Acknowledging that the public reception of "our solution for the Pacific has been gratifying," Marshall replied that he hoped that "mischievous cogitations and suggestions are now a thing of the past."[18]

Six days later, Franklin Roosevelt died.

Douglas MacArthur and Franklin Roosevelt had long cloaked their personal feelings for each other in gratuitous public pronouncements protecting their individual agendas and in gracious correspondence filled with dubious expressions of personal affection. And it is possible that after their final meeting, at Pearl Harbor in July of 1944, both men came away with some measure of new respect for the rigors the other had endured.

MacArthur had always wanted Roosevelt's job, however, and—his public protestations to the contrary—he had been convinced that he could perform it better than Roosevelt. Roosevelt had frequently found MacArthur to be a thorn in his side, but he adroitly used him, as he did most people, in support of his broad political objectives. If Bonner Fellers, MacArthur's onetime intelligence officer and military secretary, is to be believed, MacArthur let his mask of presidential cordiality slip upon learning of Roosevelt's death.

Riding together from MacArthur's headquarters to his residence in Manila, they talked of those who had passed on since the beginning of the war, but especially about Roosevelt. As MacArthur got out of the

car, he turned toward Fellers and said: "Well, the old man has gone—
a man who never told the truth if a lie would suffice!"[19] If MacArthur
truly made this comment, the irony is that many of his critics would
have said the same of him.

Having been given command of all army forces in the Pacific, MacArthur
sought to make the most of it. Hardly was the ink dry on the JCS orders of
April 3—cautioning a slow transition without disrupting ongoing Okinawa operations—when Sutherland, still MacArthur's chief of staff,
despite having had his wings clipped, Chamberlin, and Kenney swept
into Nimitz's headquarters on Guam. It was not a friendly meeting.

In his usual grating manner, Sutherland pushed for a firm schedule
detailing when army units under Nimitz's command, including those
on Okinawa, would pass to MacArthur. This rigid approach had not
been the intent of the Joint Chiefs. Nimitz and his staff found Sutherland's manner particularly galling because they were only two weeks
into the Okinawa campaign, and it was proving tough and unpredictable. Transfers from the logistics chain of army service units that were
interwoven with Nimitz's operations throughout the central Pacific,
especially on Guam and Saipan, were even more problematic.[20]

Kenney tried to brush off the resulting impasse by noting in his
account of the meetings that the "jurisdictional problems involved...
were so complicated that the dates and methods of transferring them
from the jurisdiction of one theater commander to the other could not
be settled at that conference."[21] Nimitz was blunter in his report to King.

Sutherland's mission to secure command for MacArthur was "con-
suming valuable time and delaying constructive planning" on operational matters, Nimitz told King. Nimitz stood firm about what he
would and would not release to MacArthur and when. Most distressing, Nimitz told King, was that "very little useful discussion has taken
place concerning invasion plans [for Japan] and preparations, and the
SWPA party was apparently not prepared for such discussion." Sutherland was nevertheless able to state categorically what Nimitz termed
"an interesting sidelight," namely, that "MacArthur will land in Kyushu
about D+3, stay a short time and then return to Manila until time for
the Honshu landing."[22]

With little accomplished, Sutherland and his party returned to Manila, while King took Nimitz's concerns straight to George Marshall. Sometimes it is more informative to read the drafts of unsent messages than the final text of those sent. Witness the message to MacArthur prepared by Marshall's War Department staff in response. "Disturbing information has reached me from Admiral King," the draft began, that "would appear to indicate a complete lack of understanding on Sutherland's part," including Sutherland's assertions that unity of command was unworkable and that after Okinawa "no Army troops would be allowed to serve under an Admiral."

"It is very embarrassing for me to feel compelled to take up with you a question of the employment of your staff officer," the draft continued, "but I seriously doubt the advisability of utilizing Sutherland in further negotiations with the Navy." Then came a broadside that King might well have delivered: "Our experience with Sutherland here in the War Department and certainly the Navy experience with him has been that, whatever his natural ability in many ways, he appears to be totally lacking in the faculty of dealing with others in negotiations on difficult matters."

The draft ended by noting, "After long and trying negotiations covering months we have reached a basis for resolving the command situation in the Pacific so as gradually to arrive at a solution which would be not only workable but acceptable to both War and Navy Departments." That said, further negotiations on that solution "would present extraordinary difficulties if conducted for you by Sutherland."[23]

The letter that Marshall chose to send instead may say more about Marshall's command style in dealing with MacArthur than the suggested draft reveals about the War Department's bitter feelings toward the general's chief of staff. "After considering the messages concerning the progress being made in the reorganization in the Pacific," Marshall began, "I believe that you personally should meet with Admiral Nimitz in the near future in a personal effort to resolve between yourselves the problems which have arisen rather than depending upon your respective staff officers."

Hinting that it was important to resolve these matters prior to the Joint Chiefs issuing orders to MacArthur to execute landings on

Kyushu, Marshall deftly played to MacArthur's ego and concluded: "I feel certain that you personally can handle the situation and avoid a breach that might well have tragic consequences." No specific mention was made of Sutherland.[24]

The result was that, as he had done two years previously with Halsey and, before that, with Nimitz, MacArthur once again rolled out the red carpet. It was impossible, he said, for him to leave his headquarters in Manila, but he bade Nimitz a cordial welcome there. Ever the salt of the earth, Nimitz flew to Manila on May 16 and worked out the details of the Joint Chiefs' April 3 charge directly with MacArthur. Sutherland's brash talk of no army troops serving under an admiral was brushed aside. Most significant, the procedure that had long been employed in SWPA campaigns—that an admiral would command the amphibious phase until such time as a general established suitable headquarters ashore—was confirmed. Other points of agreement included marine air and ground units operating under army control when they were part of landing forces or when they were acting in close concert.[25]

These agreements between MacArthur and Nimitz were positive, but they didn't end all rivalries or jockeying for position. When Marshall suggested to MacArthur a few weeks later that King was strongly in favor of MacArthur's being at Nimitz's headquarters on Guam during the naval buildup for the Kyushu landings to foster coordination, MacArthur was emphatic in his reply. "This suggestion is impracticable of accomplishment," he wrote Marshall. "Please tell Admiral King," MacArthur went on, "that I disagree totally with his concept and that a long campaign experience has convinced me that if there is any one feature of a field commander that must be left to his sole judgment it is the location of his command post and the actual disposition of his own person."[26]

This was MacArthur's rationale for his whereabouts over the course of the war. One moment he was seemingly intractably anchored to his headquarters—whether in Brisbane, Tacloban, or Manila—and the next he was off on wide-ranging frontline visits, frequently out of communication with his superiors and subordinates, to locations such as Los Negros, Morotai, and Leyte. In this instance, there was simply no way that MacArthur was going to allow himself to be headquartered, however briefly, in Nimitz's domain. It was a question of ego, not a question of his ability to leave Manila. Even as he penned these lines to Marshall, MacArthur had just returned from a conqueror's tour of the southern Philippines and northern Borneo, and ten days later he would not hesitate to embark on more of the same.

MacArthur's orders from the Joint Chiefs announcing his role in the invasion of the Japanese home islands left much room for discretion regarding the remainder of the Philippines. They instructed him to complete the occupation of Luzon and conduct "such additional operations in the Philippines as required for the accomplishment of the overall objective in the war." Strictly speaking, "such additional operations" were to be undertaken only if they were essential to Japan's defeat.[27] But when issued, this directive was already well behind MacArthur's activities in the field.

Given that he was so concerned about having command of the push northward to Japan, as well as his increasingly acclaimed tactic of island-hopping past strongholds, MacArthur nonetheless sent Eichelberger's Eighth Army south from Luzon, even as Manila was barely secure, to attack isolated garrisons throughout the southern half of the archipelago. These targets were of dubious strategic value to "the overall objective in the war," and instead the Eighth Army might well have supported Krueger's Sixth Army against Yamashita's Shobu and Shimbu Groups, which were putting up strong resistance in northern Luzon and, arguably, still posed a threat to Manila.

Nonetheless, Eighth Army operations south of Luzon included landings at Puerto Princesa, on Palawan, on February 28; Zamboanga, in western Mindanao, on March 10; Iloilo, on Panay, on March 18; Cebu on March 27; Tawi Tawi and Jolo, in the Sulu Archipelago, on April 2 and 9 respectively; and Cagayan, in central Mindanao, on May 10. These pretty well covered the entire Philippines.

To be sure, MacArthur had multiple genuine reasons for conducting these operations, including the urgent need to liberate POW camps and rescue the general populace from last-ditch Japanese reprisals, but when MacArthur had said, "I shall return," the man who in the fall of 1941 had convinced the War Department that he could defend the

480

Pacific Operations 1945

50°N

Bering Sea

U.S.S.R.

Sea of Okhotsk

Aleutian Islands

Kuril Islands

La Pérouse Str.

Sea of Japan

Hokkaido

KOREA

JAPAN

Tokyo

PACIFIC

OCEAN

International Date Line

Kyushu

Proposed Nov 1945

CHINA

East China Sea

Okinawa

Iwo Jima

Feb–Mar

Formosa

Apr–Jun

20°N

Mariana Islands

FRENCH INDOCHINA

South China Sea

PHILIPPINES

Saipan

Guam

Wake Island

Manila

Apr–May

Jun 10

Philippine Sea

Eniwetok

Marshall Islands

Caroline Islands

Kwajalein

Truk

Brunei

Mindanao

Palau Islands

Makin

Gilbert Islands

Tarakan

May 1

Jul 1

Kwajalein

Tarawa

0°

Borneo

Balikpapan

Hollandia

Admiralty Islands

Equator

Java

NEW GUINEA

Rabaul

Solomon Islands

Timor

NETHERLANDS INDIES

Port Moresby

Guadalcanal

Darwin

Coral Sea

New Hebrides

Fiji

Townsville

20°S

Nouméa

New Caledonia

AUSTRALIA

Brisbane

Perth

Canberra

NEW ZEALAND

Melbourne

40°S

0   1000 Miles

Wellington

120°E

140°E

160°E

180°

entire archipelago meant that he would return and free every last island. Quite simply, he wanted to be seen as the liberator of *all* the Philippines.

The result was that by the time MacArthur was given command of all army units in the Pacific and he was pointed at last toward Japan itself, he had already done far more than was necessary, in a strategic sense, in the Philippines. He even was preparing for additional operations in Borneo and the Netherlands East Indies—again despite the dubious nature that late in the war of their strategic importance to the ultimate defeat of Japan.[28]

On June 3, 1945, MacArthur sailed from Manila on the *Boise* to make a victory lap—a "grand tour," as Eichelberger called it—of these recent and pending operations. With a party that included Egeberg, Fellers, and Eichelberger, MacArthur watched a blazing sunset as the *Boise* cruised past Corregidor and headed south, first to Mindoro. The next stop was Cagayan, on Mindanao.

The *Boise* would double back north for other ports of call on Cebu, Negros, and Panay, but the purpose of this straight shot to Cagayan went without saying. The ship was retracing almost to the mile MacArthur's harrowing ride aboard PT-41 as he escaped from Corregidor. Among the points MacArthur wanted to visit was the old Del Monte plantation house, where he and his family had hunkered down awaiting B-17s. All that was left of it were bombed-out foundations overgrown with vegetation.

Eichelberger temporarily left the party at Iloilo, on Panay, while MacArthur headed west across the Sulu Sea on June 8 for Puerto Princesa, on Palawan. MacArthur had tried to persuade Kenney to accompany him on the entire tour, saying the rest would do him good, but Kenney begged off and promised to join up with him on Palawan, which he did.[29]

Together they would then observe the landings at Brunei Bay, on the northwest coast of Borneo. MacArthur had gotten his way and was pushing into the Netherlands East Indies, but he could not have done so without notable assistance from the Australian forces that he had relegated to supporting roles ever since New Guinea.

*   *   *

For well over a year, there had been growing criticism in Australia's press as well as its Parliament over MacArthur's use of Australian forces. From their perspective, not only had the Allied commander assigned them mop-up operations in bypassed areas that had proved much more heavily defended than MacArthur's communiqués suggested, he also had given them meager supplies and secondhand equipment with which to accomplish the missions.

This Australian disgruntlement was tightly managed under MacArthur's strict censorship. Verbose as his headquarters was on some matters, it clamped the lid tightly on matters unfavorable to him. As the *Canberra Times* snidely put it at the beginning of 1945, "Will anyone knowing the whereabouts of Australian soldiers in action in the South-West Pacific Area please communicate at once with the Australian Government?"[30]

While MacArthur had resisted getting involved in Java in the dark days of 1942, he subsequently tried to convince the Joint Chiefs of the political importance of freeing the Netherlands East Indies to keep faith with the Dutch government. This argument had little to do with the overall strategic objective of defeating Japan by moving north, and the Joint Chiefs were not swayed by it.

Admiral King, however, wanted to provide the British fleet, which Churchill was determined to deploy in the Pacific, with a port far removed from the US Navy's general area of operations. Brunei Bay fit the bill perfectly — never mind that the British were told of the plan only belatedly and rejected it. Then when MacArthur insisted that East Indies operations could be undertaken with Australian forces and that the Australians were upset because their troops were not in action, northern Borneo was added to MacArthur's charge.[31]

The first assault in the Borneo campaign, by a brigade of the Australian Ninth Division, came on May 1 against the small island of Tarakan, off the northeast coast. Its primary objective was to secure an airfield that could be used to support the Brunei Bay landings as well as assaults farther south against oil fields around Balikpapan. While Allied air and naval forces shepherded these troops ashore with little opposition, Japanese ground defenders once again proved more tenacious than anticipated.

Amphibious chief Dan Barbey stoked Aussie resentment by claiming that the Australians were behind the times in landing operations and that the Japanese wouldn't have been able to move inland and fortify themselves so strongly had the attackers moved more expeditiously. The Australian brigade commander replied that the problem was that the soldiers had to perform too much manual labor as a result of having inadequate equipment.

Joseph "Ben" Chifley, the acting Australian prime minister, appointed in the wake of John Curtin's rapidly declining health, took up the refrain and complained to MacArthur. The Allied commander replied tartly that he was "entirely at a loss to account for any criticism of the Tarakan operation. It has been completely successful and has been accomplished without the slightest hitch. The equipment and methods were essentially the same as those used in nearly forty amphibious landings in this area, all of which have been victorious."

As Curtin had over the years, Chifley bowed to MacArthur's version of the situation and assured the Australian Parliament that he deplored "these irresponsible criticisms which are unfair to the Supreme Commander, in whom the Government has entire confidence."[32]

But Chifley's pronouncement did not quell Aussie criticisms about the value of excursions south through Borneo as well as the manner in which they were executed. Chifley asked MacArthur to divert the veteran Australian Seventh Division northward from operations in Borneo — even if it meant delaying or dropping the planned Balikpapan invasion. Simply put, the Aussies wanted to participate in the invasion of Japan.

MacArthur claimed no knowledge of any plans for Australian troop deployments directly against Japan — they were, of course, his to make — and lectured Chifley in return that the Borneo campaign had been authorized by the Joint Chiefs under its charge from the Combined Chiefs of Staff. Unless the Australian government elected to withdraw its Seventh Division from his command, it would follow his orders or risk disordering not only the immediate plan but also the long-term strategy. Once again, Chifley acquiesced and responded that his government absolutely intended to support the SWPA agreement of 1942 and that of course the Seventh Division could be used at Balikpapan.[33]

A few weeks later, on June 10, two brigades of the Australian Ninth Division, which had been in the thick of things at Sanananda and Finschhafen, landed on the northwestern coast of Borneo off Brunei Bay as MacArthur and Kenney watched from the deck of the *Boise.* As was becoming the norm, the initial landings were largely unopposed, but Japanese troops withdrew inland and established tough defensive positions in the surrounding hills. This time, no one seems to have questioned the utility of the Australian troops.

MacArthur, Kenney, and their party went ashore and conducted one of MacArthur's patented walkabouts. After a photographer standing next to MacArthur was struck by a sniper's bullet, Kenney, Fellers, and Egeberg attempted to persuade the general to return to the *Boise,* but he insisted upon continuing. Finally he came face-to-face with an unimpressed Australian colonel who brashly told the five-star general that he was impeding his combat operations and asked him to leave the area.

Back aboard the *Boise,* MacArthur indulged in a chocolate sundae and cranked out a communiqué praising the Brunei landing with his usual superlatives, including the assertion that it and the one on Tarakan "took the enemy by surprise." He further asserted that the Japanese were "unprepared to offer effective resistance, and consequently our casualties have been negligible."[34]

Wartime casualty totals for the Southwest Pacific Area versus the Central Pacific Area do not square, however, with MacArthur's standard claims of having accomplished more with less of everything and in the process having sustained lower casualties. Allied casualties in ground campaigns in the Pacific totaled 196,661, of which 48,490 were deaths, in MacArthur's Southwest Pacific Area and 108,906 casualties, of which 28,716 were deaths, in Nimitz's South Pacific and Central Pacific Areas. MacArthur's losses included 9,353 Australian deaths.

For air, ground, and sea casualties, the US Army and Army Air Forces calculated 160,276 casualties in the Pacific campaigns, of which 55,145 were deaths, and the US Navy and Marine Corps estimated casualties of 127,294, of which 48,426 were deaths, for a total killed of

103,571. Approximately one in three of these American deaths (39,137) occurred on the ground in MacArthur's theater. Whatever else MacArthur's operations accomplished, they did not produce comparably few casualties, as he routinely claimed.[35]

The grand tour continued. *Boise* cruised eastward and called at Jolo, in the Sulu Archipelago, where Eichelberger rejoined him for visits to Davao, on the southern coast of Mindanao, and Zamboanga. Along the way, MacArthur confided to Eichelberger that he did not believe "there were four thousand Japanese left alive on Mindanao." According to Eichelberger, the surrender figures at war's end—twenty-three thousand soldiers—"show how wrong he was."[36]

Eichelberger remained in Zamboanga to oversee continuing operations in the southern islands, and MacArthur sailed into Manila on June 15. He did not plan to stay long. On June 27, he embarked again with his usual retinue, this time on the light cruiser *Cleveland,* and sailed south for Borneo. The first stop was Tawi Tawi, followed by a rendezvous with the amphibious force bound for Balikpapan.

MacArthur had long stressed the importance of cutting Japan's lifeline to Borneo's oil fields, particularly Balikpapan, the second-largest oil center in the East Indies. Halsey's Third Fleet and submarine operations had pretty well severed this lifeline by then, but an impressive array of land defenses remained. MacArthur responded by ordering sixteen days of air and naval bombardment prior to the Australian Seventh Division going ashore, the longest preassault bombardment of World War II.[37]

When the Aussies finally landed, they met little resistance but also found little of value left at Balikpapan's refineries. In contrast to the circumstances surrounding the Tarakan landings, the strong showing of American naval, air, and logistics in support of the Seventh Division blunted criticism of these specific Borneo operations even as Australians generally continued to question their overall strategic intent. The Borneo operations did not appear to be a case of island-hopping or bypassing enemy strongholds.

The real irony was pointed out by the Australian official history of the war, which reminded one and all that, this late in the war, in 1945, there were still considerable Australian forces that had been "left behind" to clean up MacArthur's bypassed pockets all the way back to the Solomons. Without the concentration of American air and naval power that MacArthur was directing in his van, they were the ones who had been left to operate on the proverbial shoestring MacArthur had long railed about. As Australian historian Gavin Long observed, "An Australian corps in Bougainville and an Australian division in New Guinea were fighting long and bitter campaigns (whose value was doubted) in which they were short of air and naval support."[38]

On July 1, MacArthur and his party went ashore at Balikpapan as usual, this time around an hour after the first wave had hit the beach. As Egeberg remembered it, he had just returned from fetching two chocolate sundaes—MacArthur seems to have developed an insatiable taste for them—and "an eager-beaver, excited idiot" rushed in to inform MacArthur, "You can't go ashore now, General. The enemy is putting a heavy barrage on the beach." According to Egeberg, "That ended our sundaes." MacArthur put his down and two minutes later signaled Barbey that he intended to go ashore immediately.[39]

Barbey tried to dissuade him, but finding that impossible, he rushed a landing craft to embark MacArthur, a few of his staff, some war correspondents, and a camera crew. "As usual," wrote Barbey, who remained the rumpled and approachable "Uncle Dan" to his officers and men, "MacArthur was immaculately dressed with well-pressed khaki trousers carrying light tan gloves." Coming upon a hardened and dirty lot of Seventh Division veterans, MacArthur asked, "How goes it, gentlemen?" and was met with stupefied looks. MacArthur moved on in uneasy silence.[40]

That night, the *Cleveland* weighed anchor and steamed back to Manila, arriving there on the afternoon of July 3, but these junkets through the southern Philippines and around Borneo illuminated two telling aspects of MacArthur's command persona—even if they were not fully recognized at the time.

The first was the strategic necessity and authorization for the operations themselves. By the time the Joint Chiefs issued their April 3, 1945, directive approving operations in the southern Philippines and on Borneo, MacArthur had already undertaken eight of eleven planned amphibious operations to secure the territory. He was well ahead of his superiors and moving in a direction opposite the main thrust against Japan. Far from bypassing enemy strongholds, the reputed island-hopper attacked them directly.[41]

Indeed, MacArthur's fixation on the entire Philippines and points in the East Indies is a key negative in evaluating MacArthur as a strategist. In the confines of strategy in the Pacific, MacArthur rightly appreciated the importance of cutting Japan's lifeline of natural resources from the East Indies. But after American submarines and carrier raids largely severed that pipeline, and after B-29s leveled the homeland industries it fed, MacArthur continued to press this point as justification for his campaigns against the southern Philippines and the East Indies. Out of his commitment to return to the entire Philippines, MacArthur refused to isolate and bypass major garrisons even after tough fighting on Leyte and Luzon. Instead he undertook operations during 1945 that were almost linear island-by-island campaigns.

The second aspect of these trips was MacArthur's continued personal excursions into combat zones and his seemingly flagrant disregard for his own safety as well as that of his party. That late in the war, that close to victory, such ventures had no military or morale-boosting purpose. They evidenced a disconcerting mix of fatalism and invincibility that can only be characterized as selfish aggrandizement. Nonetheless, at the time, the Joint Chiefs were not inclined to question or curb MacArthur's geographic expanses, and war correspondents' reports of his exploits ashore only served to burnish his warrior image with the general public. He was indeed the conquering hero, one who was about to have his greatest moment.

CHAPTER TWENTY-FIVE

"These Proceedings Are Closed"

Two days after MacArthur returned to Manila from the Balikpapan landings, his headquarters issued one of his patented communiqués— premature in its report of total victory and exaggerated in its character- ization of the strategic importance of his operations. "The entire Philippine Islands are now liberated and the Philippine Campaign can be regarded as virtually closed," it began. Never mind that the "isolated action of a guerrilla nature" of which MacArthur spoke was in fact large-scale resistance still opposing Krueger's Sixth Army on Luzon and Eichelberger's Eighth Army throughout the southern islands.

MacArthur characterized the Philippines as a wedge in the Japanese center from which strategic drives would continue both to the north and to the south and compared the archipelago to the British Isles as a gigan- tic base for future Allied operations. MacArthur indeed had plans for further operations into the Netherlands East Indies, particularly against Java. But by then, the Joint Chiefs had ordered both MacArthur and Nimitz to prepare for the invasion of Kyushu around November 1, and long before Okinawa was secured, late in June, there was no question that this operation—certainly not Java—would be the major focus.[1]

Left unreported was a July 1 operations summary from Krueger that his Sixth Army troops had counted 173,000 Japanese dead to that point on Luzon, and the enemy was still fighting in strength. The casualties "may be of interest to you," Krueger told MacArthur, because they were twenty thousand more than the number of Japanese troops Willoughby estimated to be on Luzon when the first wave of American troops splashed ashore in Lingayen Gulf.[2]

Despite the increasing sophistication of Ultra intercepts, Willoughby's interpretations of them remained suspect. As recently as the landings at Tarakan, Willoughby became distraught when an Australian general disagreed with him over the size of the Japanese garrison there. Later hard fighting proved the Australian right in his larger numbers.[3]

MacArthur supposedly once claimed that there had been "only two outstanding intelligence officers in all of military history and mine is not one of them."[4] Willoughby is a prime example that MacArthur was not always well served by his staff, but his loyalty to them, especially if they were part of the Bataan Gang, frequently caused him to overlook their individual weaknesses. Willoughby would remain with MacArthur until Korea.

The track record of MacArthur's chief intelligence officer did not bode well for the campaign against Kyushu. Throughout the spring, War Department plans for this direct stab at the Japanese homeland had been kept fluid by the continuing debate over blockade versus invasion as the final strategic move of the Pacific war. Although Admirals Leahy and King generally favored a blockade with continued air assault, they acquiesced to Marshall's arguments that only troops on the ground could subdue fanatical resistance, and, in any event, Kyushu was essential to both tightening a blockade and increasing the bombing campaign against Honshu. But what sort of resistance would they face on the ground?

Throughout the summer, Ultra intercepts showed increasing numbers of Japanese forces on Kyushu, including a massing of the type of kamikaze-style aircraft that had given Nimitz's fleet so much grief off Okinawa. Nimitz admitted to King that his support for an invasion was wavering and that, given the length and cost of the Okinawa campaign, "it would be unrealistic to expect that such obvious objectives as southern Kyushu and the Tokyo Plain will not be as well defended as Okinawa."[5]

Not only did Ultra show huge numbers of reinforcements pouring into Kyushu, including the large kamikaze air component, it also revealed the Japanese to be heavily fortifying the three primary beachheads that the Americans had selected for the invasion. Even Willoughby tried to backtrack and raise his estimates of Japanese defenders, but MacArthur would not hear of it. When Marshall questioned MacArthur directly on Ultra revelations, MacArthur's reply, according to Ultra historian Edward Drea, "typified a classic bullheaded operations officer determined to press boldly ahead regardless of intelligence reports highlighting potential hazards."

First, MacArthur claimed that the Ultra intelligence was greatly exaggerated, and he discredited the heavy strength reported in southern Kyushu. Second, even if the Japanese were massing in southern Kyushu, MacArthur said that Allied airpower would immobilize ground forces and crush them before the invasion, an assertion that flew in the face of their experience at Leyte and on Luzon, where air operations proved no guarantee of quick victory against large numbers of fortified troops. Finally, MacArthur told Marshall that his G-2 — ultimately, Willoughby — had invariably overestimated the enemy in every situation when just the opposite had generally been true.

Drea is pointed in his conclusion: "Flush with victory, convinced of his destiny, and poised to culminate his military career by leading the greatest amphibious operation history ever witnessed, MacArthur reasoned away intelligence that contradicted his plans for bringing down the curtain on World War II."[6]

Marshall's concerns about Kyushu defenses and MacArthur's haughty assurance not to worry played right into the hands of Admiral King, who had long been planning — the Joint Chiefs' recent decision notwithstanding — to revisit the blockade-versus-invasion issue before committing his fleet to operations that would likely include another furious kamikaze onslaught. Knowing that Nimitz had similar concerns, King decided to send Marshall's query and MacArthur's response to Nimitz for comment and instructed him to copy MacArthur in his reply.

If Nimitz reiterated his growing concerns about the Kyushu operation, as King assumed he would, it would give King the perfect opportunity to revisit the entire invasion plan with the Joint Chiefs. At the same time, of course, such backpedaling would be a major blow to MacArthur's plans and the army-navy cooperation that both MacArthur and Nimitz had been directed to nurture. Nimitz no doubt understood that King was putting him in a bit of a box, and he decided to take his time responding.[7] His delay proved shrewd, as the rush of events in early August of 1945 overshadowed the Kyushu plans and left all parties talking about the impact of dropping atomic bombs as well as the Soviet Union's long-awaited declaration of war against Japan.

The preliminary to dropping the first atomic bomb on Hiroshima was the Potsdam Declaration. Issued by representatives of the United States, Great Britain, and China meeting in postwar Germany—the Soviet Union was present but technically still neutral vis-à-vis Japan— it called for Japan's immediate and unconditional surrender to avoid complete destruction. When factions within the Japanese government dallied, some of them blindly hoping the Soviet Union might broker better terms, President Harry Truman ordered an atomic bomb dropped whenever weather permitted after August 3. The Twentieth Air Force carried out this directive on August 6.[8]

Much would be made of MacArthur's subsequent views on the unconditional surrender requirement of the Potsdam Declaration and the use of the atomic bomb. At the time, however, he was not consulted about the former and largely ignorant of the latter. Unlike the unconditional surrender pronouncement against Germany at the end of the Tehran conference, the Potsdam Declaration was made with some input from the military. Marshall and the Joint Chiefs were proponents, although Marshall did not ask MacArthur's advice as a field commander. In hindsight, MacArthur would say that he would have insisted that the Japanese be assured of their emperor retaining a central role.[9]

As for the atomic bomb, a War Department representative briefed MacArthur on the bomb's existence in late July, mostly in the context of making certain that Kenney's air operations avoided cities designated as likely targets. Dr. Karl T. Compton, president of MIT and a member of the presidential advisory committee on the bomb's use, visited Manila and briefed MacArthur more fully on its capabilities the day after the Hiroshima attack.

In later years, MacArthur claimed that the use of the bomb had been "completely unnecessary from a military point of view" because Japan was about to surrender, but that differs from his repeated assertions at the time that a ground invasion would be needed to bring about a final capitulation. Some of MacArthur's subsequent views may have been colored by his not having been consulted about the unconditional surrender clause or told earlier about the bomb. Then, too, the bomb kept him from command of what likely would have surpassed the Normandy invasion as history's greatest amphibious operation.[10]

The afternoon before news of the Hiroshima bomb reached Manila, MacArthur held an off-the-record briefing for around two dozen correspondents at his headquarters. As usual with these gatherings, it proved to be an hourlong discourse by MacArthur on a range of subjects. James J. Halsema, then a reporter for the *Manila Daily Bulletin,* was among the journalists in attendance. Halsema had been the editor of the paper's Baguio edition before the war and endured three years of captivity in Bilibid prison.

Off the record or not, Halsema kept detailed notes on what he called MacArthur's "amazing range of subjects." Among them were the general's opinions that the war might end sooner than many expected, that the Japanese navy was impotent and their shipping destroyed, and that the Japanese army was still large but it would be impossible to arm the civilian population effectively against an invasion.

There was, however, one old refrain that MacArthur couldn't resist singing once again — perhaps it had by then simply become a matter of habit. Despite facts proving that there had been a massive inflow of men and equipment into the Southwest Pacific Area and the entire Pacific theater, MacArthur expressed the hope that "the Balikpapan landing would be the last show he had to pull on a shoestring."

As for Kyushu, he gave no public hint of when the landings might occur, but it was generally assumed that any invasion of Japan's main islands would not take place until the fall. Nonetheless, MacArthur said he planned to go north shortly. As for the Russians, he welcomed their expected participation in the war and noted that it had been "planned since the days when we were much less sure of the outcome than we are now." Talking about a major Russian encirclement of Manchuria, the general added, "Every Russian killed was one less American who had to be."[11] Two days later, the Soviet Union indeed declared war on Japan.

*　　*　　*

While Roosevelt and Churchill had long recognized and valued the Soviet Union's contribution to the war in Europe, what the Russian bear would do—and when—against its old adversary in the Far East had been a matter of lengthy conjecture. Stalin's promise at Tehran in late 1943 that Russia would enter the war against Japan after Germany's defeat was little more than a hint of his intentions. At Yalta in February of 1945, he finally put forth a timetable of two to three months after Germany's defeat. Germany finally surrendered to Eisenhower on May 7.[12]

MacArthur, who, it will be remembered, was once briefly considered as a possible ambassador to Russia to get him out of the Pacific command cauldron, was on record multiple times throughout the war as favoring a Russian second front in the Pacific. Once again, however, his postwar hindsight—particularly as the Cold War deepened—would attempt to modify or even refute this position.

It was easy enough to explain his interest in Russian intervention as a potential diversion of Japanese attention from his theater in the dark days of 1942, but by February of 1945, he was on record still pressing this point in meetings with secretary of the navy Forrestal and Brigadier General George A. Lincoln, of Marshall's staff. The latter's visit to Manila after Yalta is particularly instructive, because Marshall sent one of his inner circle, as he had done after all previous strategic conferences, to report the decisions related to the Pacific—one more example of the fact that, far from ignoring or isolating MacArthur, Marshall went to great lengths to keep him informed.

MacArthur's response to the Yalta conversations on this occasion was to tell Lincoln that every effort should be made to get Russia into the war before any invasion of Japan took place. MacArthur pointed out that the Russians wanted a warm-water port, likely Port Arthur. He considered it impracticable to deny it because of their military power, so in return, he thought it "only right they should share the cost in blood in defeating Japan." Far from believing that Russian intervention was by then "superfluous," as he later wrote in his memoirs, he continued to espouse support for Russian intervention to the Joint Chiefs as late as June 18 and clearly hoped that Russian operations in

Manchuria would divert Japanese attention away from his proposed Kyushu landings.[13]

In the rush of events during midsummer, the Joint Chiefs, who had also been encouraging Russian involvement, suddenly came to grips with the prospect of a rapid Japanese collapse. If this occurred, Russian troops making huge territorial gains in Manchuria, and even invading Hokkaido, was a possibility. The chiefs had only to look to the territorial race in Germany that spring to gauge its likelihood. Evidence made public after the 1989 collapse of the Soviet Union revealed that, noncommittal though Stalin may have appeared to Roosevelt and Churchill, he indeed had ambitions in the Far East in 1945 that extended well beyond Manchuria and Korea to Japan itself.[14]

Predicting some of this, the Joint Chiefs sent MacArthur a message while they were still at Potsdam warning him that it might be necessary for him to take prompt action on the Japanese mainland, possibly before a Russian entry into the war. The chiefs also asked War Department staff to provide information on MacArthur's plans for occupying Japan in the event of a rapid Japanese collapse. Told that MacArthur was prepared to land occupation forces against moderate opposition twelve days after Japan's surrender, the chiefs advised MacArthur and Nimitz that coordination of their plans in the event of the same "is now a pressing necessity."[15]

When the Soviet Union declared war on Japan on August 8 and unleashed its troops along the Manchurian border, MacArthur's statement at the time remained unequivocal: "I am delighted at the Russian declaration of war against Japan," his press release of August 9 proclaimed. "This will make possible a great pincer movement which cannot fail to end in the destruction of the enemy."[16]

But it was rapidly becoming a dicey ballet: the United States wanted the Soviet Union to get involved in order to save American lives and speed the end of the war, but Soviet moves in Europe had already telegraphed that the peace would be adversarial. As the British embassy in Washington reported in its weekly dispatch to London, "It becomes daily more evident that the United States of America sees Soviet Russia as its only rival for world supremacy and at the same time has no desire to become embroiled with her."[17]

495

*   *   *

On August 10, the day after a second atomic bomb was dropped, this time on Nagasaki, the Japanese government agreed to the Potsdam terms on the condition that the sovereignty of the emperor would be preserved. Acting for the Allies, the United States accepted this accommodation provided it was understood that the authority of the emperor and the Japanese government would be subject to an appointed supreme commander for the Allied powers, who would take whatever steps were necessary to effectuate the unconditional surrender terms.[18]

There was never much question about who the supreme commander would be. The wheels had been set in motion the previous spring, when MacArthur was appointed commander in chief of US Army forces in the Pacific. Short of someone being dispatched from Washington, which no one seems to have seriously considered, the only other likely candidate was Nimitz. Despite Nimitz's qualifications and accomplishments, MacArthur had two major considerations in his favor. Not only would the occupation of Japan require ground forces, but MacArthur had also led Allied troops and been designated an Allied commander in chief. This was an easy decision, lacking the angst frequently associated with MacArthur, and President Truman made it on August 12.

Three days later, on what would be designated V-J Day—August 15, 1945—MacArthur received his formal orders as supreme commander for the Allied powers. He alone was to accept Japan's signed surrender document on behalf of the United States, China, the United Kingdom, the Soviet Union, and "the other United Nations at war with Japan," thus making it clear to the Russians that their request to preside as coequals was firmly denied.

MacArthur was further to require Imperial General Headquarters to issue such orders as necessary to arrange the surrender of Japanese forces in the field. There was to be no question that the authority of the emperor and Japanese government would be subject to MacArthur's directives and that he would exercise supreme command over all land, sea, and air forces of the Allied powers engaged in the occupation. By any standard, it was a sweeping delegation. Lest the US Navy feel slighted, the same directive appointed Fleet Admiral Chester W. Nimitz to represent the United States at the surrender ceremony.[19]

MacArthur acknowledged his orders promptly, telling Truman, "I am deeply grateful for the confidence you have so generously bestowed upon me...I shall do everything possible to capitalize this situation along the magnificently constructive lines you have conceived for the peace of the world."[20] Having sent Eisenhower the original of Roosevelt's directive appointing him to command Overlord, Marshall then sent MacArthur Truman's signed original of the directive designating him supreme commander for the Allied powers.[21]

MacArthur, however, had little time to celebrate. On August 19, a sixteen-man delegation headed by Lieutenant General Torashiro Kawabe, vice chief of the Imperial Japanese Army general staff, flew to Manila on MacArthur's instructions and delivered extensive data on Japanese army, airfield, and naval facilities as well as POW camps. Giving a hint that the Japanese were not the only ones with an emperor largely unseen behind the palace moat, MacArthur never met directly with this delegation. Instead it was Sutherland, along with Dick Marshall, Willoughby, Chamberlin, and others, who undertook the negotiations about how and when American forces would land in Japan.[22]

By their own admission, the Japanese were worried about unrest and disobedience among their troops, especially kamikaze pilots at Atsugi Naval Air Base, near Yokohama, where advance units of the Eleventh Airborne Division were scheduled to land. Sutherland agreed to postpone their landing from August 23 to August 26; the remainder of the division was to land two days later.

Turning to a Washington-drafted proclamation for Emperor Hirohito to read, the Japanese were disturbed to find an informal pronoun used for "I" in the phrase "I, Hirohito, Emperor of Japan," instead of the formal pronoun. Told this was of critical importance to their countrymen's acceptance of the surrender and future cooperation, Sutherland took the matter up with MacArthur, who readily agreed to the change, demonstrating the sensitivity to Japanese traditions he would employ during the years of occupation.[23]

As busy as the days of August were for MacArthur, there were moments of introspection that ran the gamut of the emotions he routinely held in check. Part of it was a melancholy, not unlike that experienced by many senior officers at the close of World War II, that ensued when he realized he had passed the great watershed of his life.

Two days after the first atomic bomb was dropped, veteran war correspondent Theodore H. White called on MacArthur in Manila. White was hurrying back to his post in China, but he wanted to get MacArthur's appraisal of what it meant. White reported that MacArthur was "no longer roaring as he used to roar" as he discussed the bomb. "White," MacArthur asked, "do you know what this means?" It meant, the general said, that "wars were no longer matters of valor or judgment." As he paced back and forth, MacArthur lamented, "Men like me are obsolete."[24]

There were other poignant moments as well. Jonathan Wainwright, who had long thought himself disgraced by the loss of Bataan, was liberated from a POW camp in Manchuria by Russian troops. Marshall cabled MacArthur and suggested that it might be appropriate to have Wainwright present at the surrender ceremony. Public opinion in the United States favored it, Marshall said, and MacArthur, despite his private contempt for Wainwright's actions in 1942, had little choice but to acquiesce. Marshall went on to arrange the Medal of Honor for Wainwright, which MacArthur's earlier objections had quashed.[25]

Overriding everything else, however, was the expectation of the journey to Japan that MacArthur had contemplated for three and a half years. Sutherland's agreed timetable was pushed back two additional days when a typhoon roared through southern Japan and turned the airfield at Atsugi into a muddy quagmire. On the morning of August 27, ships of Halsey's Third Fleet began moving into Sagami Bay, south of the airfield, in preparation for entering Tokyo Bay itself. The next day, an advance detachment of 150 engineers and communications technicians landed at Atsugi.[26]

MacArthur would not be far behind. It was MacArthur's judgment that if Emperor Hirohito ordered his armed forces and the general population to lay down their arms, they would not only do so, they would also treat the victors with respect and do their best to ensure their safety. Many on MacArthur's staff were skeptical, but they could not convince him otherwise.[27]

On August 29, it was finally time for MacArthur to fly north. Dusty Rhoades had picked up a brand-new C-54 some months before in the

States and had been keeping it primed and ready for MacArthur's use. This aircraft also bore the name *Bataan*. As the flight lifted off from Nichols Field, near Manila, Rhoades permitted one deviation from standard operating procedure. Theretofore he had never allowed MacArthur and Sutherland to fly on the same plane. This time, MacArthur overruled Rhoades and insisted that Sutherland accompany him, evidence that despite the testiness between them during the previous year, they still shared a deep professional bond.

North of Manila, en route to an overnight stop on Okinawa, MacArthur wanted an aerial tour of the Luzon battlefields, where the Japanese had fought to the very last. The next day at 9:00 a.m., *Bataan II* took off from Okinawa bound for Atsugi Naval Air Base. MacArthur spent most of the flight in the cockpit, especially after the white cone of Mount Fuji came into view. By making a wide turn over Tokyo Bay, Rhoades was able to land exactly on schedule, at 2:00 p.m.[28]

Throughout the day, wave after wave of C-54s had been landing the bulk of the Eleventh Airborne Division. The division band was on hand to strike up a lively march, but as MacArthur appeared alone at the door of his plane, a cluster of photographers captured one indelible image. His trademark sunglasses adorned his face, and the battered cap that had survived his escape from Corregidor perched atop his head. Corncob pipe clenched in his teeth, MacArthur started down the stairs—clearly in command but not defiant, magisterial but not regal. Eichelberger, commander of Eighth Army, which would garrison postwar Japan, met him at the bottom of the steps. "Bob," said MacArthur to the man he had once told to take Buna or not come back alive, "this is the payoff."[29]

From the airport, the general was driven with only a minimal escort twenty miles into Yokohama to the Hotel New Grand, which served briefly as his quarters. Eichelberger claimed that he "did not draw an easy breath" until MacArthur was safely ensconced there, but there were no incidents.[30]

MacArthur's landing within hours of the first troops proved far more dramatic to the Japanese people, as well as to others around the globe, than if he had come ashore behind ten or twenty divisions. His avowed understanding of the Japanese psyche aside, MacArthur might easily have become the target of fanatical Japanese resistance.

According to Willoughby, Winston Churchill later professed, "Of all the amazing deeds of bravery of the war, I regard MacArthur's personal landing at Atsugi as the greatest of the lot."[31] That may well have been Willoughby's standard pro-MacArthur hyperbole, but there is no question that the action was risky and that MacArthur had repeatedly shown he did not lack personal courage.

An attribute that Douglas MacArthur had shown on rare occasions was his mastery of understatement. He was about to display this par excellence. Indeed, for all the criticism of MacArthur—deserved and undeserved—his performance while presiding over the Japanese surrender ceremony met with universal acclaim. It may well have been one of the very few moments in his life when he was able to walk the middle ground.

At 7:20 a.m. on Sunday, September 2, after a breakfast of eggs, bacon, toast, jam, and coffee, MacArthur and a party that included Doc Egeberg and Dusty Rhoades made the five-minute ride from the Hotel New Grand through the bombed-out center of Yokohama to the customs house pier. There they went aboard the destroyer *Buchanan* for the six-mile trip out to Halsey's flagship. Named for the first superintendent of Annapolis, the nimble destroyer was a well-worn veteran of the Pacific, having seen action from the Solomons campaign through the Admiralties to Iwo Jima as well as carrier operations off the Philippines.

In a nod to the US Navy—in addition to Nimitz signing for the United States—secretary of the navy Forrestal had lobbied for the surrender ceremony to take place on the battleship *Missouri*. MacArthur raised no objections, and the shipboard location proved far more dramatic than a few tables in a hangar at Atsugi or even the old American embassy in Tokyo would have been. What better statement of American might, as well as the Allied power MacArthur had just been given, than an 887-foot, forty-five-thousand-ton battleship riding at anchor in Tokyo Bay?

Over the previous several days, MacArthur had written and rewritten the words he would read on this historic occasion. After the *Buchanan* came alongside the *Missouri,* MacArthur strode briskly up the starboard forward gangway, followed by Sutherland, and was greeted on deck with salutes and handshakes, first from Nimitz and then from Halsey. From the halyards flew two flags with five stars each—MacArthur's insignia on a field of red and Nimitz's on a field of blue.

Nimitz gestured MacArthur in the direction of the ceremonies but realized that he was on MacArthur's right. Strict protocol gave MacArthur that spot as the ranking officer. Slipping briefly behind him, and with a gentle pat on MacArthur's left side, Nimitz steered the general to the right as they walked along the deck. Halsey followed, and they went to his cabin to await the arrival of the Japanese delegation.[32]

A launch brought Minister of Foreign Affairs Mamoru Shigemitsu and chief of the Imperial Japanese Army general staff Yoshijiro Umezu, along with their attendants, alongside the *Missouri* a few minutes before 9:00 a.m. Having lost a leg to an assassin's bomb in Shanghai years before, Shigemitsu wore an artificial limb. He moved with some difficulty with a cane onto the deck and up the ladder to the surrender site, below the number 2 gun turret. Told where to stand, the Japanese delegation waited before the assembled throng of Allied officers for around four minutes, until MacArthur, Nimitz, and Halsey emerged on deck and MacArthur moved purposefully to the microphone, clutching the pages of his well-honed remarks in his left hand.

"We are gathered here," he slowly began, "representatives of the major warring powers, to conclude a solemn agreement whereby peace may be restored. The issues, involving divergent ideals and ideologies, have been determined on the battlefields of the world and hence are not for our discussion or debate.... As supreme commander for the Allied powers, I announce it my firm purpose in the tradition of the countries I represent to proceed in the discharge of my responsibilities with justice and tolerance while taking all necessary dispositions to ensure that the terms of surrender are fully, promptly, and faithfully complied with.

"I now invite the representatives of the emperor of Japan and the Japanese government and the Japanese Imperial General Headquarters to sign the instrument of surrender at the places indicated."[33]

Shigemitsu came forward first, moving slowly on his prosthesis, and with some difficulty sat down on a chair at the table before MacArthur upon which two copies of the surrender instrument were spread—the Japanese copy, bound in black, and the Allied copy, bound in green.

Shigemitsu removed his silk hat and white gloves and looked at the papers in front of him with a puzzled look of uncertainty. According to Kenney's account, there was dead silence until MacArthur's voice snapped through the air "like a pistol shot."

"Sutherland," he barked. "Show him where to sign."

Sutherland stepped forward and pointed to the correct line. It was near the top of the second page of the document, and Shigemitsu stood to reach forward and sign both copies. He then returned to his place as General Umezu stepped forward. Umezu deliberately reached into his uniform pocket and removed his eyeglasses from their case. He produced his own pen and, without sitting down, signed with barely a glance at MacArthur.[34]

Then it was MacArthur's turn. Saying that he would sign for the Allied powers, he beckoned Jonathan Wainwright and British lieutenant general Arthur Percival, who surrendered Singapore and had also been a POW, to stand behind him. MacArthur sat down at a chair on the opposite side of the table from where the Japanese had signed and produced a number of pens. The exact number and to whom MacArthur gave them would vary with the telling, although most accounts agree that he gave the first two to Wainwright and Percival.

Next came Chester Nimitz, signing for the United States, while Rear Admiral Forrest Sherman, Nimitz's chief of staff, looked over his left shoulder. Halsey joined this ensemble, and MacArthur put his left arm around Halsey's shoulders, the two old warhorses whispering a few words. Then MacArthur called forward the representatives of the other Allied powers to sign in their turn.

As the final Allied representative, Air Vice Marshal Leonard Isitt, of New Zealand, wrote his signatures, a dull roar could be heard in the distance. It grew louder and louder and came closer and closer. In uncanny choreography that MacArthur himself could not have staged better, the overcast of that morning parted to reveal upwards of 450 American planes flying in precise formation through the skies overhead. "None of us knew then," correspondent Theodore H. White later wrote in his memoirs, "that this was the last war America would cleanly, conclusively win. We thought it was the last war ever."[35]

On this climactic day, the dual drives across the Pacific, a strategy that had caused MacArthur so much angst, now appeared to have served the purpose of keeping the Japanese war machine off balance. By the time the titanic sea battles long planned by both sides occurred—in limited measure in the Philippine Sea off the Marianas and in full force aimed against MacArthur at Leyte—the bulk of Japan's airpower had been decimated and its army and navy overwhelmed on both the Southwest Pacific and Central Pacific fronts.

Perhaps most remarkable was the speed with which fortunes had changed as a result of the tremendous outpouring of America's industrial infrastructure and the sacrifices of its men and women at home and abroad. In less than four years, from utter despair on December 7, 1941, the United States had crafted the most powerful array of army, navy, and air forces that the world had ever seen—or would see again. That speed may not have been evident to a soldier slogging through the mud of the Kokoda Trail, an airman flying the lonely skies, or a sailor standing another watch. Perhaps it was never evident even to MacArthur. But on September 2, 1945, no one could deny the result.

Douglas MacArthur looked once more to the papers he held in his hand and read the final words he had written. "Let us pray," he earnestly said, "that peace be now restored to the world and that God will preserve it always. These proceedings are closed."[36]

It may well have been his finest hour.

A Study in Superlatives

O n that September morning on the deck of the *Missouri,* just as on December 8, 1941, Douglas MacArthur's career was far from finished. The full measure of his legacy was still not written. But during his four years at war, starting from the honorable though hardly heralded place in history he held in December of 1941, he had indeed become one of the best-known generals in not only American history but also world history. Whether he was one of the greatest is another question.

There was never much middle ground with Douglas MacArthur. The adjectives used to describe him—whether by his admirers or detractors—were never bland. They were superlatives of either adulation or disdain and emblematic of the superlatives that always would catalog the contradictions of his personality and define the hallmarks of his career.

He was praised for "the breadth of his views, the lucidity of his arguments, and the unerring way he puts his finger on the essentials of a problem," but he was also questioned for the "unmistakable evidences of an acute persecution complex at work...[that] produces an obviously unhealthy state of mind."[1]

The wildest superlatives at both ends of the spectrum were false: he was not the omnipotent master of any situation—"MacArthur the magnificent," as Bob Considine styled him—nor was he a coward devoid of personal courage, as his most vigorous detractors claimed.

He appeared brooding, thoughtful, and weighty in his inner

deliberations, but no one could know for certain what he was really thinking. Some came away from his presence convinced that if he was not God, he was as close as anyone was going to get. Others were certain he was a master charlatan and "the greatest 'ham actor' of all time."[2]

He was not collegial, but he could play the role of welcoming, ingratiating host. He appeared to most outsiders as remote, aloof, even mystical, yet by all accounts he was an adoring father to Arthur, a devoted husband to Jean, and a loyal, considerate, and even compassionate acquaintance — if not outright friend — to those closest to him, including George Kenney and Roger Egeberg.

"Luckiest" is not a superlative usually ascribed to him, but an errant wave against the hull of PT-41, an immediate Japanese counterattack on the beaches of Los Negros, or a determined enemy sniper on Leyte or Luzon might have made for a different ending.

His record was generally solid, but for him that was never enough. His own memoirs and those biographers who sought at his behest to win his approval by penning glowing tributes did him a disservice. There was plenty of glory and accomplishment in his record — the Clark Field surprise, Bataan food shortages, and Buna delays notwithstanding — without self-serving puffery, selective presentation of facts, and supersensitive paranoia.

No one ever claimed that MacArthur had a sense of humor, certainly not when it came to himself. His ego could not admit even the remotest possibility that he had been wrong or done something ill-advised. His worst side showed when he tried to cover up inevitable missteps, such as the reports of the Bismarck Sea victory.

Although there are stories of people, usually with hulking personalities such as Halsey and Kenney, standing up to MacArthur, rare were those who did. With plenty of ego and an outsize perception of himself, it was only natural for him to ask, why not he as president instead of Roosevelt or any other political leader?

He would go on to a widely lauded stewardship of postwar Japan. It was much more a political role than a military one, just as his initial role in 1942 Australia had been to exude confidence and rally political support. His subsequent actions in Korea, however, would underscore a critical point evident throughout his military career. Douglas MacArthur never acknowledged the basic tenet of American constitutional government: that the military is subordinate to civilian control. He moved quite easily between civil and military worlds because he saw himself at the apex of both.

Indeed, Douglas MacArthur fought many military and political battles over the course of his career—winning some, losing others—but his greatest loss came in a campaign he waged his entire life: the one against himself. He was brilliant, charismatic, and decisive, but he was also manipulative, deceitful, and as egocentric as any military leader in American history—the "George trio" of George McClellan, George Armstrong Custer, and George S. Patton being his only close competition.[3]

Ironically, during four years of war, MacArthur may have owed the most to the very people he was certain were out to discount and disparage him. While never among his fans, Franklin Roosevelt and George Marshall nonetheless consistently supported MacArthur within the framework of their global priorities, from the first efforts to resupply the Philippines to MacArthur's appointment as Allied supreme commander. Even then, where would MacArthur's Southwest Pacific Area agenda have been had not Ernie King urged the Joint Chiefs to pour resources into the Pacific and wage a two-ocean war?

On September 2, 1945, after four years at war, one thing was certain about Douglas MacArthur and his place in history. His rhetoric, however hyperbolic at times, and his characterization of events, however embellished his facts, had served to generate an enormous rallying cry for the American and Australian people in the dark days of 1942. Responsible though he was for much of the debacle in the Philippines, he had miraculously escaped on presidential orders, and the great majority in the Allied world was left with no doubt that he would return. He was their inspiration, their hope, and their synonym for victory over Japan. They saw only his stage-managed resolve, not the man behind the curtain.

"The United States would not send its greatest contemporary soldier to a secondary war zone," the Melbourne *Herald* exulted as MacArthur arrived on Australian shores in 1942, "and the fact that it regards

Australia as a sphere of supreme importance is by far the most heartening circumstance."[4]

"MacArthur," acknowledged an American commentator early in 1944, "provided his countrymen with a badly needed idol at a time when the military altar was almost bare of icons."[5]

And the American public continued to embrace him even as other heroes joined him on the altar. Asked in March of 1945 to name "the greatest United States army general in the war," 43 percent of respondents chose MacArthur. Eisenhower came in second, with 31 percent, and Patton third, with 17 percent. George Marshall, Courtney Hodges, Joseph Stilwell, and Omar Bradley lagged far behind with around one percent each.[6]

Where, then, does Douglas MacArthur stand three-quarters of a century after the four-year period of both his greatest military triumphs and defeats?

MacArthur always carried with him an indomitable will to win. It was ingrained in his genes. It was his most laudable quality. There is, as he would say, no substitute for victory, a concept that was much clearer in World War II than it would become even five short years later in Korea. He fit the times perfectly.

Douglas MacArthur's most important contribution to history was to be the hero who rallied America and its allies when they were at a low ebb and to become the symbol of determined resolve so desperately needed in the grim months of 1942. It was the role of a lifetime and, publicly, he played it brilliantly. That he came to believe more strongly through this experience in his perception of himself, and through this adulation judged it to be unequivocal, is to his discredit.

George Marshall may well have sighed at the results of the March 1945 poll — not at his own place but at MacArthur's. Marshall, more than most, knew the whole story of MacArthur's war. It is a mark of Marshall's own greatness that he so deftly managed MacArthur's fiery comet and unselfishly used its brilliance to accomplish the objectives of a global war.

Acknowledgments

Any work on Douglas MacArthur must start with acknowledging the foundation laid by D. Clayton James. His three-volume biography is a guiding light at many levels, particularly when it comes to insights and sources. While I never had the pleasure of meeting Dr. James, I have come to respect and admire the depth of his scholarship on MacArthur and his times.

The other essential acknowledgment for any work on MacArthur is James W. Zobel, the longtime archivist at the MacArthur Memorial Library and Archives in Norfolk, Virginia. Mr. Zobel is a wealth of information and a very competent guide to the ever-growing MacArthur-related collections under his stewardship. I greatly appreciate his friendly and knowledgeable assistance on my visits to Norfolk.

I also appreciate generous assistance from Jeffrey M. Flannery and the staff of the Manuscript Division of the Library of Congress; Jeffrey S. Kozak and the George C. Marshall Library, Lexington, Virginia; Donisha Smiley and the Special Collections of the Mississippi State University Library (repository of the D. Clayton James papers); William Baehr and the Franklin D. Roosevelt Presidential Library; and the staffs of the Firestone Library at Princeton University, the Norlin Library at the University of Colorado, the Hoover Institution at Stanford University, the Arthur Lakes Library at the Colorado School of Mines, and the Denver Public Library. Thanks as well to the interlibrary loan services of the Estes Valley Library, the best small-town library in America.

Once again, David Lambert has lent his cartographic skills and enthusiasm to one of my books, and I am in his debt for the maps.

Acknowledgments

Those who read and commented on portions of the manuscript or discussed MacArthur and operations in the Pacific with me in detail include: John Bruning, Dr. John Floyd, Jerry Keenan, historian Richard B. Meixsel at James Madison University, and Australian historian Peter Williams.

As witnessed by the dedication to this book, my greatest debt is to Paul L. Miles, Rhodes Scholar, retired US Army colonel, and distinguished professor at both West Point and Princeton. As an acknowledged expert in twentieth-century military and diplomatic history, Paul was invaluable in reading the manuscript, suggesting many improvements, and discussing the many facets—"warts and all," as he frequently put it—of MacArthur's evolution as a commander and his place in American military history. I greatly appreciate his efforts on my behalf as much as I cherish our friendship and many hours of conversation.

The same can readily be said of my longtime agent, Alexander C. Hoyt. We've done another one together, Alex, and I owe you an enormous debt for my professional success. You always have my back, and I greatly value your wise counsel and advice.

Finally, I have good things to say about Little, Brown as a publisher and its entire staff: first and foremost, my highly esteemed editor, John Parsley (this book is number three together), as well as Malin von Euler-Hogan, Carrie Neill, Zea Moscone, Mike Noon, and Barbara Clark. Thanks, too, to publisher Reagan Arthur for her commitment to history in general and my efforts in particular.

Appendixes

A. Chiefs of Staff, US Army, 1906–1948

Major General J. Franklin Bell	1906–1910
Major General Leonard Wood	1910–1914
Major General William W. Wotherspoon	1914
Major General Hugh L. Scott	1914–1917
General Tasker H. Bliss	1917–1918
General Peyton C. March	1918–1921
General of the Armies John J. Pershing	1921–1924
Major General John L. Hines	1924–1926
General Charles P. Summerall	1926–1930
General Douglas MacArthur	1930–1935
General Malin Craig	1935–1939
General of the Army George C. Marshall	1939–1945
General of the Army Dwight D. Eisenhower	1945–1948

B. World War II Global Strategy Conferences

First Washington Conference: December 1941, Washington, DC (Arcadia)

Second Washington Conference: June 1942, Washington, DC (Argonaut)

Casablanca Conference: January 1943, Casablanca, Morocco (Symbol)

Third Washington Conference: May 1943, Washington, DC
   (Trident)
First Quebec Conference: August 1943, Quebec City, Quebec
   (Quadrant)
Cairo Conference: November 1943, Cairo, Egypt (Sextant)
Tehran Conference: November 1943, Tehran, Iran (Eureka)
Second Quebec Conference: September 1944, Quebec, Canada
   (Octagon)
Yalta Conference: February 1945, Yalta, Soviet Union (Argonaut)
Potsdam Conference: July 1945, Potsdam, Germany (Terminal)

C. Code Names for Major Pacific Operations

Buccaneer, plans for amphibious operations in Andaman
   Islands, 1943
Cartwheel, convergent SWPA/SOPAC operations against
   Rabaul, 1943
Coronet, initial plans for invasion of Honshu and Tokyo Plain, 1946
Dexterity, landings on western New Britain Island, December 1943
Elkton, series of plans for encirclement of Rabaul, 1943
Flintlock, invasion of Marshall Islands, February 1944
Forager, invasion of Mariana Islands, June 1944
Galvanic, invasion of Gilbert Islands, November 1943
Iceberg, invasion of Okinawa, April 1945
King-Two, invasion of Leyte, Philippines, October 1944
Musketeer, invasion of Luzon, Philippines, January 1945
Olympic, plans for invasion of Kyushu, 1945
Providence, plans for occupying Buna before Japanese, 1942
Reckless, invasion of Hollandia, April 1944
Reno, series of plans for New Guinea advance to Philippines, 1943
Watchtower, invasion of Guadalcanal and Tulagi, August 1942

Notes

Abbreviations

AFPAC refers to the army forces in the Pacific.

CCS refers to the Combined Chiefs of Staff.

CG USAFIA refers to the commanding general, United States Army Forces in Australia.

CINCPAC refers to the commander in chief of the Pacific Fleet.

CINCSWPA refers to the commander in chief of the Southwest Pacific Area.

COMINCH is an abbreviation for commander in chief, US Fleet.

FECOM refers to the Far East Command.

JCS refers to Joint Chiefs of Staff.

RG refers to record group numbers in the MacArthur Memorial Archives and Library, Norfolk, Virginia.

SCAP refers to the supreme commander for the Allied Powers.

SEAC refers to the South East Asia Command.

SWPA refers to the Southwest Pacific Area.

USAFFE refers to the United States Army Forces in the Far East.

USAFPAC refers to the United States Army Forces in the Pacific.

Sources for Epigraphs

Part One

MacArthur to Marshall, RG 2, box 2, folder 1.

Henry Lewis Stimson Papers, Manuscripts and Archives, Yale University Library.

Part Two

David Horner, *Inside the War Cabinet: Directing Australia's War Efforts, 1939–45* (St. Leonards, Australia: Allen & Unwin, 1996), 223.

William Edward Brougher, *South to Bataan, North to Mukden: The Prison Diary of Brigadier General W. E. Brougher* (Athens: University of Georgia Press, 1971), 32.

Part Three

David Horner, "MacArthur and Curtin: Deciding Australian War Strategy in 1943," in Peter J. Dean, ed., *Australia 1943: The Liberation of New Guinea* (Port Melbourne, Australia: Cambridge University Press, 2014), 42.

Christopher Thorne, *Allies of a Kind: The United States, Britain, and the War Against Japan, 1941–1945* (New York: Oxford University Press, 1978), 370n39.

Part Four

Arthur H. Vandenberg, "Why I Am for MacArthur," *Collier's*, February 12, 1944.

Daniel E. Barbey, *MacArthur's Amphibious Navy: Seventh Amphibious Force Operations, 1943-1945* (Annapolis: United States Naval Institute, 1969), 183.

Part Five

SEAC War Diary, July 12 and 14, 1945, quoted in Thorne, *Allies of a Kind*, 649.

George H. Johnston, "How Good Was MacArthur?" *Australasian* (Melbourne), February 16, 1946.

Prologue: Monday, December 8, 1941

1. The account of the telephone ringing, MacArthur answering it, and MacArthur's response is widely reported, but in an interview, Jean MacArthur recalled that she answered the telephone, heard Sutherland ask for the general, and "put the General on." Jean MacArthur Oral History, June 24, 1984, RG 13, Papers of Mrs. Douglas MacArthur, box 15, folder 5.

Chapter 1: First Charge, First War

1. Roy Morris Jr., *Sheridan: The Life and Wars of General Phil Sheridan* (New York: Crown, 1992), 144–45.
2. Douglas MacArthur, *Reminiscences* (New York: McGraw-Hill, 1964), 8–9.
3. MacArthur, *Reminiscences*, 4–6; William Manchester, *American Caesar: Douglas MacArthur, 1880–1964* (Boston: Little, Brown, 1978), 17–18.
4. D. Clayton James, *The Years of MacArthur*, vol. 1, *1880–1941* (Boston: Houghton Mifflin, 1970), 13–18.
5. James, *Years of MacArthur*, 1:23–24.
6. MacArthur, *Reminiscences*, 14.
7. Ibid., 16.
8. MacArthur, *Reminiscences*, 5. Arthur III had been old enough during the hardship years at Fort Wingate to eschew any possibility of his own military service in such a rough post and thus chose the navy.
9. James, *Years of MacArthur*, 1:62, 65, 641n. Arthur senior died on August 26, 1896.
10. James, *Years of MacArthur*, 1:30–31, 63, 66; Annual Report of the Superintendent, United States Military Academy (Washington, DC: Government Printing Office, 1899), 4. Otjen represented Wisconsin's Fourth Congressional District.
11. James, *Years of MacArthur*, 1:68–71. Hazing became so severe that a cadet died from the abuse during MacArthur's second year, and MacArthur, while not a hazer himself, was among those called to testify before a congressional committee.
12. James, *Years of MacArthur*, 1:76–77; Edgerton obituary, *New York Times*, June 25, 1904.
13. James, *Years of MacArthur*, 1:79; MacArthur, *Reminiscences*, 26–27; William F. Halsey and J. Bryan III, *Admiral Halsey's Story* (New York: McGraw-Hill, 1947), 6.
14. James, *Years of MacArthur*, 1:78.
15. MacArthur, *Reminiscences*, 27–28.

16. MacArthur, *Reminiscences,* 29–30. Whether MacArthur met Quezon this early is open to doubt. See, for example, Richard Bruce Meixsel, "Manuel L. Quezon, Douglas MacArthur, and the Significance of the Military Mission to the Philippine Commonwealth," *Pacific Historical Review* 70, no. 2 (May 2001), 260–61n.

17. James, *Years of MacArthur,* 1:91–94.

18. Roosevelt to Taft, March 7, 1904, in Elting E. Morison, ed., *The Letters of Theodore Roosevelt,* vol. 4, *The Square Deal* (Cambridge, MA: Harvard University Press, 1951), 744.

19. James, *Years of MacArthur,* 1:41–43.

20. Ibid., 1:96.

21. Ibid., 1:99–100, 650n.

22. MacArthur, *Reminiscences,* 34; James, *Years of MacArthur,* 1:99, 101, 103–4. Among those who crossed his path there were George C. Marshall, Walter Krueger, and Billy Mitchell.

23. MacArthur, *Reminiscences,* 36.

24. James, *Years of MacArthur,* 1:115.

25. MacArthur, *Reminiscences,* 42.

26. James, *Years of MacArthur,* 1:123–26. It was a different time for medals; their awards in 1914 pale when judged against the deeds of recipients in World War II. The US Navy alone awarded forty-six Medals of Honor for the Veracruz operation.

27. MacArthur, *Reminiscences,* 46–47.

28. Henry J. Reilly, *Americans All: The Rainbow at War—Official History of the 42nd Rainbow Division in the World War* (Columbus, OH: F. J. Heer, 1936), 26.

29. MacArthur, *Reminiscences,* 46.

30. MacArthur, *Reminiscences,* 53; James, *Years of MacArthur,* 1:148–49.

31. Mary MacArthur to Baker, October 6, 1917, Newton Diehl Baker Papers, box 3, Manuscript Division, Library of Congress, Washington, DC.

32. Mary MacArthur to Baker, June 7, 1918, and Baker's reply, June 11, 1918, Baker papers, box 7.

33. Mary MacArthur to Pershing, June 12, 1918, John J. Pershing Papers, box 121, Manuscript Division, Library of Congress, Washington, DC.

34. James, *Years of MacArthur,* 1:164, 181.

35. *New York Times,* June 29, 1918; Pershing to Mary MacArthur, July 12, 1918, Pershing papers, box 121.

36. MacArthur, *Reminiscences,* 59; James, *Years of MacArthur,* 1:187–89.

37. MacArthur, *Reminiscences,* 64; James, *Years of MacArthur,* 1:206–8.

38. MacArthur, *Reminiscences,* 66; James, *Years of MacArthur,* 1:217.

39. James, *Years of MacArthur,* 1:223.

40. MacArthur, *Reminiscences,* 70.

41. James, *Years of MacArthur,* 1:238–41. MacArthur was in command of the Forty-Second Division from November 11 to November 22, 1918.

42. James, *Years of MacArthur,* 1:256.

Chapter 2: West Point to the Philippines

1. See, for example, MacArthur's undated letter to Pershing, circa July 1918, upon MacArthur's promotion to brigadier general, and MacArthur's letter to Pershing of May 14, 1921, upon Pershing's appointment as chief of staff: Pershing papers, box 121.

2. James, *Years of MacArthur,* 1:261.

3. MacArthur's brigadier general rank became permanent in January of 1920.

4. MacArthur, *Reminiscences,* 81.

5. James, *Years of MacArthur,* 1:274–75, 279. To stimulate discussion, MacArthur invited visiting lecturers, including Brigadier General Billy Mitchell, who regaled the corps on January 20, 1920, with stories of the developing might of airpower just two weeks before he went before Congress and boasted that bombers could sink battleships.

6. MacArthur, *Reminiscences,* 81–82; MacArthur explained his reasons for composing the quotation in a letter he wrote on April 18, 1939: RG 1, Records of the Military Advisor to the Philippine Commonwealth, 1935–1941, box 2, folder 8; also see MacArthur to Pershing, November 19, 1919, Pershing papers, box 121; Army-Navy football game results, https://en.wikipedia.org/wiki/Army–Navy _Game, accessed October 1, 2015

7. James, *Years of MacArthur,* 1:270.

8. George C. Kenney, *The MacArthur I Know* (New York: Duell, Sloan and Pearce, 1951), 246–47.

9. James, *Years of MacArthur,* 1:285–86.

10. For DOGS, see William Addleman Ganoe, *MacArthur Close-up* (New York: Vantage, 1962), 54.

11. Pershing to MacArthur, November 22, 1921, Pershing papers, box 121.

12. For Louise's background, see *New York Times,* February 15, 1922 (marriage to MacArthur); June 18, 1929 (divorce from MacArthur); June 8, 1930 (subsequent marriage); June 1, 1965 (obituary).

13. William Allen White, *The Autobiography of William Allen White* (New York: Macmillan, 1946), 572–73.

14. *New York Times,* January 15, 1922, February 15, 1922. For their approximate meeting date, see their personal letters in Joseph M. Maddalena, ed., *The Passionate and Poetic Pen of Douglas MacArthur: The Letters of Douglas MacArthur to His First Wife, Louise (Cromwell) Brooks,* (Beverly Hills, CA: Profiles in History), number 13 in a series of auction catalogs available from Maddalena's gallery.

15. *New York Times,* February 8, 1922, February 10, 1922. Pershing's wife and three young daughters died tragically in a fire in their quarters at the Presidio in San Francisco in 1915 while Pershing was on duty in Texas; only a son survived.

16. *New York Times,* January 31, 1922; Ganoe, *MacArthur Close-up,* 157, 160; James, *Years of MacArthur,* 1:293.

17. James, *Years of MacArthur,* 1:293, 296.

18. Manchester, *American Caesar,* 133–34.

19. Mary MacArthur to Pershing, circa August 1924, Pershing papers, box 121.

20. James, *Years of MacArthur,* 1:305–6.

21. MacArthur, *Reminiscences,* 85–86; James, *Years of MacArthur,* 1:64–65. There should have been some question of MacArthur's impartiality in the case. Mitchell's father, John L. Mitchell, was a comrade in arms of MacArthur's father from the 24th Wisconsin and as a United States senator from Wisconsin had written letters of recommendation for Douglas during his efforts to secure a presidential appointment to West Point. Douglas did not know Billy Mitchell well from Milwaukee, but their

paths had crossed at Fort Leavenworth, and Mitchell had been a guest lecturer at West Point. After the decision, President Coolidge amended Mitchell's sentence to half pay, but Mitchell, knowing his career was over, chose to resign.

22. James, *Years of MacArthur,* 1:328.

23. Ibid., 1:322–23.

24. MacArthur, *Reminiscences,* 88.

25. James, *Years of MacArthur,* 1:333. It is hard to believe now, but the governor-generalship of the Philippines was a major post during the early twentieth century.

26. *New York Times,* April 21, 1929.

27. MacArthur, *Reminiscences,* 83.

28. James, *Years of MacArthur,* 1:341.

29. Ibid., 1:343, 674–75n.

30. *New York Times,* August 6, 1930, August 7, 1930; Herbert Hoover, *The Memoirs of Herbert Hoover,* vol. 2, *The Cabinet and the Presidency 1920–1933* (New York: Macmillan, 1952), 339; Meixsel, "Manuel L. Quezon," 264–65.

31. MacArthur, *Reminiscences,* 89.

32. "Between World Wars," in *American Military History,* ed. Spencer Conn, et al. (Washington, DC: Center of Military History, United States Army, 1989), 409, http://www.history.army.mil/books/AMH/amh-19.htm, accessed July 11, 2013; James, *Years of MacArthur,* 1:381.

33. Annual Report of the Chief of Staff for the Year Ending June 30, 1932, quoted in Frank C. Waldrop, ed., *MacArthur on War* (New York: Duell, Sloan and Pearce, 1942), 143, 148.

34. James, *Years of MacArthur,* 1:379–80. Stimson refused to believe MacArthur's extreme position until he repeated it in Stimson's presence. Although upset, Stimson recognized that MacArthur was being driven by the need to save money on an area that accounted for 25 to 35 percent of his budget and the then-popular notion that banning or retarding new weapons would somehow make the next war less destructive.

35. James, *Years of MacArthur,* 1:369–71.

36. Walter R. Borneman, *The Admirals: Nimitz, Halsey, Leahy, and King—The Five-Star Admirals Who Won the War at Sea* (New York: Little, Brown, 2012), 147, 154–55.

37. Dwight D. Eisenhower, *At Ease: Stories I Tell to Friends* (Garden City, NY: Doubleday, 1967), 213.

38. James, *Years of MacArthur,* 1:390; MacArthur, *Reminiscences,* 90.

39. MacArthur, *Reminiscences.* 92.

40. James, *Years of MacArthur,* 1:384–85.

41. Eisenhower, *At Ease,* 216–18.

42. MacArthur, *Reminiscences,* 93.

43. Manchester, *American Caesar,* 149; James, *Years of MacArthur,* 1:388.

44. Rexford G. Tugwell, *The Democratic Roosevelt: A Biography of Franklin D. Roosevelt* (Baltimore, MD: Penguin Books, 1969), 349.

45. Richard B. Frank (*MacArthur: Lessons in Leadership* [New York: St. Martin's, 2009]) is among those agreeing with my evaluation.

46. James, *Years of MacArthur,* 1:416.

47. See, for example, MacArthur, *Reminiscences,* 101; for Marshall's name, see Forrest C. Pogue, *George C. Marshall,* vol. 1, *Education of a General, 1880–1939* (New York: Viking, 1963), 323.

48. Annual Report of the Chief of Staff for the Year Ending June 30, 1933, quoted in Waldrop, *MacArthur on War,* 175; James, *Years of MacArthur,* 1: 427–28.
49. MacArthur, *Reminiscences,* 101. MacArthur was successful in having Roosevelt amend his cuts to only $51 million. Among his victories was saving Pershing's pension from being cut—an action that got him a letter of thanks from Pershing and seems to refute any deep enmity between the two. See James, *Years of MacArthur,* 1:428; Pershing to MacArthur, February 27, 1933, Pershing papers, box 121.
50. Franklin D. Roosevelt, *Complete Presidential Press Conferences of Franklin D. Roosevelt* (New York: Da Capo Press, 1972), 4:268.
51. *New York Times,* May 17, 1934.
52. Manchester, *American Caesar,* 156 (including the Leahy quote, apparently garnered from interviews); Geoffrey Perret, *Old Soldiers Never Die: The Life of Douglas MacArthur* (New York: Random House, 1996), 168–70, relying in part on the papers of Pearson's attorney, Morris Ernest, at the University of Texas. Robert S. Allen was Pearson's regular coauthor and a codefendant in the suit.

Chapter 3: Manila Before the Storm

1. Francis Bowes Sayre, second draft of "Freedom Comes to Philippines," Francis B. Sayre Papers, box 8, Manuscript Division, Library of Congress, Washington, DC.
2. Francis Bowes Sayre, *Glad Adventure* (New York: Macmillan, 1957), 207–8.
3. MacArthur to Quezon, December 4, 1934, enclosing suggested draft, RG 18, Records of the Chief of Staff, United States Army, 1934–1935, box 1, folder "Correspondence: Philippines"; for an analysis of Quezon's motivations for this offer, see Meixsel, "Manuel L. Quezon," 255–92.
4. Carol Morris Petillo, *Douglas MacArthur: The Philippine Years* (Bloomington: Indiana University Press, 1981), 170; Memorandum of the Terms of Agreement for Military Adviser to the President of the Philippine Commonwealth Government, 1935, RG 1, box 1, folder 2; Adjutant General to MacArthur, September 18, 1935, RG 1, box 1, folder 2. Available present-day dollar value calculated to 2012 at http://www.measuringworth.com/uscompare/result.php?year _source=1937&amount=40500&year_result=2012.
5. MacArthur to Quezon, June 1, 1935, RG 18, box 1, folder "Correspondence: Philippines."
6. MacArthur to Roosevelt, September 9, 1935, quoted in James, *Years of MacArthur,* 1:489.
7. Drum to MacArthur, June 29, 1936, RG 10, VIP correspondence, box 3, folder 86. Drum addressed his letter "Dear Mac."
8. Roosevelt to MacArthur, September 19, 1935, Elliott Roosevelt, ed., *F.D.R.: His Personal Letters, 1928–1945* (New York: Duell, Sloan and Pearce, 1950), 1:507–8; War Department Special Orders No. 22, September 18, 1935, quoted in James, *Years of MacArthur,* 1:484–85.
9. Eisenhower, *At Ease,* 223.
10. MacArthur to Roosevelt, Woodring, Craig, and Surles, October 2, 1935, RG 1, box 1, folder 2.
11. MacArthur, *Reminiscences,* 103; James, *Years of MacArthur,* 1:485 regarding Hutter.
12. *New York Times,* January 24, 2000.

13. Clark Lee and Richard Henschel, *Douglas MacArthur* (New York: Henry Holt, 1952), 67–68.

14. James, *Years of MacArthur,* 1:513, 553–55. Jean MacArthur recounted her first visit to West Point to Colonel Paul Miles on one of her subsequent visits; author interview with Miles, May 13, 2014.

15. Forbes to Summerall, October 17, 1927, quoted in James, *Years of MacArthur,* 1:335–36.

16. Grace Person Hayes, *The History of the Joint Chiefs of Staff in World War II: The War Against Japan* (Annapolis, MD: Naval Institute Press, 1982), 4–5.

17. Hayes, *Joint Chiefs,* 6.

18. James, *Years of MacArthur,* 1:503–4; Meixsel, "Manuel L. Quezon," 271n. MacArthur's plans to make the Philippines "invasion proof" by constructing "a fleet of tiny, high-speed fighting craft" were even reported in the *New York Times,* May 30, 1936.

19. James, *Years of MacArthur,* 1:504; Eisenhower, *At Ease,* 225.

20. Krueger to Craig, February 16, 1938, quoted in James, *Years of MacArthur,* 1:546–47.

21. MacArthur to Quezon, June 1, 1935, RG 18, box 1, folder "Correspondence: Philippines."

22. Craig to MacArthur, August 6, 1937, RG 44a, Selected Papers of Brigadier General Bonner F. Fellers, USA, Military Secretary to General MacArthur, SWPA, SCAP, 1913–1972, box 3, folder 23; James, *Years of MacArthur,* 1:521; for a discussion that MacArthur's rhetoric in regard to military preparations in the Philippines had not played well in Washington during his spring 1937 visit, see Meixsel, "Manuel L. Quezon," 287–88.

23. MacArthur to Craig, September 16, 1937, RG 1, box 1, folder 5.

24. Dwight D. Eisenhower interview, RG 32, Oral History Collection, box 6.

25. James, *Years of MacArthur,* 1:500.

26. Woodring to Roosevelt, January 21, 1938, quoted in James, *Years of MacArthur,* 1:525.

27. Eisenhower, *At Ease,* 225–26.

28. James, *Years of MacArthur,* 1:537–38; Sayre, *Glad Adventure,* 209.

29. Eisenhower interview, in James, *Years of MacArthur,* 1:564.

30. James, *Years of MacArthur,* 1:565–67.

31. Pogue, *Education of a General,* 107, 175, 281–82, 294–96, 401n.

32. MacArthur to Early, March 21, 1941, Official File 400, Appointments, Philippine Islands, High Commissioner, Franklin D. Roosevelt Papers, Franklin D. Roosevelt Library, Hyde Park, New York.

33. Watson to MacArthur, April 15, 1941, RG 1, box 2, folder 33.

34. Marshall to MacArthur, June 20, 1941, RG 1, box 2, folder 35.

35. Roosevelt to Ickes, July 1, 1941, in Roosevelt, ed., *F.D.R. His Personal Letters,* 2:1173–74.

36. Marshall to MacArthur, July 26, 1941, RG 1, box 2, folder 36.

37. Quezon to MacArthur, July 27, 1941, RG 10, VIP files; Sayre, *Glad Adventure,* 217.

38. MacArthur to O'Laughlin, October 6, 1941, John Callan O'Laughlin Papers, Manuscript Division, Library of Congress, Washington, DC.

39. Hayes, *Joint Chiefs,* 8–12.

40. Hayes, *Joint Chiefs,* 17; Louis Morton, *Strategy and Command: The First Two Years,* vol. 1 of *The United States Army in World War II: The War in the Pacific* (Washington, DC: Center of Military History, United States Army, 1962), 86–91.

41. Marshall to MacArthur, November 28, 1941, RG 15, Materials Donated by the General Public, box 13, folder 4; for an example of MacArthur's optimism, see MacArthur to Marshall, October 28, 1941, RG 2, Records of Headquarters, US Army Forces in the Far East (USAFFE), 1941–1942, box 2, folder 1. Stimson called "the contagious optimism of General Douglas MacArthur" one of the two leading causes—the other being the reliance on B-17s—for the shift in American policy to defend the Philippines aggressively and "make it foolhardy for the Japanese to carry their expansion southward." Henry L. Stimson and McGeorge Bundy, *On Active Service in Peace and War* (New York: Harper & Brothers, 1947), 388.

Chapter 4: Lost Hours

1. MacArthur, *Reminiscences,* 128.

2. Louis Morton, *The Fall of the Philippines,* vol. 2 of *The United States Army in World War II: The War in the Pacific* (Washington, DC: Center of Military History, United States Army, 1993), 24, 49.

3. William H. Bartsch, *December 8, 1941: MacArthur's Pearl Harbor* (College Station: Texas A&M University Press, 2003), 427; Morton, *Fall of the Philippines,* 42. The latter count may include older planes used for training in the Philippine Air Corps; it is also possible that deliveries of newer planes contribute to the discrepancies.

4. Morton, *Fall of the Philippines,* 42.

5. James, *Years of MacArthur,* 1:608.

6. Ibid., 1:527, 594.

7. Ibid., 1:531–33, 591.

8. Morton, *Fall of the Philippines,* 69. MacArthur divided his USAFFE command into four operational groups: the North Luzon Force, commanded by Wainwright, which included the principal American division in the islands; the South Luzon Force, commanded by Brigadier General George M. Parker Jr.; the Visayan-Mindanao Force, commanded by Colonel William F. Sharp, which included almost half the Philippine army scattered throughout the islands south of Luzon; and the Manila Bay and Subic Bay coastal defenses, commanded by Brigadier General George F. Moore.

9. James Leutze, *A Different Kind of Victory: A Biography of Admiral Thomas C. Hart* (Annapolis, MD: Naval Institute Press, 1981), 212, 334n.

10. Leutze, *Hart,* 216–17.

11. Hart diary, November 8, 1941, quoted in Leutze, *Hart,* 217.

12. Leutze, *Hart,* 217; James, *Years of MacArthur,* 1:615.

13. Leutze, *Hart,* 218. Lest anyone think it was politics, both Hart and MacArthur were ardent Republicans.

14. Leutze, *Hart,* 218; *Time,* November 24, 1941. The same disparity in rank existed in Hawaii between Admiral Husband Kimmel and Lieutenant General Walter Short, but it did not seem to affect their relationship, despite whatever shortcomings in their coordination became obvious after December 7.

15. Leutze, *Hart,* 163–64, 218. The other naval officer who would always be in that category was William D. Leahy, another Annapolis classmate of Arthur III's and,

until 1939, Roosevelt's chief of naval operations; Leahy was then ambassador to Vichy France, and Arthur III's son Douglas II was on his staff.

16. Hart diary, February 7, 1940 quoted in Leutze, *Hart,* 164.
17. MacArthur, *Reminiscences,* 102, 128.
18. Leutze, *Hart,* 219–20; Hayes, *Joint Chiefs,* 18; James D. Hornfischer, *Ship of Ghosts: The Story of the USS Houston, FDR's Legendary Lost Cruiser, and the Epic Saga of Her Survivors* (New York: Bantam, 2006), 32, 35.
19. Marshall to MacArthur, November 27, 1941, quoted in Morton, *Fall of the Philippines,* 71.
20. Morton, *Fall of the Philippines,* 71–72.
21. Sayre, *Glad Adventure,* 221.
22. MacArthur to Marshall, November 28, 1941, quoted in Morton, *Fall of the Philippines,* 72.
23. Office Log, October–December 1941, RG 2, box 3, folder 4.
24. Leutze, *Hart,* 224–25.
25. Ibid., 225–26.
26. Jonathan M. Wainwright, *General Wainwright's Story* (New York: Doubleday, 1946), 17.
27. MacArthur to Arnold, December 6, 1941, quoted in Lewis H. Brereton, *The Brereton Diaries: The War in the Air in the Pacific, Middle East, and Europe, 3 October 1941–8 May 1945* (New York: William Morrow, 1946), 36–37.
28. For a solid biography of Brereton, see Roger G. Miller, "A Pretty Damn Able Commander: Lewis Hyde Brereton, Part I and II," *Air Power History* 47, no. 4 (Winter 2000), 4–27, and 48, no. 1 (Spring 2001), 22–45.
29. Bartsch, *December 8, 1941,* 218.
30. Ibid., 218–19, 473n.
31. Brereton, *Brereton Diaries,* 32; Walter D. Edmonds, "What Happened at Clark Field," *The Atlantic* (July 1951), 32; Bartsch, *December 8, 1941,* 211; William H. Bartsch, "Was MacArthur Ill-Served by his Air Force Commanders in the Philippines?" *Air Power History* 44, no. 2 (Summer 1997), 44–63.
32. Bartsch, *December 8, 1941,* 230, 474–475nn3–4; Brereton, *Brereton Diaries,* 34–35.
33. Bartsch, *December 8, 1941,* 238, 243, 476n19.
34. Ibid., 244–49, 427.
35. Brereton, *Brereton Diaries,* 38; Bartsch, *December 8, 1941,* 249, 478n43.
36. Morton, *Fall of the Philippines,* 79.
37. Samuel Eliot Morison, *History of United States Naval Operations in World War II,* vol. 3, *The Rising Sun in the Pacific* (Boston: Little, Brown, 1948), 168–69.
38. Morton, *Fall of the Philippines,* 79n9.
39. Morison, *Rising Sun,* 169.
40. Morton, *Fall of the Philippines,* 79.
41. Gordon W. Prange, *At Dawn We Slept: The Untold Story of Pearl Harbor* (New York: Penguin 1991), 527.
42. Marshall to MacArthur, December 7, 1941 (12:05 p.m.), RG 2, box 3, folder 1; Prange, *At Dawn We Slept,* 553.
43. Marshall to MacArthur, December 7, 1941 (3:22 p.m.), RG 2, box 3, folder 1.
44. Bartsch, *December 8, 1941,* 260.
45. Brereton, *Brereton Diaries,* 38.

46. Bartsch, *December 8, 1941*, 276–77, 483 n28.
47. Bartsch, *December 8, 1941*, 277, 483n29; Brereton, *Brereton Diaries*, 38–39.
48. Barstch, *December 8, 1941*, 277, 280,–81, 483nn30, 39–40; Edmonds, "What Happened at Clark Field," 24.
49. Bartsch, *December 8, 1941*, 282.
50. Ibid., 260–61.
51. Ibid., 283, 484n46.
52. Ibid., 284, 485n49.
53. Ibid., 283, 484n45.
54. Ibid., 261, 287.
55. Ibid., 292–94, 296.
56. D. Clayton James, *The Years of MacArthur*, vol. 2, *1941–1945* (Boston: Houghton Mifflin, 1975), 15.
57. Bartsch, *December 8, 1941*, 297, 303–4.
58. Ibid., 298–303.
59. Ibid., 308–9.
60. Bartsch, *December 8, 1941*, 264–66. The four Japanese reconnaissance planes returned to Formosa later that morning, but fog forced them to land at bases farther north.
61. Saburo Sakai, *Samurai! Flying the Zero in WWII with Japan's Fighter Ace* (New York: Ballantine, 1957), 49.
62. Bartsch, *December 8, 1941*, 425.
63. Sakai, *Samurai!*, 50.

Chapter 5: Blame and Bataan

1. Aircraft and personnel losses at Clark and Iba Fields on December 8 have always been a matter of debate; some differences may stem from planes subsequently repaired. See, for example, Morton, *Fall of the Philippines*, 88; Bartsch, *December 8, 1941*, 409, 439, 442; and James, *Years of MacArthur*, 2:4.
2. MacArthur to Marshall, December 8, 1941, quoted in Bartsch, *December 8, 1941*, 263.
3. Gerow [Marshall] to MacArthur, December 8, 1941, RG 2, box 3, folder 1.
4. Adams [Arnold] to MacArthur, December 8, 1941, RG 2, box 3, folder 1.
5. MacArthur to Marshall, December 8, 1941, quoted in Bartsch, *December 8, 1941*, 263, 480n15.
6. *New York Times,* September 28, 1946; Edmonds, "What Happened at Clark Field," 32. For more on Sutherland's differing recollections, see Morton, *Fall of the Philippines,* 82n17, n19, and James, *Years of MacArthur,* 2:10–11, quoting MacArthur's answers to the February 8, 1954, Morton questionnaire.
7. *New York Times,* September 28, 1946.
8. H. H. Arnold, *Global Mission* (New York: Harper & Brothers, 1949), 273; Brereton, *Brereton Diaries*, 50.
9. MacArthur to Arnold, December 10, 1941, RG 2, box 3, folder 1.
10. Arnold, *Global Mission*, 272; Bartsch, *December 8, 1941*, 263.
11. Claire L. Chennault, *Way of a Fighter: The Memoirs of Claire Lee Chennault* (New York: G. P. Putnam's Sons, 1949), 124.
12. Edgar D. Whitcomb, *Escape from Corregidor* (Chicago: Henry Regnery, 1958), 23.

13. Forrest C. Pogue, *George C. Marshall,* vol. 2, *Ordeal and Hope, 1939–1942* (New York: Viking, 1966), 234.
14. James, *Years of MacArthur,* 2:20; Leutze, *Hart,* 233. Saburo Sakai commented that torrential rains on December 9 interrupted Japanese operations; *Samurai!,* 52.
15. Morton, *Fall of the Philippines,* 146n.
16. Pogue, *Ordeal and Hope,* 235, 470n9.
17. Diary, December 14, 1941, Henry Lewis Stimson Papers, Manuscripts and Archives, Yale University Library.
18. Pogue, *Ordeal and Hope,* 236.
19. Dwight D. Eisenhower, *Crusade in Europe* (Garden City, NY: Doubleday, 1949), 18, 21–22.
20. Morton, *Fall of the Philippines,* 60, 98. Japanese planners had assumed that the airfield at Aparri was operational and suitable for heavy bombers. Indeed, this had been MacArthur's long-range plan, but time had gotten the better of him, and facilities there were limited and largely unoccupied.
21. Brereton, *Brereton Diaries,* 53–56.
22. Ibid., 62.
23. Ibid., 63–64.
24. Morton, *Fall of the Philippines,* 154–55.
25. Stark to Marshall, December 23, 1941, quoted in Morton, *Fall of the Philippines,* 155.
26. Hart Memorandum on Last Two Interviews with General MacArthur, quoted in James, *Years of MacArthur,* 2:21.
27. Leutze, *Hart,* 242.
28. Stark to Hart, December 17, 1941, quoted in Leutze, *Hart,* 242.
29. Hart memorandum, quoted in James, *Years of MacArthur,* 2:21.
30. Leutze, *Hart,* 241–43; for a full account of American submarine actions in the Philippines, see Clay Blair Jr., *Silent Victory: The U.S. Submarine War Against Japan* (Philadelphia, PA: Lippincott, 1975).
31. Leutze, *Hart,* 240.
32. Leutze, *Hart,* 244–46; Blair, *Silent Victory,* 130; MacArthur Proclamation, December 24, 1941, RG 2, box 2, folder 2.
33. MacArthur to Marshall, December 27, 1941, RG 2, box 2, folder 6.
34. James, *Years of MacArthur,* 2:23–24.
35. Morton, *Fall of the Philippines,* 139.
36. James, *Years of MacArthur,* 2:24–25. Selleck became one of MacArthur's harshest critics, telling James that his doctor had "forbidden me to talk about subjects which will raise my blood pressure." Of MacArthur, Selleck said only: "My relations with him were ugly, and I bitterly disliked the man." Oral Reminiscences of Colonel Clyde A. Selleck, RG 49, D. Clayton James Collection.
37. James, *Years of MacArthur,* 2:27–28.
38. MacArthur, *Reminiscences,* 125.
39. MacArthur, *Reminiscences,* 124. For troop estimates, see Morton, *Fall of the Philippines,* 162n.
40. Morton, *Fall of the Philippines,* 164.
41. Sid Huff, *My Fifteen Years with General MacArthur* (New York: Paperback Library, 1964), 38.

42. MacArthur Headquarters Diary, December 24, 1941, RG 3, Records of Headquarters, Southwest Pacific Area (SWPA), 1942–45, box 1, folder 4; Manuel Luis Quezon, *The Good Fight* (New York: D. Appleton–Century, 1946), 213–14; Sayre, *Glad Adventure,* 230.

43. Huff, *My Fifteen Years,* 39.

44. *New York Times,* December 25, 1941.

45. James, *Years of MacArthur,* 2:30–31, James, *Years of MacArthur,* 1:607–8.

46. Alvin P. Stauffer, *The Quartermaster Corps: Operations in the War Against Japan* vol. 5, bk. 3, of *The United States Army in World War II: The Technical Services* (Washington, DC: Center of Military History, United States Army, 1990), 10.

47. Morton, *Fall of the Philippines,* 165n; James, *Years of MacArthur,* 2:30–31. According to the *New York Times* of December 28, 1941, a German broadcast claimed that the Japanese military did not recognize Manila as an open city "because the decision was taken by General [Douglas] MacArthur without consultation with the Philippine population."

48. Stauffer, *Quartermaster Corps,* 9, 11; James, *Years of MacArthur,* 2:31–33.

49. Stauffer, *Quartermaster Corps,* 9; E. B. Miller, *Bataan Uncensored* (Little Falls: Military Historical Society of Minnesota, 1991), 75.

50. James, *Years of MacArthur,* 2:36–37.

51. MacArthur, *Reminiscences,* 130.

Chapter 6: Dugout Doug

1. Morton, *Fall of the Philippines,* 166–67, 178.

2. Ibid., 180, 180n, 181.

3. Ibid., 126, 182.

4. Ibid., 183, 199–201.

5. MacArthur Headquarters Diary, December 31, 1941, RG 3, box 1, folder 4.

6. Morton, *Fall of the Philippines,* 208–10, 215.

7. MacArthur to Marshall, January 7, 1942, RG 2, box 2, folder 6.

8. MacArthur to Marshall, January 1, 1942, and Marshall to MacArthur, January 2, 1942, quoted in Morton, *Strategy and Command,* 186–87.

9. Marshall to MacArthur, January 11, 1942, quoted in Morton, *Strategy and Command,* 168–71.

10. Gerow to Marshall, January 3, 1942, quoted in Morton, *Strategy and Command,* 187.

11. Pogue, *Ordeal and Hope,* 245.

12. Eisenhower, *Crusade in Europe,* 25.

13. Morton, *Fall of the Philippines,* 395–96.

14. Don Lohbeck, *Patrick J. Hurley* (Chicago: Henry Regnery, 1956), 164.

15. See James, *Years of MacArthur,* 2:54 for Brigadier General Milton A. Hill's recollection of a later visit by MacArthur "to one of the corps headquarters." This may in fact have been a subsequent visit by Sutherland.

16. James, *Years of MacArthur,* 2:48–49.

17. Ibid., 2:52–53.

18. MacArthur Headquarters Diary, January 10, 1942, RG 3, box 1, folder 4; Oral Reminiscences of General Harold K. Johnson, 11, RG 49, box 1.

19. Quezon, *The Good Fight,* 245; for leaflets, see *New York Times,* January 31, 1942.

20. MacArthur, *Reminiscences,* 131.

21. Ibid., 132.
22. Miller, *Bataan Uncensored,* 193–94.
23. James, *Years of MacArthur,* 2:57.
24. Morton, *Fall of the Philippines,* 290; MacArthur to Marshall, January 23, 1942, RG 2, box 2, folder 4.
25. Robert H. Ferrell, ed., *The Eisenhower Diaries* (New York: W. W. Norton, 1981), 44; Morton, *Fall of the Philippines,* 291n.
26. Sutherland to Chynoweth, February 1, 1942, quoted in James, *Years of MacArthur,* 2:60; Morton, *Fall of the Philippines,* 325. Chynoweth became another of MacArthur's harshest critics, particularly over the issue of food and ammunition being "highly over-centralized" and not distributed to the southern islands. As for MacArthur's command presence, Chynoweth rated him "a very poor soldier in the technical sense [because] he wasn't interested in it. He never visited. He didn't get out. He never went to see anybody. He was the most remote commander that I've ever known." Oral Reminiscences of Brigadier General Bradford G. Chynoweth, RG 49, box 2, 5–6.
27. James, *Years of MacArthur,* 2:60–61; Morton, *Fall of the Philippines,* 261–62.
28. Matome Ugaki, *Fading Victory: The Diary of Admiral Matome Ugaki, 1941–1945* (Pittsburgh, PA: University of Pittsburgh Press, 1991), 101.
29. Whitcomb, *Escape from Corregidor,* 36–37.
30. Ibid., 46–47.
31. Ibid., 41–42.
32. Luce to MacArthur, December 6, 1941, Clare Boothe Luce Papers, box 104, folder 12, Manuscript Division, Library of Congress, Washington, DC. Shortly before leaving Manila, Luce told Charles Willoughby, MacArthur's intelligence chief, with whom she had an affair, that "MacArthur would either never be heard of again, or he would one day return to the U.S.A. while the whole American people yelled, 'Hail MacArthur.'" Sylvia Jukes Morris, *Rage for Fame: The Ascent of Clare Boothe Luce* (New York: Random House, 1997), 540n25.
33. *Life,* December 8, 1941; *Time,* December 29, 1941.
34. James, *Years of MacArthur,* 2:89.
35. MacArthur to Marshall, March 7, 1942, RG 15, box 23, folder 23. Regarding the report of Homma's suicide, MacArthur said that he could not "completely substantiate this report," but nonetheless urged Marshall to "initiate publicity in this matter."
36. Diller interview, James, *Years of MacArthur,* 2:90.
37. Excerpts from radiograms from Coordinator of Information, Washington, DC, pertaining to General Douglas MacArthur, RG 2, box 2, folder 4.
38. Drew Pearson and Robert S. Allen, "The Real General MacArthur," *Liberty,* March 7, 1942, 20–22. Despite the complimentary nature of the article, George Van Horn Moseley, MacArthur's acerbic and reactionary deputy chief of staff during the 1930s, could not forgive the authors' earlier actions and scrawled on his copy: "A poor article written by two skunks."
39. MacArthur was, Eisenhower said, "the only commander I recall who used the heading bearing his own name for official messages and communiqués—'MacArthur Headquarters.'" Eisenhower interview, RG 32, box 6.
40. Whitcomb, *Escape from Corregidor,* 40.

Chapter 7: Ordered Out

1. James, *Years of MacArthur,* 2:91–92.
2. Quezon to Roosevelt, January 13, 1942, RG 4, Records of Headquarters, US Army Forces in the Pacific (USAFPAC), 1942–1947, box 15, folder 1.
3. Quezon to MacArthur, January 28, 1942, RG 2, box 2, folder 4.
4. Roosevelt to MacArthur, January 30, 1942, RG 2, box 2, folder 4.
5. Marshall to MacArthur, February 3, 1942, RG 2, box 3, folder 1. A public opinion poll conducted among Americans on January 5, 1942, found them evenly split (at 42 percent each) on whether, if the Philippines should fall, "the government should get General MacArthur out beforehand so he can fight again, or have him stay with his troops to the end." In Hadley Cantril, ed., *Public Opinion, 1935–1946* (Princeton, NJ: Princeton University Press, 1951), 428.
6. Ferrell, *Eisenhower Diaries,* 46 (January 29, 1942).
7. MacArthur to Marshall, February 4, 1942, RG 2, box 3, folder 1.
8. Marshall to MacArthur, February 8, 1942, RG 2, box 3, folder 1. Eisenhower was less gracious in his diary: "Another long message on 'strategy' to MacArthur. He sent in one extolling the virtues of the flank offensive. Wonder what he thinks we've been studying for all these years. His lecture would have been good for plebes." Ferrell, *Eisenhower Diaries,* 47 (February 8, 1942).
9. Quezon to Roosevelt, dispatched as part of MacArthur to Marshall, February 8, 1942, RG 4, box 15, folder 1. Quezon discussed the neutrality option and the embarrassment of collaborators with Commissioner Sayre; see Memorandum of conversation between High Commissioner Sayre and President Quezon re general situation in Philippines, February 8, 1942, box 9, folder "Quezon," Sayre papers.
10. MacArthur to Marshall, February 8, 1942, RG 4, box 15, folder 1.
11. Stimson diary, February 8 and 9, 1942; Pogue, *Ordeal and Hope,* 248. A handwritten annotation in Stimson's diary termed this the "fight to the finish" order for the Philippines.
12. Ferrell, *Eisenhower Diaries,* 47 (February 9, 1942). Eisenhower had already speculated in his diary: "MacArthur is losing his nerve"; February 3, 1942.
13. Roosevelt to Quezon, February 10, 1942, RG 2, box 3, folder 1.
14. Roosevelt to MacArthur, February 10, 1942, RG 2, box 3, folder 1.
15. MacArthur to Roosevelt, February 11, 1942, RG 2, box 3, folder 1.
16. MacArthur to Marshall, February 10, 1942, RG 2, box 3, folder 1; Roosevelt to MacArthur, February 11, 1942, RG 2, box 3, folder 1.
17. Marshall to MacArthur, circa February 11, 1942, RG 2, box 3, folder 1.
18. MacArthur to Marshall, February 12, 1942, RG 2, box 3, folder 1; MacArthur, *Reminiscences,* 138–39.
19. Versions of their discussion and Jean MacArthur's answer appear in many places, including in Frazier Hunt, *The Untold Story of Douglas MacArthur* (New York: Devin-Adair, 1954), 253; also see MacArthur to Roosevelt, February 11, 1942, RG 2, box 3, folder 1.
20. Huff, *My Fifteen Years,* 8; Marshall to MacArthur, February 14, 1942, RG 2, box 2, folder 4.
21. Wavell to MacArthur, February 19, 1942, RG 2, box 2, folder 4.
22. For an account of the Java Sea battles, see Jeffrey R. Cox, *Rising Sun, Falling Skies: The Disastrous Java Sea Campaign of World War II* (Oxford: Osprey, 2014).

23. Blair, *Silent Victory,* 152; Allied Warship Commanders, Chester Carl Smith, USN, http://uboat.net/allies/commanders/3225.html, accessed September 8, 2013; Diary of Basilio J. Valdes, February 20, 1942, https://philippinediaryproject .wordpress.com/1942/02/20/february-20-1942-friday/, accessed September 9, 2013; MacArthur to Riggs, February 23, 1942, RG 2, box 2, folder 4. The *Swordfish* also embarked the staff of the Asiatic Fleet's submarine command when Hart evacuated Manila.

24. MacArthur, *Reminiscences,* 139–40; MacArthur to Pershing, February 15, 1942, and Pershing to MacArthur, no date, Pershing papers, box 121.

25. MacArthur to Hurley, February 9, 1942, RG 2, box 2, folder 4.

26. Hurley to Marshall, February 21, 1942, quoted in Morton, *Fall of the Philippines,* 353.

27. Ferrell, *Eisenhower Diaries,* 49 (February 22, 1942).

28. Ferrell, *Eisenhower Diaries,* 49 (February 23, 1942).

29. Marshall to MacArthur, February 23, 1942, RG 2, box 2, folder 4.

30. See for example, MacArthur, *Reminiscences,* 140; Hunt, *Untold Story,* 256–57; Lee and Henschel, *Douglas MacArthur,* 156.

31. MacArthur to Marshall, February 24, 1942, quoted in Morton, *Fall of the Philippines,* 358.

32. Marshall to MacArthur, February 25, 1942, RG 4, box 15, folder 1; MacArthur to Marshall, February 26, 1942, RG 2, box 2, folder 4.

33. Memorandum of the Terms of the Agreement Between the President of the Philippine Commonwealth and General MacArthur, undated, RG 1, box 1, folder 2; Adjutant General to MacArthur, September 18, 1935, RG 1, box 1, folder 2.

34. Executive Order No. 1, January 3, 1942, RG 30, Papers of Lieutenant General Richard K. Sutherland, USA, Chief of Staff, SWPA, 1941–1945, box 2, folder 12; Paul P. Rogers, "MacArthur, Quezon and Executive Order Number One: Another View," *Pacific Historical Review* 52, no. 1 (February 1983), 93–94; 2012 values based on CPI at http://www.measuringworth.com/uscompare/relativevalue.php.

35. Carol Petillo, "Douglas MacArthur and Manuel Quezon: A Note on an Imperial Bond," *Pacific Historical Review* 48, no. 1 (February 1979), 114; Petillo, *The Philippine Years,* 208, 278n112–13, 279n115; MacArthur to Chase National Bank (via Adjutant General), February 15, 1942, RG 2, box 3, folder 7. A letter of thanks mentioning but not describing this executive order is in Quezon to MacArthur, February 20, 1942, RG 2, box 3, folder 7. According to Petillo's research, of the four recipients, only Sutherland "left any retrievable record of this event," and Sutherland may have done so "either intentionally or negligently."

36. Petillo, "Douglas MacArthur," 115n, 116n. For Stimson's criticism of MacArthur, see, for example, Stimson diary, March 23, 1942.

37. Ferrell, *Eisenhower Diaries,* 63, 404–5n (June 20, 1942).

38. Marshall to MacArthur, March 6, 1942, RG 2, box 2, folder 4.

39. MacArthur to Brett, March 1, 1942, RG 4, box 15, folder 1.

40. James, *Years of MacArthur,* 2:74–75; MacArthur, *Reminiscences,* 141.

41. Rockwell to Bulkeley, March 10, 1942, RG 4, box 15, folder 1.

42. Charles [sic] Bulkeley interview, RG 32, box 6, Oral History Interviews folder, number 19, page 14.

43. Huff, *My Fifteen Years,* 51–52.

44. Ibid., 55.
45. Jean MacArthur interview, RG 13, box 15, folder 6.

Chapter 8: Waltzing Matilda

1. MacArthur, *Reminiscences,* 144.
2. There are many accounts of this voyage, and many of them conflict on the details. This account is generally from George W. Smith, *MacArthur's Escape: John "Wild Man" Bulkeley and the Rescue of an American Hero* (St. Paul, MN: Zenith Press, 2005).
3. W. L. White, *They Were Expendable: An American Torpedo Boat Squadron in the U.S. Retreat from the Philippines* (New York: Harcourt, Brace, 1942), 137.
4. Huff, *Fifteen Years,* 63–64.
5. Manchester, *American Caesar,* 262.
6. John Bulkeley interview, RG 32, box 6. MacArthur recommended Bulkeley for the Medal of Honor. His award citation spoke generally about Bulkeley's bravery leading Motor Torpedo Boat Squadron Three from December 7, 1941, to April 10, 1942, and did not specifically mention the Corregidor evacuation. Bulkeley and the MacArthurs remained close, and the general did all he could to advance Bulkeley's career. He retired a vice admiral.
7. MacArthur to Marshall, March 14, 1942, quoted in Morton, *Fall of the Philippines,* 360. Contrary to MacArthur's doubts and despite a lack of brakes, Pease's B-17 made it back to Australia.
8. Jean MacArthur Oral History, RG 13, box 15, folder 6.
9. Blair, *Silent Victory,* 170–71. Whatever MacArthur's reasons for not waiting to depart Corregidor by submarine were, they did not include a lack of space for his party on the *Permit.* When the *Permit* arrived at Corregidor, the senior naval officer ordered Chapple to take on eight officers and thirty-two enlisted men, most of them from the Cast code-breaking unit. These forty, plus Schumacher, six of his crew from PT-32 (eight others were offloaded there), and Chapple's regular crew meant that 111 were crowded on board. The submarine headed for Australia, but Chapple was astonished to receive orders to conduct a war patrol just south of Manila en route. He did so, tangling with three destroyers and enduring a savage depth-charge attack. When he finally arrived in Australia after twenty-three days at sea with 111 people on board, he received an unexpected reprimand stating that, as the commanding officer, he should have "protested the carrying of a total of one hundred eleven persons in his ship."
10. Huff, *Fifteen Years,* 66–67.
11. Paul P. Rogers, *The Good Years: MacArthur and Sutherland* (New York: Praeger, 1990), 193.
12. Huff, *Fifteen Years,* 67.
13. Rogers, *The Good Years,* 193–94; Huff, *Fifteen Years,* 67–68.
14. James, *Years of MacArthur,* 2:108; Lee and Henschel, *Douglas MacArthur,* 160.
15. Huff, *Fifteen Years,* 72.
16. *The Argus* (Melbourne), January 3, 1955.
17. *Chronicle* (Adelaide), March 26, 1942.
18. Ibid.
19. Roosevelt, *Complete Presidential Press Conferences,* 19:208–9, March 17, 1942.

20. *New York Times,* March 18, 1942. In just four days, from March 16–19, 1942, the *Times* featured MacArthur in a total of twenty-one articles.
21. Editorial, *New York Times,* March 18, 1942.
22. *New York Times,* March 18, 1942.
23. Ferrell, *Eisenhower Diaries,* 51 (March 19, 1942).
24. Special Arrangements for General MacArthur's Arrival, RG 36, Selected Papers of Lieutenant General Stephen J. Chamberlin, USA, 1942–1946, box 1, folder 10.
25. *The Argus* (Melbourne), March 23, 1942.
26. John Hersey, *Men on Bataan* (New York: Knopf, 1944), 306.
27. MacArthur Press Statement, March 21, 1942, RG 4, box 49, folder 1.
28. Ugaki, *Fading Victory,* 106 (March 23, 1942).
29. *The Argus* (Melbourne), March 23, 1942.
30. MacArthur to Marshall, March 21, 1942, Henry Harley Arnold Papers, Manuscript Division, Library of Congress, Washington, DC.
31. John Jacob Beck, *MacArthur and Wainwright: Sacrifice of the Philippines* (Albuquerque: University of New Mexico Press, 1974), 167.
32. Ferrell, *Eisenhower Diaries,* 49 (February 23, 1942).
33. War Department to Sutherland, January 31, 1942, RG 4, box 15, folder 1.
34. Sutherland to Marshall, March 23, 1942, RG 30, box 2, folder 9.
35. Pogue, *Ordeal and Hope,* 254.
36. Marshall to Sutherland, March 25, 1942, RG 2, box 2, folder 4; Pogue, *Ordeal and Hope,* 253–54, 471n51–52.
37. MacArthur to Wainwright, March 29, 1942, RG 30, box 2, folder 9.

Chapter 9: CINCSWPA

1. Gavin Long, *MacArthur as Military Commander* (London: B. T. Batsford, 1969), 52.
2. James, *Years of MacArthur,* 2:78; Oral Reminiscences of Major General Richard J. Marshall, RG 49; "The Man Behind MacArthur," *Time,* December 7, 1942.
3. For one version of Willoughby's life, particularly his political persuasion, see Frank Kluckhohn, "Heidelberg to Madrid—The Story of General Willoughby," *The Reporter,* August 19, 1952.
4. Roosevelt, *Complete Presidential Press Conferences,* 19:156, February 24, 1942; James, *Years of MacArthur,* 2:86.
5. James, *Years of MacArthur,* 2:87.
6. Ferrell, *Eisenhower Diaries,* 53, (March 31, 1942).
7. Eisenhower interview, RG 32, box 6. Eisenhower went on to say: "Later General Marshall tried to initiate a Medal of Honor for me after the North African landings, but I told him that I would refuse to accept it and thought that all men in high command and headquarters jobs should be excluded from that honor."
8. H. R. 6649, 77th Congress, 2nd session, February 23, 1942. Hill was not reelected.
9. Executive Order No. 9096, 42 Fed. Reg. 2195, March 12, 1942.
10. Borneman, *Admirals,* 260–61.
11. Morton, *Strategy and Command,* 243, 246.
12. Hayes, *Joint Chiefs,* 100–101.
13. Directive to the Supreme Commander in the Southwest Pacific Area (CCS 57/1) March 30, 1942, in Morton, *Strategy and Command,* 614–15.

14. Directive to the Commander in Chief of the Pacific Ocean Area (CCS 51/1) March 30, 1942, in Morton, *Strategy and Command,* 617–18.
15. Hayes, *Joint Chiefs,* 102–3, 766n66; Morton, *Strategy and Command,* 251. Hayes says that no Marshall reply was found as of 1982.
16. MacArthur to Shedden, April 13, 1942, quoted in James, *Years of MacArthur,* 2:844n.
17. Morton, *Fall of the Philippines,* 422.
18. MacArthur to Marshall, April 8, 1942, quoted in Morton, *Fall of the Philippines,* 441.
19. MacArthur to Wainwright, April 4, 1942, quoted in Morton, *Fall of the Philippines,* 452.
20. Wainwright to MacArthur, April 8, 1942, quoted in Morton, *Fall of the Philippines,* 453.
21. Morton, *Fall of the Philippines,* 455–56.
22. Ibid., 458n18.
23. Wainwright to MacArthur, April 9, 1942, quoted in Beck, *MacArthur and Wainwright,* 194–95.
24. Morton, *Fall of the Philippines,* 467.
25. MacArthur to Fellers, June 18, 1943, RG 44a, box 3, folder "Correspondence."
26. Long, *MacArthur as Military Commander,* 83.
27. *Time,* March 30, 1942. MacArthur was no stranger to newspapers. During his tenure as chief of staff and his years in the Philippines, the *New York Times* ran hundreds of MacArthur articles and reported his activities, from the social—giving his deceased brother's daughter away in marriage—to the professional, including speculation about his successor as chief of staff and his Hyde Park luncheon with FDR. By 1940, those reports increasingly chronicled his supervision of Philippine defenses and occasionally noted his views on world events, such as his call for supporting Great Britain. *New York Times,* June 26, 1935 (Mary MacArthur wedding); May 1, 1937 (his wedding); September 4, 1935 (FDR luncheon); September 16, 1940 (Great Britain support).
28. *Time,* April 20, 1942.
29. George Clark, "The Neighbors" cartoon, April 13, 1942, found as a clipping in George Van Horn Moseley Papers, Library of Congress, box 9, folder 14.
30. Bob Considine, *MacArthur the Magnificent* (London: Hutchinson, 1942), 14–15, 128.

Chapter 10: Saving Australia
1. MacArthur to Marshall, March 21, 1942, Arnold papers.
2. James, *Years of MacArthur,* 2:121–22; Pogue, *Ordeal and Hope,* 375, 479n; Dudley McCarthy, *South-West Pacific Area—First Year: Kokoda to Wau,* Australia in the War of 1939–1945, ser. 1, vol. 5 (Canberra: Australian War Memorial, 1959), 29; Peter J. Dean, *The Architect of Victory: The Military Career of Lieutenant-General Sir Frank Horton Berryman* (Port Melbourne, Australia: Cambridge University Press, 2011), 210; David Horner, *Inside the War Cabinet: Directing Australia's War Efforts, 1939–45* (St. Leonards, Australia: Allen & Unwin, 1996), 114.
3. "General Hal George, 2nd Lt. Robert D. Jasper, & War Correspondent Mel Jacoby Killed in a Kittyhawk Ground Accident at Batchelor Airfield on 29 April

1942," in http://www.ozatwar.com/ozcrashes/nt105.htm, accessed October 20, 2013. Twenty-five-year-old Jacoby had recently married Annalee Whitmore, who became a celebrated World War II correspondent in her own right. They had been honeymooning in Manila before evacuating by boat on New Year's Eve.

4. *Chronicle* (Adelaide), March 26, 1942, 26.

5. Ugaki, *Fading Victory,* 68 (January 5, 1942).

6. Report of Prime Minister and Chiefs of Staff to Emperor, March 13, 1942, in Morton, *Strategy and Command,* 611–13. This report also called the prospects of any peace between its ally, Germany, and Germany's former ally, the Soviet Union, "utterly hopeless" and concluded that any attempt to mediate that dispute "would be detrimental" to Japan's relations with each.

7. Samuel Milner, *Victory in Papua,* vol. 4 of *The United States Army in World War II: The War in the Pacific* (Washington, DC: Center of Military History, United States Army, 1989), 3; Horner, *Inside the War Cabinet,* 97–98, 108.

8. Milner, *Victory in Papua,* 12–13; Steven Bullard, "Japanese Strategy and Intentions Towards Australia," in Peter J. Dean, ed., *Australia 1942: In the Shadow of War* (Cambridge: Cambridge University Press, 2013), 129–137.

9. Milner, *Victory in Papua,* 6–8. Part of the reason that Admiral Leary resisted Brett's first request for his newer B-17s to transport MacArthur from Del Monte was that they were busy bombing Japanese troop concentrations at Rabaul.

10. John B. Lundstrom, *Black Shoe Carrier Admiral: Frank Jack Fletcher at Coral Sea, Midway, and Guadalcanal* (Annapolis, MD: Naval Institute Press, 2006), 92–95; Milner, *Victory in Papua,* 10–11.

11. Marshall to CG USAFIA, April 27, 1942, RG 4, box 15, folder 3.

12. "Australia's Prime Ministers," National Archives of Australia, at http://primeministers .naa.gov.au/primeministers/curtin/in-office.aspx, accessed July 26, 2014.

13. *Sydney Morning Herald,* December 29, 1941.

14. Wilkinson journal, October 19, 1942, quoted in Christopher Thorne, *Allies of a Kind: The United States, Britain, and the War Against Japan, 1941–1945* (New York: Oxford University Press, 1978), 260.

15. Dean, *Australia 1942,* 185.

16. Churchill to Roosevelt, April 29, 1942, in Milner, *Victory in Papua,* 28–29.

17. Marshall to MacArthur, April 30, 1942, RG 4, box 15, folder 3.

18. MacArthur to Marshall, May 3, 1942, RG 4, box 15, folder 3.

19. Roosevelt to MacArthur, May 6, 1942, RG 4, box 15, folder 3. Stimson was harsher in his criticism of MacArthur's Australian lobbying. From Australian sources, he learned that "MacArthur is talking very disloyally to the Australians about the plans of his superiors here. In short, he is arguing very strongly and really egging the Australians on to try to make the Australian theatre the main theatre of the war and to postpone what we are trying to do in regard to fighting Hitler first." Stimson diary, May 13, 1942.

20. The standard works on King are Thomas B. Buell, *Master of Sea Power: A Biography of Fleet Admiral Ernest J. King* (Boston: Little, Brown, 1980), and Ernest J. King and Walter Muir Whitehill, *Fleet Admiral King: A Naval Record* (New York: Norton, 1952).

21. The standard biography of Nimitz, who declined to write his memoirs, is E. B. Potter, *Nimitz* (Annapolis, MD: Naval Institute Press, 1976).

22. King to Roosevelt, memorandum, March 5, 1942, Safe Files, box 3, Franklin D. Roosevelt Library.
23. Marshall to MacArthur, April 30, 1942, RG 4, box 15, folder 3.
24. MacArthur to Marshall, May 1, 1942, RG 4, box 15, folder 3.
25. Edward J. Drea, *MacArthur's ULTRA: Codebreaking and the War Against Japan, 1942–1945* (Lawrence: University Press of Kansas, 1992), 15–16, 36; Edwin T. Layton, *"And I Was There": Pearl Harbor and Midway—Breaking the Secrets* (New York: William Morrow, 1985), 389–90.
26. Lundstrom, *Black Shoe Carrier Admiral,* 125–27.
27. Milner, *Victory in Papua,* 35.
28. Lundstrom, *Black Shoe Carrier Admiral,* 138–39.
29. Milner, *Victory in Papua,* 36; James, *Years of MacArthur,* 2:159–60.
30. George Hermon Gill, *Royal Australian Navy, 1942–1945,* Australia in the War of 1939–1945, ser. 2, vol. 2 (Canberra: Australian War Memorial, 1968), 47–50.
31. Samuel Eliot Morison, *History of United States Naval Operations in World War II,* vol. 4, *Coral Sea, Midway, and Submarine Actions* (Boston: Little, Brown, 1988), 39; James, *Years of MacArthur,* 2:161. Morison's take on this action was to write: "Ship recognition comes hard to the 'fly-fly boys' of every nation; let those who have tried it from 10,000 feet, without previous training, cast the first stone!"
32. Samuel Eliot Morison, *The Two-Ocean War: A Short History of the United States Navy in the Second World War* (Boston: Little, Brown, 1963), 143–44; Lundstrom, *Black Shoe Carrier Admiral,* 168.
33. Borneman, *Admirals,* 248–49.
34. Gill, *Royal Australian Navy,* 154–55; SWPA press release (May 8, 1942), communiqué no. 20 (May 8, 1942), and communiqués no. 21 and 22 (May 9, 1942), RG 4, box 47, folder 1.
35. Marshall to MacArthur, May 9, 1942, quoted in James, *Years of MacArthur,* 2:166.
36. MacArthur to Marshall, May 10, 1942, quoted in James, *Years of MacArthur,* 2:166–67.
37. Roosevelt to King, May 18, 1942, in Roosevelt, *F.D.R.: His Personal Letters,* 2:1320–21.
38. MacArthur to Nimitz, May 19, 1942, quoted in James, *Years of MacArthur,* 2:162–63.
39. Robert H. Van Volkenburgh interview, in James, *Years of MacArthur,* 2:162.

Chapter 11: Kokoda Trail

1. Ferrell, *Eisenhower Diaries,* 54 (May 6, 1942).
2. Morton, *Fall of the Philippines,* 360–65.
3. MacArthur to Sharp, May 9, 1942, quoted in Morton, *Fall of the Philippines,* 575; Wainwright to Sharp, May 7, 1942, RG 2, box 2, folder 4; Morton, *Fall of the Philippines,* 466, 562, 569–73.
4. Pogue, *Ordeal and Hope,* 258.
5. MacArthur to Marshall, August 1, 1942, RG 4, box 15, folder 4.
6. Appreciation by the [Australian] Chiefs of Staff, February 27, 1942, quoted in Milner, *Victory in Papua,* 23.

7. Appreciation by the [Australian] Chiefs of Staff, February 27, 1942, quoted in Milner, *Victory in Papua,* 24.
8. Milner, *Victory in Papua,* 12–13. The Japanese army nixed suggestions to invade Ceylon for the same reason it opposed an invasion of Australia—the operation would tie up too many men and resources.
9. David Horner, "MacArthur and Curtin: Deciding Australian War Strategy in 1943," in Peter J. Dean, ed., *Australia 1943: The Liberation of New Guinea* (Port Melbourne, Australia: Cambridge University Press, 2014), 41; Long, *MacArthur as Military Commander,* 95.
10. Curtin to MacArthur, May 16, 1942, quoted in Milner, *Victory in Papua,* 24. The March 26, 1942, minutes of the Australian Advisory War Council—a more political group than Curtin's war cabinet but with considerable overlap—paraphrase MacArthur as saying: "It is doubtful whether the Japanese would undertake an invasion of Australia as the spoils here are not sufficient to warrant the risk. From a strategic point of view, invasion of Australia would be a blunder." Minutes of Advisory War Council Meeting, Canberra, 26 March, 1942, quoted in Horner, *Inside the War Cabinet,* 225.
11. Long, *MacArthur as Military Commander,* 95–96, quoting, in part, an April 25, 1942, SWPA communiqué.
12. McCarthy, *Kokoda to Wau,* 82.
13. *Sydney Morning Herald,* May 9, 1942.
14. MacArthur to Curtin, October 6, 1942, quoted in Milner, *Victory in Papua,* 24.
15. SWPA communiqué, March 18, 1943, quoted in Long, *MacArthur as Military Commander,* 94–95.
16. MacArthur to Curtin, November 6, 1943, quoted in Milner, *Victory in Papua,* 25.
17. Curtin to Blamey, November 16, 1943, quoted in Morton, *Strategy and Command,* 255.
18. MacArthur to Smith, March 5, 1953, quoted in Morton, *Strategy and Command,* 255.
19. MacArthur, *Reminiscences,* 152; Courtney Whitney, *MacArthur: His Rendezvous with History* (New York: Knopf, 1956), 64–65; Charles A. Willoughby and John Chamberlain, *MacArthur: 1941–1951* (New York: McGraw-Hill, 1954), 67.
20. Milner, *Victory in Papua,* 27, 39.
21. Ibid., 26, 41–42.
22. Ibid., 41.
23. MacArthur to Blamey, June 9, 1942, quoted in Milner, *Victory in Papua,* 43.
24. Milner, *Victory in Papua,* 44.
25. For the best recent accounts of the Battle of Midway, see Craig L. Symonds, *The Battle of Midway* (New York: Oxford University Press, 2011), and Jonathan Parshall and Anthony Tully, *Shattered Sword: The Untold Story of the Battle of Midway* (Washington, DC: Potomac Books, 2007), particularly 63–66, regarding the impact of the *Shokaku* and *Zuikaku* missing Midway.
26. MacArthur to Nimitz, June 8, 1942, RG 4, box 49, folder 1.
27. John Miller Jr., *Guadalcanal: The First Offensive,* vol. 3 of *The United States Army in World War II: The War in the Pacific* (Washington, DC: Center of Military History, United States Army, 1995), 9.
28. MacArthur to Marshall, June 8, 1942, RG 4, box 15, folder 4.

29. James, *Years of MacArthur,* 2:185–86; Marshall to MacArthur, June 23, 1942, and MacArthur to Marshall, June 24, 1942, RG 4, box 15, folder 4.
30. Rogers, *The Good Years,* 245.
31. James, *Years of MacArthur,* 2:188.
32. D. Clayton James, "American and Japanese Strategies in the Pacific War," in Peter Paret, ed., *Makers of Modern Strategy from Machiavelli to the Nuclear Age* (Princeton, NJ: Princeton University Press, 1986), 731.
33. MacArthur to Marshall, June 24, 1942, RG 4, box 15, folder, 4.
34. MacArthur to Marshall, June 28, 1942, RG 4, box 15, folder 4.
35. Marshall to MacArthur, June 29, 1942, RG 4, box 15, folder 4.
36. Joint Directive for Offensive Operations in the Southwest Pacific Area Agreed Upon by the United States Chiefs of Staff, 2 July 1942, in Morton, *Strategy and Command,* 619–20.
37. Marshall to MacArthur, July 4, 1942, RG 4, box 15, folder 4.
38. Miller, *Guadalcanal,* 7–8.
39. Milner, *Victory in Papua,* 3.
40. Milner, *Victory in Papua,* 51–55; James, *Years of MacArthur,* 2:191–93.
41. James, *Years of MacArthur,* 2:13–14.
42. Rogers, *The Good Years,* 276–78.
43. Arnold, *Global Mission,* 331. The extent of the MacArthur-Brett enmity is evidenced by an episode involving Brett's use of a B-17 for his return to the United States after his recall. MacArthur maintained that he had given Brett permission to take the plane only as far as Hawaii and ordered him to "return it without delay to Australia." According to MacArthur, "I specifically ordered that under no circumstances whatever was this plane to proceed beyond Hawaii." Telling Marshall that Brett had "acted in direct violation of a mandatory order," MacArthur recommended that "appropriate action be taken with regard to General Brett's deliberate disobedience of a lawful order." Marshall, who had his hands full with far weightier matters, responded: "General Brett is firmly of the opinion that you approved memorandum he presented to you authorizing him to bring this plane to the United States. The present situation is obviously a misunderstanding. The plane needed overhauling badly and will go in the shops here. Accordingly desire that the whole matter be dropped. Naturally this plane will be replaced as an attrition loss." MacArthur to Marshall, September 1, 1942, and Marshall to MacArthur, September 2, 1942, Arnold papers, reel 158.
44. Thomas E. Griffith Jr., *MacArthur's Airman: General George C. Kenney and the War in the Southwest Pacific* (Lawrence: University Press of Kansas, 1998), 1–6.
45. Griffith, *MacArthur's Airman,* 14–16.
46. Ibid., 17, 42.
47. Ibid., 46, 56.
48. Marshall to MacArthur, July 7, 1942, and MacArthur to Marshall, July 7, 1942, RG 4, box 15, folder 4.
49. George C. Kenney, *General Kenney Reports: A Personal History of the Pacific War* (Washington, DC: Office of Air Force History, 1987), 9, 11.
50. Kenney, *General Kenney Reports,* 26–27.
51. Kenney, *General Kenney Reports,* 28–29. In 2015, the MacArthur Museum Brisbane occupies this space with exhibits and archives related to the general's

wartime activities. The insurance company continued to use a portion of the building throughout the war despite its accommodation to MacArthur. See www .mmb.org.au.

52. Kenney, *General Kenney Reports*, 29–30.

Chapter 12: "Take Buna, Bob..."

1. Milner, *Victory in Papua*, 62–65.
2. Ibid., 70.
3. King to Marshall, July 31, 1942, quoted in Milner, *Victory in Papua*, 72.
4. MacArthur and Ghormley to Marshall and King, July 8, 1942, RG 4, box 15, folder 4.
5. King to Marshall, July 10, 1942, quoted in James, *Years of MacArthur*, 2:202.
6. MacArthur and Ghormley to Marshall and King, July 8, 1942, RG 4, box 15, folder 4.
7. Milner, *Victory in Papua*, 58, 65–66, 70.
8. Ibid., 66–68, 72, 77. The Kawaguichi Detachment, sent to Guadalcanal, would be decimated in heavy fighting on Bloody Ridge.
9. Ibid., 76–77, 80–81.
10. Ibid., 86–87.
11. SWPA communiqué no. 140, August 31, 1942, quoted in Charles Willoughby, et al., eds., *Reports of General MacArthur: The Campaigns of MacArthur in the Pacific*, vol. 1 (Washington, DC: Chief of Military History, 1994), 70.
12. Milner, *Victory in Papua*, 89–91.
13. Ibid., 92.
14. The Kenney alcohol story comes from Griffith, *MacArthur's Airman*, 25. Eichelberger didn't remember this story until Kenney told him in New Guinea in 1942, according to Robert L. Eichelberger, *Our Jungle Road to Tokyo* (New York: Viking, 1950), xv. Biographies of Eichelberger include J. F. Shortal, *Forged by Fire: General Robert L. Eichelberger and the Pacific War* (Columbia: University of South Carolina Press, 1987), and Paul Chwialkowski, *In Caesar's Shadow: The Life of General Robert Eichelberger* (Westport, CT: Greenwood Press, 1993).
15. Chwialkowski, *In Caesar's Shadow*, 52–53; "Richardson's intense feelings," Marshall to MacArthur, July 30, 1942, RG 4, box 15, folder 4.
16. Rogers, *The Good Years*, 317.
17. Eichelberger, *Our Jungle Road*, 11–12; Milner, *Victory in Papua*, 92, 133. Part of the problem was that troops trained in large measure by officers and NCOs without combat experience had yet to meet wartime reality. According to the official Australian history, "The Australian soldier lived hard during training; in battle he was in many respects no more uncomfortable than he had often been before. The American formations on the other hand tended, in Australian opinion, to clutter themselves up with inessential paraphernalia, and thus to increase the difference between camp life and battle conditions to such an extent that contact with the latter was bound to produce a rude shock, even to the most high-spirited." See McCarthy, *Kokoda to Wau*, 33.
18. Kenney, *General Kenney Reports*, 53.
19. Kenney, *General Kenney Reports*, 97–99; Milner, *Victory in Papua*, 95.
20. Milner, *Victory in Papua*, 97–100.

Notes

21. Kenney, *General Kenney Reports,* 11–12. Whitehead would remain Kenney's right arm throughout the war. Walker was reportedly killed in January of 1943 while leading a bomber raid against Rabaul, despite Kenney's orders to stay out of combat. Some speculation exists that Walker survived a crash landing only to die as a prisoner of war.

22. See, for example, Kenney's interview recollections in James, *Years of MacArthur,* 2:246–247, and Rogers, *The Good Years,* 329.

23. MacArthur to Kenney, September 6, 1942, quoted in Griffith, *MacArthur's Airman,* 89.

24. MacArthur to Marshall, September 16, 1942, RG 4, box 16, folder 1.

25. MacArthur to Marshall, September 30, 1942, RG 4, box 16, folder 1.

26. James, *Years of MacArthur,* 2:226, 231.

27. Marshall to MacArthur, September 21, 1942, RG 4, box 16, folder 1.

28. MacArthur to Marshall, September 17, 1942, RG 4, box 16, folder 1.

29. Marshall to MacArthur, September 11[?], 1942, RG 4, box 16, folder 1.

30. MacArthur to Marshall, September 22, 1942, RG 4, box 16, folder 1.

31. Marshall to MacArthur, September 23, 1942, RG 4, box 16, folder 1; Kenney, *General Kenney Reports,* 115.

32. Borneman, *Admirals,* 294–97. Hap Arnold took part in the Nouméa conference after having been in Australia to meet with MacArthur and inspect Kenney's air operations. In his diary, Arnold gave Kenney high praise—"a real leader and has the finest bunch of pilots I have seen"—and MacArthur mixed reviews: "Thinking it over, MacArthur's two hour talk gives me the impression of a brilliant mind, obsessed by a plan he can't carry out; frustrated to the extreme, much more nervous than when I formerly knew him, hands twitch and tremble, shell-shocked." See John W. Huston, ed., *American Airpower Comes of Age: General Henry H. "Hap" Arnold's World War II Diaries* (Maxwell Air Force Base, AL: Air University Press, 2002), 1:394.

33. Eichelberger to MacArthur, September 29, 1942, RG 30, box 1, folder 6.

34. James, *Years of MacArthur,* 2:173; Kenney, *General Kenney Reports,* 101.

35. McCarthy, *Kokoda to Wau,* 280; James, *Years of MacArthur,* 2:232–33; Kenney, *General Kenney Reports,* 105.

36. Milner, *Victory in Papua,* 104–6, 110, 113, 115, 121, 214, 413; for MacArthur's report of Horii's death, see SWPA press release, December 21, 1942, RG 4, box 49, folder 1.

37. SWPA press release, November 18, 1942, RG 4, box 49, folder 1.

38. Milner, *Victory in Papua,* 125–27.

39. McCarthy, *Kokoda to Wau,* 310.

40. Eichelberger, *Our Jungle Road,* 23.

41. Ibid., 34.

42. James, *Years of MacArthur,* 2:241.

43. Halsey to MacArthur, November 28, 1942, RG 4, box 10, folder 2.

44. MacArthur to Marshall, November 29, 1942, RG 4, box, 16, folder 1.

45. Eichelberger, *Our Jungle Road,* 15–16.

46. Sutherland to Chamberlin, November 29, 1942, Selected Papers of Lieutenant General Robert L. Eichelberger, USA, Commanding General, Eighth Army, SWPA, USAFPAC, FECOM, 1942–1948, RG 41, box 1, folder 3.

536

47. Eichelberger, *Our Jungle Road,* 20–21.
48. Kenney, *General Kenney Reports,* 157–58; "absolute nadir," Frank, *MacArthur,* 63.
49. Eichelberger, *Our Jungle Road,* 21–22; Milner, *Victory in Papua,* 205n.
50. Eichelberger, *Our Jungle Road,* 22.
51. For "inspired leadership," see Eichelberger to Sutherland, December 3, 1942, RG 41, box 1, folder 2; Harding to MacArthur, December 7, 1942, RG 30, box 1, folder 6. Harding went on to minor commands in the Canal Zone and the Caribbean before overseeing the army's official history of the war.
52. Eichelberger to Sutherland, December 13, 1942, RG 41, box 1, folder 2.
53. MacArthur to Eichelberger, December 13, 1942, RG 41, box 1, folder 2.
54. MacArthur to Eichelberger, December 25, 1942, RG 41, box 1, folder 2.
55. Rogers, *The Good Years,* 341.

Chapter 13: Finishing Buna, Looking Ahead

1. *Fortune,* November 1942, 8, 14. In the segregationist manner of the time, *Fortune* broke the results into "White students" and "Negro students." The latter named Roosevelt first, followed by Joe Louis, MacArthur, and George Washington Carver.
2. *Pittsburgh Press,* June 5, 1942; *Portland Guardian* (Victoria), June 13, 1942; James, *Years of MacArthur,* 2:171.
3. Blamey to MacArthur, January 28, 1943, and MacArthur to Blamey, February 12, 1943, RG 4, box 6, folder 2. Among the reasons for the friction were "the spectacle of American troops with Australian girls, particularly the wives of absent soldiers, and the American custom of caressing girls in public [and] boasting by some American troops, and their tendency to draw guns or knives in a quarrel." See McCarthy, *Kokoda to Wau,* 625–26.
4. Long, *MacArthur as Military Commander,* 118.
5. Ibid., 119.
6. *Time,* July 6, 1942.
7. MacArthur to Marshall, August 8, 1942, RG 4, box 15, folder 4.
8. Marshall to MacArthur, August 10, 1942, RG 4, box 15, folder 4; *Washington Post,* August 7, 1942.
9. MacArthur to Marshall, August 11, 1942, RG 4, box 15, folder 4.
10. Huston, *American Airpower,* 1:392–93, September 25, 1942.
11. Edward V. Rickenbacker, *Rickenbacker: An Autobiography* (Englewood Cliffs, NJ: Prentice-Hall, 1967), 327, 337, 376.
12. For such speculation, see, for example, Frank, *MacArthur,* 59; W. David Lewis, *Eddie Rickenbacker: An American Hero of the Twentieth Century* (Baltimore: Johns Hopkins University Press, 2005), 414–15, 443–44, 622n; Finis Farr, *Rickenbacker's Luck: An American Life* (Boston: Houghton Mifflin, 1979), 241.
13. For one person's speculation about Sutherland's thoughts, see Rogers, *The Good Years,* 342.
14. Eichelberger to American Troops in the Buna Area, January 3, 1943, RG 41, box 1, folder 3.
15. SWPA communiqué no. 271, January 8, 1943, quoted in Willoughby, et al., *Reports of General MacArthur,* 1:98.
16. MacArthur to Eichelberger, January 8, 1943, RG 41, box 1, folder 3.

17. Miller, *Guadalcanal,* 348.
18. Jay Luvaas, ed., *Dear Miss Em: General Eichelberger's War in the Pacific, 1942–1945* (Westport, CT: Greenwood Press, 1972), 62.
19. Eichelberger, *Our Jungle Road,* 57; *Courier-Mail* (Brisbane), January 8, 1943.
20. Milner, *Victory in Papua,* 330, 347, 358, 361–62.
21. Eichelberger to Sutherland, January 16, 1943, RG 41, box 1, folder 3.
22. Order of the Day, January 22, 1943, quoted in Milner, *Victory in Papua,* 365.
23. Eichelberger, *Our Jungle Road,* 22.
24. Mitsuo Koiwai postwar testimony, quoted in Milner, *Victory in Papua,* 374.
25. SWPA communiqué no. 291, January 28, 1943, RG 4, box 47, folder 3.
26. Milner, *Victory in Papua,* 370–72.
27. Miller, *Guadalcanal,* 350. These numbers do not include air or naval losses, the latter of which totaled more than four thousand American sailors in the naval engagements around Guadalcanal.
28. Milner, *Victory in Papua,* 372.
29. SWPA press release, January 24, 1943, RG 4, box 49, folder 1.
30. SWPA press release, January 9, 1943, RG 4, box 49, folder 1.
31. James, *Years of MacArthur,* 2:275–76. After the North African campaign, Marshall recommended Eisenhower for a Medal of Honor after he had seen far less frontline action than Eichelberger. Eisenhower refused to be considered for it, thinking it an undeserved combat decoration and—according to what Eichelberger claimed Eisenhower told him after the war—"because he knew of a man who had received one for sitting in a hole in the ground—meaning MacArthur" on Corregidor. See Luvaas, *Dear Miss Em,* 76n15.
32. Michael Schaller, *Douglas MacArthur: The Far Eastern General* (New York: Oxford University Press, 1989), 69.
33. *Life,* February 15, 1943, 17–18; *Saturday Evening Post,* February 20, 1943, 22.
34. Luvaas, *Dear Miss Em,* 65.
35. Ibid.
36. MacArthur, *Reminiscences,* 157; Luvaas, *Dear Miss Em,* 65.
37. It has generally been reported by historians that the British had their way on the first two points and that the Americans prevailed on the latter. Given the indirect nature of the first two against Germany, it has even been argued that they combined with the third to create "a de-facto Pacific-first strategy in the face of direct presidential orders to the contrary." See Mark A. Stoler, *Allies and Adversaries: The Joint Chiefs of Staff, the Grand Alliance, and U.S. Strategy in World War II* (Chapel Hill: University of North Carolina Press, 2000), 101.
38. Arnold to Marshall, October 6, 1942, quoted in Hayes, *Joint Chiefs,* 265.
39. Streett to Wedemeyer, October 9, 1942, and Wedemeyer to Streett, October 11, 1942, quoted in Hayes, *Joint Chiefs,* 265. The War Plans Division became the Operations Division, War Department General Staff, effective March 23, 1942.
40. Streett to Handy, October 31, 1942, quoted in Hayes, *Joint Chiefs,* 265–66.
41. *New York Times,* February 23, 1942; Stimson diary, December 10, 1941; Huston, *American Airpower,* 1:392–93, September 25, 1942.
42. For a further discussion of the myth—or reality—of unity of command, see Phillip S. Meilinger, "Unity of Command in the Pacific During World War II," *Joint Force Quarterly* 56 (2010), 152–56.

43. Stimson and Bundy, *On Active Service,* 507.
44. Hayes, *Joint Chiefs,* 266–67.
45. Ibid., 269–71.

Chapter 14: "Skipping" the Bismarck Sea

1. MacArthur and Ghormley to Marshall and King, July 8, 1942, RG 4, box 15, folder 4.
2. MacArthur to Marshall, January 27, 1943, RG 4, box 16, folder 2.
3. King to Marshall, February 6, 1943, quoted in Hayes, *Joint Chiefs,* 309.
4. Hayes, *Joint Chiefs,* 311, 821n30.
5. John Miller Jr., *Cartwheel: The Reduction of Rabaul,* vol. 5 of *The United States Army in World War II: The War in the Pacific* (Washington, DC: Center of Military History, United States Army, 1959), 34–36.
6. Drea, *MacArthur's ULTRA,* 67; Miller, *Cartwheel,* 36–38.
7. Drea, *MacArthur's ULTRA,* xii.
8. Drea, *MacArthur's ULTRA,* 68; Miller, *Cartwheel,* 40. Based on Ultra, Kenney's bombers disrupted an earlier attempt to reinforce Lae, sinking two transports, damaging another, and eliminating six hundred soldiers who might have made the difference at Wau. Ultra was not, however, infallible. Because of a temporary blackout caused by a change of cipher key, cryptanalysts missed the move of ten thousand men of the Twentieth Division from Palau to Wewak. See Drea, *MacArthur's ULTRA,* 66.
9. Drea, *MacArthur's ULTRA,* 69–71, 251n22; Miller, *Cartwheel,* 40–41; "We went in," *New York Times,* March 7, 1943.
10. SWPA communiqué no. 326, March 4, 1943, RG 4, box 47, folder 3. There were no cruisers in the immediate Bismarck–Huon Gulf area, although large destroyers were routinely misidentified as light cruisers by both sides.
11. Diller interview, quoted in James, *Years of MacArthur,* 2:295.
12. SWPA communiqué no. 329, March 7, 1943, RG 4, box 47, folder 3.
13. *Washington Post,* April 14, 1943.
14. Ibid., April 14, 1943.
15. Wedemeyer to Marshall, April 15, 1943, quoted in James, *Years of MacArthur,* 2:297.
16. Wesley Frank Craven and James Lea Cate, eds., *The Pacific: Guadalcanal to Saipan, August 1942 to July 1944,* vol. 4 of *The Army Air Forces in World War II* (Washington, DC: Office of Air Force History, 1983), 147–49.
17. Marshall to MacArthur, September 7, 1943, RG 3, box 1, folder 7.
18. MacArthur to Marshall, September 7, 1943, RG 3, box 1, folder 7.
19. Marshall to MacArthur, September 8, 1943, RG 3, box 1, folder 7; Kenney to Arnold, September 14, 1943, RG 4; box 6, folder 1; James, *Years of MacArthur,* 2:299. The air force historical office accepted the lower losses.
20. *Washington Post,* September 4, 1945.
21. James, *Years of MacArthur,* 2:300.
22. MacArthur, *Reminiscences,* 171; Kenney, *General Kenney Reports,* 205; Whitney, *Rendezvous with History,* 85; Willoughby, *MacArthur,* 111.
23. Kenney, *The MacArthur I Know,* 91. This book was released in the wake of MacArthur's firing by Truman and essentially reiterated pro-MacArthur accounts from *General Kenney Reports.*

24. Kenney interview, quoted in James, *Years of MacArthur,* 2:301–2; Samuel Eliot Morison, *History of United States Naval Operations in World War II,* vol. 6, *Breaking the Bismarcks Barrier* (Boston: Little, Brown, 1950), 64.
25. James, *Years of MacArthur,* 2:303.
26. Drea, *MacArthur's ULTRA,* 71–72.
27. *Washington Post,* September 4, 1945.
28. Rickenbacker, *Rickenbacker,* 332–33.
29. Maurice Matloff, *Strategic Planning for Coalition Warfare, 1943–1944,* vol. 4 of *United States Army in World War II: The War Department* (Washington, DC: Center of Military History, United States Army, 1994), 92n62.
30. Matloff, *Strategic Planning,* 93.
31. Hayes, *Joint Chiefs,* 313–14; Matloff, *Strategic Planning,* 92n61, 97; Richard M. Leighton and Robert W. Coakley, *Global Logistics and Strategy, 1940–1943* vol. 5 of *United States Army in World War II: The War Department* (Washington, DC: Center of Military History, United States Army, 1995), 694.
32. Kenney, *General Kenney Reports,* 211–12.
33. Hayes, *Joint Chiefs,* 315–16.
34. Memo, Sutherland, Spruance, and Browning to JCS, "Offensive Operations in the South and Southwest Pacific Areas during 1943," March 20, 1943, quoted in Hayes, *Joint Chiefs,* 326.
35. Hayes, *Joint Chiefs,* 327.
36. Joint Chiefs of Staff Directive: Offensive Operations in the South and Southwest Pacific Areas During 1943, 28 March 1943, in Morton, *Strategy and Command,* 641.

Chapter 15: Meeting Halsey

1. Borneman, *Admirals,* 43–48, 78; "had the time," Halsey, *Admiral Halsey's Story,* 33; for a full-length biography of Halsey, see E. B. Potter, *Bull Halsey: A Biography* (Annapolis, MD: Naval Institute Press, 1985).
2. Borneman, *Admirals,* 156–58, 177–78; Halsey, *Admiral Halsey's Story,* 66.
3. MacArthur to Halsey, February 9, 1943, RG 4, box 10, folder 2.
4. Halsey to Nimitz, February 13, 1943, William Frederick Halsey Papers, Manuscript Division, Library of Congress, Washington, DC, box 15, file folder "Special Correspondence, Nimitz, 1941–April 1943."
5. Halsey, *Admiral Halsey's Story,* 154.
6. MacArthur to Nimitz and Halsey, January 13, 1943, RG 4, box 10, folder 2. Despite his "Allied" command, MacArthur seems to have been loath to have the Australian Blamey preside over SWPA in his absence.
7. Marshall to MacArthur, January, 1943, RG 4, box 16, folder 2.
8. Potter, *Bull Halsey,* 215.
9. Halsey, *Admiral Halsey's Story,* 154–55.
10. MacArthur, *Reminiscences,* 173–74.
11. Nimitz to Halsey, May 14, 1943, Chester W. Nimitz Papers, series 13, box 120, Naval History and Heritage Command, Washington, DC.
12. The Elkton III plan is reproduced in Morton, *Strategy and Command,* 675–85; James, *Years of MacArthur,* 2:315–16; Miller, *Cartwheel,* 26.
13. James, *Years of MacArthur,* 2:317.

14. MacArthur to Marshall, June 12, 1943, RG 4, box 16, folder 3.
15. An extract from the final report of the Trident Conference, approved May 25, 1943, is reproduced in Morton, *Strategy and Command,* 648–49. The invasion of the Gilbert Islands, and what would prove to be bloody Tarawa, was not added as a step to precede the Marshall invasion until the Quadrant Conference in late August.
16. MacArthur to Marshall, June 24, 1943, RG 4, box 16, folder 3.
17. MacArthur to Marshall, June 20, 1943, RG 4, box 16, folder 3.
18. Forrest C. Pogue, *George C. Marshall: Organizer of Victory, 1943–1945* (New York: Viking, 1973), 253.
19. *Sydney Morning Herald,* May 14, 1943; Potter, *Bull Halsey,* 219–20, 400n. Apparently for security reasons, it took almost a month for reports of their conference to appear in newspapers in Australia and the United States.
20. James, *Years of MacArthur,* 2:320–21; Borneman, *Admirals,* 315–16, 517-18n.
21. MacArthur, *Reminiscences,* 174–75.
22. For biographical material about Barbey, see Daniel E. Barbey, *MacArthur's Amphibious Navy: Seventh Amphibious Force Operations, 1943–1945* (Annapolis, MD: United States Naval Institute, 1969), and Paolo E. Coletta's chapter on Barbey in William M. Leary, ed., *We Shall Return! MacArthur's Commanders and the Defeat of Japan* (Lexington: University Press of Kentucky, 1988).
23. Morison, *Breaking the Bismarcks Barrier,* 130, 134.
24. Barbey, *MacArthur's Amphibious Navy,* 24.
25. Ibid., 232.
26. For biographies of Krueger, see Kevin C. Holzimmer, *General Walter Krueger: Unsung Hero of the Pacific War* (Lawrence: University Press of Kansas, 2007), and William M. Leary's chapter about Krueger in Leary, *We Shall Return!* "Doctrine knits," Holzimmer, *General Walter Krueger,* 42; "love to try," ibid., 97. Halsey did a similar exchange stint at the Army War College while Krueger was at Jefferson Barracks.
27. MacArthur to Marshall, January 11, 1943, quoted in Willoughby, et al., *Reports of General MacArthur,* 1:107n.
28. Holzimmer, *General Walter Krueger,* 101–2; Leary, *We Shall Return,* 66; "What [Kreuger's] seniors," Barbey, *MacArthur's Amphibious Navy,* 27.
29. Luvaas, *Dear Miss Em,* 67.
30. Chart of the command organization, Southwest Pacific Area, July 1943, in Morton, *Strategy and Command,* 409.
31. Morison, *Breaking the Bismarcks Barrier,* 133.
32. Barbey, *MacArthur's Amphibious Navy,* 42, 57.
33. "Biggest anti-Navy agitator," Tarbuck to Barbey, May 19, 1961, quoted in Gerald E. Wheeler, *Kinkaid of the Seventh Fleet* (Washington, DC: Naval Historical Center, 1995), 362; Drea, *MacArthur's ULTRA,* 61.
34. Craven and Cate, *Guadalcanal to Saipan,* 178–79.
35. SWPA press release, August 18, 1943, RG 4, box 49, folder 1.
36. MacArthur to Halsey, August 23, 1943, and Halsey to MacArthur, August 25, 1943, Halsey papers, box 15, folder "MacArthur."
37. Miller, *Cartwheel,* 202–5.

Chapter 16: Bypassing Rabaul

1. Miller, *Cartwheel,* 224.
2. Marshall to MacArthur, July 21, 1943, RG 4, box 16, folder 3.
3. MacArthur to Marshall, July 23, 1943, RG 4, box 16, folder 3.
4. Halsey notes, April 2, 1951, Halsey papers, box 35.
5. Extract of the Final Report of the Combined Chiefs of Staff to the President and Prime Minister at the Quadrant Conference, 24 August 1943 (CCS 319/5), in Morton, *Strategy and Command,* 650–53.
6. Miller, *Cartwheel,* 225; Marshall to MacArthur, October 2, 1943, RG 4, box 16, folder 4.
7. Willoughby, et al., *Reports of General MacArthur,* 1:121.
8. James, *Years of MacArthur,* 2:324.
9. Miller, *Cartwheel,* 191.
10. Kenney, *General Kenney Reports,* 288–89.
11. MacArthur, *Reminiscences,* 179.
12. Kenney, *General Kenney Reports,* 289. According to Kenney's interview with D. Clayton James, he was in the lead B-17, and MacArthur was in the number three plane. George C. Kenney interview, RG 49, box 1.
13. Kenney to Arnold, September 7, 1943, quoted in Craven and Cate, *Guadalcanal to Saipan,* 185. The numbers of aircraft are Kenney's and differ slightly from squadron reports. See Craven and Cate, *Guadalcanal to Saipan,* 724–25n95.
14. Kenney, *General Kenney Reports,* 293; MacArthur, *Reminiscences,* 179; SWPA communiqué no. 541, October 4, 1943, RG 4, box 47, folder 1.
15. MacArthur, *Reminiscences,* 179.
16. Craven and Cate, *Guadalcanal to Saipan,* 186.
17. Miller, *Cartwheel,* 212–13; Japan's National Defense Zone, September 1943, plate 57 in Willoughby, et al., *Reports of General MacArthur,* 2:227.
18. Miller, *Cartwheel,* 217–18. Adair to Barbey, August 5, 1960, quoted in Leary, *We Shall Return!,* 219.
19. James, *Years of MacArthur,* 2:329; Willoughby, et al., *Reports of General MacArthur,* 2:229.
20. SWPA communiqué no. 541, October 4, 1943, RG 4, box 47, folder 4.
21. David Dexter, *The New Guinea Offensives,* Australia in the War of 1939–1945, ser. 1, vol. 6 (Canberra: Australian War Memorial, 1961), 483.
22. Miller, *Cartwheel,* 272–73n2.
23. Kenney to MacArthur, October 10, 1943, quoted in Miller, *Cartwheel,* 273.
24. Miller, *Cartwheel,* 273–74.
25. Whitehead to Kenney, November 11, 1943, Craven and Cate, *Guadalcanal to Saipan,* 329–30; Kenney, *General Kenney Reports,* 326–27.
26. Kenney, *General Kenney Reports,* 327; Barbey, *MacArthur's Amphibious Navy,* 100.
27. Miller, *Cartwheel,* 274–75.
28. For biographies of Kinkaid, see Wheeler, *Kinkaid of the Seventh Fleet,* and Wheeler's chapter on Kinkaid in Leary, *We Shall Return!*
29. Wheeler, *Kinkaid of the Seventh Fleet,* 273–86; see also John B. Lundstrom, *The First Team and the Guadalcanal Campaign: Naval Fighter Combat from August to November 1942* (Annapolis, MD: Naval Institute Press, 1994), 353, 356–459.

30. MacArthur's displeasure with Carpender, evidently exacerbated by Sutherland's and Kenney's routine antagonism of the navy, is referenced in Buell, *Master of Sea Power*, 319–20; D. Clayton James, *A Time for Giants: The Politics of the American High Command in World War II* (New York: Franklin Watts, 1987), 110; Wheeler, *Kinkaid of the Seventh Fleet*, 343; and James, *Years of MacArthur*, 2:357–58, 866n18. As MacArthur put it: "[Carpender] is not especially fitted to serve in a mixed command due to his concentration upon his own service channels rather than the broader concept of inter-service integration of outlook." MacArthur to King, June 17, 1943, RG 4, box 10, folder 3.

31. MacArthur to Marshall, October 27, 1943, Marshall to MacArthur, October 27, 1943, MacArthur to Marshall, October 28, 1943, RG 4, box 16, folder 4.

32. Wheeler, *Kinkaid of the Seventh Fleet*, 345, 349.

33. George McMillan, *The Old Breed: A History of the First Marine Division in World War II* (Washington, DC: Infantry Journal Press, 1949), 168–70; Miller, *Cartwheel*, 278; James, *Years of MacArthur*, 2:343.

34. Barbey, *MacArthur's Amphibious Navy*, 89.

35. Leary, *We Shall Return!*, 221.

36. Miller, *Cartwheel*, 279, 284, 291–92.

37. Willoughby and Chamberlain, *MacArthur*, 139.

38. Morison, *Breaking the Bismarcks Barrier*, 377–78.

39. Krueger to MacArthur and MacArthur to Krueger, December 28, 1943, RG 4, box 14, folder 3.

40. James, *Years of MacArthur*, 2:335.

Chapter 17: One General to Another

1. *Courier-Mail* (Brisbane), September 27, 1943, quoting in part the *New York Herald Tribune* and *Army and Navy Journal*.

2. Whitehill interview with King, August 29, 1949, box 7, file folder 28, Naval Historical Collection, Naval War College, Newport, RI; Eisenhower's corroboration of King's account is in Eisenhower, *Crusade in Europe*, 196.

3. William D. Leahy, *I Was There: The Personal Story of the Chief of Staff to Presidents Roosevelt and Truman Based on His Notes and Diaries Made at the Time* (New York: Whittlesey House, 1950), 201–2.

4. Ibid., 207–8.

5. Leahy, *I Was There*, 209; Charles F. Brower, *Defeating Japan: The Joint Chiefs of Staff and Strategy in the Pacific War, 1943–1945* (New York: Palgrave Macmillan, 2012), 83–84.

6. Brower, *Defeating Japan*, 86–87. King was among those who questioned in hindsight what impact the decision to scrap Operation Buccaneer had on postwar China and the eventual collapse of Chiang Kai-shek's government. See King and Whitehill, *Fleet Admiral King*, 525–26.

7. Overall Plan for the Defeat of Japan: Report by the Combined Staff Planners, in Morton, *Strategy and Command*, 668–69. Had Operation Buccaneer gone forward, it might have required closer cooperation between American and British commands.

8. Paul P. Rogers, *The Bitter Years: MacArthur and Sutherland* (New York: Praeger, 1991), 57.

9. Ibid.
10. Jean MacArthur acknowledged MacArthur's habit of rehearsing speeches, particularly "Duty, Honor, Country." Paul Miles, in discussion with the author, January 31, 2014, recounting conversations with Jean MacArthur and William C. Westmoreland.
11. For Paul Rogers's insights into Sutherland's transformation, which should be taken cautiously, see *The Bitter Years,* 58–59.
12. Morton, *Strategy and Command,* 537–38, 541–42.
13. Hayes, *Joint Chiefs,* pp. 506-507.
14. Eisenhower, *Crusade in Europe,* 206–7. According to Marshall, the president told him, "Well I didn't feel I could sleep at ease if you were out of Washington." As Marshall's chief biographer put it, "The prominent part taken by the Chief of Staff in current meetings…must have made the President realize anew the necessity of retaining him in the Allied councils." Pogue, *Organizer of Victory,* 320–21.
15. Weldon E. "Dusty" Rhoades, *Flying MacArthur to Victory* (College Station: Texas A&M University Press, 1987), 137.
16. Rhoades, *Flying MacArthur,* 160; Pogue, *Organizer of Victory,* 322–23.
17. Rhoades, *Flying MacArthur,* 160–61.
18. Ibid., 162–65.
19. Pogue, *Organizer of Victory,* 323. There has been some speculation over the years about Marshall's motives in traveling to the Pacific. Bruce Mangan, a retired American intelligence officer, quoted Frank McCarthy, Marshall's aide, secretary of the General Staff, and later the producer of the films *Patton* and *MacArthur,* as saying, in a conversation around 1979, that " 'taking the long way home' was Marshall's way of getting through the disappointment" of not having been given command of Operation Overlord. However, McCarthy told Pogue in earlier letters that Marshall gave "no indication of despair" in not getting the post. Marshall would have had to harbor particular bitterness if the tonic he chose to ease it with was a visit with Douglas MacArthur, who, after all, had been the cause of considerable stomach acid! Bruce Mangan, e-mail message to author, January 31, 2014; Pogue, *Organizer of Victory,* 325, 641n62.
20. Hunt, *Untold Story of Douglas MacArthur,* 313–14. MacArthur apostles Charles Willoughby and Courtney Whitney did not mention Marshall's visit in their books.
21. Kenney, *General Kenney Reports,* 333; Rogers, *The Bitter Years,* 61.
22. Kenney, *General Kenney Reports,* 333–34; James, *Years of MacArthur,* 2:370-371; Pogue, *Organizer of Victory,* 323–24; Rogers, *The Bitter Years,* 61; Wheeler, *Kinkaid of the Seventh Fleet,* 354–55.
23. MacArthur, *Reminiscences,* 183–84.
24. Marshall to MacArthur, December 23, 1943, RG 15, box 13, folder 5.
25. Hunt, *Untold Story of Douglas MacArthur,* 314.
26. James, *Years of MacArthur,* 2:374. As noted earlier, MacArthur had been the direct beneficiary of King's constant calls for more resources in the Pacific. There is one other myth that grew out of the brief MacArthur-Marshall meeting on Goodenough Island that must be dismissed. Writing in *American Caesar,* William Manchester quoted Marshall as interrupting MacArthur when he

referred to "my staff" by retorting, "You don't have a staff, General. You have a court." While at some levels that might have been an accurate characterization, it is hardly in keeping with Marshall's widely acknowledged persona for him to have said it. No less an authority than Forrest Pogue took Manchester to task for citing as its source Pogue's own biography of Marshall. Pogue vehemently disclaimed responsibility for the quote and doubted Marshall made it. Pogue went on to say that he knew of no one who would take authorship of yet another sentence in Manchester's footnoted paragraph. It took a swipe at Marshall by noting, as if it were somehow related, that "the Chief of Staff had been off horseback riding when the Japanese attacked Pearl Harbor, and tactful officers never reminded him of it." Manchester, *American Caesar,* 352, 729n156; Forrest Pogue, "The Military in a Democracy—A Review: *American Caesar,*" *International Security* 3, no. 4 (Spring 1979), 65.

27. Matloff, *Strategic Planning,* 399.
28. Ibid., 396–97.
29. Table 5—U.S. Overseas Deployment: 31 December 1943, in Matloff, *Strategic Planning,* 398.
30. MacArthur to O'Laughlin, October 26, 1943, RG 3, box 1, folder 7.
31. Table 6—Strength, U.S. Forces in the Pacific, 31 December 1943, in Morton, *Strategy and Command,* 538; Australian estimate from John Robertson, *Australia at War 1939–1945* (Melbourne: Heinemann, 1981), 124.
32. Table 7—Major U.S. Combat Forces in the Pacific, 31 December 1943, and Table 8—Major U.S. Combat and Air Forces in Pacific and European Areas, 31 December 1943, in Morton, *Strategy and Command,* 539–40.
33. Morton, *Strategy and Command,* 521–22; Matloff, *Strategic Planning,* 317; James, *Years of MacArthur,* 2:353.
34. Matloff, *Strategic Planning,* 400–401.
35. James, *Years of MacArthur,* 2:352.
36. Barbey, *MacArthur's Amphibious Navy,* 100.
37. Robert W. Coakley and Richard M. Leighton, *Global Logistics and Strategy, 1943–1945,* vol. 6 of *United States Army in World War II: The War Department* (Washington, DC: Center of Military History, United States Army, 1989), 246.
38. Table 21—Shipbuilding in 1944: Evolution of the Program in 1943, in Coakley and Leighton, *Global Logistics and Strategy,* 258.
39. MacArthur to Duncan, March 3, 1944, RG 10, box 3, folder 92.
40. Drea, *MacArthur's ULTRA,* 61–62.

Chapter 18: Gambling in the Admiralties

1. Barbey, *MacArthur's Amphibious Navy,* 128.
2. Miller, *Cartwheel,* 302–4.
3. Drea, *MacArthur's ULTRA,* 92–93.
4. Borneman, *Admirals,* 348, 350–53.
5. Halsey, *Admiral Halsey's Story,* 186.
6. Draft of letter from Halsey to "My dear John" (whose identity is unknown), April 2, 1951, Halsey papers, box 35. Why King included Rabaul in his question when he was well aware of the bypass decision is uncertain, but that's the way Halsey remembered the exchange.

7. Miller, *Cartwheel,* 308. For more on the January 27–28, 1944, conference at Pearl Harbor, particularly the erroneous perception reported to MacArthur that Nimitz and his staff suddenly leaned toward supporting the New Guinea axis over the central Pacific, see Matloff, *Strategic Planning,* 455–57; Hayes, *Joint Chiefs,* 546–47; and Borneman, *Admirals,* 360–61.

8. Miller, *Cartwheel,* 315.

9. John Miller Jr., "MacArthur and the Admiralties," in Kent Roberts Greenfield, ed., *Command Decisions* (Washington, DC: Center of Military History, United States Army, 1987), 295.

10. Ibid., 296–97.

11. Kenney, *General Kenney Reports,* 359–60.

12. Miller, "MacArthur and the Admiralties," 298–99; Drea, *MacArthur's ULTRA,* 102.

13. Miller, *Cartwheel,* 317.

14. Kinkaid to Miller, November 16, 1953, quoted in Miller, "MacArthur and the Admiralties," 299.

15. MacArthur to Marshall, February 2, 1944, quoted in Hayes, *Joint Chiefs,* 548–49.

16. Hayes, *Joint Chiefs,* 550.

17. MacArthur to Marshall, February 27, 1944, RG 4, box 16, folder 6.

18. Marshall to MacArthur, March 9, 1944, RG 4, box 16, folder 4.

19. Rhoades, *Flying MacArthur,* 189. Rhoades flew the *Bataan* to Port Moresby to await their return.

20. Miller, "MacArthur and the Admiralties," 300; Kenney, *General Kenney Reports,* 361.

21. Roger Olaf Egeberg, *The General: MacArthur and the Man He Called "Doc"* (New York: Hippocrene, 1983), 15–17, 25.

22. Miller, "MacArthur and the Admiralties," 300.

23. SPWA press release, March 1, 1944 (10:00 p.m.), RG 4, box 49, folder 3.

24. MacArthur, *Reminiscences,* 188.

25. Egeberg, *The General,* 30.

26. Ibid., 33–34.

27. SWPA press release, March 1, 1944, RG 4, box 49, folder 3.

28. Rhoades, *Flying MacArthur,* 190.

29. Miller, *Reduction of Rabaul,* 330–32.

30. SWPA press release, unknown date, RG 4, box 49, folder 3.

31. Miller, *Cartwheel,* 324, 343, 348–49; SWPA communiqué no. 700, March 10, 1944, RG 4, box 48, folder 1.

32. Halsey, *Admiral Halsey's Story,* 189–90.

33. Leahy, *I Was There,* 224.

34. Ibid., 229–30.

35. MacArthur to Leahy, December 28, 1949, RG 10, VIP files.

36. Leahy to MacArthur, January 5, 1950, RG 10, VIP files.

37. Leahy, *I Was There,* 228.

38. Truk had an undeserved reputation as a "Gibraltar of the Pacific" but was more important than Rabaul as a linchpin in Japanese naval operations. Discussions about bypassing Truk or taking it by direct assault went on for months, although

because it was located in the Central Pacific Area, MacArthur was not directly involved.

39. Memo, Naval Bases in South Pacific Areas for Supporting Future Operations, March 27, 1944, quoted in Hayes, *Joint Chiefs,* 564–65.
40. Marshall to MacArthur, March 19, 1944, RG 15, box 13, folder 5.

Chapter 19: Hollandia—Greatest Triumph?

1. Drea, *MacArthur's ULTRA,* 94–95, 104, 232.
2. MacArthur to Marshall, March 5, 1944, RG 4, box 16, folder 4.
3. Kenney, *General Kenney Reports,* 369–70; Griffith, *MacArthur's Airman,* 158, 294n12. Griffith deems it unlikely that Kenney would have proposed such a move.
4. Halsey to unknown recipient (draft of letter), April 2, 1951, Halsey papers, box 35.
5. Fellers to Barbey, August 3, 1960, RG 44a, box 1, folder 3. The aide was likely Roger Egeberg or Larry Lehrbas. According to Fellers, the navy and air force planners were Captain Ray Tarbuck and Colonel Royden E. Beebe Jr.
6. Fellers to Barbey, August 3, 1960, November 9, 1965, and November 17, 1965, RG 44a, box 1, folder 3. See Hunt, *Untold Story of Douglas MacArthur,* 325. Fellers told Barbey that Hunt's account was "accurate." Willoughby apparently sided with Chamberlin: see Willoughby, *MacArthur,* 104, about "Steve Chamberlin's account," claiming Chamberlin proposed Hollandia at a conference that included MacArthur, Kenney, and Dick Marshall.
7. Barbey to Fellers, July 29, 1960, RG 44a, box 1, folder 3.
8. Fellers to Chamberlin, March 20, 1944, RG 44a, box 1, folder 8.
9. JCS to MacArthur and Nimitz, March 12, 1944, quoted in Hayes, *Joint Chiefs,* 559–60; see also Matloff, *Strategic Planning,* 458–59.
10. Leahy, *I Was There,* 230.
11. MacArthur to Nimitz, March 15, 1944, RG 4, box 10, folder 6.
12. Nimitz to MacArthur, March 15, 1944, RG-4, box 10, folder 6.
13. Potter, *Nimitz,* 290–91. Halsey did not attend this conference because he had just seen MacArthur and was occupied with wrapping up the Emirau operation.
14. Kenney, *General Kenney Reports,* 373–74, 377; Potter, *Nimitz,* 290.
15. Nimitz to King, April 2, 1944, quoted in James, *A Time for Giants,* 178.
16. Barbey, *MacArthur's Amphibious Navy,* 162.
17. Robert Ross Smith, *The Approach to the Philippines,* vol. 8 of *The United States Army in World War II: The War in the Pacific* (Washington, DC: Center of Military History, United States Army, 1996), 22.
18. Barbey to Fellers, August 19, 1960, RG 44a, box 1, folder 3.
19. Craven and Cate, *Guadalcanal to Saipan,* 592–95; Kenney, *General Kenney Reports,* 373–74, 379–81.
20. Eichelberger, *Our Jungle Road,* 9, 100, 102. One of Eichelberger's strangest experiences that year came on MacArthur's sixty-fourth birthday—January 26, 1944—when MacArthur visited Eichelberger's training camp at Rockhampton. A photo of the two was circulated with the caption "General MacArthur and General Eichelberger at the New Guinea Front." Eichelberger claimed that the dead giveaway was "the unmistakable nose of a Packard motorcar in one corner of the picture [and] there weren't any Packards in the New Guinea jungle in early 1944" (page 99).

21. Rhoades, *Flying MacArthur,* 217; James, *Years of MacArthur,* 2:450. These two sources, as well as Egeberg's, differ as to who piloted which aircraft.
22. Smith, *Approach to the Philippines,* 30–31.
23. Barbey, *MacArthur's Amphibious Navy,* 169–70.
24. Wheeler, *Kinkaid of the Seventh Fleet,* 365.
25. Barbey, *MacArthur's Amphibious Navy,* 167–69; Eichelberger, *Our Jungle Road,* 102–3; Smith, *Approach to the Philippines,* 48–49.
26. Barbey, *MacArthur's Amphibious Navy,* 169; Smith, *Approach to the Philippines,* 52.
27. Eichelberger, *Our Jungle Road,* 105.
28. James, *Years of MacArthur,* 2:448; Smith, *Approach to the Philippines,* 53–54.
29. Smith, *Approach to the Philippines,* 55–58.
30. Barbey, *MacArthur's Amphibious Navy,* 172.
31. Smith, *Approach to the Philippines,* 78–79.
32. Barbey, *MacArthur's Amphibious Navy,* 173; Eichelberger, *Our Jungle Road,* 107.
33. SPWA press release, April 24, 1944, RG 4, box 49, folder 3; Rhoades, *Flying MacArthur,* 219.
34. Barbey, *MacArthur's Amphibious Navy,* 178–79.
35. MacArthur, *Reminiscences,* 192.
36. GHQ SPWA, Communiqué No. 745, April 24, 1944, RG 4, box 48, folder 1.
37. William Manchester, *Goodbye Darkness: A Memoir of the Pacific War* (New York: Little, Brown, 1979), 243. See also Manchester's characterization of it as "a military classic." Manchester, *American Caesar,* 344.
38. Smith, *Approach to the Philippines,* 577.
39. Marshall to MacArthur, June 8, 1944, RG 15, box 13, folder 5.
40. Kenney interview, in James, *A Time for Giants,* 200.
41. MacArthur to Marshall, June 18, 1944, RG 4, box 17, folder 1.
42. Marshall to MacArthur, June 24, 1944, RG 4, box 17, folder 1. For an appraisal of Marshall as a global strategist, see Paul L. Miles, "Marshall as Grand Strategist," in Charles F. Brower, ed., *George C. Marshall: Servant of the American Nation* (New York: Palgrave Macmillan, 2011).

Chapter 20: Presidential Ambitions, Presidential Summons

1. MacArthur to Wood, May 7, 1914, quoted in James, *Years of MacArthur,* 1:121; MacArthur to Pershing, circa July 1918, Pershing papers, box 121; *New York Times,* April 21, 1929; Drum to MacArthur, June 29, 1936, RG 10, box 3, folder 6. As to the first point, it is my observation that those who suggest the presidency for others are merely hoping to have similar suggestions fall their own way.
2. MacArthur to Carver, January 10, 1938, RG 1, box 1, folder 10.
3. Wendell Willkie, "Let Us Do More Proposing Than Opposing," *Vital Speeches of the Day* 8, no. 8 (March 1, 1942), 299.
4. *New York Times,* May 20, 1942. Following MacArthur in the top five were Wendell Willkie, Thomas E. Dewey, Henry A. Wallace, and Donald M. Nelson.
5. *Time,* November 9, 1942, 21–22.
6. *The Argus* (Melbourne), October 30, 1942.
7. Stimson diary, October 29, 1942.

8. Huff, *Fifteen Years,* 89; Arthur H. Vandenberg Jr., ed., *The Private Papers of Senator Vandenberg* (Boston: Houghton Mifflin, 1952), 77–78.

9. MacArthur to Vandenberg, April 13, 1943, *Private Papers,* 77.

10. Schaller, *Douglas MacArthur,* 77–78, quoting from Wilkinson journal entries of November 1, 1942, and January 14 and February 13, 1943.

11. Wilkinson recorded Stuart's perceptions in his journal on January 26, 1943; a copy of the journal from Churchill College, Cambridge, is in RG 15, box 15, folder 2.

12. James, *Years of MacArthur,* 2:427–28.

13. Franklin D. Roosevelt press conference, October 5, 1943, #920, pages 9–11, http://www.fdrlibrary.marist.edu/_resources/images/pc/pc0153.pdf, accessed January 15, 2015; James, *Years of MacArthur,* 2:361–62.

14. Vandenberg to Wood, November 5, 1943, *Private Papers,* 82–83. For Willoughby's role, see, for example, Vandenberg to Willoughby, August 17, 1943, RG 10, VIP files.

15. John McCarten, "General MacArthur: Fact and Legend" *American Mercury* 58 (January 1944), 7–18. The Army War College's library service recommended the McCarten article in its monthly bulletin describing materials distributed to unit libraries; D. Clayton James noted that it was "the only published article about him" that was placed in his personnel file. James, *Years of MacArthur,* 2:413, 871n12.

16. Arthur H. Vandenberg, "Why I Am for MacArthur," *Colliers,* February 12, 1944, 14, 48–49.

17. McCarthy to chief of staff, February 16, 1944, RG 15, box 13, folder 5.

18. Editorial, "MacArthur and the Censorship," *Harper's Magazine* 188 (May 1944), 537.

19. *New York Times,* May 6, 1944.

20. The situation closest to this was that of General George B. McClellan during the Civil War. Dodderer that he was during the Peninsula campaign, McClellan had held no major command for the better part of two years before he challenged Lincoln in the 1864 election while still nominally on active duty. Democrat James K. Polk was uncomfortable with the presidential ambitions of his two top generals during the Mexican-American War—Whigs Winfield Scott and Zachary Taylor—but Polk had made it clear that he would serve but one term, and Scott and Taylor remained generally silent on their presidential interests.

21. McCarten, "General MacArthur: Fact and Legend," 8; see also Vandenberg to Willoughby, August 17, 1943, *Private Papers,* 80, outlining the plan to do "absolutely nothing of a promotional nature which would involve 'our campaign' in any ordinary political atmosphere or involve us in any of the usual preconvention methods."

22. MacArthur to Fellers, December 29, 1939, RG 44a, box 3, folder 23.

23. Miller to MacArthur, September 18, 1943, RG 10, VIP files; MacArthur to Miller, October 2, 1943, reproduced in *New York Times,* April 14, 1944.

24. Miller to MacArthur, January 27, 1944, RG 10, VIP files; MacArthur to Miller, February 11, 1944, reproduced in *New York Times,* April 14, 1944.

25. Cantril, *Public Opinion,* 626, 632. The August 17, 1943, poll showed MacArthur with only 7 percent, but the question was asked of all voters. The other samplings were among Republicans.

26. Cantril, *Public Opinion,* 634. It is further telling that in all the polls reported by *Public Opinion* during 1943 and 1944, MacArthur's is the only military name to appear regularly. One cannot find Marshall, Eisenhower, Somervell, or any other name save that of Harold Stassen, who started as a politician.
27. Vandenberg to Wood, April 10, 1944, *Private Papers,* 83–84.
28. SWPA press release, April 17, 1944, RG 4, box 49, folder 3.
29. SWPA press release, April 30, 1944, RG 4, box 49, folder 3. General William Tecumseh Sherman started the art of absolute denial in politics when he professed in 1872, "I hereby state, and mean all that I say, that I never have been and never will be a candidate for President; that if nominated by either party, I should peremptorily decline; and even if unanimously elected I should decline to serve."
30. Vandenberg to MacArthur, June 6, 1944, RG 3, box 1, folder 8.
31. Marshall to MacArthur, July 6, 1944, RG 4, box 17, folder 1.
32. MacArthur to Marshall, July 18, 1944, and Marshall to MacArthur, July 18, 1944, RG 4, box 17, folder 1.
33. Leahy, *I Was There,* 247–48.
34. Rhoades, *Flying MacArthur,* 249, 252–53 (July 10 and 15, 1944). Despite MacArthur's routinely reported vitality and the fact many Allied leaders, including the president's wife, had been crisscrossing the globe in support of the war effort, for a man of sixty-four, twenty-six hours in the air was a taxing trip.
35. Rhoades, *Flying MacArthur,* 256–58, July 26, 1944. Why Roger Egeberg didn't accompany MacArthur as his physician is not known. Chambers was likely the doctor instrumental in getting Egeberg assigned to MacArthur. Rhoades noted his amusement at the fact that some newsmen erroneously reported that MacArthur arrived in Hawaii in the *Bataan.*
36. Schedule from daily log at FDR Library at http://www.fdrlibrary.marist.edu/daybyday/daylog/july-26th-1944/, accessed July 14, 2014.
37. Leahy, *I Was There,* 249–50.
38. Newspaper clippings, Chester W. Nimitz Collection, section 8, Naval History and Heritage Command.
39. MacArthur, *Reminiscences,* 199.
40. Egeberg interview, October 18, 1976, quoted in Manchester, *American Caesar,* 368.
41. MacArthur, *Reminiscences,* 197–98.
42. Leahy, *I Was There,* 251.
43. William D. Leahy diary, July 29, 1944, William D. Leahy Papers, Manuscript Division, Library of Congress, Washington, DC.
44. Leahy, *I Was There,* 250–51.
45. Ibid., 250.
46. Rhoades, *Flying MacArthur,* 260–61 (July 29, 1944).
47. Roosevelt, *Complete Presidential Press Conferences,* 24:33, July 29, 1944.
48. Leahy, *I Was There,* 255. This meeting occurred on August 22. Nothing in the record suggests that the chiefs considered Leahy's report of Roosevelt's comments in the Luzon–Formosa debate as a directive to take Luzon first. Hayes, *History of Joint Chiefs,* 875n34.

Chapter 21: Toward the Philippines

1. Bonner Fellers draft of Pearl Harbor conference notes, page 7, RG 44a, box 3, folder 16.
2. King to MacArthur, July 21, 1944, RG 4, box 10, folder 6. A messenger delivered this letter to MacArthur on the evening of MacArthur's arrival in Honolulu.
3. MacArthur to King, August 5, 1944, RG 4, box 10, folder 6.
4. Roosevelt to MacArthur, August 9, 1944, RG 15, box 23, folder 23.
5. MacArthur to Roosevelt, August 26, 1944, RG 15, box 23, folder 23.
6. Pogue, *Organizer of Victory,* 453.
7. Marshall to MacArthur, September 12, 1944, RG 4, box 17, folder 2. It should be noted in Great Britain's defense that the British always anticipated that any operations in the SWPA—unless boundaries changed—would be under MacArthur's supreme command, just as American troops in the CBI theater were under Mountbatten's supreme command.
8. Roosevelt to MacArthur, September 15, 1944, RG 15, box 23, folder 23.
9. Thorne, *Allies of a Kind,* 479.
10. Ibid., 480. New Zealand had little to do with MacArthur because it was in the South Pacific Area.
11. Ibid., 481.
12. Ibid., 484.
13. Ibid., 479. Nonetheless, in one of his many tirades about lack of American support for his theater, MacArthur once let a ray of truth show through and told John O'Laughlin: "If I had not had the Australians I would have been lost indeed." MacArthur to O'Laughlin, October 26, 1943, RG 3, box 1, folder 7.
14. Dean, *Architect of Victory,* 272–74; Peter J. Dean, "MacArthur's War: Strategy, Command and Plans for the 1943 Offensives," in Dean, *Australia 1943,* 57. As Australia's official war history described it, MacArthur's sidelining of Australian troops was "achieved by stealth and by the employment of subterfuges that were undignified and at times absurd." Gavin Long, *The Final Campaigns: Australia in the War of 1939–1945,* ser. 1, vol. 7 (Canberra: Australian War Memorial, 1963), 599.
15. Marshall to MacArthur, August 9, 1944, RG 4, box 17, folder 2. The Ninety-Third Division was a segregated unit that had served with distinction in France during World War I and had recently been reactivated.
16. MacArthur to Marshall, August 9, 1944, RG 4, box 17, folder 2.
17. Matloff, *Strategic Planning,* 483–85.
18. As D. Clayton James noted in an article on strategy after the completion of his MacArthur trilogy: "The recurring piecemeal nature of Japanese ground, sea, and air defensive operations demonstrated a serious lack of coordination and cooperation between the army and navy commands that made American inter-service rivalries appear mild in contrast." James, "American and Japanese Strategies," 718.
19. Robert Ross Smith, *Triumph in the Philippines,* vol. 10 of *The United States Army in World War II: The War in the Pacific* (Washington, DC: Center of Military History, United States Army, 1993), 9–10; Hayes, *Joint Chiefs,* 614–16. The fourth member of the Joint Chiefs, Hap Arnold, commanding general of the US Army Air Forces, was no longer too concerned with the prospects of bomber

bases in China because B-29s were about to start flying against Japan's home islands from safer and more reliably supplied bases in the Marianas. That proved a good thing, because as Chinese resistance weakened, Japanese forces overran air bases in southern China previously planned for B-29 use.

20. Hayes, *Joint Chiefs*, 616–20; Matloff, *Strategic Planning*, 486–87. The islands in the Palau archipelago, including the tiny atoll of Peleliu, lie near the center of a circle encompassing Hollandia, Mindanao, the Marianas, and Truk. With Truk isolated, Palau was a natural springboard to the Philippines as well as a center for land-based air.
21. Rhoades, *Flying MacArthur*, 287 (September 19, 1944).
22. For more on Spruance's role at the Battle of the Philippine Sea, see Borneman, *Admirals*, 364–68.
23. MacArthur to Halsey, undated, Halsey papers, box 15, folder "MacArthur."
24. Halsey to MacArthur, June 10, 1944, RG 10, VIP file.
25. Halsey, *Admiral Halsey's Story*, 198–200.
26. Halsey, *Admiral Halsey's Story*, 200; M. Hamlin Cannon, *Leyte: Return to the Philippines*, vol. 9 of *The United States Army in World War II: The War in the Pacific* (Washington, DC: Center of Military History, United States Army, 1993), 8–9.
27. Borneman, *Admirals*, 385. A regimental combat team occupied Ulithi and its fine anchorage without opposition on September 23, a week after the Peleliu invasion.
28. MacArthur to Joint Chiefs, September 15, 1944, RG 4, box 17, folder 2; Pogue, *Organizer of Victory*, 453–54, quoting Marshall's biennial report to the secretary of war. Despite the intrigue over a larger role for the British in the Pacific, including the deployment of the British fleet, the American Joint Chiefs appear to have made this decision without consulting their British counterparts—another indication that the Americans continued to consider the Pacific their domain.
29. James, *Years of MacArthur*, 2:488–89, 800; Egeberg, *The General*, 59; SWPA press release, September 15, 1944, RG 4, box 49, folder 3.
30. MacArthur to Sutherland, September 16, 1944, RG 4, box 10, folder 6.
31. Hunt, *Untold Story of Douglas MacArthur*, 341.
32. Rogers, *The Bitter Years*, 160.
33. Kenney, *General Kenney Reports*, 432.
34. JCS to MacArthur, September 13, 1944, quoted in Hayes, *Joint Chiefs*, 621.
35. Kenney, *General Kenney Reports*, 434; Rogers, *The Bitter Years*, 161–62.
36. Rogers, *The Bitter Years*, 162.
37. Sutherland likely told Marshall he was acting for MacArthur.
38. Rhoades, *Flying MacArthur*, 285.
39. *The Argus* (Melbourne), March 27, 1944, 6; Rogers, *The Bitter Years*, 65–68.
40. Rhoades, *Flying MacArthur*, 209.
41. Rogers, *The Bitter Years*, 81–85.
42. Ibid., 91–92.
43. Rogers, *The Bitter Years*, 147, 149; Egeberg, *The General*, 59.
44. Rogers, *The Bitter Years*, 163–66; Rhoades, *Flying MacArthur*, 283, 285. Sutherland told Rhoades that he wanted Clarke returned to Brisbane on the *Bataan* along with MacArthur but that under the circumstances it "was not possible." He directed Rhoades to arrange other transportation for her.
45. Hayes, *Joint Chiefs*, 623–24.

Chapter 22: Sixty Minutes from Defeat

1. MacArthur's office itinerary is reported in James, *Years of MacArthur*, vol. 2, appendix B. James, page 494, gives a total night count at Hollandia of four, assuming that MacArthur boarded the *Nashville* on the evening of September 12 instead of sleeping in his quarters ashore. In any event, he was there for a portion of only six days.
2. Willoughby and Chamberlain, *MacArthur*, 187–88; Rogers, *The Bitter Years*, 148.
3. Kenney, *The MacArthur I Know*, 92–94.
4. Huff, *Fifteen Years*, 95.
5. MacArthur, *Reminiscences*, 212.
6. Marshall to MacArthur, September 27, 1944, RG 4, box 17, folder 2.
7. CINCPAC to CINCSWPA, September 15, 1944, RG 4, box 10, folder 6.
8. Eichelberger, *Our Jungle Road*, 156–57, 164.
9. Cannon, *Leyte*, 24.
10. Ibid., 25–27.
11. "Cool and very aggressive," Krueger to MacArthur, July 2, 1944, quoted in Holzimmer, *General Walter Krueger*, 188–89.
12. Cannon, *Leyte*, 25, 28–30.
13. James, *Years of MacArthur*, 2:545, 547–48.
14. Rhoades, *Flying MacArthur*, 289 (September 24, 1944).
15. Ibid., 290, September 30, 1944; for one reprise of the MacArthur-Curtin relationship, see Robertson, *Australia at War*, 118–20.
16. MacArthur to Jean MacArthur, October 15, 1944, RG 10, VIP files.
17. Rhoades, *Flying MacArthur*, 293 (October 14–15, 1944).
18. MacArthur, *Reminiscences*, 214.
19. Robertson, *Australia at War*, 167.
20. James, *Years of MacArthur*, 2:553–55.
21. MacArthur, *Reminiscences*, 216–17.
22. Kenney, *General Kenney Reports*, 448.
23. James, *Years of MacArthur*, 2:559–60.
24. SWPA special communiqué, October 20, 1944, RG 4, box 48, folder 2.
25. SWPA communiqué no. 927, October 21, 1944, RG 4, box 48, folder 2.
26. Roosevelt to MacArthur, October 21, 1944, RG 4, box 17, folder 2.
27. Halsey to MacArthur, October 21, 1944, RG 10, VIP file.
28. C. Vann Woodward, *The Battle for Leyte Gulf: The Incredible Story of World War II's Largest Naval Battle* (New York: Skyhorse, 2007), 19–20.
29. Borneman, *Admirals*, 387–91; Woodward, *Battle for Leyte Gulf*, 14, 32, 42, 90, 159.
30. Wheeler, *Kinkaid of the Seventh Fleet*, 396–98; Borneman, *Admirals*, 391–92.
31. Halsey, *Admiral Halsey's Story*, 214.
32. Halsey to King via Nimitz, November 13, 1944, Action Report Third Fleet, Enclosure A, 28, 31, Halsey papers, box 35.
33. Woodward, *Battle for Leyte Gulf*, 216.
34. United States Strategic Bombing Survey Summary Report (Pacific War), (Washington, DC: United States Government Printing Office, 1946), 8.
35. Akin to Sutherland, October 25, 1944, RG 4, box 6, folder 4. MacArthur was not the only one seeking information, as Barbey sent Captain Ray Tarbuck to the *Wasatch* to get similar clarification on the enemy situation. See Barbey, *MacArthur's Amphibious Navy*, 255.

36. COM Third Fleet to CINCPAC, CINCSWPA, COM Seventh Fleet, COMINCH, October 25, 1944, RG 4, box 10, folder 6.
37. This quote by Grant is well circulated, and it is not entirely clear whether it stems from Grant's legend or subsequent MacArthur family lore.
38. Evan Thomas, *Sea of Thunder: Four Commanders and the Last Great Naval Campaign, 1941–1945* (New York: Simon and Schuster, 2006), 325, quoting Sutherland papers.
39. Pogue, *Organizer of Victory,* 168.
40. Kenney, *The MacArthur I Know,* 170.
41. Pogue, *Organizer of Victory,* 626n23, quoting Stimson diary, November 22, 1944.
42. MacArthur to Nimitz and MacArthur to Halsey, October 29, 1944, RG 4, box 10, folder 6.
43. MacArthur, *Reminiscences,* 230.

Chapter 23: Return to Manila

1. James, *Years of MacArthur,* 2:566–67.
2. SWPA press release, November 3, 1944, RG 4, box 49, folder 3.
3. James, *Years of MacArthur,* 2:567–69; Wesley Frank Craven and James Lea Cate, *The Pacific: Matterhorn to Nagasaki, June 1944 to August 1945,* vol. 5 of *The Army Air Forces in World War II* (Washington, DC: Office of Air Force History, 1983), 386; Cannon, *Leyte,* 306; Kinkaid to MacArthur, November 1, 1944, and MacArthur to Kinkaid, November 13, 1944, RG 4, box 6, folder 4.
4. Cannon, *Leyte,* 276.
5. Sixth Army Report, quoted in James, *Years of MacArthur,* 2:572.
6. Craven and Cate, *Matterhorn to Nagasaki,* 385.
7. Ibid., 390.
8. Kinkaid to MacArthur, November 30, 1944, RG 4, box 6, folder 4.
9. Wheeler, *Kinkaid of the Seventh Fleet,* 411–13; James, *Years of MacArthur,* 2:606–7; Rogers, *The Bitter Years,* 209.
10. Smith, *Triumph in the Philippines,* 22–25.
11. Hayes, *Joint Chiefs,* 657–58.
12. SWPA communiqué no. 975, December 8, 1944, RG 4, box 48, folder 2.
13. Cannon, *Leyte,* 362.
14. Smith, *Triumph in the Philippines,* 45–46.
15. Smith, *Triumph in the Philippines,* 47–48; Borneman, *Admirals,* 409–11.
16. Public Law 482, 78th Congress, December 14, 1944.
17. MacArthur to Roosevelt, December 16, 1944, RG 5, Records of General Headquarters, SCAP, 1945–1951, box 1, folder 10.
18. MacArthur to Rear Echelon GHQ, December 16, 1944, RG 26, Service Record and Papers of General Douglas MacArthur, USA, 1903–1964, box 1, folder 2A.
19. Egeberg, *The General,* 91.
20. Rhoades, *Flying MacArthur,* 322–23 (November 23, 1944).
21. Ibid., 324–25, November 24 and 30, 1944.
22. Egeberg, *The General,* 92–93.
23. Rogers, *The Bitter Years,* 211.
24. Rhoades, *Flying MacArthur,* 333 (December 18, 1944).
25. Rogers, *The Bitter Years,* 213–17.

26. Rhoades, *Flying MacArthur,* 337–38 (December 29, 1944).
27. SWPA communiqué no. 993, December 26, 1944, RG 4, box 48, folder 2.
28. Sixth Army Reports, quoted in Cannon, *Leyte,* 361.
29. Cannon, *Leyte,* 367–68.
30. Eleventh Airborne Division history, quoted in James, *Years of MacArthur,* 2:602.
31. Eichelberger, *Our Jungle Road,* 181–82.
32. Drea, *MacArthur's ULTRA,* 180.
33. Ibid., 180–85.
34. Smith, *Triumph in the Philippines,* 29–30.
35. Marshall to MacArthur, February 27, 1945, RG 15, box 13, folder 6.
36. MacArthur to Jean MacArthur, January 8, 1945, RG 10, VIP files.
37. James, *Years of MacArthur,* 2:619–20; MacArthur, *Reminiscences,* 240.
38. James, *Years of MacArthur,* 2:620–21.
39. MacArthur, *Reminiscences,* 241.
40. SWPA communiqué no. 1008, January 10, 1945, RG 4, box 48, folder 3.
41. James, *Years of MacArthur,* 2:622; Smith, *Triumph in the Philippines,* 52–53.
42. Clyde Eddleman interview, RG 49, "Oral Reminiscences II, Eddleman."
43. Walter Krueger, *From Down Under to Nippon: The Story of the Sixth Army in World War II* (Washington, DC: Zenger, 1979), 227.
44. Smith, *Triumph in the Philippines,* 94–97.
45. Egeberg, *The General,* 115.
46. MacArthur, *Reminiscences,* 244.
47. Smith, *Triumph in the Philippines,* 171, 181, 184–85; James, *Years of MacArthur,* 2:627.
48. Smith, *Triumph in the Philippines,* 211–12.
49. Smith, *Triumph in the Philippines,* 212–13; MacArthur, *Reminiscences,* 244.
50. James, *Years of MacArthur,* 2:630; Wheeler, *Kinkaid of the Seventh Fleet,* 422–23; Nimitz to MacArthur, February 7, 1945, and MacArthur to Kinkaid, February 8, 1945, Nimitz "gray book"; MacArthur, *Reminiscences,* 245.
51. MacArthur, *Reminiscences,* 246; James, *Years of MacArthur,* 2:631–33; confirmation of the Palawan massacre appeared in the *Canberra Times,* March 5, 1945.
52. SWPA communiqué no. 1035, February 6, 1945, quoted in James, *Years of MacArthur,* 2:637, 889n14.
53. Griswold papers quoted in Max Hastings, *Retribution: The Battle for Japan, 1944–45* (New York: Knopf, 2007), 232.
54. Smith, *Triumph in the Philippines,* 240–44.

Chapter 24: Hail the Conquering Hero
1. MacArthur, *Reminiscences,* 248.
2. Rogers, *The Bitter Years,* 253–54. Of the men MacArthur took with him off Corregidor, Brigadier General Harold H. George had been killed in a runway accident in 1942 and Lieutenant Colonel Joe R. Sherr lost his life in an air crash in India in 1943.
3. Krueger to MacArthur and MacArthur to Krueger, February 17, 1945, RG 4, box 14, folder 3.
4. Rogers, *The Bitter Years,* 265.
5. James, *Years of MacArthur,* 2: 645–46; MacArthur, *Reminiscences,* 247.

6. James, *Years of MacArthur,* 2:650; for the difficulties and advisability of using an air drop against Corregidor, see Smith, *Triumph in the Philippines,* 335–39, 344.
7. Egeberg, *The General,* 144–51.
8. MacArthur, *Reminiscences,* 250; James, *Years of MacArthur,* 2: 651–52; MacArthur to Pershing, February 6, 1945, Pershing papers, box 121.
9. H. G. Nicholas, ed., *Washington Despatches, 1941–1945, Weekly Political Reports from the British Embassy* (Chicago: University of Chicago Press, 1981), 511–12 (February 11, 1945).
10. MacArthur to Marshall, December 17, 1944, RG 4, box 17, folder 2.
11. Marshall to MacArthur, December 19, 1944, Larry I. Bland and Sharon Ritenour Stevens, eds., *The Papers of George Catlett Marshall,* vol. 4, *"Aggressive and Determined Leadership,"* June 1, 1943–December 31, 1944 (Baltimore and London: Johns Hopkins University Press, 1966), 701; MacArthur to Marshall, December 22, 1944, RG 4, box 17, folder 2.
12. Draft of MacArthur to Marshall, December 22, 1944, marked "NOTE: This has *not* been used" in type and initialed "Dick [presumably Sutherland, but possibly Marshall] — Hold for future use, MacA." RG 4, box 17, folder 2.
13. MacArthur to Marshall, December 22, 1944, RG 4, box 17, folder 2.
14. Stimson diary, December 27, 1944.
15. Hayes, *Joint Chiefs,* 684–85, 688–92.
16. Leahy to MacArthur, December 11, 1944, RG 10, VIP file; Walter Millis, ed., *The Forrestal Diaries* (New York: Viking, 1951), 31 (February 28 and March 10, 1945); Forrestal had a habit of calling at Leahy's residence to discuss important matters; see Leahy, *I Was There,* 338.
17. Hayes, *Joint Chiefs,* 692–93. The exhaustive back-and-forth between army and navy planners that preceded this decision can be found in the George C. Marshall Papers, George C. Marshall Foundation, Lexington, Virginia, reel 119, item 2931, "Command in the Pacific, December 29, 1944, to September 1945."
18. MacArthur to Marshall, April 5, 1945, and Marshall to MacArthur, April 6, 1945, RG 15, box 13, folder 6.
19. Fellers to Kimmel, March 6, 1967, RG 44a, box 5, folder 28, "Pearl Harbor." Fellers related this in an "anti-Roosevelt" letter about prior knowledge of the attack on Pearl Harbor. MacArthur made no reference to Roosevelt's passing in *Reminiscences.*
20. James, *Years of MacArthur,* 2:726; Potter, *Nimitz,* 378–79.
21. Kenney, *General Kenney Reports,* 537.
22. Nimitz to King, quoted in Millis, *Forrestal Diaries,* 45–46.
23. Draft of Marshall to MacArthur, marked "message was not sent," April 15, 1945, RG 15, box 13, folder 6.
24. Marshall to MacArthur, May 4, 1945, RG 15, box 13, folder 6.
25. Nimitz to King, et al., May 19, 1945, reporting "agreements reached in conference between CinCAFPac and CinCPac at Manila on May 16, 1945," George C. Marshall Papers, reel 119, item 2926; Potter, *Nimitz,* 380.
26. Marshall to MacArthur, June 6, 1945, and MacArthur to Marshall, June 19, 1945, RG 15, box 13, folder 6.
27. Hayes, *Joint Chiefs,* 693.

28. See, for example, James, *Years of MacArthur,* 2:738–41. As the US Army's official history put it: "The remaining islands — including Mindanao east of the Zamboanga Peninsula — had no strategic importance in the campaign for the recapture of the Philippines and the East Indies, but pressing political considerations demanded their immediate recapture as well.... They were designed for the purpose of liberating Filipinos, re-establishing lawful government, and destroying Japanese forces." Smith, *Triumph in the Philippines,* 584–85.

29. Eichelberger used "Grand Tour" as a chapter title in *Our Jungle Road,* describing these events; schedule from MacArthur's office diary in James, *Years of MacArthur,* 2:803; for two accounts of these travels, see Eichelberger, *Our Jungle Road,* 240–42, and Kenney, *General Kenney Reports,* 550–51.

30. *Canberra Times,* January 10, 1945; Robertson, *Australia at War,* 174.

31. Hayes, *Joint Chiefs,* 696–97; Horner, *Inside the War Cabinet,* 179–83.

32. Chifley to MacArthur, May 9, 1945, and MacArthur to Chifley, May 10, 1945, and Chifley's statement to the Australian Parliament, May 10, 1945, RG 4, box 8, folder "Australian Government, Apr–Aug, 1945."

33. Chifley to MacArthur, May 18, 1945, and MacArthur to Chifley, May 20, 1945, quoted in Long, *Final Campaigns,* 389; Dean, *Architect of Victory,* 294.

34. SPWA communiqué no. 1162, June 12, 1945, RG 4, box 48, folder 3.

35. Frank, *MacArthur,* 123–25.

36. Eichelberger, *Our Jungle Road,* 244.

37. James, *Years of MacArthur,* 2:756, 761.

38. Long, *Final Campaigns,* 547.

39. Egeberg, *The General,* 178.

40. Barbey, *MacArthur's Amphibious Navy,* 319–20; Egeberg, *The General,* 178.

41. James, *Years of MacArthur,* 2:745, and generally, see, for example, D. Clayton James, "MacArthur's Lapses from an Envelopment Strategy in 1945," in William M. Leary, ed., *MacArthur and the American Century: A Reader* (Lincoln: University of Nebraska Press, 2001), 173–79.

Chapter 25: "These Proceedings Are Closed"

1. SWPA communiqué no. 1185, July 5, 1945, quoted in *MacArthur Reports,* 1:357; Hayes, *Joint Chiefs,* 706.

2. Drea, *MacArthur's ULTRA,* 200.

3. Edward J. Drea, "Military Intelligence and MacArthur," in Leary, *MacArthur and the American Century,* 195.

4. Eddleman interview, RG 49. "General MacArthur," the *Washington Post and Times-Herald* noted ten years after the war, at the time of Willoughby's gushing biography, "always has managed to collect a certain number of sycophants around him, some of whom with his help have sought to embellish his reputation beyond what the historical records have established." *Washington Post and Times-Herald,* August 14, 1955.

5. Richard B. Frank, *Downfall: The End of the Imperial Japanese Empire* (New York: Random House, 1999), 147, 212.

6. Marshall to MacArthur, August 7, 1945, and MacArthur to Marshall, August 9, 1945, RG 9, box 160, folder "War Dept 3 Aug–4 Sept 45"; Drea, "Military Intelligence and MacArthur," 195–96; Frank, *Downfall,* 274–75.

7. Frank, *Downfall,* 276, 419–20n.
8. James, *Years of MacArthur,* 2:772–73; Frank, *Downfall,* 232–35.
9. Hayes, *Joint Chiefs,* 722; Brower, *Defeating Japan,* 140–45.
10. James, *Years of MacArthur,* 2:775–76, 898n; Frank, *MacArthur,* 120; MacArthur, *Reminiscences,* 262. Marshall told King about the atomic program in 1943; King told Nimitz in February of 1945. Marshall did not tell MacArthur any earlier, perhaps in part because the necessary air bases for B-29s delivering the bombs were in Nimitz's area and Marshall was well aware of MacArthur's frequent indiscretion in handling sensitive information.
11. Halsema to James, November 16, 1970, quoted in James, *Years of MacArthur,* 2:773–74. Halsema's father, E. J. Halsema, had long been an American official in Baguio. Detained but allowed to live outside an internment camp because of his age, the senior Halsema was killed during an American air attack on Baguio on March 15, 1945. According to Halsema family lore, E. J. Halsema introduced MacArthur to Jean Faircloth en route to Manila in 1935.
12. Hayes, *Joint Chiefs,* 668, 682–84; Leahy, *I Was There,* 318.
13. James, *Years of MacArthur,* 2:763–64; Millis, *Forrestal Diaries,* 31 (February 28, 1945); MacArthur, *Reminiscences,* 261–62. At the height of the Cold War, longtime MacArthur aide Bonner Fellers acknowledged to historian Harry Elmer Barnes that "for some time I have known of a report going the rounds that in January 1945 General MacArthur sent a long cablegram to Washington urging that Russia not be brought into the war in the Pacific." Fellers nonetheless noted that he had been with MacArthur almost "night and day throughout this time" and that he had "no knowledge of such a study and I believe I would have known it had it been written at this time." Fellers to Barnes, March 2, 1960, RG 44a, box 1, folder 4.
14. Frank, *Downfall,* 322–24.
15. Ray S. Cline, *Washington Command Post: The Operations Division,* vol. 2 of *The United States Army in World War II: The War Department* (Washington, DC: Center of Military History, United States Army, 1990), 348–49.
16. AFPAC press release, August 9, 1945, RG 4, box 49, folder 4.
17. Nicholas, *Washington Despatches,* 603, August 18, 1945.
18. Frank, *Downfall,* 302.
19. Directive to SCAP, August 15, 1945, RG 15, box 13, folder 6; Marshall to MacArthur, August 15, 1945, RG 9, box 160, folder "War Dept 3 Aug–4 Sept 45."
20. MacArthur to Truman, August 15, 1945, RG 5, box 2, folder 2.
21. Marshall to MacArthur, August 15, 1945, RG 10, VIP files.
22. James, *Years of MacArthur,* 2:778. The Japanese delegation flew from Tokyo to Ie Shima, near Okinawa, in two Betty bombers specially painted white and marked with green crosses. There they boarded an American C-54 for the flight to Manila.
23. James, *Years of MacArthur,* 2:778–79. For MacArthur's postwar administration of Japan, see D. Clayton James, *The Years of MacArthur,* vol. 3, *Triumph and Disaster, 1945–1964* (Boston: Houghton Mifflin, 1985), and Seymour Morris Jr., *Supreme Commander: MacArthur's Triumph in Japan* (New York: HarperCollins, 2014).
24. White, Theodore H. *In Search of History: A Personal Adventure* (New York: Harper & Row, 1978), 224.

25. Pogue, *Ordeal and Hope,* 259.

26. James, *Years of MacArthur,* 2:780, 784.

27. MacArthur, *Reminiscences,* 270; Whitney, *MacArthur,* 214.

28. Rhoades, *Flying MacArthur,* 356, 441, 443–44. Sutherland had been in the States when news of the Japanese surrender came, and MacArthur insisted that he return to take part in the surrender ceremony. Sutherland had flown east on the original *Bataan,* and the B-17 was by then undergoing a major overhaul at Wright Field, in Ohio, so Sutherland commandeered another B-17 for his return.

29. Eichelberger, *Our Jungle Road,* 262.

30. Ibid., 263.

31. Willoughby, *MacArthur,* 295. Churchill reportedly made this remark to Winthrop Aldrich, the American ambassador to Great Britain from 1953 to 1957.

32. Egeberg, *The General,* 206, 209; James, *Years of MacArthur,* 2:788–89; United News newsreel, "Japanese Sign Final Surrender," at https://www.youtube.com/watch?v=vcnH_kF1zXc, accessed December 24, 2014. Later, Nimitz sent MacArthur the general's flag as a gift.

33. "Japanese Sign Final Surrender" newsreel.

34. Kenney, *The MacArthur I Know,* 187–88.

35. White, *In Search of History,* 228.

36. "Japanese Sign Final Surrender" newsreel.

Epilogue: A Study in Superlatives

1. Sir Charles Gairdner to Hastings Ismay, May 30, 1945, quoted in Thorne, *Allies of a Kind,* 650; Robert E. Sherwood, *The White House Papers of Harry Hopkins* (London: Eyre & Spottiswoode, 1949), 867.

2. George H. Johnston, "How Good Was MacArthur," *Australasian* (Melbourne), February 16, 1946, 13. Johnston was a veteran Australian war correspondent who reported on MacArthur from Australia through New Guinea, Manila, and Tokyo. Writing in Melbourne's weekly *Australasian* six months after the Japanese surrender, Johnston asked "How Good Was MacArthur?" in an article he penned as if looking back from the vantage point of two centuries.

   In 1946, Johnston acknowledged in a preface, "the figure of MacArthur is shrouded in mystery, entangled in diametrically opposed opinions." But what would people think in 2146? "During a four-year period millions of words were written about MacArthur," Johnston purported to report from 2146, "although no two writers seemed to agree upon the real character of the man. To some he was the greatest soldier of history; to others he was a sinister, megalomaniac insatiable for power and praise."

   Two centuries had not cleared the view, Johnston wrote, but he repeated a theme recognized in 1946 and he deemed it ever clearer as the years had passed: "MacArthur was deliberately and artificially molded into a world figure and a national hero (even though, at the time, he was a defeated general), because he was the opiate the United Nations needed to distract their minds from the catastrophe of Pearl Harbour." Afterward, Johnston claimed MacArthur remained "an heroic and legendary figure, partly because of his later brilliant conquests, but largely because of the indefatigable efforts of his publicity men...."

3. Contrasting MacArthur with Patton, Williamson Murray and Allan Millett's landmark study of World War II notes: "[MacArthur's] emotional balance was

precarious. These personal foibles, which made George Patton look normal, diverted attention from what should have been the real issue: MacArthur's professional military competence. His erratic performance in the Philippines should have led to his relief and retirement, but, instead, the Medal of Honor and a flood of media attention, encouraged by Roosevelt, diverted attention from America's military disasters. Then, having created a monster, FDR and the Joint Chiefs had to live with MacArthur and his powerful friends." Williamson Murray and Allan R. Millett, *A War to Be Won: Fighting the Second World War* (Cambridge, MA: Belknap Press of Harvard University Press, 2000), 205.

4. *Herald* (Melbourne), March 18, 1942, quoted in David Horner, "An Australian Perspective," in Leary, *MacArthur and the American Century,* 110.

5. John McCarten, "General MacArthur: Fact and Legend," *The American Mercury* 58, no. 241 (January 1944), 8.

6. Cantril, *Public Opinion,* 263–64.

Bibliography

Official Histories

Cannon, M. Hamlin. *Leyte: Return to the Philippines.* Vol. 9 of *The United States Army in World War II: The War in the Pacific.* Washington, DC: Center of Military History, United States Army, 1993.

Cline, Ray S. *Washington Command Post: The Operations Division.* Vol. 2 of *The United States Army in World War II: The War Department.* Washington, DC: Center of Military History, United States Army, 1990.

Coakley, Robert W., and Richard M. Leighton. *Global Logistics and Strategy, 1943–1945.* Vol. 6 of *The United States Army in World War II: The War Department.* Washington, DC: Center of Military History, United States Army, 1989.

Craven, Wesley Frank, and James Lea Cate. *The Pacific: Guadalcanal to Saipan, August 1942 to July 1944.* Vol. 4 of *The Army Air Forces in World War II.* Washington, DC: Office of Air Force History, 1983.

———. *The Pacific: Matterhorn to Nagasaki, June 1944 to August 1945.* Vol. 5 of *The Army Air Forces in World War II.* Washington, DC: Office of Air Force History, 1983.

Dexter, David. *The New Guinea Offensives.* Australia in the War of 1939–1945, ser. 1 (Army), vol. 6. Canberra: Australian War Memorial, 1961.

Gill, George Hermon. *Royal Australian Navy, 1942–1945.* Australia in the War of 1939–1945, ser. 2 (Navy), vol. 2. Canberra: Australian War Memorial, 1968.

Greenfield, Kent Roberts, ed. *Command Decisions*. Washington, DC: Center of Military History, United States Army, 1987.

Leighton, Richard M., and Robert W. Coakley. *Global Logistics and Strategy, 1940–1943*. Vol. 5 of *The United States Army in World War II: The War Department*. Washington, DC: Center of Military History, United States Army, 1995.

Long, Gavin. *The Final Campaigns*. Australia in the War of 1939–1945, ser. 1 (Army), vol. 7. Canberra: Australian War Memorial, 1963.

Matloff, Maurice. *Strategic Planning for Coalition Warfare, 1943–1944*. Vol. 4 of *The United States Army in World War II: The War Department*. Washington, DC: Center of Military History, United States Army, 1994.

Matloff, Maurice, and Edwin M. Snell. *Strategic Planning for Coalition Warfare, 1941–1942*. Vol. 3 of *The United States Army in World War II: The War Department*. Washington, DC: Center of Military History, United States Army, 1999.

McCarthy, Dudley. *South-West Pacific Area—First Year: Kokoda to Wau*. Australia in the War of 1939–1945, ser. 1 (Army), vol. 5. Canberra: Australian War Memorial, 1959.

Miller, John, Jr. *Cartwheel: The Reduction of Rabaul*. Vol. 5 of *The United States Army in World War II: The War in the Pacific*. Washington, DC: Center of Military History, United States Army, 1959.

———. *Guadalcanal: The First Offensive*. Vol. 3 of *The United States Army in World War II: The War in the Pacific*. Washington, DC: Center of Military History, United States Army, 1995.

Milner, Samuel. *Victory in Papua*. Vol. 4 of *The United States Army in World War II: The War in the Pacific*. Washington: Center of Military History, United States Army, 1989.

Morton, Louis. *The Fall of the Philippines*. Vol. 2 of *The United States Army in World War II: The War in the Pacific*. Washington, DC: Center of Military History, United States Army, 1993.

———. *Strategy and Command: The First Two Years*. Vol. 1 of *The United States Army in World War II: The War in the Pacific*. Washington, DC: Center of Military History, United States Army, 1962.

Smith, Robert Ross. *The Approach to the Philippines*. Vol. 8 of *The United States Army in World War II: The War in the Pacific*. Washington, DC: Center of Military History, United States Army, 1996.

——. *Triumph in the Philippines*. Vol. 10 of *The United States Army in World War II: The War in the Pacific*. Washington, DC: Center of Military History, United States Army, 1993.

Stauffer, Alvin P. *The Quartermaster Corps: Operations in the War Against Japan*. Vol. 5, bk. 3, of *The United States Army in World War II: The Technical Services*. Washington, DC: Center of Military History, United States Army, 1990.

Personal Memoirs and Diaries

Alanbrooke, Field Marshal Lord. *War Diaries 1939–1945*. Edited by Alex Danchev and Daniel Todman. Berkeley: University of California Press, 2001.

Arnold, H. H. *Global Mission*. New York: Harper Brothers, 1949.

Barbey, Daniel E. *MacArthur's Amphibious Navy: Seventh Amphibious Force Operations, 1943–1945*. Annapolis, MD: Naval Institute Press, 1969.

Bland, Larry I., ed. *George C. Marshall Interviews and Reminiscences for Forrest C. Pogue*. Lexington, VA: George C. Marshall Foundation, 1991.

Bland, Larry I., and Sharon Ritenour Stevens, eds. *"Aggressive and Determined Leadership": June 1, 1943–December 31, 1944*. Vol. 4 of *The Papers of George Catlett Marshall*. Baltimore: Johns Hopkins University Press, 1966.

——. *"The Right Man for the Job": December 7, 1941–May 31, 1943*. Vol. 3 of *The Papers of George Catlett Marshall*. Baltimore: Johns Hopkins University Press, 1991.

Brereton, Lewis H. *The Brereton Diaries: The War in the Air in the Pacific, Middle East, and Europe, 3 October 1941–8 May 1945*. New York: William Morrow, 1946.

Brougher, William Edward. *South to Bataan, North to Mukden: The Prison Diary of Brigadier General W. E. Brougher*. Athens, GA: University of Georgia Press, 1971.

Chandler, Alfred D., Jr., ed. *The Papers of Dwight David Eisenhower: The War Years,* vol. 1. Baltimore: Johns Hopkins University Press, 1970.

Chennault, Claire L. *Way of a Fighter: The Memoirs of Claire Lee Chennault.* New York: G. P. Putnam's Sons, 1949.

Egeberg, Roger Olaf. *The General: MacArthur and the Man He Called "Doc".* New York: Hippocrene, 1983.

Eichelberger, Robert L. *Our Jungle Road to Tokyo.* New York: Viking, 1950.

Eisenhower, Dwight D. *At Ease: Stories I Tell to Friends.* Garden City, NY: Doubleday, 1967.

———. *Crusade in Europe.* Garden City, NY: Doubleday, 1949.

Ferrell, Robert H., ed. *The Eisenhower Diaries.* New York: W. W. Norton, 1981.

Halsey, William F., and J. Bryan III. *Admiral Halsey's Story.* New York: McGraw-Hill, 1947.

Harsch, Joseph C. *At the Hinge of History: A Reporter's Story.* Athens, GA: University of Georgia Press, 1993.

Hoover, Herbert. *The Cabinet and the Presidency 1920–1933.* Vol. 2 of *The Memoirs of Herbert Hoover.* New York: Macmillan, 1952.

Huff, Sid. *My Fifteen Years with General MacArthur.* New York: Paperback Library, 1964.

Huston, John W., ed. *American Airpower Comes of Age: General Henry H. "Hap" Arnold's World War II Diaries.* Maxwell Air Force Base, AL: Air University Press, 2002.

Kenney, George C. *General Kenney Reports: A Personal History of the Pacific War.* Washington: Office of Air Force History, 1987.

———. *The MacArthur I Know* New York: Duell, Sloan and Pearce, 1951.

King, Ernest J., and Walter Muir Whitehill. *Fleet Admiral King: A Naval Record.* New York: W. W. Norton, 1952.

Krueger, Walter. *From Down Under to Nippon: The Story of the Sixth Army in World War II.* Washington, DC: Zenger, 1979.

Layton, Edwin T. *"And I Was There:" Pearl Harbor and Midway— Breaking the Secrets.* New York: William Morrow, 1985.

Leahy, William D. *I Was There: The Personal Story of the Chief of Staff to Presidents Roosevelt and Truman Based on His Notes and Diaries Made at the Time.* New York: Whittlesey House, 1950.

Luvaas, Jay, ed. *Dear Miss Em: General Eichelberger's War in the Pacific, 1942–1945.* Westport, CT: Greenwood Press, 1972.

MacArthur, Douglas. *Reminiscences.* New York: McGraw-Hill, 1964.

Maddalena, Joseph M., ed. *The Passionate and Poetic Pen of Douglas MacArthur: The Letters of Douglas MacArthur to His First Wife, Louise (Cromwell) Brooks.* Beverly Hills, CA: Profiles in History, n.d. Number 13 in a series of auction catalogs available from Maddalena's gallery.

Miller, E. B. *Bataan Uncensored.* Little Falls, MN: Military Historical Society of Minnesota, 1991.

Millis, Walter, ed. *The Forrestal Diaries.* New York: Viking, 1951.

Morison, Elting E., ed. *The Square Deal.* Vol. 4 of *The Letters of Theodore Roosevelt.* Cambridge, MA: Harvard University Press, 1951.

Quezon, Manuel Luis. *The Good Fight.* New York: D. Appleton–Century, 1946.

Rhoades, Weldon E. "Dusty." *Flying MacArthur to Victory.* College Station: Texas A&M University Press, 1987.

Rickenbacker, Edward V. *Rickenbacker: An Autobiography.* Englewood Cliffs, NJ: Prentice-Hall, 1967.

Rogers, Paul P. *The Bitter Years: MacArthur and Sutherland.* New York: Praeger, 1991.

———. *The Good Years: MacArthur and Sutherland.* New York: Praeger, 1990.

Roosevelt, Elliott, ed. *F.D.R.: His Personal Letters, 1928–1945.* New York: Duell, Sloan and Pearce, 1950.

Roosevelt, Franklin D. *Complete Presidential Press Conferences of Franklin D. Roosevelt.* New York: Da Capo Press, 1972.

Sakai, Saburo. *Samurai! Flying the Zero in WWII with Japan's Fighter Ace.* New York: Ballantine, 1957.

Sayre, Francis Bowes. *Glad Adventure.* New York: Macmillan, 1957.

Stimson, Henry L. *The Diaries of Henry Lewis Stimson in the Yale University Library.* New Haven: Yale University Library, 1973.

Stimson, Henry L., and McGeorge Bundy. *On Active Service in Peace and War.* New York: Harper & Brothers, 1947.

Ugaki, Matome. *Fading Victory: The Diary of Admiral Matome Ugaki, 1941–1945.* Pittsburgh, PA: University of Pittsburgh Press, 1991.

Vandenberg, Arthur H., Jr., ed. *The Private Papers of Senator Vandenberg.* Boston: Houghton Mifflin, 1952.

Wainwright, Jonathan M. *General Wainwright's Story.* New York: Doubleday, 1946.

Waldrop, Frank C., ed. *MacArthur on War.* New York: Duell, Sloan and Pearce, 1942.

Whitcomb, Edgar D. *Escape from Corregidor.* Chicago: Henry Regnery, 1958.

White, William Allen. *The Autobiography of William Allen White.* New York: Macmillan, 1946.

Willoughby, Charles, et al., eds. *Reports of General MacArthur: The Campaigns of MacArthur in the Pacific.* Washington, DC: Center of Military History, United States Army, 1994.

Secondary Sources

Bartsch, William H. *December 8, 1941: MacArthur's Pearl Harbor.* College Station: Texas A&M University Press, 2003.

Beck, John Jacob. *MacArthur and Wainwright: Sacrifice of the Philippines.* Albuquerque: University of New Mexico Press, 1974.

Blair, Clay, Jr. *Silent Victory: The U.S. Submarine War Against Japan.* Philadelphia: Lippincott, 1975.

Borneman, Walter R. *The Admirals: Nimitz, Halsey, Leahy, and King—The Five-Star Admirals Who Won the War at Sea.* New York: Little, Brown, 2012.

Brower, Charles F. *Defeating Japan: The Joint Chiefs of Staff and Strategy in the Pacific War, 1943–1945.* New York: Palgrave Macmillan, 2012.

Buell, Thomas B. *Master of Sea Power: A Biography of Fleet Admiral Ernest J. King.* Boston: Little, Brown, 1980.

Buhite, Russell D. *Douglas MacArthur: Statecraft and Stagecraft in America's East Asian Policy.* Lanham, MD: Rowman & Littlefield, 2008.

Cantril, Hadley, ed. *Public Opinion, 1935–1946.* Princeton, NJ: Princeton University Press, 1951.

Chwialkowski, Paul. *In Caesar's Shadow: The Life of General Robert Eichelberger.* Westport, CT: Greenwood Press, 1993.

Considine, Bob. *MacArthur the Magnificent.* London: Hutchinson, 1942.

Cox, Jeffrey R. *Rising Sun, Falling Skies: The Disastrous Java Sea Campaign of World War II.* Oxford: Osprey, 2014.

Davies, Robert B. *Baldwin of the Times: Hanson W. Baldwin, a Military Journalist's Life, 1903–1991.* Annapolis, MD: Naval Institute Press, 2011.

Dean, Peter J. *The Architect of Victory: The Military Career of Lieutenant-General Sir Frank Horton Berryman.* Port Melbourne, Australia: Cambridge University Press, 2011.

———, ed. *Australia 1942: In the Shadow of War.* Port Melbourne, Australia: Cambridge University Press, 2013.

———. *Australia 1943: The Liberation of New Guinea.* Port Melbourne, Australia: Cambridge University Press, 2014.

Drea, Edward J. *MacArthur's ULTRA: Codebreaking and the War Against Japan, 1942–1945.* Lawrence: University Press of Kansas, 1992.

Farr, Finis. *Rickenbacker's Luck: An American Life.* Boston: Houghton Mifflin, 1979.

Frank, Richard B. *Downfall: The End of the Imperial Japanese Empire.* New York: Random House, 1999.

———. *MacArthur.* New York: Palgrave Macmillan, 2007.

Ganoe, William Addleman. *MacArthur Close-up.* New York: Vantage, 1962.

Gordon, John. *Fighting for MacArthur: The Navy and Marine Corps' Desperate Defense of the Philippines.* Annapolis, MD: Naval Institute Press, 2011.

Greenfield, Kent Roberts. *American Strategy in World War II: A Reconsideration.* Baltimore: Johns Hopkins University Press, 1963.

Griffith, Thomas E., Jr. *MacArthur's Airman: General George C. Kenney and the War in the Southwest Pacific.* Lawrence: University Press of Kansas, 1998.

Hastings, Max. *Retribution: The Battle for Japan, 1944–45.* New York: Knopf, 2007.

Hayes, Grace Person. *The History of the Joint Chiefs of Staff in World War II: The War Against Japan*. Annapolis, MD: Naval Institute Press, 1982.

Hersey, John. *Men on Bataan*. New York: Knopf, 1944.

Holzimmer, Kevin C. *General Walter Krueger: Unsung Hero of the Pacific War*. Lawrence: University Press of Kansas, 2007.

Hoopes, Townsend, and Douglas Brinkley. *Driven Patriot: The Life and Times of James Forrestal*. New York: Knopf, 1992.

Horner, David. *Inside the War Cabinet: Directing Australia's War Efforts, 1939–45*. St. Leonards, Australia: Allen & Unwin, 1996.

Hornfischer, James D. *Neptune's Inferno: The U.S. Navy at Guadalcanal*. New York: Bantam, 2011.

———. *Ship of Ghosts: The Story of the USS* Houston, *FDR's Legendary Lost Cruiser, and the Epic Saga of Her Survivors*. New York: Bantam, 2006.

Hunt, Frazier. *The Untold Story of Douglas MacArthur*. New York: Devin-Adair, 1954.

Hurley, Alfred F. *Billy Mitchell: Crusader for Air Power*. Bloomington: Indiana University Press, 1975.

James, D. Clayton. *A Time for Giants: The Politics of the American High Command in World War II*. New York: Franklin Watts, 1987.

———. *The Years of MacArthur*. 3 vols. Boston: Houghton Mifflin, 1970–85.

Karnow, Stanley. *In Our Image: America's Empire in the Philippines*. New York: Random House, 1989.

Leary, William M., ed. *MacArthur and the American Century: A Reader*. Lincoln: University of Nebraska Press, 2001.

———. *We Shall Return! MacArthur's Commanders and the Defeat of Japan*. Lexington: University Press of Kentucky, 1988.

Lee, Clark, and Richard Henschel. *Douglas MacArthur*. New York: Henry Holt, 1952.

Leutze, James. *A Different Kind of Victory: A Biography of Admiral Thomas C. Hart*. Annapolis, MD: Naval Institute Press, 1981.

Lewis, W. David. *Eddie Rickenbacker: An American Hero in the Twentieth Century*. Baltimore: Johns Hopkins University Press, 2005.

Lohbeck, Don. *Patrick J. Hurley.* Chicago: Henry Regnery, 1956.

Long, Gavin. *MacArthur as Military Commander.* London: B. T. Batsford, 1969.

Lundstrom, John B. *Black Shoe Carrier Admiral: Frank Jack Fletcher at Coral Sea, Midway, and Guadalcanal.* Annapolis. MD: Naval Institute Press, 2006.

———. *The First Team and the Guadalcanal Campaign: Naval Fighter Combat from August to November 1942.* Annapolis, MD: Naval Institute Press, 1994.

Manchester, William. *American Caesar: Douglas MacArthur, 1880–1964.* Boston: Little, Brown, 1978.

———. *Goodbye, Darkness: A Memoir of the Pacific War.* New York: Little, Brown, 1979.

Masuda, Hiroshi. *MacArthur in Asia: The General and His Staff in the Philippines, Japan, and Korea.* Translated by Reiko Yamamoto. Ithaca. NY: Cornell University Press, 2012.

McMillan, George. *The Old Breed: A History of the First Marine Division in World War II.* Washington, DC: Infantry Journal Press, 1949.

Miles, Paul L., Jr. "American Strategy in World War II: The Role of William D. Leahy." PhD diss., Princeton University, 1999.

Morison, Samuel Eliot. *Breaking the Bismarcks Barrier: 22 July 1942–1 May 1944.* Vol. 6 of *History of United States Naval Operations in World War II.* Boston: Little Brown, 1950.

———. *Coral Sea, Midway and Submarine Actions: May 1942–August 1942.* Vol. 4 of *History of United States Naval Operations in World War II.* Boston: Little, Brown, 1988.

———. *The Rising Sun in the Pacific: 1931–April 1942.* Vol. 3 of *History of United States Naval Operations in World War II.* Boston: Little Brown, 1948

———. *The Two-Ocean War: A Short History of the United States Navy in the Second World War.* Boston: Little, Brown, 1963.

Morris, Roy, Jr. *Sheridan: The Life and Wars of General Phil Sheridan.* New York: Crown, 1992.

Morris, Seymour, Jr. *Supreme Commander: MacArthur's Triumph in Japan.* New York: HarperCollins, 2014.

Morris, Sylvia Jukes. *Rage for Fame: The Ascent of Clare Boothe Luce.* New York: Random House, 1997.

Murray, Williamson, and Allan R. Millett. *A War to Be Won: Fighting the Second World War.* Cambridge, MA: Belknap Press of Harvard University Press, 2000.

Nicholas, H. G., ed. *Washington Despatches, 1941–1945, Weekly Political Reports from the British Embassy.* Chicago: University of Chicago Press, 1981.

Parshall, Jonathan, and Anthony Tully. *Shattered Sword: The Untold Story of the Battle of Midway.* Washington, DC: Potomac Books, 2007.

Perret, Geoffrey. *Old Soldiers Never Die: The Life of Douglas MacArthur.* New York: Random House, 1996.

Petillo, Carol Morris. *Douglas MacArthur: The Philippine Years.* Bloomington: Indiana University Press, 1981.

Pogue, Forrest C. *George C. Marshall: Education of a General, 1880–1939.* New York: Viking, 1963.

———. *George C. Marshall: Ordeal and Hope, 1939–1942.* New York: Viking, 1966.

———. *George C. Marshall: Organizer of Victory, 1943–1945.* New York: Viking, 1973.

Potter, E. B. *Bull Halsey: A Biography.* Annapolis, MD: Naval Institute Press, 1985.

———. *Nimitz.* Annapolis, MD: Naval Institute Press, 1976.

Prange, Gordon W. *At Dawn We Slept: The Untold Story of Pearl Harbor.* New York: Penguin, 1991.

Reilly, Henry J. *Americans All: The Rainbow at War—Official History of the 42nd Rainbow Division in the World War.* Columbus, OH: F. J. Heer, 1936.

Roberts, Andrew. *Masters and Commanders: How Four Titans Won the War in the West, 1941–1945.* New York: Harper, 2009.

Robertson, John. *Australia at War 1939–1945.* Melbourne: William Heinemann, 1981.

Sarantakes, Nicholas Evan. *Allies Against the Rising Run: The United States, the British Nations, and the Defeat of Imperial Japan.* Lawrence: University Press of Kansas, 2009.

Schaller, Michael. *Douglas MacArthur: The Far Eastern General.* New York: Oxford University Press, 1989.

Sherwood, Robert E. *The White House Papers of Harry L. Hopkins.* Vol. 2, *January 1942–July 1945.* London: Eyre & Spottiswoode, 1949.

Shortal, John F. *Forged by Fire: General Robert L. Eichelberger and the Pacific War.* Columbia: University of South Carolina Press, 1987.

Smith, George W. *MacArthur's Escape: John "Wild Man" Bulkeley and the Rescue of an American Hero.* St. Paul, MN: Zenith Press, 2005.

Spector, Ronald H. *Eagle Against the Sun: The American War with Japan.* New York: Free Press, 1985.

Stoler, Mark A. *Allies and Adversaries: The Joint Chiefs of Staff, the Grand Alliance, and U.S. Strategy in World War II.* Chapel Hill: University of North Carolina Press, 2000.

Symonds, Craig L. *The Battle of Midway.* New York: Oxford University Press, 2011.

Thomas, Evan. *Sea of Thunder: Four Commanders and the Last Great Naval Campaign, 1941–1945.* New York: Simon and Schuster, 2006.

Thorne, Christopher. *Allies of a Kind: The United States, Britain, and the War Against Japan, 1941–1945.* New York: Oxford University Press, 1978.

Tugwell, Rexford G. *The Democratic Roosevelt: A Biography of Franklin D. Roosevelt.* Baltimore: Penguin Books, 1969.

Weigley, Russell F. *The American Way of War: A History of United States Military Strategy and Policy.* New York: Macmillan, 1973.

Wheeler, Gerald E. *Kincaid of the Seventh Fleet.* Washington, DC: Naval Historical Center, 1995.

White, Theodore H. *In Search of History: A Personal Adventure.* New York: Harper and Row, 1978.

White, W. L. *They Were Expendable: An American Torpedo Boat Squadron in the U.S. Retreat from the Philippines.* New York: Harcourt, Brace, 1942.

Whitney, Courtney. *MacArthur: His Rendezvous with History.* New York: Knopf, 1956.

Willoughby, Charles A., and John Chamberlain. *MacArthur, 1941–1951*. New York: McGraw-Hill, 1954.

Woodward, C. Vann. *The Battle for Leyte Gulf: The Incredible Story of World War II's Largest Naval Battle*. New York: Skyhorse, 2007.

Zobel, James W. *MacArthur: The Supreme Commander at War in the Pacific*. Mechanicsburg, PA: Stackpole Books, 2015.

Articles

Bartsch, William H. "Was MacArthur Ill-Served by his Air Force Commanders in the Philippines?" *Air Power History* 44, no. 2 (Summer 1997): 44–63.

Edmonds, Walter D. "What Happened at Clark Field." *The Atlantic* (July 1951): 32.

Harper's Magazine. "MacArthur and the Censorship." May 1944: 537.

James, D. Clayton. "American and Japanese Strategies in the Pacific War." In *Makers of Modern Strategy from Machiavelli to the Nuclear Age*. Edited by Peter Paret. Princeton, NJ: Princeton University Press, 1986.

Johnston, George H. "How Good Was MacArthur." *Australasian*, February 16, 1946.

Kluckhohn, Frank. "Heidelberg to Madrid—The Story of General Willoughby." *The Reporter*, August 19, 1952.

McCarten, John. "General MacArthur: Fact and Legend." *American Mercury* 58 (January 1944): 7–18.

Meilinger, Phillip S. "Unity of Command in the Pacific During World War II." *Joint Force Quarterly* 56 (1st Quarter 2010): 152–56.

Meixsel, Richard Bruce. "Manuel Quezon, Douglas MacArthur, and the Significance of the Military Mission to the Philippine Commonwealth." *Pacific Historical Review* 70, no. 2 (May 2001): 255–92.

Miles, Paul L. "Marshall as Grand Strategist." In *George C. Marshall: Servant of the American Nation*. Edited by Charles F. Brower. New York: Palgrave Macmillan, 2011.

Miller, Roger G. "A Pretty Damn Able Commander: Lewis Hyde Brereton." Pts. 1 and 2. *Air Power History* 47, no. 4 (Winter 2000): 4–27; 48, no. 1 (Spring 2001): 22–45.

Pearson, Drew, and Robert S. Allen. "The Real General MacArthur." *Liberty,* March 7, 1942: 20–22.

Petillo, Carol M. "Douglas MacArthur and Manuel Quezon: A Note on an Imperial Bond." *Pacific Historical Review* 48, no. 1 (February 1979): 107–17.

Pogue, Forrest. "The Military in a Democracy: A Review: *American Caesar.*" *International Security* 3, no. 4 (Spring 1979): 58–80.

Rogers, Paul P. "MacArthur, Quezon and Executive Order Number One: Another View." *Pacific Historical Review* 52, no. 1 (February 1983): 93–100.

Stoler, Mark A. "The 'Pacific-First' Alternative in American World War II Strategy." *International History Review* 2, no. 3 (July 1980): 432–52.

Vandenberg, Arthur H. "Why I Am for MacArthur." *Colliers,* February 12, 1944: 48–49.

Willkie, Wendell. "Let Us Do More Proposing Than Opposing." *Vital Speeches of the Day* 8, no. 8 (March 1, 1942): 297–99.

Personal Papers and Manuscript Collections

Henry Harley Arnold Papers. Manuscript Division, Library of Congress, Washington, DC.

Newton Diehl Baker Papers. Manuscript Division, Library of Congress, Washington, DC.

Robert L. Ghormley Papers. Special Collections Department, J. Y. Joyner Library, East Carolina University, Greenville, NC.

William Frederick Halsey Papers. Manuscript Division, Library of Congress, Washington, DC.

D. Clayton James Papers. Mississippi State University, Starkeville.

Ernest Joseph King Papers. Manuscript Division, Library of Congress, Washington, DC.

Ernest J. King Papers. Naval Historical Collection, Naval War College, Newport, RI.

William D. Leahy Diary. William D. Leahy Papers. Manuscript Division, Library of Congress, Washington, DC.

Clare Boothe Luce Papers. Manuscript Division, Library of Congress, Washington, DC.

MacArthur Memorial Archives and Library, Norfolk, VA.

RG 1: Records of the Military Advisor to the Philippine Commonwealth, 1935–1941

RG 2: Records of Headquarters, U.S. Army Forces in the Far East (USAFFE), 1941–1942

RG 3: Records of Headquarters, Southwest Pacific Area (SWPA), 1942–1945

RG 4: Records of Headquarters, U.S. Army Forces Pacific (USAFPAC), 1942–1947

RG 5: Records of General Headquarters, Supreme Commander for the Allied Powers (SCAP), 1945–1951

RG 9: Collection of Messages (Radiograms), 1945–1951

RG 10: General Douglas MacArthur's Private Correspondence, 1848–1964

RG 13: Papers of Mrs. Douglas MacArthur

RG 15: Materials Donated by the General Public

Papers of Vice Admiral John D. Bulkeley, USN, Motor Torpedo Boat Squadron 3

Papers of PhM, 1/c, Elmer G. Heck, USN

RG 18: Records of the Chief of Staff, United States Army, 1934–1935

RG 23c: Selected Papers of Major General Charles A. Willoughby, USA, 1943–1954

RG 26: Service Record and Papers of General Douglas MacArthur, USA, 1903–1964

RG 29: Papers of Major General Richard J. Marshall, USA, Deputy Chief of Staff, SWPA

RG 30: Papers of Lieutenant General Richard K. Sutherland, USA, Chief of Staff, SWPA, 1941–1945

RG 32: Oral History Collection

RG 34: Diary of Brigadier General Lewis C. Beebe, USA

RG 36: Selected Papers of Lieutenant General Stephen J. Chamberlin, USA, 1942–1946

RG 41: Selected Papers of Lieutenant General Robert L. Eichelberger, USA, Commanding General, Eighth Army, SWPA, USAFPAC, FECOM, 1942–1948

RG 44a: Selected Papers of Brigadier General Bonner F. Fellers, USA, Military Secretary to MacArthur, SWPA, SCAP, 1913–1972

RG 46: Papers of Lt. Paul P. Rogers, USA, Chief Clerk, GHQ, SWPA, 1941–1989.

RG 49: D. Clayton James Collection

RG 79: Papers of Major General Spencer B. Akin, USA, Chief Signal Officer, USAFFE, SWPA

RG 107: Papers of Colonel Joseph R. Sherr, USA, Signal Corps, GHQ, SWPA, 1941–1943

George C. Marshall Papers. George C. Marshall Library and Archives, Lexington, VA.

Samuel Eliot Morison Papers. Manuscript Division, Library of Congress, Washington, DC.

George Van Horn Moseley Papers. Manuscript Division, Library of Congress, Washington, DC.

Admiral Chester W. Nimitz Collection. Operational Archives Branch, Naval History and Heritage Command, Washington, DC.

John Callan O'Laughlin Papers. Manuscript Division, Library of Congress, Washington, DC.

John J. Pershing Papers. Manuscript Division, Library of Congress, Washington, DC.

Franklin D. Roosevelt Papers. Franklin D. Roosevelt Library, Hyde Park, NY.

Francis Bowes Sayre Papers. Manuscript Division, Library of Congress, Washington, DC.

Andres Soriano Papers. Manuscript Division, Library of Congress, Washington, DC.

Government Documents and Publications

Annual Report of the Superintendent of the United States Military Academy. Washington: United States Government Printing Office, 1899.

Exec. Order 9096. F.R. Doc. 42-2195, Mar. 12, 1942.

H. R. 6649. 77th Cong., 2nd Sess., Feb. 23, 1942.

"Nimitz Gray Book." Naval History and Heritage Command. Online at http://www.ibiblio.org/anrs/docs/D/D7/nimitz_graybook5.pdf.

Public Law 482. 78th Cong., Dec. 14, 1944.

"United States Strategic Bombing Survey Summary Report (Pacific War)." Washington, DC: United States Government Printing Office, 1946.

Online Resources

"Allied Warship Commanders: Chester Carl Smith, USN." Uboat.net. Accessed September 8, 2013. http://uboat.net/allies/commanders/ 3225.html.

"Army-Navy Game." *Wikipedia*. https://en.wikipedia.org/wiki/ Army–Navy_Game.

"Australia's Prime Ministers." National Archives of Australia. Accessed July 26, 2014. http://primeministers.naa.gov.au/primemi nisters/curtin/in-office.aspx.

"Between World Wars." in *American Military History*: 409. Center of Military History, United States Army. Accessed July 11, 2013. http://www.history.army.mil/books/AMH/amh-19.htm.

"Diary of Basilio J. Valdes, February 20, 1942." The Philippine Diary Project. Accessed September 9, 2013. https://philippinediaryproject .wordpress.com/category/diary-of-basilio-j-valdes/page/8/.

"Franklin D. Roosevelt Day by Day": July 26, 1944. Pare Lawrence Center at the FDR Presidential Library. Accessed July 14, 2014. http://www.fdrlibrary.marist.edu/daybyday/daylog/july-26th-1944/.

Franklin D. Roosevelt press conference, October 5, 1943. Franklin D. Roosevelt Presidential Library and Museum. Accessed January 15, 2015. http://www.fdrlibrary.marist.edu/_resources/images/pc/ pc0153.pdf (page 127).

"General Hal George, 2nd Lt. Robert D. Jasper, & War Correspondent Mel Jacoby Killed in a Kittyhawk Ground Accident at Batchelor Airfield on 29 April 1942." Peter Dunn's Australia @ War. Accessed October 20, 2013. http://www.ozatwar.com/ozcrashes/nt105.htm.

"Japanese Sign Final Surrender!" United Newsreel Corporation. Accessed March 29, 2011. http://www.youtube.com/watch_popup?v=vcnH_kF1zXc&feature=player_embedded.

Newspapers and News Magazines

The Argus (Melbourne)
Canberra Times
Chronicle (Adelaide)
Courier-Mail (Brisbane)
Evening Star (Washington, DC)
Fortune
Life
Melbourne Herald
New York Herald Tribune
New York Times
Pittsburgh Press
Portland Guardian (Victoria)
Saturday Evening Post
Sydney Morning Herald
Time
Washington Post
Washington Post and Times-Herald

Index

Index

WALTER R. BORNEMAN is the award-winning author of eight works of nonfiction, including *1812, The French and Indian War, Polk, American Spring,* and the national bestseller *The Admirals.* He lives in Colorado.